Russian Media Law and Policy in the Yeltsin Decade

Essays and Documents

Communications Law and Policy in Transition

Volume 1. **Russian Media Law and Policy in the Yeltsin Decade: Essays and Documents**
Edited by Monroe E. Price, Andrei Richter, and Peter K. Yu

Programme in Comparative Media Law & Policy
Center for Socio-Legal Studies, University of Oxford

Russian Media Law and Policy in the Yeltsin Decade

Essays and Documents

Edited by

Monroe E. Price

Benjamin N. Cardozo School of Law
Yeshiva University
New York, U.S.A. and
Programme in Comparative Media Law & Policy
Centre for Socio-Legal Studies
University of Oxford
Oxford, U.K.

Andrei Richter

School of Journalism
Moscow State University
Moscow Media Law & Policy Center
Moscow, Russia

and

Peter K. Yu

Benjamin N. Cardozo School of Law
Yeshiva University
New York, , U.S.A. and
Programme in Comparative Media Law & Policy
Centre for Socio-Legal Studies
University of Oxford
Oxford, U.K.

KLUWER LAW INTERNATIONAL
THE HAGUE / LONDON / NEW YORK

Published by:
Kluwer Law International
P.O. Box 85889, 2508 CN The Hague, The Netherlands
sales@kli.wkap.nl
http://www.kluwerlaw.com

Sold and Distributed in North, Central and South America by:
Kluwer Law International
101 Philip Drive, Norwell, MA 02061, USA
kluwerlaw@wkap.com

Sold and Distributed in all other countries by:
Kluwer Law International
Distribution Centre, P.O. Box 322, 3300 AH Dordrecht, The Netherlands

Library of Congress Cataloging-in-Publication Data
Russian media law and policy in the Yeltsin decade: essays and documents/edited by Monroe E. Price, Andrei Richter, and Peter K. Yu.
p. cm.—(Communications law and policy in transition; v. 1)
Includes bibliographical references and index.
ISBN 9041188770 (alk. paper)
1. Mass media—Law and legislation—Russia (Federation)—History. 2. Press law—Russia (Federation)—History. 3. Freedom of the press—Russia (Federation)—History. 4. Mass media policy—Russia (Federation) I. Price, Monroe Edwin, 1938- II. Richter, Andrei. III. Yu, Peter K. IV. Series.

KLB3482 .R87 2002
343.4709'9—dc21

2002022235

Printed on acid-free paper

ISBN 90 411 8877 0

Kluwer Law International incorporates the imprint of Martinus Nijhoff Publishers

To Wade Greene

Contents

II. Statutes and Decrees

Preface

This book is tied to the history of the *Post-Soviet Media Law and Policy Newsletter*. The *Newsletter* came into being in 1993 after one of the editors, Monroe Price, had been appointed as a public interest member of the Commission on Radio and Television Policy, an unusual entity co-chaired—for most of its existence—by former President Jimmy Carter and Eduard Sagalaev, a Russian broadcasting executive. The purpose of the Commission was, ostensibly, to exchange views between the U.S. and (at first) Soviet policymakers and executives in the broadcasting field. The Commission was established in the late days of Glasnost and Gorbachev and sought to assist Gorbachev's policy of openness and change. By the time the Commission was operative, Gorbachev was almost part of history—as was, of course, the Soviet Union.

The *Newsletter* came into being because there was then a thirst for more complete information about changes in the administration of Russian (and other post-Soviet) media policy, shifting directives, alterations in President Yeltsin's modes of dealing with television. Sources were little known, nor was it clear how issues should be defined.

For six years, the *Newsletter* was published almost monthly. It was circulated to a hardy band of subscribers and, through the miracle of still-new technology, was put on the Internet. The *Newsletter* had helped develop a community, provide material for scholars, and assist in building or enriching a discipline of comparative media law and policy studies.

In 1999, the *Newsletter*, for all practical purposes, was transmutated into *Communications Law in Transition Newsletter*, partly because of the existence, through the Internet, of a wide variety of sources for information about media policy in the post-Soviet world. One of the editors, Andrei Richter, invented what became a widely-read Russian-language version of the *Newsletter*, wholly separate in editorial content and in audience. The Russian counterpart remains vital, at the time of this publication, and has a number of regional editions.

Among those who must be thanked or acknowledged are the following. Wade Greene of the Rockefeller Family Fund, who saw the need for supporting the *Newsletter*; Edith Bjornson, then of the Markle Foundation, who was responsible for placing one of the editors, Professor Price, as a member of the Carter Commission; Peter Krug, who, from the beginning, was Associate Editor of the *Newsletter* and a frequent contributor; Aleksei Simonov of the Glasnost Defence Foundation, who was an architect of a number of enterprises that contributed to a strong critical culture in Moscow (including the *Newsletter*). Eric Johnson of Internews brought a muscular legal perspective to post-Soviet media developments that only an intelligent and committed non-lawyer can bring. Stefaan Verhulst, the former director of the Programme in Comparative Media Law and Policy at the University of Oxford, provided intellectual and moral support and was a constant source of useful suggestions. Helen Darbishire of the Open Society Institute provided a small grant that would ensure circulation of the book to a broad audience. Bethany Davis was responsible for taking the project in hand at a critical point in its development and ensuring that the manuscript would be crisper, more pointed, and within the publisher's guidelines.

The Benjamin N. Cardozo School of Law of Yeshiva University, and its Howard M. Squadron Program in Law, Media and Society, was the home of the *Newsletter* and allowed it to be published, nourished, and distributed. The Jacob Burns Institute for Advanced Legal Studies provided generous support of the *Newsletter* as well as other related projects conducted under the auspices of the Squadron Program.

Under the direction of one of the editors, Peter Yu, students at the Law School were able to assist in the preparation and production of the periodical. Karen Underwood, as an assistant to Professor Price, also helped to ensure that the *Newsletter* was published. And Timothy Hamilton and Michael Kassner have made invaluable contribution for making the *Newsletter* available online.

The *Newsletter* could not have been published without the existence of BBC Worldwide Monitoring. This invaluable tool is too little known, but it provides a chronicle of important political and economic decisions that affect media all over the world. *The Moscow Times*, ITAR-TASS, and Interfax also are reliable sources of information.

This volume does not capture the way in which the *Newsletter* sought to provide information on breaking events. Rather, it tries to furnish a broad overview of media during the Yeltsin years. Those who wish to look at the *Newsletter* archives should visit http://www.vii.org/monroe/. The Russian-language Newsletter is available at http://www.medialaw.ru/.

Russian Media Law and Policy in the Yeltsin Decade

Essays and Documents

Part I

Essays

I.

An Introduction

The Russian Press After Perestroika*

Andrei Richter

Introduction

The demise of Communist rule in the USSR, followed by the disintegration of the Soviet Union itself, brought a collapse and restructuring of most of the basic elements in Russia. Partly caused by mass media activity, it also brought the fall of the old system of press and broadcasting. Glasnost, which originated as an official Communist Party policy directed to open a critical discussion of the country's past and of ways to improve socialism in the USSR, broke the bonds of censorship and spread beyond all possible limits toward freedom of speech and press. Perestroika, the restructuring of the Soviet economy and society, which took place between 1985 and 1991, created new material circumstances for the development of the press and broadcasting. This article, first published in 1995, addresses legal regulations, economic conditions, and information sources of the Russian press between 1992 and 1994. It provides a background for this volume's larger discussion of what occurred in Russian media during the Yeltsin years. This chapter also focuses on steady trends that are likely to determine the future of Russian press in the years to come.

Legal Regulation of Mass Media

Among the most important events of the three years between 1992 and 1994 was the establishment of a legal basis for freedom of speech and information. Until then, the Communist Party's bodies and functionaries regulated mass media. Retrospectively, the legal decisions made during those years were in conformity with the Decree on the Press signed by Vladimir Lenin on October 27, 1917. That Decree introduced "temporary and extraordinary measures to stop the flow of dirt and slander," but was never revoked during the seven decades of Soviet rule. The "full freedom within the limits of responsibility before the court," promised in its text, that would be realized by "a broad and progressive . . . legislation" only occurred with the promulgation of the USSR Law on the Press and Other Mass Media ("USSR Press Law") (August 1, 1990) and the Russian Federation Law On the Mass Media (February 8, 1992). Although governmental and local bodies attacked these laws during much of the nineties, they were serious legal guarantees of media activity that were in accordance with democratic principles.

Freedom of mass information as fixed in Russian law means unlimited (except by existing legislation) freedom to seek, obtain, produce, and disseminate information; to found, own, use, and manage mass media outlets; and to prepare, acquire, and operate

* 20 Canadian Journal of Communication 7 (1995).

technical devices and equipment, raw goods, and materials intended for the production and distribution of mass media products. Russian law reinforces inadmissibility of censorship, originally proclaimed in article 1 of the USSR Press Law.

Another noteworthy legal act is the *Law of the Russian Federation* of March 21, 1991, which introduced specific administrative and criminal penalties for creating obstacles to the professional activity of journalists and for other violations of the mass media legislation. Its punishments are important because they provide concrete specifications within a system of haphazard and sometimes contradictory laws, decrees, and regulations that are aggravated by a lack of coordination between lawmaking and law-enforcement bodies. The State Inspectorate to Protect the Freedom of the Press and Mass Information was created in September of 1991 with the mandate to petition government, founders, and editors of publications, as well as TV and radio stations, when violations of the law are committed. It can also file a court suit to close a media organization. The new Russian Constitution adopted by national referendum on December 12, 1993, is the latest and probably the most important act that guarantees freedom of press and speech. Confirming the ban on censorship, it states (in article 29) that "[e]veryone has the right to freely seek, obtain, transmit, produce, and disseminate information by any legal method."

The Fall of the Central Press

Until about 1990, newspapers in the USSR had a stable hierarchy. The so-called "central press" was the leader. It consisted of Moscow-based, nationally distributed newspapers and magazines that presented the official policy of the Communist Party, the government, and different central bodies, both state and public. Although in 1990 the central press comprised just 3 percent of the total number of newspapers, their circulation was 73 percent of the total.

Paramount in the central press were *Pravda* (*Truth*), the daily newspaper of the Communist Party's Central Committee, and *Izvestiia* (*News*), the Supreme Soviet's paper. The Central Committee also published magazines and newspapers on communist theory and practice, as well as on industry, agriculture, culture, international affairs, and so forth. Leadership of the Young Communist League (Komsomol) owned a youth affairs paper, *Komsomolskaia Pravda* (*Young Communists' Truth*). The Trade Unions' Central Council ran *Trud* (*Labor*) for worker collectives; the Board of the Writers' Union had *Literaturnaia Gazeta* (*Literary Gazette*) for the intelligentsia; the Union of Movie Workers published *Sovetski Ekran* (*Soviet Screen*), a magazine for movie fans; while the State Sports Committee had *Sovetski Sport* (*Soviet Sport*), a daily for sports fans; and so on.

Below the national level this scheme was repeated in the capitals of the Soviet republics, with newspapers and magazines of the same character as those published in Moscow. Although there was no overt subordination of these publications to the central publications, direct command links between the bodies governing them presupposed some kind of master-servant relationship.

The system was reproduced again at the regional level, where the party and Soviet bodies usually merged their efforts to run joint publications to cut production costs; then, once more, at the municipal level, and, again, at the district level in the countryside, at industrial enterprises, and so forth. Although the tip of the pyramid was small, national publications were the most popular in the country. These newspapers were of very similar content, often with the same "opinions" and editorials that not only explained party view on political issues but also reinforced the newspaper's role, in the best Leninist tradition, as a "collective propagandist, collective agitator, and collective organizer." Magazines had some liberties as "second-class press" and had more liberties in style and ratio of propaganda to entertainment stories.

From 1986 to 1988, Mikhail Gorbachev installed editors loyal to his policies, and the central press became instrumental in his reforms. Because of their large readership, national publications were used to appeal directly to the people over the heads of the opposition. Their letters-to-the-editor sections presented a way for people to participate in *perestroika*.

Soon after this period, unexpected events began to occur. The USSR Press Law demanded that all publications be officially registered with state bodies. In fact, this procedure let the editorial staffs look for and register "founders" that could be different from their old masters, or even register the newspapers as their own. This practice created the first practical threat to the pyramid by freeing newspapers from previous subordination. At the same time, enterprising editors and the newly rich launched publications at the periphery.

The next blow to the bureaucracy occurred in August of 1991 with the ban of the Communist Party and nationalization of its property. Because the governing party had ceased to exist as the dominant structure some of the ex-communist papers, mainly provincial ones, took different names. Such words as "kommunist," "Pravda," and "sovetski" went out of fashion. Other papers took a different editorial line.

In some cases the state tried to imitate the old system by creating a similar structure of governmental and Soviet press in Moscow and in the republics. They allowed an atmosphere of greater autonomy for local administrations and did not exercise political control over the editorial content of the newspapers. True, economic levers in the form of subsidies were still in the hands of the state, but their impact is worthy of special discussion below.

On the surface, the pyramid still seemed to be in place by the mid-nineties, but inside the puppet-strings had been destroyed. Nobody viewed the national Moscow-based papers as a central press, or looked for propagandist trends and organizational instructions in its pages. With public interest shifted to community issues, the local press appeared to have become the most stable part in a shattered structure.

Local Press: Sources of Stability

The years following perestroika, 1989 and 1990, were the peak of popularity for mass media (see Table 1). The population was truly interested in the political scene. Sessions of the Congress of Peoples' Deputies were watched live on television and listened to on radio with such intensity that a sharp fall in industrial production figures occurred. In a way, that was a time of glasnost "intoxication." The next three years were characterized by a growing distrust of media against a backdrop of general political apathy and severe economic crises. The latter was a factor, which led many families to abandon their traditional subscriptions to five or six publications and limit themselves to just one. The media were no longer viewed by the population as a source of help and hope, or a channel to express their opinions.

Table 1: Circulation of Major Newspapers (Millions)

Title	1985	1986	1987	1988	1989*	1990	1991	1992†	1992‡	1993†	1993‡	1994†	1994‡
Dailies:													
Trud	16.7	18.2	18.2	19.0	19.8	21.4	18.5	13.6	12.5	4.0	1.4	1.8	1.3
Komsomolskaia Pravda	13.2	14.6	17.0	17.6	17.6	22.0	17.9	13.5	2.5	3.7	1.2	1.7	1.2
Pravda	10.5	10.8	11.1	10.7	9.6	7.7	2.6	1.4	1.4	0.5	0.6	0.4	0.1
Izvestiia	6.7	6.9	8.0	10.4	10.1	10.3	4.7	3.8	3.8	1.1	0.7	0.8	0.8
Moskovski Komsomolets	—	—	—	—	—	1.4	1.5	1.6	1.7	1.3	1.2	1.4	1.2
Nezavisimaia Gazeta	n/a	n/a	n/a	n/a	n/a	n/a	0.3	0.2	0.2	0.1	0.1	0.1	0.1
Weeklies:													
Argumenti i Fakti	1.4	1.9	3.2	9.1	20.5	33.2	24.2	25.7	26.2	12.1	5.1	6.1	3.5
Moskovskie Novosti	—	—	1.0	—	—	—	1.8	1.0	0.8	0.8	0.3	0.3	0.2

* subscription only † first half of year ‡ second half of year

In 1988, the local press began to be preferred over the central press. Initially, those Union republics where the "national idea" dominated peoples' minds demonstrated this tendency. With increasing independence from Moscow, the demand for national stories gave way to interest in local news, practical information, entertainment, and stories of day-to-day life. Polls said that concern for world affairs or national politics had dropped dramatically in a couple of years. The majority of Russians wanted to read about such issues as the cost of living and crime—exactly what the local press provides. Among the least popular topics were ethnic issues, life in other republics of the former USSR, and foreign policy—all prominent in the national press.

This resulted in relative stability in the local publications' circulations. During the subscription campaign for the second half of 1993, local newspapers managed to preserve 84 percent of their readers and magazines 100 percent; meanwhile, national newspapers kept 63 percent of their subscribers and magazines just 66 percent. Overall, in 1993 the combined print runs of the local press exceeded those of the Russian national publications, although to a large extent this is attributed to the high popularity of cheap or free tabloids containing classified ads and TV listings. Another reason for the stability of the local press, a purely economic one, was their comparatively low distribution costs.

Who Owns the Press?

As was stated above, the press in the USSR was owned by the Soviets, the state apparatus, and public organizations controlled by the Communist Party, by the party directly, or by a combination of these three institutions. With the collapse of communist rule, the Soviets and state bodies became the major owners, especially at the local level. Between themselves they had or shared (usually with journalists) ownership of 2,140 out of a total of 12,000 publications.

Party non-communist press had barely begun in Russia in the early nineties, mostly due to the infancy of the political parties, which began emerging in 1990. Its popularity and circulation were low. In 1993, there were about 200 party papers, twelve of them published in Moscow and eighteen in St. Petersburg. Most of the parties succeeded in publishing just a few issues of their newspapers or newsletters before publication lapses. In a climate of political apathy and distrust for politicians, it was hard to expect growth or stability in the political parties' press.

A rough evaluation of the ownership structure of the Russian press suggests that 29 percent of national newspapers were federally owned, 30 percent belonged to public organizations and parties, and 41 percent were private; 21 percent of regional newspapers were federally owned, while 22 percent were private; as to the municipal press, 85 percent of it was municipally owned, while the rest was private and public. Of all new papers registered in Russia in 1993, 57.1 percent were private property, 23.1 percent belonged to the state (5.8 percent being municipal property), and 19.8 percent were owned by public organizations and political parties. There were no private chains of newspapers or even plans to set them up. Commercial companies and banks were more active in the sphere of broadcasting, although one of them, the Most (Bridge) firm, alongside a major broadcasting company, NTV, ran the popular *Segodnia* (*Today*) newspaper and eventually became a substantial owner of Russian media.

A Prescription to Survive

In 1991, the press went from being a major profit-maker for the Communist Party and the state to becoming a source of serious financial losses. Moreover, the larger the print run a publication had, the heavier the financial loss. The explanation for this lay in skyrocketing printing and newsprint costs and distribution rates, while subscription fees set and paid several months in advance could not cover the unpredictably increased expenses: newspapers were losing money with every additional copy printed. Cautious of the inflation rate, newly bruised editors only allowed subscriptions to be paid six months in advance (in Ukraine it was only three months). Pocketbook considerations caused managers of the publications to begin to look for alternative distribution schemes, better deals with paper producers and printers, cuts in the number of foreign and national correspondents, sublets of their office space, and so forth.

In 1994, the breakdown of production expenses was the following: distribution (32 percent), printing (21 percent), newsprint (20 percent), salary and honoraria (12 percent), office rent, transportation, repairs, stationery, and so forth (11 percent), wire services (4 percent). (These data came from *Moskovskie Novosti* (*Moscow News*) with 240 editorial workers—sixty of them journalists—but the percentages were similar to those of other publications.)

Of the more typical sources of income, advertising made up the biggest share of revenues for major publications. At *Argumenti I Fakti,* for example, advertising income covered 70 percent of all expenses of the newspaper. At *Moskovskie Novosti,* 60 percent of revenues came from ads, while 37 percent more were brought in by subscriptions, and the remaining 3 percent came from street sales. They also started to look for ways to earn money on the side. *Argumenti i Fakti* (*Arguments and Facts*), a weekly, invested its capital, gained at the end of the 1980s, into the construction of brick-producing factories, book publishing, and a telecommunications business in the city of Nizhni Novgorod; it also started to deal in shares and securities. *Pravda* combined its dwindling resources with those of a Greek communist businessman to create a joint-stock company, Pravda International. *Moskovski Komsomolets* (*Moscow Komsomol Member*) created several trade companies with stores of their own, and began to provide high interest loans to different businesses. *Kommersant* (*Businessman*) published its weekly version in English, distributed for hard currency in the United States and among the foreign community inside Russia.

Nezavisimaia Gazeta (*Independent Newspaper*), alongside *Kommersant*, was one of the few Russian publications that still had an English version on sale in the West. That edition maintained a circulation of approximately 40,000 sold for about $2.00 a copy (read mainly by intellectuals and university professors), which brought in much-needed foreign currency. It also ran an advertising agency, RENEZA, which offered Russian companies an opportunity to place their ads in *The Washington Times* for rubles, and NEGA news service, comprised of *Nezavisimaia*'s correspondents and stringers in the ex-USSR. *Ogoniok* (*Little Flame*), the most popular weekly magazine of the glasnost era, launched *The Echo*, the first Russian-British newspaper, run together with a French-British publication *L'Echo*. This commercial venture, dedicated to the spread of the English language among Russians as "a guarantee of a real freedom and success in the West," was designed to back the maternal magazine with its profits.

Izvestiia was among the first publications to do business with a Western press company. Since 1989, it co-ran an advertising agency with the German publisher, Burda Verlag, Burda-Izvestiia. Together with *The Financial Times* of London, *Izvestiia* ran *Finansovie Izvestiia* (*Financial News*) weekly, sharing profits from the ads that foreign firms placed in it. Advertisements seemed to be a major source of revenue for *Izvestiia*; they occupied up to 25 percent of its pages. Finally, *Komsomolskaia Pravda* went even further: it gave up to 43 percent of its space to advertisements. Its innovation (followed by *Argumenti i Fakti, Pravda,* and others), though, lay in the practice of putting local ads into its editions published in various Russian cities and provinces, as well as in Ukraine, Belarus, and Kazakhstan. This way the newspaper attracted local advertisers interested in a targeted audience. By adding local news, television listings, and weather forecasts to these editions, *Komsomolskaia Pravda* gained a significant portion of subscribers.

This list could be extended, but through these examples it is obvious that there was no single prescription for survival. Though all these methods may not have been perfect they permitted presses of different and opposite views to stay afloat on the dwindling information market, letting the audience choose among many sources of news and opinion. For the majority of newspapers and magazines the reason they did not close down during those years lay in the fact that they received government subsidies. Some provincial presses had no business opportunities to pursue and so had no choice but to request government subsidies. Others did not care to pursue business opportunities while subsidies underwrote their bills.

State Subsidies

The issue of subsidies presents the most complex and delicate aspect of the relationship between the state and mass media in Russia. On the one hand, financial reliance of the press on the state gives serious grounds to question political independence of media, their objectivity, and balance of reporting. On the other hand, some say that the press and broadcasting, if viewed not just as political instruments or commercial enterprises, but also as institutions for the cultural and educational benefit of the population, should be able to enjoy the patronage of the state.

Since 1991, distribution subsidies became the main preoccupation of the Russian Ministry of Press and Information, and the first head of the Ministry was Mikhail Poltoranin. Ideally, priority was given to papers for children, disabled persons, national minorities, and literary and cultural magazines. At the same time, by separate decisions of the government, huge donations were given to mass circulation newspapers that were working for the so-called "common information space" in the former Soviet Union, namely *Trud* and *Komsomolskaia Pravda.* Among the criteria for singling out these two publications was the personal preference of President Boris Yeltsin.

Just a few publications, *Moskovskie Novosti*, *Kommersant*, and *Kuranty* among them, categorically rejected any state help on the grounds that "the free press must save itself by its own means." Most newspapers accepted state help, viewing themselves as "indispensable informational and psychological support weapon[s] of the reforms." Faced with a wave of open and covert cries for help, the government was quick to learn that economic pressure provided as effective a tool for control over editorial policies. For example, a source says that *Komsomolskaia Pravda* was "mildly" forced in early 1993 to abandon its year-long practice of monthly front-page interviews with Mikhail Gorbachev by a call from the Ministry of Press and Information. From the beginning, Poltoranin did not hesitate to limit the sphere of state protectionism and material support only to the publications "that work for a rebirth of Russia."

During the brief tenure of Dr. Mikhail Fedotov, one of the authors of the USSR and Russian media laws, as the Minister of Press and Information from December 1992 to August 1993, a transformation of Poltoranin's policy of subsidies was initiated. To begin with, Fedotov declared that budget money would not be given to publications subsidized by private businesses or foreign capital, press digests, religious or commercial newspapers, bulletins of advertisements, or the erotic press. Regarding the local press, the Ministry planned to support just one publication in every area, and that would be the most "important and popular newspaper" of the territory. Preference was to be given in accordance with a petition by the provincial governor and after an accord of the municipal or regional Soviet. The money was to be allocated once for the whole year with advice to secure it by purchasing shares of a printing shop, or by putting it into a local bank. "Thus, the necessity of subsidies will disappear in one or two years . . . . All other local publications must exist by the rules of the market and either be unprofitable or profitable depending on their concept, professionalism, and the financial efficiency of their leaders," outlined a Fedotov report.

Other conditions were implied for those who might have been recipients of budgetary infusions. A publication was required to undergo an audit that might result in compulsory recommendations to cut staff, lease a portion of its editorial offices, and so forth. Only after execution of the advice would a petition for the money be granted. According to estimates, around 200 publications would eventually be granted subsidies under these severe terms.

The exact figures of subsidies from this period are inconsistent. For one thing, they were constantly reviewed due to inflation of just under 1 percent per day. Moreover, different governmental functionaries provide different figures. Also, recipient publications preferred to understate the figures, or to say that they could not get the allocated sums, while their competitors tended to inflate them. For example, the original sum allocated in 1992 for *Izvestiia* was 55 million rubles, but according to its rival *Rossiiskaia Gazeta* it received 858 million rubles that year.

Federal subsidies, which started at several dozen million rubles in 1991, continued on a much larger scale in 1992 and were spread among at least 300 publications, 42 of them local. A report based on data from the Ministry of Press and Information and presented for parliamentary hearings on state policy in the sphere of mass information in the summer of 1992 said that 80 percent of the subsidies were coming from the federal budget, while the remaining 20 percent were taken from local administration sources. The 1992 figure of total subsidies from the national budget was to comprise 5.11 billion rubles, but the projected inflation was expected to increase it to some 9.553 billion rubles. *Moskovskie Novosti* reported that 12.318 billion rubles were allocated for "more than three hundred" publications in 1992, 85 percent of the sum coming from the federal budget, and 15 percent from local budgets.

Other figures for 1992—eight billion rubles for 501 publications—were quoted in a ministerial memorandum prepared a posteriori in early 1993, while the same Ministry's Department for Mass Media spoke of nine billion rubles allocated to 400 newspapers from the federal budget. Thus, the actual figures for 1992 are difficult to determine.

As for the figures for 1993, the federal draft budget prepared by the government in March envisaged federal subsidies for the press in the amount of 11-12 billion rubles, although as much as 54 billion rubles were requested by the Press Ministry to keep print media afloat. During 1993, though with a heavy emphasis on its last two quarters, the Ministry of Finance did provide 24.580 billion rubles (which almost equals the original sum, taking into account the inflation rate) distributed among some 600 publications. In comparison, subsidies to state television in the same year totaled more than 100 billion rubles (about U.S. $90 million).

The Russian government's policy in 1994 did not decrease doubts regarding the desirability of direct state subsidies to the press. More appropriate government actions, as almost everyone from editors to the Minister agreed, would have been unlocking hard currency accounts of newspapers in the state Vnesheconombank (locked there along with other business and private accounts in 1990 due to the shortage of hard currency), providing tax benefits and favorable loans to the press, providing privileged tariffs for the use of telecommunications and postal services, providing privileges in lease holdings, and denationalization and demonopolization of newsprint production, printing, and distribution industries.

Stop the Presses?

Printing plants in Russia in the early nineties were basically museums of newspaper and book production technology because of their obsolete equipment. The technical level of the machinery manufactured in the country for the industry was fifty years behind that of the Western world. Color printing of newspapers and electronic layout were still a novelty for Russian publications. Even that outdated equipment could not satisfy the demand, due to a shortfall of production that reached 42 percent in late 1980s. Half of the types of equipment needed to be imported, and there were never enough dollars for that.

Most of the best printing plants belonged to the state, but they work on a self-accounting basis. Newsprint was purchased by publications directly from paper mills, while inks and other materials were sold through deals between the factory and the editors. After payment of taxes and other bills, the factory spent revenues without state intervention. In most cases, the printing houses and the periodicals did not have common owners, nor did they own one another. While the newspapers were interested in maintaining good relations with the printers, the latter could always switch to producing other printed materials: flyers, booklets, and so forth. Therefore, it was common for editors to receive only a one-week advance notice informing them of a sharp increase in costs for printing services.

The fall in circulation figures inflicted a blow on the printers as well, since it was easier to produce, for example, one million copies of one newspaper than a hundred thousand of copies of each of the ten papers.

Paper Mills: No More a Monopoly

The state of the paper producing plants was even worse than that of the printing shops. Six out of every ten plants were in operation since the turn of the century. Sixty-five percent of the equipment used had exceeded its expected productive life; some of it was installed as part of reparations paid by Germany after World War II and was manufactured as early as 1928. With the largest forests in the world, Russia produces six times less cellulose and eight times less paper than the United States. Until the early nineties, the state supported the price of newsprint. Then the prices became "liberated" (see Table 2). This reversed the situation in the newsprint market from a very high demand to a very low one. The customers of paper producing factories did not want to and could not afford to pay huge sums of money because of bad economic conditions among the populace and a general fall in demand. This situation led the mills to sell as much newsprint as possible abroad for dollars, while the government, inspired by the press, started to raise obstacles on this road to easy profits. In 1993, Russia turned out one million tons of newsprint compared to 1.8 in 1988. The biggest paper mills in Russia—Kondopoga, Solikamsk (both state-owned) and Balakhna (a stock company)—competed to attract orders from different publications. As a result, the hike in newsprint prices was modest compared with that for the distribution and publishing services.

Table 2: Newsprint Price Dynamics (Thousands of rubles per ton)

Price	**1990**	**1991**	**Jan. 1992**	**May 1992**	**Nov. 1992**	**Apr. 1993**	**Aug. 1993**	**Jan. 1994**
State wholesale	0.29	0.88	4.2	n/a	n/a	n/a	n/a	n/a
Market deals	n/a	5-7	12-20	15-20	25-30	78	100	300

Distribution System: On the Road to Collapse

National distribution of the press in Russia was a monopoly. It belonged to *Rospechat* (*Russia Press*), a semi-independent agency under the Ministry of Communication. Its predecessor in USSR times, *Soiuzpechat* (*Union Press*), had at the peak of its activity in the 1980s 833 small shops, 37,700 newsstands and kiosks, and 9,900 newspaper vending machines to sell publications in the Soviet Union. It sold and provided subscriptions to almost every newspaper, magazine, and journal, using its branches in every district of the country and every post office nation-wide (about 47,000 in 1993). *Rospechat* was also a major publisher of catalogues of publications. Naturally, it had profound expertise, advanced computing machinery, and facilities to do its business. As a monopoly, the agency dictated the sum taken from the publications for distribution both by subscription and street sales. This commission amounted to 73 percent of the selling price of a publication for the second half of 1993, having risen from

52 percent in the first half of that year and from 20 percent just a couple of years before that. The cost of the press for subscribers in 1993 grew 26.5 times compared to the end of 1992, or 90 times compared to 1991. According to *Obshchaia Gazeta* (*Common Newspaper*), the dynamics of the subscription rates in 1993 outstripped those of per capita income, minimum wage, exchange rate, and other economic indicators.

Editors vigorously protested against such "robbery" by petitioning the government with requests to tamper with the agency, or to underwrite the publications' expenses. In rare cases they tried to establish distribution companies of their own. Although at the local level some publications did succeed in street sales and subscriptions, at the national level they did not have the resources even to start such a business. This was no wonder, since a calculation of the sum necessary to create an alternative agency, done in the summer of 1991, totaled 11 billion rubles, U.S. $400 million at the then rate of exchange.

When called upon to respond, *Rospechat* explained the high tariffs for its services by citing increased rent for its branch premises, transportation costs, electricity bills, and so forth. The just argument here was that *Rospechat*, viewed by the state bodies as an ordinary business enterprise, paid for all its services at the same tariffs as, for example, a profitable restaurant or a hotel for foreign tourists.

In the early nineties three categories of publications seemed capable of weathering the storm. They were small-scale local (mainly municipal) newspapers that were not engaged in wide distribution schemes, or could develop their own tiny agencies, large newspaper companies that were able to attract nation-wide (ex-USSR) readership and could recover the losses by making profits in other spheres of the economy, by selling their pages to foreign advertisers, by means of joint ventures with foreign companies, or by successfully selling their editions abroad, and governmental, parliamentary, or local administration publications that could survive with the help of budgetary money.

News Agencies

Until the early 1990s the system of news agencies in the USSR consisted of TASS (Telegraph Agency of the Soviet Union) with its 14 subsidiaries in the Union republics, and Novosti Press Agency. By the mid 1990s, Russia alone had 400 news agencies. TASS, with the collapse of the USSR, became the Information Telegraph Agency of Russia, ITAR-TASS, keeping the TASS abbreviation as a familiar trademark only. For decades following its 1925 founding, TASS was under the jurisdiction of the Council of Ministers of the USSR, later under the USSR President, who appointed his former press-secretary Vitali Ignatenko as its director general in 1991. At its peak in the mid-1980s, TASS had bureaus and correspondents in 110 foreign countries (later in just 75 countries), and was the main information source for the Soviet people on life abroad and on domestic affairs; it was one of the "Big Five" world agencies. At that time TASS had a staff of almost 5,000 workers, one-fifth of them journalists.

As the 1990s progressed the financial deficit led ITAR-TASS to cut its workforce to about 3,500, of which 900 are journalists, including 115 working abroad. ITAR had three regional branches, in St. Petersburg, Vladivostok, and Khabarovsk, as well as numerous bureaus all over Russia and the republics of the former Soviet Union. It had 120 clients in foreign countries and sold its services to every state TV and radio company and to the majority of national and regional publications inside Russia. It remained the semi-official outlet used by the Russian government to make its views known to the world public, as well as to distribute official documents.

Before 1991, Novosti, created as a public company in 1961 to "sell" the Soviet Union to foreign countries, published propaganda magazines (as many as 29 monthlies, 7 bimonthlies, and 10 weeklies), brochures, and books in 34 foreign languages for distribution in 125 countries of the world. Then, in July of 1990, Boris Yeltsin, the new chairman of Russia's legislature, suggested that *Novosti* be put under the control of the republican parliament and re-organized as a champion of liberal forces. In response, President Mikhail Gorbachev initiated a series of transformations of the agency, putting it under different jurisdictions, splitting it, merging it with other media outlets, and so forth. Due to economic pressures, the agency also suffered from the closure of most of its bureaus abroad, including those in the former Soviet republics. The dwindling company became the Russian Information Agency ("RIA") Novosti, which was under the direct control of the Kremlin. RIA provided more news on business affairs, entertainment, arts, culture, and sports. However, those attempts to break from old propaganda did not prevent a substantial loss in the number of subscribers. In subscribers RIA fell far behind TASS, its only state competitor.

The obvious leader among the non-state agencies is Interfax. Founded in September of 1989 as a faxed bulletin of Moscow Radio and *Interkvadro*, a Soviet-French-Italian joint venture, Interfax was re-registered as a news agency after the breakup of the international venture in October 1990. It became a closed stock company chaired and directed by Mikhail Komissar, a former radio correspondent and engineer. Although on the surface Interfax was known for its political news and scoops, its business and economic information distributed in Russian and English was valued the most. In 1994, it ran 21 periodical bulletins of general and business news with a staff of 220 employees (sixty to eighty of whom are journalists) at its Moscow headquarters and 200 more elsewhere in the former Soviet Union. With some sixty foreign subscribers, it expanded and had business affiliates in London (Interfax-Europe), Denver, Colorado (Interfax-USA), as well as news affiliates Interfax-Ukraine in Kiev and Baltfax (a joint company with the Baltic News Service) in Tallinn. It also planned to open affiliates: Interfax-Asia in Almaty and Tashkent, Interfax-Siberia in Novosibirsk, Interfax-Far East in Vladivostok, and Interfax-Belarus in Minsk.

Most of the new wire services were non-state, their common peculiar feature being an almost total dependence on Western subscribers due to an inflated exchange rate: even a small fee paid in dollars allowed them to cover expenses and gain strength. Until the end of the 1980s there were no provincial news agencies in Russia. In the 1990s they appeared and died at a high frequency, although some became well established: Severo-zapad (North-West) in St. Petersburg, Ural-accept in Yekaterinburg, and Sibinform in

Novosibirsk. Usually created by a group of newsmen from a local paper, they tried to serve the world with information from their regions. However, unless their region was a conflict area, it was hard for them to find clients rich enough to pay for the services. Among obstacles to the growth of provincial news agencies were bad communication lines with the outside world; a demand for "packaged information," not just news from Nagorno-Karabakh or Abkhazia; and lack of expertise or trustworthiness on their side.

In the last years of the 1980s the Russian press gained a level of freedom unprecedented in its almost three-centuries-long history; some analysts even call the *perestroika* years its "golden age." But, since 1990, circumstances for the print media have worsened owing to economic pressure and their growing dependence on government subsidies. By the mid-1990s, only a handful of publications had obtained financial independence from the state or politically biased groups that viewed them (in the old tradition of the country) as pipelines to the public and tools of political control. The task of constructing and strengthening democratic society, a prerequisite for real and lasting freedom, was more responsible and consequential than that of overturning the communist machine. This task seemed to be the biggest challenge for Russian journalists during the turbulent 1990s. With 59 percent of the population reading newspapers every day (compared with 61 percent listening to the radio and 86 percent watching television) their target was within reach.

The following articles address whether we shall remain as proud of our press as we were during the "golden age."

After the Bloodshed: Survey of the Russian Press from 1993 to 1995*

Jamey Gambrell

In the two years after the bloodshed of October 1993, when anti-Yeltsin factions backed by Vice President Alexander Rutskoi attempted to take over the Ostankino television station by force and Yeltsin's own government imposed temporary censorship on Moscow newspapers, the Russian press continued to be the subject of major political battles.[1] In the wake of the December 1993 elections, the nightly news produced by government-owned television became noticeably more tendentious in its coverage of government policies; both left and right regularly denounced the press for "destabilizing" the political situation in the country. Defamation suits against journalists and papers became the harassment of choice by political opponents (Vladimir Zhirinovsky, an ultra-nationalist and head of the Liberal Democratic Party, for instance, filed over one hundred such suits), and accusations of editorial corruption and irresponsible reporting are heard from all sides of the political spectrum, as well as from inside journalistic ranks.[2]

While some Moscow papers prospered with independence, many publications staved off bankruptcy only by virtue of government subsidies. On the other hand, continuing government monopolies, particularly in distribution networks, made the cost of shipping prohibitive, leading to a severe decline in the subscription lists of the central papers and to a consequent loss of income. More often than not local authorities still directed the provincial press. These authorities often controlled a paper's access to offices, printing presses, and even bank accounts. The occupation of journalist became more and more dangerous: seven journalists were killed in the October 1993 events.

* 13 Cardozo Arts & Entertainment Law Journal 781 (1995).

[1] This article is an updated version of an essay originally written in the fall of 1994. Since then, the bureaucratic reorganization of government structures dealing with the press continued. The most controversial of these was the "privatization" of Ostankino, the first channel of Russian television, which still reaches most parts of the former Soviet Union. In late 1994, President Yeltsin, by decree, transformed Ostankino into Public Russian Television (known as "ORT" after its Russian acronym). A substantial minority interest was transferred to a consortium of Russian banks, while the majority was split between the government and Goskomimushchestvo. Vladislav Listyev was appointed to head the new company, and it was widely believed that his decision to suspend, temporarily, all advertising on ORT, led to his assassination. In any event, heated protests were organized against the new company, and the Duma tried several times, unsuccessfully, to override the decree and pass legislation regulating the privatization of state mass media. On June 7, 1995, Yeltsin vetoed Duma and Federation Council legislation annulling ORT; subsequently Duma deputies sought relief from the Constitutional Court. On November 4, 1995, however, the saga appeared to come to an end when the Constitutional Court refused to hear the Duma's challenge to the decree.

[2] Zhirinovsky won a suit against Egor Gaidar, Member of Parliament and former Prime Minister of the Russian Federation, who referred to him as a "fascist" in *Izvestiia*.

Journalists' vulnerability to the growing reach of politically and economically motivated crime was tragically illustrated on October 17, 1994, when Dmitrii Kholodov, a twenty-seven-year-old reporter for *Moskovskii Komsomolets*, who was investigating corruption in the military, was killed by a bomb blast. Seven months later, the nationally known television journalist Vladislav Listyev was gunned down in front of his apartment building on March 1, 1995, shortly after he was appointed head of the newly organized Public Russian Television station.

Yeltsin's administration's failure to articulate and implement in legislation a consistent press policy kept much of the press in economic limbo, left the door wide open for political manipulation of press issues, and seemed to reflect a deep philosophical unwillingness to fully relinquish the old Soviet controls. Between the fall of the Soviet Union in 1991 and 1995, the press ministry was reorganized and renamed a number of times, and there had been a succession of "ministers." But the bureaucratic reshuffling of ministries and organizations charged with "curating" the media did little to ensure the independence of the Russian press. Crucial issues—like the licensing of television and radio frequencies and the privatization of government printing presses and radio and television stations—remained unresolved. In fact, as the December 1995 parliamentary and June 1996 presidential elections approached, it seemed clear that the issue of the press's "independence" was being used by liberals and conservatives alike to further their own immediate political agendas.

One such shuffle—exemplary in nature—came after the virtual defeat of Russia's Choice in the 1993 elections. The Yeltsin government dissolved the Information Ministry of the Russian Federation (temporarily headed during the elections by Vladimir Shumeiko, former Chairman to the Federation Council, or Russian senate) and distributed its previous management and regulatory functions between two non-ministerial level organizations: the Federal Service on Radio and Television Broadcasting, headed by Yegor Yakovlev (who was also named to head the state television company Ostankino in the wake of the October 1993 events), and Roskompechat (the Press Committee of the Russian Federation), headed by Boris Mironov. In addition, the special Arbitration Tribunal established to resolve media disputes and monitor press coverage of the 1993 elections was formalized as a part of the president's administration and was renamed the Presidential Judicial Chamber for Information Disputes. After the December elections, the Press Committee was charged with overseeing the periodical print media and textbook publishing, managing government-owned printing presses, distributing government subsidies to newspapers and journals, and dealing with violations of the Press Law.

In 1994, as the summer lull in Russian politics came to an end, conflicts over the role and status of the press and its relationship to the government hit the front page once again. On September 2, 1994, Yeltsin signed a decree firing Boris Mironov, Chairman of the Press Committee. Mironov was not well known to the journalistic community at the time of his appointment. A *Pravda* employee for many years, he had served as a consultant for the Ministry of Press and Information under former minister Mikhail

Poltoranin, and had most recently been director of the government publishing company Russian Book. He was known to be a protegé of Poltoranin, a member of Russia's Choice who was chairman of the Duma's Press and Information Committee (indeed, Poltoranin was the model for the hero of a novel Mironov wrote). In meetings with journalists, and in a series of interviews and articles, Mironov's chauvinistic views soon gave the liberal press cause for alarm. Furthermore, his clear reluctance to issue warnings to nationalist-oriented and anti-Semitic newspapers for blatant violations of article 4 of the Russian Mass Media law (which forbids "fomenting ethnic hatred") created serious conflicts within the committee itself. Protests over his appointment began to sound almost immediately.

Tensions escalated dramatically through 1994. In June, apparently in response to reproaches from nationalist colleagues, Mironov published a lengthy manifesto in the official government paper *Rossiiskaia Gazeta*, titled *Russia Yearns for Ideals*. In convoluted language that tellingly combined old Soviet denunciatory rhetoric with the humiliated and injured tropes of the new Russian nationalism, Mironov called for a new state ideology based on "the Orthodox faith, conscience, and loyalty to Russia" that would be capable of keeping a "perfected" Russia on the true path and preventing her from being "buffeted by the troubled sea of political passions." Claiming that journalists had forgotten their "duty to bring the reader peace and wisdom," he stated:

> [U]nder the slogan of the press's "democraticness," a frenzied licentiousness and permissiveness is developing . . . the journalist is appointed to carry the word through newspapers, radio, and television, but this does not mean that he is allowed to use this word to create evil, moral oppression in society, divisiveness, and malice . . . to sow rumor and spread calumny, destroy the stability of the state, the symbols of whose strength and unity are the Coat of Arms, the Anthem, the Flag, and the President.

In Mironov's view the press and politicians refused to leave the government in peace to get on with its work, and the government must take steps accordingly:

> The state must—and herein lies its obligation to society—defend itself, from the moral terror of newspapers, radio, and television . . . . It is obliged in the name of strengthening the state, protecting the nation, to demand that its citizens [take responsibility] for the consequences of their actions, and journalists can be no exception.

This declaration did not go unnoticed by the press: Viktor Loshak, editor of the *Moscow News* wrote, for example, that

> in Mironov's writings "Pravda" jumps out in every line. He doesn't confer, share or inform—he insists: Russia must, the people must, Russians need . . . the author is a professional lover of the Motherland, and like every patriot who's managed to scramble his way to the platform, he knows precisely what program will save the people.

Though rumors of Mironov's imminent dismissal began to circulate after this article appeared, he remained in place throughout the summer of 1994. In mid-July, the Judicial Chamber for Information Disputes requested that the Press Committee issue warnings against a number of right-wing nationalist papers for publications violating article 4 (after two such warnings a paper could be closed by the courts, though was rarely enforced).[12] Mironov was traveling at the time, and the warnings were issued by one of his deputies, Sergei Gryzunov. According to Gryzunov, Mironov was furious and asked him to resign; Gryzunov refused and called instead for Mironov's resignation.

Then, in August, on a tour of the provinces, Mironov made a series of inflammatory statements to regional newspaper editors that eventually made their way back to the Moscow press. In Stavropol, Kazan, and Orenburg, he called for rigorous control of the press and government appointment of provincial editors, saying that it was "natural" for editors to be "called on the carpet" by government officials. "We were unpardonably early in rejecting the words that the newspaper is the collective agitator, the propagandist and the organizer—they are more pertinent now than ever before," Mironov said, paraphrasing Lenin's views on the press. In Orenburg, he was reported as saying that "if Russian nationalism is fascism, then I'm a fascist."

The liberal press reacted with an unusually coordinated campaign: virtually all of the major newspapers (with the exception of *Komsomolskaia Pravda* and *Trud*) published attacks on Mironov almost simultaneously. The *Moscow News* ran his photo on the cover under the headline "The Fascist Minister in Chernomyrdin's Government,"[15] and *Moskovskii Komsomolets*' front page juxtaposed Mironov's statements with quotes from Hitler under the banner "Hello, Doctor Goebbels." In a front page editorial *Segodnia* editor Dmitrii Ostalsky wrote that "when something is said by a minister of a government that pretends to be one of the first liberal (at least democratic) governments, and this "something" more closely resembles Hitler's speeches . . . then either the government should resign, or the minister."[16] Yeltsin's decree firing Mironov was signed on September 2, 1994.[17]

---

[12] The Judicial Chamber could make its own findings and recommendations in disputes, request that the Press Committee issue warnings, or refer a case to the prosecutor. It only considered press disputes when the "social good" was at stake, i.e., it did not handle most defamation suits. While in theory it was an innovative and needed institution, and indeed served a fruitful purpose during the December elections, it had insufficient legal status to enforce its decisions, and its actual effect on journalistic practice was unclear. *Rossiiskaia Gazeta* was required to publish its decisions, but the conservative editorial staff regularly published them side by side with tendentious, mocking replies. President Putin dissolved the Judicial Chamber in June 2000.

[15] Technically speaking, Mironov did not have minister status and was not in the cabinet, since the Russian Press Committee, successor to the Press Ministry, was not a cabinet post.

[16] The escalation of the Mironov scandal coincided with an international conference on the role of the press in a democratic society co-hosted by the Ministry of Foreign Affairs and the European Council. Print and television coverage of the conference emphasized that the existence of an independent press was one of the main criteria for Russian admission to the Council, which may have had something to do with

The firing of Mironov marked the first time that a concerted press effort succeeded in pressuring the government into removing a cabinet-level functionary. All sense of elation on the part of the liberal press, however, was tempered by the fact that one of Mironov's personally chosen deputy ministers, Vladimir Volodin, who was believed to hold similar views, was appointed acting chairman. Like Mironov, Volodin was also once a member of Poltoranin's staff, and, as an article in the English-language *Moscow Times* remarked, "all trails in this story lead back to . . . Mikhail Poltoranin." As Evgeny Kiselev noted in his prestigious weekly news program "Itogi" on NTV:

> [we must not] rush to the conclusion that the press has finally acquired the strength of a fourth estate . . . in the wake of Mironov's resignation, a fierce struggle for his chair will ensue, all the more so since there exists a project to merge the Press Committee and the Federal Agency for TV and Radio Broadcasting into a single, powerful agency, such as was the Ministry of Press and Information under Poltoranin . . . [who may be] one of the main pretenders to the leadership position of the new agitprop.[19]

Press commentary generally agreed that the Mironov affair was symbolic of a greater power struggle—both among concrete political figures and factions, as well as on a larger, philosophical level. "Mironov was the incarnation of certain powers," said Gryzunov, "the so-called 'patriots' and supporters of Russian 'statehood.' He simply overstepped certain boundaries." "Why did the press minister and those who are with him need an agitprop machine?" asked *Moscow News* in its attack on Mironov, "Isn't it so that when the elections come it will all go like clockwork?" "Everything that's happened [with the press] in recent days," said Gryzunov at a press conference held to discuss the Mironov affair shortly after the minister's firing, "has to be seen in the light of the 1996 pre-election campaign, which has already started." Anatoly Vengerov, Chairman of the Judicial Chamber, and others pointed out, "the problem of the leadership of the Press Committee arose long before Mironov was appointed. It reflects a crisis in support and subsidies for the mass media."

Mironov's dismissal. The Council declined to admit Russia in early October, however, citing widespread human rights abuses by the police and bad prison conditions.

[17] Mironov was succeeded by Gryzunov who held the office until mid-1995 when he was followed by Ivan Laptev. Gryzunov, among other things, was a critic of the government's handling of the Chechen crisis, a fact that did not endear him to the government.

[19] Kiselev and many others saw the Mironov affair as resulting from Mikhail Poltoranin's attempts to raise his status with Yeltsin after the December elections by "building a bridge" between the nationalists and reformers. Kiselev went on in his "Itogi" commentary to detail Poltoranin's connections to Mironov, and recall the controversy last spring over anti-Semitic remarks made by Poltoranin in two interviews, one on Russian TV and the other with the Jordanian newspaper *Ar-Rai*. Among other things, Poltoranin apparently characterized the language of the independent Russian press as "labor-camp Hebrew" and told the Jordanian correspondent that a Zionist lobby was trying to isolate Yeltsin from the people and control the mass media in Russia. According to "Itogi," the interview was published in *Ar-Rai* on March 29, 1994.

This statement was made during a time when the majority of the most prestigious Moscow papers—including *Izvestiia*, *Moskovskii Komsomolets*, *Moskovskie Novosti*, and *Argumenti i Fakti*—were not receiving subsidies (*Kommersant* and *Segodnia* have always been financed by private capital). However, government subsidies were not a thing of the past. According to Gryzunov, who headed Roskompechat's Subsidy Distribution Committee, for the second half of 1994 the government allocated 111.4 billion rubles (approximately $50 million).[24] Theoretically, subsidies were given only to money-losing papers; priority was given to special interests such as children's literature, pensioners, veterans, and invalids. Publications of political parties were not eligible for funds. Nonetheless, half of the above-mentioned sum went to support a small number of government papers like *Rossiiskaia Gazeta*, *Rossiiskie Vesti*, and the magazine *Rossiia*; the remainder was divided up among 800 newspapers and 300 journals.

In the wake of Mironov's firing, debate over the press crisis shifted focus to several major pieces of long-pending legislation on the financing, regulation, and privatization of the print press, radio, and television. Attempts to settle the tangled property legacy of the Soviet past and stabilize the precarious economic position of the press, seemed increasingly to be guided by the political considerations of the moment. In the summer of 1994, the Duma passed a prescriptive draft law—sponsored by Poltoranin's Committee on Information Policy—that would have regulated both the quantity and quality of radio and television coverage of government activity.[26] The law detailed the number of minutes government-owned stations would be required to devote to presidential decrees and Duma activities, and forbade any commentary on them. It would, in effect, have established a potential censorship mechanism and thus met with wide protest in liberal journalistic circles.

But attached to the Duma's first version of this draft was an amendment to the existing Press Law forbidding government organizations from serving as founders of periodical publications—a measure that liberal defenders of press freedom in Russia considered crucial if the press was to become truly independent.[28] The Federation Council (the upper chamber of Russian Parliament, which was chaired by Russia's Choice representative Vladimir Shumeiko) immediately voted down the draft law, not, it is thought, because the Council objected to the attack on press freedoms, but because the ban would have restricted the present government's influence on the print media. In the provinces, the local administrations and president-appointed governors, mindful of elections at all times, largely control the press.

---

[24] Subsidy Distribution Committee members included, among others, Konstantin Bogdanov, head of the Journalists Union; Yassen Zassoursky, dean of the journalism school at Moscow State University; and Vyacheslav Kostikov, who was Yeltsin's press secretary at that time.

[26] The draft law also regulated the amount of space that could be devoted to advertising in the print media.

[28] Mikhail Fedotov originally proposed these measures during his short tenure as Press Minister; Fedotov was removed as Press Minister after lobbying by the regional press, and Mikhail Poltoranin was installed in his place.

In October 1994, however, the Duma garnered the two-thirds vote necessary to override the Council's veto, and sent the amendment regarding government founding of the press straight to Yeltsin for his signature. It seemed clear that the Duma was not motivated by an overwhelming love for freedom of speech either, but that the anti-Yeltsin majority saw the ban on government-sponsored print media as an opportunity to limit the Yeltsin administration's access to the press. In response to the Duma's action, Vladimir Shumeiko wrote to Yeltsin, urging him to veto the bill. According to *Rossiiskaia Gazeta*, "Shumeiko feels that today . . . a rejection of government participation [in the press] would open the door to the destruction of the Russian information system and facilitate the transfer of the mass media to the control of representatives of the shadow economy."[29]

The situation also revealed contradictions within the Yeltsin administration. For all intents and purposes, it in effect advocated a government-controlled press. In the most generous interpretation, the administration gave extremely mixed signals regarding freedom of the press. In early October 1994, Yeltsin's chief of staff, Sergei Filatov, met with the President's regional envoys to discuss the inability of provincial media to properly explain government policies. Russian television coverage noted that "[i]n view of the forthcoming elections, the participants felt also that it would be appropriate to transfer control over the media's financial resources from the governors to the president's representatives." On January 13, 1995, President Yeltsin signed into law the statute On Rules for Coverage by State Mass Media of the Activity of Bodies of State Power, which includes duties imposed on state-owned media to disseminate reports by various officials and government agencies.

Another major piece of legislation being discussed at that time in the Parliament caused even more uproar, and engendered numerous counter proposals. The draft law on "Government Support of the Mass Media,"[32] proposed by the Duma's Informational Policy Committee (headed by former press minister Mikhail Poltoranin) sought to eliminate the system of government subsidy by providing substantial tax breaks for the press. But it also wanted to regulate the "privatization" of the major printing presses (which were still federal government property): fifty-one percent of the stocks would remain the property of the federal government; twenty percent would be sold to workers of the printing presses; and twenty-nine percent would be divided proportionate to usage among the newspaper and publishing collectives that had used the presses for at least three years.[33]

---

[29] During his brief tenure as Press Minister, Shumeiko advocated a "new state ideology" and said that there was no censorship during the October events, but that Moscow papers were just looking for publicity.

[32] The draft law, O Gosudarstvennoi Podderzhke Sredstv Massovoi Informatsii Rossiiskoi Federatsii, was published in *Rossiiskaia Gazeta* on June 18, 1994.

[33] The scheme was much the same for radio and television, though the division of stocks differed somewhat.

Some of these provisions—particularly the tax breaks—were long called for by journalists as an alternative to government subsidy that would place all publications on an equal footing. Many observers argued that ownership of offices and at least partial ownership of printing presses needed to be transferred to newspapers if they were to survive independently. In the provinces, in particular, local papers are often housed in the offices of the local administration, and thus were easily subject to political blackmail. Furthermore, given the small advertising market and high transportation costs, newspapers were generally unprofitable; printing presses, however, made a handsome profit on commercial work, and thus could subsidize otherwise unprofitable newspapers.

But one section of the draft law created enormous controversy. It provided for the creation of a "super-fund," a National Fund for the Development of the Mass Media. This fund was to be managed by an "oversight committee" created and appointed by the Federation Council, the Duma, and the President, which would in turn appoint a director and a board to run it. According to the published text of the draft law, "government means of mass communication" would be "turned over to the foundation for management," as would the fifty-one percent of stocks remaining in government hands after "privatization" of printing presses. The National Fund would have the right to form commercial subsidiaries, invest in other businesses, accept budgetary funds from the government, and found its own banks. The oversight committee would be responsible for issuing credits to publications, printing presses, and radio and TV stations, and for distributing financial aid to the press. Furthermore, all government orders would be negotiated through the Fund, which would give it a huge potential for indirect subsidy through economic favoritism.

The draft law made no mention of including journalists or other non-governmental professionals on the oversight committee or board, nor did it spell out the mechanisms and criteria by which "financial aid" would be awarded to the press. This law would have, in effect, institutionalized a new version of state capitalism by commercializing the function of a press ministry, and blurring the still fragile boundaries between the private and public sector, and financial and political interests. Many critics called it "a monster monopoly" that would have created a press ministry with wide ranging leverage over newspapers, television, and radio. It also would have resulted in a press with a vested financial interest in dependence on the government.

The lower chamber of the parliament (the Duma) supported the law, though it, too, was vetoed by the Federation Council; and it was widely thought that Yeltsin would not have signed it even if it had passed both houses. Opposition to Poltoranin's draft law spawned numerous counter projects, however none of them questioned the very principle of government funding for the press.

Some voices spoke out for a different approach, however, though few politicians or journalists addressed the issue as directly as the vastly popular weekly *Argumenti i Fakti* ("*AiF*") did in its front-page editorial on the Mironov affair: "What Do We Need a Press Ministry for?" In bold-face type *AiF* declared that "[i]n order for the press to become genuinely independent, it doesn't need handouts in the form of subsidies, which thinly disguise the desire to keep the press on a hook," but tax breaks and other favorable conditions. "By the way," the editorial continued (also in bold type), "press ministries exist only in third world countries, where the governments keep vigilant control over the mass media. In civilized countries there are no such institutions, just as there are no government newspapers." In the newspaper *Segodnia*, Mikhail Leontiev, noting the recurrent efforts of a series of press ministers to bring both print and electronic press under one institutional roof, argued that the press ministry should in fact be a "Ministry of Privatization of the Mass Media, whose goal would be to prepare and carry out a mission of self-destruction in a relatively short period, for example, to liquidate both the parasitical institute of official media, as well as the office that controls them." Analyzing the situation, Evgeny Kiselev pointed out, however, that,

> The political establishment still thinks it should control the mass media. But they can't say it quite so openly . . . . Mironov did and he was "punished"—but another person in his position might be trickier, more circumspect . . . . It's a particularly Russian phenomena—whether people are liberal or not, they will think ten times before letting go of the media. Regardless of party affiliation—everyone from Communists to anti-Communists wants to have a "pocket press."

The greatest battles, however, were waged over government monopolies and the regulation of the electronic media. Though the Press Law of 1990 called for the creation of a licensing commission, by mid-1995 this crucial institutional mechanism had not yet been established, and a series of stop-gap measures further confused the legal situation. As a result, according to Alexei Simonov of the Glasnost Defense Fund, and former chairperson of one such temporary committee, no licenses had been granted for over a year, and there was a backlog of nearly a thousand applications. Even ORT and RTV, the two main government channels, do not hold proper licenses. And the position of the ambitious, private station NTV was still far from secure. Again, with the 1996 elections approaching, these issues only grew in importance, since unlicensed channels were more vulnerable to political pressure and reprisals from local and federal authorities, as well as to law suits from candidates unhappy with their coverage. Furthermore, a system of double licensing of frequencies existed, whereby two licenses were granted by separate agencies for the same frequency: one to the programmer and one to the owner of the broadcasting equipment. It was hardly surprising to learn that the Ministry of Communications, which issues the licenses to equipment owners, itself owned approximately ninety-five percent of the broadcasting equipment in the country.[38]

[38] The situation with the Ministry of Communications is further complicated by the fact that Ostankino (ORT), Russian TV, and other programmers owed the ministry over 410.5 billion rubles (approximately $205,250,000 at that time) as of September 1, 1994. The Ministry has been regularly threatening to block transmission of everything but news programs on government television if the debt is not paid immediately in full. Both government television and independent television have complained that the Ministry's monopoly on transmission has led them to charge exorbitant, unfair rates.

Against this background of legal, regulatory, and economic chaos, the potential for manipulation of the media—particularly television—by criminal and political interests had everyone worried. Corruption and ethical misconduct on the part of journalists was a growing problem—particularly in television, where fee-skimming, "hidden advertising," conflicts of interest and kickbacks, among other things, were rampant. The Ostankino and RTV nightly news programs, for instance, often included short subjects on businesses that smacked of advertising—but it was nearly impossible to prove such claims.[39] Furthermore, the political and economic perils posed by the lack of advertising regulation became abundantly clear in the summer of 1994 when the MMM pyramid scheme collapsed, causing tens of thousands to lose their savings.[40] (Russia had no "truth in advertising" laws at that time, though a draft law on advertising was being considered by the Duma).[Ed1]

Unfortunately, the debate on issues of corruption and government control of the press was often clouded by warring political interests: there was much dark talk of the "shadow economy" taking over media (as in Shumeiko's statement above), but what was meant by such phrases usually depended on the political affiliations of the accuser. Communist and nationalist factions, for instance, generally lumped all private capital—the new, powerful Russian banks and oil companies—together with criminal "mafia interests." Many journalists from reformist oriented papers accused their privately financed—and much better paid—competitors of being "bought" by "big capital," though the problem with journalistic corruption is hardly limited to privately held papers.[41] Most

---

[39] This was a big issue during the campaign leading up to the 1993 elections as well; many newspapers, in search of income, added to the blurring of editorial and advertising material by printing paid-for interviews with candidates.

[40] MMM's wildly popular, brilliant ads, produced in the form of a mini-soap opera, had convinced millions of people to invest their money in the firm. When the company's director Sergei Mavrodi was arrested, the ads continued on television for quite some time; irate MMM stockholders demonstrated throughout Moscow, and eventually formed a political party, which demanded that the government reimburse them for the loss of their stocks' value, free Mavrodi, and resign. On October 2, 1994, a group of MMM stockholders marched to the White House—under green banners—a hundred or so yards behind nationalist and communist contingents in the demonstrations held to mark the first anniversary of the October 1994 events. Mavrodi was released from prison (still uncharged) in early October because he had filed as a candidate for the Duma and Russian law gave both candidates and elected officials immunity from prosecution; he was elected to the Duma at the end of October, apparently with some support from Zhirinovsky's party.

[Ed1] Decree No. 1183 On Consumer Protection Against Unfair Advertising was passed on June 10, 1994.

[41] This accusation is, in conversation at least, most frequently lodged against the prestigious independent television company NTV and the newspaper *Segodnia*, which are financed largely by Most Bank. Most Bank, owned by businessman Vladimir Gusinsky, is closely connected to Moscow Mayor Yuri Luzhkov. It is a widely recognized, but unwritten, rule among Moscow papers that while Yeltsin and the federal government may be criticized freely, Luzhkov cannot be touched—otherwise the paper may find its lease suddenly canceled, or its rent quadrupled, since the municipal government still controls Moscow real estate. Kiselev, however, in responding to these accusations in an interview with me, said: "We run a news program. We need events and facts, not rumors. If we have an event, we will cover it."

people felt that, ultimately, the impetus for responsible journalism needed to come from individual journalists themselves.[42] In the Russian atmosphere at the time, however, one often heard not only right-wing nationalists, but also die-hard liberals come to the paradoxical conclusion that only government control could guarantee the freedom and honesty of the press. However, as Alexei Simonov, head of the Glasnost Defense Fund, remarked, "whenever you've got a center that has influence on the press, we have not left the USSR far behind."

When Gusinsky's bodyguards were attacked in December 1994 by members of Yeltsin's special guard, the political purpose of the attack was generally seen as two-fold: a warning to Gusinsky, because of NTV's daring coverage, and a warning to Luzhkov, who was believed to have presidential ambitions.

[42] The 27 journalists who founded the Moscow Journalists' Charter last year, for instance, all signed a declaration of journalistic ethics. The Moscow Charter has received seed funds from George Soros to implement a program of practical money to journalists: the members themselves receive no aid, but have established a program that includes buying bullet-proof vests for journalists working in "hot spots"; purchasing subscriptions to Reuter's or Interfax news agency and the TASS data bank for provincial papers that cannot afford it; financial aid to journalists injured in the line of duty; and, eventually—they hope, an independent analysis of the accuracy of Moscow's polling institutes. The Charter is also fund-raising for these programs among Moscow businessmen.

II.

Freedom of Speech and Democracy

Law, Force, and the Russian Media*

Monroe E. Price

Introduction

Looking at the development of mass media law in post-Soviet Russia is like examining the wrists of a recently freed prisoner where the marks of the chains are still present. The very claims for freedom and the guarantees of change bespeak past injustices and old allocations of power. In the short period that has transpired, issues of law in the defining of communication have already had a dramatic cycle: the rule of law has been followed by the assertion of military force and bloodshed, and force, in its turn, has been followed again by a clumsy reaffirmation of law. Television has been an arena for bitter struggle, political and armed. In this context, the evolution of rules for the organization and governance of the press has reflected changes in political and economic powers in a society seeking definition and stability. The forms of a media law—its words, its constructions, its hermeneutics—cannot be understood without its embedded context. Like other laws, those concerning broadcasting can be studied like shards from an archeological site, as clues to the nature of their social and political origins.

In conducting this inquiry, the problem of defining independence is approached from different vantage points. The formal language of statutes and judicial decisions cannot be understood without some insight into the historic origin of words and concepts. These transition states have a specific legacy in which a complex terminology and elaborate doctrine have had extraordinary sway; some familiarity with that legacy is necessary to understand the transfer of mind to a new set of jurisprudential expectations. In addition, the turbulent aspect of inventing independence is a human function as well as a legal one; some insight into the aspirations, motivations, and capacities of those who have been pioneers of independence is essential. All media transitions build not only on the innovators, but on those who were previously in control, the existing pool of journalists, and the existing journalistic tradition. An important aspect of these processes of law reform is the effort by Western entities—governments, foundations, private entrepreneurs—to expend passion, treasure, and talent to further the concept of independence. It will be useful, in understanding the evolution of media law in the transition states, to have a greater grasp of the objectives and efforts of these doctors of free speech.

In the Republics of the former Soviet Union, declarations of media independence proliferate at the same moment as the states themselves grope for a definition of their own power in a radically different world. Just before the break-up of the Soviet Union,

---

* 13 Cardozo Arts & Entertainment Law Journal 795 (1995).

Moscow's Second Channel, representing the fierce identity of Russia, announced independence from its parent, Gosteleradio, but became immediately dependent on the Russian Federation. In the summer of 1992, a group of Russian businessmen, led by Eduard Sagalaev, announced a joint venture with Turner Broadcasting System (of CNN fame) to create the first private sector, independent television station in Russia. That same year, Boris Yeltsin, President of Russia, appeared on television with a group of editors to reaffirm his commitment to the freedom of the press, and, in particular, the "independence" of *Izvestiia* from the state; but the paper remained dependent on the state for newsprint and access to printing facilities. *Pravda* declared independence from the Communist Party, but a year later was suspended by the government for its advocation of the violent overthrow of the constitutional order. Debates between President Yeltsin and Parliament, before its 1993 dissolution, were most vituperative over which institution most supported press independence. A strong commercial entrant, NTV, backed by a banking group which sought widespread media influence, declared itself, in 1993, the first truly independent entity with extensive news programming. In January 1994, newspapers, as a group, threatened a strike to maintain their independence; but, in their demands for continued subsidies and other protections, the need for old relationships was clear. Despite abundant declarations, the sense persisted that the elixir that produced autonomy had not yet been discovered.

These varying formulations of independence are indicators that absolute independence—coupled with financial security—is usually chimerical. Most journalists, though independent of the state, are dependent on a publisher or an editor. Most publishers and editors are dependent on advertisers, banks, or other funding sources. Perhaps only the willfully poor or boisterously successful are persistently independent. Robert Karl Manoff has addressed these definitional aspects of independence, challenging common formulations. The media in the former Soviet Union, he has written, can achieve a certain measure of political independence, but at the cost of increased dependency on non-state institutions. "To put the matter simply, one needs to weigh carefully the consequences of trading dependence on government, party, administration, and the state for dependency on captains of industry and individual commercial enterprises." For Manoff, the "independence" of the media, even in long-standing Western democracies, is not absolute. Everywhere, including in established, functioning democracies, the relationship among the media, politicians, and government is an ambiguous one. Governments control and allocate the broadcast spectrum; they grant and rescind preferred postal rates for printed matter; they pass and enforce official secrets acts, alien and sedition acts, and national security legislation.

At its simplest, the essence of independence is independence from something or someone. In the American vocabulary, independence means immunity from government, particularly from government-sponsored inculcation of national identity. A report of the Commission on Radio and Television Policy, an unusual consortium headed by former President Jimmy Carter and concerned with the development of broadcasting policy in the former Soviet Union, sought to establish goals and define conditions for broadcasting autonomy. These goals included ferreting out truth "without fear or favor"; empowering ordinary members of the public in the democratic process; gaining credibility so as to minimize citizen alienation and encourage participation in democratic processes; controlling abuses of power by government through exposing misdeeds and establishing a countervailing center of power; providing a forum for ordinary people effectively to press their interests upon and command resources from powerful institutions including government; and providing access to means of self-expression.

Definitions like those of the Carter Commission center on freedom from accountability to government, freedom to maximize economic profits, and freedom for broadcasters to pursue any goals they choose, disciplined only by the pressures and incentives of a competitive free economic market. While this approach is laudable, like so much that vaunts independence and autonomy, it has a built-in weakness: there is too little evident relationship between the goals articulated for society and the specific immunity demanded from societal regulation. The prophets of independence and supporters of free television assume that the societal goals of discourse and individual empowerment will be realized through the growth of independent broadcasters. It is hardly clear, yet, whether these assumptions are realizable.

I. The Russian Mass Media Law of 1991

The Russian Mass Media Law, signed by President Yeltsin just two days after the formal dissolution of the Soviet Union in December 1991, was practically the first effort throughout all of the transition societies to enact a modern framework for communications policy. Drafted by journalists and academics in a time of dramatic change, the law is an awkward version of an ideal, a sometimes apolitical formulation of the proper relationship between the media and the state. The Russian Mass Media Law is not a statute that begins with language glorifying the state, or in which the state is even the central actor. The idea of the statute is to involve the state as little as possible, to move toward autonomous information providers that have rights against the state, rather than the other way around. As an embodiment of Western traditions of independence, the statute might be an emblem of democratization—an ingredient, like a new flag of a new national identity—rather than the means to implement or require aspects of loyalty.

Censorship provisions have such significance and scope that their treatment deserves closer attention as an example of how law is deployed as an engine of reform and, simultaneously, as a badge of power. The opening chapter of the 1991 Russian Mass Media Law is a basic guarantee of freedom from censorship for "instruments of mass information." There, and in the media laws of each transition state, an explicit prohibition of censorship has been important to proclaim. But the obligatory post-Soviet declaration is accompanied by another form of law, namely what is specifically excluded from the sweep of anti-censorial zeal. Article 4 of the Russian Mass Media Law lists the permissible content prohibitions, and by doing so defines the proper zone of national concern with the shaping of public consciousness. Instruments of mass information, for example, are prohibited from calling for a change in the existing constitutional order by force; from arousing religious animosities; from fomenting social, class, or national intolerance; or from proliferating war propaganda. These exceptions, these nodes of sensitivity, recall areas of exclusion in article 10(2) of the European Convention for the Protection of Human Rights and Fundamental Freedoms and articles 19(3) and 20 of the International Covenant on Civil and Political Rights.

In the turbulent post-Soviet environment, however, the excessive dependence on the words of law are expressive, also, of the overriding concerns of an insecure officialdom. The law's prohibition against a call for revolution in the existing constitutional structure tells of remembered wounds and an institutional aspiration for stability, the preservation of basic elements of the status quo, for a political debate that has important bounds. The state has a duty to defend against the promulgation of messages that could be destructive to the process of openness. A prohibition against arousing religious animosities revealed the sensitivities that, in 1991, were already evident and affirmed a new role for the state as fostering, not suppressing religious organizations. Sanctions against speech fomenting social, class, or national intolerance denoted an important role for the state in ameliorating the harsh schisms and ancient hatreds among ethnic groups. Finally, a statutory prohibition against "war propaganda" could be understood as a footnote to past dogma that a private, capitalist press, the press of the future, could use to stir the people into unwarranted aggression.

The Russian Mass Media Law demonstrates, in article 3, an effort to alleviate the onerous requirements of pre-publication registration and discretionary approval of instruments of mass information. The drafters knew too well how power could influence the question of who should be registered and who should not. Such measures historically invited substantive intervention from the state. Here, too, there is faith in words. The Russian Mass Media Law contains registration requirements, but seeks to make the scheme less intimidating by limiting the discretion of the registration authority. It also provides the skeletal framework—anticipating a supplement that has long been in gestation—for the issuance, regulation, and annulment of television and radio broadcast licenses.

Limitations that seem automatic, not requiring the exercise of dangerous discretion, are built into the design of the law. Because article 7 places limits on who can be the founder of an instrument of mass information, authorities can refuse registration under article 13 if the ownership or structure is improper. Article 7 denies foreign citizens and persons without citizenship who do not live continuously within the boundaries of the Russian Federation from establishing a mass media outlet. Registration is a tool for enforcing this rule. Much more troublesome is the power under article 13(3) to deny an applicant's registration when the registering authority claims to know in advance that the content of a new publication would violate the law (for example, that it would foment class or national intolerance). Even factors that once seemed clear can become fuzzy, and the power to register can easily be abused. As media ownership becomes more complicated, as relationships with foreign broadcasting entities and press investors become more common, the simple structure that looked adequate in 1991 begins to flounder.

National power to register—to legitimate—implies a power to take away registration, to close, to delegitimate. The relationship between a publication and the state, and the capacity of the state to influence content (often not so subtly), are functions of this harshest of sanctions: the power of the government, already, as we shall see, exercised in the post-Soviet era, actually to close a newspaper. Law, in this sense, limits, but it also empowers and legitimates state activity. One could conceive of a statutory scheme that had no power to close an instrument of mass information, relying, if necessary, on the ordinary authority of the state to punish individuals for criminal acts, or to collect taxes, or to impose damages for injuries inflicted. In this respect, the Russian Mass Media Law has the beguiling appearance of liberalization, but also the more than implicit threat that the government can step in when something is deemed dreadfully wrong. Under article 16, a section too-often invoked in the years since 1991, the Ministry of Press and Information, later succeeded by the Committee on the Press, could and did force closure of a publication, if, in the view of officialdom, it persisted in violating statutory prohibitions, such as promoting conflict. The requirement that there be a prior court order was only sometimes respected.

Restrictions concerning ownership of the media provide another set of insights into how law incorporates or limits dreams and establishes visions of identity. In the 1991 Russian Mass Media Law, ownership restrictions, especially in a context where the institutions of official power had an earlier monopoly, are an index to the dedication to pluralism, to assumptions about the future role of the state in shaping national identity, and to the pace of change. The Russian Mass Media Law, as in all transitions, was to determine whether the government, directly or indirectly, would be able to establish and operate a substantial subset of instruments of mass information. The statutory approach was, therefore, an important determinant of the nature of the state and its potential for shaping public opinion and fostering loyalties.

The 1991 law permitted, in article 7, any "state organ" to found a mass media outlet. This provision signifies continuity with the environment of the past, a situation in which great powers in the society—the Communist Party, ministries, trade unions, even Parliament—could be founders of newspapers or broadcasting entities, a legacy of the principles that reached far back in Soviet history. The shift from public to private, one of the most difficult aspects of any transition, was shaped by this provision. State broadcasters and print media form a crucial element in Russia's mixed system of state and private mass media outlets, and state-owned mass media became hotly-contested focal points of conflict between the executive and legislative branches—a conflict that erupted in October 1993. In the fall of 1994, the State Duma had approved a draft law, On Amendments and Additions to the Existing Law on the Mass Media, which would prevent federal and regional bodies of power from being founders of mass media except for those which published only official documents. The question of severely curtailing the power of state organs to participate actively in the direction of the media as founders or publishers remained a matter of much debate.

The Russian Mass Media Law, like many of the first generation of media laws throughout the region, is a time-bounded monument to the experience of new freedoms and the traumas of transformation. Transition laws, as a group, are idealistic in construct and artifacts of a new order still being born. But in their idealism, many of these early laws, including the 1991 Russian law, did not adequately address what should occur to the previously all-powerful state broadcasting authorities or the encouragement of private competition at the margin. The law did not address whether the media should, substantively, incorporate and offer a voice for the many voices rising in Russian society, including those with agendas very different from those of the ruling authorities. Financial necessities quickly put much of the newly private press at risk and made them increasingly dependent on government subsidies. As to these issues, the 1991 Russian Mass Media Law, like many other mass media statutes, was tantalizing and complex in its enshrinement of aspects of independence but not sufficiently detailed to ensure that independence would actually ensue.

Organic to the vision of this transitional statute was the preservation (and modification) of the idea of the founder from its important historical setting, in which the Party, Party organs, and the state were the traditional and exclusive sponsors of mass media. The transition to another form of collective ownership had to take place, in the view of the drafters, through the creation of a new kind of sponsoring organization, not the full equivalent, yet, of private publishers. Consequently, the device of "founder" was reinvented, as an intermediary between government and Party on the one hand and journalists on the other. Part of the complex notion of "founder" and a law-driven definition of independence is contained in articles 16 through 24. These sections provide a detailed program for the internal organization of mass media activities. The explicit state direction is not censorship, to be sure, but meticulous concern with the way editorial (primarily newspaper) ventures are organized.

The statute illustrates its preoccupation with any authority, even the authority of a newspaper's internal hierarchy, by requiring an agreement between the founder and the editor-in-chief, and, beyond that, setting forth arrangements, both editorial and functional, between the editor-in-chief and the journalists. Independence, or the capacity to act freely, becomes the function of a code of law.[19] Article 26, for example, allocates power from the publisher or founder to the editor by mandating that a publication can be distributed only after its editor-in-chief has given permission. The Russian statute, like

[19] The Russian Mass Media Law presupposes a formal arrangement, at least for newspapers, with an "editorship" that includes the editor-in-chief and the journalists' collective. Article 19 states that the editorship performs its tasks "on the basis of professional independence," and article 18 prohibits the founder from interfering with the editorship except for pre-agreed conditions. A status agreement must exist between the editorship and founder; and articles 16 and 20 set forth components of such an agreement. These include setting forth the circumstances under which the founder may close the newspaper and how the editor-in-chief is appointed and removed.

many of its transitional contemporaries, differs in this respect from United States law, which does not, normally, order that there be a particular design for the internal structure of a newspaper organization or a television network. In the United States, as in many national systems, there is no guarantee that an editor will be "independent" of a publisher, however desirable the goal. To the extent that an editor is independent, it is a result of tradition, and, in rare instances, contract, but not a constitutional or statutory right. In the same vein, the Russian Mass Media Law uses the forms of law to accord greater rights than are typical in the West to those who work for the mass media. Under article 20, the journalists collectively have the right to approve the editorial charter—the mass media outlet's by-laws or regulations—by a majority vote, provided that no less than two-thirds of its membership is present and that the regulations are also approved by the founder. These regulations would cover the manner of appointing the editor-in-chief, the manner for ceasing operation, and the manner by which founders or publishers could be changed. In the United States it is unusual, unless reflected in the ownership structure, for journalists, as a body, to have rights independent of collective bargaining agreements.

Emblematic of past frustrations, the 1991 Mass Media Law in articles 38 through 40 guarantees access to government reports and provides for audiences or press conferences with officials. Because the Russian Mass Media Law confers special privileges on journalists, the category of those so blessed must be legally differentiated. Article 49 provides a code of behavior: journalists are obliged to verify the reliability of information reported to them, protect confidential sources, honor requests for citation by those who provide information, obtain prior permission when it appears that a news report will be an invasion of privacy, notify those persons whose pictures have been taken, keep superiors informed of possible lawsuits, and refuse assignments that might entail violation of the law. If a journalist does all this, article 49 states, the government then "guarantees the journalist protection of his honor, dignity, health, life and property" as a person who performs a public duty.

As meritorious as these ethical goals for reporters might be, the imposition of such government standards suggests a relationship between journalist and government that is reminiscent of the sometimes velvet, sometimes steel, prison of the past. Journalists are, in article 47, provided special rights of access, including a kind of post-Chernobyl right to visit calamities, catastrophes, and places of "mass unrest and mass gatherings of citizens, as well as areas in which a state of emergency has been declared . . . ." Somewhat chillingly, they are burdened with responsibilities as well. If journalists fail (for example, if they distribute false information which defames the honor and dignity of a state organ), article 48 provides that they can be stripped of accreditation by that agency. Because article 47 provides journalists with a right of access, there must, as a result, be a defined category of "journalist" who has more of a right than others to enter prisons, rummage through government files, or see what is going on in defense installations. Article 51 provides that the journalist is forbidden to use his or her privileged position to cover up falsification of information, to transmit rumors under the guise of truth, to collect information for unauthorized persons or organizations, or to distribute information "for the purpose of defaming a citizen or individual categories of citizens exclusively on the basis of sex, age, racial or national affiliation, language, attitude toward religion, profession, place of residence and work, or in connection with their political convictions . . . ." Articles 59 and 60 provide a list of potential sanctions for journalists who are not true to these responsibilities.

The Russian Mass Media Law of 1991 remained an experiment in the use of the statutory form—laws arrayed on a page—as a way of fashioning a transition from control to greater pluralism. But the forms of law without a commitment to the rule of law is not sufficient. Dedication to complex terminology could not alter reality in the absence of institutions in which law could be interpreted and enforced by government officials and judges with a common commitment to pluralistic goals. Clumsy formulations, lengthy recitations, and awkward adjustments of old ways to new political realities could not suffice to ensure the evolution of a free press. The Russian Mass Media Law of 1991 was a breakthrough—a shining example of the move toward law as a means of assuring an altered public sphere and a more pluralistic national identity. The victory of passage, however, was followed by the recognition of the hardships of adjustment.

II. From Law to Force

In the brutal year after the dissolution of the Soviet Union, during adjustment to new realities, perspectives on the nature and function of law substantially altered. Deepening conflict over the distribution of power in the society meant that the dreamed of paradigm, a non-manipulated press, the hope of the media law, was impossible of immediate achievement. Like similar laws being considered elsewhere in transition societies, the 1991 law was largely about press immunity from government intervention, focusing on the rights of journalists against their publishers and editors, and the rights of citizens and journalists against the state. But the earthquakes within the ruling order—the disputes for control among interest groups and institutions—meant that the goal of immunity was unrealizable. In the first years after passage, it was hardly independence, hardly the structuring of a public sphere that took center stage. Instead, reallocation of control of the media, especially television, became the harsh focus of struggle and political division.

Nothing in the 1991 law dealt explicitly with the allocation of power between branches of government, between the President and Parliament. But as the intense division among competing forces for public loyalty took place, the media was a flashpoint. Controversy over the media's role in society contributed to President Boris Yeltsin's calling for new elections and the closing down of Parliament. Disputes over the division of media power, unresolved by law, would disintegrate into the storming of the great production facility that housed Ostankino, the massive factory of state central television. The text of law and the institutions for its interpretation could not hold the hostile energy within competing camps. Law and force alternated in defining the control of the media. As had proved to be true elsewhere in the transition societies, the appointment and dismissal of the chief officers of the state broadcasting service became levers for violent disagreement and the reimposition of state influence.

Private newspapers, freer than broadcasting, were also an arena for battles for control. As paper and printing costs skyrocketed in the post-Soviet period, government subsidies became necessary for survival for most publications. The 1991 Mass Media Law did not address the tensions that would arise in determining which journals would be favored by government largesse. Here, too, a dispute arose between the President and Parliament as to the criteria for distribution. An assertive Parliament sought to impose a legislative standard with the appearance of political neutrality, and suspicion mounted between that institution and the Ministry of Press and Information.

A dramatic example of the struggle for control was the status of the great newspaper *Izvestiia.* Established as its organ at the dawn of Revolution, the Supreme Soviet of the Soviet Union always had the newspaper under its direction and control. With the dissolution of the Soviet Union, the question of succession arose. Journalists voted to claim the paper for themselves, invoking the spirit, if not the letter, of the 1991 Media Law. Here was a test of the rights of journalists against the historic "founders" of instruments of mass information. For *Izvestiia*, as with much of the Russian press of the post-Soviet period, daily life consisted of the transformation of institutions which were the projections of political entities to institutions which would be independent of such organs and subject to owners, investors, and subscribers. The Russian Parliament claimed that as inheritor of the mantle of the Supreme Soviet, it controlled the editorial direction of the paper. The issue became especially important because, at a critical moment in the constitutional life of the nation, the influential paper, though once the child of the legislative branch, favored the President over the views articulated by the Parliament and its Speaker, Ruslan Khasbulatov. "Freedom of the Press" became a rallying cry for those supporting the journalists and opposing greater parliamentary power. But a vote for freedom, here, as elsewhere, was also decidedly a vote for one side in a power struggle. The journalists succeeded, and the victory was marked as a tribute to greater press autonomy. In fact, the outcome was also a measure of shifting political power.

The battles over control of the media escalated in 1992 and early 1993, reflecting the deadly enmity between the President and Parliament, an enmity that produced governmental crisis after crisis. The crises served as a major justification for a national referendum on April 25, 1993, throughout the Russian Federation and the narrow adoption of a new constitution in December 1993. But the run up to the referendum itself produced an aggravation of government-media relations and the conclusion of the electoral contest did not improve matters. The April referendum tested the commitment of the President and Parliament to a truly free press, though the flag of independence was waved by all sides, and the commitment was found wanting. Both the forces behind Boris Yeltsin and the forces of the opposition maneuvered for control of television, radio, and print media.

President Yeltsin's first decree, announced during the spring campaign, established a new effort to "protect" the mass media, under the President, as "the supreme official personage of the state" and as "guarantor of the rights and liberties of the individual." His opponents saw the decree as a law designed to compel press loyalty. Citing its authority under the 1991 Law on the Mass Media, President Yeltsin's Ministry of Press and Information, a few days prior to the April 25 referendum, initiated court action to close down two opposition newspapers, *Sovetskaia Rossiia* (*Soviet Russia*), and *Den* (*The Day*), on the grounds that they were abusing that law by fomenting inter-ethnic conflict and violence against the state. In St. Petersburg, local authorities, who are supporters of the President, temporarily removed television commentator Aleksander Nevzorov from the air in late March, claiming that his calls for volunteers to defend the Motherland against Yeltsin's "anti-constitutional coup" were a violation of the Mass Media Law's prohibition against appeals for armed insurrection.

Just a month before the April vote, in the mid-sized city of Saratov on the Volga, local deputies, who are opponents of the President, marched into the local television station and seized the microphone from a surprised reporter. According to a Moscow news account of the Saratov incursion, journalists during the old regime were instructed not to show empty wheat fields, or to show workers on their knees so that the wheat looked taller. These journalists fear that this may happen again.

Yeltsin's decree ordering that the press be guarded from hostile abusers of media rights was mild compared with the activities of the legislative branch and the President's opponents. The Congress of People's Deputies (the super-Parliament), angered by perceived imbalances in news coverage of the crisis that favored Yeltsin, passed its own Resolution, before the referendum, requiring the formation of its own supervisory councils (the membership to be chosen by federal and local legislative bodies) in order to "ensure objective coverage" and "prevent political monopolization" of broadcasting. In addition, the Congress ordered government agencies to transfer to the Supreme Soviet their powers to start and partially supervise media activity. Aleksei Simonov, the head of the Glasnost Defense Foundation, said at the time that Russian television was only frailly an example of "fantastic pluralism." He cautioned against reading too much into the clash of opinions and the presentation of different sides of the great constitutional questions. According to Simonov, pluralism is the result of uncertainty about the future. Television remains government-controlled, but it is difficult to identify "government." Simonov observed further that the relationship between television and the state is governed by people and loyalties, rather than by law and constitution.

Typical of the Russian media war, and similar contests in other transition societies, was the invocation on all sides of the duty to protect the freedom of the press. Parliament strengthened and extended the power of supervisory councils it had established in the name of guaranteeing freedom. Oleg Poptsov, Chairman of the All-Russian TV and Radio Company, condemned, however, the "extraordinary hostility of the [Supreme Soviet] committee on mass media towards the mass media." The President's Minister of Press and Information, Mikhail Fedotov, resigned on August 21, calumnizing parliamentary observation councils that he claimed had already been set up and started to operate throughout the regions. "They are already dividing up air time. They are deciding who is to be shown and who isn't. Lists of desirable and undesirable speakers are being compiled . . . . The whole purpose of the game is to call freedom censorship and censorship freedom."

The continuing duel among institutions brandishing competing media laws was one of the principal zones of bitterness between the President and the Supreme Soviet during the summer and fall of 1993. Finally, President Yeltsin's September 21 dramatic suspension and later disbanding of the Parliament led to the immediate institution of censorship. At least ten newspapers in Moscow were closed down following the violent events of early October, and, at the outset, all newspapers were subject to censorship, having to submit material for government review before publication. On September 23, citing the Mass Media Law, the Council of Ministers ordered the suspension of additional media, namely the newspapers, magazines, and radio and broadcast programs of the Supreme Soviet. The Council's resolution declared that with the Parliament suspended, a new "founder" for its publications was needed, and the successor would be the government itself. Shortly after the September 23 Council of Ministers' action, the government installed a new editor-in-chief at the newspaper *Rossiiskaia Gazeta*, Natalia Ivanovna Polezhaeva, who initiated radical changes in personnel and editorial directions. These actions brought her into conflict with the journalists on the paper who, in a September 27 meeting, voiced their unanimous objection to the takeover and claimed that the substitution of founders had been illegal.

The shift from law to force was epitomized by the bloody battle at Ostankino, one of the last acts in the conflict between the President and Parliament. Except for the White House, home of the Parliament, and the Comecon building, housing the Moscow Mayor's offices, Ostankino was the only major site of massive struggle. An October night of violence left at least sixty-two people dead and scores wounded, members of the television staff and foreign journalists included. Cameras panning through the corridors and studios showed scenes of rubble and destruction. In doing so, the cameras revealed something else: that the control that comes from law is just a thin overlay beneath which the armed march, the terrorist act, the seizure of transmission towers, and the arbitrariness of censorship are ready to emerge.

III. Strengthening of the Rule of Law

After the battle of Ostankino, a condition resembling the rule of law was reasserted. With increasing speed, new institutions were put in place and decrees issued re-employing the language of independence and free speech. Even the earlier acts of censorship were justified on the basis of law. The October close down of several newspapers had, as indicated, been based not only on the President's "emergency powers," but also article 4 of the Mass Media Law (authorizing closure if a publication engages in appeals for seizure of power; for violent change in the constitutional order or integrity of the state; or incitements to national, class, social, or religious prejudice or intolerance), as well as international human rights law.

In an obeisance to the reinstitution of law, President Yeltsin, who had just months earlier suspended the Constitutional Court, also established a new "arbitration tribunal" that would ultimately be transformed into a unique instrument for deciding and mediating information disputes. With the disbanding of the Russian parliament and the announcement of elections to a new Federal Assembly, to be held December 12, 1993, the already-contentious question of media access became an issue of great concern among potential candidates. In response to critics who argued that the press was predominantly pro-Yeltsin and that the government continued to treat state-owned television as its own propaganda tool, Yeltsin included a provision in the Statute on Elections aimed at providing equal access to the media. According to article 28 of this statute, all mass media

> whose founding agencies include a state body, organization, or institution, or a body of local self-government, or mass media whose financing comes even partially from state funds or the funds of bodies of local self-government [were] obliged to afford equal opportunities with respect to pre-election campaign presentations to all candidates for deputy to the state Duma. Article 28 soon was expanded in the Statute on Information Guarantees, adopted October 29. In addition to dealing with questions of equal access and other matters, the new tribunal created by the Statute could issue warnings to candidates who in their campaigning made false statements "demeaning the honor, dignity [or] business reputation of candidates [or] their agents." Both the Arbitration Tribunal and the Russian Electoral Commission in early December rejected the demand by First Deputy Premier Vladimir Shumeiko that the Communist and Democratic parties be removed from the election lists because they declared themselves against the proposed constitution.

In December 1993 and January 1994, President Yeltsin and other officials issued a series of additional decrees relating to mass media, largely designed to establish a legal framework for a free press. These included a renewed commitment of financial benefits for the state broadcasting apparatus, including, temporarily, substantial outlays for signal distribution. A decree of January 10, titled Issues Ensuring Publication and Dissemination of the Mass Media and Printed Matter, called for preferential taxation of the print mass media, a system of state subsidies and improved access to printing facilities. A decree guaranteeing citizens' rights to information, issued December 31, 1993, ordered news programs of state radio and television to "inform citizens without fail of the principal provisions of legal acts and decisions of state bodies on fundamental domestic and foreign policy questions on the day they are issued." Of course, the order to promulgate government decrees, while increasing citizen access to information, raised the possibility of greater intervention in day-to-day editorial decisions made by state entities.[49]

In the wake of the December elections, Vyacheslav Bragin, who had been the head of Ostankino, was ousted—a reminder of the relationship between the forms of law and the exercise of power. Bragin's downfall was partly attributable to the results of the election in which nationalists had done surprisingly well and the results had not been as favorable to the government as had been hoped. Television was supposed to have the aura of fairness, but when it counted those in power wanted the unifying quality of television, its persuasive capacity, to be used in a way that would redound to the benefit of the Yeltsin reformers. In a move of considerable importance for the development of a pluralistic broadcasting system in Russia, linked perhaps to the failure of state television during the elections, President Yeltsin ordered the granting of a television broadcasting license to a private entity, NTV. The cause of pluralism and access was advanced, but the rule of law was nicked: the just recently established mode of awarding valuable channel rights seemed to be circumvented so that a favored (and talented) broadcaster would prevail.

Intense societal conflict, threatening the existence of legal institutions, was felt throughout early 1994, with the legitimacy of many of the new bodies (including the Duma and Federal Council) very much at issue. In the spring of 1994, President Yeltsin, to achieve a moratorium among contending forces, put forward a Treaty of Civic Accord, a novel instrument that was more a public relations device than a binding agreement among its signatories. The Treaty sought to place a frame around a debate that had, a few months earlier, erupted into battle. The Treaty could also be seen as an effort by those in a broad status quo position to establish standards of discourse that might discredit their most radical challengers. The Treaty provided that "the parties . . . consider that the grandeur of Russian history, with its heroic and tragic pages, obliges one to avoid simplified or insulting appraisals of the past and to prevent the distortion of historical fact." In addition, under the Treaty,

> the parties . . . stress that love for the fatherland, freedom and moral duty to society, creative labor, all the values common to the whole of mankind, spiritual and moral traditions of the multiethnic people of the Russian Federation should become the basis for its revival. The parties to the treaty pledge to uphold, in word and deed, the norms of moral behavior in politics, the economy and public life. To render clearer the relationship of the press to this process of establishing a consensual social order, the Treaty provided that "a special role in all of this belongs to the mass media . . . the efforts of which should be supported by the state and society."

---

[49] A year later, in late 1994, the State Duma sought to establish a set of rules, On the Procedure for State Run Media to Cover the Activities of State Power, to assure more regular and more fixed coverage of legislative activities. A "Parliamentary Hour" program was reinstated.

By the summer of 1994, the Duma was also able to develop a draft statute on radio and television broadcasting to supplement and build on the 1991 Mass Media Law. Passed on first reading by the Duma on October 26, the draft statute not only maintained its rhetorical commitment to prohibiting censorship, but it also imposed on the state the obligation to employ the media for "the defense of public morals and morality, the strengthening of the family, and the confirmation of a healthy lifestyle." Under the bill, government ought to ensure that broadcasters "satisfy the variegated informational needs of viewers and listeners" and encourage the "wide distribution of education and culture." The language of the bill also foresaw as an underlying principle of broadcasting "creating the requisite conditions for the maintenance and development of national culture" and cooperating "in the formation of a law-based state."

More unusual was a proposed law prepared in the summer of 1994 to take in hand, rearrange, normalize, and shift control of elements of state underpinning for financing the media. The draft, On State Support of the Mass Media, was the creation of Mikhail Poltoranin, the powerful chair of the relevant Duma committee and former Minister of Press and Information, and it sought to address a number of demands and concerns of the emerging independent press. The proposal sought to reduce publishers' dependence on state printing monopolies and substitute indirect subsidies (such as tax relief) for existing, more onerous programs. The bill, as reported from its committee, like the government's earlier decree, was designed to provide favorable tax treatment for profits earned by editorial offices of mass media, publishing houses, news agencies, television and radio broadcast companies, and similar enterprises. Video equipment and printing presses could be brought into Russia free of duty. Media institutions would be able to keep foreign currency and use it to acquire equipment and materials. Favorable postal rates and special rents for the use of public buildings would be established. Equally important, the bill provided a scheme for the systematic transformation of all state-owned printing facilities used in newspaper, book, and journal output. Such enterprises would be privatized: up to thirty percent of the stock would remain in federal hands for three years, with the rest distributed to workers in the enterprises, newspapers, magazines, and book publishers that historically used the printing facilities. A certain amount would be reserved for the general public as investors.

The most creative innovation of Poltaranin's proposal was the establishment of a National Fund for Media Development that would hold, for a limited time, the government's own stock in printing enterprises. This Fund would accumulate and invest funds to strengthen the printing and distribution structure for mass media and book publishing. It would be a vehicle which would manage funds and control stock in privatized mass media assets, such as printing press and book publishing operations. The Fund would work with the state as it determined its own "needs . . . for the solution of nationwide tasks in the spheres of upbringing education, culture, science and technology as well as the development of new printing technologies."

In this respect, the Poltoranin approach sought to redefine a state role in ways that mediated between an American hands-off tradition and the practices of the Soviet past.

The state would redefine its requirements in terms of purchases of books for libraries and educational establishments, in terms of encouragement of manufacturing, and in the redeployment of existing subsidies. The Fund was attacked by Sergei Gryzunov, the head of the government's Committee on the Press, who criticized the Fund as a new approach to monopolization, which accumulates and redistributes money according to those who are liked as opposed to those who are disliked.

Seizing the language of free enterprise, in the fall of 1994 President Yeltsin approved the privatization of Ostankino in a manner that seemed to equip it to compete more effectively with private entrants while, at the same time, maintaining control in government hands. Under the decree, signed November 30, 1994, approximately fifty percent of the company would be owned by the State Committee for the Management of State Property, with the remaining stock distributed among a dozen handpicked major companies. The "privatization" took place against the threat of the merger of the once-proud first channel into what had once been its mere appendage. The alternative to privatization and the injection of new financing was, for Ostankino, a slow and depressing decline and death. The increasingly combative Poltoranin attacked the plan on grounds clearly linked to national identity concerns.

While the resolution of control over the great instruments of state television seemed to become settled, elements of strength among new independent competitors became more prominent. A joint venture in which Turner Broadcasting System was linked to Russian partners dissolved as those in Moscow found more favorable financing at home. Under the direction of Igor Malashenko, a young hero of television in the Gorbachev period, NTV, financed by Moscow bankers, posed a threat to central television's domination of the news, so much so that the government threatened to withdraw its license because of unfavorable coverage of Yeltsin's military campaign in Chechnya.

Notwithstanding the rhetoric of independence, there seemed to be a systematic discouragement of the growth of nongovernmental television even five years after the dissolution of the Soviet Union. Local and regional governments proliferated efforts to use television to produce and distribute information themselves, thereby increasing their control over the messages available to the public. A 1994 draft statute on the coverage of the Duma provided that the legislative body would have its own production capability and command time, at least on the state channels. Many municipalities and other local or regional bodies were gaining their own channels or participating in private channels as joint ventures. Enforcement of copyright law lessened the power of independents, depriving them of their ill-gotten lifeblood: pirated American films and cartoons. Discriminatory pricing of government-controlled transmission facilities and discriminatory taxes on equipment purchases inflated costs. In addition, the government, in the spring of 1994, ordered that the state channels should restrict the time independent entities were given as "windows" to broadcast their material. The market for advertising was being manipulated to injure small independents as the large state channels expanded the number of minutes they would sell. Independents saw the boundless appetite for advertising at Ostankino or Russian Television as a purposeful threat.

In this environment, official, philanthropic, and business entities from the West sought to buttress whatever they deemed to be moves to "independence," sometimes with little concern about the relationship among different forms of privatization, control, and political divisions. By the fall of 1994, USAID was moving to implement its Russian American Media Partnerships to foster independent television, radio, and the press, in theory because of the role they could play in enhancing and reinforcing democracy. These partnerships would help non-government Russian media organizations become independent, self-supporting institutions. In terms of objectives, the Agency provided three justifications for the United States' aid to the internal press of a third country: First, a financially viable and politically independent non-government media sector is a mechanism crucial to government accountability; second, such a sector is useful in ensuring that the existing state media remains honest; and third, such a sector safeguards freedom of the press. The USAID wished to diminish the leverage that the state continued to exert over the non-governmental press, because of its economic control of printing presses, distribution, and information networks.

IV. The Future Role of the State

Defending his aggressive position in fashioning new media laws, Mikhail Poltoranin argued in fall 1994 that the strategic objective of Russia's information policy should be to "deepen democracy." With the destruction of the totalitarian regime, "the importance of its mouthpieces—the central newspapers—fell off as well." He blamed a decline in support for central television on its "propaganda for spiritual emptiness." Society, he argued, "has grown tired of boundless freedom for impudence and slander, of freedom for instigation and political foppishness." The state, Poltoranin argued, could no longer "continue a policy of peaceful nonresistance to evil." He recalled how Ostankino and Tass "assailed" Yeltsin and his associates from every point in 1990, leading to the creation of the All-Russian State Television and Radio Company and the Novosti Russian News Agency to "break the information blockade." Now it was time for a new set of alternate forces to break a new information blockade.

. . . .

Comparing Broadcast Structures: Transnational Perspectives and Post-Communist Examples*

Monroe E. Price

I. Thinking Transnationally

Enough activity is taking place, in terms of research and advice on broadcasting structures in Central and Eastern Europe and the former Soviet Union, that it is worthwhile to step back and think about the formidable process of shaping transnational perspectives. What is in the wardrobe of public or private concerns that motivates cross-cultural communications studies? In these extraordinary times of trying to manufacture liberal democracies from national pasts and the detritus of command economies, are these advising activities productive? How should one measure effectiveness? Who are the interested parties and what is the basis of their interests?

Governments, including those of the United States, the United Kingdom, and France, provide financial support for travel, research, and the interaction of journalists and scholars; American foundations and universities provide critical encouragement. The outline of a small industry, made up partly of communications scholars from the West and academics and broadcasters from the East, is taking shape. It will be possible—maybe not now, but certainly at some future time—to establish a production chart: who are the manufacturers of new laws? Who are those engaged in research and development? Who are the retailers? Who are the installers and repairmen? And finally, if things do not work out, who will collect the debris?

At this nascent industry's most basic level, there is the project of chronicling specific statutory drafts and laws country by country, organizing them by category, and engaging in a textual analysis that compares the proposed and achieved shifts in one state to those in another. Various categories for analysis and archiving automatically come to mind; e.g., prior censorship, frequency allocation, extent of privatization, journalists' rights, viewers' rights, appointment of chief executive officers of public service broadcasters, composition and appointment of supervisory or regulatory bodies, and judicial review of regulatory decisions. Yet, in the post-modern, post-critical, post-legal-realist world we are more than naturalists with stuffed cabinets of statutes pinned like butterflies under glass. The mere text of laws, and certainly drafts, can be misleading, especially if the purpose of examining these is to reveal the evolution of the relationship between broadcasting structures and society. Without a sense of context, these drafts and statutes are evidence not of broadcasting practices, but of political divisions, possible aspirations, societal compromises, local confusions, or international fashions. The

* 11 Cardozo Arts & Entertainment Law Journal 275 (1993).

purpose of this essay is to provide that context, which will facilitate examination of the evolution in this relationship.

To measure actually the expansion of democratic values, the mere examination of documents is far from sufficient. Travel, meetings, and discourse must take place. There is a kind of odd intercourse here, reminiscent of European exploration of exotic lands. Western journalists and scholars travel to Central Europe or the former Soviet Union, where they spend time conducting interviews; a mosaic of their impressions provides some insight into what is taking place. Czechs, Poles, Russians, and Slovenians are flown to London, Washington, and Paris, like Native exemplars of a distant past; they perform and are studied to provide a basis for Western academics, governments, and businesses to determine the lay of the land. Meetings take place in castles and conference centers, or by fax and phone.

But what is communicated, even face-to-face? The problems of communication are probably similar to those that plagued eighteenth- and nineteenth-century scholars and civil servants. Formal language difficulties aside, a fundamental hurdle is the uncertainty about transferability of concepts. We cannot really know how rooted in a particular history and flow of experiences a set of practices might be. No matter how sophisticated we are, how schooled in the relativism of anthropology and sociology, it is too easy to conclude that laws and institutions come in ready-made, almost modular packages (though sometimes they must). What we must take into account is not merely the translation of words, or even of concepts, but the translation of deeply ingrained administrative environments. One cannot talk of "judges," of "neutral principles," or of "accountability of government officials to the rule of law" without sensitivity to the complexities of adjustment. Dynastic memory makes some forms of power and hierarchy more acceptable in the East than in the West. Even simple concepts, such as those involved in the implementation of broadcasting alternatives, may have complex counterparts. On the other hand, tacit acceptance of the limitations that bar modular transformations will render the Western observer almost useless, for the implementation of Western ideals is critical to the development of liberal democracies. What should be sought, but is difficult to achieve, is the project of interpretation. Such interpretation comprises a critical study of the statutes and laws drafted in the transitional states, the construction of a set of narratives about the reshaping of broadcasting systems, and a journey into the dark forest of hermeneutics.

Only through the lens of differences—differences which have their origins in disparate internal histories—can the transferability of concepts be perceived; and the quintessential example of central historical differences is in the meaning attached in a given society to "freedom of expression"—the relationship between the political state and the media—the bellwether of differences in how states regulate the distribution of information. Internal histories of free speech are hardly laboratory—pure, however. They are made through the absorption of other histories: histories of violence and war, of idealism and cynicism; histories that have become more complex with the expansion of international trade. It is this trade, not only in images and in goods but in the very concept of how pictures, thoughts, and words are regulated, that underscores the importance of the search for national identity in the transition states. The tasks of interpreting new statutes and constructing a new broadcasting system are rendered more coherent by trying to locate, in each instance, the role of the state as a shaper of national identity.

In a world trained to think of itself as immersed in the "information era," the relationship between the nature of any given political system and the structure of its communication systems is of great importance. For the political scientist Karl Deutsch, one way of understanding the political essence of a society is to examine and calibrate its internal web of message-sending.[7] He offers what he calls a "functional definition of nationality," a predictive model for the behaviors of nations that relies on gauging the coherence of its communication systems. For Deutsch, "the range and effectiveness of social communication . . . may tell us how effectively [a community] has become integrated, and how far it has advanced, in this respect, toward becoming a nation." He added that the limits of selfhood of a group of people "will be the limits of its effectiveness in transmitting and circulating information."

Conversely, any study about the regulation of television must be more comprehensive, not focusing on just a single aspect of a general system, but touching questions concerning the nature of the entire communications and political structure. Of course, this is a difficult task. Television itself is mesmerizing, powerful, and ubiquitous, with an immediate glamour and presence that makes it the first, and strangely isolated, object of interest and study—a kind of demon of modern life. Indeed, the role of television may be shifting in its relationship to other media, including computers and radio. For example, the increase of global programming, partly a consequence of the improved capacity of satellite transmission and cable distribution, may mean that television is a progressively weaker instrument for the making of national identities. Regardless, the regulation of television receives enormous attention. It may not, however, be the kind of attention that fully takes into account all the necessary factors to be considered in defining the relationship between the media and society.

Part of the problem is that scholars are condemned to compare societies that have had almost opposite histories of communications structures—some moving toward liberal democracy from autocratic command approaches, some seeking to increase the diversity of content and the ease of access in an already relatively-free communications structure. Some societies have asserted the power to use communications networks totally to shape or control loyalties, while others have encouraged competition against the state and have also limited the state's role. There is a spectrum here, not necessarily of democracy versus authoritarianism, but of active state involvement in the construction of a public sphere and of sustaining a national identity on the one hand, or pretending to leave these questions to the market on the other. Only by being reflective about these more complex

[7] Karl W. Deutsch, Nationalism and Social Communication: An Inquiry into the Foundations of Nationality (2d ed. 1966).

issues—and not focusing solely on a single model of the democratic state—can Western observers and counselors constructively participate in the task of attempting to democratize and provide greater freedom for broadcasting structures in former socialist states.[11]

II. Speech, Political, and Economic Structures

An obvious and critical element in reviewing the patterns of a restructured media involves sources of financial support, the essence of the relationship with the state. In the Soviet *ancien regime*, the goal of the monopoly broadcasters, as instruments of the state, was relatively clear, and the source of financing to perform the prescribed functions was also clearly established. The transformation of the once-formidable First Channel of the Soviet Union, virtually the official voice of the Soviet Union, provides an example. Secure in its financing, it was secure in its purpose. In the post-Soviet world, however, it suddenly had an ambiguous status and mandate, and that ambiguity was reflected in the insecurity of financing. With the loosening of the imperial ties, the Channel was seeking to be pan-Republican, the soft unifier of the "Commonwealth of Independent States," of the "Newly Independent States," of the territories of the former Soviet Union, or of some other geo-political mass.[13] This alternative was not necessarily consistent with the political goals of the new Republics, and ambiguity in role leads to ambiguity in financing. An informal agreement among the presidents of the Republics to maintain and finance the Channel provided shaky assurance. It was not clear whether the First Channel's purpose was to provide a Russian language signal to the large numbers of Russian nationals who inhabited the new states, to provide a common information sphere, to establish a new sense of linkage between a different center and a different periphery, or merely to maintain a flow of entertainment at a difficult economic period while the several state television networks were still weak and inexperienced.

To determine whether there is a model for a pan-Republic service is to assume important questions about what cultural, communications, and economic links there will be among the component parts of the Union. Ukrainian officials and others complain that the Channel maintains the tradition of Russification, and that it continues to be a voice of the Russian empire, though perhaps more subtly. What should the policy of the First Channel be? Who should appoint its chief? How are these questions considered from the perspective of free speech ideas? Programming changes were evident in the early 1990s

---

[11] The problem of expression is closely bound with specific pasts. In Bulgaria, for example, in early 1992, a fervent group—calling itself the "Ten Words Are Enough Movement"—sought to adopt a minimalist approach to the role of the state in defining a broadcasting system. Ten words, declaring that the media must be free, were believed sufficient to lead a new liberal democratic world. Perhaps this movement should have been embraced. However, the group was attacked as reactionary, linked to the Communist past, and as championing the status quo ante. The portability of the words of the First Amendment to the United States Constitution is a perilous matter, both for scholars and policymakers.

[13] The very confusion over nomenclature, depending on whether adherents to the Commonwealth, former Republics, the Balkans, or other areas are included in a political grouping, underscores the problem of ambiguity of purpose and financing.

as the First Channel sought to attract an audience with demographic features attractive to advertisers. Consequently, programming content that would not insult its now more diverse political constituency was necessary. An MTV look replaced the more somber presidium aesthetic. In what would probably be a temporary compromise, the Russian Federation seemed to underwrite the Channel's program costs prior to 1993 (though trying to decentralize transmission costs), partly as a reflection of the view in other Republics that the Channel espouses a Russian, not a regional, perspective.

Patterns of financing are more commonly a matter of concern in development of the print media than they are in television. An official state television network, financed by the state, is taken for granted in ways that a state-financed newspaper is not. As a result, questions involving the allocation and subsidization of newsprint are ubiquitous. Perhaps, in many of these structures, the state must underwrite civil society and its zone of discourse. Nonetheless, withdrawing subsidies from television may mean a steady decline to a diet of the shabbiest programming and the elimination of television as a source of culture, information, and discourse, just as it may mean a deterioration of the supply of information through newspapers. Transaction costs, including obstacles imposed by the assertion of intellectual property rights, can impede the growth of strong public service or independent broadcasters. Indeed, in some contexts, the adoption of a copyright regime may protect better-heeled state television monopolies from the competition of non-state broadcasters.[14] Non-enforcement or slack enforcement of copyright can be seen as a kind of subsidy that discriminates in favor of independent broadcasters. Almost universally, advertising has become an acceptable, if not mandatory, source of revenue. In societies where people are trying to be consumers, but where demand for consumer goods is not high and the supply is problematic, developing a market for advertising is quite difficult. Much advertising (off, more than on, television) is used to develop brand identification so that when the market matures particular competitors will have built a franchise for themselves.

Redefinition of concepts of "independence," (as in "independent broadcaster") is a frequent aspect of the narratives of transformation. Westerners are always looking for "independent" journalists or "independent" producers, rarely stopping to examine the context of independence. In Ukraine, for example, where "independent" television services are beginning, they not only use the state transmitter and the state studio facilities, but they broadcast pursuant to rights that seem to be governed by the state television service itself. One can see the hazards looming, but whether outside experts can merely fit the proper piece into the machinery of regulation is unclear. A sign of the difficult passage to independence could be witnessed during the early 1990s in Kiev as

[14] The policy of the United States is to assure that the copyrights in motion pictures are respected and that films are not pirated. But most so-called infant "independent" television stations in the transition societies (primarily the Newly Independent States) were reliant on bootlegged films and similar product for a competitive edge. In some markets, these pirate-based independents were accounting for almost fifty percent of the audience market. Thus, it may be in the interest of the state broadcasters to choke off the supply of product to these competitors by joining in the insistence on compliance with copyright law.

the state television service physically manifested its endurance. A gleaming new television facility, started as a monument during the statist days of a decade ago, was prepared for occupancy. Perhaps architecture, not legislation, demonstrates the role of the state in broadcasting—a physical symbol of the continuing relationship of state interest to non-state originated communications. Often things are not as they appear to be to the foreign observer; this makes long-distance reliance on formal language, or even casual narrative, extremely perilous as a guide to transformations.

III. Interpreting Texts

A substantial distinction still exists between approaches to broadcasting structures in post-Communist and Western societies. In the transitional societies, perhaps primarily in the former Republics of the Soviet Union, the state's role in both establishing national identity and rendering the idea of the state more coherent has continued. The background factors—the social, economic, and political contexts—are clear. But what about text? Do the emerging texts of press and broadcasting laws reflect these differences? In the United States, Great Britain, and in Europe, the modern state appears—with some cyclical moves—to cope with competing demands for the loyalty of its citizens through the vocabulary of deregulation; i.e., the appearance of as little governmental intervention as possible and, to the extent possible, a continuing diminution in that intervention. For example, in the summer of 1992, President Mitterand of France was precluded from establishing a publicly-funded television advertising campaign to convince French voters to ratify the Maastricht Treaty on European Union. Government use of its resources for the overt shaping of national identities through the media is considered less and less acceptable, and to the extent it takes place, it should be openly articulated and its structure should be transparent.[19] During the early 1990s, the situation was otherwise in the republics of the former Soviet Union and the states of Central and Eastern Europe. War (or the threat of war), irredentism, fierce immigration debates, and the general instability of economic transformations, meant that the competition for loyalties was extraordinary. The very definition of the state was often at issue. Therefore, government intervention in the cultivation of national identity was developing at a fevered pitch.

Of course, there is much—perhaps too much—that the formal statutory language, and even the process leading to enactment of the statute, does not disclose. Where does technology come in? How much is regulatable? And how much is determined by the entry of satellite and cable technology rather than by the articulated desires of lawmakers? The formal language does not disclose the power of the audience, nor how it reads what is on the screen, nor what changes in its viewing patterns ensued from the entry of new competitors who are often outside the formal framework. Nor does the formal wording indicate patterns of conformity between the aspirations of law and the action of officials, much of what is called the "rule of law." And aside from verbal

[19] How and whether these goals have been achieved or whether it is, in fact, an objective, is the subject of a larger project which touches upon such complex issues as funding for public broadcasting, subsidy policy with respect to the arts, and structures of access during political debates.

aspirations, which mirror some adopted notion of democracy, the infrastructure for transformation (i.e., existence of a consumer market, availability of capital, and incentives for investment) may be wildly out of kilter with the established model. The language of statutes may have the purpose of camouflage, or may be designed to placate an international community rather than to guide conduct. The purpose here is not to determine what the law "is" or what conduct is proscribed or permitted; rather, it is to look at statutes in the same way that an archaeologist looks at shards to help decipher, decode, and explain an ancient civilization—as narrative text about the society.

All this said, studying the language of legislative provisions, proposed and enacted, that deal with the relationship between the media and the state is a way to search for the vocabulary of change. Laws and lawmaking are clues as to the nature of the transformations—whether, for example, they represent a revolution of rights, or as Andras Sajo has argued, an attempt to restore some hard-to-locate pre-Socialist order of an imagined national past. Broadcasting legislation might be the actual working out of conflicts, or it may be evidence of inexorable anxieties that plague the society. Some parts of the new broadcasting laws may be drafted not as a reflection of internal realities, but rather of the compulsion, inducement, or idealized hopes of outside models—a mirror pointed outside toward the face of the West. Some parts show the scars of the past; they can be read mainly as articulated triumphs over some seemingly rejected torturous practice, retained in the very act of forceful repression. Broadcasting statutes reflect the definition of power in the new societies and the competition between assertions of legislative, executive, judicial, and personal authority. As they reveal the ambivalence toward the shift in ownership from public to private, the statutes and the statutory process involve the debate over the state monopoly for loyalties. There are residual prohibitions on those outside the state: glasnost with limitations, restrictions on ownership, and limitations on the range in which hostility to the very idea of the state can be expressed. During the current period of change, these new legal texts provide some insight into the new conceptions of the state, of government, and of democracy that their drafters hold.

. . . .

IV. Conclusion: Searching for Standards

Given the bewildering complexities inherent in evaluation, one might ask whether absolute norms can be expressed, or whether Western observers are doomed to come to the task of advice and evaluation with their objectives wholly suppressed or only half-articulated. An effort to make more transparent the standards used by those who are engaged in the process of change could be useful. Some obvious formal norms are Article 19 of the Universal Declaration of Human Rights, Article 10 of the European Convention on Human Rights, Articles 19 and 20 of the International Covenant on Civil and Political Rights, and the First Amendment to the United States Constitution. These norms, part of the consensus for the new discourse, are superficially advocated, transferred, and transported—even enforced—as a condition of providing financial assistance. But what motivations provide the underpinnings of this consensus? Why do the messengers from the West seem so committed to particular free-speech practices, which are familiar to them but are sometimes difficult to translate in exact terms across formerly impenetrable borders? We need to unpack the surface ideas of these concepts and determine what bases exist for giving individual and governmental support to advocacy of the vital speech aspects of liberal transformations. Given the basic context of this discussion—namely, that of Western observers studying transformations said to be from authoritarianism to greater political involvement—measuring the formal adoption of Western words in media statutes and in constitutional forms ought not be considered sufficient. In thinking about transformations in these transitional societies, it is useful to ask whether the same objectives exist for intervening Westerners that consciously or unconsciously underlie their appraisal of speech regulation in their own countries. Are these champions of arguments grounded in domestic political theory, in self-realization, and in the protection of dissent at home restricted to similar arguments in considering reform abroad? Is it enough to say that the desired restructuring of the broadcasting system contributes in fact to a more pluralistic, democratic society? If the motivation of the Western advisors is not merely to replicate their home ambitions, how can their goals be articulated? Several sources of motivation can be contemplated, if not for those who advise, then for those who recruit and dispatch the advisors.

What might be called the "missionary basis" is altruistic. Its source is a profound moral and political belief in human dignity, and a concurrent duty, philosophical and almost religious in origin, to ensure that others see the light. It is the understandable desire to make a common bond with people similarly situated who can be assisted in reaching shared goals. Academics devote their time to writing and advising about the transformation of broadcasting structures because they fundamentally believe in freedom and want to extend its reach. Like many of their fellows in and out of government, academics may be caught up with the hope for an ideal that is unrealized in their own countries. Free speech is fundamental to a democratic society; in some respects it is the centerpiece of a secular religion with a strong and productive priesthood. There are variants on this missionary theme. Some find it more congenial to preach their doctrine abroad than at home. There is a romantic illusion that in a transforming society, hurdles that seem insurmountable in the structured home environment might be overcome elsewhere. To the extent that free speech is the celebration of dissent against authority, the advocacy of broadcasting reform abroad can be the consequence of frustration with battling against an entrenched establishment at home. This time, they hope, a society will get it right.

Even if change, in text and practice, appears to contribute little to these goals in the short run, an iron variant can be articulated: broadcasting reform is designed to create a safety net for democratic political change. By placing talent trained outside the government's immediate control together with a kind of technology of independence, the sustainability of democratic dissent is perpetuated. The immediate historical setting for this argument is the famed August 1991 coup in Moscow. The inability of its perpetrators to gain immediate control of radio and other means of communication was said to be an important element in its downfall. Permeable information frontiers, including a network of domestic independent transmitters (in both senses of the term), provide a resource for continued discourse and criticism. In times of emergency, they provide an alternate source for representations of truth and calls to action.

Of course, even this standard is full of complexity—since pluralism and democracy can be at odds—and much of the debate (or lack of debate) in the region is about the pace of change itself. "Progress" against this standard seems to involve three sub-tests: (1) is there a greater flow of information to the citizenry than before? (2) is there a larger zone for public discourse than before? (3) And is there a capacity for a broad diversity of views, including the unfettered opportunity to criticize the government? The relationship between this cluster of standards and the new and proposed broadcasting structures is a difficult one. That the absence of censorship increases the availability of information and affords a greater diversity of views is axiomatic. But in what distribution? Though other segments of the population now have quicker access to greater quantities of the world's information store, are there large segments that are more deprived of information now than before? Assumptions about how much news (biased and unbiased) was available under the *ancien regimes* of the newly emerging states may be far wide of the mark. In the absence of competition, news programs may have been watched more consistently by a greater range of the population. New economic differentiation may mean greater access to information by the rich or middle class, and less access by the working class. This will be particularly true if state broadcasting diminishes or if its subsidies and quality decline. The modern trend in the West is to move away from requirements that a substantial percentage of time be devoted to news and documentary programming. Arguably, in the transformed, advertising-supported structure of the media, the zone of public discourse—of argumentation and establishment of opinion outside the umbrella of government—is far more likely to exist in newspapers than in television (with radio falling somewhere in between). With regard to minorities, television may become a place for the mere parading of diversity—a pluralism structured by the state, as opposed to a forum for a sharp diversity of views or sources of information. Those rendering advice are thus often involved in an odd cultural bind: either recommending a free-market approach in which increased entertainment crowds out news and cultural programming, or recommending output-based structures (more news, more education) that are superficially inconsistent with trends in their own countries. Most proposed broadcast structures seem to have more substantial public service requirements than is currently fashionable in the market-based structures of the West.[96]

[96] There is also the question of differing determinations of what constitutes "news." In some instances, such as the Hungarian draft, there is a requirement that the news be objective. What constitutes "news" is a politically charged subject and is substantially affected, in most of these loci of transformation, by government policies. "News," as the consequence of a command structure, will differ, it is assumed, from "news" that is the product of a market; but how—other than in terms of the potential for criticism of the government—is rarely clear.

A frequently articulated national defense argument is related, but problematic, i.e., free speech yields a democratic state, and democratic neighbors are less likely to engage in war; reason prevails where discourse is open and unencumbered. Nevertheless, free speech can also subvert governments and destroy, as well as promote, democratic forms. For American foreign policy, piping truth behind the Iron Curtain was sometimes considered therapeutically destabilizing. Among the shaky neophyte republics (now friends), the destabilizing aspects of truth may not continue to be of such high priority. From a defense perspective, then, free speech becomes double-edged. The time may come when Western passions no longer demand the adoption of speech codes that tolerate the widest range of criticism and diversity. Destabilizing speech can come from neo-Nazis, fundamental religionists, ethnic separatists, or advocates of the old totalitarian way of life.

Altruism, commitment to democracy, and the creation of stable democratic societies—these are the major tropes of reform. But other motivations can be briefly canvassed. One is that an enhanced world market relies on the expansion of efficient national markets, and that both require broadly available uncensored information. The capacity to distribute information to potential consumers, whether retail or manufacturing, is vital to nurturing demand. Moreover, unencumbered access to information concerning societal activities—whether it is the plans of government, the political tendencies of the citizenry, or aspects of behavioral change—is profoundly important for those who take risks (e.g., entrepreneurs and producers). Late twentieth-century ideas of free speech include substantial opportunities for advertising and commercial messages, as well as for corporate influence over the structure of taste and consumption. Accordingly, the West is a net exporter of the products that accompany free speech—its paraphernalia and programming. Enhanced networks of communication become the infrastructure for substantial developments in trade.[97] In these terms, a standard to be applied in evaluating reform is whether the broadcasting transformation contributes to the strengthening of a market economy, both by enhancing the market for information and ideas, and by enhancing the market for other goods and services. Privatization of the broadcast media is often put forward as a measure for acceptable movement, but this point must be analyzed further. In most of the countries, the pace of privatization of television—in the sense of taking state services and turning them over to private entities—has been quite slow, although the process is speedier for newspapers and radio. There are few, if any, examples of fully privatizing a major television service (i.e., sale to a private entity unconnected with the government).

[97] There is a more cynical view of the link between the messengers of democratic reform and developments in trade. The patina of democracy, including the freedom associated with broadcasting reform, compensates for injurious developments in the economic sphere. In some transforming societies, according to this view, chaos, flights of capital, disappearance of natural resources, and declining quality in the fundamentals of the standard of living are articulated as transitional, with the new freedoms serving as partial, and perhaps sufficient, compensation.

Another standard not often articulated by Western observers—and possibly in conflict with those more frequently stated—is whether a transformation contributes to establishing a more secure and enduring national identity. Some draft statutes (e.g., Slovenia's and Bulgaria's) reinforce the new national identity and duty of the broadcasting enterprise. There is no objective national identity, however, and it thus falls to the government or to the broadcaster (as a surrogate) to define which national identity should be projected. Certainly, unstable regimes rely on the state-controlled media to help strengthen their power. These are often states in the process of being "invented," to use Hobsbawm's term,[99] or "imagined," to use Benedict Anderson's term.[100] The role of the broadcasting system in this process is an important priority. In Kiev, a special effort has been made to find and promulgate a Ukrainian national identity. Perhaps it is no accident that the Crimean Parliament, largely Russian, declared that the substitution of its channel for the Russian Channel from Moscow was one ground for its short-lived declaration of independence. But certainly, a fundamental problem in the translation of concepts concerns the way in which the state defines the role of the broadcasting system. National quota provisions and statutory obligations to reflect the cultures of specific national minorities are frequent characteristics of the new identity-oriented legislation that is typical of our time. More important than these formal provisions, however, is the internalized idea of the broadcasting system. Perhaps by definition, the *ancien regime* treated the mass media as an instrument of the state, dedicated to its own perception of what was needed to strengthen the public cause. Even now, it is hard for this concept to disappear, and for those who try to cross the borders of understanding, comprehending this concept may be important.

We have come to think of broadcasting as part of "the press" or part of "speech" and, therefore, specially privileged. But in terms of generating images of national identity, broadcasting institutions have to be seen among other media that perform similar functions. Educational systems are the prime example. Many of the debates about the purpose and content of public education (or the public financing of private education) turn on the state's role in reproducing itself, in delineating itself, and in projecting itself in certain ways. In some countries—England among them—the connections between the role of the state in education and its role in broadcasting have been quite evident. Perhaps what is occurring in Central and Eastern Europe and the former Soviet Union is the formation of a complex market for individual and group loyalties—a market that can be defined in the same manner as the market for capital, labor, automobiles, or sugar. If there is such a market, the government certainly plays a role both as a creator and as a participant. One can look at proposed structures in these countries (or at international conventions and existing structures) as methods of articulating the particular rules that apply to this competitive marketplace. These rules, by measuring out the rights of individuals to receive and impart information, delimit the state's power to coerce an

[99] The Invention of Tradition (Eric J. Hobsbawm and Terence Ranger eds., 1983).

[100] Benedict Anderson, Imagined Communities: Reflections on the Origin and Spread of Nationalism (1991).

unfair advantage in the competition for loyalties. Most Western structures similarly impose constitutional norms that deny government the power to monopolize the market for national identities. What they do not do, however, is preclude the state from acting as one of the competitors. For example, the First Amendment to the Constitution of the United States, which precludes Congress from abridging the freedom of speech and the press, forbids the government from using the force of law to block competition in the market for loyalty and national identity. The First Amendment does not disable the government from participating as a seller in the market for loyalties, except in one particular way—by establishing a church. The European Convention on Human Rights also provides for an open market for loyalties in Article 10, but it provides very specific and relevant exceptions. Governments may restrict their competitors when regulation "is necessary in a democratic society in the interests of national security, territorial integrity or public safety."[103]

As the struggling governments of Central and Eastern Europe enter this market for loyalties, one can look at their statutory drafts from this analytical framework. What competition for loyalties is permitted? Does the state have a monopoly both in broadcasting and the press? Does a competitive and vital newspaper market make a concentrated and government-oriented broadcasting structure more tolerable? Does the march toward privatization and commercialization mean that broadcasting will be less of a forum for public discourse and competition than might otherwise be the case? Additionally, as these countries are dedicating themselves to transforming broadcasting structures, important global transformations come into play that may render a viable and effective national system impossible. The increasing permeability of borders to signals and information from abroad means that purposive efforts to control discourse may be increasingly ineffective. Besides, given the depth and persistence of basic ideas of identity held by national subgroups (as we see bursting forth everywhere: the Slovaks out of Czechoslovakia, the Russians in the Ukraine, the Germans in Kazakhstan, the dismemberment of Yugoslavia), it is not clear that the talent, skill, and insight involved in using broadcasting to build counter-identities—identities of cohesiveness—can be effective. Perhaps broadcasting can reinforce and inflame, but not shift, deep-seated popular identities. Finally, the entry of advertising creates new, and potentially more effective, competitors for loyalty. These are forces that shift individual identities from those of citizens to a new status as consumers, who believe not in their flag, but in their commercial hopes and fantasies. The Western observer comes on the scene of Eastern transformations at a time when, for him, the positive function of the state in preserving and communicating the idea of the center has diminished. Both the BBC in Great Britain and the Public Broadcasting Service in the United States have been under fire recently

[103] The state may also restrict (or impose conditions or penalties) for the protection of health or morals, for the protection of the reputation or rights of others, for preventing the disclosure of information received in confidence, or for maintaining the authority and impartiality of the judiciary. The British government, in a case that was arguably about national identity, cited the confidentiality protection provision in seeking an injunction against a former member of the British Security Services.

because of doubts about whether government should generate (or subsidize the generation of) images of national identity. If allowed, what images they should be permitted to so generate?[104]

Every state holds a conversation with its subjects as to the legitimacy of its existence. In this conversation, the state is engaged in self-justification, in making the case for the continuation and improvement of the state, and in seeking the loyalty of its citizens. Governments generate images that reinforce the relationship between its subjects and itself for many reasons. Indeed, national identity, so theatrical and compelling a concept, may be nothing more than that collection of images that the government (or a series of interest groups) manufactures or encourages to keep itself in power. The state may claim to intervene in defense of its culture, and that may be a valid and relevant ground for the intervention. But those in power may use the machinery of the state to encourage a world outlook—grounded components of a "national identity"—which, to reinforce their dominance, is consonant with their political status. Some states may have so weak a franchise (absent force and fiction), that the creation and propagation of a narrative of legitimacy is all-consuming, pervasive, and devastatingly revealing of the regime. Even in democratic societies, however, the necessity for generating and maintaining a narrative of community is an important occupation. What is significant is that these ideas and images are part of every state's definition.

[104] One might wonder whether there is or should be a jurisprudence of transformations; whether there is a way of looking at the process of restructuring of legal systems at the time of paradigm shifts—from capitalism to socialism, from feudalism to the modern state, from an authoritarian society to a democratic one. Looking across examples of these vast changes, are there similarities from which we can predict the process of change? What might be interesting would be to ask this question: if there were such a jurisprudence of transformation, what would it tell us about the complexities of restructuring broadcasting systems? Or, put differently, given the experience that is accumulating in the process of restructuring, what can we infer from it that will help articulate or foreshadow such a jurisprudence of transformation?

Izvestiia as a Mirror of Russian Legal Reform: Press, Law, and Crisis in the Post-Soviet Era[*]

Frances H. Foster

The mass media are a mirror of society. Blaming the mirror is a fruitless occupation.

— Andrei Sharipov[1]

Introduction

On the evening of March 20, 1993, Boris Yeltsin stunned the world by announcing the introduction of emergency presidential rule in Russia. He cited his "duty as a citizen, as a patriot, and as a human being" to protect the Russian populace and reform process from an antidemocratic, obstructionist parliament. In succeeding days, President Yeltsin, Supreme Soviet Chairman Khasbulatov, and Constitutional Court Chairman Zorkin waged a veritable battle of the titans. All three framed their competing claims to legitimacy in legal and democratic rhetoric, yet ran roughshod over formal legal rules and processes.[5] Indeed, the eventual resolution of the crisis required resort to extra-constitutional measures.

The March power struggle provides dramatic evidence of Russia's failure to realize the "democratic, law-based state" it pledged at Alma Ata in December 1991. In fact, however, it is only symptomatic of a larger problem—the "breakdown of all legal authority" in post-Soviet Russia.

Why have Russian leaders had such difficulty translating promise into reality? What practical and theoretical factors explain this stunted progress toward a democratic, law-based state? Why has law in post-Soviet Russia failed to meet its ultimate challenge as a force for stabilization in a period of profound national change and crisis?

This Article attempts to provide some preliminary answers to these crucial questions. It seeks to identify major structural, procedural, and attitudinal obstacles to Russian legal reform efforts in the post-Soviet era. The Russian legal system is in such flux as to make conventional scholarly examination of "law on the books" irrelevant, if not futile. Accordingly, this Article takes a "law in action" approach and considers the general course of legal reform through the experience of one entity, the newspaper *Izvestiia*.

---

[*] 26 Vanderbilt Journal of Transnational Law 675 (1993).

[1] Andrei Sharipov, *Necha Peniat* [*Nothing to Blame*], Rossiiskaia Gazeta, Dec. 4, 1992, at 2.

[5] Interestingly, Boris Yeltsin admitted that all three branches of government had acted contrary to the Constitution. Valerii Zorkin received sharp criticism for his immediate denunciation of Yeltsin's decrees as unconstitutional.

If history is instructive, a free press will be important for the development of democracy in Russia. In other contexts, the press has acted as a major force to advance and safeguard democratic values, institutions, and procedures. In fact, one United States scholar has posited that "it is possible to have a democracy without judicial review, though not without freedom of the press."[12]

Russia's Soviet heritage is markedly different. Even at the height of Gorbachev's *glasnost* reforms, the approved functions of the press were to communicate and facilitate central communist party and state directive and ideology. Soviet leaders derived significant authority from control of information and greeted calls for the most minimal relaxation of restrictions with suspicion and hostility.

In post-socialist Russia, then, there likely will be considerable tension between notions of the press as an instrument of the party or state and as an independent "bulwark of liberty." The devolution of central control over information promises to be a matter of particular sensitivity and potential conflict.[16] Thus, an examination of the evolving status and rights of the Russian press should give some indication of the overall problems in Russia's democratic and legal reform.

Izvestiia provides an ideal case for studying post-Soviet developments. In the brief period since its self-declared emancipation in August 1991, this newspaper has directly collided with many key elements of the Russian legal system. As a result, it offers important insights into lawmaking norms and rules; economic regulation in the transition from command to market economy; formal and practical enforcement mechanisms; and the relationship between press, law, and crisis in the post-Soviet era.

I. The *Izvestiia* Experience

Izvestiia's past gave little intimation of its future role as gadfly and advocate for change. Founded in 1917, it served for seventy-four years as the official mouthpiece of the Soviet legislature and "active assistant" of the Communist Party. Its very name,

---

[12] Lucas A. Powe, Jr., The Fourth Estate and the Constitution: Freedom of the Press in America 294 (1991).

[16] Yeltsin issued as his first emergency decree the Presidential Decree On the Protection of the Freedom of Mass Information (Mar. 20, 1993). This was a response to what Yeltsin perceived to be a "real threat to the freedom of speech" by the Russian legislature. The decree stipulated "strict accountability" of all officials of state organizations and public associations for interference in mass media activity. It also provided for the Ministry of Internal Affairs to guard media facilities and for the Council of Ministers to create a State Inspectorate for the Protection of the Freedom of the Press and Mass Information. On March 28, the Congress responded by declaring illegal the Russian Federal Information Center that Yeltsin had established on December 25, 1992, to "ensure . . . the timely and broad dissemination of accurate and true information about the course of reforms in Russia and the clarification of Russian Federation state policy through the press and mass media." In addition, the Congress introduced so-called "observers' councils" to monitor mass media activity. Approximately 100 deputies petitioned the Constitutional Court for review.

Izvestiia Sovetov Narodnykh Deputatov SSSR [*News of the Soviets of USSR People's Deputies*] ("*Izvestiia SSSR*") proclaimed its subordinate status.

In the waning months of the Gorbachev regime, however, *Izvestiia* journalists increasingly chafed under central party and state domination.[19] With the attempted coup of August 19-22, 1991, *Izvestiia* finally was able to assume a new role and voice. From then on, it tested the limits of Russian democratic and legal reforms.

A. *Izvestiia*'s "Coup Within a Coup"

On August 20, 1991, *Izvestiia* announced its rebirth with a flourish. In open defiance of its editor-in-chief, it published Boris Yeltsin's "Appeal to the Citizens of Russia," a denunciation of the coup and call for a general strike. In so doing, *Izvestiia* enjoyed the distinction of being the only central newspaper to brave the wrath of the ruling junta.

Two days later, *Izvestiia*'s editorial office and journalists' collective formally confirmed their newspaper's new direction. Citing acts of omission and commission during the coup, they unilaterally proclaimed independence from their legal founder, the Presidium of the USSR Supreme Soviet, and fired their editor-in-chief.[24] They justified these radical steps as fully conforming with recent Russian presidential decrees and implementing resolutions regarding the treatment of coup participants.[26]

On August 23, *Izvestiia* received a certificate of re-registration from the Russian Ministry of the Press and Information ("Press Ministry"). This document officially recorded the newspaper's change in name (from *Izvestiia SSSR* to *Izvestiia*) and in founder (now the *Izvestiia* journalists' collective). On the same day, *Izvestiia*'s staff unanimously adopted a new charter and, for the first time in history, elected its own editor-in-chief.[28]

[19] In February 1991, Nikolai Efimov, *Izvestiia*'s editor-in-chief, attempted to remove several of the newspaper's journalists including first deputy editor-in-chief, Igor Golembiovskii. The *Izvestiia* staff, infuriated by the action, intervened in favor of Golembiovskii and suggested that Efimov step down from his position. Efimov remained editor-in-chief, nonetheless. In June 1991, on the direction of USSR Supreme Soviet Chairman Anatolii Lukianov, Efimov announced new appointments to the editorial staffs of *Izvestiia* and its supplement *Nedelia*. *Izvestiia* journalists protested this decision as directly violating the rights of the Presidium as founder of *Izvestiia* and *Izvestiia*'s Editorial Office as founder of *Nedelia*.

[24] In August 1990, the USSR Supreme Soviet Presidium officially founded and registered the newspaper *Izvestiia Sovetov Narodnykh Deputatov SSSR* in accordance with the recently enacted USSR Law On the Press and Other Mass Information Media. *Izvestiia SSSR* received the first registration certificate.

[26] The Decision specifically cited Yeltsin's Decree No. 61 of August 19, 1991, which characterized the coup as an unconstitutional "crime against the state" and called for removal from office and criminal prosecution for all officials who implemented decisions of the ruling junta.

[28] Igor Golembiovskii was the unanimous choice for editor-in-chief.

In a symbolic break with the past, *Izvestiia* reappeared on August 24, under a different masthead as well as title.[29] Over the following months, its editors and journalists repeatedly emphasized the newspaper's independent status and line. For example, on September 5, they explicitly rejected *Izvestiia*'s traditional, statutorily prescribed function as official publisher of legislative materials. They served notice that *Izvestiia* would no longer mechanically reproduce legislation on instruction from above but, rather, would print only those documents "of interest to readers." Soon thereafter, *Izvestiia*'s editorial office also renounced the newspaper's longstanding role as conduit between the citizenry and authorities. It stated unequivocally that henceforth *Izvestiia* would neither reply to readers' letters nor forward them to government organs "for action."

There was a marked change as well in the content and tone of *Izvestiia* articles. Reporters paraded their liberation from party and state sponsorship in pieces that openly criticized even the highest Soviet and republic leaders and bodies. There was an immediate response from readers and authorities—a noticeable increase in retail sales and bans on circulation by several republic governments.

Despite these dramatic departures from previous practice, *Izvestiia*'s staff members insisted that the newspaper was "the direct heir and rightful successor" of *Izvestiia SSSR*. They described their publication as the "renewed" version of its predecessor. They deliberately selected both a title and a numbering scheme that would reflect this linkage to the past.[38] On October 17, 1991, *Izvestiia*'s claim to succession received legislative support in a USSR Presidium resolution entitled On the Transformation of the Newspaper-Publishing Complex 'Izvestiia' into the Economic Amalgamation Concern 'Izvestiia.'

Over the following months, *Izvestiia* took an increasingly harsh stance toward the Russian parliament and its chairman, Ruslan Khasbulatov. The newspaper featured the Russian Supreme Soviet's latest foibles and procedural irregularities. It held up for criticism and ridicule Khasbulatov's colorful expressions and heavy-handed management of legislative sessions.

On March 17, 1992, *Izvestiia* stepped up its attack. It published an exposé of Khasbulatov's alleged involvement in the expulsion of ethnic Chechens from Moscow hotels and subsequent persecution by the Moscow militia. The author accused the parliamentary chairman of abuse of power and violation of fundamental constitutional and human rights guarantees. She even reported ongoing proposals and proceedings for Khasbulatov's removal from office. This article proved to be the catalyst for direct confrontation between Russia's First and Fourth Estates during the latter half of 1992.

[29] The slogan "Workers of the world, unite!" was conspicuously absent from the masthead.

[38] The August 24 issue was published as number 202 (for 1991) and number 23468 (since the original date of *Izvestiia SSSR*'s founding).

B. Early Economic Challenges

During its first year of existence, *Izvestiia* waged a desperate struggle for economic survival. It rapidly discovered that independence came with a heavy price—loss of funding and preferential treatment from the Communist Party and state. *Izvestiia*'s staff suddenly was forced to deal with the stark realities of economic enterprise and competition. It was ill-equipped for these new tasks, in terms of both experience and financial resources. Because of party and state sponsorship, the newspaper had long been insulated from the practical problems of supply, production, and distribution. Moreover, when *Izvestiia*'s journalists' collective formally assumed control on August 23, it acquired only the "intellectual structure" of the newspaper and none of its more tangible assets. A separate entity, the Publishing House *Izvestiia* of Soviets of USSR People's Deputies (*Izvestiia* Publishing House), remained the legal owner of all editorial offices, production facilities, equipment, and the like. *Izvestiia* used this property under a contractual arrangement with *Izvestiia* Publishing House.

In the fall of 1991, per custom and mandate from the Ministry of Communications, Russian newspapers, including *Izvestiia*, launched a drive for 1992 subscriptions. They raised prices substantially to compensate for the rapidly escalating costs of newsprint, publishing materials, delivery, and distribution. As a result, most publications experienced a considerable decline in subscriptions and faced imminent bankruptcy. *Izvestiia* emerged relatively unscathed from the 1992 subscription campaign.[54] Within a month, however, it too was "on the brink of financial crisis." The precipitating factor was the introduction of Boris Yeltsin's market reforms in early 1992.

On January 2, 1992, the Russian government instituted widespread price liberalization. This policy had a staggering impact on Russian newspapers. With the lifting of price controls, the cost of newsprint alone rose from 300 rubles per ton to 13,000 rubles per ton. *Izvestiia* reported an increase in overall production expenses of as much as 200 times previous charges.

To make matters worse, nearly all of the essential publication services remained under government monopoly. This situation raised particular difficulties in the distribution and transportation sectors, both controlled by agencies of the Ministry of Communications. In mid-January, the central newspaper distribution organization, *Rospechat'* (formerly *Soiuzpechat'*), suddenly presented the Russian print media with an ultimatum—either raise prices to an amount preset by *Rospechat'* or lose all access to retail sales. The proposed "minimum prices" were astronomical, well beyond the means of most Russian readers. *Izvestiia*, for example, faced a 400-500 percent price hike. The Moscow Post Office soon followed suit and imposed a substantial tariff for delivery of mailed subscriptions.

---

[54] *Izvestiia* retained 71.81% of its subscription rate of the previous year as compared to *Literaturnaia Gazeta*'s and *Pravda*'s rates of 26.11% and 39.33%, respectively.

The combined effect of price liberalization and monopolization led to the virtual "collapse of the newspaper empire." Subscription fees collected in late 1991 at state-controlled prices were woefully inadequate to offset the spiraling expenses of 1992. As a result, many publications were forced to cease operations either temporarily or permanently. Even *Pravda* suspended publication in mid-March, a matter of considerable embarrassment to Russian leaders. *Izvestiia* in the first quarter alone suffered a 400 million ruble loss from subscriptions. By July, the situation had deteriorated to the point that *Izvestiia* was actually subsidizing its subscribers in the amount of more than two rubles per issue.

Throughout this period, representatives of *Izvestiia* and other prominent Moscow newspapers appealed to the Russian government for assistance. The response, exemplified by Boris Yeltsin's February 20, 1992, Decree On Additional Measures of Legal and Economic Protection for the Periodical Press and State Book Publishing, took two forms—subsidies and measures designed to mitigate the effect of market reforms. As will be described below, both approaches proved problematic but provided some immediate relief to publications on the edge of bankruptcy.[71]

Beginning in the spring of 1992, *Izvestiia* faced an additional, more direct threat to its continued existence, this time from the political arena. The Russian legislature set out to accomplish what economic reform had not—the total destruction of *Izvestiia*.

C. Conflict with the Russian Legislature

Ruslan Khasbulatov delivered the opening volley at a March 30 meeting with members of the Supreme Soviet Mass Media Committee. He attacked the major publications as "corrupt," "subversive" tools of the Yeltsin government. He placed particular emphasis on *Izvestiia*'s anti-legislative bias and "ungrateful, uncivil role."[73]

At the subsequent Congress of People's Deputies, Khasbulatov intensified his offensive. On April 10, he announced from the rostrum a proposal to revoke *Izvestiia*'s status as an independent publication and to "restore" it as official organ of the Russian soviets. In support, Khasbulatov cited numerous complaints from deputies regarding *Izvestiia*'s inaccurate reporting and poor financial management. In addition, he stated that *Izvestiia* had accumulated a debt of over one billion rubles and had lost its readership. Following this speech, Khasbulatov had an appropriate resolution drafted for

[71] *Izvestiia*'s survival, however, was due more to its own efforts than to government assistance. It adapted to changing market conditions in a variety of traditional and innovative ways. Like other Russian publications, it made deep cuts in staff, salaries, deliveries, copies, and local editions. It also launched re-subscription campaigns at higher prices to offset escalating expenses. *Izvestiia* diversified its operations by adding new publications, including a joint venture weekly *My/We* with Hearst. It was one of the first newspapers to make extensive use of advertising, locate unofficial sources of newsprint, and contract directly with distributors. *Izvestiia* even reorganized its management structure, creating two limited liability companies.

[73] Khasbulatov warned journalists: "The press should not harbor any illusion of being the Fourth Estate! You are of no significance!"

congressional consideration. On the final day, deputies voted to instruct the Supreme Soviet to reexamine the legal position of the mass media at its next session.

These events provoked a storm of indignation from the Russian mass media. Journalists contended that any unilateral legislative alteration of *Izvestiia*'s status would violate the letter and spirit of Russian legislation.[79] *Izvestiia* went even further. It publicly refuted Khasbulatov's allegations of a one billion ruble debt as an "all-out lie." After consultation with Russian and Western lawyers, the newspaper took legal action. It filed a slander suit against Khasbulatov demanding both moral and material damages.

Khasbulatov failed to appear in court either personally or through legal representation to answer *Izvestiia*'s charges. As he explained subsequently, "it is not convenient for a . . . chairman of the Supreme Soviet to go to court over every petty insult or piece of vulgarity." Instead, he responded by turning to the Russian procuracy to compile a convincing case against *Izvestiia*.

The procuracy conducted an intensive one-month investigation into the creation and operations of the *Izvestiia* newspaper and its spin-off entities, *Izvestiia* Concern and *Izvestiia* Editorial Office.[85] In its official report, the procuracy asserted five major claims: (1) the August 1991 suspension of *Izvestiia SSSR* and establishment of *Izvestiia* violated the USSR Law On the Press and Other Mass Media ("USSR Press Law");[86] (2) the formation of *Izvestiia* Concern and *Izvestiia* Editorial Office contravened USSR and Russian enterprise legislation;[87] (3) the October 17, 1991 USSR Presidium resolution was legally ineffective to convey *Izvestiia SSSR* to *Izvestiia*;[88] (4) the use of *Izvestiia* Publishing House property by *Izvestiia* Concern and *Izvestiia* Editorial Office violated Russian ownership law; and (5) by "unfortunate oversight," the official committee for liquidation of USSR Supreme Soviet property failed to inventory and transfer *Izvestiia*

---

[79] Specifically, they cited articles of the Russian Mass Media Law that allowed re-registration or termination of a registered publication only by decision of the founder or by court order. They also denounced the proposed bill as inconsistent with constitutional guarantees and public aspirations for genuine freedom of expression and an independent press.

[85] According to the official "Explanatory Note" submitted by the heads of *Izvestiia*, *Izvestiia* Publishing House, and *Izvestiia* Concern, *Izvestiia* Concern was a seven-person enterprise formed by *Izvestiia* Publishing House and *Izvestiia*'s editorial staff "to fulfill a very narrow range of tasks: to resolve contradictions that arise, hold talks of a commercial nature, and so forth." *Izvestiia* Editorial Office was established by *Izvestiia* Concern and the *Izvestiia* newspaper. The goal was to give the editorial staff formal legal status as a juridical person and, hence, "rectify" the earlier improper founding and registration of *Izvestiia* Concern.

[86] The report cited article 13 of the USSR Press Law, which provided that only the founder, registering organ or court had the authority to make a decision on suspension or publication of a mass media organ.

[87] The major problem in both cases was the fact that one of the founding parties was not a recognized juridical person for purposes of the USSR and Russian enterprise laws (the *Izvestiia* editorial staff in the case of *Izvestiia* Concern and the *Izvestiia* newspaper in the case of *Izvestiia* Editorial Office). The Soviet and Russian enterprise laws require more than one legal founder of a limited liability company.

[88] The report contended that the Presidium exceeded its legal competence by creating an *Izvestiia* newspaper publishing complex. Under Soviet and Russian enterprise laws, only enterprises have the right to form amalgamations.

SSSR to the Russian Supreme Soviet in December 1991. As a result of these findings, the procuracy filed a formal protest regarding the registration of *Izvestiia* Concern, recommended "further study" of the other entities created by *Izvestiia*, called for Presidium "examination" of *Izvestiia* Publishing House property, and pronounced "essential" an immediate correction of the liquidation committee's "error."

Despite numerous procedural and substantive objections from *Izvestiia*, the procuracy submitted the report to the Presidium and published it in *Rossiiskaia Gazeta*, the official organ of the Russian Supreme Soviet. The Presidium swiftly endorsed the findings. On July 13, 1992, it departed from the agenda to approve for Supreme Soviet consideration the Draft Resolution On the Newspaper *Izvestiia Sovetov Narodnykh Deputatov SSSR* ("Draft *Izvestiia SSSR* Resolution"). This bill declared that *Izvestiia*'s August 1991 establishment and registration were contrary to the USSR Press Law and that the Russian Supreme Soviet was the "legal successor" to the USSR Supreme Soviet Presidium, the injured founder of the suspended *Izvestiia SSSR*. Accordingly, the resolution called for publication of a newspaper of Russian "representative organs of power" "on the basis of" the *Izvestiia* Publishing House and *Izvestiia SSSR*. Furthermore, it directed the Russian Press Ministry to "assist" *Izvestiia* in "bringing its founding documents and registration into line with legal requirements and to allocate necessary premises for normal operations."

The draft bill received sharp criticism from all sides. Members of the Russian mass media, government, and legislature loudly denounced the proposed law as a threat to the very future of *glasnost'* and freedom of the press. Boris Yeltsin himself pledged his "unequivocal and resolute support" for *Izvestiia*. The Supreme Soviet Mass Media Committee formally condemned the bill and proclaimed its adoption by the legislature "impossible."[100] Consequently, the committee recommended removal of the Draft *Izvestiia SSSR* Resolution from Supreme Soviet consideration and further study of *Izvestiia* Concern's formation.

These combined protests initially appeared successful. The *Izvestiia* issue disappeared from the Supreme Soviet agenda. Nonetheless, late in the evening of July 17, it suddenly reemerged. After a spirited debate over the legality of the procuracy investigation and the draft bill, Ruslan Khasbulatov cut short deputy discussion and called for immediate action. He then proceeded to dictate from the rostrum the following two point "formula": "*Izvestiia* is the newspaper of the Russian Federation Soviets of

---

[100] The committee cited internal contradictions, violations of established procedures, and the "patently political character" of the Khasbulatov-*Izvestiia* conflict. It even questioned the very basis of the proposed law—Russian Supreme Soviet inheritance of the USSR Presidium's founding status. The Mass Media Committee stated that the status of a newspaper founder is "not a property matter." Thus, it argued that mass media, not ownership laws, governed any succession to status. The committee cited article 18 of the Russian Mass Media Law, which provided that upon abolition or reorganization of the founder, "its rights and duties are transferred in full to the editorial office." The Mass Media Committee concluded, accordingly, that *Izvestiia*'s editorial office had properly exercised its rights in August 1991. Moreover, it noted that the USSR Supreme Soviet, the legal founder of the *Izvestiia SSSR*, filed no protest at the time.

People's Deputies. The Ministry of the Press, the Ministry of Justice . . . considering the serious violations during registration, should be directed to legalize this newspaper in the appropriate manner." Deputies promptly approved their chairman's resolution sight unseen by a recorded vote of 136 to 23 (with twelve abstentions).

After a mysterious, nearly two-week delay, *Rossiiskaia Gazeta* published the official text of the Russian Federation Supreme Soviet Resolution On the Newspaper *Izvestiia* ("*Izvestiia* Resolution"). Surprisingly, the final version bore scant resemblance to the Khasbulatov text adopted by the deputies on July 17 (or, for that matter, to the original draft bill). The *Izvestiia* Resolution began with a detailed indictment of *Izvestiia* for its creation, registration, and continuing use of the state publishing house and other state property. It asserted that the applicable legislation was the USSR Press Law and not the Russian Federation Law On the Mass Media (Russian Mass Media Law), because the latter did not enter into force until February 8, 1992. The law then cited previous Russian Congress decisions to authorize "resumed" publication of a newspaper *entitled Izvestiia Sovetov Narodnykh Deputatov Rossiiskoi Federatsii* [*News of the Soviets of People's Deputies of the Russian Federation Supreme Soviet*] ("*Izvestiia RF*") "on the basis of" the *Izvestiia* Publishing House and the former *Izvestiia SSSR*. It called upon the Russian Press Ministry and the Supreme Soviet Mass Media and Legislation Committees to "bring *Izvestiia*'s founding and registration documents into line with existing legislation." Lastly, this final version of the *Izvestiia* Resolution declared itself effective upon publication.

To *Izvestiia*, at least, both the authorship and rationale of this reworked law were evident. *Izvestiia* detected in the deliberately vague, ambiguous language the fine hand of that "esteemed lawyer," Ruslan Khasbulatov. The newspaper argued that the resolution represented nothing less than Khasbulatov's final response to *Izvestiia*'s slander suit: "The best way to silence a plaintiff is to nail him into a coffin and send him to the graveyard."[113]

[113] It should be noted that throughout this period the Supreme Soviet was also engaged in the formulation of a general resolution on the mass media, per instructions of the April Congress of People's Deputies. There were reports of serious disagreement on the so-called Temporary Drafting Commission. By Khasbulatov's personal order, Mass Media Committee Chairman Viacheslaw I. Bragin was removed as chairman of the Temporary Commission, and Nikolai T. Riabov, chairman of one of the legislative chambers (the Soviet of the Republic), assumed responsibility for preparation of the resolution. Under its new leadership, the Temporary Commission produced the Draft Resolution On State Policy in the Field of the Mass Media. This bill included a provision instituting an "observers' council" to monitor the mass media, with extensive authority over personnel and financing of Russian television, radio, and newspapers. The Mass Media Committee sharply criticized the draft and prepared its own variant. Legislators eventually hammered out a compromise version, which one deputy characterized as "toothless but balanced." The final text, re-titled The Resolution On Economic Support and Legal Guarantees for Mass Media Activity, established procedures for state subsidies to the mass media, recommended "concessions analogous to those granted to cultural institutions and organizations," and called on the Russian government to address such critical issues as future subsidies, material and technical development, equipment production, and demonopolization of the printing and delivery sectors. The

D. Aftermath

Izvestiia received an outpouring of domestic and foreign support. Journalists, scholars, politicians, readers, and professional and public associations lambasted the *Izvestiia* Resolution as devoid of even the "semblance of legality."[114] The *Izvestiia* Resolution raised serious enforcement problems as well. Press Minister Mikhail Poltoranin announced that his ministry would not carry out the "unlawful" *Izvestiia* decision and would appeal to the Constitutional Court for relief. *Izvestiia* refused to comply on grounds that to do so would violate the Russian Mass Media Law adopted only months earlier by the Supreme Soviet. According to Chairman Viacheslav Bragin, the Russian Mass Media Committee was "put in a very awkward position" of having to implement a resolution it consistently had declared illegal.

These concerns culminated in a formal request for Constitutional Court review on August 3, 1992. The petitioners, three people's deputies,[119] claimed that the *Izvestiia* Resolution violated constitutional provisions on separation of powers,[120] human rights,[121] Russian Federation republic sovereignty,[122] and legislative procedure.[123] They asked the Constitutional Court for three forms of relief: (1) recognition of the *Izvestiia* Resolution as unconstitutional and ineffective from the date of entry into force; (2) retroactive

---

resolution also instructed the Mass Media and Legislation Committees to prepare draft laws on television and broadcasting and on appropriate amendments to Russian criminal and administrative violations codes, respectively. Thanks to a last-minute concession from Khasbulatov, there was no mention of an observers' council in the final text.

[114] Critics cited the blatant disregard of lawmaking procedures, flaws in statutory language and content, and lack of legislative competence. Most critics focused on contradictions with constitutional separation of powers. Others emphasized violations of the rights of other former Soviet republic legislatures as heirs of the USSR Supreme Soviet. Many critics were disturbed by the broader implications for freedom of speech and democracy. Some extended their attack on the *Izvestiia* Resolution into a challenge of the very legitimacy of the legislature. It should be noted that the legislature did have defenders in its actions against *Izvestiia*.

[119] The deputies were Sergei Sakhrai, Aleksander Kotenkov, and Igor Berzukov. The Russian Press Ministry was unable to petition the Constitutional Court because it was not one of the parties specified by article 59 of the Constitutional Court Law.

[120] They contended that the legislature had improperly exercised judicial powers by resolving questions regarding transfer of property and registration of a mass media organ. Moreover, it had encroached on the exclusive jurisdiction of the executive branch by issuing mandatory instructions to a government body (the Press Ministry).

[121] Specifically, the petitioners argued that the attempt to subordinate *Izvestiia* and, hence, destroy its objective coverage of legislative work, constituted a threat to citizens' constitutional rights to seek, receive, and disseminate information freely. In addition, they asserted that because a resolution is not subject to judicial appeal, the legislature effectively deprived the *Izvestiia* journalists' collective of the constitutional guarantee of legal protection of rights and interests.

[122] The petitioners contended that the Supreme Soviet had violated constitutional and Federation Treaty provisions by adopting a resolution relating to soviets throughout Russian Federation territory without any consultation or consent of the affected republics.

[123] The deputies claimed unconstitutionality on grounds of improper legislative procedures, citing voting irregularities on July 17, 1992, and the marked inconsistency between approved and final texts.

invalidation of any subsequent acts based thereupon; and (3) temporary suspension of the resolution pending Constitutional Court examination.

The Constitutional Court swiftly issued the requested suspension.[125] The legislative response came on August 17, an application for registration of a newspaper entitled *Izvestiia RF*.[126] Reportedly, Khasbulatov personally initiated this action without any prior consultation or clearance from the Mass Media Committee, Presidium, Supreme Soviet, or local soviets. In a press conference on August 17, Khasbulatov only reinforced his determination to subordinate *Izvestiia* to legislative control. He warned all assembled to "[w]ait for a development in the situation." Khasbulatov gave a preview of his next move by placing particular emphasis on the need to resolve "ownership questions" regarding building and printing facilities. From that point on, the legislative offensive against *Izvestiia* shifted from an attack on the newspaper's independent status to an assault on its economic base.

E. The Battle for Control of *Izvestiia* Publishing House

Boris Yeltsin launched a preemptive strike on August 22, 1992. He issued an ordinance instructing the Russian Federation State Committee for Management of State Property (*Goskomimushchestvo*) "to examine the question of assigning in accordance with established procedure, the property of the publishing complex *Izvestiia Sovetov Narodnykh Deputatov SSSR* to its successor—the *Izvestiia* newspaper publishing complex."

On August 24, Fikriat Tabeev, the chairman of the Russian Property Fund, countered with his own ordinance. This document claimed for his organization legal ownership of all *Izvestiia* Publishing House property until Supreme Soviet confirmation as founder. Five days later the battle of ordinances continued. Goskomimushchestvo Chairman Anatolii Chubais formally proclaimed the creation of the *Izvestiia* State Newspaper-Publishing Complex (*Izvestiia* Complex). This new entity included *Izvestiia* Concern, *Izvestiia* Editorial Office, *Izvestiia* Publishing House, and all subordinate structures. The Goskomimushchestvo ordinance recognized *Izvestiia* Complex as the successor to *Izvestiia* Publishing House and appointed Igor Golembiovskii as the interim general director.

A sharp debate ensued over the respective property claims and spheres of operation of Goskomimushchestvo and the Federal Property Fund. Both sides bolstered their cases with frequent citations to Russian Federation laws regarding disposition and privatization of state property. In fact, however, the controversy really represented a battle by proxy between Yeltsin and Khasbulatov. Goskomimushchestvo was an executive agency under Yeltsin's command, and the Federal Property Fund was a body

[125] It should be noted that the Constitutional Court has no legal authority to mandate suspension of legislation pending consideration of the case. It has the power only to "request" such action.

[126] The newspaper was registered in mid-September under the title *Izvestiia Narodnykh Deputatov Rossiiskoi Federatsii* [*News of the Russian Federation People's Deputies*].

subordinate to the Russian parliament. In the fall of 1992, the two principals became directly involved in the *Izvestiia* Publishing House conflict.

On September 7, the Supreme Soviet Presidium met in closed session. The main order of business was consideration of a draft resolution transferring *Izvestiia* Publishing House to the jurisdiction of the Russian Supreme Soviet. Khasbulatov reportedly prepared this bill in virtual secrecy, without the knowledge of the Mass Media Committee or the "overwhelming majority" of Presidium members. In violation of established legislative procedures, Khasbulatov proposed immediate adoption of the resolution without discussion. Deputies balked and voted for postponement of draft consideration until September 14 to permit examination by the relevant parliamentary committees. Khasbulatov warned legislators that if they failed to "find a solution" in one week's time, he would unilaterally determine *Izvestiia* Publishing House's fate with his own decree.

The following week, the Mass Media Committee formally denounced the draft resolution and recommended its removal from the legislative agenda. Deputies initially followed the committee's suggestion. Once again, however, Ruslan Khasbulatov intervened and threatened to ensure personally the "appropriate" disposition of *Izvestiia* Publishing House property. This time, the deputies heeded their chairman's warning. They re-voted in the desired fashion and officially added the *Izvestiia* Publishing House question to the agenda. By a substantial majority, the two parliamentary chambers officially adopted Khasbulatov's bill on October 19 and 20.[144]

On October 21, the legislature sent an unmistakable message regarding its determination to seize control of *Izvestiia*'s economic base. Deputy Chairman Yuri Voronin issued an ordinance "in fulfillment" of the *Izvestiia* Publishing House Resolution, which named a director for *Izvestiia* Publishing House and called for preparation of a new character. Even more ominously, it instructed both the *Izvestiia* financial administration and the so-called "guards of the supreme bodies of state authority and government," a 5000-person armed unit under Ruslan Khasbulatov's command, to "ensure preservation of material and technical valuables, buildings, and structures" of *Izvestiia* Publishing House.

In succeeding days, a powerful coalition of government, legislative, and media forces developed in opposition to the Supreme Soviet and its chairman, Khasbulatov. On October 27, representatives met at a Mass Media Committee session to discuss appropriate strategies to resist parliamentary "maneuvers" regarding *Izvestiia*. The most tangible results were the Mass Media and Legislation Committee's joint appeal to their deputy colleagues to reexamine the *Izvestiia* issue and petition to the Constitutional Court to review the *Izvestiia* Publishing House Resolution. Press Minister Poltoranin concluded that "the time has come for the president to have a say in the solution of this problem."[150]

---

[144] As in the case of the *Izvestiia* Resolution, there were serious questions regarding the validity of the final tally of votes.

[150] It should be noted that Mikhail Poltoranin was engaged in a personal struggle with Ruslan Khasbulatov. He publicly attacked Khasbulatov's attempt to seize control of *Izvestiia* as the "fuse [that]

Ironically, on the very day of the Mass Media Committee meeting, the Supreme Soviet leadership decided to back up its demands with force by dispatching its troops to the shared premises of *Izvestiia* Publishing House and *Izvestiia* Editorial Office. At this point Boris Yeltsin reentered the arena. In a presidential directive of October 27, he declared the parliamentary guards an "illegal armed formation" and ordered their immediate disbandment. After a brief skirmish between governmental and parliamentary forces, Khasbulatov's guards withdrew from the *Izvestiia* facilities, thus avoiding a potentially bloody confrontation between the executive and the legislature. Shortly thereafter, the *Izvestiia* Publishing House voluntarily acknowledged the Russian Federation Supreme Soviet as its founder and reregistered accordingly. Thus far, there has been no serious objections raised by the Russian president or media.

For the next six months, *Izvestiia*'s fate hung in the balance. On May 19, 1993, the Constitutional Court finally issued its long-promised decision and ruled in favor of *Izvestiia* on all counts. Russian executive and legislative branches remain at loggerheads. Indeed, in recent months their battle over *Izvestiia* has rapidly escalated into all-out warfare for control of the Russian mass media and the very destiny of Russia itself. Thus, the *Izvestiia* case is far more than a single, isolated struggle for survival in post-Soviet Russia. It is a revealing precursor of the current constitutional crisis of power and a "touchstone" by which to judge the overall process of Russian legal reform.

II. Lawmaking in Post-Soviet Russia

Izvestiia's experience reveals a number of serious problems in Russian lawmaking approaches and techniques. These anticipate and help explain the recent confrontation between Russia's president, legislature, and Constitutional Court.

A. Governing Law

The Russian parliament initially framed its attack on *Izvestiia* as a challenge to the newspaper's independent status, centering on the August 1991 termination of *Izvestiia SSSR* and registration of *Izvestiia*. Both sides subsequently contended that the key to resolution of the case was determination of the applicable law. The Supreme Soviet leadership argued that the relevant legislation was the June 1990 USSR Press Law, the statute in force at the time of *Izvestiia*'s "rebirth" as an independent newspaper. It maintained that *Izvestiia*'s editorial office and journalists' collective's unilateral suspension of *Izvestiia SSSR* violated Article 13 of the USSR Press Law. Pursuant thereto, only a founder, court, or registering organ possessed the requisite legal authority to cease publication of a mass media organ. None of these specified bodies did so. As of August 1991, the USSR Supreme Soviet Presidium, not the *Izvestiia* journalists'

might wreck the situation in Russia." He also accused parliamentary chairman of inordinate personal ambitions and dictatorial tendencies, even drawing a parallel with Stalin. Khasbulatov responded by officially requesting that Boris Yeltsin remove Poltoranin from his positions as Press Minister and Vice Premier.

collective, was the official founder of *Izvestiia SSSR*. Accordingly, the Russian Supreme Soviet concluded that as "successor" to the USSR Presidium it was fully justified in taking measures to "restore the original situation."

Izvestiia, by contrast, declared the governing law to be the December 1991 Russian Mass Media Law, in effect at the time of the Russian parliamentary offensive against *Izvestiia*. Article 6 stipulated that this legislation applied to all mass media "founded in the Russian Federation." Although strictly speaking, no "Russian Federation" existed in August 1991, the Russian Mass Media Law implementing resolution granted ex post facto recognition to existing Russian entities previously registered in accordance with the USSR Press Law. *Izvestiia* maintained that its August 1991 founding and registration complied with all of these statutory requirements. Its founder, the *Izvestiia* journalists' collective, had submitted the appropriate documentation to government authorities. Shortly thereafter, the collective received an official certificate of registration from the Russian Press Ministry, which never expressed any objection to *Izvestiia*'s establishment. Thus, *Izvestiia* contended that for Russian Mass Media Law purposes, the journalists' collective, and not the USSR Supreme Soviet Presidium, was the newspaper's legal founder. Under this interpretation, the December 1991 Russian statute effectively cut off any claims of a previous founder to challenge the newspaper's status.

The conflict between union and republic laws is by no means solely a post-Soviet phenomenon. As early as June 1990, the first Russian Congress of People's Deputies asserted the primacy of its own Constitution and legislation on Russian territory and proclaimed its authority to suspend operation of all USSR laws that contravened RSFSR sovereign rights. Despite strong opposition from Gorbachev, Russian leaders subsequently extended these claims to require explicit Russian confirmation of all USSR legislative, administrative, and presidential acts. This created a serious "war of laws" between federal and republic authorities and contributed to the ultimate collapse of the USSR.

With the dissolution of the Soviet Union in December 1991, the conflict between federal and republic law once again came to the fore. Recognizing the virtual impossibility of creating overnight a new legislative scheme, the Russian leadership opted for a temporary continuation of USSR legislation. In its formal ratification of the Agreement On Establishment of the Commonwealth of Independent States, the Russian Supreme Soviet set out the following general rule: "[P]ending the adoption of appropriate RSFSR legislative acts, the norms of the former USSR shall apply on RSFSR territory, insofar as they do not contradict the Constitution of the RSFSR, the legislation of the RSFSR, and the Agreement." The *Izvestiia* case reveals the real difficulties of applying this broad principle in actual practice.

The coup of August 1991 and subsequent introduction of emergency rule by Boris Yeltsin further complicated the *Izvestiia* debate over governing law. These events inspired what might be called the "illegitimate lawmaker" argument. In essence, *Izvestiia* claimed that the USSR Supreme Soviet Presidium had so discredited itself during the coup that it had lost any moral or legal right to remain the newspaper's founder. In support, *Izvestiia* cited specific Yeltsin decrees and Russian Supreme Soviet resolutions that unilaterally suspended existing Soviet legislation and institutions. Many of Yeltsin's emergency decisions, however, later were challenged as unconstitutional.[176]

On balance, then, the *Izvestiia* journalists' collective and editorial office clearly violated the USSR Press Law when they terminated the legally registered mass media organ *Izvestiia SSSR*. The only colorable defense is that they acted in accordance with special emergency enactments that were themselves of dubious legality. The more likely view is that *Izvestiia* journalists and staff took advantage of a chaotic situation to liberate themselves from Soviet party and state control. The dissolution of the USSR legislature and its Presidium in December 1991, however, rendered *Izvestiia*'s troubled beginnings fundamentally irrelevant. From that point on, there no longer existed an entity with the legal standing to sue as founder of *Izvestiia SSSR*. The Russian Supreme Soviet claim to succession is questionable at best, as it is based solely on the laws regarding inheritance of USSR Supreme Soviet property, not status. This may well explain why Khasbulatov eventually chose to end his attack on the *Izvestiia* newspaper and pursue far stronger claims to the ownership of its material base, the *Izvestiia* Publishing House.

Nonetheless, the *Izvestiia* debate over governing law has important implications for the present and future. Recent experience with constitutional drafting only confirms the difficulties of integrating legal regimes from two markedly different periods of history. The Russian legislature thus far has resisted proposals for adoption of an entirely new constitution to reflect the concrete needs and realities of the post-Soviet era. Instead, it has chosen to make over 300 amendments to the original Russian Constitution of 1978. The result is a "patched up" document riddled with inconsistencies and fundamentally unsuited for resolution of current political and economic problems.

Even more interestingly, the "illegitimate lawmaker" defense has resurfaced in recent months. It was in fact Boris Yeltsin's very justification for instituting special presidential rule by decree in March 1993. In his March 20 announcement, Yeltsin explained that the Russian legislature at its recent Eighth Congress of People's Deputies had acted in such an unconstitutional, reactionary, and undemocratic fashion that he as president was "compelled to assume responsibility for the country's future." To reinforce this claim of parliamentary illegitimacy, Yeltsin characterized the legislature as a CPSU-controlled entity intent upon the restoration of communism in Russia. In so doing, he recast the Russian executive-legislative conflict as a Manichean struggle between the

[176] The most criticized decrees were those directed against the mass media and the communist party. Yeltsin ultimately lifted his mass media suspensions. On November 30, the Constitutional Court upheld Yeltsin's ban on the party, but ruled that low-level party cells were legal and that property claims should be resolved by the Russian judiciary.

forces of good and evil, a characterization that proved highly persuasive, at least to Western audiences.[185]

B. Lawmaking Procedure

[O]ne of the most significant lessons of the Gorbachev-era "perestroika parliament" was its demonstration of the critical importance of legislative procedure. From 1989-1990, the reformed Soviet legislature discovered through practice that regularized rules can promote legislative professionalism, enhance public participation in the lawmaking process, protect parliamentary minorities, and restrain control from above. The *Izvestiia* case affirms the continued validity of these conclusions for Russia today.

The *Izvestiia* experience suggests that, if anything, the level of procedural observance has only deteriorated in the post-Soviet period. This case reveals a consistent pattern of disregard of legislative rules. One illustration is the *Izvestiia* Resolution, enacted in an accelerated, truncated process that violated the letter and spirit of the Supreme Soviet Standing Orders in every lawmaking stage.[187] This flexible approach to

---

[185] In fact, many Western commentators took this a step further and declared both the legislature and the Constitution void *ab initio* because they were created in the communist era. Yale Law School Professor Bruce Ackerman even compared Boris Yeltsin's "end run" around the "communist" Constitution to George Washington's "radical action" at the Constitutional Convention and praised his move as a "model" for Eastern Europe.

[187] The basic rules governing Supreme Soviet lawmaking procedure are set out in the Standing Orders of October 24, 1990. This statute is nearly a verbatim reproduction of its USSR counterpart. The troubled passage of the *Izvestiia* Resolution began with its anonymous formulation behind closed doors. This was contrary to efforts by Soviet and Russian reformers since 1989 to transform the pre-initiation phase into a more open and participatory process. The draft "turned up" unexpectedly at the July 13 Presidium session without any formal mention in the published agenda or accompanying documentation as required by statute. In violation of articles 62 through 64 there apparently was no clear identification of the bill's authors or official "initiator." Nevertheless, the Presidium swiftly approved the text for direct submission to the Supreme Soviet. In so doing, it bypassed the traditional "preliminary examination" by "relevant" committee(s) [here, the Mass Media Committee] and the Legislation Committee. (It should be noted, however, that in June 1992, the Russian legislature amended this article to give the Presidium blanket authority to determine drafting committees, stages, and conditions. There was no longer any specific requirement of submission to "relevant" committee(s) and the Legislation Committee.)

When the Supreme Soviet gave "due regard for the findings" of the Mass Media Committee and refused to include the bill on its agenda, it acted in accordance with article 68 of the Standing Orders. Despite this decision, however, the *Izvestiia* issue resurfaced on the last day of the Supreme Soviet session. From then on, there occurred an extraordinary series of Standing Orders' violations. Deputies proceeded directly to draft consideration and vote, thus effectively nullifying statutory guarantees for the participation of parliamentary committees and the concerned public in preparation, discussion, and revision of legislation. Supreme Soviet discussion of the *Izvestiia* Resolution was a parody of established procedures. Chairman Khasbulatov interrupted speakers at will, provided unsolicited personal commentary and direction, limited the duration and scope of deputy discussion, and finally dictated his own text. Ironically, one of the formal functions of the chairman is to monitor compliance with the Standing Orders. The voting stage was equally defective. In marked contrast with the Standing Orders' norm of "two readings" per bill, deputies gave final approval "sight unseen" to Khasbulatov's bill. Even the recorded tally of votes was dubious because it included names of absent deputies.

statutory creation and enactment rapidly became the rule rather than the exception in Russian legislative practice. By the fall of 1992, a special task force of the Legislation Committee reported that leadership infractions of procedural rules had reached the point of an unconstitutional abuse of power by the Supreme Soviet Presidium and its chairman.

Lack of procedural regularity had far-reaching consequences. One result was effective insulation of lawmaking from public, and even legislative committee, knowledge, input, and accountability. It also encouraged hasty, unsystematic preparation of statutes, which contributed to the low quality and sporadic production of Russian legislation. Most significantly, nonobservance of legislative procedures removed any restraints on the chairman's direction of parliamentary discussion and action. This allowed Khasbulatov to disregard the rights and views of legislative opponents and even to reconstitute "unsuitable" legislative committees.

Throughout this period, Khasbulatov took a variety of measures to reinforce his de facto control of the legislative process. He unilaterally redefined his personal powers as chairman and expanded the size and functions of his staff. Moreover, he revived the tradition of authoritarian "leadership" by the Presidium and legislative apparatus.

By March 1993, Congress and Supreme Soviet sessions had degenerated into "constant and gross breaches" of the Standing Orders. On occasion, apparatus officials reportedly cast votes for deputies. The Presidium regularly supplanted the Russian legislature as lawmaker. For example, in direct violation of the Constitution, it formulated questions for national referendum.

To make matters worse, there were major flaws as well in the executive branch's approach to creation and adoption of laws and regulations. Unlike the legislative context, here the fundamental problem was not disregard of established lawmaking rules and channels but the virtual absence of any such procedures. There was no formal drafting body with the assigned responsibility for supervising the language, content, and consistency of proposed laws with existing presidential, administrative, and legislative acts. Executive, especially presidential, lawmaking was largely an ad hoc process. Decrees generally appeared in reaction to recent developments rather than as part of an integrated program. The *Izvestiia* case provides several examples. These include the Yeltsin and Goskomimushchestvo ordinances on *Izvestiia* Publishing House and the presidential edict banning Khasbulatov's parliamentary guard.

Executive lawmaking occurred behind a shroud of secrecy, with limited opportunities for public comment, participation, or information regarding the authors, content, or timing of acts. Disorganization and delay were common at even the highest levels of the Russian executive branch. One particularly dramatic instance was the "sad

---

The ultimate procedural infringement was publication of an official text that diverged substantially from the adopted version. Only one month earlier, the Supreme Soviet had amended its Standing Orders to add the following language: "After the Russian Federation Supreme Soviet has adopted a law as a whole, it is impermissible to introduce into the text of the law any changes whatsoever, including stylistic."

lot" of the Russian Government resolution on mass media registration levies. As directed by the December 1991 Russian Mass Media Law, the Press Ministry readied this document for publication in February 1992. It dispatched the final text to the Finance Ministry for endorsement. Unfortunately, the resolution mysteriously disappeared there "among all the other papers." After a lengthy search, officials located the document. In the interim, however, the Russian mass media were unable to register new publications.

A recent trend will likely exacerbate these internal bureaucratic problems. In late 1992 and early 1993, there has been a rapid proliferation of presidential agencies and staff directly accountable to and in some cases funded by Yeltsin. This has already raised considerable uncertainty and tension as to which bodies—presidential or governmental—are ultimately responsible for executive branch lawmaking and enforcement. Khasbulatov has overtly encouraged these "contradictions" by word and deed. He has emphasized repeatedly the existence of two "parallel" and "competing" governments, the legitimate Russian government headed by the Council of Ministers and the unconstitutional presidential administration. Under Khasbulatov's tutelage, the Russian legislature introduced constitutional amendments calculated to drive a further wedge between top government and presidential authorities. These significantly expanded the scope and lawmaking powers of the Council of Ministers at the expense of the presidency.[209]

Yeltsin has recognized the grave flaws in executive lawmaking. He has issued a series of measures designed to introduce procedural regularity, specificity, and predictability into the process. The most notable of these is his January 14, 1993 Decree On the Procedure of Lawmaking by Central Federal Executive Bodies and the Russian Federation Presidential Administration. This law provides guidelines regarding draft preparation, adoption, and publication.

Yet, the events of March 1993 reveal the stubborn persistence of traditional lawmaking attitudes and techniques. The package of Yeltsin emergency decrees originated in the deep, impenetrable recesses of Yeltsin's personal bureaucracy. There was no direct public access or information regarding the initiation, preparation, discussion, and approval of these crucial documents.[211] Despite recent procedural requirements to the contrary, Yeltsin never cleared his decrees with the Ministry of Justice. Moreover, he reported their existence on March 20 but published them in only a piecemeal fashion over succeeding days, with no explanation proffered for the delay. The key act even diverged markedly from the announced text.

Earlier this year Yeltsin's new chief of staff, Sergei Filatov, recommended a more formal approach to presidential lawmaking. He called for the institution of a "rigorous procedure for the passage of drafts of all presidential documents" and "expert legal study

[209] This resolution put into immediate effect the constitutional amendments that had been enacted by the Seventh Congress but never implemented because of the December compromise agreement.

[211] Even after Yeltsin's March 20 speech Russian leaders and the populace were unable to view the actual text of the decree.

before they ever reach the president's desk." The March experience confirms the wisdom of this proposal.

C. Competence

The *Izvestiia* case reveals that the constitutionally prescribed "separation of powers" is a myth in post-Soviet Russia. In practice, the lines between legislative, executive, and judicial jurisdictions are blurry if not invisible. For example, the Supreme Soviet in its *Izvestiia* Resolution clearly displayed no hesitation whatsoever in intruding into executive and judicial preserves. Despite its lack of authority to do so, the parliament issued mandatory directives to executive agencies. Over the formal objections of Mass Media Committee members, other deputies, and legal experts, it opted to supplant the courts and deal with the issue directly by legislative fiat. Indeed, the consistent use of the "resolution" format was indicative of parliamentary attitudes toward the other branches of power. Unlike laws, resolutions are immune from presidential veto and judicial review.

Russian President Yeltsin similarly displayed a marked preference for unilateral rule by decree on virtually any subject act imaginable. The general expectation of Yeltsin and *Izvestiia* proponents was that presidential edict would automatically and conclusively settle disputed matters. In fact, however, this technique often led to greater confusion and tension. A prime illustration was Yeltsin's August ordinance on the *Izvestiia* Publishing House, which effectively called for a transfer of state property to a nonexistent entity. The result was a total of five separate, inconsistent laws on *Izvestiia* Publishing House—by President Yeltsin, the Federal Property Fund, Goskomimushchestvo, the Supreme Soviet, and Deputy Chairman Voronin. Not only did Yeltsin's ordinance fail to accomplish the definitive resolution anticipated, but it actually led to armed confrontation between the executive and legislative branches. Ironically, the entire dispute over *Izvestiia* Publishing House never belonged in the hands of the president or legislature in the first place. Instead, the issue clearly fell within the competence of the judiciary.

The *Izvestiia* case also suggests the fundamental irrelevance of inter- and intra-republic jurisdictions and interests. The Russian executive and parliamentary leaderships consistently have pledged to observe the rights of other former USSR republics and of republics within the Russian Federation. Yet, they gave little consideration of these interests in the battle over *Izvestiia*. *Izvestiia*, after all, originated as a Soviet, not a Russian, central press organ. Even in its "renewed" form, the newspaper openly proclaimed its intent to publish throughout the Commonwealth of Independent States and the Russian Federation. In fact, this was the very reason the Supreme Soviet cited for acquiring an additional legislative newspaper—*Izvestiia* covered a broader territory and audience than existing parliamentary papers.[225] Nevertheless, both legislature and

[225] Parliamentary leaders contended that, as a result of the March 1992 Federation Treaty, the Supreme Soviet suddenly needed an additional newspaper.

president attempted to decide *Izvestiia*'s fate without consultation, let alone the consent, of interested republic constituencies.

The *Izvestiia* experience highlights in bold relief the grave consequences of a failure to differentiate lawmaking jurisdictions. One result was a pattern of uncoordinated, inconsistent regulation, of which the *Izvestiia* Publishing House war of laws stands as the most obvious example. As will be described below, the bewildering maze of legislative, presidential, and administrative regulations addressing the economic support of the mass media was also illustrative of this problem.

Another adverse consequence was the increasingly unrestrained conflict between branches of government. By mid-1992, this had reached the point of no deference or recognized lines of authority. The *Izvestiia* case reveals how problems at the top of the governmental structure can have a spillover effect at lower levels. In the summer of 1992, an executive agency, the Press Ministry, repeatedly refused to implement legislation it deemed unconstitutional. Likewise, a subordinate legislative body, the Federal Property Fund, without compunction issued an ordinance that directly contradicted a presidential instruction. The end result was an impasse between the executive and legislative branches.

These problems were only compounded by the leadership's rejection of any notion of continuity or supremacy of law, including the Constitution itself. In a September 1992 interview, Ruslan Khasbulatov proclaimed that "the supreme legislative body is entitled to solve any problem." When asked whether this included the right to alter adopted legislation at will to conform with changing circumstances, he responded, "But of course, how can it be otherwise?" Yeltsin's actions suggested a similar devaluation of continuity and supremacy of law. He issued presidential decrees on an ad hoc basis without any real commitment to ensuring their compatibility with existing legislative or constitutional norms.

As the *Izvestiia* experience indicates, this lack of theoretical or practical constraints on lawmaking only encourages continued rule by law rather than rule of law. It permits the use of law as an instrument to further the personal ambitions and agenda of the individual lawmaker. The *Izvestiia* case provides a particularly egregious example—Ruslan Khasbulatov's overt manipulation of the legislative process to retaliate against a troublesome critic. At the same time, the *Izvestiia* experience shows a more subtle form of personal lawmaking. Both Khasbulatov and Yeltsin frequently invoked the specter of harsh, unilateral action as a bludgeon to secure desired resolution of an issue by more conventional means.

The recent constitutional crisis, then, is the logical culmination of trends identified in the *Izvestiia* case. Like *Izvestiia*, the Russian populace and reform process became hostage to the "whim" of the lawmaker. Lack of coordination and eventually open conflict between executive and legislative branches made it impossible for Russia to construct the legal framework essential for national modernization. By late 1992, the situation had deteriorated to the point of a total paralysis of lawmaking and overall governing authority. At the December Seventh Congress of People's Deputies it became painfully obvious that there existed no effective legal standard or mechanism to break the deadlock between Russia's president and parliament. Only extra-constitutional "conciliation" by Constitutional Court Chairman Valerii Zorkin rescued Russia from the brink of disaster.

The collapse of this temporary truce took the familiar form of an executive-legislative struggle over jurisdictional authority spearheaded by Boris Yeltsin and Ruslan Khasbulatov. Unlike the *Izvestiia* case, this was no longer a war by proxy. On March 12, the Russian legislature once again unilaterally redefined constitutional boundaries. This time, however, it directly challenged and limited presidential authority. Most notably, in its Resolution On Measures for the Implementation of the Constitutional Reform, the Congress gave the Supreme Soviet the immediate legal right to suspend presidential decrees and orders pending Constitutional Court review and to terminate presidential powers following any attempt to dissolve legally elected state bodies.

The Russian president's response was also consistent with past practice. On March 20, Yeltsin threatened to resolve the crisis by personal fiat. The key difference was that Yeltsin now openly proclaimed supremacy of presidential edict over contrary legislative enactment and declared strict vertical control of Russian regional authorities.

As in the *Izvestiia* case, this potentially disastrous confrontation between executive and legislative branches eventually ended in stalemate. Yeltsin retreated from his announced introduction of emergency presidential rule. President and Parliament reached an uneasy, unworkable compromise and Russia braced itself for the inevitable next round.

III. Enforcement of Law in Post-Soviet Russia

Izvestiia's final and most profound lesson is the inadequate enforcement of law in post-Soviet Russia. The case reveals significant statutory, institutional, and attitudinal obstacles and barriers. This has serious implications for future Russian legal reform efforts. It suggests that even the most meticulously designed legal provisions will remain ineffective without accompanying enforcement mechanisms and, most importantly, societal and leadership commitment to their adherence.

A. Statutory Gaps

The *Izvestiia* experience indicates that one explanation for Russian difficulties in enforcement has been the failure to stipulate concrete mechanisms and procedures within the four corners of the laws to be applied. After enactment of the *Izvestiia* Resolution and *Izvestiia* Publishing House Resolution, commentators and authorities specifically identified this "acute question." The result was considerable uncertainty about the practical effect of the new law, a fact that only fueled existing tensions.

Izvestiia's defamation action against Ruslan Khasbulatov was particularly illustrative of this problem. The newspaper sought two remedies, retraction and monetary damages. It rapidly discovered, however, that despite explicit statutory guarantees for "defense of honor and dignity," it was, in fact, "virtually unprotected from slander and defamation." Due to gaps and inconsistencies in current Russian law and practice, there are no clear-cut standards or enforceable rights to damages for injury to business reputation.[286] Not surprisingly, *Izvestiia*'s suit was ultimately dismissed in October 1992.

A review of recent statutes reveals that enactment of "toothless" legislation is common in post-Soviet Russia. One example of this phenomenon is the much vaunted Russian Mass Media Law, which has proven to be essentially a dead letter for precisely this reason. All sides now are engaged in a competition to introduce "specific legal levers" to ensure "suitable" implementation of the statute.

Similar defects exist in presidential and administrative acts. The problem is compounded in this context, however, by the absence of any formal structures to implement presidential measures. In recent months, both President Yeltsin and the Council of Ministers have taken steps to improve enforcement of their respective acts. On April 30, 1993, Yeltsin formally created a "Control-Observation Council" and "Control Department" to monitor executive fulfillment of presidential instructions. The Council of Ministers also has announced formation of a special supervisory council to promote lower-level compliance with administrative regulations.

B. Institutional Obstacles

One of the most striking features of the *Izvestiia* case is the virtual absence of the judiciary. Under both Soviet and Russian mass media legislation, the initial conflict over newspaper formation and registration was an issue for court, not legislative or presidential, determination. Likewise, the subsequent disputes regarding use of state property, creation of limited liability spin-off companies, and leadership-initiated liquidation and reorganization of existing economic entities were matters specifically within the statutorily designated competence of Russian courts and arbitrazh tribunals. Yet, president and parliament consistently chose to bypass formal dispute resolution channels and deal with *Izvestiia* by direct fiat. This lack of deference suggests that even in the post-Soviet era, the judiciary remains Russia's weakest branch of government.

[286] One major problem in pursuing the case was uncertainty regarding the applicability of the Fundamentals of Civil Legislation of the USSR and Union Republics. This law, which specifically provided in its article 7 for material damages, was slated to enter into force on January 1, 1992. By that time, however, the USSR had ceased to exist. On March 3, 1993, the Supreme Soviet issued a resolution providing specifically for the applicability of the Fundamentals of Civil Legislation to violations occurring after August 3, 1992. An American lawyer suggested that another obstacle for *Izvestiia* might be judicial tolerance for politicians' nonobservance of property rights.

The *Izvestiia* experience also offers some disturbing insights into the evolving role and functions of the Russian procuracy. According to Russian legislation, the procuracy is a neutral, independent institution whose tasks include "ensuring supremacy of law and strengthening of legality, [and] the socioeconomic, political, and other rights and freedoms of citizens." The *Izvestiia* case suggests a marked divergence between law and reality. It reveals a pattern on the part of the procuracy of increasing receptivity to political pressure, subordination to parliamentary dictate, and inattention to legal procedures and guarantees. These trends have only intensified in recent months. The procuracy has rapidly emerged as the de facto investigatory arm of the Russian legislature. Parliament now claims the powers to appoint the procuracy's highest officer, determine its salary scale, direct its work, and even extend to it special legislative protection services. In the process, executive authorities have turned to their own agencies to carry out assigned procuratorial duties. There are even reports of future plans to abolish the procuracy altogether or subordinate it to executive control.

Furthermore, the *Izvestiia* case indicates the inadequacy of existing structures to enforce inter-republic rights. Interestingly, shortly after adoption of the *Izvestiia* Resolution, the Guild of Parliamentary Journalists formally appealed to signatories of the Agreement On Establishment of the CIS Inter-Parliamentary Assembly. The Guild requested immediate convocation of the Assembly for purposes of resolving relations between state organs and the mass media. *Izvestiia* ultimately received no assistance, however, from the Assembly or any other CIS institution.

Since its formation in December 1991, the CIS has proven to be largely an empty shell. Due to sensitivity regarding republic sovereignty and fears of Russian dominance, CIS members have deliberately rejected mandatory supranational mechanisms in favor of voluntary coordination and consultation among republic leaders. In its first year of existence, the CIS produced over 200 accords, few of which have been implemented. In January 1993, CIS heads of state met in Minsk to develop more effective legal and organizational structures. Included in the agenda were proposals to activate the CIS Economic Court and to create a special Interstate Court for resolution of ethnic and inter-republic conflicts. It is an open question whether either body will become a meaningful forum.

Similarly, the *Izvestiia* case highlights a serious problem with enforcement of intra-republic rights and interests. Recent events have reinforced this lesson. President and parliament have repeatedly issued acts directly violating the republic guarantees set out in the 1992 Federation Treaty. The only republic recourse has been nonobservance or appeal to central legislative and executive authorities or to the Constitutional Court to repeal such measures. Republic leaders have identified as the major source of this difficulty Russia's failure to institute the appropriate machinery for enforcing Federation Treaty provisions. Accordingly, at the Eighth Congress on March 10, 1993, the Council of Heads of Republics formally called for creation of a commission to prepare a draft law on principles and mechanisms for Federation Treaty implementation. Less than three weeks later, at the Ninth Congress, deputies from Nizhnii Novgorod proposed the rapid establishment of a powerful Council of the Federation. Some leaders also have recommended including the Federation Treaty within the text of the new Russian Constitution to give it highest legal status and force. The drafts published by President Yeltsin and the Constitutional Commission, in fact, followed this suggestion. If past practice is any guide, however, mere enshrinement in the Constitution is unlikely to secure in and of itself genuine recognition of republic sovereignty.

On a more positive note, the *Izvestiia* case points to one apparently promising development in post-Soviet law enforcement, the emergence of the Constitutional Court as a potential check on unconstitutional lawmaking activity. It is impressive that throughout the case all parties—newspaper staff, legislators, and administrative authorities—invoked Constitutional Court intervention. This trend has continued in 1993. Despite complaints about possible Constitutional Court bias, President and parliament alike have repeatedly turned to the Court to review the key contentious documents. Perhaps, Chairman Zorkin is justified, then, in describing the Court as a "little island of arbitration."

Moreover, the Constitutional Court ruling on *Izvestiia* is encouraging. The Court went beyond obvious separation of powers violations to take a surprisingly sweeping stand in defense of citizens' rights. Most notably, it cited and upheld the broad constitutional guarantee of freedom of expression. It is regrettable that the Court did not also take advantage of the opportunity to condemn infractions of legislative procedures and to establish a constitutional standard of due process of lawmaking. Constitutional Court judges apparently discussed the issue in hearings but ultimately chose to address it only indirectly in the final opinion.

At the same time, however, the *Izvestiia* experience reveals some of the limitations of the Constitutional Court. The most obvious of these was the lengthy delay in consideration of the case. The Constitutional Court promised a decision in late 1992, but failed to issue its opinion until May 1993, after the dispute had become essentially moot. This delay reflects the Court's heavy case load and inefficient organizational structure and procedures. In early May 1993, the Constitutional Court reported a backlog of 200 petitions and appeals. To remedy this situation, the Court has recommended a significant overhaul of existing Constitutional Court legislation. For instance, it has called for reduction of its quorum requirement, establishment of special chambers for resolution of individual complaints, and a prerequisite of at least fifty deputy signatures on petitions for consideration of parliamentary conflicts.

Another serious problem in the present scheme is the absence of concrete mechanisms to implement Constitutional Court decisions. For example, in the *Izvestiia* case, the Constitutional Court could only request, not mandate, Supreme Soviet suspension of the *Izvestiia* Resolution pending review. The legislature never responded to the request or even discussed it in formal session. On the contrary, it proceeded to form and register its own publication, *Izvestiia* RF. This practice continues today. The executive and legislative branches consistently ignore Constitutional Court directives and execute laws under Constitutional Court consideration. Yet, the Court lacks effective legal or practical means or sanctions to secure compliance.

A final and potentially fatal flaw is the growing official and public perception of Constitutional Court politicization. Since December 1992, the Court and, most visibly, its chairman, Valerii Zorkin, have become increasingly embroiled in the executive-legislative struggle for power.[334] This has led to considerable debate about the Court's ability to operate as a neutral, disinterested tribunal.[335] It remains to be seen what will be the full impact of this political involvement on the Constitutional Court's stature, credibility, and effectiveness in the difficult days ahead.

C. Attitudinal Impediments

The blatant disregard of law and legal institutions by Russia's highest officials was a consistent theme in the *Izvestiia* case. Indeed, the legal system proved virtually irrelevant. Personal intervention by Yeltsin and Khasbulatov, not formal legal channels or organs, ultimately determined the fates of the *Izvestiia SSSR*, *Izvestiia*, and the *Izvestiia* Publishing House.

At the height of the *Izvestiia* dispute, Khasbulatov proclaimed that "the supreme legislative body is entitled to solve any problem." This included the right to assume judicial, even Constitutional Court, functions because "we defined court laws ourselves." In recent months, Yeltsin has echoed these sentiments. He has openly asserted the authority to supplant legal institutions that fail to uphold his notion of legality. Some of his supporters have gone still further to insist that Yeltsin himself is now the sole "guarantor" of the democratic, law-based state. Others have completely rejected existing enforcement mechanisms in favor of direct popular implementation of law.

Leadership devaluation of law has already had a demonstrable effect on post-Soviet Russia. In March 1993, it brought the country to the brink of civil war. At the March 26 emergency session of the Congress of People's Deputies, Valerii Zorkin reminded president and legislators that the "main reason for the conflict is not only and not so much the text of the Constitution but authorities' failure to abide by the Constitution." Unfortunately, his words fell on deaf ears. In their recent "war of constitutions," president and parliament have continued to focus on constitutional text rather than observance. As a result, a reenactment of the March confrontation appears imminent.

In a less immediate sense, the Russian leadership's negative attitude toward law threatens to undermine the very goal it espoused for its new order in December 1991—establishment of a democratic, law-based state. As Russian and Western scholars have

[334] For example, Valerii Zorkin played a prominent role at the Seventh, Eight, and Ninth Congresses. He frequently provided public personal commentary in the mass media on legislative and presidential actions.

[335] It should be noted that there have been intense legislative and executive efforts to influence and/or undermine Constitutional Court actions.

noted, the essential prerequisite for success in this endeavor is the development of a national legal consciousness and, eventually, legal culture. This requires a concerted effort to inculcate in Russian officials and citizenry a genuine respect and confidence in legal norms, values, institutions, and processes. With the "barren legal culture" of the Russian and Soviet past and the crisis environment of the post-Soviet present, this is an extraordinarily difficult task. At the very least it demands clear, uncompromising leadership example and commitment. Presidential and parliamentary actions of the past few months fly in the face of this reform effort and put it in serious jeopardy. As Soviet of Nationalities Chairman Ramazan Abdulatipov recently remarked, "Seeing the president or a deputy 'overthrowing' the Constitution almost daily, is there any kind of law in which man ought to have faith? If a law adopted by the Supreme Soviet means absolutely nothing to top politicians, how can you force the man in the street to obey this document?"

IV. Concluding Reflections: Press, Law, And Crisis

As Russia lurches from crisis to crisis, its leaders have reached accord on a single point, the dire necessity for a "stabilizing body." In the United States, two mechanisms that have answered this need are the press and the legal system. As the *Izvestiia* case has illustrated, neither has emerged as a force for stabilization in the Russian context. This raises challenging questions about the relationship between press, law, and crisis in the post-Soviet era.

A. Press and Stabilization

The initial Russian justifications for freedom of the press were strikingly similar to their United States counterparts. Proponents argued that an independent Fourth Estate would expose and check potential abuses and "mistakes" by executive, legislative, and judicial branches; provide the citizenry with the "full and objective" information essential for democratic self-governance; assist in the spiritual liberation of the populace from the shackles of socialism; offer a forum for introduction, comparison, and debate of reform proposals; and "consolidate" Russian citizens in support of their embattled government during "a time of most difficult sociopolitical changes and economic trials." Russian leaders have promised unswerving defense of the Fourth Estate and have even recognized it as an essential prerequisite for establishment of a democratic, law-based state.

Yet, reality has diverged markedly from these high-sounding phrases. As the preceding study has shown, there has been a pattern of increasing leadership attempts to influence and to subordinate the Russian mass media by direct and indirect, political and economic means.[354] The post-Soviet era has witnessed a rapid implementation of prior restraints on publication, restrictions on press access to information, numerous criminal and civil actions against media organs and personnel, and introduction of draft legislation

[354] The *Izvestiia* case provides a graphic illustration of how economic factors can impact actual exercise of press rights. In the words of one commentator, the experience demonstrates that "ownership is power."

to expand liability for disclosure of state secrets, insulting of top officials, attacks on constitutional organs of power, and violations of Russian Federation "integrity." Some Russian commentators have detected an ominous correspondence between recent proposals and the most repressive, "antidemocratic" provisions of the Soviet-era criminal code.

Foreign and domestic observers generally attribute this backlash to the Russian leadership's unfamiliarity with, sensitivity to, and, ultimately, intolerance of Fourth Estate criticism and opposition. The *Izvestiia* experience provides strong support for this argument. After all, the original catalyst for the dramatic events that followed was *Izvestiia*'s open, direct challenge to the authority, legitimacy, and public image of the Russian parliament and its chairman. Interestingly, in the midst of the *Izvestiia* case when Yeltsin too received unfavorable press coverage, there was immediate speculation that president as well as parliament would turn against the media.

A closer look, however, suggests an additional, less obvious explanation. The recent moves against the media may reflect not only the early success of the Russian press as an embryonic Fourth Estate, but also its fundamental failure as a force for societal consolidation and moderation during a period of profound national crisis.

One of the most compelling but least cited United States defenses for freedom of expression relates precisely to the issue of crisis management that confronts Russia today. In the words of Thomas Emerson, "freedom of expression . . . is an essential mechanism for maintaining the balance between stability and change."[362] In the United States context, the press has traditionally promoted this equilibrium in two main ways. It has acted as a "safety valve" for the release and "domestication" of popular discontent and frustration. Equally importantly, it has communicated to and persuaded the United States citizenry that established political and legal institutions and processes are both predictable and flexible enough to accommodate change.

In post-Soviet Russia, enhanced press independence has led to very different results. The Russian press has played a destabilizing, not moderating, role. Its debate of competing strategies and objectives has contributed to public disunity. Its unrelenting criticism and exposure of personal and systematic failings has eroded rather than fostered public confidence in the post-socialist Russian leadership and evolving norms, rules, institutions, and procedures. Thus, the press has demystified and delegitimized the present as well as the past.

A central tenet of the United States rationale for broad expressive rights is that "an open society will be the stronger and more cohesive one." The early experience in post-Soviet Russia, however, suggests the opposite conclusion. In his examination of United States freedom of expression, Thomas Emerson identified two limitations that may help explain this apparent contradiction between general theory and Russian practice: (1) "society must be committed to democratic procedures or rather in the process of

[362] Thomas I. Emerson, The System of Freedom of Expression 7 (1970).

committing itself," and (2) "men [must] have learned to function within the law."[369] The *Izvestiia* experience provides ample evidence that Russia has thus far failed to satisfy either of these requirements. The case casts serious doubts on the level of current commitment to democratic procedure and indicates grave problems in enforcement and observance of law. This prompts a perplexing question that has far-reaching implications for the reform process in Russia and other former socialist states. Is conventional wisdom correct that press freedom is a precondition for the democratic, law-based state? Or is the democratic, law-based state a precondition for press freedom?

B. Law, Culture, and Communication

In their quest for a way out of crisis, Russian officials and commentators have frequently lamented the absence of a "legal" mechanism to contain and resolve conflict. The preceding study has painted a discouraging portrait of post-Soviet legal reform efforts. It has highlighted concrete procedural, institutional, and attitudinal problems that are likely to present continuing obstacles in the future. In the final analysis, however, the greatest threat to Russian stability and legality may lie elsewhere.

In his pioneering work *The Electronic Media and the Transformation of Law*, M. Ethan Katsh remarked, "[m]odern law promotes stability and limits the process of societal change by placing a heavy emphasis on maintaining links with the past."[375] He later noted that, to fulfill these functions, law relies heavily on mass communication and belief in words and symbols.

This analysis may provide two further explanations for the failure of law to manage change in the post-Soviet era. First, the Russian legal system lacks the essential moorings to the past. It can invoke few accepted cultural or historical standards or traditions of legality, justice, and due process. This reflects the overall "cultural despair" of present-day Russia, a country currently in search of a national identity and past. Second, there is no "rhetoric for mediating and muting . . . conflicts." During both socialist and post-socialist eras, Russia's leaders have frequently reinterpreted, redefined, and repudiated such terms as constitutionality, democracy, and rule of law. As a result, in Russia today "the most sacred words have lost their true meaning." This effacement of language and symbols has deprived Russia of an important instrument to secure voluntary compliance and trust in legal structures, rules, and procedures.

This, then, raises serious concerns about the Russian leadership's current emphasis on the formulation of a new Constitution, elimination of "antidemocratic," obstructionist institutions and officials, and uncritical importation of Western political and legal values and forms. It suggests that, even if implemented, these largely cosmetic changes are unlikely to lead to successful establishment of a stable, democratic, law-based state. As a

---

[369] Thomas I. Emerson, *Toward a General Theory of the First Amendment*, 72 Yale Law Journal 877, 884 (1963).

[375] M. Ethan Katsh, The Electronic Media and the Transformation of Law 13 (1989).

Russian commentator recently observed, "In the heat of the struggle, the initial aims are somehow forgotten."

In the end, the most effective solution to Russia's "constitutional crisis" may indeed be constitutional—not a "modern" post-socialist Constitution, however, but a fundamental constitution and reconstitution of Russian legal tradition, culture, and language. If past practice is any guide, the Russian press has the potential to play a major role in this endeavor, as a force for mediation, articulation, and development of a national and popular legal consciousness. In so doing, it could shatter its age-old image as a passive mirror of Russian reality and emerge as an active and essential component of the post-Soviet legal reform process.

Freedom and Responsibility in the Russian Media*

Yassen N. Zassoursky

Media have been in transition in Russia since the spring of 1986, and their transition from an administrative-bureaucratic model toward the market and democratization has been closely connected with the transition of Russian politics from Soviet authoritarianism to democratic pluralism. During *perestroika* of 1985 to 1991, continuing with the establishment of new democratic political institutions from 1992 to 1995 and culminating in the arrival of financial and corporate clans during the presidential election of 1996 the political scene transformed itself. After 1996, the new financial powers seemed to participate directly in the media and have influence over various decision making activities.

The political structuralization of the Russian society brought about new roles for the media in democratic procedures. They began to participate in elections and public debates among other political processes. The state and other private parties have demonstrated their desire to promote political aims through state-controlled and independent private television channels and press.

The emergence of "offizios" (officieux, semiofficial) in the private media who express views close to those of the government is characteristic of the developments in the media in 1996 when Patrick Henry described NTV, an independent television channel, as "increasingly the Kremlin voice" in *The Moscow Times*. Now political pressures on the media are often channeled through the private media outlets of Vladimir Gusinsky and Boris Berezovsky.

One of the reasons for this new trend is the turbulent economy. Unfortunately, the media were the first to feel the influence of the market. The price for newsprint, printing, and distribution increased dramatically in 1992. As a result of this, prices of newspapers and magazines rose sharply, leading to drastic cuts in press circulation. The circulation of Moscow national dailies dropped from 90 million in 1990 to 8 million in the first half of 1996. Now *Komsomolskaia Pravda*, with 1.4 million, has one of the biggest circulation among the dailies. However, in 1990, it had a circulation of 24 million copies. Subscription prices are too expensive for many Muscovites, and they buy their newspapers at newsstands.

The changes in the political power structures in Russia, and the difficulties in the development of the civil society are reflected in the changing roles of the media in Russian politics. At the local newsstand near my home I was told that they sell fifteen titles of dailies. The most popular newspapers here are *Moskovskie Komsomolets*,

---

* Post-Soviet Media Law & Policy Newsletter, Feb. 27, 1997, at 11.

Izvestiia, *Komsomolskaia Pravda*, *Nezavisimaia Gazeta*, *Sovetskaia Rossiia*, *Segodnia*, and *Kommersant Daily*. These seven newspapers have different political orientations and readerships. Four of these newspapers were established in the Soviet Period: *Moskovski Komsomolets* was published by the Moscow branch of the Young Communist League; *Izvestiia* was the paper of the Supreme Soviet of Russia; and *Sovetskaia Rossiia* was the Communist Party newspaper for the Russian Federation. Present day *Moskovski Komsomolets* and *Komsomolskaia Pravda* have both changed substantially; *Moskovski Komsomolets* seems to be right of the center while *Komsomolskaia Pravda* is left of the center. *Izvestiia* is an independent daily, centrist in its politics. *Sovetskaia Rossiia* remains the newspaper of the Communist Party of Russia and retains its old rhetoric.

The other three papers were set up during *perestroika*. *Kommersant Daily* targets financial and business circles. It has twelve to sixteen pages, making it the biggest of the Moscow papers. It covers finance and business and has an excellent cultural page on Saturdays. The paper was set up in 1990 as a continuation of the original *Kommersant* which was published from 1909 to 1917 when it ceased publication because of the October Revolution. It is believed to be supported by the Stolichni Bank. Its publishers own a chain of magazines, including *Kommersant Weekly*.

Nezavisimaia Gazeta (*The Independent*) was launched in 1990 on the model of *Le Monde* and *The Independent* with the motto: *Sine ira et studio* (without anger and prejudice). Its editor, Vitali Tretyakov, tried to sustain financial independence, but failed and had to rely on the support of Boris Berezovsky's LogoVAZ corporation. However, this paper has the best interpretative journalists. *Segodnia* (*Today*) newspaper was set up by former journalists of *Nezavisimaia Gazeta*, who disagreed with Vitali Tretyakov. It is financed by the Most Bank group and has a very broad cultural approach to the news though it has recently started moving towards business journalism.

Four other papers should be mentioned to make the picture more complete, *Trud*, *Zavtra*, *Pravda*, and *The Moscow Times*. *Trud*, a daily, originally owned by Trade unions, is now independent from them. It is now partially owned by the Gazprom corporation. It has retained its readership among employees and workers and has the biggest circulation of 1.44 million.

Zavtra (*Tomorrow*), a weekly, is the most notorious extremist newspaper. It calls itself the newspaper of the Russian state. It has nationalist, very close to xenophobic, inclinations.

Pravda was the most authoritative and authoritarian newspaper in the Soviet Union, but it has lost readership even among the Communists. Its present circulation is about 200,000 as compared with more than 10 million copies in 1990. Now it is owned by a Greek millionaire.

The problem of ownership in Russian media is very complicated. The very notion of "owner" does not exist in the press law, because the law was adopted before Russia started to move toward a market economy. After getting rid of state and Party controls, most media became independent and were put into the hands of the journalists. However, the economic realities of the media industry require capital, and in search of funding journalists turned to banks, corporations, the state, and private individuals for money. The state tried to subsidize the press, but it did not have enough money. The banks and corporations began to finance the media industry, and now Russia has its own media tycoons. Most prominent among them are bankers and financiers Boris Berezovsky and Vladimir Gusinsky.

Boris Berezovsky's media empire includes investments in the *Ogoniok* weekly magazine, ORT and *Nezavisimaia Gazeta.* Vladimir Gusinsky, the former head of the Most Bank, created the largest Russian media corporation, which includes the *Segodnia* newspaper, the NTV television channel, *Itogi* newsmagazine (published in cooperation with *Newsweek*), Echo of Moscow radio, and the *Seven Days* (*Sem Dnei*) television weekly. His approach to the media is expressed in the phrase, "the race for sensation, which is maximally hot and interesting." For him media "are super profitable." As for journalists, their attitude was well formulated by Albert Plutnik of *Izvestiia*: "the free word is becoming a hostage of the financial dependence of the press."

Besides Gusinsky and Berezovsky, owners of the media include Gazprom, which invested in the NTV television, *Komsomolskaia Pravda*, *Trud*, and other media enterprises. It is not clear whether Russian media tycoons get big financial profits, but clearly they achieve political gains, and through them they may achieve profitable business ventures. Igor Malashenko, the director general of the NTV Television, flatly stated in his interview with *Nezavisimaia Gazeta* that corporations, by investing in media, "do not seek exclusively commercial gains, for them the concerns of prestige are important." Berezovsky's and Gusinsky's media clans supported Yeltsin in the Presidential election campaign, and both were rewarded: Gusinsky's NTV channel got the daytime share (from 6 a.m. to 6 p.m.) of the fourth Russian state-owned channel for just $730; and Berezovsky was appointed to the position of deputy secretary of the Security Council of Russia.

Aside from experiencing economic troubles the media has also succumbed to political pressure. The election campaigns of 1995 and 1996 revealed important difficulties in the development of Russian democratic media. For the sake of supporting President Yeltsin, who seemed to represent the only viable alternative to the Communist, Gennadi Zyuganov, many journalists sacrificed their professional democratic attitudes and principles. As prominent Russian investigative journalist Yevgeniia Albats put it during a debate at the European Center of the Freedom Forum on June 28, 1996, the media was faced with "a choice between bad and very bad."

The Presidential election team was joined by the director general of the NTV. It was a difficult decision for Igor Malashenko to join Yeltsin's election camp, but he made it because he thought that a Zyuganov victory meant an end to all independent media. Ironically, his decision drew Malashenko's NTV television closer to the President, to the Government, and to the state.

During the election process, the Russian media which supported Mr. Yeltsin became extremely selective in their news coverage and their comments. Even the popular puppet show "Kukly" (Dolls), broadcast on the NTV channel, lost its satirical fervor. The television critic Lidiia Polskaia wrote in the *Moskovskie Novosti*: "Before the elections 'Kukly' chose soft irony, acting according to certain rules of politeness, which often turned into elementary dullness." Television "was prejudiced in favor of democracy," wrote Vsevolod Vilchek, a prominent television expert. And *Moscovskie Novosti* published a story about the election under the title: "Corruption Better Than Communism."

The presidential election campaign was free of any restraints and was often conducted on the pattern of an information war. Yevgeni Krasnikov of the *Moskovskie Novosti* writes that two principles were taken up: "à la guerre comme à la guerre" and "the aim justifies the means." The program of public opinion management, conducted by the Fund of Effective politics and headed by Gleb Pavlovski, staged events, disrupted Mr. Zuganov's press conferences, and distorted the views of opponents. Gleb Pavlovski closely cooperated with Igor Malashenko and leading television anchors.

In less regulated Russian media, self-censorship is practiced even by respectable newspapers. For example, *Izvestiia* refused to publish Sergey Kovalev's Open Letter to President Yeltsin accusing the President and Mr. Lebed of failing to fulfill their pre-election promises though this newspaper did attack the lack of progress to implementing the President's election program. Self-censorship of this sort diminishes freedom of the press, because the media forsakes its social responsibility and bows to political pressures and political convenience.

The election campaign confronted Russian media with a difficult choice between a mouthpiece and a mirror, as *Kommersant Daily* put it in the article on the role of television in the Presidential elections in Russia. To a large degree, Russian media became an instrument of political advertising, the mouthpiece in many cases winning over the mirror. Such developments make the road to the freedom of the Russian media very rocky indeed. That road must travel from Soviet style propaganda-agitation-organization press to free and diverse information.

The presidential election campaign exposed the dangers of reinstating state control over the media and of turning it into vehicles of support for the President, the Government, and the state. The return to the practices of independent, free and pluralistic journalism will take some time, but hopefully it will be realized. The difficult emergence of the new democratic media culture is nonetheless irreversible, though there are various pressures to substitute freedom for responsibility instead of promoting freedom and responsibility.

The development of free media in Russia has its difficulties and paradoxes, but nonetheless Russian journalism has become a formidable force. And this can be seen by the example of the most popular Moscow daily, *Moskovski Komsomolets*, with a circulation of about one million copies, distributed predominately in Moscow. The paper covers local Moscow news, sports, entertainment, popular music, crime, and accidents, but it is also involved in national politics. It publishes investigative reports, which often go beyond local scandals. It was this newspaper which exposed corruption in the Russian Army. One of its investigative reporters, Dmitri Kholodov, who was covering the Ministry of Defense, was murdered by a bomb in 1994, just before the beginning of the Chechen war.

The latest political sensation of *Moskovski Komsomolets* was the publication of a tape of a secret conversation during the presidential election battle between Anatoly Chubais, who is now the head of President Yeltsin's administration, Victor Ilushin, the first vice-premier, and Sergei Krasavchenko, an advisor to Yeltsin. According to the published version of the tape, the three leading members of President Yeltsin's campaign plotted to cover up the use of U.S. dollars from unknown sources to promote Yeltsin's victory in the elections.

The three leading politicians denied that they ever had such a conversation. The State Duma, the lower house of the parliament, referred the case to the prosecutor-general. Alexei Mitrofanov, a member of the Duma from Zhirinovski's Liberal-Democratic Party, called the publication "a crime against the State" and said that the journalist who wrote the story, Khinstein, should be "put into prison once and for all." We have a full amount of freedom of press and of expression; but there are people in high places who would like to control and manipulate the media. I must add to this that *Moskovski Komsomolets* supports President Yeltsin and does not in any way belong to the opposition, but it is strongly against corruption.

Izvestiia is a much more prestigious daily. It has a circulation of 556,000 copies and is distributed throughout Russia. *Izvestiia* attracted public attention by publishing a series of articles about the appointment of prominent Russian banker and financier Boris Berezovsky to the position of deputy to the Secretary to the Russian Security Council Ivan Rybkin. *Izvestiia* disclosed that Boris Berezovsky had double citizenship: of Russia and of Israel. Berezovsky denied the allegations at first, then after another publication in the *Izvestiia* Berezovsky admitted that he had Israeli citizenship, but had withdrawn it. *Izvestiia* went on with their investigation, revealing that the Israeli authorities had not received an application from Berezovsky to cancel his Israeli citizenship. Moreover his name was still in the computer of the Ministry of the Interior as a citizen of Israel. Certainly Berezovsky is a very bright man—he is a banker, a financier, a prominent academic, an economist, and a media mogul, who controls a substantial part of the Russian media, but he did not hesitate to deny evident facts and to mislead the public.

This wave of accusations and revelations, which can be compared to the Watergate scandal, received its name in Russian, "compromatball"—where the compromising facts are taken as a ball in a game, or rather a feud of financial and political clans. The *Moscow Times* described it as the "Kremlin sleaze war."

The cases of both *Moskovski Komsomolets* and *Izvestiia* are characteristic of the media situation in Russia—media are free to criticize and to expose, but the Government and the courts are free to ignore these criticisms, revelations, and exposures. It is important to note, however, that the television channels belonging to Berezovsky's and Gusinsky's empires ignored these revelations. These new information policies led the *Obshchaia Gazeta* journalist Anatoly Khimenko to the conclusion about new and also very old methods of controlling Russian television formulated in the title of his article, *New Agitprop? Tele-preachers and Their Flock.* And finally the Russian public and the world at large know very well about the corruption in Russia, but corruption remains. The Russian media are like Cassandra, who was prophetic, but never heeded.

For the last decade Russian media have been in transition from an administrative-bureaucratic model to the market and democratization—the Fourth Estate model; now they are facing new difficulties as the government and private corporations attempt to use the media as instruments, tools, and sources of power.

Changes in the political power structures in Russia and the difficulties in the development of the civil society are reflected in the changing roles of the media in Russian politics. Ethical and professional standards are becoming just as important as media independence and autonomy. On the other hand we have pluralistic print media, independent regional and local broadcasting, and growing access to the Internet and satellite television (CNN and other networks), which contribute to counter this trend. And while it is true that control over the national television has certainly increased, they have not yet become absolutely sterile.

Information and the Problem of Democracy: The Russian Experience*

Frances H. Foster

Leading First Amendment scholars claim that free speech is a threat to democracy. Authors spanning the entire political spectrum decry the effects of uncontrolled individual expression on traditional American political values and notions of democratic governance. They provide evidence that free speech has deepened gender, racial, and ethnic divisions, silenced women and people of color, and effectively excluded such groups from the political process. They demonstrate that a laissez-faire approach to expression has led to capture of government by the wealthy and powerful. They present the chilling conclusion that free speech has created an apathetic, self-centered, and cynical populace that has lost both the interest and the will to fulfill its democratic mission of citizen sovereignty.

These scholars' prognosis for the future is grim. They see evolving communication and information technology as only accelerating the demise of American democracy. Their solution is a new (or perhaps old) vision of the First Amendment, one that would permit a few "narrow" restrictions on individual rights of expression to ensure dissemination of information conducive to American democratic aspirations.

The tension between democracy and free speech is by no means a purely American concern. It is a global phenomenon. So too is the impulse to rescue democracy by exalting the community's need for "beneficial" information over the individual's claim to untrammeled expression.

This article examines the efforts of one country, Russia, to develop a framework of collective information rights to reconcile the competing interests of democracy and freedom of expression. I conclude that the Russian experiment is ambitious but ultimately unsuccessful. Nonetheless, it provides valuable cautionary lessons for others intent on following a similar path.

In Parts I-IV, I set out four distinct approaches to information explored by Russia since the dissolution of the Soviet Union in December 1991. I have labeled these the informed citizenry theory, the defense of democracy theory, the popular mandate theory, and the parental theory. I examine the basic principles of each theory, specific impact on the mass media, and practical applications.

In Part V, I argue that all four theories are fundamentally flawed. First, I consider why Russia's democratic model of information rights has become a formula for authoritarian rather than popular control. I find the explanation in two common features

* 44 American Journal of Comparative Law 243 (1996).

of four otherwise divergent theories of information: their formulation of information as a collective, not individual, right and their insistence on the utilitarian value of information for democracy. I argue that these definitions have rendered Russian information rights meaningless and unenforceable without significant outside interpretation and intervention.

Second, I contend that Russian information theories were doomed to failure because they were grounded in an outdated understanding of information processing and technology. I challenge in particular their flawed assumption that closed information systems remain viable in today's "information age." I show that Russian leadership attempts to filter information even for the most laudable of reasons have proven to be both futile and dangerous. Citizens have easily circumvented these measures through access to independent information services and foreign media technology and development of their own unofficial information channels. The end result has been considerable cost to the credibility and stability of the post-Soviet government and its democratic program.

I conclude that despite its very different political, legal, and cultural context the Russian experience raises troubling questions for recent United States First Amendment scholarship. The Russian case confirms that "movements for democratization throughout the world . . . are far from irrelevant to current reform efforts in the United States."

I. The Informed Citizenry Theory

Throughout the post-Soviet era, the right to information has been established constitutional law in Russia. The Constitution of 1978, which remained in effect until December 1993, guaranteed each citizen the "right to seek, receive, and disseminate information freely." Likewise, the current Constitution stipulates that "[e]veryone has the right to seek, receive, pass on, produce, and disseminate information freely by any legal means."

In official and unofficial discourse, there have emerged four different interpretations of the rights to information. The informed citizenry theory is the earliest and most expansive of these. It provides a sweeping guarantee to the Russian populace of "full" and "independent" information. This theory rests on a concept of post-Soviet democracy as a system of genuine citizen sovereignty over the state.

A. Theory

Under the informed citizenry theory, comprehensive popular information is essential as a "democratic" check on governing authorities. It is necessary to lift the "shroud of secrecy" that long insulated official organs and personnel from public scrutiny and accountability and that perpetuated Soviet authoritarianism. It is vital to ensure continuous citizen oversight and "correction" of evolving post-Soviet institutions as well. Popular information can even assist the leadership in keeping itself on a democratic course. As Russian Information Agency General Director Andrei Vinogradov pointed out, "How will [government] see itself without a mirror to look into?"

The informed citizenry theory also emphasizes the role of information in "consolidation" and "stabilization" of a democratic government. It views full, truthful, and independent information as a prerequisite for public confidence in and support of a leadership and its policies. Its basic argument is that "[k]nowledge unites people and increases the ranks of . . . supporters, whereas ignorance disunites and alienates." The informed citizenry theory predicts a dire fate for a Russia without popular information—failure of the reform process, social "explosion," and eventual collapse of Russia's first "democratic" government.

B. Exaltation of the Mass Media

The informed citizenry theory accords the mass media the highest possible status. It highlights the invaluable "informing" function of a free and independent media in collecting and disseminating information to the Russian populace. The informed citizenry theory lauds the media as the "fourth estate," a coequal and "democratic" counterweight to the executive, legislative and, to a lesser extent, judicial branches. Not surprisingly, then, throughout the post-Soviet era, representatives of the mass media have been among the most vocal proponents of the informed citizenry theory.

C. Applications

There have been five major uses of the informed citizenry theory in post-Soviet Russia. First, it has been an argument for affirmative official action either to preserve the media from economic and/or political extinction or to safeguard information and expressive rights in general. Supporters have consistently cited the media's role in informing Russian society as grounds for blanket exemption from free market principles and for specific preferences such as state subsidies, tariff reductions, and tax concessions. Likewise, the informed citizenry theory has figured prominently in appeals to Yeltsin and the Constitutional Court to rescue print and electronic media from legislative attempts at censorship and control. Occasionally, it has been invoked as well by Yeltsin's opponents to encourage legislative action against pro-presidential media. The informed citizenry theory also has been extended beyond the media context to become a standard argument to induce Yeltsin to redress legislative encroachment on freedoms of information and expression.

Second, the informed citizenry theory has been a justification for unexpurgated media coverage of the negative as well as positive aspects of post-Soviet Russia. It has been a defense for relentless media criticism and ridicule of Russian leaders, institutions, and processes. It has licensed media exposure of the seamy side of post-Soviet life—corruption, organized crime, prostitution, alcoholism, nationalistic hatred, and the like. Under the informed citizenry theory, journalists have disseminated potentially destabilizing, even unsubstantiated reports of individual officials' ill health, misconduct, ethnic prejudices, and ambitions for power and rumors of forthcoming leadership resignations or dismissals.[42]

The most highly publicized example of this second use of the informed citizenry theory occurred in March 1994 when *Obshchaia Gazeta* published a detailed description of an alleged coup plot to overthrow Yeltsin, which the newspaper itself acknowledged to be of questionable reliability. The newspaper defended its decision as promoting an informed Russian citizenry. *Obshchaia Gazeta*'s position was eventually vindicated by the Judicial Chamber for Information Disputes, a quasi-legal tribunal established by Yeltsin.

Third, the informed citizenry theory has served as an argument for expanded public and media access to official sources and channels. It has been cited in calls to open up the Russian lawmaking and decision-making processes to public scrutiny. It has been the standard under which the media have attempted to obtain specific unpublished documents, to attend closed meetings, or to question individual officials. While this third application of the informed citizenry theory has been widespread throughout the post-Soviet era, it has reached its height in periods of local or national states of emergency. A prime example was Yeltsin's coup of September/October 1993. During the tense two-week standoff between president and parliament, executive authorities severely restricted media access to government officials, legislative foes, and the scene of the ongoing hostilities. Opponents of these restrictions responded by invoking the informed citizenry theory to condemn Yeltsin's actions as violations of the Russian Constitution.

Similarly, the informed citizenry theory has been a central theme in the campaign to reduce the government stranglehold over dissemination of "state secrets," especially by former employees. Post-Soviet authorities have retained virtually complete discretion to determine what constitutes protected government information. Even the most recent legislative and executive acts on state secrets have made few inroads into this broad power. Under the informed citizenry standard, critics have contended that lack of a clear-cut definition of "state secrets" undermines citizens' constitutional guarantee of independent information, shields official incompetence and misconduct, and sets limits on effective investigative journalism.

Fourth, the informed citizenry theory has been a defense against direct government interference with freedoms of expression and information. For example, in the media context it has appeared in efforts to resist or protest official attempts to monitor, censor, and mandate expression. It has also been a frequent defense against government criminal, civil, and extralegal actions against individual media organs.

---

[42] Boris Yeltsin has been a frequent target of media exposés. Newspapers have even created special columns to report and investigate rumors, under such titles as *Checking Up on Rumors* and *Rumor and Authoritative Sources*." Russian authorities have directly contributed to this climate of rumor and innuendo by deliberately leaking stories of possible leadership changes or policy decisions as "test balloons."

Fifth, the informed citizenry theory has been a political instrument in the struggle for supremacy of post-Soviet Russia. Both Yeltsin and his parliamentary rivals have cited their role as "staunch" defenders of freedom of information to justify ad hoc legal and extralegal strikes against the other. This has led to considerable confusion and uncertainty regarding the precise contours of the constitutional right to information. At the most extreme, there have been periods of "parallel" executive and legislative regulation of information rights, when both sides used the informed citizenry theory to assert unilateral control over information access, content, and channels.

II. The Defense of Democracy Theory

The defense of democracy theory is the most restrictive interpretation of information rights. It competed with the informed citizenry theory throughout the First Russian Republic and finally achieved official endorsement during the coup of September/October 1993. This theory views democracy as an established system of power besieged by hostile forces intent on its destruction.

A. Theory

The defense of democracy theory defines the constitutional right to information as a public right to "constructive" information. In marked contrast to the informed citizenry theory, it views "full" information as an essential threat to the democratic system. It emphasizes the potential destabilizing effects of information.

According to the defense of democracy theory, information can alienate citizenry from government. Exposure of official frailties to public cynosure discredits government in the eyes of the citizenry (and world community). It delegitimitizes the democratic system as a whole and encourages popular distrust, apathy, and nonparticipation in the political process.

"Irresponsible" dissemination of information can also exacerbate political and ethnic divisions. Incessant reports of even the most inconsequential disagreements between branches of power fuels political tensions and inhibits compromise. Similarly, coverage of small-scale ethnic conflicts creates a dangerous atmosphere of ethnic discord and hostility throughout society.

In addition, information can undermine the moral foundations of democracy. As one Russian official explained, "Aggressive amorality with its degrading influences is no lesser danger to society than Fascism." Not surprisingly, then, a consistent theme of the defense of democracy theory is the public right not to be assaulted by "offensive" information.

According to the defense of democracy theory, full information can also undercut, rather than promote, reforms undertaken by a democratic government. For example, reports regarding potential risks and negative aspects of voucher privatization discouraged public confidence and involvement in the program and imperiled the overall effort to move Russia from command economy to market economy.

Finally, open public access and information regarding government activities can lead to paralysis in the decision making process. Under the defense of democracy theory, official secrecy is both desirable and essential for preservation and effective operation of a democratic system. The appropriate extent of such secrecy varies according to changing governmental needs and challenges. During periods of national crisis when an embattled democracy is fighting for its very existence, maximum secrecy is vital. This affords authorities the necessary flexibility, freedom of action, and element of surprise to annihilate "antidemocratic" forces. In more ordinary day-to-day decision making situations, a lower level of secrecy is in order. Even at such times, however, there must be sufficient official insulation from public scrutiny to allow serious, frank debate and resolution of contentious issues.

B. Demonization of the Mass Media

The defense of democracy theory regards the mass media as a dangerous adversary. It argues that the media exalt abstract constitutional rights above the concrete interests of state and citizenry. In so doing, they jeopardize the evolving democratic process and cause serious harm to society. Under the protective banner of freedom of press, expression, and information, the media bombard the populace with a barrage of false, distorted, offensive, and negative news. They unleash "psychological war," discredit organs of power, "torpedo" reforms, inflame an already tense atmosphere, and contribute to public dissatisfaction and despair.

Under the defense of democracy theory, the notion of an independent Fourth Estate is anathema. It views the proper role of the media instead as conduit between government and citizenry. Like the informed citizenry theory, the defense of democracy theory recognizes the value of an "informing" media for democracy. Its understanding of this function is fundamentally different, however. The defense of democracy theory limits the media to "constructive," "responsible," "balanced," and "objective" dissemination of information. This entails unswerving support for a democratic leadership and its policies, respect for official access and publication/broadcasting boundaries, and, above all, communication of the positive accomplishments of the democratic government and reform process.

C. Applications

Throughout the post-Soviet era, the defense of democracy theory has served as the principal rationale for strict limitations on information access and dissemination. The 1993 coup was an extreme example. In September/October 1993, officials declared Russian democracy under attack and proclaimed that "this [was] not the time for the whole truth." These "dangerous days for democracy" weighed particularly heavy on the Russian mass media. In defense of democracy, executive authorities suspended parliamentary and opposition publications and broadcasts, fired newspaper editors-in-chief, and imposed censorship on both print and electronic media coverage of the crisis and its aftermath.[82] The Yeltsin regime introduced a virtual information blackout. Government press services and public relations departments provided minimal news regarding ongoing developments and "fenced off" Russian officials from media inquiries. Enforcement organs restricted press access to parliamentary leaders and premises, resorting to arrests and physical violence to restrain the more persistent members of the Fourth Estate.

Even during more peaceful periods, the defense of democracy theory has been the inspiration for a series of political, economic, and legal measures to curtail expression and information. These include political reprisals against "disloyal" journals and officials; award of subsidies according to the content, posture, and "social importance" of individual media organs; mandates on publication and prior restraints; suspension and termination of journals; media and public access restrictions; and post-publication criminal and civil actions. The defense of democracy theory has also figured prominently in the preparation of legislation to expand liability for state secrets, insulting of top officials, attacks on constitutional organs of power, violations of Russian Federation "integrity"; to prevent "pollution" of the airwaves; and to establish media oversight bodies.

III. The Popular Mandate Theory

The popular mandate theory was the guiding principle for the fall 1993 election and constitutional referendum campaigns. It exalts citizens' constitutional rights to information. However, it defines the role of information narrowly as an instrument to activate public participation in the electoral process. Its basic tenet is that the "highest measure of democracy" is formal endorsement and legitimization by the citizenry in fair and open elections.

A. Theory

The popular mandate theory views public political apathy as the greatest threat to democracy. It argues that indifference to politics is a direct function of insufficient and inappropriate information. To remedy the problem, the popular mandate theory calls for a significant increase in the flow of political information to the electorate. The general expectation is that exposure to and understanding of the issues and candidates translate automatically into a higher turnout at the polls.

[82] On October 4, 1993, Yeltsin declared a state of emergency in Moscow. Pursuant to this decree, the Ministry of Press and Information suspended all publications whose founders participated in illegal acts in Moscow or that supported such illegal acts. These journals included *Pravda*, *Sovetskaia Rossiia*, *Den'*, *Rabochaia Tribuna*, *Glasnost'*, *Narodnaia Gazeta*, *Ruskii Poriadok*, and *Ruskii Vestnik*. The most visible example of censorship occurred on October 5 when *Nezavisimaia Gazeta* and *Segodnia* were published with blank spaces, indicating articles removed by censors.

The popular mandate theory also promises voters a genuine comparison and choice among competing candidates and approaches. It requires dissemination of "diverse" views and guarantees participants in the electoral process "equal opportunities" to address the citizenry. The popular mandate theory grants all candidates, irrespective of wealth or status, "equitable access" to mass communication and information media. Moreover, it calls for full and fair presentation of positions and forbids any outside manipulation or distortion.

Finally, the popular mandate theory demands serious, "civilized," and constructive election campaigns and coverage. It prohibits "unethical," "defamatory," and "improper" criticism of opponents (or even the Constitution itself). It contends that such behavior endangers the democratic process as a whole. Candidate "mudslinging" dampens voter enthusiasm and participation in elections and sets a negative precedent for post-election parliamentary deliberation and decision making.

B. "Excommunication" of the Mass Media

Under the popular mandate theory, the exclusive function of the mass media is to provide a free and neutral platform for communication of political information. This theory regards the print and especially electronic media as the most efficient mechanisms for rapid transmission of key facts, issues, and views to the electorate. Like the defense of democracy theory, it contends that the media can best facilitate democracy in their capacity as conduits of information, rather than as independent Fourth Estate.

The popular mandate theory views active media involvement in campaigns with suspicion. It emphasizes the power of journalists to skew political information, processes, and outcomes. As Vice Premier Vladimir Shumeiko explained, "a smart commentator can destroy a candidate with literally two words in the course of his presentation."

To prevent media manipulation and interference in elections, the popular mandate theory permits only objective, nonpartisan and unfiltered reporting of campaigns. It "rules out" any analysis, comparison, and criticism of candidates and positions that could unduly influence voters' perceptions and decisions. Instead, it "instructs" journalists and broadcasters to serve as impartial moderators to ensure fair, equal, and civilized presentation of all points of view.

C. Applications

The popular mandate theory has served first and foremost as a stimulus for government to bombard its citizens with political information (primarily through the media). In the interests of democracy, it has allowed officials to ignore or supersede audience preferences for lighter fare. This use of the popular mandate theory had a discernible impact on Russian media content during the fall of 1993. Campaign speeches, platforms, and rebuttals, as well as general summaries of the draft Constitution, dominated newspaper columns and flooded the airwaves. Political monologues and advertisements often preempted popular programming.

The "diversity" and "equality" principles of the popular mandate theory have inspired affirmative measures to regulate conditions for dissemination of political information and access to mass information media. These have included assignment of free air time by lot in equal blocks to all registered candidates; limitations on fees and opportunities for paid political advertisement; and provision of free newspaper space for publication of candidate and party platforms. The Russian government has also sought to reduce the distorting effects of status on the electoral process by monitoring and restricting media use by government officials, heads of television and radio companies, and journalists who are candidates or candidates' representatives.

The popular mandate theory's concern with fair and full presentation has translated into extensive legal and extralegal prescriptions on potentially "distorting" practices and coverage. For example, post-Soviet Russia has banned public opinion polls and "agitation" for or against candidates immediately prior to or during voting. It has also issued detailed directives regarding the approved format, content, and scope of election-related broadcasts. Under the popular mandate theory, the Russian leadership has made a concerted effort to eliminate "covert political advertising" by the media. In the process, it has denied journalists the rights to comment on election speeches or positions; express support or preference for particular candidates, parties, and programs; present facts that might discriminate against a specific candidate; and use an "ironic" tone in describing a campaign speaker or platform.

Finally, the popular mandate theory's emphasis on "civilized" information has been a central theme in post-Soviet Russian election policy and practice. Under this strand of the popular mandate theory, officials have refused "dangerous" political parties "complete freedom of propaganda," prohibited criticism of the Constitution and defamation of rivals, and banned subversive and inflammatory political statements. Leaders have applied moral as well as legal principles, techniques, and sanctions to ensure compliance. For example, under official direction, candidates have concluded "gentlemen's agreements" to refrain from unethical campaign conduct and have publicly confessed "impolite" behavior. The popular mandate theory has also been the rationale for establishing special extralegal organs to monitor and enforce dissemination of "civilized" information. The most notable of these has been the Information Arbitration Tribunal, a quasi-judicial body created by Boris Yeltsin to safeguard information guarantees in elections. During its brief tenure in November and December 1993, the Information Arbitration Tribunal invoked both law and morality in censuring candidates, journalists, and officials for campaign misconduct.

IV. The Parental Theory

The parental theory was Yeltsin's response to the election debacle of December 12, 1993. Low voter turnout, unenthusiastic popular endorsement of the Constitution, and decisive repudiation of reformist candidates, parties, and platforms were blamed in large part on a failed information policy. This experience also led to a fundamental reevaluation of the short-term prospects for democracy in Russia. Under the new view, Russia is "immature and unprepared for democracy."

According to the parental theory, the role of information is to nurture democracy. Its function is to create the two necessary conditions for future development of a democratic system—"social accord" and "political culture." The parental theory guarantees the populace constructive, reliable, and educational information.

A. Theory

Under the parental theory, the populace is unsophisticated, credulous, and gullible. It is unable to discriminate truth from falsehood or salutary from harmful information. It is easily duped and manipulated by unscrupulous and subversive forces. The parental theory seeks to remedy this popular naïveté and inexperience with an information policy that is protective and educational.

As a protective measure, the parental theory categorically rejects the notion of a free market of competing ideas. It views such a scheme as detrimental to the interests of both individuals and society.[149] The parental theory calls instead for a preliminary filtering out of false, deceptive, negative, divisive, and immoral contaminants to ensure the flow of only pure, trustworthy, and positive information to the populace.

On the educational side, the parental theory highlights the role of information in inculcating in the populace new norms and patterns of political behavior. Its immediate goal is to create the "social accord" and "mature" political culture required to expedite Russia's transition to democracy. Its long-term objective is to train the populace for its future role as citizenry of a democratic state.

To promote popular political education the parental theory requires increased efforts by officials and media to explain government activities and accomplishments in terminology comprehensible by ordinary citizens. It also envisions extensive notification and involvement of citizens in supervision and enforcement of government programs.[155]

Most importantly, the parental theory calls for extensive use of information media and techniques to instill in the populace the values of a "civilized" political system—consensus, compromise, moderation, and, above all, commitment to national welfare. It seeks to instruct citizens in appropriate ethical principles and conduct through the glare of publicity. A favored technique is to provide the populace with concrete examples for

[149] A prime example is the July 1994 collapse of the MMM pyramid scheme. Organizers lured an estimated ten million unsophisticated investors with glossy advertisements promising three thousand percent annual dividends, Paris apartments, California vacations, and the like.

[155] Two examples are proposals for the public to monitor signatories' compliance with the April 1994 Social Accord Treaty and to supervise authorities' observance of human rights guarantees in implementation of anticrime edicts.

emulation or censure. Under this approach, both positive and negative role models are brought to public notice. Thus, one politician is praised for "civilized" behavior while another is subjected to "public trial."

B. Domestication of the Media

The parental theory defines the media as public guardian or trustee—an objective reporter, official mouthpiece, link between state and society, and, above all, purveyor of information that serves the public interest. Under this view, the primary function of the media is to assist the leadership in raising the political, educational, and cultural standards of the populace. This includes the critical task of creating a national identity to "unite" citizens, "fill a spiritual vacuum and inspire confidence in tomorrow."

The parental theory rejects the previous "opposition role" of the media as "outdated" and obstructive of current efforts to promote social stability and democratic development. It contends that in a pluralistic party system there is no longer any need for the media to serve as gadfly and democratic check on authorities. Instead, it calls for "civilized" relations between media and government.

The parental theory's ideal is a "cultured, civilized and professionally and ethically mature" media. It regards as truly "democratic" media those that voluntarily adopt and observe ethical limitations on their constitutional rights to access and dissemination of information. The parental theory contends that today's media diverge markedly from this model. It claims that irresponsible journalists manipulate the public consciousness through unsubstantiated rumor, "black propaganda," and misinformation. The parental theory concludes that, if unchecked, the media "cause material as well as psychological damage" to the audience and "shatter" society and the evolving democratic reform process.

C. Applications

The parental theory has been the rationale for significant reforms in the process of collection and distribution of information. Under its direction, authorities have created or reorganized presidential, administrative, and legislative outlets to feed the media and citizenry predigested information suitable for popular consumption. They have reinforced these structural controls with formal and informal restrictions on press and public access to official personnel and to discussions, texts, details, or even direct confirmation of draft laws, decrees, and policy decisions.

The parental theory has been invoked as well in official efforts to regulate the content of information disseminated to citizens. Both protective and educational objectives have sparked executive and legislative measures to guarantee a flow of information in the "public interest." Under the protective rubric, authorities have sought to restrict harmful information through, inter alia, bans on fascist and erotic literature and on "unscrupulous" advertising. Under the educational standard they have promoted increased dissemination of "beneficial" information, primarily in the political sphere. Measures have included guidelines for prompt, equal, and objective media coverage of executive, legislative and judicial branch activities; mandates for publication of official documents, policies, and speeches; and directives for production of articles and broadcasts of "an educative nature" on political, cultural, and "socially significant" issues.

The parental theory has also served as the principal justification for official restraints on the media. Authorities have employed a panoply of direct and indirect legal, political, and economic means to curtail media activities. Some of these have targeted specific organs or personnel deemed insufficiently trustworthy, conscientious, and public-spirited in their approach to dissemination of information. Thus, under the parental theory, authorities have attempted to suspend or appropriate recalcitrant publications, have refused to circulate documents and barred entry to official meetings to representatives of disfavored media organs, and have threatened reprisals against individual "unreliable" journalists. A broader approach has been use of economic levers to "domesticate" the media. Economic subsidies, which for most Russian media spell the difference between economic survival or collapse, have been a particularly popular means to encourage obedience to official directives.

Finally, the parental theory has inspired a series of extralegal norms, bodies, and sanctions to implement "information guarantees" and to ensure "civilized," "ethical" journalism. Under both protective and educational rationales, authorities have effectively elevated ethical standards over legal, even constitutional, rights of expression and information. They have relied heavily on extralegal mechanisms and methods to ensure "proper" exercise of such rights and to punish deviations with the "most powerful sanction of moral impact," publicity. A prime illustration of these trends is the Judicial Chamber for Information Disputes, an extralegal tribunal formed on December 31, 1993, to "assist" the President in upholding information rights and freedoms. This body has the sweeping responsibilities of guaranteeing objectivity, authenticity, equality, and pluralism in the mass media; protecting the moral interests of children and adolescents; settling disputes among parliamentary factions regarding allocation of air time; and correcting factual errors in media reports. Consistent with the parental theory, the Judicial Chamber has emerged in practice as a moral guardian, educator, and stern disciplinarian rather than neutral forum for resolution of information-related issues.

V. The Failure of Information Theory in Russia

Throughout the post-Soviet era, Russian Constitutions have proclaimed a broad guarantee of freedom of information. Yet, the actual contours of this constitutional right have varied significantly over time. In a brief three-year history, Russian authorities have explored four distinct approaches to information with qualitatively different theoretical underpinnings and practical applications. The tenure of each has been short-lived. Each has proven easily discarded and replaced by a new or revived theory more consonant with changing leadership needs and challenges. The result has been considerable uncertainty, inconsistency, and fluctuation in the scope and definition of constitutional rights of expression as well as information. Nowhere could this be more evident than in the mass media context. Russian mass media have experienced a marked decline in fortune—from exaltation as independent Fourth Estate to vilification as dangerous adversary of state and society, excommunication from the political process, and subordination as conduit of government-filtered information to the populace. With each change in status have come new legal and extralegal redefinitions and constraints on media rights to access and dissemination of information.

Russia's failure to develop a coherent, effective approach to information rights raises two troubling questions. Why have "democratic" theories of information rights reinforced traditional authoritarian approaches to Russian populace, media, and dissemination of information? Why have "democratic" theories ultimately undermined, not generated, popular support and confidence in Russia's self-styled "democratic" leadership and its reform program?

A. From Information Liberty to Information Diktat

Three factors may explain why Russia's "democratic" theories of information rights have become formulae for authoritarian rather than popular control. These are indeterminacy of underlying constitutional text, adoption of a collective standard of information rights, and interpretation of information rights through the lens of democracy.

1. Constitutional Text

Frederick Schauer has noted the "majestic indeterminacy" of constitutional provisions on expressive and information rights worldwide. The result, he has argued, is that "definition does not and cannot come from the text of the constitution itself," but "must come from elsewhere."[192]

Russian Constitutions are consistent with this pattern. The much-amended Constitution of 1978 and its 1993 successor set out expressive and information rights in broad, indeterminate language. Both guarantee individuals "freedom of thought and speech," and the right to "seek, receive, and disseminate information freely." The Constitutions contain textual qualifications that are equally sweeping and indeterminate. For example, the 1978 Constitution subjects information guarantees to "restrictions established by law." The 1993 Constitution prohibits "propaganda of social, racial, national, religious, or linguistic supremacy." As Schauer predicts, definition of these provisions has indeed come from "elsewhere." In Russia's case, textual indeterminacy

---

[192] Frederick Schauer, *Free Speech and the Cultural Contingency of Constitutional Categories*, *in* Constitutionalism, Identity, Difference and Legitimacy 353, 356 (Michel Rosenfeld ed., 1994).

has translated into a license for officials to manipulate the content and flow of information.

Textual indeterminacy does not necessarily undermine legitimacy or enforceability of constitutional rules. Nor need it lead inexorably to authoritarian control of speech and information. As Thomas Franck has observed in the international law context, "lack of textual determinacy may be redressed by process determinacy."[197] Franck suggests two possible remedial devices. These are "clarification by an authority recognized as legitimate by those to whom the rule is addressed" and "common community understanding of the rule's complex context." Frederick Schauer identifies three potential sources of "credible" interpretation and delineation: influence of United States constitutional doctrine, internal development within the legal/constitutional organs of the relevant legal/constitutional system, and cultural categorization.[201]

In post-Soviet Russia, however, none of these has offered a viable challenge or alternative to authoritarian monopoly on interpretation of constitutional text. Foreign example (Western European perhaps even more than American) has clearly influenced Russian constitutional and legal norms and rules on speech, media, and information. Nonetheless, its current and long-term impact is limited at best in an era of rising nationalist sentiment. Politicians and populace alike now blame much of Russia's economic, political, and social ills on misguided, mechanical transplantation of foreign models.

To compound the problem, Russia possesses no executive, legislative, or judicial body with the "pedigree," experience, competence, or popular respect to clarify, articulate, and apply constitutional rules in a clear and consistent manner. Initially, it appeared as if the Constitutional Court might assume this function. In the early days of the post-Soviet era, the Court began the difficult process of developing from scratch constitutional method and jurisprudence. It soon abandoned this task, however, to become embroiled in the internecine struggle between the Russian president and parliament. This politicization of the Court compromised its credibility, independence, and legitimacy and eventually resulted in its suspension and reorganization. A reconfigured Constitutional Court finally resumed operations in 1995 after a one and one-half year hiatus.[207]

Furthermore, Russian cannot draw on a common community or cultural understanding to supply meaning and legitimacy to constitutional guarantees of free speech and information. As I have noted elsewhere, post-Soviet Russia is a country in the grips of profound "cultural despair." It is currently seeking a new national identity and past. Moreover, Russia emerged from the Soviet period without a popular legal consciousness, let alone legal culture. It "can invoke few accepted cultural or historical standards or traditions of legality, justice, and due process." Absence of legal and

[197] Thomas M. Franck, The Power of Legitimacy Among Nations 80 (1990).
[201] Schauer, *supra* note 192, at 361-67.
[207] The Constitutional Court issued its first major decision on March 23, 1995.

constitutional culture, tradition, and language has created a serious void, one that has allowed Russian authorities to appropriate interpretation of constitutional text. As will be seen below, information theories have only reinforced this position by defining information rights in utilitarian communal terms.

2. Collective Definition of Information Rights

One of the most striking developments in the post-Soviet era has been the rapid shift in official and unofficial discourse from an emphasis on individual rights of expression to collective rights to information. In the process, constitutional rights to information have emerged from relative obscurity first to buttress expressive liberties and then to restrain, even supplant, these rights. Post-Soviet interpretations of information rights have consistently made community not individual their central concern. This is reflected in all four information theories. It is most obvious in the defense of democracy and the parental theories. These theories expressly place societal welfare above individual rights and limit dissemination and receipt of any potentially harmful, destabilizing, or immoral information. In a more subtle but equally pervasive manner, this concern also animates the informed citizenry and the popular mandate theories. Both theories grant constitutional rights and protections to the individual solely in his/her capacity as citizen-participant in democratic self-government. They "reduc[e] [the individual] to his or her citizenship" and "mere membership in a democratic collective."

Interestingly, constitutional rhetoric as well as theory has underscored the supremacy of community over individual. The 1978 and 1993 Constitutions guarantee "each person" (*kazhdii*) rights to information. Yet, proponents of every information theory have consistently restated these individual rights as collective rights of "citizens" (*grazhdane*), "society" (*obshchestvo*), "Russians" (*Rossiiane*), and "the people" (*narod*).

This communal focus has introduced a significant theoretical and practical constraint on information (and expressive) rights—exercise in the "public interest." Yet Russian information theories have not provided concrete definition of what information promotes or endangers the public interest nor have they established an arbiter or procedure to do so. Rather, they refer to abstract, overarching standards of "fairness," "morality," "truth," "objectivity," and the like. As a result, all four schemes render information rights effectively unenforceable without outside interpretation and guidance. This has proven to be an open invitation to authorities to filter information in the name of society.

3. The Problem of "Democracy"

Russian information theories have further exacerbated the need for external interpretation by adopting a utilitarian or "instrumental" justification for information rights. All four theories take as their basic premise that information must serve "democracy."

Tying constitutional rights to "democracy" would be problematic in any context. It requires some shared understanding of the term "democracy" to ensure stable and consistent definition and application of constitutional guarantees. Yet, as a vast literature has demonstrated, there is little consensus worldwide on what constitutes "democracy." In the United States, for example, there are at best "competing visions" of democracy.

For Russia, the problem of "democracy" is not contested meaning but absence of meaning. During the Soviet and post-Soviet eras, the term has been used in such inconsistent, even dramatically opposite, ways as to lose any practical or symbolic content or value.

As has been shown above, this "democratic" rationale has resulted in considerable fluctuation in the scope and protection of constitutional rights to information in the post-Soviet era. Russia's self-proclaimed "democratic" authorities have expanded or contracted information rights at will in accordance with their current evaluation of Russia's stage and form of democracy. Under this approach, information rights threaten to become as malleable and meaningless as "democracy" itself.

B. The Limits of Propaganda in an Information Age

Since Yeltsin's coup of September 1993, Russian authorities have made a concerted effort to manage information in order to mold Russian populace into "democratic" citizenry, loyal to "democratic" leadership and reform program. In their campaign to transform public attitudes and behavior, they have placed particular emphasis on central control of mass media (especially television) access and output.[220] Russian government and parliament have adopted two distinct approaches to information. Both of these have failed because they were based on an outdated understanding of information processing, communication, and technology.

1. Information and Democratic Participation

The first approach, exemplified by the popular mandate theory and recently, to a lesser degree, by the parental theory, has sought to bombard Russian populace with "objective" political information. Its basic premise is that political apathy is the product of inadequate information. Thus, it prescribes a concentrated dosage of direct exposure to "democratic" actors, institutions, and processes to stimulate popular interest and involvement in "democratic" politics. This scheme is government-dictated rather than consumer-driven. It rejects consumer preferences for entertainment-oriented programming as merely reflecting the low political culture and educational level of the masses. It requires strict, central regulation of information access and dissemination to ensure equal, fair, and, above all, neutral communication to citizens of a diversity of

[220] This focus on regulation of television is hardly surprising. Television is regarded as the most effective medium for rapid dissemination of information in post-Soviet Russia.

views. It relegates the mass media to the status of transmitters of political information and prohibits media interference, distortion, or even commentary.

As discussed above, the first attempt to implement this approach, during the fall 1993 election campaign, ended in failure. An information model intended to activate public political participation actually had the opposite effect. It contributed to further popular indifference and alienation from "democratic" politics. According to Russian commentators, the cause was "excessive tutelage" and "overregulation" by authorities. They argue that the architects of Russia's "democratic" information policy forgot a key player—the audience.

Russian critics view the 1993 election experience as a disastrous attempt to force-feed political information to an electorate already "overfed" with politics. Numerous polls have recorded public satiation with politics as have statistics regarding selection of television programs and newspaper subscriptions. Indeed, when Russia's first tabloid hit the stands in November 1993, it promised readers crossword puzzles, horoscopes, sports, crime reports, erotica, "super-investigations by journalists," "[a]nd most important—no politics!"

Russian commentators also castigate officials for treating voters to a steady diet of "facts" without presentation. They target guidelines for television coverage of election campaigns as particularly defective. They contend that strict regulations on format, content, and media involvement prevented debate, comparison of views, and professional analysis or criticism. These rules also provided little opportunity for audience, feedback, participation, or commentary. The result was "flat," dull programming that failed to engage the viewing public. As one Russian explained on the eve of the elections, "all I feel is boredom, because all around me are the bare facts or juggling with the facts but nothing more—no who? where? or for whom?"

According to Russian analysts, official information regulations further turned off voters by encouraging "self-advertising" monologues by political candidates rather than dialogues or polylogues. As the campaign proceeded, candidates increasingly used their reserved air times for bombastic, demagogic, and slanderous attacks on political opponents. This only intensified popular cynicism and distaste for "democratic" politics. To Russian critics, then, low voter turnout was inevitable. As an *Izvestiia* author predicted in November 1993, the electorate's ultimate response to all its "suitors" was: "Go away, fools!"

These conclusions are consistent with current literature on information processing and mass communication. Recent research demonstrates that the media are "more effective in reinforcing existing attitudes than in changing them." It suggests that the media have the least impact on topics that have "already reached a 'saturation' level in the public's mind." A number of studies highlight the critical importance of audience receptivity to media message. This work challenges the previous model of an automatic stimulus-response relationship between media and audience. It suggests that a strategy directed solely at increasing output of political information is unlikely to create an informed and involved citizenry.

Under the current view, the "sine qua non" for successful communication of information is "sensitivity to what the audience wants or needs to know." Presentation is a key determinant of audience reception of information. Studies reveal that one of the least effective communication techniques is to bombard the public with raw data. They indicate that attractive "packaging," organization, and interpretation are essential prerequisites for audience interest, processing, and understanding of new information. These findings have led researchers to two conclusions that will not surprise critics of Russia's 1993 election campaign. First, rigid insistence on "objective," nonpartisan media coverage may actually discourage popular concern, learning, and involvement in the political arena. Second, inattention to audience preferences also may disserve the "democratic" goal of citizen self-government. Boredom, alienation, and/or "distaste for media offerings" are powerful contributors to popular political apathy, cynicism, and nonparticipation.

2. Propaganda and Loyalty

Under the second approach to information, represented by both the defense of democracy and parental theories, Russian authorities have attempted to dictate the content as well as format of information disseminated to the Russian populace. In a classic example of what Monroe Price has called a "market for loyalties,"[249] Russian leaders have sought to assert monopoly control over communication "to exclude a range of destabilizing narratives," to project their own images of national identity, and to generate popular unity, support, and loyalty to the "democratic" regime and its vision of Russia's future.

Consistent with Price's paradigm, Russian authorities have taken affirmative measures to "restrict supply" of information and to "establish barriers to entry" by potential competitors. They have subsidized "constructive" messages, censored "harmful" messages, and have become a "vocal contributor" of their own messages. Government treatment of the ongoing conflict in Chechnya is illustrative.

From the start, intense official secrecy has cloaked the Chechen operation. Authorities dispatched troops into Chechnya without public announcement or explanation by president or prime minister. Executive and military personnel and organs, including "information" directorates, have suppressed unfavorable news and refused to respond to critical questions or reports. Russian government and military authorities have taken

[249] Monroe E. Price, *The Market for Loyalties: Electronic Media and the Global Competition for Allegiances*, 104 Yale Law Journal 667 (1994).

drastic measures to restrict media coverage[256] and have resurrected Soviet-style propaganda bodies and techniques.[257]

Throughout the Chechen conflict, authorities have compelled state mass media to carry government press service reports. On January 11, 1995, in a move distinctly reminiscent of the past, the state television company Ostankino even interrupted regularly scheduled programming on orders from above to air a patriotic, government-commissioned film on the Chechen war. The film featured "touching pictures" of "magnificent" young Russian soldiers to the stirring accompaniment of Wagnerian music and a narrator's inspirational words about Russia's "character" and "greatness."

These efforts to manage information have been unsuccessful. Russian authorities have been consistently stymied by public access to alternative information media and channels. One such source has been independent Russian information outlets. Due to private financing, some organizations have been able to operate without state subsidies. In so doing, they have been exempt from most indirect and direct governmental controls of their activities.[262] The result has been increased dissemination of stories and pictures that undermine, even contradict, the official line. For example, during the Chechen conflict, independent television channels have broadcast reports of "secret" Russian troop movements and have offered viewers visual proof of continued bombings and civilian casualties in Groznii despite government announcements to the contrary. NTV, Russia's only private national television company, has been a particular thorn in the side of Russian authorities. It has provided extensive critical coverage of events in Chechnya and has earned a reputation among the Russian public as the most "trusted" source of news on Chechnya. In late December 1994, NTV introduced new satellite transmitters that will potentially expand its broadcast area to reach an audience of 100 million viewers. According to reports from Kremlin insiders, however, NTV's independent coverage and status may be in jeopardy. Boris Yeltsin apparently is considering a "reorganization" of the company with the Russian government as a founder and holder of a 51% controlling interest.

Russian citizens have also circumvented their government's efforts to control information by developing their own formal and informal information channels. As

[256] Actions against journalists include, *inter alia*, restrictions on access to the combat zone and to Russian troops, confiscation of film and audio-cassettes, cutting of telephone lines to prevent transmission of live reports, and denials of accreditation, expulsions, physical assaults, and shootings of Russian and Western correspondents.

[257] These have included the Provisional Information Center, a Russian "analogue to the Ministry of Truth," and the revived television show "Vremia," complete with familiar theme music and smiling announcer to supply viewers with the approved government version of events in Chechnya.

[262] Throughout the post-Soviet era, Russian authorities have been able to exercise indirect control over media content and format through their power to grant or withhold economic subsidies on a selective basis. Moreover, most of the key mass media regulations apply to "state mass media," a term that has been defined as embracing any publication or television or radio company that receives financial support from the Russian government. Private funding frees independent media organs from both types of controls.

human rights activist Aleksei Smirnov explained, "If the authorities close people's access to the truth, people begin to publish information themselves." One example is the new samizdat bulletin *Ne Znat,' Ne Slushat,' Ne Ponimat'* [*Without Knowing, Hearing, and Understanding*]. Its purpose is to provide comprehensive, uncensored coverage of events in Chechnya. A less organized but pervasive source of popular information is rumor. As discussed earlier, Russia is rife with rumors on every imaginable topic, from the personal habits of politicians to alleged coup attempts. A number of newspapers even devote special columns to investigating the latest rumors. Throughout the post-Soviet era, rumor has consistently undermined Russian authorities' efforts to withhold, censor, or dictate information.

Another nongovernmental source of information has been foreign information networks. Advances in communications technology, in the form of satellites, computers, fax machines, and the like, have significantly expanded public access to outside information media. This has eroded the Russian government's capacity to contain "dangerous" information. Even during crisis situations, such as the 1993 coup and current Chechen conflict, foreign journalists have defeated domestic information blackouts.[273] They have broadcast out of Russia via satellite live reports, pictures, and statements by regime opponents, which have then been retransmitted to the Russian audience.[274]

Foreign information services have disclosed government "secrets" to Russian populace. For example, in October 1994, the *New York Times* reported that an oil spill had occurred three weeks earlier in the Russian Republic of Komi. The story was rapidly disseminated into Russia, where it caused a "furor." Subsequent investigation revealed that regional and federal departments had had prior knowledge of the disaster but had deliberately concealed it from Russian and world public. Russian commentators saw distinct parallels with past Soviet cover-ups (especially Chernobyl) and concluded that "one thing is clear: were it not for the article in the *New York Times* nobody would have known about the accident."

Foreign sources have also undercut statements by official Russian personnel. A recent illustration involved Defense Minister Pavel Grachev. The embattled Grachev proclaimed on Russian television that he enjoyed wide support among the military and provided as evidence a stack of messages to Yeltsin and Krasnaia Zvezda from military units, districts, and labor collectives. Radio Liberty responded with a report, which was subsequently carried by Russian newspapers, that the messages were in fact the product of a carefully orchestrated campaign by the Defense Ministry. Signatories included two daughters of a high-ranking general and another general who wrote: "According to Defense Minister Pavel Grachev's order, I announce my support for Pavel Grachev."

[273] In fact, foreign media also played a major role in defeating the 1991 coup attempt, which led to the dissolution of the Soviet Union and propelled Boris Yeltsin to power.

[274] For example, in January 1995, the German newspaper *Bild Am Sonntag* conducted a telephone interview with Chechen leader Dzhokhar Dudaev. The interview was beamed via satellite to Germany, published by *Bild Am Sonntag*, and then retransmitted into Russia.

The failure of Russia's second approach to information management is hardly surprising. It assumed the continued viability of closed information systems, an obsolete model in today's "information age." This experience is consistent with general trends worldwide. As Monroe Price has noted, "The new technologies and the mechanisms that are evolving for their exploitation are reducing the capacity of existing states to regulate political discourse."[283]

In Russia's case, however, the government effort to become the "monopoly supplier" of information to its citizenry has proven to be not only futile but harmful. Once again, the effect has been the opposite of that anticipated by its architects. Regulations to contain, filter, and dictate information have actually exacerbated societal instability, discord, and distrust in government.

The Chechen information policy reveals the very real dangers of Russia's second approach to information. Official efforts to conceal or suppress information have fueled societal tension. They have generated widespread public concern that Russia is moving in an authoritarian direction towards a police state. Formal and informal restrictions on access and dissemination have created hostile media that are now "waging war on their own state." They have also tarnished the image of Russian democracy in the eyes of Russian liberals and the West.

Government propaganda on Chechnya has also proven counterproductive. As discussed earlier, independent eyewitness accounts have repeatedly contradicted official statements, revealing their distortions, inaccuracies, and "blatant lies." According to January polls, only 14% of the Russian audience trust government reporting on Chechnya. Russians are turning in droves to alternative sources of information. Russian leaders as well as information services have lost credibility with the public. Indeed, recent reports suggest that Boris Yeltsin may be the ultimate casualty of the Chechen information policy. With an approval rating plummeting to 8%, Yeltsin is in a battle for his political future.

The Chechen situation highlights a surprising lesson of the post-Soviet era: suppression of potentially "harmful" information may be more dangerous than its expression, even in a transitional or fragile democratic system. The Russian experience suggests that restrictions on information may eliminate an important "safety valve" for the release or "domestication" of societal discontent and frustration. A *Komsomol'skaia Pravda* journalist expressed this notion of "stress reduction" best in his criticism of government closure of the opposition newspaper *Den'*: "A deeply suppressed mania leads to paranoia. Hatred to B. Yeltsin should be articulated—then it becomes less dangerous."

The Russian case also indicates that efforts to contain information may prevent advance warning of impending disaster. The Judicial Chamber for Information Disputes recognized this risk in defending *Obshchaia Gazeta*'s March 1994 publication of the

[283] Price, *supra* note 249, at 704-05.

unsubstantiated coup "version No. 1": "world history has known of cases where a leak of information has resulted in state upheaval but dismissal of such information has led to tragedy."

Official secrecy and silence regarding unflattering or controversial matters may create an "information vacuum," which only encourages rumor and instability. For example, in September 1994, official spokespersons refused to comment on reports of Yeltsin's alleged misconduct abroad. The response was immediate public speculation that the presidential administration was preparing another "surprise" for Russians. Coup is the "natural offspring" of official secrecy.

As amply demonstrated in the 1993 coup and Chechen conflict, restrictions on information access and dissemination may antagonize a potential force for national stabilization, the mass media. Foreign experience has shown that the media can perform a valuable function in promoting societal consolidation and moderation during periods of national crisis. As I have noted elsewhere, they can "persuade . . . citizenry that established political and legal institutions and processes are both predictable and flexible enough to accommodate change." A hostile media, in contrast, may only further undermine popular confidence in the legitimacy and stability of political institutions and leaders.

Finally, the Russian experience suggests that official propaganda, at least that of the "direct," "open," and "centralized" variety, may be of limited value in an era of rapidly evolving communications technologies. Alternative sources of information easily circumvent government attempts to filter and dictate information and expose official omissions, distortions, and lies. In Russia's case, this has caused authorities to "lose substance" in the eyes of the public. It has reached the point where Russians have no faith in official statements or documents. Even more troubling, the Russian citizenry is now convinced that its "democratic" government "lies even when it tells the truth."[307]

Conclusion: Lessons from Russia

Post-Soviet Russian authorities have experimented with four theories for the role of information in democracy and each has failed. The informed citizenry theory posits that the citizenry should receive the information it needs to monitor, check, and correct governing authorities. The theory failed in the Russian context because it lacked definition. Rival political forces ended up competing over what information the citizenry requires and who is the best "guarantor" of its dissemination. By negative implication, the theory became an excuse for regulating information rights and asserting official

[307] For example, beginning in May 1994, Russian authorities issued warnings to the public regarding deceptive advertisements for risky investment schemes. These were targeted in particular at potential investors in the MMM joint stock company, a pyramid scheme that ultimately collapsed on July 29, 1994. Russian investors discounted both the advance warnings and subsequent charges against MMM as "[l]ies, out-and-out slander, juggling of facts."

control over the channels for distribution of information. It rapidly yielded to the second failed theory, the defense of democracy theory.

The defense of democracy theory holds that the citizenry needs only "constructive" political information. It views full information as a threat to democracy itself. The theory led to strict limitations on information access and dissemination, heavy censorship of the media, and, ultimately, to popular rumor, suspicion, and dependence on outside news sources.

The popular mandate theory explores the opposite extreme. It bombards the citizenry with raw, unanalyzed political information to encourage public interest and involvement in the political arena. This theory entails extensive government regulation to ensure proper format and conditions for information transmission, to override audience preferences, and to prevent media interference. The popular mandate theory also proved unsuccessful in Russian practice. A steady stream of raw, unanalyzed political information bored the public and only intensified popular political apathy, alienation, and nonparticipation. This theory was immediately replaced by yet another failed theory, the parental theory.

The parental theory views the public as unsophisticated, credulous, and gullible. It seeks to shield citizens from harmful information and to provide only educational and salutary messages. It undertakes to serve them essentially by telling them what and how to think. This theory failed in Russia because it grossly underestimated the audience. It encouraged government dissemination of information that lacked credibility and inspired rebellion. In the end, the citizenry rejected both the information and its supplier.

Thus, all four "democratic" theories led to reassertion of authoritarian control over information. This result appears to proceed from three causes. First, the right to information as expressed in Russian law and Constitution is highly indeterminate and, therefore, subject to manipulation by the various branches of government. This is true as well of the right to information in the United States and elsewhere. The difference is that Russia has neither the legal traditions nor institutions necessary to give content to the vague expressions. Second, the concept of "democracy" is equally indeterminate and subject to manipulation. Russian leaders could plausibly deny the citizenry information on the grounds that they were thereby serving the interests of democracy.

Third, contrary to the express wording of the Russian Constitution itself, each of these theories defines the right to information as a collective right of the citizenry rather than as a right of citizens individually. This approach has both theoretical and practical flaws. Theoretically, it grants the majority of citizens, acting through its elected government, the right to deny even the most essential information to individuals. Practically, it gives authorities the right to control information. In other words, a collective right to information expressed indeterminately implies the necessity for an arbiter to define the scope of the right.

Russian officials assumed the role of arbiter and attempted to manage the flow of information to suit their own political purposes. From their efforts we learn two important lessons for other democracies wrestling with information policy. First, public disinterest in the kinds of information government wants them to have is a very real limitation on government. Information diktat is unsuccessful. Second, official propaganda, at least in the blunt, artless forms practiced in post-Soviet Russia, is ineffective and potentially destructive. It is easily subverted by the alternative channels available in our modern information age. Moreover, it breeds rumors, cynicism, and distrust of government.

Ultimately, the solution to the information problem of democracy may be to redefine the right to information in individual rather than collective terms. The concept of information as an individual right finds some expression in United States law but not at the constitutional level. Prevailing First Amendment theory, particularly in the scholarly literature, defines the right to information vaguely and in collective terms. Theories in which the right to information is an individual right are largely untested, but they may be our future. Nothing else seems to work.

III.

Evolving Regulation

A. Elections

Free Speech and the Mass Media in Russia: Lessons from the December 1993 Election and Constitutional Referendum*

Melissa Dawson

Introduction

On December 12, 1993, Russian voters approved a new constitution, the first Russian constitution to be adopted since the collapse of communism in August 1991. This constitution proclaims a commitment to freedom of thought and speech and forbids censorship, thus elevating principles already embodied in Russian law to the constitutional level. It also provides that citizens may not be compelled to express opinions and guarantees the right to seek out, obtain, and transmit information (not including state secrets). At the same time, the Russian constitution prohibits "propaganda or campaigning that instigates social, racial, national or religious hatred and enmity," as well as "propaganda of social, racial, national, religious or linguistic superiority." It allows for the adoption of federal constitutional laws restricting speech in a state of emergency or when otherwise "necessary to protect the foundations of the constitutional system, morals, health and rights and legitimate interests of other persons, and to ensure the defense of the country and the security of the state." Thus, the Russian constitution envisions drawing a balance between free speech and other competing values. This balancing process will be heavily influenced by the particular vision of democracy held by those entrusted with interpreting the constitution.

The decisions and recommendations issued by the Information Arbitration Tribunal ("IAT") provide a valuable opportunity to learn about the Russian conception of the role of free speech in a democracy. The IAT was a quasi-judicial body formed specifically to address issues relating to the media and speech which arose during the period leading up to the December 12, 1993, election. This election was called after the dissolution of the Russian parliament earlier that fall in order to select a new parliament and to ratify the draft constitution.

At the time the IAT was created, Boris Yeltsin faced a tense political situation. Many were critical of Yeltsin's handling of the crisis that followed his dissolution of the parliament in September, which in early October culminated in a bloody confrontation between the army and a group of deputies who refused to disband. In particular, critics pointed to the temporary imposition of censorship and the shutting down of several newspapers at the time of the crisis as an indication that Yeltsin had strayed from the

* 13 Cardozo Arts & Entertainment Law Journal 881 (1995).

democratic path.[9] Many also believed that Yeltsin's success in a referendum held the previous April, reaffirming popular support for his presidency, was attributable to the strong pro-Yeltsin bias in the media.[10] Thus, it was important for Yeltsin to ensure the legitimacy of the December election by guaranteeing that the media treated candidates fairly.

In the Statute on the Election of Deputies to the State Duma, which set forth the general parameters for the election of deputies to the lower house of the new Russian Parliament, Yeltsin included several provisions guaranteeing candidates equal access to the media and forbidding unlawful government interference with media coverage of the election campaign. These provisions were expanded in the Statute on Information Guarantees for the Election Campaign, adopted October 29, 1993. According to its preamble, this statute was to protect

> [f]ree, democratic elections and the citizens' exercise in full measure of their right to vote, [which] demanded that all candidates and parties be assured of the opportunity freely to set forth their viewpoints through the use of the mass media and also of the prevention of unlawful interference in the activity of the editorial offices of the media during the period of the election campaign.

This statute provided detailed guidelines governing the behavior of the candidates and the mass media during the election campaign and created the nine-member Information Arbitration Tribunal to ensure adherence to these guidelines.

The Statute on Information Guarantees was developed by a long-standing advocate of the protection of free speech rights, Yuri Baturin, along with a group of law students who specialized in the legal rights of the mass media. Baturin participated in the

---

[9] Censorship was introduced during a brief state of emergency, between October 4 and 18, under the Law on the State of Emergency. Yeltsin's government also closed down a number of newspapers in the aftermath of the October events, announcing that it would file criminal charges against them for "direct calls for bloodshed which contributed to destabilization and rebellion." Among the newspapers which were closed down were *Den'*, *Russkii Poriadok* (*Russian Order*), and *Russkoe Slovo* (*Russian Word*). According to Vladimir Shumeiko, who was appointed as Minister of the Press soon after the October events, "[a]ll these newspapers [had] a fascist orientation and their suspension [was] perfectly in line with . . . the [Russian Law On the Mass Media]." In addition, *Pravda*, *Sovetskaia Rossiia*, and *Narodnaia Pravda* were temporarily closed because, according to Shumeiko, the chief editors of these newspapers had called for the overthrow of legitimate bodies of state power. Thus, these newspapers were allowed to reopen when they agreed to install new editors-in-chiefs.

The effects of the October events were felt in television as well. Aleksandr Nevzorov's anti-Yeltsin (and many would argue, fascist) show "600 Seconds" was pulled off the air, and the popular television anchors Aleksandr Lubimov and Aleksandr Politkovsky were fired from the Ostankino television company after telling people to go home and go to bed rather than heeding the call of Yegor Gaidar to rally around the Moscow City Soviet building in support of Yeltsin during the October confrontation with parliament.

[10] According to one source, in the weeks leading up to the April 25 referendum, 80% of television programming was pro-Yeltsin, while only 20% represented the views of parliament.

writing of both the Soviet Press Law of 1990 and the Russian Law On the Mass Media of 1991. Similarly, many of the individuals appointed by Yeltsin to the IAT were well-known advocates of free speech rights.

Because the IAT did not have any binding authority, its power derived largely from the legitimacy of its decisions. Thus, the IAT sought to base its decisions on widely held Russian values concerning the role of the media in a democracy. At the same time, the IAT was expected to play a more active role than a traditional court in monitoring the Russian media. Rather than waiting for disputes to be brought before it, the IAT had the power to consider a wide range of issues at its own discretion without receiving a complaint from any of the parties involved. The IAT members were "to watch and listen day and night, day and night, to listen and to read." The IAT also had the option of referring criminal violations to the public prosecutor's office.

This Paper will examine the conception of the role of free speech in a democracy that emerges from the IAT's decisions. I will compare the IAT's approach to that of Alexander Meiklejohn and a growing number of students of the First Amendment who question the market-oriented, laissez-faire approach that the United States Supreme Court has taken toward free speech during recent decades. Following in the tradition of Meiklejohn, who focused on the social value of free speech and its importance for achieving enlightened self-governance, these scholars argue that certain types of regulation which the Court considers antithetical to the First Amendment in fact are permitted, if not required, by the First Amendment. Further, these "new Meiklejohnians" point out that the legal framework which has evolved in the United States with respect to free speech is poorly equipped to address the issues of access to the mass media and the effects of disparities in economic resources among potential speakers.

The decisions of the IAT reflect certain fundamental values that are consistent with the democratic vision of Meiklejohn and his followers. In particular, the IAT focused on the social value of free speech rather than on free speech as an individual right. Thus, it emphasized the listener's right to hear rather than the speaker's right to express himself. To the extent that the IAT protected free speech, it sought to ensure a healthy deliberative process and wise decision-making in the election, primary goals of free speech in the Meiklejohnian model of democracy. Consistent with the Meiklejohnian approach, the IAT condemned the efforts of local Russian officials to suppress the speech of certain candidates and sought to provide all candidates with an opportunity to be heard in the mass media.

Even as the IAT appeared to be motivated by goals that were consistent with the Meiklejohnian vision of democracy, some of the means by which it sought to ensure a constructive deliberative process were seriously at odds with the Meiklejohnian approach to speech. One of the most striking examples of this was the IAT's efforts to eliminate journalistic bias, which led it to become heavily involved in scrutinizing the content of journalists' speech, censuring a great deal of speech that would be considered valuable in the Meiklejohnian model. These decisions raise a question as to whether free speech in a political campaign is supposed to protect journalists or candidates.

Further, in seeking to prevent the pre-election debate from degenerating into mudslinging between the candidates, the IAT advanced a notion of civility that arguably impeded discussion of important political issues. In some cases, the IAT made pronouncements that amounted to accusations of sedition. The IAT's involvement in making content-based determinations as to what speech is useful and what is not is troubling from a democratic perspective because of the potential for governmental abuse of such power.

After briefly discussing the Meiklejohnian approach to free speech, I will examine the IAT's decision-making in two areas. First, I will address the provisions and decisions aimed at ensuring fair treatment of candidates and parties by the media, including positive access rights, government censorship, and media bias. Secondly, I will address the speech limitations that the IAT imposed on the candidates during their campaigning. Finally, I will discuss some of the theoretical and practical issues that the Russian model of free speech raises for those concerned with the role of free speech in a democracy.

I. The Governmental Process Model

A. The Meiklejohnian Model

The governmental process model derives its approach to speech from the fundamental principle that in a democracy, the citizens themselves, rather than an "alien" government, must make decisions concerning public policy. Alexander Meiklejohn, one of the key figures in this school of thought, argues that in order to make wise public policy decisions, citizens must be provided with all possible perspectives on the issues and be given the opportunity to deliberate. The emphasis, then, is on the right of the listener to become informed about the issues, rather than on the right of the speaker to express himself. According to this approach, the judiciary must play an active role in protecting free speech in order to ensure a democratic political process. So long as the political process is democratic, the economic policy choices made by the citizens will be valid, allowing the judiciary to defer to them.

In contrast to those who argue that an adversarial marketplace of ideas ultimately will lead to the discovery of truth, Meiklejohn envisions citizens as deliberating with the objective of achieving the common good. He rejects the notion that the common good will result from an adversarial process in which all simply fight to advance their own personal preferences, and argues that the marketplace metaphor is destructive because it provides citizens with a justification for ignoring the general welfare in their political decision making. Further, he notes that the goal of free speech is not so much to produce new truths as to allow citizens to deliberate and inform themselves in order to participate effectively in the process of democratic self-government.

Meiklejohn draws on the metaphor of democracy as a town meeting to illustrate his approach to speech. Like a town meeting, all are free to come, and all come as political equals, with a "duty to think [their] own thoughts, to express them, and to listen to the arguments of others." This town-meeting approach also contains built-in limits to speech:

> The final aim of the meeting is the voting of wise decisions. The voters, therefore, must be made as wise as possible . . . . As the self-governing community seeks, by method of voting, to gain wisdom in action, it can find it only in the minds of its individual citizens . . . . What is essential is not that everyone shall speak, but that everything worth saying shall be said.[29]

Thus, the moderator of a town meeting may refuse to give the floor to someone who will merely make a point that has been made already, but he must not refuse the floor to a speaker because the idea which that speaker will express is distasteful to the moderator or to the community. Further, speech that is abusive or threatening should be suppressed, as this is likely to hinder fruitful debate rather than contribute to it. However, with respect to the criticism of public officials, Meiklejohn recognizes that the crime of sedition is inconsistent with democratic self-governance.

The narrowness of the limits to freedom of speech that may arise from the governmental process approach are clearly demonstrated in the work of Robert Bork. Based on Meiklejohn's argument that freedom of speech is intended to protect the governmental process, Bork argues that "the protection of the First Amendment must be cut off when it reaches the outer limits of political speech." Thus, he would decline the invitation of Meiklejohn and many others to extend protection of speech to "[f]orms of thought and expression within the range of human communications from which the voter derives the knowledge, intelligence, sensitivity to human values: the capacity for sane and objective judgment which, so far as possible, a ballot should express."[34]

B. Meiklejohn's Followers

Alexander Meiklejohn wrote in an era in which government suppression of dissent was the main threat to free speech in the United States. Thus, in *Political Freedom*, Meiklejohn expresses deep concern about the implications of McCarthyism on democracy and devotes much of his attention to refuting the arguments of those who seek to suppress "dangerous" speech. Although stating that the First Amendment does not preclude Congress from legislating to "enlarge" or "enrich" speech, Meiklejohn devotes little attention to the issue of positive regulations to enrich speech. While at one point he comments that commercial radio does not deserve the First Amendment's protection

[29] Alexander Meiklejohn, Political Freedom: The Constitutional Powers of the People 26 (1948).

[34] Robert Bork, *Neutral Principles and Some First Amendment Problems*, 47 Indiana Law Journal 1, 26 (1971) (quoting Alexander Meiklejohn, *The First Amendment Is an Absolute*, 1961 Supreme Court Review 245, 256-57 (1961)).

because it is in the business of making money, he does not satisfactorily address the implications for his model of the impact of economic factors on speech. Arguing that the Constitution allows either as much or as little government regulation to achieve the common good as the citizenry desires, Meiklejohn shows little concern with these issues.

As the threat of direct government suppression of speech has declined under the Supreme Court's strict standard in *Brandenburg v. Ohio*,[37] issues involving the relationship between speech and property rights have begun to receive increased attention from some First Amendment scholars. Many of these scholars have drawn on Meiklejohn's self-governance model, but have criticized the failure of Meiklejohn and of the entire "Free Speech Tradition" to address the negative impact upon the democratic process of disparities in wealth among speakers. Shifting their attention away from the traditional focus on government suppression of speech, these scholars emphasize the positive role that government can play in enacting regulations to enrich the democratic deliberation process by, for example, adopting campaign finance reforms or guaranteeing media access in specific circumstances. They suggest that "what seems to be government regulation of speech actually might promote free speech," while "what seems to be free speech in markets might, in some selected circumstances, amount to an abridgement of free speech." Thus, these scholars are critical of Supreme Court decisions striking down Congressional attempts to make the deliberative process more fair and to redress inequalities in citizens' abilities to make their message heard due to disparities in wealth.

Among the scholars who have explored these issues in some depth is Cass Sunstein, who shares many of Meiklejohn's basic beliefs concerning free speech. Like Meiklejohn, Sunstein argues that in order to understand the role of free speech in a democracy, one must look to the placement of sovereignty in the people rather than in the government. Free speech in a democracy allows for meaningful popular sovereignty by giving citizens the opportunity to become fully informed on issues of public policy and to engage in broad debate, which provides a foundation for wise decision-making. In order for free speech to accomplish these objectives, Sunstein argues, certain conditions must be met. Among these conditions are "adequate information; a norm of political equality, in which arguments matter but power and authority do not; an absence of strategic manipulation of information . . . and a broad public orientation toward reaching right answers rather than serving self-interest, narrowly defined."[44]

Sunstein, like Meiklejohn, sees the crime of sedition as inconsistent with freedom of speech in a democracy because it prevents citizens from becoming fully informed concerning the relative merits of candidates for public office. Also like Meiklejohn, Sunstein recognizes that his focus on popular sovereignty means affording speech relevant to public affairs a greater degree of protection than other types of speech. However, in contrast to Meiklejohn, Sunstein does not equate free speech with a lack of government interference. He points out that even when the government ostensibly does

[37] 395 U.S. 444, 447 (1969).

[44] Cass R. Sunstein, Democracy and the Problem of Free Speech 19 (1993).

not regulate speech at all, by upholding existing economic and legal structures that have significant impact on the relative ability of different speakers to be heard, the government is in fact regulating speech. Thus, the relevant question becomes not whether the government should regulate speech but rather how it should regulate speech.

Focusing mainly on the mass media, Sunstein answers that speech should be regulated in order to achieve a broad debate that will best realize the principal of popular sovereignty. Regulation of the media is necessary to achieve this objective, he argues, because public information and broad debate are public goods that will be under provided if left to market forces. Sunstein recognizes that some types of regulations may pose a danger to the deliberative process rather than enhancing it. For instance, he is cautious about direct regulation of content, noting the risk of government abuse of such regulation. He is also critical of "command-and-control" regulation, and instead advocates incentive-based strategies that do not entirely suppress the market. Ultimately, however, the regulation should seek to influence media content in order to foster broader and more fruitful debate than would result from a market-based media system. Thus, he argues that pornography and hate speech should not be protected forms of speech because they actually impede healthy debate. He also advocates the provision of free media time to all political candidates in periods leading up to elections and favors guaranteeing rights of reply for both candidates and commentators.

Sunstein is not alone in arguing that the United States market-based approach to free speech leads to distortion in the democratic deliberation process. For instance, Mark Graber argues that "individuals have the constitutional right to convert their material resources into expression as long as the average member of the community can afford to invest similarly in politics."[56] Further, citizens have the right to combine their resources to afford more expensive means of communicating their ideas. However, "[n]o one has a constitutional right to use economic privilege to magnify otherwise relatively weak political skills." He continues, "[a]ffluent Americans have no First Amendment right that permits them to achieve political success through constant repetition of relatively unwanted ideas." Similarly, Judge Skelly Wright argues that the government should regulate campaign spending in order to ensure that elections are not skewed by disproportionate financial resources.[59] He contends that "when media mastery weighs more heavily than appeals to judgment, when opportunities to communicate with voters are extremely unequal, the result is a cynical distortion of the electoral process." These arguments rely on the assumption that it is the role of the government to manage societal debate in order to protect political equality and thereby ensure robust debate and wise, democratic decision making.

---

[56] Mark A. Graber, Transforming Free Speech: The Ambiguous Legacy of Civil Libertarianism 232 (1991).

[59] J. Skelly Wright, *Money and the Pollution of Politics: Is the First Amendment an Obstacle to Political Equality?*, 82 Columbia Law Review 609, 642-45 (1982).

II. Fair Media Treatment of Candidates During the Russian Election Campaign

One of the main goals of the IAT was to ensure that all candidates received fair treatment by the media. This goal was embodied in two types of provisions in the Statute on Information Guarantees and the Statute on Elections (hereinafter referred to collectively as the "election statutes"). First, these statutes contained provisions regulating the terms on which candidates and parties could gain access to the media, especially television and radio. Second, the statutes included provisions aimed at ensuring that the coverage itself would be fair and objective by eliminating media bias and government interference.

A. Access to the Media

1. Television and Radio

An important question with respect to free speech is when, and on what terms, an individual should have the opportunity to appear on television or radio in order to advance his political views or respond to an attack. In the Anglo-American context, advocates of positive access rights such as Cass Sunstein argue that a fair political process requires that all groups be given an equal chance to present their views in the mass media. Opponents argue that such rights entail too much government interference with the editorial choices of the media and therefore pose a threat to free speech. In the Russian case, however, this debate must take into account the fact that the vast majority of television and radio companies are state-owned or -subsidized, with many key positions occupied by government appointees. As a result, a failure to grant positive access rights to candidates in the 1993 election campaign probably would have meant that pro-Yeltsin candidates would have received a great deal of media coverage while opposition candidates were shut out.

The election statutes sought to counteract this imbalance by giving each candidate and political party one free broadcast on state-owned television and on state-owned radio, to be used during the course of the election campaign as the candidate or party chose. Candidates and parties were entitled to at least twenty minutes for each broadcast. The Statute on Elections also required that between November 22 and December 12, state-owned television and radio companies devote an additional hour of free air time every morning and evening to parties and candidates, to be administered in such a way that each party would receive the same amount of air time on equal terms.

All candidates and parties also were entitled to purchase a limited amount of additional air time which was to be offered to them on equal terms. In order to assure that access was affordable, article 6 of the Statute on Information Guarantees stipulated that the rates charged for broadcasting election-related speeches, press conferences, interviews, debates, and round tables could not exceed the broadcasting company's costs. However, in the case of private television companies, it provided for compensation from the state budget for any disparity between this rate and the company's usual rate.

In addition to negotiating with the major state television and radio companies to work out the scheduling of free air time devoted to candidates and parties, the IAT addressed numerous complaints from candidates alleging that they had been wrongly denied the free air time on public television and radio stations to which they were entitled. These complaints were generally upheld by the IAT, except in cases in which candidates had not met the basic requirements for receiving free air time; for example, where the candidate was not included on the official all-Russia list of candidates.

The IAT also issued a number of clarifications and recommendations concerning the provision of free air time to candidates. For instance, the IAT declared that a candidate should not be denied free air time to which he was entitled as an individual candidate merely because he also appeared in a broadcast that aired as part of his party's free air time.

The IAT also explained that for the purpose of determining which broadcasting companies were required to offer free air time to candidates, state-funded media included any media that had received funding from a state or local budget in the last quarter of 1993. Finally, the IAT emphasized on a number of occasions that candidates had the right to use their free air time as they wished, without interference from the television or radio company, so long as candidates did not violate the "legal and ethical norms" governing the election campaign.

Further, the IAT issued several clarifications with respect to the terms on which paid air time would be available to candidates. For instance, it held that article 6 of the Statute on Information Guarantees did not apply to "political advertisements." Article 6 provided that in the case of paid air time to be used for the broadcast of debates, round tables, and interviews related to the election, television and radio companies could charge only the cost of their expenses. But in its decision the IAT did not provide a specific test to distinguish political advertisements from other election material presented during air time purchased by candidates and parties. Article 2 of the Statute on Information Guarantees defined a political advertisement as "material paid for by the candidate, election association, or other person acting in the interests of the candidate, prompting and calling on the citizens to perform proposed actions." However, as campaigning is almost by definition the act of prompting citizens to vote for a candidate, this definition might well be applied to any of the activities described in article 6. Unfortunately, no published IAT decisions address the line between political advertising and campaign activities that fall under article 6.

In addition to protecting the rights of access to the broadcast media specifically granted in the election statutes, the IAT also addressed the right of a candidate to air time in order to rebut untrue information broadcast about him. In Decision 4, the IAT addressed a case in which three television companies (Ostankino, Russian Television, and a local television station) broadcast information that candidate V.N. Diankov had been removed from the official list of candidates because of a finding that many of the signatures offered in support of his candidacy were falsified. Although Diankov had in fact been removed from the list of candidates, this decision was later canceled by the election commission, which placed Diankov back on the list several hours before the broadcasts. The IAT awarded Diankov the same amount of air time on the three channels to rebut the negative publicity as had been devoted to the negative material by each station.

2. Newspapers and Periodicals

In contrast to its approach to the broadcast media, the Statute on Information Guarantees did not grant candidates free access to space in newspapers and periodicals. The Statute on Information Guarantees did, however, require newspapers receiving state funds that granted column space to one candidate also to grant space to all other candidates on the same terms. (Privately owned newspapers that did not receive any government support, a small minority of publications, were not subject to this requirement.) The Statute did not address the question of paid advertising in newspapers, setting no upper limit on political advertising in the print media. Because candidates were not entitled to any free access to the print media under the election statutes (in contrast to television and radio) only a few of the IAT's decisions involved access to newspapers and periodicals. The IAT did hold that newspapers could devote as much space to paid political advertising as they chose, but upheld the requirement that periodicals offer space to all candidates on the same terms.

The IAT denied positive access rights in two cases where candidates sought apologies or retractions by a newspaper. In one of these cases, the IAT found that the newspaper *Izvestiia* had printed an article that insulted a candidate two days before the election in violation of article 30 of the Statute on Elections. The IAT required *Izvestiia* to publish its decision declaring that *Izvestiia* had violated the Statute on Information Guarantees. The IAT also recommended that the editor of *Izvestiia* place the journalist who wrote the article on leave for the duration of the election campaign (only two days). However, the IAT did not grant space directly to the candidate to rebut the article, in contrast to the Diankov case, in which it granted equal air time to the candidate to rebut incorrect information broadcast about him.

In another case, the IAT declined to require that *Izvestiia* print a public apology to candidate Andrei Razin, who claimed that the newspaper had printed an article that placed him in "an unequal position with respect to the other candidates." The court said that without evidence showing that the article was untrue, there was no basis for the complaint. It added that if *Izvestiia* received material in response to the article from Razin, it was up to the editorial board to decide if it wanted to provide space in the newspaper for the material.

Although these cases can be distinguished from the Diankov case in that the first involved an insult rather than incorrect information and the second was held to be unfounded, the failure of the IAT to require that *Izvestiia* grant space to either candidate suggests that it may have been more reluctant to grant positive access rights in the print media than in the broadcast media. One possible reason for this reluctance was a perception by the framers of the election statutes and IAT members that such rights were less necessary in the print media than in the case of television and radio. Whereas Russian television and radio are still quite centralized and are largely state-run, Russian print media are more independent from the government, even though the majority receive government subsidies. Thus, there is a proliferation of newspapers and periodicals in Russia representing a wide spectrum of political views. On the other hand, the IAT's decision in the Razin case was based on the fact that Razin submitted no evidence at all that the article in question was false, suggesting that perhaps if he had, the IAT's response might have been different. Thus, the distinction between the IAT's approach to rebuttal rights in the broadcast media as opposed to the print media should not be exaggerated.

B. Objective Coverage of Candidates

1. Journalistic Bias

One of the most unusual aspects of the IAT's approach to speech, from the perspective of democratic theory, was the approach it took toward the role of journalists in the election campaign. The election statutes included numerous provisions designed to ensure that coverage of the elections would not be distorted by journalistic bias, in many cases suppressing journalistic commentary about the election altogether. Journalists were forbidden in their coverage of the elections to express support for a particular candidate or to provide more favorable coverage to one candidate than another. Journalists were also required to suspend their journalistic activities during the course of the election campaign if they were running as candidates in the election. Another provision required news programs to provide all election-related information at the beginning of their broadcasts in a block, without any commentary. Finally, to avoid distortion of the election results, the Statute on Elections prohibited the dissemination by the mass media of results from opinion polls in the ten days immediately preceding the election.

In carrying out these provisions, the IAT became deeply involved in evaluating the content of media coverage to determine when coverage was biased. In its decisions, the IAT identified a number of journalistic practices it found objectionable. For instance, in one decision it criticized journalists for violating the Statute on Information Guarantees by inserting their own opinions of the candidates and parties in their coverage. It offered as an example a case in which candidate Nikolai Travkin was making an election trip to the Russian provinces. Instead of simply reporting that Travkin had left on a campaigning trip, the journalist also provided statistics concerning the low level of support for Travkin's party in the region Travkin was visiting. Although the IAT gave no hint that this statistical information was incorrect, it blamed the journalist for biased coverage because the statistics "clearly discredit[ed]" the candidate.

As an additional example of a journalist inserting his own opinion into his coverage, the IAT cited a case in which, after broadcasting a speech by candidate Arkadii

Volski in favor of "stability, honesty and progress," a commentator appeared and proceeded to criticize the speech. Again, the IAT gave no indication that the commentator uttered any false or insulting statements about the candidate. Rather, the mere fact that the journalist had expressed negative opinions about the candidate's speech was considered objectionable.

As a particularly egregious example of media bias, the IAT singled out for criticism the decision of the Ostankino television company to air a film about candidate Vladimir Zhirinovsky on the eve of the election. The film, "The Hawk," used archival footage and interviews in order to expose Zhirinovsky's ultra-nationalism, anti-Semitism, and xenophobia. The IAT held that Ostankino had violated article 30 of the Statute on Elections, prohibiting the dissemination of material that damaged the honor and dignity of a candidate within seven days prior to the election.

The IAT also deplored the practice of turning news coverage into "hidden political advertisements." In particular, it noted that journalists often used interviews of officials who were also running as political candidates to give the official an opportunity to campaign on behalf of his or her party under the guise of news. As an example, the IAT pointed to a case in which, while being interviewed in his capacity as a government official, Deputy Prime Minister Alexander Shokhin was asked a question about his relationship with the Party of Russian Unity and Accord, a party which was advancing Shokhin as a candidate in the election. In the eyes of the IAT, this question was not a legitimate question to pose to a government official running in an election and reflected the interviewer's bias in favor of Shokhin. The IAT's confidence that it could determine what constituted appropriate contents of media coverage could also be seen in its criticism of the practice of running stories about candidates that were unrelated to the themes of the television programs on which they were shown. According to the IAT, such broadcasts were also hidden political advertisements.

As in the case of political advertising in general, the IAT was unable to provide a satisfying definition for "hidden political advertisement." In attempting to define the term, the IAT said that hidden political advertisements had "all the characteristics of political advertisements" described in article 2 of the Statute on Information Guarantees but were not designated as advertisements. Given that this definition included any paid material that promoted a particular candidate, it encompassed a wide variety of material, especially as the IAT applied the term "hidden political advertisement" to material that was not paid for by the candidate, removing the possibility of a bright-line test based on whether the candidate had paid to air the material.

In fact, the IAT's decisions reflected a "we'll-know-it-when-we-see-it" approach that appeared to be based on its instincts as to the motivations of journalists in particular cases. The IAT was particularly suspicious (and perhaps rightly so) of journalists who, in violation of the Statute on Information Guarantees, continued to work as journalists while also running as candidates in the elections. The IAT blamed much of the bias in the media on these journalists, singling out in particular Viacheslav Bragin, who was appointed by Yeltsin to head the Ostankino television company and continued to hold his position while campaigning as a candidate.

2. Government Interference

The IAT also scrutinized the behavior of government officials to determine when their acts constituted unacceptable interference with the media. In addition to prohibiting government authorities or government bodies from "influencing or exerting pressure on a journalist for the purpose of inducing him to present biased coverage of the activity of candidates and election associations," the Statute on Elections prohibited public officials from even endorsing candidates, considering such endorsements to constitute an unacceptable influence on the election campaign.

In censuring local officials for interference, the IAT went beyond cases of blatant interference, such as the shutting down of a private television company by local authorities in the Primorskii region. It also criticized local government officials for attempting to influence the outcome of the elections by expressing their own opinions with respect to the candidates. In its final assessment of the campaign, for instance, issued just after the election, it noted that many officials had campaigned actively for and against candidates, in spite of the prohibition in article 26 of the Statute on Elections. It gave as an example a case in which a local official had accused a candidate of having committed a criminal act. In another example, the IAT censured a judge who commented in the press about the merits of a civil case brought by one of the candidates.

Thus, the IAT's decisions reflected a broad definition of interference, encompassing not only acts of censorship or attempts by officials to explicitly pressure the media, but also more subtle interference, in the form of endorsements of candidates by public officials or even the expression of opinions about candidates by public officials.

III. Limits on the Speech of Candidates

In addition to monitoring the media's treatment of candidates, the IAT interpreted and applied provisions in the election statutes limiting candidates' speech. For instance, one provision required that the bulk of a campaign speech made by a candidate during free air time be used to lay out his or her own platform. Another provided that candidates would be subject to legal sanctions for abusing the "right to engage in campaigning" by disseminating material "not corresponding to reality and demeaning the honor, dignity and business reputation of other candidates." Similarly, article 30 of the Statute on Elections prohibited the dissemination of material that damaged the honor and dignity of a candidate within seven days prior to the election. Finally, the IAT invoked the language of article 4 of the Russian Law On the Mass Media (although not actually citing it), prohibiting the use of the mass media "for . . . inflaming national, class, social, religious intolerance or hatred, or for the propaganda of war." This principle was also embodied in article 29 of the draft constitution. Below, I will address the decisions of the

IAT limiting candidates' speech in three areas: criticism of the draft constitution, criticism of other candidates, and speech inflaming racial and national hatred.

A. Limits on Criticism of the Draft Constitution

In late November, the IAT was faced with a new challenge when Yeltsin, along with members of his government, sought to limit criticism of the draft constitution by political candidates. At a meeting called by Yeltsin that included representatives of the thirteen political parties competing in the election, Yeltsin reportedly asked the candidates "not to touch" the constitution and threatened to take away their free air time if they deviated from their own platforms to criticize the constitution. Officials of Yeltsin's State and Law Administration went even further, saying that political parties and candidates who criticized the constitution in the mass media would not only lose their free air time, but also have to withdraw from the elections.

According to the head of the State and Law Administration, Aleksander Kotenkov, in collecting signatures to participate in elections to a body created by the draft constitution, the parties and candidates had essentially promised those who signed in their support that they would uphold the new constitution. Thus, calls for the electorate to vote against the draft constitution would be a "distortion of the electorate's will expressed during the signature collecting campaign and [a] formal refusal to stand in elections to the new legislature." The same argument was made by First Deputy Prime Minister and Minister of the Press Shumeiko (also a deputy candidate), who filed an official complaint with the IAT and the Central Election Commission asking that both the Communist Party and the Democratic Party of Russia be eliminated from the election campaigns because of their criticism of the draft constitution in the mass media. Shumeiko also asked for "clarification" with respect to four other parties whose members had publicly criticized the draft constitution.

Those who called for limits on criticism of the constitution also argued that they were necessary to avert the instability that might result if a new Federal Assembly was elected while the constitution that created that body was rejected. Yeltsin repeatedly warned that "the future of peace and tranquility in Russia" depended on the adoption of the draft constitution. The specter of civil war was raised by many others as well, especially within the Yeltsin government. Prime Minister Viktor Chernomyrdin warned of "new shocks and rising tension" if the draft constitution were rejected. Sergei Stankevich, a prominent Moscow politician, said that postponing the adoption of a new constitution would mean "mounting crime and uncontrollable conflicts."

But this scenario was rejected by many. Grigorii Yavlinsky, one of the leaders of the Yavlinsky-Boldyrov-Lukin bloc (a key competitor against Russia's choice for the democratic vote) dismissed the danger of rejecting the draft, saying, "I do not believe that anything supernatural or awful would take place [if it were rejected]." And one of the framers of the draft constitution sharply criticized the attempts to limit discussion of it, saying it would be "political hypocrisy" to hold the referendum on the constitution without allowing real debate. Further, numerous parties openly rejected the constitution, arguing that its adoption would do more harm than good. Among these were the Christian Democratic Movement of Russia, the Russian Communist Party, headed by Ziuganov, and numerous small parties. Conversely, the constitution was supported by Zhirinovsky's Liberal Democratic Party not so much out of a fear of civil war, but because of the strong presidency it would create.

The IAT also apparently rejected the argument that any criticism of the draft constitution posed a threat of civil war sufficient to justify limiting debate, unanimously holding that merely criticizing the draft constitution did not disqualify candidates from participating in the election. The IAT reiterated the right of candidates to determine the contents of their campaigning as they chose, including using some of their free air time to criticize the draft constitution. At the same time, it made clear that it did not expect candidates to devote an inordinate amount of time to criticizing the draft constitution, reminding candidates that they were required under article 18 of the Statute on Information Guarantees to devote the bulk of their campaign speeches to their own platforms. In addition, the IAT drew on the language of the Law On the Mass Media in cautioning that criticism of the draft constitution was not to inflame national or religious enmity, appeal for civil war, or disclose state secrets.

But the IAT went beyond the explicit requirements of the election statutes and the Law On the Mass Media by imposing the additional requirement that criticism of the constitution should also be "well-founded" and that candidates who criticized the draft should "provide the voters with the candidate's or party's concrete proposals concerning the content of the constitution." It went even further by adding that candidates should not engage in "vulgar" criticism of the constitution. As an example of such vulgar criticism, it cited an earlier decision in which it had censured candidate Stanislav Govorukhin of the Democratic Party of Russia for saying during a television appearance that the draft constitution was "stained by the blood spilled October 4 [during the storming of the Russian parliament building]."

In imposing these limits on criticisms of the draft constitution, the IAT once again involved itself in drawing subtle distinctions between different types of speech based on what it considered the usefulness of its content and the tastefulness of its phrasing. The IAT provided little guidance for determining when criticism was well-founded or vulgar, but seemed to assume that these terms were understandable to all.

B. Civility and Limits on Criticism of Candidates and Officials

The negative reaction of the IAT to official attempts to limit discussion of the constitution was in marked contrast to its response to efforts by Yeltsin and many candidates to encourage more "civilized" campaigning, a goal which the IAT shared. Thus, in a number of decisions the IAT invoked article 25 of the Statute on Information Guarantees, which prohibits abuse of the right to campaign through dissemination of false information that demeans the honor or dignity of other candidates and parties, in order to censure candidates whose campaigning crossed the bounds of civility. In some of these decisions, the IAT also relied on article 18 of the Statute on Information Guarantees, requiring that candidates devote the bulk of their speeches to their respective platforms.

In one case involving civility, the IAT found a violation of article 25 of the Statute on Information Guarantees when candidate Yegor Gaidar said that candidate Vladimir Zhirinovsky had gone beyond the "Hitler of Soviet films" to become the "real Hitler of 1992." The IAT said in its decision that even though it was unable to determine whether the statement was false (one of the requirements of article 25), it could say that the statement was an insult to Zhirinovsky, and therefore violated article 25. In reaching this conclusion, the IAT simply presumed the statement was false and placed the burden of proving truth on the speaker. Thus, a violation of article 25 existed when the speaker could not rebut this presumption. Still, the IAT did not require Gaidar to apologize to Zhirinovsky, saying that the IAT did not have the power to do this, even though the Statute on Information Guarantees gave the Tribunal the power to make recommendations to candidates concerning the content of their campaigning.

In another decision, the IAT found that several candidates had violated article 25 of the Statute on Information Guarantees by insulting one another. Among the politicians who were warned were Stanislav Govorukhin, Nikolai Travkin, and Vladimir Zhirinovsky. In this decision, the IAT provided no details about the actual insults and did not seek to determine whether any of them might be true. Once again, in applying article 25, the IAT seemed much more concerned about the insulting nature of the statements than their falsity.

In the same decision, the IAT also expressed concern about the violation of article 18, requiring that candidates devote the bulk of their speeches to their own platforms. In invoking article 18, the IAT pointed out that the candidates had denied voters "the constitutional right . . . to receive essential and reliable information about the platforms of the candidates and parties" and to gain an understanding of how each of the candidates planned to implement his or her program. There was no indication that the IAT had actually measured the time devoted by the candidates to insulting each other or calculated the percentage of each candidate's time devoted to criticizing one another. Rather, the IAT's reliance on article 18 appeared to reflect its sense that the election campaign should be devoted to debate over issues rather than personal insults.

Finally, in another decision the IAT found that statements by candidates Vladimir Zhirinovsky, Alexander Nevzorov, and Yuri Kuznetsov violated ethical norms by insulting President Yeltsin and other members of his government. As none of the statements were quoted in the decision, it is difficult to assess the seriousness of the insults. However, in singling out insults directed at the president as a discrete ethical violation, the IAT's decision suggested that it saw no need to relax the requirements of civility with respect to public officials.

C. Limits on Inflammatory Speech

The IAT also frequently reminded candidates that in their campaigning they must not make appeals for civil war or engage in speech that inflamed nationalist or racial enmity. In particular, it warned that criticism of political opponents or of the draft constitution should not be used for any of these purposes. The prime offender in this area appears to have been Vladimir Zhirinovsky, who was criticized for "inflaming nationalist animosity" and "inciting to infringe on human rights." Candidates Bondarik, Nevzorov, and Kuznetsov were also criticized for using their free television air time for "the propaganda of nationalist discrimination and inflaming of nationalist animosity." In its decision, however, the IAT did not cite the language it found to be offensive, thus failing to provide examples that would help to define the sweeping terms of the prohibition. Rather, the IAT seemed to assume that all could recognize inflammatory speech.

IV. Problems and Issues Raised by the IAT's Approach to Free Speech

In the decisions discussed in the sections above, the IAT's approach to free speech generally reflected a commitment to ensuring high-quality debate that would allow voters to become as well informed as possible about the candidates and issues in order to make wise political choices on election day. This is a crucial goal of free speech for Alexander Meiklejohn, and many of the methods used by the IAT to accomplish it, including guaranteed access rights for candidates and limited rights of rebuttal, were similar to the types of regulations advocated by followers of Meiklejohn, such as Cass Sunstein. As discussed below, the Russian experience in the fall of 1993 illustrates some of the difficult issues that those who advocate these types of regulations must address. Other decisions adopted by the IAT, however, ran directly against the basic tenets of the governmental process model and raised questions about some aspects of the IAT's vision of democracy. Among these decisions were the IAT's efforts to eliminate journalistic bias, its statements that criticism of the draft constitution must be well-founded and not "vulgar," and its protection of the "honor and dignity" of candidates.

A. Fair Media Treatment

1. Access to Media

The IAT protected three types of positive access rights for candidates with respect to the Russian mass media. First, it protected the right of all candidates to each receive a free television and radio appearance of at least twenty minutes during the campaign, with a certain amount of additional free air time during morning and evening broadcasts devoted to the campaign in the last three weeks of the election. Second, it allowed candidates to purchase limited amounts of air time for only the cost to the television or radio station of the broadcast. Third, it granted air time to rebut incorrect information that had been broadcast about a candidate. It might have been willing to grant such a right of rebuttal in the print media if a case had arisen in which there was evidence that a printed statement about a candidate was false.

In protecting these three types of positive access rights, the IAT sought to ensure a degree of political equality among the candidates and foster diverse debate. Nonetheless, the IAT was not entirely satisfied with the results of its efforts. In his final assessment of the election coverage, for instance, the head of the IAT, Anatolii Vengerov, expressed disappointment at the infrequency with which candidates used free and low-cost air time for debates in the form of moderated round-tables. The negative reaction of the IAT to what it perceived to be mere "political advertisements," as opposed to more substantive messages, reflected a similar dissatisfaction with candidates' use of their free air time.

The failure of positive access rights to live up to the expectations of the IAT in the fall 1993 election campaign suggests that the provision of positive access rights to candidates does not by itself necessarily guarantee the kind of fruitful debate that is often advanced as a justification for such rights. One of the dangers of guaranteed access rights is that they will be used to convey slick but superficial messages instead of contributing to serious, high-quality debate. This raises a question for advocates of positive access rights in the United States as to whether these rights can be structured so as to avoid this phenomenon, perhaps by conditioning them on a requirement of face-to-face debate among candidates. If this approach were taken, however, the government would become a moderator in almost a literal sense, posing a question concerning who sets the agenda for societal debate.

Another difficult issue is raised by the IAT's approach to rebuttal rights. If candidates are to be granted a right of rebuttal when false information has been broadcast or printed about them, who decides when information is false? Although this determination appeared relatively straightforward in the Diankov case, there are numerous scenarios in which a decision concerning the truth or falsity of information broadcast or printed about a candidate would require that subjective conclusions be drawn from a particular set of facts. In the world of Alexander Meiklejohn, it is the role of the electorate to draw its own conclusions concerning what is true and what is false. To vest the power to make such determinations in the government is, in a sense, to undercut the electorate's right in a democracy to draw its own conclusions concerning what is true or false. It could be argued that this problem would be avoided if rebuttal rights were granted whenever a candidate was criticized, regardless of truth or falsity. Such a broad right of rebuttal, however, would entail a significant loss of editorial control and might well lead the mass media to avoid criticizing political candidates, thereby chilling much valuable discussion of candidates. This dilemma needs to be addressed by those who argue for a right of rebuttal in the United States.

Finally, it is interesting to note that although the IAT's approach to access rights reflected a commitment to political equality, the Tribunal did not insist upon complete equality of media access. Instead, it was willing to tolerate the inequality that arose in the broadcast media from unequal financial resources by allowing parties and candidates to purchase air time. In fact, a number of commentators expressed concern about the inequality in media access resulting from disparate financial resources. One warned that

> there is not going to be equality between the candidates or between the blocs, and . . . given the desire and a certain degree of ability, one bloc is going to be rolling in bags of money while another is going to have to rest content with pennies, and we will see some candidates on television around the clock but only get a brief glimpse of others or never see them at all.

These commentators warned that paid political advertising would allow candidates to buy the election.

2. Objective Coverage

Beyond providing access to the candidates so that their messages could be heard by the Russian electorate, the IAT also sought to ensure that voters would have the opportunity to evaluate the candidates without being influenced by government interference or media bias. Thus, the IAT condemned not only government censorship, but also any expression of personal political views concerning the candidates by government officials and journalists. This aspect of the IAT's approach to free speech represents a significant deviation from the governmental process model, although the commitment to allowing citizens to draw their own conclusions about the candidates at first seems consistent with the spirit of that model. From the Meiklejohnian perspective, the problem with this approach is that it suppresses core political speech by focusing on the speech of candidates while providing little protection for the speech of journalists. As a result, the IAT's approach denied the electorate the opportunity to be fully informed of all information and opinions worth hearing.

In treating the mass media (particularly the broadcast media) as a mere conveyor belt for transmitting the messages of candidates, the IAT denied Russian journalists a role in the election debate and deprived Russian voters of potentially valuable commentary. As Vsevelod Vilchek, head of Ostankino's Sociology Center complained, "television journalists [were] virtually excluded from the airwaves and deprived of the right to perform their professional duty as seekers of the truth and exponents of the audience's interests." Rather than playing a watch-dog role, as they had in the era of glasnost, during the fall 1993 election campaign the broadcast media were expected simply to convey information and refrain from actively engaging in the societal deliberation process.

The IAT's approach to media bias is disturbing from the perspective of the governmental process model not only because it limited valuable debate, but also because of the intimate government involvement it entailed in evaluating the speech of journalists. As the Travkin decision illustrates, the determination of what constitutes bias is highly subjective. Even the presentation of facts without any overt expression of opinion may constitute bias because of the journalist's selection of facts. Thus, it is almost impossible to formulate a bright-line rule for evaluating bias. As a result, any effort on the part of the government to eliminate bias will involve the government in evaluating the content of each particular case, with little possibility for consistency and great danger of abuse. The government, after all, has its own interests in the outcome of the election that may not coincide with those of the electorate as a whole.

On the other hand, the IAT's approach to the involvement of government officials in the election reflected concern about government interference with societal debate. In many regions of Russia, local officials remain powerful and sometimes corrupt. By limiting the speech of government officials with respect to candidates, the IAT may have been acting on the belief that even an endorsement by an official of a particular candidate could discourage those whose livelihood depended on that official's from criticizing that candidate or openly supporting another candidate. At the same time, by silencing government officials, the IAT deprived voters of information that may have been an important consideration.

B. Limits on Candidates' Speech

1. Criticism of the Draft Constitution

The IAT rejected attempts to ban all criticism of the draft constitution, thus allowing Russian society to carry on some degree of debate concerning the constitution's merits. However, while the IAT upheld the right of candidates to criticize the draft constitution, it made clear that criticism should be well-founded and should not be vulgar. In imposing such a requirement, the IAT took upon itself the role of evaluating the validity of criticisms of the constitution, thus restricting speech in a manner that was inconsistent with the governmental process model. The governmental process model does not allow government to limit speech because it does not like its content. As it did in cases involving media bias, the IAT limited core political speech in the name of ensuring a fair and constructive debate.

2. Civility

While the protection of a minimal level of civility is required to allow for orderly debate under Meiklejohn's model of free speech, the protection of the honor and dignity of candidates by the IAT goes far beyond what is envisioned by the governmental process model. By placing such limits on criticism of candidates for public office, the IAT essentially sought to enforce a law against sedition. Under the governmental process model, it is recognized that no such crime can exist in a democracy because it means limiting debate concerning a crucial policy choice, the selection of public officials. Because it is so important for the electorate to be as informed as possible about its elected officials, limits on speech that might harm the dignity and honor of political candidates are impermissible.

Further, the IAT's presumption of falsity in defamation cases under article 25 of the Statute on Information Guarantees made it even more difficult to criticize a candidate without censure. Because of this presumption, any insult that could not be proven true was considered to be in violation of the statute. Given the evident political content of insults such as Gaidar's comparison of Zhirinovsky with Hitler, it is very likely that this approach led to the suppression of political speech. Proponents of the public discourse model would also point out that limits on speech that harm the honor or dignity of candidates are detrimental to democracy because they involve the imposition of a single, governmental conception of civility. As a result, no opportunity exists for competition between different notions of civility in society and the ability of society to define itself is limited.

Finally, the IAT's insistence that candidates must devote the bulk of their speeches to their own platforms rather than to criticism of other candidates was often used by the IAT to impose its views concerning what speech was useful and what was not. In seeking to control the focus of public debate, the IAT again imposed its own conception of what constituted valuable debate, rather than allowing Russian society to set the agenda for political debate. Although such an agenda-setting role on the part of the government may sometimes be acceptable to Meiklejohn and his followers, who allow the government to act as a moderator of public debate, the Russian case raises the question of whether the government, in acting as moderator, may sometimes become too actively involved in framing political issues.

3. Limits on Inflammatory Speech

In a number of decisions, the IAT criticized candidates for racist or nationalist speech that "inflame[d] national enmity" or "provoke[d] civil war" but did not include examples of such speech. As a result, it is difficult to know the limits of these categories and how much speech the IAT is willing to suppress on these bases. Nevertheless, the IAT's decisions indicate that it apparently accepts the concept of group libel as a valid one. Group libel is a troubling concept from the perspective of the public discourse model. In this model, one of the dangers of group libel is its effect of imposing conceptions of group identity rather than allowing groups to define their own identities through public discourse. These constantly changing identities may be frozen by government imposition of official group identities, thereby preventing the healthy development of democratic society. Although limits on speech that inflames nationalist enmity might be justified in the public discourse model to the extent that such speech poses a real and immediate threat of civil war, there is no indication that the IAT imposes any requirements of imminent threat or incitement to action.

In contrast, the limits imposed by the IAT on speech that inflamed nationalist enmity are consistent with the governmental process model, to the extent that that model aims at ensuring the expression of diverse viewpoints by different groups within society. Because racist speech by one group may impede the ability of another group to engage in public debate, such speech may decrease the ability of society to make wise political choices. This result, in turn, signifies a reduction in the degree of democracy in society, according to the public discourse model. Thus, the IAT's approach to inflammatory speech is beneficial to democracy, from the perspective of the governmental process model.

Conclusion

The IAT's implementation of the election statutes during the fall 1993 election campaign marked the first attempt of the Russian government to deal comprehensively with media and speech issues arising during the course of a democratic election. (The election was the first general election held since the collapse of communism in August 1991.) The common theme running through the IAT's decisions was the importance of ensuring constructive debate in order to allow citizens to make informed choices at the polls. Free speech was considered important for advancing societal welfare rather than the individual interests of speakers. Thus, at a general level, the IAT's approach was consistent with the philosophy underlying the governmental process model. Further, in many ways, the IAT was a success for democracy in Russia. Although the body was created by Yeltsin and filled with government appointees, it did not give in to the government's position that all who criticized the draft constitution should be disqualified from the election. The IAT also ensured that all candidates had the opportunity to convey their messages in the mass media, and appeared to carry out its mission in an even-handed manner.

However, the IAT was unwilling to tolerate what it viewed as the excesses of free speech—vulgarity, insults, and unfounded opinions. In limiting these types of speech, the IAT deviated from a fundamental tenet of Alexander Meiklejohn's model that voters should have the opportunity to be exposed to all possible positions concerning issues of public importance and make their own determinations about the validity of those positions. The IAT's experience illustrates the risk that certain types of government regulation of the mass media may detract from rather than enhance the electorate's ability to make its own determinations on issues of public importance. In particular, the IAT's close involvement in evaluating the content of speech most likely chilled important political debate during the election campaign. In fact, a poll carried out by Russian Television found that only thirteen percent of viewers had found the political broadcasts useful. Vsevelod Vilchek expressed concern that "no mechanisms were provided for in the broadcasting structure [to protect the voter]; rather, mechanisms against demagoguery, lies and manipulation of viewers' minds by all kinds of commercial advertising and political propaganda have been deliberately blocked."

Alexander Meiklejohn characterized citizens in a democracy as "courageous, self-reliant men, with confidence in the power of free and fearless reasoning applied through the processes of self-government." It is possible that citizens must gain experience with democracy in order for this confidence to develop. It was not until 1964, after all, that the crime of sedition was finally rejected outright by the United States Supreme Court. In Russia, it is likely that this confidence will build slowly, especially in light of the political instability throughout the former Soviet Union and the very real threats of pro-government bias and abuse by government officials resulting from the media's dependence on government subsidies.

However, we should not expect Russia to follow a path to democracy that is identical to that of the United States. The decisions of the IAT suggest a vision of free speech that is more limited than that of Meiklejohn and his followers, allowing a greater role for government in regulating the content of speech and restricting the voices that can be heard by Russian voters. At the same time, the dissatisfaction of many Russian commentators with the fall 1993 election coverage could lead to a revision of the government's approach to free speech in the next Russian election. The lesson of the fall election campaign may be that Russian society must continue to develop an approach to free speech that will satisfactorily accommodate its vision of democracy with competing values and practical concerns.

Information Tribunal Made Permanent Under President's Supervision*

Peter Krug

Re-shaping and embracing institutions to monitor and supervise the mass media, President Yeltsin has transformed the once-temporary Information Arbitration Tribunal into a permanent fixture within his administrative apparatus. In so doing, he has broadened its agenda to include, among other new duties, the guaranteeing of objectivity and the morality of children's programming, as well as the issuing of warnings to mass media outlets.

The Tribunal was created in late October [1993] to supervise the use of mass media during the December 12 election campaign. Yeltsin has concluded that the Tribunal, which issued about a dozen decisions, played a constructive role and gained "positive experience" in a new and difficult electoral process.

In a December 31 decree, Yeltsin placed the body directly under his administration and endowed it with a new name—*Sudebnaia Palata Po Informatsionnym Sporam Pri Prezidente Rossiiskoi Federatsii*—which we translate as the Presidential Judicial Chamber for Information Disputes.

The Chamber, we believe, will have jurisdiction over all mass media including independent broadcasters and the press. Its predecessor, the Tribunal, issued opinions concerning newspapers, and nothing in the language of the December 31 decree appears to limit its scope to a particular medium or to state entities.

The decree named seven members to the new Chamber, five of whom served on the nine-member Tribunal: Law Professor Anatoli Vengerov, who continues to serve as Chairman; Igor Yeremin, a member of the Mass Media Committee of the former Supreme Soviet, who will serve as Deputy Chairman; Aleksander Kopeyka, also a member of the Mass Media Committee of the Regional (Northwestern Russia, including the City of St. Petersburg) State Inspectorate for Defense of Freedom of the Press and Mass Information of the Russian Federation; and Marian Panyarskaya, a law student at the Mass Communications School in Moscow. The two new members of the Chamber are Yuri Feofanov, legal affairs commentator for *Izvestiia* and editor of the journal *Zakon* ("*Law*"), and Igor Ivanov, chief specialist of the Central Electoral Commission's department for electoral arbitration and preparation of normative documents. Tribunal members who were not named to the new Chamber are: Aleksei Simonov, Vladimir Sukhomlinov, Aleksei Voinov, and Anatoli Yezhelev.

---

* Post-Soviet Media Law & Policy Newsletter, Jan. 27, 1994, at 1.

The Chamber will have a broader range of responsibilities than its predecessor and its role will be multi-faceted, although the December 31 decree is silent as to the Chamber's powers of enforcement. When it was formed pursuant to the October 29 Regulations on Information Guarantees and the Election Campaign, the Tribunal's scope of responsibility was limited to the December 12 parliamentary election campaign: the resolution of disputes arising from violations by editors, journalists, moderators, candidates, and electoral commissions of the Regulations. Under article 30 of the Regulations, the Tribunal received authority to make recommendations on improvements in mass media campaign coverage and content of partisan campaign material, consider complaints against broadcasting companies and journalists, provide explanations regarding application of the Regulations, and present expert findings to courts of law on matters arising out of the Tribunal's consideration of complaints submitted to it. In early November, Tribunal chairman Anatoli Vengerov characterized the Tribunal as not a juridical but an "ethical-legal structure" which would use public opinion as its primary weapon.

In contrast, the duties assigned to the new Chamber in Yeltsin's December 31 decree suggest that the Chamber will expand upon its former activities to assume a number of new functions. Some of the Chamber's activities will combine investigation and decision making, such as the guaranteeing of objectivity and authenticity in news reports, and the more closely-defined correction of factual errors—functions that are reminiscent of those assigned to the controversial supervisory councils established last summer by the Supreme Soviet. Some decision-making functions will mix elements of adjudication and policy determination, such as the resolution of disputes about allocation of broadcast air time between parliamentary factions and the guaranteeing of pluralism in broadcast news and public affairs programs. Still others will involve the Chamber in norm creation, such as the protection of the moral interests of children and adolescents.

Other new duties of the Chamber will incorporate elements from the Russian Constitutional Court (suspended from mid-October to mid-January) and the soon-to-be disbanded Ministry of Press and Information. For example, the Chamber will presumably be called upon to issue advisory opinions on matters that may include constitutional interpretation. The December 31 decree cites article 29 of the new Russian constitution (which in subsection 4 guarantees citizens the right to "seek, receive, transfer, produce and disseminate information by any lawful means") and specifies as one of the Chamber's duties the rendering of assistance to the President in "upholding rights and freedoms in the mass information sphere."

Finally, in performing at least one of its designated duties—the issuance of warnings to mass media outlets under article 16 of the Law On the Mass Media—the Chamber will approach the role of prosecutor. It is in this function, inherited from the Ministry of Press and Information (slated for dissolution in February) that the Chamber's standing as an impartial arbiter will perhaps be most severely tested. Under article 16, the Ministry's issuance of written warnings to a media outlet concerning alleged violations of Aricle 4 of the Mass Media Law ("Inadmissibility of misuse of the freedom of mass information") is the essential pre-condition for court-ordered termination of the mass media outlet's activity.

Although the December 31 decree does not explicitly say so, it must be assumed that the new Chamber—given the power to issue warnings—will also inherit the Ministry's power under article 16 to seek a court order terminating an outlet's activity.

Will the Chamber use this considrable power to enhance its overall enforcment authority in order to sanction broadcasters and publishers who engage in activities unfavorable to the administartion, as well as the specific acts prohibited by article 4? Will the Chamber find itself applying article 16 to limit coverage, for example, of political opponents such as Vladimir Zhirinovsky? It is noteworthy that among its resolutions during the Decmebr 12 electoral campaign, the Tribunal charged Zhirinovsky with "repeatedly" making announcements which "stirred national differences and incited violations of human rights" on December 6 and 7 and making televised statements which were intended to "not only stir up national hatred, but intergovernmental conflicts as well, and to provoke a civil war" on December 8. The Tribunal resolution added that Zhirinovsky and others "allowed themselves to insult the President and other government officials, and openly defied other generally accepted ethical norms." At the same time, the Tribunal on December 17 upheld Zhirinovsky's complaint that Ostankino's showing of the documentary of "The Hawk" in the eve of election was unlawful.

There is nothing in the December 31 decree to suggest that the Chamber will operate as an independent judicial organ. The decree states that the Chamber will be "attached to" the President and will not be part of the Russian Federation's federal court system. In addition, in establishing the Chamber's secretariat as a "working apparatus" within the President's administration, the decree assigns to the Presidnet's chief of staff the responsibility of approving the structure and size of the secretariat. Thus, the jobs (or at least salaries) of Chamber administrative personnel will be dependent on the allocation of the President's budge. It should also be noted that Chairman Vengerov has expressed his agreement with Yeltsin's broad cosntitutional goals. He appeared on national television immediately after the December 12 election, welcoming the adoption of the new constitution. In an interview last May, Vengerov, who was cited as an expert who took part in prepartion of an earlier draft constitution establishing strong presidential authority, spoke of the need for such provisions, stating that "Russia has always needed strong executive authority at major turning points in its history."

In sum, given its broad mandate in the December 31 decree, the Presidential Judicial Chamber for Information Disputes may be expected to play a major role in the evolution of mass media law and policy in Russia. In so doing, the Chamber will probably soon face the dilemma of seeking to serve the President's interest and at the same time mainiting respect as an impartial authority. While giving Yeltsin more direct influence over the Chamber's activities, the move creates the risk of destroying the Chamber's credibility as an impartial decisionmaker.

Professor Frances Foster's article in the ensuing section discusses in depth the various decisions issued by the Judicial Chamber for Information Disputes. Part II of this volume collects a selection of these decisions.

B.

Content Control

Of Founders and Emergencies: Euphemizing Censorship*

Peter Krug

It is a little tricky to dignify censorship within the rule of law, or bring legal analysis to moments of revolution, but here is how we understand the statutory justifications for the fairly draconian events after the dissolution of the Parliament and violence of October 3. Recall that on September 23, after suspension of the Parliament, the Council of Ministers also ordered the suspension of newspapers, magazines, and radio and broadcast programs of the Supreme Soviet. And on October 4, the government suspended a group of "extreme" newspapers, including *Pravda*, *Sovetskaia Rossiia*, and *Den*, on the grounds that their founders were organizations that participated in the Moscow uprising.

The government also asserted prior censorship for two days over other publications including *Nezavisimaia Gazeta* and *Segodnia*. A St. Petersburg daily, *Chas Pik* ("*Rush Hour*"), published a report by Pavel Gutiontov, Chair of the Committee on Defense of Freedom of Speech and Rights of Journalists. He reported that one censored item was a short report on the suspension of a number of newspapers founded by the organizations responsible for the "events in Moscow." What the censors found condemnatory was not the report itself, but "the lack of exaltation" about the decision. "It is hard to call these actions a brave step towards democracy," Gutiontov concluded.

A complicated, and interesting explanation for the September 23 action resides in the murky area of Russian law concerning the power of "the founder" of newspapers and other instruments of mass information. Remember that only publications for which the Supreme Soviet was the founder were closed in late September. In a sense, the Council of Ministers' resolution declared that, with the Parliament suspended, a new "founder" for its publications was needed, and the successor would be the government itself. Under article 16 of the Mass Media Law, a founder may, under certain circumstances, close its publications down without having to seek a court order (as otherwise required by statute). Those circumstances are limited to authorizations found either in the editorial charter or an agreement between the founder and the editor-in-chief of the publication.

The October 4 terminations and suspensions were based on the President's emergency powers, but even there, the interpretation of these powers seemed to relate to the prohibitions of article 4 of the Mass Media Law (authorizing censorship if a publication engages in appeals for seizure of power, for violent change in the constitutional order or integrity of the state, or incitements to national, class, social, or religious prejudice or intolerance). In an October 5 interview, the chief of the State Inspectorate for the Protection of the Press, Yuri Luchinskii, justified the closure of

* Post-Soviet Media Law & Policy Newsletter, Oct. 20, 1993, at 3.

Pravda, *Den*, and other newspapers by equating their communism with fascism and their common relationship to article 4 criteria. Earlier, on September 22, Luchinskii had warned that all publications calling for abolition of the Presidency or the removal of the President would be regarded as contravening article 4, with "all the implications" that entailed.

St. Petersburg's *Vedomosti* ("*The Record*") published details on the suspension of the Aleksander Nevzorov's virulently anti-Yeltsin television program "600 Seconds." The order, which was signed by Deputy Minister of Press and Information O. Yusitkov and chief of the State Inspectorate for Protection of the Press Yuri Luchinksii, was received on October 5 by Bella Kurkova, chair of the television company. The full text of the order (implemented by Kurkova) was as follows:

> In accordance with the introduction of the emergency rule in the city of Moscow by the Decree of the President of the Russian Federation No. 1578 of October 4, the Ministry of Press and Information of [the Russian Federation] has been instructed to provide, starting from October 4, 1993, the execution of Article 23(b) of the Law on Emergency Rule. Since the program "600 Seconds" on St. Petersburg's Channel 5, retransmitted in Moscow, stirs up ethnic, class, social, religious intolerance and enmity, we require you to stop its transmission to Moscow pending the lifting of emergency rule. If you cannot do it technically, you must suspend airing of TV program "600 Seconds" until our special instruction.

The authority of the "founder" or the existence of an emergency become important analytical tools. In normal circumstances, the law requires government to follow certain extremely important procedural requirements if it seeks to enforce article 4.[**] These procedural safeguards stipulate that a mass media outlet may be terminated or suspended but only upon judicial review and only after proof of repeated violations during the prior twelve months and the prior issuance of written warnings. For example, as mentioned above, the government had taken *Den* to court earlier, and had negotiated a settlement in which the government dropped its civil action and *Den* promised not to violate article 4. But—and this is the magic of law—these procedural safeguards do not apply if the action is taken by the "founder" as the Council asserted in its September action or pursuant to emergency powers, as the President argued in October.

The powers and problems of asserting foundership can be found in the takeover and reorientation of the newspaper *Rossiiskaia Gazeta*, a paper for which the Parliament had been the founder. Shortly after the September 23 Council of Ministers' action, the

[**] Regarding its obligations under international agreements, Russia is a party to the International Covenant on Civil and Political Rights which, in article 19, guarantees the right to receive and impart information. However, article 19(3)(b), not often cited, permits restrictions—provided by domestic law—deemed necessary for "the protection of national security or of public order." Article 4(1) of the Covenant also permits parties to derogate from their article 19 responsibilities "in time of public emergency which threatens the life of the nation and the existence of which is officially proclaimed."

government installed a new editor-in-chief, Natalia Ivanovna Polezhaeva, who initiated radical changes in personnel and editorial directions. These actions brought her into conflict with the journalists of the paper who, in a September 27 meeting, voiced their unanimous objection to the takeover and claimed that the substitution of founders had been illegal.

Pornography, Pluralism, and the Russian Press*

Brian McNair

In general, the Russian press remains a politically committed, partisan press, declamatory and subjective. This is a hangover not merely from the Soviet system, but of pre-Soviet journalistic traditions. If there is partisan commitment, however, there is also pluralism, covering the spectrum from Thatcherite free marketeers to fascists and neo-Nazis.

While many Russians are understandably concerned about the appearance of the latter, others argue that the survival of press diversity is more important at the current stage of Russian political evolution than the imposition of a politically correct, but authoritarian conformity. To the extent that the Russian press contain excesses and extremism of various kinds, argues one senior journalist, they reflect the reality of contemporary Russian society, in itself a necessary if discomforting social role. "Without them the picture would be distorted and limited, and the construction of civil society and a lawful state impossible."

Whether one agrees with such a liberal view or not, anti-Semitic and other materials associated with fascism will continue to appear in the Russian press, largely because the legal system is not functioning effectively. The Soviet system has disappeared, but has not yet been replaced by a legitimate Russian system.

Another consequence of the legal "black hole" at the heart of Russian society is the emergence of explicit pornography on the kiosks and newsstands. In principle, the press law prohibits such material. The law is simply ignored, however, in the apparent knowledge that it will not be enforced.

Some of this material is educational in intention, addressing what is widely acknowledged to be the ignorance of the Russian male about matters of sexuality, and introducing previously taboo topics, such as masturbation and the female orgasm, into public discourse. The situation echoes the development of post-Franco Spain, in which the artificial and austere puritanism of an authoritarian regime produces, when that regime collapses, a rush to uncover the forbidden and catch up with the rest of the world. In this respect the explosion of pornography is indicative of Russia entering its "striptease" phase of cultural development, peeling away the layers of sexual repression and guilt accumulated during the Soviet era.

Russian pornography is as yet cheaply produced, usually in black and white on poor quality newsprint. Much of it is imported from Latvia. Higher quality porn is available through imported eastern European magazines (Polish, Yugoslavian, etc.), and

* Post-Soviet Media Law & Policy Newsletter, June 3, 1994, at 16.

in the Russian-language edition of Penthouse, which launched at the beginning of 1993. Similar in most respects to the American edition of the magazine, Russian Penthouse presents a glossy mix of misogynistic soft-porn and features dealing with such matters as prostitution in Moscow, and the opening of new strip-clubs. It also features a Russian "Girl of the Month."

Alongside the emergence of porn, the Russian press has developed an extensive tabloid sector, characterized by an editorial focus on crime, political scandal, agony columns, entertainment and lifestyle. Publications such as the curiously named SPEED ("SPEED" being the Russian acronym for AIDS) resemble the British Tidbits with their combination of topless females, stories about western movie and rock stars, and gossip columns. Others, such as *Megapolis Express* and *Sovershenno Sekret* (*Absolutely Secret*) adopt a revelatory, sensational approach to crime and political affairs.

Viewing these publications, one receives the impression of a press experimenting with the possibilities of editorial control, and frequently failing to correctly draw the lines of taste and decency in accordance with the prevailing cultural level of the population. Many Russians, particularly of the older generation, reared in Soviet cultural traditions, find it disturbing to be confronted with pornography on their newsstands, or to find once staid and safe newspapers suddenly addressing such subjects as incest, drug abuse and political corruption. In *Pravda* in June 1993 an old communist wrote nostalgically of the days when the Soviet press could be trusted not to shock, but instead "gloried labour and exposed bureaucrats." Now, he complained, the press had been "set loose" and had developed "a permanent preoccupation with sex, relentless anti-communism, and trivia. It's no accident," he suggested, "that people shy away from newspaper kiosks."

Such comments can be viewed as the predictable complaints of a generation for whom the status quo of Soviet society will always be preferable to what is now emerging in Russia, but similar concerns are voiced by younger, more liberal commentators, such as the deputy editor of *Moskovskoe Novosti*, who asserts that "press freedom in post-Soviet Russia has not meant giving full and objective information to the reader. Infected by the decay of communism it has turned into freedom of abuse and insult; freedom to pursue private ideological wars; freedom to unleash any dirt on the page and on air—in a word, freedom to do anything, without limits."

Such views, and the debate about press standards to which they contribute, are not exclusive to Russia. But in Russia the debate is driven with particular intensity due to the suddenness of the change from one press culture to another, fuelled by the economic pressures working on newspapers and journalists. In such circumstances it is inevitable that some publications should follow the tabloid path, seeking to maximize readers with precisely the same techniques and strategies perfected by western companies. As is the case with television, the absence of effective legal regulation allows the barriers of acceptability to be pushed further and faster than might otherwise have been suggested by the traditional puritanism of a Soviet-influenced culture. On the other hand, many publications, such as the aforementioned *Sovershenno Sekret*, skillfully use tabloid techniques to attract readers to what is often a highly political content. Political coverage has by no means disappeared from the Russian press, but as is to be expected in a harsh and competitive market place, its style and presentation have changed markedly, and not always for the worse.

Even the more extreme expressions of press freedom, in the spheres of politics and sexuality, as already suggested, may be viewed as the necessary reflection of a society in which difference and transgression were for so long suppressed. Despite the offensive nature of much of this material, it arguably plays an important role in the continuing evolution of Russian political culture towards a state of tolerance and diversity.

There is, in any case, no going back for the Russian press, even if going back were thought to be desirable. Western observers may hope that they will avoid some of the mistakes made by media organizations in the advanced capitalist societies. In the end, it will be for Russian media workers, and their audiences, to decide how far and how fast the "striptease" shall be allowed to proceed.

Parental Law, Harmful Speech, and the Development of Legal Culture: Russian Judicial Chamber Discourse and Narrative[*]

Frances H. Foster

I. Introduction

Throughout history, scholars have asserted that a developed legal culture is a precondition for establishment of the rule of law. Yet, they have failed to offer any concrete blueprint for creating such a culture. For post-Soviet Russia this is not a theoretical concern but a practical imperative. With a "barren legal culture" as its legacy from its imperial and socialist past, Russia confronts the enormous challenge of constructing a legal tradition, language, and culture virtually from scratch.

This Article examines Russian efforts to develop a popular legal consciousness and, ultimately, legal culture during the Second Russian Republic of January 1994 to the present. It focuses on techniques employed by the Russian Federation Presidential Judicial Chamber for Information Disputes ("Judicial Chamber"), a body specifically created by Boris Yeltsin in December 1993 to assist in effective enforcement, interpretation, and inculcation of constitutional norms and rules. [*Editor's Note: President Putin abolished the Judicial Chamber by decree on June 3, 2000.*] In its brief history, the Judicial Chamber has wrestled with issues that have challenged more developed legal institutions worldwide. These include the constitutionality of hate speech, pornography, unpatriotic speech, limits on public access to government information, and direct and indirect controls on the media by state and commercial entities.[7] In the process, it has made a concerted effort to provide a "public assessment" of information disputes and to raise citizens' "understanding" of the appropriate relationship between individual constitutional rights of free speech, press, and information and the competing interests of the Russian "democratic" community. Moreover, from the start, the Judicial Chamber has relied heavily on "publicity" as a powerful sanction and enforcement mechanism.

This Article is based on an examination of Judicial Chamber opinions published in the newspaper *Rossiiskaia Gazeta* from February 1994 through December 1996.[12] My

---

[*] 54 Washington and Lee Law Review 923 (1997).

[7] During the lengthy suspension and reorganization of the Russian Constitutional Court, the Judicial Chamber provided the closest equivalent to judicial review of the constitutionality of legislation and acts. The Constitutional Court finally resumed operations in March 1995 after a one and one-half year hiatus.

[12] I have chosen *Rossiiskaia Gazeta* because it is the official source for publication of Judicial Chamber opinions. In addition, Judicial Chamber opinions often explicitly call for publication in *Rossiiskaia Gazeta*. Nonetheless, there are problems with the use of *Rossiiskaia Gazeta* as a database. From the start,

primary interest is not in the results of these opinions but rather in the texts themselves. What do they convey to the reader about the court's definition of itself, the parties before it, its audience, and the relationship between Russian citizens and institutions? What do these texts communicate about "law in general and the Constitution in particular?" How do they contribute to development of a post-Soviet Russian legal discourse and culture?

To answer these questions I turn to a substantial literature by U.S. legal scholars on how courts attempt to "influence patterns of thought" through judicial opinions. In particular, I draw on the pioneering work and methodology of James Boyd White. Professor White has demonstrated that analysis of the discourse, rhetoric, and narrative of legal texts, including judicial opinions, can yield new insights into the U.S. legal system.[15] A key methodological goal of this Article is to offer a critical examination of the application of these analytical techniques to foreign law, an examination that explores not just the new insights these techniques can offer but also the dangers inherent in any attempt to use domestic methodologies to study foreign legal systems.

Part II briefly reviews existing U.S. scholarship on the communicative functions of judicial opinions. It introduces Professor White's metaphors of judicial opinion as "performance" and "conversation" and considers possible extensions of U.S. analytical approaches to comparative study of judicial opinions.

The remainder of the Article applies White's notions of performance and conversation in the Russian context. Part III provides the background necessary for evaluating Judicial Chamber opinions. Part IV utilizes White's performance metaphor to examine the major group of cases decided by the Judicial Chamber, those involving media dissemination of "harmful speech." I study Judicial Chamber discourse and narrative techniques by reconstructing the plots and characters of these opinions. Following Professor White's lead, I place particular emphasis on the Judicial Chamber's "self-definition" or "self-creation."

Part V poses the question White raises in the United States context: "What kind of conversation do . . . [these opinions] establish, with what relation to democracy?" Not surprisingly, Russian judicial discourse does not fall easily into either of the "democratic" or "authoritarian" categories that White uses to describe the range of American judicial discourse. To provide a more accurate picture of Russian judicial discourse, I rely on a

---

there has been an ongoing conflict between the Judicial Chamber and *Rossiiskaia Gazeta* over the newspaper's practice of selective and abridged publication of opinions. The original legislation required "mandatory publication" of Judicial Chamber recommendations and "its most important decisions" without specifying who determines which decisions are "most important." In September 1994, the Judicial Chamber issued a special decision clarifying that it had sole authority to determine which decisions fall under the "most important" category. Moreover, the Judicial Chamber has ruled against *Rossiiskaia Gazeta* in several cases. *Rossiiskaia Gazeta* has become a vocal opponent of Judicial Chamber policy and practice.

[15] *See generally* James Boyd White, Justice as Translation: An Essay in Cultural and Legal Criticism (1990); James Boyd White, When Words Lose Their Meaning: Constitutions and Reconstitutions of Language, Character, and Community (1984).

peculiarly Russian view of the role of law, specifically, the idea of "parental" law articulated by Harold Berman in 1950.

Finally, Part VI builds on the analysis of Part V to assess the rewards and risks of importing domestic legal methodology into comparative law scholarship. Although use of the sophisticated tools developed in American legal scholarship can provide valuable insights into foreign legal systems, the comparative law scholar must adapt those tools to the culture in which the scholar applies them. Uncritical application of American methodology without cultural translation distorts the foreign experience.

II. Judicial Opinion as Performance and Conversation: U.S. Perspectives

In his foreword to a recent *University of Chicago Law Review* symposium, James Boyd White invited the reader to "imagine a legal world without the judicial opinion, . . . in which judges would never explain themselves . . . . They would simply decide the cases, issuing orders reflecting their judgment."[21] With the current trend toward decreasing publication of judicial opinions, Professor White's invitation may be less a scholarly thought experiment than a preview of the American future. This adds a certain urgency and poignancy to the question White asks in his title: "What's an Opinion for?"

Professor White's response is that an opinion is more than a record of case outcome; it is also an important vehicle for the court to communicate with the parties, the legal community, and the lay audience. An opinion "translates" non-legal language and experience into the "language of the law" and, at the same time, makes legal language, texts, and acts "intelligible." It is a "claim of authority" and "meaning" for the court, its vision of the world, its "invocation" of the past, and its modes of thought, expression, and reasoning. Thus, White concludes that the form as well as result of an opinion are of critical importance since an opinion "deeply affects and shapes . . . the imaginations, minds, and feelings of those who live with the law."

In his earlier work, Professor White has offered two metaphors to assist us in understanding how courts communicate through opinions. His first metaphor is judicial opinion as "performance," one that is political and ethical as well as legal in nature. Under this view, the court/author creates an elaborate cast of characters in lead and supporting roles. It "gives itself an ethos, or character, and does the same for both the parties to a case and for the larger audience it addresses—the lawyers, the public, and other agencies in government." The court fashions complex, disparate facts and events into a coherent plot that leads to an inevitable denouement. The vehicle may be a tragedy, comedy, farce, or "virtual morality tale." The performance occasionally receives critical acclaim but more often than not plays to an empty house.

White's second metaphor is judicial opinion as "conversation." Under this interpretation, an opinion is a "form of responsive discourse" between judge/speaker and

---

[21] James Boyd White, *What's an Opinion for?*, 62 University of Chicago Law Review 1363, 1363 (1995).

reader/listener. It creates through language and rhetoric a "discoursing community" (of judge, reader, and other people discussed in the opinion) with distinctive values and culture. Each opinion is not an isolated conversation, however, but rather a "stage" in the larger conversation that we know as the law. Thus, an individual opinion's "constitutive rhetoric" and mode of engaging the reader in "law talk" may have broader political, ethical, and legal implications.

Invoking John Dewey's claim that "[d]emocracy begins in conversation,"[40] Professor White proposes a new standard for evaluating a judicial opinion: "Is this an invitation to a conversation in which democracy begins (or flourishes)? Or one in which it ends?" In his application of this test to U.S. Supreme Court opinions, he finds "democratic" and "authoritarian" conversations. A democratic conversation is one in which the judge addresses the reader as an equal and invites all to participate in an "open" dialogue about the law, premised on shared values and "human conditions" and in language accessible to every citizen. An authoritarian conversation, in contrast, is one that "demands simple and total obedience of its reader" to the judge's characterization of fact and law.

An impressive array of scholars and judges from across the ideological spectrum share White's view that judicial opinions perform essential communicative functions. As a rapidly growing literature attests, White is also not alone in his concern for how as well as what a court communicates. Armed with techniques borrowed from other disciplines (primarily linguistics and literary criticism), U.S. academics, practitioners, and judges have produced a substantial body of work on the rhetoric, discourse, and style of judicial opinions, with close attention to the use of language, word order, metaphor, hyperbole, tone, and the like.

What has emerged in the process is a recognition of the important role of judicial "storytelling" or "narrative" as a communicative device. This has led to a new appreciation of the extent to which judges engage in "fact-spinning," "master narratives," and other storytelling techniques to make outcomes appear unavoidable, to elicit empathy, to organize precedent, to humanize abstract legal theories and norms, to palliate harsh results, to reinforce the legal and moral authority of the decision and decision maker, and to exclude alternative arguments, interpretations, and perspectives.

This application of discourse and narrative analysis to judicial opinions has had considerable value. It has enabled scholars to go beyond examination of the merits and resolution of the case at hand and explore broader issues, such as how a court defines its own authority and mission, its relationship to its audience and external legal actors and texts, and the language, meaning, and reach of the law. In so doing, these approaches may also help shed light on the very nature of law itself. As Robert Cover observed in his seminal article *Nomos and Narrative*: "Once understood in the context of the narratives that give it meaning law becomes not merely a system of rules to be observed,

[40] Dialogue on John Dewey 58 (Corliss Lamont ed., 1959).

but a world in which we live."[66] Moreover, if John Dewey is correct that democracy begins in conversation, then the study of the "conversation" between judge and reader that White urges may even provide signals about the overall status and prospects for democracy in a given society.

Despite the potential contributions of discourse and narrative analysis, the techniques are seldom employed in comparative law scholarship on judicial opinions. This may in large part reflect the formidable challenge of linguistic and cultural translation. As substantial U.S. literature reveals, legal scholars and practitioners find the problems they encounter within their own system daunting and humbling. These difficulties are, of course, only magnified in the comparative law context. Yet, the few scholarly efforts to negotiate these linguistic and cultural differences have confirmed the value of studying foreign as well as U.S. opinions through the prism of discourse and narrative analysis. For example, two recent articles published in the *Yale Law Journal* and *Wisconsin Law Review* used these techniques to debunk long-held comparative law perceptions of the French judiciary as "passive applicator" of code provisions and to offer new perspectives and approaches to hate speech based on a comparative study of Canadian and U.S. narratives.[71]

Thus far, scholarly attempts to apply discourse and narrative analysis in the comparative law context have tended to focus on established Western legal systems with familiar judicial organs and materials that are relatively accessible to the foreign observer. In post-Soviet Russia, this Article confronts a very different situation—a foreign legal system that is in flux, a quasi-judicial organ that defies categorization, and opinions that are published sporadically and are unavailable in translation. Perhaps, then, it is not surprising that when this Article asks questions developed in the U.S. context, it finds new answers, answers that can be explained only by the distinctive features of Soviet/Russian law.

III. Setting the Stage: The Author and Its Opinions

On December 31, 1993, Boris Yeltsin issued a presidential decree establishing a permanent Judicial Chamber for Information Disputes. The new body was the successor to the short-lived Information Arbitration Tribunal, a quasi-judicial organ instituted in October 1993 to monitor and ensure fair, full, and equal media coverage of Russia's fall 1993 election and constitutional referendum campaigns.

The Judicial Chamber consists of a panel of seven media specialists under the chairmanship of law professor Anatolii Borisovich Vengerov. Judicial Chamber

[66] Robert M. Cover, *The Supreme Court, 1982 Term—Foreword: Nomos and Narrative*, 97 Harvard Law Review 4, 4-5 (1983).

[71] *See* Mitchel de S.-O.-l'E. Lasser, *Judicial (Self-)Portraits: Judicial Discourse in the French Legal System*, 104 Yale Law Journal 1325, 1385 (1995); Mayo Moran, *Talking About Hate Speech: A Rhetorical Analysis of American and Canadian Approaches to the Regulation of Hate Speech*, 1994 Wisconsin Law Review 1425.

members represent a wide variety of professional backgrounds and communities—academic, legislative, administrative, and journalistic. Five of the seven members served on the Information Arbitration Tribunal.

The initial presidential decree and subsequent founding Statute assign the Judicial Chamber sweeping and vaguely-defined responsibilities. The "main task" is to help the Russian President "exercise his constitutional powers as guarantor of rights, freedoms, and legitimate interests in the mass information sphere enshrined in the Russian Federation Constitution." Other duties include guaranteeing objectivity, accuracy, equality, and pluralism in the mass media, protecting the moral interests of children and adolescents, resolving disputes about allocation of air time between legislative factions, correcting factual errors in media reports, and providing mass media-related draft legislation, expert advisory opinions on application of statutes, and "rulings" on presidential decrees.[78]

The Judicial Chamber has authority to resolve "information disputes and other matters" involving norms established in the Russian Constitution, laws, and presidential edicts, "universally recognized principles and norms of international law," Russian Federation international treaties, "journalistic ethics," and "generally-accepted ethical norms." Thus far, the Judicial Chamber has concentrated on two major issues—media dissemination of allegedly harmful materials and government interference with mass media activities.[80] There are only two express limitations on Judicial Chamber competence. It cannot examine disputes that are "assigned by law to the jurisdiction of Russian Federation courts" or those pertaining to information protected by law as a "state, commercial, or other secret."[82]

Despite its broad charter to monitor, implement, and create norms in the mass information sphere, the Judicial Chamber's prescribed enforcement powers are modest. According to the Statute on the Judicial Chamber, it has the authority to reprimand officials and journalists, to order rectification of factual errors, and to "raise" with the "appropriate" organs or personnel the need for more stringent remedies, such as written warnings, administrative or criminal proceedings, or termination of media outlets.[83] The

---

[78] Interestingly, the original presidential decree also authorizes the Judicial Chamber to issue warnings to the mass media. This "function" is omitted in the Statute on the Judicial Chamber.

[80] A study of Judicial Chamber statements and recommendations suggests that there may be a third major category of claims emerging—those dealing with intellectual property issues.

[82] The Judicial Chamber has consistently read these jurisdictional restrictions narrowly. For example, it has repeatedly claimed competence to hear disputes involving slander or libel of public officials, matters that arguably fall exclusively within the jurisdiction of Russia's ordinary court system. It has asserted jurisdiction on grounds that such cases are not purely private civil actions but also constitute "information disputes that have a public-legal character and social significance."

[83] In actual practice, the Judicial Chamber has ranged well beyond the remedies stipulated in its Statute. For example, it has directed newspapers to dismiss editors-in-chief. . . . The Judicial Chamber has proposed that official bodies repeal legislation, decrees, and decisions. In many opinions, the Judicial Chamber has also offered general recommendations and reforms inspired by the case at hand. These have included suggestions for new or amended legislation and "orderly" rules for accreditation and access of

Judicial Chamber has the right to demand "necessary" materials from government agencies and media editorial offices and written explanations of unethical actions from editorial offices, officials, and journalists. Judicial Chamber decisions are binding and not subject to appeal. Government organs and personnel "to whom a decision is addressed" must report to the Judicial Chamber within two weeks on their compliance with the decision.[86]

From the start, the status of the Judicial Chamber within the Russian legal system has been an open question. The Judicial Chamber formally operates within the presidential administration. Its staff is appointed by the President and its activities are financed out of the presidential budget. Yet, according to its Statute, the Judicial Chamber is an "independent" and "impartial body." As its Chairman Anatolii Vengerov often emphasizes, even the President himself cannot interfere in its activities.

In addition, the Judicial Chamber does not fit neatly into any existing legal or institutional category. To a certain extent, it operates as a court. It examines written petitions from claimants or brings proceedings on its own initiative.[90] It holds open hearings at which it considers evidence and oral testimony from parties and/or their "representatives," expert witnesses, and other concerned persons.[93] It evaluates factual and legal issues with extensive reference to procedural history (if any), governing Russian constitutional, statutory, presidential, and administrative provisions, and international law norms and rules.[98] It resolves disputes, prescribes remedies after considering mitigating and aggravating factors, and publishes most of its opinions.[100]

---

journalists. The Judicial Chamber has also admonished the press "to be more careful in verifying facts and information" and called for stricter government enforcement of mass media legislation. It has even offered advice regarding improvements in media content and coverage.

[86] In addition, in cases where the Judicial Chamber has sent materials to an "appropriate" organ regarding a violation of mass information rights and freedoms, that organ must report the results of its examination to the Judicial Chamber within one month.

[90] Claimants have included journalists, newspaper editors, and media organizations. The Judicial Chamber has also received numerous petitions from government officials, parliamentary deputies, and federal and regional legislative, judicial, and administrative bodies. Occasionally, special interest groups and ordinary citizens seek Judicial Chamber assistance as well.

[93] As reported in Judicial Chamber opinions, the most common forms of evidence are newspaper articles and videotaped television broadcasts. Also frequently mentioned are any prior official rulings regarding the action or parties, media founding and registration documents, and unspecified materials submitted by the parties.

[98] Most commonly cited are the Russian Constitution, Law On the Mass Media, and Presidential Decree No. 2334 of December 31, 1993, On Additional Guarantees for Citizens' Right to Information. Other cited statutes include the Law On the Status of Deputies, Fundamental Principles on Protection of Citizens' Health, and Labor Code.

[100] The Judicial Chamber also carefully notes any admissions of misconduct by the parties, and issues opinions in the form of decisions, recommendations, statements, and expert conclusions. Unfortunately, there is no statutory definition of the structure or content of these four types of opinions. According to the Statute on the Judicial Chamber, as amended, there is mandatory publication of all recommendations and the "most important decisions" in *Rossiiskaia Gazeta*. Occasionally, the Judicial Chamber also orders or

Yet, as its opinions reveal, the Judicial Chamber actually performs an amalgam of functions. It acts as court, Constitutional Court, legislative body, government agency, prosecutor, and media ethics board.[102] Even in its most formal decisions, the Judicial Chamber is not merely an arbiter of fact and law; it is an engaged and emotional participant in the process. The Judicial Chamber expresses its views of the parties and their conduct in strong, often colorful language. It uses a specific case or controversy as a springboard for a general discussion of legal and moral principles, rights, and responsibilities. It makes a conscious effort to guide and educate as well as decide and discipline. Thus, Chairman Vengerov may have captured the essence of the Judicial Chamber best when he described it as "unfamiliar, unusual, and somewhat juridically exotic."

Since its inception, the Judicial Chamber has been widely criticized as extra-constitutional and ineffective. It has even been labeled a successor to the notorious communist revolutionary tribunals, censorship bodies, and agitation and propaganda organs. It is routinely pilloried in the press, ignored by defendants, and threatened with extinction. Its future is uncertain. Nonetheless, its current contribution is considerable. As the author of more than one hundred opinions, the Judicial Chamber provides invaluable insights into evolving post-Soviet approaches to law.

IV. Judicial Chamber Performance: The Harmful Speech Opinions

Judicial Chamber opinions paint a dismal picture of a public bombarded with false, offensive, and dangerous information, yet deprived of even the most basic facts about its government's policies and actions. These cases cover a wide range of topics, from media dissemination of ethnic slurs to seductive cigarette advertisements. Despite the significant variation in content, there are marked continuities in the Judicial Chamber's depiction of the characters, issues, values, and legal principles involved. Thus, these cases provide a useful vehicle for studying the message the Judicial Chamber conveys to the reader about legal norms and discourse in post-Soviet Russia.

A. The Plots

More than two-thirds of its published opinions concern publications and broadcasts that the Judicial Chamber deems harmful for Russian society. There are six recurrent plots. The first and most prevalent involves media dissemination of information that "incites" ethnic, social, and religious "intolerance," "hatred," or

---

recommends publication of an opinion in a claimant's or defendant's newspaper. In 1995, the Judicial Chamber published a complete collection of opinions with commentary and documents.

[102] Its very name—*Sudebnaia Palata Po Informatsionnym Sporam Pri Prezidente Rossiiskoi Federatsii* [Russian Federation Judicial Chamber for Information Disputes]—reveals the multifaceted nature and ambiguous position of the Judicial Chamber. *Sudebnaia* expresses its role as a court. *Palata*, however, is a term more commonly associated with a legislative "chamber" or "house" or governmental "board." *"Pri" Prezidente* adds to the confusion further by designating the Judicial Chamber as a body "under" or "attached to" the President.

"tension." The prototypical case is Decision No. 42, an examination initiated by the Judicial Chamber of Ia. Mogutin's controversial *Novyi Vzgliad* article, *Chechen Knot: 13 Theses*. The article rejected the official account of the ongoing conflict in Chechnya as a Russian military effort to defeat armed rebellion by Chechen separatists and restore constitutional order in a Russian Federation Republic. The author argued instead that the Chechen war was the natural result of "ethnic incompatibility" and "zoological," "genetic" animosity of superior, Christian Russians for inferior, Moslem Chechens. He claimed that Chechens were "semi-savage," were famous "only for their barbarism and sullen anger," and "had made absolutely no contribution to the world other than international terrorism and the drug trade." Mogutin attacked opponents of his views. He "insulted" religious leaders, castigated intellectuals for their "anti-Russian" and "unpatriotic attitudes," and accused "democrats" of "wanting to shrink the borders of the Russia they hate."[117]

A central theme in recent opinions is media dissemination of fascist and anti-Semitic materials. In the words of the Judicial Chamber, it "has addressed this subject often." For instance, in January 1995, the Judicial Chamber made a special expert assessment of publications in the Volgograd newspaper *Kolokol* as "abuses of freedom of mass information." *Kolokol* articles blamed Russia's current ills on "purposeful destruction by Zionist groups of the West and a fifth column of Zionists in Russia," characterized Jews as enemies of the Russian people who controlled "all key positions in Russia," and even "tested" the family names of local leaders for possible Jewish origins.

The second major plot concerns media dissemination of information that "discredits" state institutions, personnel, and legislation. The Judicial Chamber has examined and censured publications and broadcasts ridiculing the federal legislature as a "farce" and its deputies as "clowns" and "buffoons." It has denounced materials accusing government officials of corruption, abuse of power, and falsification of educational and military credentials. President Yeltsin has also figured prominently in Judicial Chamber opinions. Indeed, in April 1994, the Judicial Chamber was moved to issue a special statement condemning a *Zavtra* journalist for attempting to "discredit, diminish, and injure the Russian Federation president with profoundly immoral and malicious speculations on the subject of his health in an effort . . . to introduce into the public consciousness the impression that the chief of state is an incapable and incapacitated politician."

In addition, the Judicial Chamber has focused on another form of information that subverts the Russian political process—"improper" media coverage of election campaigns. It has identified several negative media practices. These include "premature" dissemination of election campaign literature and speeches; publication and

[117] The Judicial Chamber held that Mogutin's article violated the Constitution, Law On the Mass Media, and ethical norms. It sent its decision to the Russian Press Committee (the registering body) with instructions to suspend or terminate *Novyi Vzgliad* and to the procurator's office to determine whether or not to press criminal charges.

broadcasts of offensive, slanderous, and inflammatory statements by candidates; incomplete, unreliable, and biased commentary; and "clear political preferences" and support for candidates that go "beyond the bounds of the permissible."

Judicial Chamber decisions also deal with materials that "disparage" Russian legislation. The most notable of these is Decision No. 43, an action brought against several central Moscow newspapers for their "inaccurate," "tendentious," and "biased" critiques of the draft advertising law. The Judicial Chamber supported the claimant's contention that these articles discredited individual statutory provisions and their conceptual basis, insulted the drafters, and undermined public support for enactment of the law.

The third plot involves media dissemination of information that discriminates on the basis of gender. *Rossiiskaia Gazeta* has published two key Judicial Chamber decisions on the topic, Decision No. 5 and Decision No. 30. The first case declared unconstitutional newspaper publication of advertisements for job openings limited to male applicants only. The second case dealt with a very different type of discriminatory publication—articles that targeted female legislators for "disrespect" and "humiliation." At issue were two *Sobesednik* articles that allegedly insulted and discredited the professional activity of female deputies through the use of sexual innuendo and other "inappropriate" methods. For example, one article contended that the "Women of Russia" parliamentary faction had called upon Russian women to withhold sex from "their husbands and boyfriends until order is restored in Russia." Another article's title asked "How Much Is the Honor of 22 Female State Duma Deputies Worth?"

The fourth recurrent plot concerns information that undermines public morality. A prime illustration is Decision No. 7, the Judicial Chamber's determination that several *Novyi Vzgliad* articles constituted a threat to the moral interests of Russian children and adolescents. *Novyi Vzgliad* had published grotesque accounts of "pathological" criminal and sexual "perversions" under such provocative titles as "Cannibal-Lover," "Breasts in a Pastry," and "Serial Murders." Because of lax distribution policies, *Novyi Vzgliad* apparently had reached the tender eyes of Russian adolescents and had become a topic of wide discussion among schoolchildren.

In a similar vein, a much-publicized recent decision ruled that the "Wild Field" television program "disseminat[ed] . . . information [that] weakens moral principles and has the potential to cause moral injury and destroy family relations." The broadcast, an exposé of allegedly rampant lesbianism in Russian prisons, contained close-up shots of women prisoners who had not consented to being filmed.

The fifth plot concerns media dissemination of information that causes physical harm. The best example is Recommendation No. 1, issued by the Judicial Chamber in May 1994. This opinion, entitled "On Advertisements Disseminated by the Mass Media That Are Hazardous to Life and Health," provided a critical analysis of newspaper and television advertisements that encourage public consumption of alcoholic beverages and tobacco products. It also denounced media advertising and "propagandizing" of unapproved medicinal remedies and uncertified practitioners of "nontraditional methods of treatment." Recent opinions suggest that advertisement of "unhealthful" products remains a serious problem despite stiff new legal prohibitions against it.

The sixth and final plot concerns information that causes financial harm to citizens. The key case is Decision No. 16, the Judicial Chamber's ruling against the allegedly fraudulent, illegal, and unlicensed television lottery Game "05." One of the founders, a television journalist, advertised the lottery on his Sunday television program. Game "05" organizers promised TV viewers large sums of money for telephoning in the correct answers to "relatively simple questions." They neglected to mention, however, the expense of each telephone call. As a result, most callers received for their efforts the taped message "your number has not been chosen by the computer" and a high telephone bill. In all, the Moscow telephone company sent out 600 million rubles worth of bills to Game "05" participants.

Several subsequent Judicial Chamber opinions have only confirmed the threat of "unscrupulous," "misleading," and "concealed" advertisements to Russian consumers. For example, in a June 1995 decision, the Judicial Chamber targeted the "deceptive" and "unfair" practices of the Federal Investment Fund for Social Protection. Even though it was a purely commercial entity, the Fund had included in its television advertisements shots of Russian legislative buildings, sessions, and chairman as well as pictures of the state flag and state emblem. According to the Judicial Chamber, the goal was to lure potential investors with the false promise that the Fund was a state organization, backed by the full faith and credit of the Russian legislature.

B. The Characters

Judicial Chamber opinions feature a large and varied cast of characters. Those with recurring roles are society, the speaker, the publisher, the audience, the target, the state, and, of course, the Judicial Chamber itself.

1. Society

The dominant image in Judicial Chamber opinions is that of a fragile post-Soviet "democratic" society and reform process. Their fate hangs by a thread. "Irresponsible" journalism threatens to rend the moral fabric of society and destroy the already tenuous credibility and legitimacy of Russia's "young institutions of statehood." Conditions are so precarious that even the most minor media deviation from legal or ethical principles could trigger a "social explosion" and plunge Russia into anarchy, chauvinism, and immorality.

Judicial Chamber rhetoric underscores the gravity and sensitivity of the situation. The watchword of Judicial Chamber opinions is "danger." Dissemination of "extremist views" poses a "high degree of social danger." Fascism is a "real social danger." Seductive advertisements for cigarettes and alcoholic beverages are "dangerous for life and health." Dramatic adjectives, such as "serious," "alarming," "destructive," "provocative," and "pernicious," reinforce this view of a Russian society in peril. Use of superlatives and modifying adverbs only heightens the sense of urgency. For example, one opinion described publications "fraught with the most ruinous consequences." Another condemned an author's "sharply destructive position."

References to warfare pervade Judicial Chamber opinions. "Aggressive" "enemies" menace Russian society. Publications "propagandize war," incite paramilitary armed groups, and provide recipes for Molotov cocktails and other weapons. The Judicial Chamber proposes new or improved legislation in the "battle" against fascism and abuses of the mass media.

Words of balance and weight convey the impression of a Russian society poised on the brink of disaster. The Judicial Chamber has called upon journalists to "weigh every word" and has warned of the dangers of even the "slightest imbalance" in analysis of interethnic conflicts. In its joint recommendations with the Union of Russian Journalists, the Judicial Chamber made its most extensive use of the metaphor yet. It proclaimed that media coverage of interethnic relations and interactions between federal and local authorities "must be carefully weighed on pharmacist's scales since a mistake in the dosage can make a publication a poison rather than a medicine."

2. The Speaker

The speaker, be it journalist, advertiser, or editorial staff, is generally the principal villain of the piece. In the most dramatic Judicial Chamber opinions, the speaker has deliberately set out to destroy the Russian state and incite social and ethnic discord. These opinions emphasize the fundamentally evil character of the speaker and his message. They also highlight the intentional nature of the act. Words such as "deliberately," "knowingly," and "intentionally" appear often. At the same time, the Judicial Chamber attempts to isolate the speaker and undercut the credibility of the message. It does so by depicting the speaker as mentally unbalanced and the message as "extremist" or "absurd."

Other Judicial Chamber opinions paint the speaker as unscrupulous and duplicitous. These cases involve journalists or advertisers who take advantage of public naïveté and glitches in the Russian legislative and government system for financial, personal, or political self-aggrandizement. These speakers "do not spurn the basest methods" to sell their stories, schemes, and products. Their stock in trade is deception. The Judicial Chamber brings this point home by providing a detailed list of "tricks" employed by journalists and advertisers. These include falsification of data, deliberate omission or misstatement of facts, use of quotations out of context, reference to "worthless" sociological polls, and hidden advertisements.

Another concern of Judicial Chamber opinions is the disrespectful attitude of Russian speakers toward state organs and personnel. Speakers repeatedly "slander," "libel," "mock," "deride," and "maliciously insult" even the highest leaders and government bodies. Moreover, as a June 1995 decision revealed, advertisers do not hesitate to appropriate the most sacred symbols of Russian statehood to hock their wares.

In a number of opinions, speakers appear as sloppy and inexperienced. They fail to verify facts and rumors, make numerous mistakes in their reporting of legal texts and issues and use of legal terminology, write in a "crude," "unidimensional and primitive fashion" about complex social and political problems, and are "elementarily ignorant and mistaken." Even a rare Judicial Chamber harmful speech ruling in favor of journalists, Decision No. 44, criticized authors of the television exposé "Newspaper Histories" ("Fascism in Russia. Who?") for their "use of insufficiently verified and inaccurate information."

Thus, the speaker emerges in Judicial Chamber harmful speech decisions as a "negative" influence on Russian society and democratic reform process. Whether by accident or design, authors of harmful materials repeatedly violate professional ethics, moral principles, and citizens' legal rights, interests, honor, and dignity. They insist on "unbridled" freedom of speech but are "insufficiently responsible about the possible consequences." In the final analysis, the speaker is a figure that deserves minimal protection and respect.

3. The Publisher

The Judicial Chamber reserves its harshest invective for the publisher of harmful materials. In some cases, it characterizes publishers as open and dedicated enemies of Russia. It uses the strongest possible language to condemn newspapers such as *Zavtra*, *Novyi Vzgliad*, and *Al'-Kods* for inciting social and national hatred, discrediting Russian officials and institutions, and undermining public morality. The Judicial Chamber has spoken of full-scale campaigns by some mass media organs to destroy Russia's political and social establishments, including "all-out persecution of prominent politicians and officials." It has attacked publishers of this ilk for using fraudulent means to obtain registration certificates, ignoring legal and administrative publication procedures, and persisting in their "dangerous," "impermissible" activity despite warnings from the Judicial Chamber and law enforcement organs. According to the Judicial Chamber, these publishers "flagrantly" "flout" Russian legal and ethical norms, yet remain unrepentant and intransigent. They are beyond appeal to reason or conscience.

In other cases, the Judicial Chamber focuses on publishers that place profit motive ahead of legal and ethical duties. In these opinions, publishers deliberately "distort" information for "sensation" and "popularity." They disseminate remunerative advertisements that are illegal, dangerous, deceptive, and libelous and allow major advertisers to control the content of publications and programming. Such publishers make no attempt to supply morally uplifting materials, but instead cater to the basest tastes of their audience. Moreover, they routinely exploit loopholes in the law and inadequate law enforcement for financial gain.

A constant theme in Judicial Chamber opinions is the irresponsibility of Russian publishers. They make little effort to verify published information or to supervise employees. They disseminate harmful materials and "pay no regard to the pernicious effect on the morality of society" or stability of the Russian state. When called to account for their actions, publishers either deny responsibility altogether or attempt to shift liability to authors or subsidiary units. In several cases, publishers proffer disingenuous excuses for their actions. They plead poverty, ignorance, youth, and the inexorable demands of capitalist competition. They frequently refuse to participate in Judicial Chamber sessions or they provide evasive, unconvincing answers and explanations.

Finally, publishers appear as "unprincipled and inconsistent" hypocrites. Mass media organs "speak endlessly about human rights [but] with ease and extraordinary irresponsibility trample on these rights." They laud *glasnost'* and citizens' constitutional right to receive information yet "avoid open and public discussion" and substantiation of their own "untruthful and biased" stories. Worst of all, mass media organs complain of "*diktat* of authorities" at the very same time that they themselves are attempting to establish "*diktat* of the press."

4. The Audience

In sharp contrast is the Judicial Chamber depiction of the media audience. Russian readers, viewers, and listeners are sympathetic but pitiable characters. They are naïve and gullible, easily defrauded and duped by unscrupulous journalists, advertisers, politicians, and publishers. They are undiscriminating consumers of information, unable to distinguish fact from fiction or beneficial from harmful information. Their tastes are crude and unsophisticated. They have an insatiable appetite for scandal, sensation, hyperbole, pornography, and perversion.

In Judicial Chamber opinions, the audience is not an independent actor, but a passive victim of outside forces. It is susceptible to any external influence, including those that seek to exacerbate ethnic, social, and religious divisions and to undermine public confidence in democratic institutions, officials, and legislation. Judicial Chamber language conveys this sense of passivity. Several opinions describe the audience as "led astray," "deceived," or "misinformed" by a speaker or publisher. Others refer to attempts to "introduce into the public consciousness" a certain idea, to "cause" readers to have a negative attitude, impression, or stereotype, or to "create insufficient public support" for specific officials or legislation.

This depiction of the naïve, credulous audience has important implications for Judicial Chamber treatment of harmful speech. It suggests the need for some sort of preliminary filter or protective device (whether it is media self-restraint, moral codes, or government supervision) to ensure dissemination of only information that benefits Russian audience and, ultimately, society.

5. The Target

The target of harmful speech appears in two guises—as complainant and as "absence." Several Judicial Chamber decisions involve claims by government or legislative personnel or groups that were allegedly defamed, humiliated, and discredited by mass media publications or broadcasts. In these opinions, the target is in the foreground, the initial impetus and focus of Judicial Chamber attention. The target is important, however, not as an individual but as the personification of his/her office. In each of these cases, the sole concern of the Judicial Chamber is the injury to state and society rather than individual. For example, in April 1995, the Judicial Chamber ruled that *Rossiiskaia Gazeta*'s article "The Thief's Hat Is on Fire," which accused Press Committee Chairman S.P. Gryzunov and his organization of illegal use of subsidies and budgetary funds, constituted "an abuse of the mass media and violation of legal and ethical norms." The Judicial Chamber defined the injury as "discredit[ing Gryzunov] as a leader of the federal administration," "undermin[ing] the professional reputation of a government institution," and "infring[ing] the rights and legal interests of citizens, especially the receipt of reliable information of social significance."

In other opinions, the target is strikingly absent from the text. Numerous cases deal with mass media dissemination of hate speech, especially ethnic slurs. Yet, there is no discussion of the actual or potential effect of such materials on the target groups or their members. Instead, the focus is exclusively on the societal implications. To the Judicial Chamber, the harm of hate speech is that it undermines government efforts to "normalize tragic interethnic conflict," foments ethnic discord and intolerance, and deepens societal cleavages.

Thus, the target emerges in Judicial Chamber opinions as, at best, a minor character. The real victim is society. The combined portrayal of target as "complainant" and "absence" only reinforces the Judicial Chamber's construction of harmful speech as nothing less than a serious threat to Russia's future.

6. The State

In the abstract, the state is idealized and sanctified. The Judicial Chamber speaks in respectful tones of the "institutions of Russian statehood" and exalts Russian legislators as "the people's representatives." It proclaims the "federal organs of power" (defined in capital letters as Russian Federation President, State Duma, and Government) off limits to media ridicule, humiliation, and attack. It is appalled by a commercial advertiser's irreverent use of "state symbols and attributes."

At a more immediate level, however, a very different picture of the Russian state emerges. The Judicial Chamber portrays actual legislative, administrative, judicial, and presidential personnel and bodies as inept, inexperienced, and overburdened. They appear fundamentally incapable of meeting the challenge of harmful speech.

Several Judicial Chamber opinions emphasize the failure of Russia's parliament to create an adequate legislative "base" to battle mass media abuses. They highlight significant gaps in such areas as dissemination of fascist materials, production of "dangerous" advertisements, and departures from registration certificates and broadcast licenses. Despite these glaring deficiencies in the lawmaking process, some legislators and legislative committees are unwilling to tolerate constructive criticism of their efforts. For example, the State Duma's Committee on Information Policy responded to Judicial Chamber "critical assessments" of its mass media-related drafts with an angry, public denunciation of the Judicial Chamber as "extra-constitutional."

The Judicial Chamber depicts the state as equally ineffective in enforcing the minimal law that does exist. Several opinions cite in particular the "insufficient control" of the mass media by government registration and procuratorial bodies. In Judicial Chamber opinions, state organs command little respect from the mass media. Publishers and authors of harmful materials act with impunity, ignoring official warnings from law enforcement authorities. To compound the problem, Russia's court system is clogged with citizens' libel and slander suits against the media.

Finally, Judicial Chamber opinions suggest that the state, in fact, contributes to the harmful speech problem. It does so by "covering up" information and denying journalists access to government meetings and personnel. The Judicial Chamber identifies as especially egregious in this regard the conduct of administrative and presidential agencies; these bodies are "more closed than former party committees." In the end, this inaccessibility of government disserves Russian state and society. It discourages proper verification of sources and leads to publication of unreliable, incomplete, and inaccurate information, bribery of officials, and outright "fabrication and conjecture."

C. Judicial Chamber Self-Definition

Thus, Judicial Chamber harmful speech opinions portray a country out of control, fast approaching social explosion and anarchy. With its gullible public, irresponsible media, and impotent state, Russia appears headed inevitably to its doom. Only immediate and decisive intervention can reverse this course. Since Russian leaders and official institutions are unable to perform this critical function, the Judicial Chamber must step into the brink as Russia's last hope. This notion of "compelled performance" is the basis for Judicial Chamber self-definition and authority.

1. Compelled Performance

The Judicial Chamber portrays itself first and foremost as a reactive institution, one that is set into motion only in response to some external stimulus. It underscores this point by beginning each opinion with direct reference to a specific triggering agent, event, or circumstance. In most cases, it cites a formal complaint or appeal from a named individual, legislative body, or government agency. Even where the Judicial Chamber itself initiated the opinion, it takes care to identify some outside impetus. For example, in its statement approving *Obshchaia Gazeta*'s publication of a fictitious coup plot, it opened with a description of widespread public concern and pleas for the Judicial Chamber "to express its attitude" toward the publication and to clarify "whether this case represented an exercise of freedom of speech or, on the contrary, an abuse of freedom of mass information."

Although the Judicial Chamber often refers to relevant Russian legislation, it defines its rulings and remedies (especially those that are most controversial) as fundamentally dictated by necessity and/or moral imperative. Thus, in its first statement, the Judicial Chamber announced that it was "necessary" to issue a formal condemnation of mass media use of unsubstantiated rumors, stories, and reports, which "fuel tragic interethnic conflict," "overt immorality," "defamation" of government institutions, and "destabilization of the sociopolitical situation." It focused particular attention on a *Zavtra* article entitled *Kremlin Secrets*. It acknowledged that its denunciation of this article would have no legal or practical impact. Nonetheless, the Judicial Chamber felt obligated to speak because it would be "wrong" to allow such an "odious publication" "to remain unheeded and unexamined."

The Judicial Chamber conveys this image of compelled performance most powerfully through its presentation of facts. In each case, it constructs the facts in a way that makes a comprehensive response by the Judicial Chamber appear both unavoidable and essential to the future of Russia. The Judicial Chamber typically starts the facts section of its opinions with a detailed and dramatic description of the allegedly harmful material at issue. It does not merely characterize the publication or broadcast as, for instance, "pornographic" or "subversive" or recapitulate the content in moderate, judicious language. Instead, it sets out the subject matter in colorful, even gory detail. It cites graphic and offensive titles and reproduces provocative and outrageous excerpts from texts and videotapes.

The Judicial Chamber makes no attempt to present the facts in a neutral fashion and to invite the reader to determine if the material is harmful or innocuous. It injects its own evaluations of publications, broadcasts, and parties throughout its opinions in blunt, unequivocal language. For example, in one decision, it introduced the facts section thus: "The publication 'Chechen Knot. 13 Theses' is obviously provocative in nature." It then proceeded to castigate a *Novyi Vzgliad* author for "delirious fabrications," "absurdity," "insulting, vile epithets," "unidimensional and primitive" style, and "misanthropic ideology."

In its construction of facts, the Judicial Chamber also makes a conscious effort to place each individual case into a broader context. It redefines the specific publication or program at issue as part of an overall harmful speech crisis that threatens Russian society, state, and democratic reform process. In so doing, it suggests that even the smallest transgression can lead to disastrous consequences. By recasting the individual harmful publication or broadcast as part of the larger threat to Russia rather than an isolated incident, the Judicial Chamber establishes a claim of authority for both decision and decision maker. The Judicial Chamber strengthens this claim in many opinions by tracing the misconduct under examination and the general harmful speech problem, in part, to official inaction. As a result, the Judicial Chamber appears to have no alternative but to respond. Anything else would be irresponsible and unthinkable.

The language, voice, and tone of Judicial Chamber opinions reinforce this impression of inevitability and compelled performance. Judicial Chamber opinions feature extensive use of words of obligation and necessity. Moreover, all published opinions are written in a univocal (or "monologic") third person singular. They are signed by Chairman Vengerov, not by individual judges.[244] There are no separate dissenting or concurring opinions that might suggest other readings of facts and law.[245] The tone is engaged, emotional, and judgmental. Opinions exude "concern," "regret," and, above all, "righteous indignation" about the case at hand and the general state of affairs in Russia. These factors combine to create a sense of unanimity and certitude. They send a clear message to the reader: There is only one possible interpretation of the facts and it is an interpretation that demands immediate and decisive action.

A prime illustration of these techniques is Decision No. 21, the Judicial Chamber's broad-scale attack on "mass media publications that incite social and nationalist intolerance." The Judicial Chamber provided a detailed description of specific racist, fascist, and anti-governmental articles with direct citation to titles and text. For example, it reproduced the title of a *Zavtra* article, "Yeltsinism-Hilterism," as evidence of that newspaper's "utter refusal to accept legitimate authority." It quoted a *Narodnoi Stroi* article's call for creation of an empire dedicated to "preservation and cultivation of the Aryan element . . . as first among Russians."

Throughout Decision No. 21, the Judicial Chamber emphasized the general societal implications of such publications. According to the Judicial Chamber, "crude and unsubstantiated attacks against . . . institutions of Russian statehood" promote "social intolerance." Publications that "create negative ethnic stereotypes" constitute a "social danger." They inspire "nationalist radicals" and "extremists" and "supply an "ideological base" for fascist armed groups.

The Judicial Chamber also made a point of noting the futile efforts of governmental authorities to control media "abuse of freedom of mass information." It castigated registration bodies, the Russian Press Committee, the procuracy, and the legislature for their inadequate responses to this critical societal problem. This led the

[244] In contrast, the Judicial Chamber Regulations call for the signature of Judicial Chamber members.

[245] According to the Statute on the Judicial Chamber and the Judicial Chamber Regulations, decisions are adopted by a majority of the total number of Judicial Chamber members (as are statements, recommendations, and expert conclusions). Reprimands and proposals to terminate media activity or to issue warnings to media founders or editorial staffs, however, must be approved by a "consensus" of Judicial Chamber members. The Judicial Chamber Regulations specifically provide that a member "who disagrees with the majority opinion can state in writing his separate opinion, which is attached to the case." No such opinions have been published thus far either in *Rossiiskaia Gazeta* or the Judicial Chamber's own collection of opinions.

Judicial Chamber to the inescapable conclusion that it must step to the fore and take action. In the words of the Judicial Chamber, "[I]t is impossible to tolerate any longer this abnormal and socially dangerous situation in which mass media publications incite social and nationalist hatred." With this claim of authority grounded in dire necessity, the Judicial Chamber concluded Decision No. 21 with a series of strikingly comprehensive proposals. It did not confine its remedies to the specific publications at issue, but rather, provided a blueprint for overall systemic reform, with the Judicial Chamber as architect, guide, and overseer. Thus, the notion of "compelled performance" is ultimately transformed into a rationale, indeed an imperative, for a highly activist Judicial Chamber.

2. Judicial Chamber Roles

The Judicial Chamber, then, assumes the mantle of Russia's savior, a position not chosen for itself but thrust upon it by sheer force of circumstances. In this capacity, it sets for itself an agenda that ranges far beyond that stipulated in its founding documents. Under the Judicial Chamber's self-fashioned program, it must do more than resolve information disputes and correct infractions of mass media legislation. It must also communicate the enormity of the harmful speech problem to spur official and public concern, identify the root causes of the problem, and offer constructive solutions.

In its least controversial role, the Judicial Chamber portrays itself as adjudicator of disputes. It tries fact and applies the law. It considers evidence, evaluates party testimony and arguments, and applies existing domestic and international law norms and rules to specific fact situations. The Judicial Chamber also speaks as a stern but fair disciplinarian. It reprimands offenders, metes out punishment, weighs mitigating factors, and when necessary, calls for further corrective action. Moreover, in several cases, the Judicial Chamber appears as special guardian of the weak and powerless. It makes particular efforts to protect the young and naïve from corruption, fraud, and deception.

In addition, the Judicial Chamber often figures as investigator and prosecutor. It scrutinizes publications and broadcasts for possible infringement of constitutional and mass media legislation and institutes proceedings on its own initiative against violators. Similarly, the Judicial Chamber independently uncovers and censures governmental misconduct in the mass media sphere.

The Judicial Chamber also speaks as dramatic raconteur. It conveys to the reader of its opinions the crisis proportions of Russia's harmful speech threat. Through the use of powerful language and imagery, it recasts each case as a morality play, part of the Manichean struggle between the forces of good and evil for control of Russia's soul and destiny.

Moreover, the Judicial Chamber portrays itself as objective and constructive outside critic of Russia's mass media system. As such, it appears uniquely qualified to conduct the full and impartial examination required to determine the sources of and contributors to Russia's harmful speech problem. In this capacity of diagnostician, the Judicial Chamber highlights fundamental systemic and attitudinal defects—a flawed and inadequate legislative base; haphazard enforcement by the state and the mass media; adverse, unintended effects of recent political, economic, and institutional reforms; and above all, the failure of Russian government, media, and public alike to "understand" the proper role of a "free press" in a post-Soviet democracy.

The Judicial Chamber defines itself as both architect and executor of an effective response to Russia's harmful speech challenge. In these functions, it assigns itself a variety of roles and responsibilities. It views itself as law creator, formulating statutory and regulatory schemes to address legislative gaps and defects in such critical areas as media registration, dissemination of fascist materials and deceptive advertisements, and media access to state personnel, meetings, and documents. The Judicial Chamber also assumes the position of economic and institutional reformer. It recommends adoption of economic policies to "strengthen" the press and limit dependence on government and commercial sponsors. Moreover, it calls for an overhaul of federal, regional, and local government procedures and bodies to improve the institutional machinery for enforcement of media rights and responsibilities.

Finally, for the Judicial Chamber, its most important and contested role is that of teacher and moral guide of Russian society. Since its inception, the Judicial Chamber has launched a massive campaign to train and educate Russian government, press, and citizenry about the appropriate status, rights, and responsibilities of a post-Soviet democratic press. It self-consciously directs its opinions toward the outside reader as well as the parties. It uses each dispute as a point of departure to interpret and explain broad constitutional and legal guarantees of speech, press, and information freedom and their legal and ethical limits.

A good example of this didactic role of the Judicial Chamber appears in Decision No. 69, the ruling against A.G. Nevzorov's television exposé of Russian women's correctional facilities. The Judicial Chamber took care to explain to the reader that "in general" media coverage of Russian penitentiaries "deserves support." It emphasized that "openness" of the prison system to the mass media and thus public opinion has practical value and explicit statutory basis. Such coverage is an "essential condition" to ensure observance of "generally-accepted principles and norms" within prisons. Moreover, "[t]he right of a journalist to collect and disseminate information, including information about the penitentiary system and its actual problems, is recognized and guaranteed by Russian legislation." The Judicial Chamber then proceeded to clarify that the media's right to information is not absolute: "However, realization of this right must not become the grounds and excuse for infringing the constitutional rights of citizens, including prisoners, to inviolability of private life." It concluded that by filming convicts without their consent, Nevzorov "flagrantly violated" constitutional, statutory, and ethical norms.

As the above example indicates, the Judicial Chamber speaks as moral arbiter as well as teacher. The Judicial Chamber, whose task consists of reminding Russian government, press, and public of the serious ethical principles and values at stake in harmful speech cases, is the conscience of the community. In virtually every opinion, it defines media infractions as violations of both law and "generally-recognized ethical norms." It conducts a public trial of the moral character and conduct of parties. It excoriates media and government defendants, holding them up as object lessons for public ridicule and censure. It also makes a point of communicating any mitigating factors, evidence of repentance, or other positive attitudes or behavior by parties. Throughout its opinions, the Judicial Chamber stresses the need to supplement legal methods with extralegal techniques. It calls upon parties to find "civilized" and "acceptable" means to settle information disputes and remedy losses informally. It urges self-regulation by professions, internal control by media and state organizations, and personal "self-restraint" by journalists. It favors extensive use of publicity as a sanction and deterrent.[282]

The Judicial Chamber's concerted effort and directive to combine legal and moral norms and techniques is the most notable and controversial aspect of its opinions and its charter for the future.[283] This blended approach is also the key feature of the Judicial Chamber's distinctive "conversation" about law, a topic that will be explored in Part V of this Article.

3. Self-Limitations

The Judicial Chamber has received little appreciation for its efforts to rescue the Russian society, state, and democracy from the harmful speech challenge. Critics commonly depict the Judicial Chamber as an extra-constitutional body that dispenses "justice" on an ad hoc basis in accordance with its own notions of law and morality. The Judicial Chamber's self-portrait is markedly different. It views its decision making and authority as subject to real procedural, factual, and legal constraints. Throughout its opinions, it makes a point of emphasizing and reassuring the reader of these limitations.

In its opinions, the Judicial Chamber conveys the impression that it operates within defined procedural and institutional parameters. It acts upon receipt of formal petitions from plaintiffs and considers counterclaims by media and government defendants. After due notice to parties, it holds "judicial hearings," in which designated "representatives" of parties participate. It acknowledges limits on its jurisdiction to hear cases. For example, in Decision No. 51, the Judicial Chamber expressly declined to provide a "legal evaluation" of a republic presidential decree, liability of a newspaper editorial office, "other questions of a property nature," and contributory actions by nonparty organizations on grounds that such matters fell outside its competence.

---

[282] The Judicial Chamber has recommended extensive media coverage of "abuses of freedom of mass information," prime offenders, and responses by law enforcement organs. It orders media to retract or "rectify" false, inaccurate, misleading, and libelous stories and often requires publication of its own critical evaluations of texts and authors.

[283] A revealing example of this "blended" approach appeared in Statement No. 1 On I. Andronov's Publication in *Zavtra* (Apr. 4, 1994): "A legal barrier should be erected against insolent, shameless, and groundless attacks on the institutions of Russian statehood, their leaders and representatives and here, ethical values should be used."

Similarly, the Judicial Chamber indicates qualified authority to remedy violations of mass media legislation. Often it confines itself to reprimanding offenders and issuing non-binding "proposals" for further action against defendants. It forwards case materials to the proper governmental and media channels and personnel "for adoption of measures stipulated by law." In many opinions, the Judicial Chamber reinforces this concern for procedural regularity by requiring formal publication in the official source for Judicial Chamber documents—*Rossiiskaia Gazeta.*

Judicial Chamber treatment of evidence and testimony points to another important constraint on decision making. It suggests that the Judicial Chamber can render judgment only after a thorough consideration of all facts, viewpoints, and circumstances. Opinions contain lengthy lists of documents and experts consulted by the Judicial Chamber. They also record the names of speakers at formal hearings (the parties, their representatives, and interested third persons). In several opinions, the Judicial Chamber discusses presentations by claimants and defendants, noting strengths and, especially, weaknesses in both sides' arguments.[294]

Judicial Chamber opinions call attention to the legal as well as factual bases of decisions. The message is that all rulings are grounded in and even dictated by law, not personal whim or subjective determination. The Judicial Chamber takes care to support its conclusions with direct citation to governing domestic and international law norms and rules. For example, in its ruling against media dissemination of discriminatory employment advertisements, the Judicial Chamber quoted verbatim guarantees of gender equality set forth in the Russian Constitution and Labor Code and the United Nations Convention on Elimination of All Forms of Discrimination Against Women. Moreover, in every opinion, the Judicial Chamber prefaces its holdings, statements, and recommendations with explicit reference to authorizing provisions in its Statute or Regulations and, occasionally, other Russian legislation.

Finally, the Judicial Chamber makes an effort throughout its opinions to persuade the reader that its approach to harmful speech cases is reasonable and balanced. For instance, in Statement No. 2 the Judicial Chamber reported that it had "refrained from hasty conclusions about the accuracy of the publication" at issue. This was due to the fact that there was an ongoing criminal investigation of the case, "the results of which [were] still unknown." The Judicial Chamber also conveys a sense of cautious, balanced decision making by emphasizing the positive as well as negative aspects of media dissemination of information. Thus, it will pledge its support for such general principles as "pluralism" and "professional creative freedom of journalists" in the same opinion that it denounces a specific case of media "abuse of freedom of mass information."

---

[294] For example, in Decision No. 11 On the Publication in *Ekspress-Gazeta* No. 5 (March 1994) of "Some People Know How to Live!" (Apr. 21, 1994), the Judicial Chamber rejected *Ekspress-Gazeta*'s argument that because it was a "young" newspaper it had to employ a sensationalistic style to "get on [its] feet" and "defeat [its] rivals." The Judicial Chamber stated that it was "impermissible to assert that one can use cheap sensations, publish untrue and insulting materials, and mock the institutions of Russian statehood for the sake of winning in the newspaper market."

An excellent illustration of this technique appears in Decision No. 43, the Judicial Chamber's ruling against "unreliable," "inaccurate," and "insulting" critiques of Russia's draft advertising law. In this opinion, the Judicial Chamber applauded "legitimate and constructive" media criticism of the bill. According to the Judicial Chamber, such publications were "justified" and could potentially "contribute to improvement of the draft law." The Judicial Chamber expressed its sensitivity to the "understandable" press "concern" about the content of the law and its implications for economic reform, the market economy, and "formation of an economic base for independence of the mass media." It then meticulously distinguished the materials before it from exemplary "objective, reliable, and professional" critiques. In so doing, the Judicial Chamber communicated that its decision should not be read as an arbitrary, blanket condemnation of all media critique but, rather, as a reasonable, narrow ruling against publications that misstated, distorted, and discredited the substance and goals of the draft advertising law.

V. Judicial Chamber Conversation: What Kind of Conversation?

In the final analysis, the Judicial Chamber defines itself as, above all, a legal institution. According to its members, it is "guided by principles of law" and subject to the "high ethical demands" of law. It defends and upholds "legal principles" even in the face of official, media, and public opposition. Its mission is not only to apply law but also to "explain," "reveal," and "create" law. Thus, Judicial Chamber opinions are as much a "conversation" about law as a "performance." They communicate to parties, legal and journalistic communities, and lay audience alike the Judicial Chamber's vision of law in post-Soviet Russia.

. . . .

B. What Kind of Conversation?

1. Rejection of White's Democratic and Authoritarian Typologies

The Judicial Chamber's conversation is a conversation about democracy yet is not "democratic" as defined by Professor White in the U.S. context. Clearly, this is not a conversation among equals. Throughout its opinions, the Judicial Chamber stakes out a position of dominance vis-à-vis its reader. Whether in the capacity of judge, teacher, moral arbiter, or disciplinarian, it claims a superior understanding of the form, substance, and goals of Russia's evolving legal system. Moreover, unlike White's democratic conversation, the Judicial Chamber explicitly excludes some individuals from participation—those journalists and publishers that are so evil or incorrigible as to be beyond redemption or appeal.

The Judicial Chamber's conversation diverges from the democratic model in other crucial aspects. The Judicial Chamber does not draw on shared values or understandings of such fundamental concepts as democracy or the rule of law. It seeks to create and inculcate such values. The Judicial Chamber also does not attempt to engage the independent judgment or critical reasoning of the reader and invite him to apply law to complex fact situations on his own. Instead, it guides and teaches the reader how to do so. Furthermore, the Judicial Chamber does not "hol[d] up its own efforts to [audience] scrutiny and criticism." It asserts and defends its authority as legal and moral actor. Indeed, it often appears hypersensitive to outside criticism.

The Judicial Chamber does not adopt the democratic format because it cannot do so. Such a conversation requires all participants to know, accept, and share basic notions of law and legality as well as a common commitment to and definition of democracy and the rule of law. With the low level of legal culture in Russia today, the Judicial Chamber addresses an audience that lacks familiarity and respect for legal norms and rules. Moreover, as repeated political and ethnic crises underscore, it speaks to an audience deeply divided by cultural, ethnic, and ideological differences, with sharply divergent views regarding Russia's past, present, and future. Thus, at this point in Russian history, a democratic conversation about law would appear to be both premature and futile.

At first glance, the Judicial Chamber's conversation seems to fit the authoritarian model identified by White in U.S. opinions. The Judicial Chamber "reduces difficulty to simplicity." It often characterizes facts and law with a "blunt and unquestioning finality" and "demands simple and total obedience" of its reader to those interpretations. It claims for itself the authority, even the obligation, to "remake" constitutional and statutory language at will.[333] It repeatedly rejects "legalistic argumentation" in favor of vague, often unarticulated ethical principles and standards. The most powerful argument to the Judicial Chamber is framed not in terms of a reasoned discussion of legal norms and rules, but rather in accordance with the Judicial Chamber's notions of responsibility and benefit to Russian society. Like White's authoritarian judge, the Judicial Chamber thus emerges as a "wise judge, entitled to act as the 'conscience' of the community." It "assert[s]" "the power of the moral, aesthetic, and civilized actor over the language and categories of the law."

Yet, as I explain in detail in the next section, the Judicial Chamber's conversation is not authoritarian in the strictest sense. The essential difference is that the Judicial Chamber does not seek to impose a vision on its audience. Instead, it makes a real effort to guide, persuade, and train its reader. In essence, its goal is to prepare its reader for participation at some future date in a genuinely open and free democratic conversation.

---

[333] The Judicial Chamber views Russia's skeletal legislative base as creating a dangerous vacuum, which facilitates widespread violations of citizens' constitutional rights and freedoms. It sees itself as obligated to fill this gap in practice. Accordingly, it independently remakes constitutional and statutory language to ensure full legal coverage of specific fact patterns and problems. For example, a common technique is to insert adjectives to modify constitutional provisions. Thus, the Judicial Chamber often restates the constitutional right to receive information as the right to receive "reliable" or "objective" information. Another approach is to expand existing statutory categories and definitions. For instance, in a number of opinions, it unilaterally extends the concept of "abuse of freedom of mass information," set out in article 4 of the Law On the Mass Media, to cases involving media critique of government officials and institutions. This permits the harshest possible penalties against offenders.

The Judicial Chamber rejects the authoritarian model because it too is incompatible with current Russian conditions. First, such a format would likely be ineffective in achieving the Judicial Chamber's principal objective—creating the new legal culture needed for a full-fledged Russian democracy ruled by law. It is impossible to change long-standing popular attitudes and customs—let alone develop a legal culture from scratch—overnight by mere fiat. Second, an authoritarian conversation would lack theoretical and popular legitimacy. Resort to authoritarian techniques would suggest historical associations with Russia's discredited Tsarist and Soviet totalitarian past and would likely generate popular resistance. Third, from a purely practical institutional standpoint, such an approach would be problematic. The Judicial Chamber has minimal enforcement powers to back up its commands. Moreover, as a new body, it is unable to draw on an historical track record or reservoir of popular respect for and compliance with its rulings. To make matters worse, because of its uncertain status in the Russian political, legal, and constitutional structure, it cannot even rely on more established government organs to implement its decisions. The Judicial Chamber without legal or practical authority could be authoritarian in name only.

Thus, neither the "democratic" or "authoritarian" models proposed by Professor White in the U.S. context adequately describe the Russian Judicial Chamber's conversation about law. As I will demonstrate in the next section, the best analytical framework for understanding Judicial Chamber opinions is the "parental" model originated by Harold Berman in 1950.

2. Parental Conversation

a. Berman's Parental Law Model

In his path-breaking study *Justice in Russia: An Interpretation of Soviet Law*,[341] Professor Berman introduced the concept of parental law to explain the distinctive features of the evolving Soviet Russian legal system. The cornerstone of the parental model is its emphasis on the "nurturing" or "upbringing" role of law.[342] This leads to a new definition of the relationship between law and the people it addresses. Law is a "parent" and "teacher" and the "subject of law" is a "child or youth to be trained, guided, disciplined, protected." The parental model views the individual primarily in terms of his/her membership in the group. It defines the legal person not as an "independent possessor of rights and duties" but as a "dependent member of the collective." As a result, the parental model places heavy emphasis on cooperation and responsibility for group welfare. It subordinates individual rights to collective interests, regarding such rights as, in essence, "conferred in trust" for society as a whole.

Another important feature of the parental model is its view of the transitional, embryonic nature of society, state, and law. Just as the legal person is "young," so too is

[341] Harold J. Berman, Justice In Russia: An Interpretation of Soviet Law (1950).

[342] The Russian term is *vospitatel'naia rol' sovetskogo prava.*

the system in which he is located. Each citizen is part of a "growing, unfinished, still immature society, which is moving toward a new and higher phase of development."

Law in the parental model has several basic goals. At the most immediate level, it seeks to "protect" the individual "against the consequences of his own ignorance." Its broader and more ambitious objective is to create the appropriate internal conditions to advance society to the next stage of development. Accordingly, under the parental model, law must help "unite and organize and educate" society. It must mold the thinking and law-consciousness of each citizen to instill a genuine belief in and respect for official legal values. At the same time, law must promote the moral education of society. It must "guide the people to virtue." In short, the parental model calls for the use of law to accomplish nothing less than the transformation of every citizen into the "new person" required for the establishment of a more advanced order.

The parental model relies primarily on "communication" and "example" to achieve these goals. It envisions widespread "propagandizing" of law, that is, a concerted effort by legal institutions and personnel to "circulate information about law" to the general populace. It also features "persuasion" and "suggestion" as tools of legal communication and socialization. Thus, in trials, it directs judges and counsel to "pay special attention to the educational effect" of court proceedings on parties, courtroom spectators, and the public at large. This includes identifying and explaining the overall "social and political aspects of the case" in order to convince immediate and outside audiences that statutory provisions are properly applied to the specific facts at issue.

The parental model also turns to "example" as a technique to make abstract legal and moral values accessible to the public. It calls for extensive use of publicity. It presents concrete role models for public approbation and emulation and "exposes" the "shame of offenders." Similarly, the parental model "induces" offenders to confess, repent, and undergo public re-education in order to inculcate and reinforce approved norms and patterns of behavior in both offenders and society as a whole.[360]

b. Application to the Judicial Chamber

The Judicial Chamber defines the participants in its conversation about law in a way that is markedly similar to that under Berman's parental model. In its opinions, the Judicial Chamber converses with an audience of youths. It speaks to the "young institutions of Russian statehood," still shaky, immature, and fundamentally unprepared to govern a post-Soviet democracy. It addresses media recently liberated from the shackles of censorship, which in their youthful exuberance commit excesses and abuses of their new-found rights and freedoms. It converses with media consumers, who are naïve and unsophisticated and require constant outside vigilance and protection "against the consequences of their own ignorance." It speaks to litigants' representatives and legal personnel with only a rudimentary knowledge of law, who elevate the letter of the law

[360] In some cases, the court's role "is reduced to that of making the accused an object lesson for others, attempting to humiliate him and to make him suffer."

over its spirit and mistake legal rights for a license to act without constraint. Finally, it addresses the public at large, unversed in democratic and legal values and in need of careful guidance, teaching, and training.

The tone of the Judicial Chamber's conversation is distinctly parental. It is loving, protective, and educative, yet also stern, moralistic, and disciplinary. Like an overwrought parent, the Judicial Chamber at times reaches the point of utter frustration with its audience's slow pace of learning and continuing misbehavior despite repeated correction. It expresses this impatience in bursts of intemperate language and occasionally retreats to lecturing rather than guiding its reader.

The basic goal of the Judicial Chamber's conversation is identical to that of the parental model. It is to create the requisite conditions for Russia to progress to the next, higher stage of development, in this case a democracy ruled by law. Through its opinions, the Judicial Chamber endeavors to raise popular law-consciousness. It attempts to familiarize the reader with the existing legal framework. It sets out applicable constitutional and statutory provisions and meticulously explains their scope and limits. It demonstrates proper application of general legal principles and rules to specific fact patterns with concrete illustrations. It also outlines necessary reforms and improvements in Russia's legal system.

The Judicial Chamber also makes a real effort through its opinions to "unite and organize" society. It attempts to create a sense of community by identifying, isolating, and excommunicating outsiders. It appeals to public patriotism and pride in Russia's victory over "German Fascism" and Soviet communism. It encourages shared commitment to the defense and further development of post-Soviet democracy. The Judicial Chamber calls upon all elements of Russian society to join in a common struggle against the forces that threaten the Russian state, society, and reform process—fascism, immorality, ethnic separatism, anti-governmental propaganda, and the like. It enlists the Russian government, professional associations, and the general public in the battle against media dissemination of harmful speech.[377] The Judicial Chamber strives to make democracy and the rule of law the common cause and unifying bond of Russian society.

As under the parental model, the Judicial Chamber relies heavily on communication and example to achieve its objectives. In communicating legal and moral norms and rules, it puts a premium on simplicity and accessibility to the reader. It recasts complex fact situations in simple, unambiguous terms. There are no gray areas or possible alternative interpretations of the facts. Similarly, in its treatment of law, the Judicial Chamber tends to paraphrase, summarize, and recapitulate statutory provisions in language accessible to the lay reader. It often removes potential uncertainties, contradictions, or inconsistencies in statutory provisions.[380] A prime example is its

[377] The Judicial Chamber calls for similar collective action to defend media rights against official interference.

[380] In some opinions, however, the Judicial Chamber deliberately points to problems in statutory language and suggests needed reforms.

approach to one of the thorniest constitutional issues worldwide—the apparent conflict between the journalist's right to speak and the audience's right not to be harmed by that speech. The Judicial Chamber dissolves this conflict by redefining the constitutional right at issue as a collective right of the citizenry to receive information rather than an individual right of the journalist to free expression.[381] It thus reduces each harmful speech case to a simple question: Was the information disseminated by the media beneficial or detrimental to the interests of Russian society as a whole? In so doing, it avoids the use of complex, multi-factored or pronged tests to balance individual and collective rights. It also eliminates the need for direct evidence and evaluation of the actual impact of a publication or broadcast on the immediate audience. The Judicial Chamber's sole concern is whether the material in question has the potential to promote or undermine public welfare in the broadest sense.

The Judicial Chamber also follows the parental model in its emphasis on persuasion and suggestion as communicative devices. It self-consciously constructs its opinions with an eye to convincing the reader of the propriety, even necessity, of its action in the case at hand. As has been discussed above, it uses a variety of techniques for this purpose. These include depiction of parties' attitudes and misconduct in stark, dramatic language, verbatim reproduction of offensive media titles and material, and extensive use of dicta. Furthermore, as under the parental model, the Judicial Chamber attempts to persuade the reader by highlighting the larger context and implications of each case. It explains the social, political, economic, and ideological causes of Russia's harmful speech problem and underscores its threat to Russian society, state, and the democratic reform process.

Finally, in conformity with the parental model, the Judicial Chamber regards "example" as a particularly effective technique to tutor its audience in new, democratic notions of law and morality. It crafts its opinions as virtual morality plays, featuring positive and negative role models. It uses party attitudes and conduct as concrete object lessons to make abstract, unfamiliar values and rules accessible to the reader. It emphasizes shame, repentance, confession, and reform. To achieve maximum educational and demonstration effect, the Judicial Chamber reprimands and corrects behavior that is not in strict violation of the law but, nonetheless, detrimental to the overall interests of Russian society. Moreover, it does not confine its inquiry to the specific litigants before it. It holds nonparties as well as parties up as examples for public edification and guidance.

The Judicial Chamber's choice of the parental format is a natural and understandable response to Russia's distinctive conditions. Parental law is a familiar approach, deeply rooted in Russian history. It seems ideally suited to the current

[381] Interestingly, the Judicial Chamber generally defines the official interference cases as well as infringements of the constitutional right of citizens to receive information rather than of expressive and press freedoms. This reinforces the image of Russian press as representative or trustee of society rather than independent actor.

transitional period. It recognizes the embryonic nature of Russian democracy and legality and the need for gradual change and development. It appropriately calls for revolution from below rather than above. It seeks to create a new legal culture by nurturing and transforming popular law-consciousness over time through education, persuasion, and guidance.

At the same time, the parental model's protective emphasis also fits today's Russia. It offers a theoretical framework for safeguarding the Russian citizenry and state from the inevitable dislocations and crises of the transitional era. In particular, it provides a rationale for swift, decisive action against those who would exploit gaps in changing legal and political structures to harm the Russian public, government, and reform process.

Yet, despite these advantages, the Judicial Chamber's parental conversation did not meet with an enthusiastic reception. Its intended audience often balked at participation. Media and government officials routinely resisted the Judicial Chamber's guidance and correction and challenged its very legitimacy and authority to act. The parental tone of Judicial Chamber opinions appears to alienate many readers. Indeed, there is some empirical evidence that contemporary Russians reacted with intense hostility and "passionate anger" to texts they considered patronizing and demeaning to their intellect. The Judicial Chamber's blending of legal and ethical norms and techniques, which is such a central feature of the parental model, seemed to be another source of sensitivity and concern. For many in post-Soviet Russia, this approach rose the specter of a return to the "dark era" of extralegal tribunals and censorship bodies. As a result, some argue that the one redeeming feature of the Judicial Chamber was its very lack of enforcement powers.

Nonetheless, the Judicial Chamber continued to receive appeals and petitions from Russian media representatives, government officials, and citizens. It issued and published opinions on a wide variety of mass media-related topics. It was the most consistent source of interpretation of constitutional provisions on expressive, information, and press freedoms. The Judicial Chamber even saw its jurisdiction expanded to include resolution of disputes arising from media coverage of national election campaigns. Thus, the Judicial Chamber's impact on Russian legal culture seems to have been extensive and worthy of note.

VI. Concluding Remarks on Comparative Law Translation of Methodology

Comparative law has long been the orphan of legal academia, its practitioners dismissed as mere translators of foreign legal phenomena and its scholarly product tagged with the lethal label of "descriptive." The result today is considerable "methodological anxiety" in the field as comparative law scholars search for the grand theory, paradigm, or model that will at long last secure respect and acceptance of their work. Not surprisingly, many scholars have turned directly to mainstream U.S. legal literature for inspiration. Recent articles on comparative and foreign law topics have applied law and economics, critical race theory, rhetorical analysis, feminist jurisprudence, and systems analysis with mixed success. This Article is no exception.

In this Article, I used two methodologies developed by U.S. legal scholars for the study of U.S. judicial opinions—narrative analysis and discourse analysis—to examine Russian Judicial Chamber opinions. Through narrative analysis, I sought to identify the recurring plots and characters in the stories told by the Judicial Chamber about media dissemination of harmful speech. Narrative analysis revealed a disturbing portrait of post-Soviet Russia as a society out of control, a naïve citizenry under constant assault from irresponsible media yet largely unprotected by a young, inexperienced government. It presented the Judicial Chamber as the reluctant savior of Russia, compelled by dire necessity to serve as the last line of defense against the barrage of subversive, immoral, deceptive, and dangerous materials that threaten the future of post-Soviet democracy.

Through discourse analysis, I sought to identify the Judicial Chamber's techniques for communicating with parties, the legal community, the media, the government, and the general public. This analysis focused on the type of conversation between the Judicial Chamber and the reader of its opinions. Initially, my goal was to choose between the two types of conversation presented by White in the American context—"democratic" or "authoritarian." I ultimately concluded, however, that neither described the Judicial Chamber's conversation nearly as well as the "parental" model developed by Berman in 1950 to explain the distinctive Russian approach to law.

In the process of applying narrative analysis and discourse analysis, I discovered some of the rewards and risks of importing U.S. legal methodology into the comparative law field. On the positive side, I found that at least two of these methodologies can be valuable tools for communicating foreign legal phenomena to lay and expert audiences alike. Both narrative analysis and discourse analysis proved successful as techniques for bringing foreign judicial opinions to life. They revealed subtle nuances, unstated premises, and larger context in a format accessible to even the lay American reader. In so doing, these methodologies furthered a central ethnographic mission of the comparative law scholar—to "render the foreign familiar."

I learned that application of U.S. methodology can yield new insights for the foreign law expert as well. Specifically, narrative analysis and discourse analysis highlighted aspects of Judicial Chamber policy and practice that more conventional research and analytical techniques might have missed—aspects that the Judicial Chamber seldom expresses explicitly in its opinions and commentaries. These include the Judicial Chamber's definition of itself, its relationship with its audience, its place in the post-Soviet political and legal systems, and its "blended" solution to Russia's "free press" problems. Focusing on the tone, language, and style of Judicial Chamber opinions was particularly useful in identifying potential tensions and conflicts in the Judicial Chamber's practice and in understanding public resistance and criticism of its efforts.

More generally, application of narrative analysis and discourse analysis to Judicial Chamber opinions helped shed light on the overall progress of post-Soviet legal reform.

The Judicial Chamber's harmful speech stories proved to be a rich source of information on Russia's concrete successes and continuing problems in implementing its new post-Soviet Constitution and legislation. In highlighting institutional, procedural, and attitudinal impediments, these stories also pointed to possible directions for future reform of the legal system. A narrative analysis of Judicial Chamber opinions offered insights as well into changing definitions and relationships between citizen, state, and media in the post-Soviet era. It suggested that Russia is still only in the early stages of transition toward its ideal democracy founded on the rule of law.

Analysis of Judicial Chamber discourse may ultimately yield even more fundamental lessons for the Russian law specialist about post-Soviet legal reform efforts. By focusing on how rather than what the Judicial Chamber communicates in its opinions, this approach revealed a surprising but consistent pattern of "parental" conversation about law between the Judicial Chamber and the reader. Discourse analysis in turn may provide important signals of how Russia's current leadership proposes to address the critical problem of creating a legal culture. Indeed, preliminary research suggests that the re-emergence of "parental law" is by no means confined to the Judicial Chamber context. For example, as I have discussed elsewhere, the Russian president and legislature have already adopted what can only be described as a parental theory of information rights. Thus, Berman's parental model may also offer the Russian law specialist the best framework for studying the evolving post-Soviet legal reform process as a whole.

On a more sobering note, however, analysis of Judicial Chamber discourse and narrative also revealed the very real dangers in applying U.S. methodology to foreign legal systems. I discovered that use of such methodology can exacerbate the comparative law scholar's already "despairingly difficult" "problem of translation." It can entail multiple layers and forms of translation, each rife with possibilities for distortion. My experience illustrates the types of translations and associated problems that a scholar may confront in using U.S. methodology in a foreign context.

In applying discourse analysis and narrative analysis to Judicial Chamber opinions, I encountered five distinct translations, each of which presented theoretical and practical difficulties. "Every act of communication . . . is an act of translation." Thus, the first translation I confronted was the central topic of this Article—the Judicial Chamber's communication with its audience through harmful speech opinions and the audience's reception of that communication. This process of communication and reception constituted a classic example of a translation within a single language and community. What was problematic was my role as analyst of this translation. In essence, my task was to evaluate how a Russian judicial body communicated through Russian-language texts with a Russian audience and the likely response of that audience. Yet, my vantage point was that of an outside observer, at a vast spatial, linguistic, and cultural distance from both the author and reader of Judicial Chamber opinions.

Only compounding these difficulties was the Article's second translation—the translation of American methodology to Russian context. This translation required the use of methodologies that had been developed for the study of U.S. judicial opinions but never tested in or adapted for specific Russian conditions. Thus, there was a real risk that application of U.S. discourse and narrative techniques would yield an inaccurate, incomplete, or even distorted picture of Russian legal phenomena. One concern was that use of these methodologies might lead me to read into Judicial Chamber opinions implicit meanings or patterns that were in fact unwarranted. Another potential danger was that I might become so locked into methodology that I could miss key points or lessons of cases. At worst, I might unconsciously distort Russian reality to fit pre-existing American methodology.

I confronted a third translation when I attempted to record the findings of my analysis of Judicial Chamber discourse and narrative. My task at this stage was to translate a peculiarly Russian experience into a language and format accessible to an American audience. As a preliminary matter, I sought to make Judicial Chamber opinions available to a non-Russian-speaking audience. This entailed two additional translations—linguistic and cultural. I had to translate Russian-language texts into English and at the same time convey discrete cultural meanings and "modes of thought." Many scholars have justly described this effort at linguistic and cultural translation as "impossible." As James Boyd White has warned, "[i]t requires . . . an attempt to be perfectly at home in two worlds, an attempt that must always fail." There is always substantial risk that "connotations" will be "added" or "lost" in the process of linguistic and cross-cultural translation. In the case of Judicial Chamber materials, translation proved particularly challenging because of the extensive use of idiomatic expressions rooted in Russian history and culture.[425] Often, there were no satisfactory English-language equivalents to capture the rich texture and range of meanings of the original Russian-language phrases.

Translation of Russian experience into the stories told in this Article also proved to be problematic. I now had to become storyteller as well as observer and translator. This new role carried with it its own potential dangers and distortions. These included the temptations to embellish or exaggerate for dramatic effect and to use material selectively to ensure a coherent storyline or uniform depiction of characters. My major concern was that by recasting the Russian experience as stories I might leave the American audience with an unintended negative impression of the Judicial Chamber and its approach to law.[428] Use of the narrative format might also trivialize this body's

[425] Idiomatic, even obscene, phrases appear most often in the Judicial Chamber's direct quotations of material from newspaper articles or broadcast videotapes.

[428] The stories told by the Judicial Chamber, of course, are not necessarily true. In attempting a comparison, one must, as Walter Weyrauch has pointed out, compare myth with myth and reality with reality. Walter Otto Weyrauch, *Oral Legal Traditions of Gypsies and Some American Equivalents (Gypsy Law Symposium)*, 45 American Journal of Comparative Law 407, 412 (1997). Hence, it would not be appropriate to compare the stories told by the Russian Judicial Chamber with the reality of contemporary American law. At the same time, it is important to remember that focusing on U.S. judicial opinions is itself problematic. Due to limited publication of U.S. opinions, narrative and discourse analyses of U.S. decisions may produce a distorted picture of American reality as well.

significant accomplishments and contributions to the Russian legal reform process. In my capacity as storyteller, I became conscious as never before of the comparative law scholar's dual responsibility to audience and foreign legal system. This responsibility weighed particularly heavy in this case where most of the audience had no access to the original Russian-language sources and, hence, no means to verify or challenge my rendition of Judicial Chamber theory and practice.

In conclusion, my experience suggests that U.S. methodologies can be useful tools for examining foreign legal systems, but that they must be applied with flexibility, caution, and, above all, sensitivity to context.[429] The ultimate lesson of this Article is that the scholar must be prepared for the unexpected—the divergences from usual patterns, the spontaneous adaptations of methodology to a foreign environment, the new answers to questions formulated in the American context. Comparative law translation of methodology, thus, may do more than render the foreign familiar. It may render the familiar foreign as well.

[429] This sensitivity to context, however, may have its own dangers.

Controlling Content on Television in Russia*

Svetlana Kolesnik

The Russian Federation legislation makes no special provisions for control over mass media content. According to article 29(5) of the Constitution, freedom of mass information is guaranteed, and censorship is prohibited.

As of this writing, there is still no broadcasting law in Russia. This media environment therefore allows for voluntary use of frequencies allocated for the radio and television services. Today, the licensing process is regulated by the Decree on Television and Radio Licensing in the Russian Federation approved by the government on December 7, 1994. This Statute creates an advisory role for the Commission on Broadcasting formed by the Federal Service of Russia on Television and Radio and by the Ministry of Communication. Specialists in broadcasting, actors, sociologists, and lawyers serving the public interest are invited to become involved with activities of the Commission.

As it considers applications, the Commission generally puts forward certain demands on the content of the proposed channel. Every license contains a channel description defining the broadcasting character. Analyzing the programming of twenty-seven radio stations in Moscow, we find at least six, or about twenty percent, that do not observe the license conditions. The situation in other regions of the country is not as well-known, as the Commission does not have the staff to monitor broadcasting outside Moscow.

Why are broadcasters so insensitive to the conditions of their licenses? Economic pressure forces them to disregard license conditions, to stop thinking about the public interest, and to generally move toward a cheaper format. For example, two private television companies in Nizhni Novgorod, "Volga" and "Nizhegorodskaya," use the format typical of many regional companies: American movies, often pirated, news items captured from foreign satellite channels, and a lot of advertisements. The absence of a proper mechanism of license observance has led to the exclusion of a tangible public interest from the mentality of Russian broadcasters.

The peculiarity of the development of broadcasting in Russia reflects the rapid move from total ideological control over the media towards the absolute absence of any control. During this period, however, the necessary and traditional role played by the state, whereby public regulators restrain the influence of capital and advertisers while securing the public interest, has not been developed. Furthermore, economic stagnation,

---

* Post-Soviet Media Law & Policy Newsletter, Sept. 5, 1996 (Supp.), at 3.

the increase in prices for signal delivery, and the lack of financial support from the state budget have brought state television close to bankruptcy.

Under this environment, financial privileges and subsides that television and radio companies receive from the state power organs eventually determine the companies' political position. Recent elections for the State Duma in 1995 and for the President in 1996 provide the best examples of politically slanted television. There are four local state television channels and two private television channels in Nizhni Novgorod. All four state channels are subsidized by the local administration, which is said to avoid direct pressure while using certain financial levers to exert influence on the channels. During the State Duma elections, Governor Boris Nemtsov promoted himself by promising a financial reward for positive coverage. Nemtsov's competitor, Mr. Rasteriiaev, appeared in television programming only when, according to the law, he was granted free time. Today, all Russian media understand the situation in this way: the refusal to cooperate with state authorities means an end to financial support as well as other potential penalties.

The Federal Service on Television and Radio recently formed the Regional Commissions on Television and Radio, which are responsible for local licensing. These licenses became an important tool in the hands of local administrations that managed to take control of these Commissions. For example, the head of the Commission in Tomsk is the Tomsk governor-adviser. If a company is not loyal to the administration, the company will not receive a license or is in danger of losing it.

At the same time, a company loyal to the administration can get a channel without licensing. NTV, a well-known property of the financial group Most, got the prime-time hours of the state-owned fourth channel two years ago without going through the licensing process. It became known, recently, that the President assured NTV that, by decree, he will grant them an entire channel. The Federal Service on Television and Radio played no formal role in this process, nor did its licensing commission. NTV's preferential treatment is widely seen as payment for the channel's vital support of Boris Yeltsin during the 1996 election campaign. During the campaign, the head of NTV, Igor Malashenko, played a key role as a presidential adviser.

The mass media's growing dependence on state structures is distorting its performance. A recent article in *The Moscow Times* by Catherine Fitzpatrick, Eurasian program coordinator for the Committee to Protect Journalists, describes the climate for the news media in Russia as "difficult, even frightening." As she noted, "paradoxically under Yeltsin, the press has suffered its most brutal attacks in decades."

Many journalists acknowledge that control over media content related to economic and political issues is very extensive and reflects strong political concerns. Mr. Malashenko controls every word in NTV's news programs. As does Ksenia Ponomareva, the head of the ORT's news program "Vremia." Before the 1996 presidential elections, ORT fired many professional journalists and hired students. "I hate the word professionals," Mr. Ponomareva said. Former "Vremia" correspondent Lilia Lashenko stated, "I cannot understand why they fired us. We were able to reelect Yeltsin." Perhaps it was a little too risky to work in the presidential campaign with the people who once contributed to building the most democratic institution of the Russian society—our mass media. These people were educated by the struggle for the freedom of the press and strove to enhance journalistic professionalism. They have opinions and are not ready to change yet again.

In 1994, the Faculty of Journalism, Moscow State University, and the Research Center of Middle Tennessee State University conducted a sociological study entitled "Freedom of Expression and Journalists." The study indicated that journalists felt rather free expressing their views in the presence of their editors-in-chief. Furthermore, there were few differences in the responses of American and Russian journalists. It would be interesting to repeat the same study today, at a time when journalists describe the atmosphere in editorial broads as one of overwhelming hostility, and where collectives are hostile to the editors-in-chief and vice versa.

The main reason for this hostility in private television is the tough control over content exercised by editors and owners. Victor Tzoi, owner of the television company Integral and radio company Prospect in the city of Habarovsk, provided perhaps the most striking illustration. During the 1996 election campaign, his companies broadcast political ads and feature stories about Mr. Tzoi, and journalists worked as public relations officers for his candidacy. Mr. Tzoi is in the State Duma and, as vice chairman of the Mass Media Committee, a significant voice in determining Russian mass media policy.

New industrial and political clans controlling the political and economic life of the Russian society exercised thorough pressure over broadcasting during the presidential campaign of 1996. The result in many cases was that journalists' freedom of expression was limited to the goal of reelecting Mr. Yeltsin. Even the ORT and NTV's choice of movies was determined by the task of the moment: to expose communists as the evil of the world.

Today, despite many achievements in the field of broadcasting in Russia, and all the guarantees of freedom of the press in the Russian Federation Constitution, we can nevertheless trace new attempts to limit freedom of expression broadcasting by the party of power. We can say that modern Russian broadcasting is treated by the new political elite as ideological institutions where journalists are considered ideological workers in service to the state and/or private owners.

C.

Advertising

The MMM Case: Implications for the Russian Media*

Frances H. Foster

The collapse of the MMM investment fund on July 29 sent shock waves throughout Russia and the world. It provided a graphic illustration of the dangers of attempting to introduce capitalism overnight into Russia. Lured by glossy television and newspaper advertisements promising 3000 percent annual dividends, California vacations, Paris apartments and the like, an estimated ten million Russian citizens invested billions of rubles in what turned out to be a classic Ponzi scheme.

The MMM case has important potential implications for the mass media. It brings to the fore the essential question of whether Russia should rely primarily on the market or on government regulation to sort out truth from falsehood in commercial information.

While the press has emphasized the continuing need for government subsidies, others have pointed out the incompatibility of such support with the ideal of an independent "Fourth Estate." Commercial advertisement has proven to be one of the most successful responses to this dilemma. The newspaper *Izvestiia* is a prime example. Due in large part to its five-year aggressive campaign for advertisements, *Izvestiia* managed to operate without state subsidies in 1993 and even showed a small profit.

It is hardly surprising, then, that most of the major Russian newspapers and television stations chose to carry MMM advertisements. MMM, named by *Izvestiia*'s Mikhail Berger as "Russia's chief advertiser," reportedly spent 10 billion rubles per day on advertising alone. Critics have charged that, as a result, the Russian print and electronic media were essentially "purchased" by the MMM company. They contend that by displaying MMM advertisements and publishing articles that expressed only the most muted criticism of the company's investment practices, mass media outlets became MMM's "accomplices" in deceiving the Russian public.

The role of advertising in the MMM case has already drawn considerable official attention. A week prior to the July 29 collapse, the Committee on Antimonopoly Policy publicly recommended that the mass media cease carrying MMM advertisements. On July 30, ITAR-TASS reported that Moscow Mayor Yuri Luzhkov had ordered a ban on all MMM advertisements pending full investigation of the company's activities. On the same day, Yeltsin's top security advisers called for a crackdown on companies with similar advertising campaigns and for the Duma to suspend its vacation and adopt emergency federal legislation on advertising.

Also on July 30, the Finance Ministry issued a statement charging the media with "unlawful promotion" of financial companies and announcing its plans to ask tax and

* Post-Soviet Media Law & Policy Newsletter, Sept. 10, 1994, at 2.

procuratorial organs to investigate media activities and confiscate "any unlawfully-derived profits." It specifically cited the MMM example in "advising" Russian citizens to seek professional guidance before purchasing securities and to be wary of "a commercial promising to pay higher than average dividends or that share values can only go up." Largely as a result of the MMM case, federal administrative and legislative authorities are currently in the process of drafting comprehensive regulations on advertising.

Media dissemination of "improper" advertisements is by no means a new issue for post-Soviet Russia. As early as December 1992 this question gained prominence when the Moscow Procurator's Office instituted criminal actions against *Moskovskii Komsomolets* and *Chastnaia Zhizn* for publishing advertisements for "intimate services" and illegal purchase and sale of convertible currency, orders, and medals. More recently the focus has been on advertisement of hazardous products and activities. For example, the May 5 Recommendation of the Presidential Judicial Chamber for Information Disputes condemned media advertisement of alcoholic beverages, tobacco products, and unlicensed practitioners of non-traditional medicine as contrary to Russian health legislation. The Judicial Chamber made two points that may be indicative of overall Russian approaches to advertising. First, it directed the media to verify that potential advertisers had obtained the requisite certification of products before agreeing to advertise such products. Second, it called for confiscation of all profits generated from illegal advertisements.

Thus far, Russian authorities have provided only rudimentary guidelines on the specific problem of advertisements for banking and financial enterprises. In April, the Central Bank issued an appeal to the mass media to confirm with the Central Bank that potential advertisers were formally licensed to do business in Russia. In May, the Finance Ministry published in *Rossiiskaia Gazeta* a letter to Russian citizens on the "critical situation" in the Russian securities market. This notice cautioned investors that "no advertisements should be trusted." In early June, *Rossiiskie Vesti* reported that former Finance Minister Boris Fedorov had submitted to the Duma a draft Law on Protecting Consumers' Rights in the Sphere of Financial Services. Fedorov proposed the creation of special inspection departments within the Central Bank and Finance Ministry to investigate and prevent deceptive financial advertising. He also recommended publication of "black lists" of unlicensed financial companies. He called for immediate suspension of these enterprises' operations and advertisements and for imposition of fines on any media outlets that "publish or broadcast an advertisement for companies that are ultimately banned."

At present, the two key legal acts are Yeltsin's decrees of June 10 and June 11, 1994: Decree No. 1183 On Consumer Protection Against Unfair Advertising and Decree No. 1233 On Protection of Investors' Interests. In brief, these decrees introduce reporting requirements for advertisers (e.g., "real" dividend and interest rates and registration information), prohibit advertisement of securities prior to registration of the prospectus, and oblige advertisers to avoid false, misleading, and unconfirmable promises regarding future performance. Sanctions include mandatory withdrawal of "unfair" advertisements, cancellation of the securities issue registration, and suspension or revocation of the advertisers' business license. The mass media, in turn, have a legal duty to require presentation by a potential advertiser of securities of its official certificate of registration. Any mass media that carry false advertisements or announcements regarding securities are obliged to publish information on the subsequent cancellation of the registration of the securities issue.

The Committee on Antimonopoly Policy and the Central Bank have already served notice that they intend to enforce these presidential decrees. For example, in late July, the Antimonopoly Committee issued implementing procedures and formally notified managers of twelve private companies of their noncompliance with the new advertising requirements. The Committee also announced plans to reduce media advertising from forty percent to twenty-five percent of printed space and from twenty-five percent to fifteen percent of broadcast time. On August 19 the Central Bank press service provided central Russian news agencies and publications with a list of more than twenty unlicensed financial firms.

Russian authorities have pledged to ensure that there will be no repetition of the MMM scandal. They have promised imminent adoption of detailed laws on securities markets, banking operations, and commercial advertising. Early indications are that these laws will introduce extensive content regulation of advertisements. Recent official statements and commentary have focused almost exclusively on the negative side of advertising—specifically, the power of major advertisers to influence, even distort, media coverage of events and to mislead and ensnare a gullible public.

It is, however, important to remember as well the potential benefits of advertising for post-Soviet Russia. To borrow a phrase from C. Edwin Baker, advertising can be the "life blood" of a democratic media. As a non-governmental "subsidy," it can liberate the media from state support and direction and, ideally, increase the media channels available to the Russian audience. Advertising can also be an effective source of commercial information and encouragement for Russian consumers. As such, it can contribute directly to development and expansion of the Russian economy, an urgent priority for the Yeltsin government.

Legal Regulation of Advertising in Russia*

William G. Frenkel

The advertising industry in Russia is fairly young and is essentially a product of the post-Soviet era. During the Soviet period, very little commercial advertising was used to market products and services, and the state had a virtual monopoly on all aspects of the advertising process, from the creative stage to production to media placement to broadcasting and other media. With the launch of pro-market reforms in the Soviet Union and subsequently in the Russian Federation, advertising rapidly became a full-fledged business providing sizable revenue to the companies involved in advertising activities. Advertising rates have climbed dramatically from the early 1990s; prime television spots in Moscow now command up to $30,000 per minute, while radio spots could cost as much as $500 for thirty seconds, and a single page of print media can cost up to $10,000. The biggest spenders in the Russian advertising market are multinational consumer goods companies, but some local companies are also utilizing advertising quite widely to promote new products and services. The total Russian advertising industry approached $7 billion in 1995, with television grabbing the biggest share of revenue, reflecting the popularity of this medium among many Russians. By way of an example, the four largest advertisers in the country spend in excess of $10 million monthly on television campaigns alone. However, other media are also gaining in advertising revenues, with outdoor advertising becoming an important medium for those advertisements for which broadcasting is either prohibited or ineffective. Direct mail marketing, on the other hand, is still quite rare because of the poorly developed postal service.

Until 1995, Russia had no comprehensive law governing advertising activities. The principal legislation was enacted on July 18, 1995, in the form of the Law On Advertising No. 108-FZ ("Advertising Law") which came into force on July 25. The law governs relations arising in the course of production, placement and dissemination of advertising of goods and services in the Russian Federation, including banking, insurance, securities and other financial services and products. The main purposes of the law include "protection from unfair competition through advertising, prevention of improper advertising capable of misleading or injuring the consumer and preservation of public interests and principles of morality and humanity." Interestingly, the law contains a clause giving it extraterritorial jurisdiction over parties violating its provisions where actions of Russian or foreign persons, whether in Russia or abroad, result in restraint of trade, confusion on the part of individuals or legal entities in Russia, or other adverse consequences in the Russian markets.

---

* 4 Parker School Journal of East European Law 129 (1997).

The Advertising Law was considered to be very controversial, and it went through many drafts before being adopted in its final form by the Russian parliament. The two principal competing drafts originated in the State Committee for Antimonopoly Policy (which secured the regulatory authority for overseeing compliance with the Advertising Law) and the Duma Committee on Information, Telecommunications and Economic Policy. Although within Russia the Advertising Law was not well received by the industry, the final text of the law was praised abroad. Some of the drafters of the law were assisted by the experts of the Organization for European Cooperation and Development, and the law was declared to be the model legislation of the year in 1995 by the European Parliament.

One explanation for the domestic controversy surrounding the law lies in the fact that the advertising business in 1994 produced an estimated revenue of $5 billion—a sizable amount for an emerging economy such as Russia's—on a relatively small capital investment. The stakes were clearly high, and given that any regulation of commercial speech normally results in a certain segment of the market losing business, intense lobbying efforts were undertaken by certain industrial sectors and mass media to prevent the regulation of advertising. The balancing act that any legislation regulating advertising is called to perform between the freedom of businesses to promote their goods and the protection of consumers from improper advertising and outright fraud is a delicate one, and in a country like Russia it touches on many legitimate and illegitimate interests of the constituencies involved. As with any other legislation, the real test of the Advertising Law is going to be in the enforcement of its provisions by the regulatory authorities and the courts over time, but one can infer that the law, like much of the recent Russian legislation, has had little "bite" in trying to discipline unruly markets. The enforcement of this admittedly well-drafted law has so far been characterized by both a heavy-handed approach in issuing flat prohibitions against certain activities that are not inherently detrimental to the consumer and in ignoring or failing to curb instances of outrageous abuse of consumers' rights.

In addition to the Advertising Law, a number of separate enactments regulate advertising activities in specific industrial sectors. For example, the Law On State Regulation of Manufacture and Distribution of Ethyl Alcohol and Alcohol Production No. 171-FZ of November 22, 1995, addresses the liquor industry (Article 17), whereas the Law On the Securities Market No. 39-FZ of April 22, 1996, regulates advertising of securities (Article 9). There is little coordination between these different laws, and this lack of harmonization presents distinct interpretive problems for advertising of certain products subject to conflicting legal requirements. Moreover, certain types of advertising are not regulated by the Advertising Law at all. For example, outdoor advertising is ordinarily regulated by local enactments, and direct marketing campaigns may require special permission from the postal authority. Advertising of erotic products is governed by article 37 of the Law On the Mass Media of December 27, 1991, and local authorities have some jurisdiction over such activities. Political advertising, specifically excluded from the scope of the Advertising Law by article 1(4), is also a subject of separate statutory provisions, primarily on the basis of the Law On Elections of June 16, 1995. These include restrictions on political advertising during certain pre-election periods, equal access rules for political candidates, recording and other requirements.

The Advertising Law contains a number of restrictions on the advertising messages, images and symbols (i.e., content) and aspects such as frequency, amount and mode of advertising (i.e., procedures for production, media placement and dissemination of commercials). In general, the same requirements apply to all media, but certain requirements are relevant only to broadcast media (such as radio and television) while others are applicable to print media.

An interesting question arises with respect to the jurisdiction of the local, regional and autonomous republic authorities under the Advertising Law. Article 3 refers only to federal government agencies and federal legislation as the exclusive source of legal regulation of advertising activities. A number of Russian jurists argued that on the basis of the Russian constitution, "subjects of the Russian Federation," or all government authorities other than those on the federal level, should be allowed to regulate advertising alongside the federal authorities, and one lawsuit is now pending in the Constitutional Court of the Russian Federation on this issue. In this suit, the municipal government of Moscow is arguing that it has the authority to regulate advertising within the city in conjunction with the federal government.

Definition of Advertising

Understanding how "advertising" is defined is obviously crucial for determining whether the Advertising Law applies to any given communication or expression. Article 2 defines advertising as "information about a physical person or a legal entity, goods, ideas and initiatives disseminated in any form and in any media, which is aimed at an undefined circle of persons (general public) and which is used to attract or maintain interest toward such person or entity, goods, ideas and initiatives and to facilitate their distribution and sale." This is the first definition of advertising in Russian law, and as such, it has not yet been interpreted by many courts or administrative agencies, which would clarify its boundaries. The definition appears to be sufficiently broad, though, to cover most commercial expression. The only explicit exception is provided by article 1(5) of the Law for individual messages (classified advertisements) placed by natural persons not engaged in business activity. Even classified advertisements and other announcements placed by legal entities may be exempt if they are not aimed at direct business activity (such as employment related advertisements). Russian commentators conclude that all other messages and communications that satisfy the above definition (i.e., those that are designed to market or sell products and services) are generally deemed advertising even if they were not conceived to be advertising. Thus, commercial retail signs may be considered advertising if they contain more than merely names, trademarks or service marks. This often comes up in the context of slogans placed on such signs.

Article 19 of the Advertising Law also defines "sponsorship," which, in contrast to 11 advertising," relates to financial or other assistance rendered to a legal entity or physical person for the purposes of publicizing the sponsor's name or its goods or services. The definition of sponsorship is as follows: "contribution by a sponsor of property, intellectual property, provision of services toward the activity of another (sponsored) person on the condition that the name of the sponsor is publicized." The law states that sponsor's contributions are deemed payment for advertising, and a sponsor is deemed an "advertiser" while the sponsored person is the "disseminator of advertising" (functionally identical to mass media or agents or intermediaries). While the law does not expressly subject sponsorship to the same standards as advertising, it uses the terms applicable to advertising, and the agencies enforcing the law have generally interpreted it in this way. Since sponsorship is in many instances virtually indistinguishable from advertising, one can conclude that all provisions of the law which directly pertain to advertising also apply to sponsorship. A number of companies in the Russian market have attempted to circumvent the provisions of the Advertising Law by masking their advertising as sponsorship. They met with poor results, since the government authorities have generally viewed sponsorship as advertising subject to the provisions of the law.

General Limitations on the Content of Advertising

Article 5 of the Advertising Law provides for a number of general limitations on all types of advertising regardless of medium. First, advertising must not be concealed as the distribution of general information or regular programming. The point of this requirement is two-fold: (i) to physically separate commercial advertisements from the rest of the programming or material (the law requires that advertisements either be clearly distinguishable from non-commercial programming or be marked as such) and (ii) to prevent advertisers from disguising their commercials as something other than advertising (for example, "infomercials"). Furthermore, mass media organizations may not require payment for what basically amounts to publicity. Although payment is not an explicit element of the statutory definition of advertising, publicity in Russia is generally interpreted as reporting on a newsworthy event involving a certain person, company, product or service, the publication of which is not solicited by the person or company being featured and is not compensated. Advertising may not be disguised as news, editorials or other non-commercial material or programs.

Second, the law requires that all advertising be in Russian unless the advertised publication, material or program itself is in a foreign language, in which case foreign language commercials arc allowed. Some cities, such as Moscow, have moved to ban retail signs in foreign languages or required their translation into Russian. Third, the law bans advertising of certain products which may not be legally manufactured or distributed in Russia. No advertising of banned products may be undertaken. Advertising of licensed products is permitted only to the extent that the advertisement discloses the license number and the name of the licensing authority. Advertising of products subject to mandatory certification must state that the product is subject to certification. As more and more products become subject to certification in Russia, this requirement is bound to affect a significant volume of advertisements. However, advertising of uncertified products appears to be possible as long as the commercial informs the public that the manufacturer is applying for certification.

Fourth, advertising may not violate the applicable copyright law. This provision may be of some assistance in combating the widespread piracy of brand names and products that afflicts the entire former Soviet Union and parts of Eastern Europe. In particular, this provision may be used in fighting deceptively similar advertising campaigns, in which the protected material, images or slogans are copied or imitated by another company in designing its own advertisements.

Finally, advertising should not prompt violence, aggression, panic or any other response which may threaten health or safety of people.

Specific Restrictions on Advertising

The Advertising Law also contains prohibitions on what the law deems "improper advertising," a collective term encompassing inaccurate, misleading, unethical, unscrupulous, intentionally false or subliminal advertising. While permitting other Russian legislation to define other types of advertising that may be improper and illegal in accordance with article 2, in article 6 of the Law, improper advertising is specifically defined to include such advertising that attempts to disparage or discredit individuals, undermines the reputation of the competitor or contains falsehoods.

Article 7 of the law prohibits misleading or inaccurate advertising. Misleading advertising is defined as that containing inaccurate or untrue information on aspects of the advertised product or service as its characteristics, availability, its price, the seller's delivery or refund policy and so on. Article 7 also specifically bans the use of superlatives such as the "best," "solely" or "exceptional" in an advertisement without documentary foundation and unfounded comparisons between the product or service being advertised and other products or services. Thus, opportunities for competitive advertising are severely limited in Russia.

Article 9 of the law prohibits false advertising. False advertising is defined as advertising that deliberately attempts to deceive the customer and clearly demonstrates the intent to deceive on the part of the advertiser. Article 10 prohibits covert advertisements, such as subliminal advertising or advertising disguised as a non-commercial message, usually within regular programming. The law addresses special video inserts and double sound tracks, but its focus also appears to be on the prominent use of products or their trademarks in non-commercial materials, such as films or television programs.

Article 8 prohibits unethical, offensive or socially unacceptable advertising. Unethical advertising includes advertising that violates generally accepted principles of morality and humanity. Such advertising is defined as advertising which offends a racial, ethnic or national group, gender, religious group, age group and other groups or affiliations on the basis of language, profession, social status, religious, political or philosophical convictions, etc.; defames the Russian Federation or another sovereign state, their official state symbols, anthems, emblems, or units of currency and religious symbols; advertising which maligns or denigrates internationally recognized works of art; and advertising which ridicules an individual, legal entity, business, trade or commodity for not using the product or service (negative advertising).

The actual list of improper, misleading or unethical advertising in the Advertising Law may be more extensive than what is provided in article 8. The boundaries of "unethical," should clearly be measured against contemporary Russian society, which in some instances is considerably more tolerant than other societies. The danger, of course, lies in the fact that the law refers to other legislation (without specifying it) which may render advertising "improper" and result in a violation. Article 8 provides some specific guidelines via references to demographic distinctions, but also employs the term "accepted morals and norms of humanism," which defies any simple interpretation. Any individual or legal entity whose dignity, reputation or business name has been discredited, or who has been personally defamed by unethical advertising, may initiate a legal action against the media organization in which the commercial was placed to demand a withdrawal of the commercial and an opportunity to refute or rebut the offending statement, message or image.

Limitations on Alcohol and Tobacco Advertising

The Russian Advertising Law, like that of many European countries, bans the advertising of alcohol and tobacco products. The United Kingdom, for example, has a total ban on advertising of alcohol and tobacco in all mass media. In 1991, there was also an attempt to ban alcohol and tobacco advertising completely in Russia. The new law replaces a presidential decree on advertising of alcohol and tobacco, which was put into force several months prior to its adoption and preempted the provisions relevant to advertising of alcohol and tobacco contained in the Fundamentals on Legislation on Protection of Health. In its place, article 16 of the law imposes a somewhat less restrictive but still quite formidable set of limitations on the advertising of alcohol and tobacco. For example, advertisements of tobacco or alcohol may not be placed in magazines on the first or last page, in newspapers on the first or last lines, in any publications targeting minors, or in regular programming on radio, television, and motion pictures, and advertising may not demonstrate or otherwise portray smoking or drinking, and may not create an impression that smoking or drinking is important to achieving success in society, sports or personal life, or improving a person's mental or physical condition.

Although it was initially prohibited under the Advertising Law to advertise alcohol or tobacco on radio or television between the hours of 7 a.m. and 10 p.m., alcohol and tobacco advertising has been completely prohibited on television broadcasts beginning

January 1, 1996. Other media may contain advertising of tobacco only if the advertisement contains a warning about adverse consequences of smoking (at least three seconds of air time for broadcast advertisements and at least five percent of advertising space for print advertising) and the above conditions are observed.

Since the Advertising Law implies that sponsorship is a form of advertising and may be subject to restrictions imposed on it, the same rules would appear to apply to alcohol or tobacco sponsorships in any medium, including broadcast media, as apply to regular advertising. Thus, alcohol and tobacco sponsorships are banned from all broadcast media, and their use in print media is subject to the same rules as direct advertising set forth above. A number of companies have been trying to get around the ban by advertising non-alcoholic beers on television with the same brand name or trademark, advertising the trademark alone, advertising the image and resorting to sports and cultural sponsorships. In many instances, such initiatives were held illegal and enforcement actions were taken against the advertisers. The result of the ban was an almost twenty-five percent drop in the total advertising revenue in Russia, although some other media, most notably outdoor advertising, reportedly picked up new business from alcohol and tobacco advertisers.

Limitations on Advertisements of Inherently Dangerous Products

The Advertising Law governs advertising of inherently dangerous products, which fall into two major categories: medical items, including pharmaceutical products, health care products and medical equipment, and firearms. Article 16 of the law bans such advertising without permission for the manufacture and sale of the advertised product and a patent for the process in the case of pharmaceutical products. If permitted, such advertising may not promote methods of medication, treatment, disease prevention, diagnosis or rehabilitation without a special permit issued by a governmental public health authority regardless of the availability of any other permissions for the marketing of such products. Instructions for using health care products and medicines sold by prescription only is allowed only through printed matter sold with the product.

Advertising of guns, weapons and military equipment is generally banned, except for hunting and sporting equipment and certain equipment whose import and export is licensed by the Russian authorities. Advertising of licensed arms and weapons is allowed only in specially licensed print publications or, if in electronic (broadcast) media, then after 10:00 p.m. Any weapons or armaments, including civil-use weapons that have military applications which must be specially licensed, may not be advertised at all if the advertisement directly or indirectly discloses military technology or applications.

Limitations on Advertisements of Financial Products and Services

The Advertising Law contains a number of limitations on advertising of financial, securities or investment services and insurance. Article 17 states that such commercials may not guarantee fixed payments or returns, advertise securities prior to the registration of the offering prospectus, refer to quantitative information that has no relation to the advertised services or securities, guarantee dividend amount on common registered shares of stock, or conceal any specific term of an investment contract if it is describing the terms of the contract. As mentioned above, the Law On Securities Markets contains additional requirements for securities advertisements.

Limitations on Advertisements for Minors

The Advertising Law attempts to protect minors from unscrupulous advertising. Article 20 prohibits advertisements where the production, placement, or circulation of advertisements of any products or services targeting youth questions the good name and experience of parents or teachers or undermines minors' respect for them, leads the minor to persuade parents or others to buy the advertised product for him or her, convinces the minor that possession of certain products makes them attractive to other minors; or suggests that the advertised product can be afforded by a family of any budget.

Procedural Limitations

The Advertising Law also limits the scheduling, timing and amount of advertising, affecting primarily broadcast media but also print and outdoors media. These "media placement" limitations are primarily the responsibility of mass media (including agents and intermediaries), which accept and disseminate advertising. Article 11 of the law restricts the interruption of programs for commercial breaks or messages. Broadcast programs lasting for less than fifteen minutes may not be interrupted. Educational broadcasts running fifteen minutes may not be interrupted more than once, and for no longer than forty-five seconds. Broadcast programs lasting from fifteen to sixty minutes may not be interrupted more than twice.

Moreover, children's radio broadcasts and religious programs may not be interrupted by advertisements at all. The law requires advertisers to obtain the consent holders of the copyright to motion pictures and radio dramas before interrupting such programs with commercials. Given the state of the Russian protection of intellectual property in general, it is unlikely that many advertisers or broadcasters will comply with this provision, but the drafters of the law have clearly expressed their interest in protecting the integrity of audio-visual works and their creators' moral rights.

Advertising of the same product, service or client may not be repeated more than twice, or longer than two minutes, any hour. On radio broadcasts that are not certified as pure advertising programs, advertisements may not take up more than twenty-five percent of the airtime. It should be noted that the broadcasters' licenses also limit their advertising time and often state that advertising will be limited to no more than fifteen minutes per hour. Print advertising is limited to forty percent of the total publication unless the publication is certified as a pure advertising service. Commercial breaks within films or videos in theatrical distributions and telephone directory services are regulated by article 13 of the law. The former are completely banned, except during intermissions, while the latter are permitted only with the permission of the subscriber. Outdoor signs are governed by article 14, which prescribes certain basic requirements for posters, billboards, illuminated signs and other commercial signs, and refers to local authorities for additional regulation. Finally, placement of advertising on automobile vehicles and mail items is regulated by article 15.

In order to counterbalance the broad obligations and extensive liability imposed on the producers of advertising and mass media, the law allows these organizations to request and receive from the advertiser information confirming the accuracy of the information used in advertisements and license or certification information pursuant to articles 22 and 23 of the Advertising Law. Furthermore, the producer of advertising is obligated to notify the advertiser if any of its requirements for advertisements violate legal norms. The producer may rescind its agreement with the advertiser and seek damages where the advertiser refuses to modify its requirements to conform to the provisions of the Advertising Law or to supply the requisite documentation supporting its claims or information used in the advertisement.

Acceptance of Public Messages

A potentially troublesome provision in the Advertising Law is article 18 concerning "social advertising" or mandatory public messages, which must be "in the interests of the state and general public and be charity oriented." This article appears to apply to all media, whether print or broadcast, as well as to producers of advertising. Social advertising may not contain information on commercial businesses, individual business people, specific products, or commodities produced by the non-profit organizations. The law states that mass media which generally accept advertising are to allow social advertising for at least five percent of their total advertising time. The same requirement applies to advertising intermediaries (agents) and advertising producers.

Although the import of article 18 is unclear, it appears that mass media organizations are obligated to accept social advertising if it is offered by potential advertisers. However, while the law appears to encourage acceptance and production of advertising on a gratuitous basis for charitable purposes, it also states that the terms of placement or production of such social advertising are subject to a contractual arrangement. This would indicate that if the potential advertiser were unwilling to pay the standard advertising rate, then there may not be an absolute obligation to accept such an advertisement for a lower rate or for free. The law does specify that the "timing and mode" of social advertising shall not be changed by the company airing, distributing or disseminating the commercial, provided that the commercial is placed with the media organization at least thirty days in advance. This appears to mean that a group placing social advertisement has the right to choose the timing and the mode of the advertisement provided that such group requests the advertisement at least thirty days in advance.

Enforcement and Penalties

The State Committee on Antimonopoly Policy of the Russian Federation ("GKAP") is charged with enforcement of the Advertising Law. The law also empowers non-governmental groups to monitor compliance with the law and bring violations of the law to the attention of GKAP, the prosecutors office, or the courts. The procedure for administrative actions by GKAP under the Advertising Law is governed by the Decree of the Antimonopoly Committee No. 147 of November 13, 1995, on the Procedure for Hearing Matters Regarding Violations of the Advertising Legislation of the Russian Federation. Presidential Decree No. 1183 On Protection of Consumers from Unfair Advertising was adopted on June 10, 1994, in the wake of one of the largest Russian financial scandals to date, the pyramid scheme. It provides additional guidance on enforcement matters, granting concurrent jurisdiction in advertising matters to government agencies other than GKAP, such as the Central Bank, Ministry of Finance, State Committee for State Property Management, Federal Insurance Supervisor, and others.

Upon detecting a violation of the Advertising Law, GKAP can require the advertiser—the company that placed the advertisement—to cease and desist from engaging in improper advertising and to counter-advertise," or issue a refutation or rebuttal of previously-run advertising. "Counter-advertising" is defined as a refutation of the illegal or improper statements previously disseminated by the violating organization in order to rectify the consequences of such an improper statement. Moreover, GKAP may protect consumers' rights through other means, including the annulment of transactions through legal actions in courts and the revocation of licenses by administrative agencies. GKAP may also seek to initiate criminal actions.

For violations of the law, GKAP can also impose civil fines of up to 200 times the minimum wage (currently about $7,000) under article 31 of the law. However, fines can be levied only after the violating entity or person had defied a specific order or directive issued by GKAP. Refusals to conduct corrective counter-advertisement or to cease illegal advertising when ordered may be punished by criminal sanctions and fines up to 5,000 times the minimum wage (currently approximately $90,000). Deliberately false or misleading commercial advertisement may also be punished according to the Russian criminal code, which has been recently amended to strengthen deterrence of white-collar crimes. Article 182 of the Criminal Code defines 'intentionally false advertising" and provides for fines and imprisonment of the people responsible for crime where the false adverting results in significant harm. GKAP also has the right to report violations of the Advertising Law to the violators licensing agency. Finally, individuals or companies that have been injured by violations of the Advertising Law are expressly entitled to private civil remedies, and may seek monetary damages, including damages for actual losses, lost or foregone profits and moral harm, from the violators of the advertising legislation.

An important threshold question arises as to who can be liable under the Advertising Law for commercials that violate its provisions. Article 30 of the law divides responsibility for violations among the "advertiser" (the company or person placing the advertisement), the "advertisement producer" (the company or person using the information to make the advertisement in full or in part), and the "advertising disseminator or agent" (the company or person disseminating the advertisement, which can include mass media organizations and advertising agencies acting as intermediaries).

Article 30 of the Advertising Law states, "the advertiser shall be responsible for violation of the advertising legislation of the Russian Federation with respect to the principal statement included in the advertisement unless it is proven that the law is violated by the advertisement Producer or advertising disseminator." This essentially means that the advertiser bears the primary responsibility for compliance with the law, however, both advertising producer and advertising disseminator or its agent may also be liable for violations of the law in certain circumstances. This places a significantly higher burden of regulatory compliance on Russian media than on its counterparts in those jurisdictions, which do not normally hold mass media and advertising intermediaries liable for violations of local law. Article 30 further states that the advertisement producer is responsible for complying with the law with reference to layout or setup, production, and advertising format. Article 30 concludes by stating that the advertising disseminator or agency is responsible for complying with the law "with respect to placing, timing and method of dissemination of the advertisement." Thus, mass media generally bear the secondary responsibility for "improper advertising" for media placement. Under Article 24, anyone involved in the advertising process is required to furnish enforcement agencies with information and documents relevant to the jurisdiction of the agency in question, upon request.

Since most mass media organizations are rarely advertisers themselves (except for self-promotion), the Advertising Law does not make them responsible for the "principal statement" of an advertising, which is the most fertile area for legal controversy. However, mass media organizations and advertising agencies are often involved in the development or production of a commercial. In those cases, they may be treated as an advertisement producer, and thus held responsible for violations of the law "with reference to placing, timing, and means of dissemination of the advertisement." It is unclear what this means or how it differs from a violation of the law in the "principal statement." However, because it may be possible to characterize violations of many of the provisions of the law as violations of the proper "format," violations of the law by commercials where the mass media or advertising agency is the advertisement maker will likely expose them to risk.

Because mass media organizations are disseminators of their own advertising, they will always be fully responsible for violations of the Advertising Law with respect to "placing, timing and means of dissemination of the advertisement." These requirements, however, are largely straightforward and do not usually involve interpretative issues of great complexity. Moreover, the law also states that advertisers, advertisement producers, and advertising disseminators are responsible for violations of the law in accordance with Russian law. Consumers and other persons whose rights have been violated by improper advertising may commence legal actions to collect damages from responsible parties. It is likely that only those parties that are responsible for violations of Article 30 are liable to pay damages in accordance with Article 31. However, because this is not explicitly stated in the law, there is some risk that a court would allow a party adversely affected by an advertisement to apply for damages against a mass media organization, even if the violation were solely related to the "principal statement" under Article 30 or were not defined as a violation under the Advertising Law.

In light of the recent vintage of the advertising legislation in Russia, there is very little interpretation of the Advertising Law and little experience with its enforcement by GKAP. Because the differences in the liability of different groups involved in the advertising process are unclear under the current law, mass media organizations should avoid airing or running any commercials that clearly violate the explicit terms of the Advertising Law. They should also consider not airing commercials that they suspect violate even the spirit of the law, especially when the mass media organization is itself the advertisement producer. It should be noted that the law states that the advertisement producer should inform the advertiser about conflicts between the provisions of the law and any proposed advertisement. The law also grants the advertisement producer and the advertising disseminator or agent the right to request documentary evidence from the advertiser proving the authenticity of the information contained in the advertisement. This suggests that the law intends for the advertisement producer and advertising disseminator to take an active role in ensuring that a given advertisement complies with the Advertising Law and other applicable advertising legislation. A mass media organization should consider asking for evidence of the authenticity of the information contained in the commercial if there is some doubt about the authenticity of any claims made in such a commercial. Finally, mass media organizations should consider including into their standard advertising contracts a provision which states that the advertiser guarantees that the principal statement in the advertisement fully complies with the Russian Advertising Law, and the advertiser takes all responsibility for non-compliance of the principal statement of the commercial with the Russian advertising law and indemnities the organization for any losses it may suffer as a result of non-compliance. Where a media organization accepts a pre-produced commercial in the making of which it played no part, it should also seek a statement that the format and production comply fully with the Russian law.

The Advertising Law also envisions participation of self-regulatory groups in the process of enforcement. Article 28 of the law vests several important functions in self-regulatory organizations, including consultation on legislation on advertising, independent evaluation of advertising to determine whether violations exist, issuance of recommendations to advertisers and mass media, assistance to GKAP in assuring legal compliance on the part of advertisers and mass media, and the right to initiate legal actions related to violations of the Advertising Law. One such self-regulatory organization already in existence is the Moscow Public Council on Advertising.

D.

DEFAMATION

Civil Defamation Law and the Press in Russia: Private and Public Interests, the 1995 Civil Code, and the Constitution*

Peter Krug

Introduction

The legal status of the Russian press has been transformed in the 1990s. Beginning in 1990, the state and Communist Party mass media monopoly has been abolished and direct pre-publication controls over content have been outlawed, fundamentally altering the nature of press-state relations.[3] Writing in 1991, the authors of the initial draft of the 1990 Press Law declared, "within a couple of years, a great leap forward has taken place—from total obedience to a degree of freedom that is hardly confined within legal limits."[7]

Meanwhile, equally fundamental changes have taken place in the press's horizontal relations with non-state parties in the sphere of individual personality rights protection. Before 1990, the press operated under an extra-legal "duty to criticize" and therefore enjoyed broad latitude to subject to public criticism and ridicule individuals for whom the legal system offered limited protection.[9] Beginning with the 1990 Press Law,[10] however, and culminating in a new Civil Code effective January 1, 1995, the press has been made subject to a comprehensive system of post-publication civil responsibility for dissemination of statements injurious to personality interests.[11] The scope of protection for individual rights of personality has been broadened incrementally to include new protected interests, such as a right to privacy, and a potent new remedy—recovery of monetary damages for non-material harm ("moral damages").[12]

---

[3] The initial changes came with enactment of the country's first press law in June 1990. The 1990 Press Law is no longer in effect as a result of the dissolution of the USSR in December 1991. In Russia, it has been replaced by legislation which became effective in February 1992 and remains in effect.

[7] Yuriy M. Baturin et al., *The Road to Freedom for the Soviet Press*, 12 Journal of Media Law & Practice 43, 43 (1991).

[9] The press's ability and mandate to criticize did not extend to publication of facts or commentary critical of Communist Party or governmental policies or leaders.

[10] Article 39 of the 1990 Press Law expanded upon the existing Civil Code provision protecting against false defamatory publications by making the press responsible for infliction of "other" non-material injuries, and introducing a remedy of monetary damages.

[11] The new Civil Code, part 1, was enacted by the Russian State Duma on October 21, 1994, and signed into law by President Yeltsin on November 30, 1994.

[12] For the purposes of this article, "moral damages" refers to the remedy of money damages for harm which cannot strictly be measured in monetary terms. According to the Russian Supreme Court, moral

This expansion of personality rights protection has been accompanied by a significant increase in the number of civil lawsuits, many of them against press defendants. Among those recognizing the new possibilities afforded plaintiffs has been State Duma Deputy Vladimir Zhirinovskii, who in a news conference candidly warned reporters:

> [I want to] inform you that those newspapers that have been trying to defame me—the latest case was that with the Moscow Guardian. The Leningradskii [district] court imposed a 10 million-ruble fine on the newspaper. The newspaper has disappeared, but we will find it abroad, and it will pay. Therefore, you should be quite cautious. I am a lawyer, and any attempts to defame the party's leader or the party itself will be immediately followed by a law suit. Before writing articles, you should check whether there is money in your coffers, in the coffers of your newspaper.

The increasing litigiousness is occurring amid widespread concern over perceived press abuses and the general level of discourse in the mass media. In June 1995, a joint declaration by the Union of Russian Journalists and the Judicial Chamber for Information Disputes, a tribunal of jurists and journalists which makes non-binding determinations in individual complaints against the mass information media, decried the widespread dissemination of inaccurate information, willful distortions, and "crude, insulting" journalistic style, warning that such publications "discredit the mass information media in the eyes of the public." The declaration cited the increased level of suits against the press as testimony to the "ease" with which the mass media irresponsibly flout human rights, vilify reputations, and engage in willful falsification.

Although issues relating to the expansion of personality rights protection have received considerable attention in the academic and professional literature, relatively little has been devoted to its impact on the press. This article examines the shift from the Soviet regime's promotion or tolerance of offensive expression in the press which might injure an ordinary citizen's reputation, sense of privacy, or personal feelings, to the Russian Federation's system favoring protection of individuals against such expression. It will focus on the defamation action—Russia's oldest and most widely invoked form of personality rights protection—which permits recovery for injury to an individual's honor or dignity.

[The first three parts of this Article] describe and analyze current civil defamation law in Russia, both in its statutory basis and as applied in judicial proceedings, and to identify the factors which have shaped its development. [The following parts] examine the textual basis for the possible application of public interest considerations, in the form of constitutional or international law norms, to that law.

---

harm is mental or physical trauma resulting from injury to protected non-material interests including personal and business reputation, individual dignity, and privacy.

I. Current Civil Defamation Law

A. The Statutory Scheme

Following a pattern common to a number of legal systems, Russia employs both criminal and civil law to regulate public discourse and provide protection of personality interests. The Criminal Code, articles 130 and 131, protects against intentional injuries to reputation by "defamation" [*kleveta*] and to self-esteem by "insult" [*oskorblenie*].[20] Although recently invoked in several highly publicized cases, these statutes have not been utilized as often as Russia's civil law system, which provides the availability of moral damages, and unlike the Criminal Code does not require a showing of defendant's intent to injure.

The statutory rules governing civil defamation actions are found in articles 151 and 152 of the 1995 Civil Code, which in cases involving press defendants is supplemented by the Mass Media Law.[25] In addition, important principles of civil defamation law have been established by the Russian Federation Supreme Court and supreme courts in the Soviet era,[26] in the form of "guiding instructions" to the lower courts as to construction and application of statutory law.[27]

The defamation provisions in article 152 protect the "honor" [chest'], "dignity" [*dostoinstvo*], and "business reputation" [*delovaia reputatsiia*] of natural and juridical persons. The statutory elements for determination of liability in civil defamation—dissemination to at least one third party of a false defamatory statement—have remained the same since the introduction into Soviet law of such a right of action in the 1960s.

Of these elements, only the showing of dissemination places an evidentiary burden of proof on the plaintiff. The law presumes that a defamatory statement is false, placing the burden of proving truth on the defendant. Whether the statement in question has a defamatory meaning is a question of law for the court to decide. The Russian Supreme Court fashioned the currently applicable definition of "defamatory meaning" in 1992:

[20] Unlike article 130, article 131 does not allow truth as a defense.

[25] The 1995 Civil Code supersedes all legislation that is inconsistent with it.

[26] The Supreme Court of the Russian Federation is the highest judicial authority on civil, criminal, and administrative cases and stands at the apex of general jurisdiction trial and appellate courts. It is a body separate from the Russian Federation Constitutional Court and has specialized jurisdiction over interpretation and application of the Constitution. In addition, a separate judicial hierarchy exists for those specialized courts that have jurisdiction over commercial law cases. It is a separate body, with different jurisdiction, from the Constitutional Court of the Russian Federation. The Supreme Court is the successor to the Supreme Court of the Russian Soviet Federated Socialist Republic. In addition, under the Soviet Union's federal structure, the highest court during the Soviet era was the USSR Supreme Court.

[27] A responsibility of the Russian Federation Supreme Court is the issuance of binding directives to the lower courts on matters of court practice, including statutory interpretation. The USSR and RSFSR Supreme Courts also issued guiding explanations.

> False communications which are defamatory are those which contain assertions about the violation by a citizen or organization of applicable legislation or moral principles (about commission of dishonorable acts, incorrect behavior in the workplace or in private life, or other statements discrediting productive economic or social activity, reputation, and so on), diminishing their honor and dignity.

However, the standard for making this determination is not altogether clear. The identification of both honor and dignity as protected interests suggests consideration of objective and subjective elements. Honor is viewed as requiring an objective appraisal of the effect on the plaintiff's reputation, whereas dignity suggests the plaintiff's own evaluation of his or her standing in the community as a result of the statement. These concepts in turn stem from the nature of honor as a matter of reputation, whereas dignity is more closely related to individual self-esteem. As a result, it is not clear whether courts are to judge defamatory meaning from the perspective of an objective "reasonable person" or by some other standard.

Available remedies against a mass media defendant include retraction, right of reply, and moral damages. As applied by the courts, moral damages are potentially available to all successful plaintiffs and there are no categorical limitations on the availability of the remedy. The courts have broad discretion as to the size of moral damages awards, although the 1995 Civil Code does set forth certain criteria: article 151(2) directs courts to take into account the degree of the defendant's fault, the depth of non-material suffering linked with the victim's individual characteristics, and "other circumstances deserving of attention."

These remedial provisions, particularly moral damages, have important implications for mass media organizations and individual journalists. In the Mass Media Law, a detailed catalog of the duties of "journalists" identifies a broad range of persons who are potentially responsible for violations of personality rights. Journalists must verify the reliability of information which they receive and more generally must "respect the rights, legal interests, and honor and dignity of citizens and organizations." In addition to journalists, mass media outlets themselves and their founders, publishers, editorial offices, and "authors" are subject to liability for violations of the statute's provisions. Whether individual members of an editorial office are subject to liability is somewhat ambiguous, although it appears that they are.[42] Although the provisions

[42] Under article 19 of the Mass Media Law, an "editorial office" [*redaktsiia*] shall be a juridical person or any other entity organized in a form permitted by law (although the definition of "editorial office" in article 2 appears to include a natural person as well). Since article 56 refers explicitly to an "editorial office" as one of the entities or persons subject to liability, editors who are natural persons (such as the "editor-in-chief" [*glavnyi redaktor*]) might arguably be relieved of responsibility. On the other hand, article 56 includes among responsible persons the category of "journalist," the definition of which clearly includes one who exercises editorial functions. Nikolaev concludes that in cases where the editorial office is not a juridical person, the proper defendants should be the founder and the responsible person at the organization that handles the mass media outlet's business affairs.

regarding responsibility are complex, it is clear that the entity most often named as a defendant, and therefore most often vulnerable to imposition of moral damages, will be the editorial office.

This complex of rules has purposes that are both retrospective and forward-looking. It provides responsibility under the remedial structure in the 1995 Civil Code and the Mass Media Law, but is also meant to deter future abuses. According to one of the legislative sponsors of the 1990 Press Law, a moral damages provision was necessary because "it is necessary to cool off pens which are too feverish."[44] Other commentators have spoken approvingly of the benefits of moral damages' deterrent effect in systems of personality rights protection generally. Given these considerations, it is presumable that journalists will be sensitive to potential litigation costs, including not only damages awards themselves, but also the costs of defense.

B. Standard of Liability

The civil defamation statutory scheme does not expressly address two questions of particular significance: the standard of liability and the treatment of statements not easily susceptible to an objective truth/falsity determination. As to the former, the 1995 Civil Code is silent, suggesting a liability without fault standard that imposes liability in all cases of false defamatory expression. The "degree of fault" criterion in article 151 relates to measurement of moral damages in individual cases, not the determination of liability itself. The Soviet courts, interpreting the existing defamation statute, concluded as far back as the 1960s that it called for a liability without fault standard—an approach never altered and grounded in the rationale that a fault-based standard was unnecessary because moral damages were not an available remedy.

The introduction of moral damages in the 1990s, however, has rendered the old rationale obsolete, and continued use of liability without fault combined with the damages remedy conflicts with a rule of statutory interpretation recently reiterated by the Russian Supreme Court. In a review of the various statutes in Russian legislation providing for moral damages, the Court stated that a condition for their imposition must be the fault of the defendant, unless expressly stated otherwise in the applicable legislation. As an example of such legislation, the Court cited the statute governing compensation for employee injuries, which contains an express liability without fault standard for injuries suffered in the course of highly dangerous work assignments.

If the Court's directive is applied to the statutes governing civil defamation, it should follow that liability resulting in moral damages must be conditioned on a finding of the defendant's fault, since neither the Mass Media Law nor articles 150 through 152 of the 1995 Civil Code contain any express contradictory provisions. Despite this, published reports of civil defamation cases in the 1990s do not give any indication that courts have considered application of standards other than liability without fault. This

[44] *Bessporнoe i Spornoe* [*Non-debatable and Debatable*], Zhurnalist, No. 1, at 8, 11 (1990) (interview with Georgii Shakhnazarov, Deputy to the Supreme Soviet).

problem would perhaps be alleviated if article 151 of the 1995 Civil Code were to make fault a condition for imposition of moral damages, and not solely a factor in determining their amount. If so, restorative remedies might be available even in the absence of fault, although moral damages would not be.

The absence of a clearly defined standard of liability, when combined with the broad discretion granted courts as to the measure of moral damages, results in a significant element of unpredictability in Russia's system of personality rights protection. In addition, the ambiguity concerning a standard serves to negate the creation of parameters for defenses as to the issue of liability itself. Addressing the availability of moral damages in 1994, a Council of Europe delegation to Russia made the following observation:

> This has been described as a provision which can be easily abused to undermine the economic viability of certain media. There appears to have been a considerable number of cases brought under this provision, and it was observed that the courts are as yet rather inexperienced in determining damages, due to lack of clear legal rules and the absence of an established case-law approved by the higher courts.

In sum, with the exception of certain limited exceptions set forth in the Mass Media Law, the law imposes liability on all disseminated defamatory statements, unless the defendant can prove the truth of the statement at issue.[54] Whether moral damages are available in all cases of liability is unclear, but it is evident that courts have not signaled any particular concern about reconciling the inconsistent aspects of this question and have continued to apply a liability without fault standard. Meanwhile, the limitation of applicable defenses to a showing of truth also raises issues in a second area not addressed in the statutes and subject to judicial interpretation: the treatment of critical commentary or defamatory opinion.

C. Defamatory Opinion: The Fascist Cases

As do all legal systems seeking to protect personality rights, Russia's confronts the choice of treating all defamatory statements alike or fashioning difficult distinctions between assertions of fact and statements of opinion. In the Russian Criminal Code, a distinction is made between false statements of fact (the subject of article 130) and insulting forms of expression for which a truth/falsity determination is not relevant (the subject of article 131). In the Soviet era, jurists debated whether some sort of distinction should also be made in the Civil Code, and in post-Soviet Russian law it appears that the question has been resolved in favor of treating all defamatory statements as susceptible to

[54] It is unclear whether this exception represents legislative balancing of the private interests of defamation plaintiffs and defendants or recognition of a public interest in the dissemination of truthful information. According to one jurist, writing in 1990: "Society is always interested in the truth, in the correct evaluation of the acts of each of its members. But if false information defaming a famous person is disseminated, this frequently entails irreparable harm to society."

a determination as to their truth or falsity. As a result, because the burden of proof in defamation lies on the defendant, the effect of such treatment is the imposition of liability even in cases where the statement at issue is arguably opinion and where an assertion of facts was not intended.

This conclusion, based in part on the absence of such a distinction in scholarly commentary on civil defamation law, is buttressed by the courts' treatment of recent cases involving defendants' use of the term "fascist" to label plaintiffs or their beliefs. These cases are among a number of high-visibility defamation lawsuits in the 1990s that have involved leading public officials or political figures as plaintiffs and in which the challenged statements were made in the context of discussion about political topics.[59]

In *Zhirinovskii v. Gaidar*, Deputy Vladimir Zhirinovskii sued former Prime Minister Egor Gaidar and the newspaper *Izvestiia*, seeking twenty-five million rubles (approximately $12,500) in moral damages for publication of a May 17, 1994, article in which Gaidar described Zhirinovskii as "a fascist populist" and "the most popular fascist in Russia." In September 1994, a Moscow district court determined that the statements were false and ordered the defendants to pay moral damages totaling one million rubles (approximately $ 500). In so ruling, the court rejected the defendants' argument that the article in question had been "a purely analytical one," investigating Zhirinovskii's "political essence," and therefore the term "fascist" was used as a "political characteristic only." The defense had also sought to refute Zhirinovskii's charge on a factual basis, introducing into evidence Adolf Hitler's *Mein Kampf*, Zhirinovskii's book *The Last Dash South*, and the *Encyclopedia of Philosophy*.

Two months later, that decision was upheld on appeal by the Moscow City Court. According to published accounts of the proceeding, the court's primary focus was upon the truth or falsity of the statement that the plaintiff was a "fascist." Zhirinovskii rejected this designation, stating instead that he considers himself a "national-socialist," and his attorney argued that the defendants' evidentiary support for their assertions was inadequate. Attorneys for the defendants, on the other hand, sought to convince the court that their clients had not intended to make a statement of fact, but rather a "political assessment" or "diagnosis." As in the lower court, they also sought to draw parallels between the plaintiff and Adolf Hitler, presenting evidence of their writings as well as historical parallels between Germany in the 1920s and Russia in the 1990s—political

---

[59] In terms of numbers, the leading plaintiff has probably been Deputy Zhirinovskii, who reportedly had filed nearly 100 suits by early July 1994. Other multi-suit plaintiffs include Moscow Mayor Iurii Luzhkov (at least 25 cases) and former Russian Federation Vice President Aleksander Rutskoi.

The tactic of multiple lawsuits has its antecedents: a member of the United States Congress, Representative Martin L. Sweeney of Ohio, filed at least 75 defamation lawsuits against publications which reported in 1939 that he opposed the appointment of a man as federal judge because the nominee was "a Jew, and one not born in the United States."

Also, the use of the defamation lawsuit as a political weapon recalls the widespread use of similar actions in Europe and the United States in the 1920s and 1930s.

assessments which the plaintiff's lawyer urged the court to ignore because they were not related to the facts.

In upholding the lower court's decision, the Moscow City Court ruled that the defendants had failed to meet their burden of proof. The court rejected the use of scholars' conclusions as evidence, stating that these conclusions represented "private opinion" and questioning the validity of claimed similarities between Zhirinovskii's writings and Hitler's *Mein Kampf.* One of the judges stated that no official documents had been presented to show that Zhirinovskii's Liberal-Democratic Party is a fascist organization.

The Moscow City Court's decision was the subject of a January 1995 protest by the Deputy Procurator General to the Civil Law Chamber of the Russian Supreme Court. The grounds for the protest were that the *Izvestiia* article was an exercise of free expression guaranteed by the Russian Constitution: a discussion of the political and ideological characteristics of the views of Deputy Zhirinovskii and an analysis of those views by means of comparing them with those of other political figures. In February, the Civil Chamber denied the protest and thereby declined to review the decision.

In addition to its rejection of the constitutional argument, the Supreme Court's denial of the protest suggests that Russian law might be incorporating into its system of personality rights protection the elements of a civil action based on "insult," or "abusive comment," as is found in certain other European legal systems and which might correspond to the crime of "insult" under article 131 of the Russian Criminal Code. The courts' statutory authority for protection of self-esteem, independent from its linkage with reputation as a protected interest in defamation, lies in the unspecified category of "other" among the protected personality interests in article 150(1) of the 1995 Civil Code. Truth is not identified in the Code as a defense against alleged invasion of article 150(1) interests. An action based on insult would be consistent with this, since the key question of whether an expression is insulting "in form" is not susceptible to a factual determination.

Whether it is more accurate to say that the courts in the fascist cases treated the use of the term "fascist" as an assertion of fact or in reality viewed it as "abusive comment," it is clear that their approach was consistent with the statutory scheme governing protection of personality rights. The conclusion that the Moscow City Court strictly followed statutory requirements in *Zhirinovskii v. Gaidar* is reinforced by the remarks of two observers, Yulia Rakhayeva and Kronid Lyubarsky. While both authors were sympathetic to the defendants and disagreed with the court's decision, they did not suggest that the panel was incompetent, or was motivated by anything other than an effort to apply the existing law. The authors' frustration with the court's decision appears to stem from the absence in the law of public interest considerations.

II. Communal Values and Private Interests: 1960s to 1995

The fact that Russian law has neither developed an explicit standard of liability linked with creation of defenses other than truth, nor attempted to fashion distinctions in the difficult area of defamatory opinion, is in large part attributable to the treatment of defamation as purely private law, devoid of public interest considerations other than protection of the interests of private victims of offensive expression. As construed by the courts in *Zhirinovskii*, for example, defamation law does not permit intervention of public interest concerns beyond perhaps the legislature's determination that truthful statements are exempt from liability. Personality rights protection cases are treated from the same perspective as private property or contract disputes, in which the courts are called upon to consider the relations between private parties and allocate their rights and duties as set forth in the Civil Code.

The status of personality rights protection in the 1990s as purely private law represents a transformation in Russia's treatment of offensive expression. To understand the reasons for this new approach it is necessary to examine its roots and the dynamics of its predecessor's component parts: the communal ethos of the Soviet era and the legal reformers' adherence to fundamental tenets of the civil law tradition. In the Soviet era, the ongoing tension between two conflicting tendencies—the regime's imposition of public values and jurists' preference for protection of private interests against outside intervention—shaped the setting for the creation and evolution of the system of personality rights protection.

A. Pre-1990

1. The Soviet Regime and Communal Values: Offensive Expression as a Public Good

The intrusion of public values, in the form of state and Communist Party interests, into private relationships was a defining characteristic of the Soviet regime and its approach to law. This theme was sounded by V.I. Lenin in 1922, when he admonished the drafters of the first civil code—jurists schooled in the civil law tradition that excluded the state as a party in private law relations—"not to adopt the old, bourgeois understanding of civil law, but to create a new one."

The primacy of public goals played an important part in the approach to offensive expression in the mass media. Critical to the public ideology and communal goals of the Soviet regime was the instrumental use of mass information, voiced both positively to publicize examples of citizens' exemplary conduct and negatively to expose anti-social acts to public ridicule. To promote the latter role, the regime imposed a "duty to criticize" on the press, espousing public criticism as a means of furthering political and social discipline.

This role of the press as an instrument of social discipline was emphasized during the Khrushchev era, when the regime sought to displace the terrorist extra-legal mechanisms of Stalinist rule by promoting communal values, associated with the parental role of law. State and Communist Party documents proclaimed proper rules of everyday social behavior, grounded in communal values, under the headings of "Rules of Socialist Community Life" and "Communist Morality." Of particular significance for the press and for personality rights protection were the directives of the 1961 Communist Party Program, which in section 5 declared the "important part" played by the mass media in the "molding of the new man" and the role of the "general public, public opinion, and extensive criticism and self-criticism" in combating "survivals of the past" such as the "remnants of private-owner psychology, superstitions, and prejudices" and "manifestations of individualism and selfishness."

Operating under such directives, the tightly controlled monopoly press regularly targeted by name private citizens and lower-level public administrators, often vilifying them with, in the words of one commentator, "coarse insults, ridicule, broad innuendoes, . . . abusive adjectives and epithets, and [with] ominous generalizations and frankly biased or cynical editorial comments." Instead of words, caricatures were often employed: for example, the case of a passenger whose face in a tram car poster was joined to the body of a pig because she was caught riding without a ticket. Citizens' private lives were considered appropriate material for such commentary.[82]

2. Russian Jurists and Codification: The Civil Law Tradition

In the last decades of tsarist rule, Russian legal scholars were developing a private law system grounded in the precepts of the continental European civil law tradition. That legal culture was marked in the early twentieth century by elements inherited from ancient Roman law and nineteenth-century laissez-faire European liberalism, including a jurisprudential emphasis on conceptualization and categorization of legal rules, a sharp distinction between private and public law, an influential role for legal scholars in elucidating legal rules, legislative supremacy under which written codes serve as the primary sources of law, and a maximum of individual autonomy in private legal relationships, including tort. The method for effectuating and safeguarding these precepts is codification, in which the legislature calibrates the proper adjustment of rights and duties in private relationships.

The Bolshevik victory did not result in eradication of this burgeoning civil law tradition. In later reform periods, under the slogans of "socialist legality" in the Khrushchev years, and a "law-based state" (*pravovoe gosudarstvo*) in the Gorbachev era, Soviet civilians promoted codification as the best mechanism for fulfilling the objectives of establishing a system based on statutory rather than administrative supremacy and respect for individual rights. In the immediate post-Stalin years, for example, proponents of socialist legality, seeking a law-based system which would limit the abuse of state

[82] This leeway did not extend to criticism of the Communist Party or governmental leadership.

power, actively participated in the intense codification activity which began in the late 1950s and included enactment in the 1960s of new Civil and Criminal Codes in the Soviet Republics.[95] It was in this setting that civil law jurists sought to create a system of personality rights protection.

3. Personality Rights Protection: 1960s to 1990

Soviet Russia's system of personality rights protection was created amid the clash of the competing tendencies of communal ethos and "socialist legality" in the Khrushchev reform era, and reflected the amalgam of these two components, the former replete with denunciations of individualism and the latter seeking to safeguard individual rights. The result was a limited system of personality rights protection imbued with communal values and providing a restorative remedy—retraction.

Within the movement for civil law reform and codification, a group of Soviet jurists renewed the effort to establish a system of personality rights protection. These efforts coincided with the post-World War II expansion of personality rights protection in other countries, marked in particular by the West German Supreme Court's recognition in 1954 of a "general right of personality" and the recognition of personality rights in certain East European countries. These developments were in large part a response to the horrors of the Nazi regime and World War II. The basic tenets of the European personality rights movement, which sought codified protection of individual autonomy from arbitrary state and third party action, were viewed by the reformers as particularly applicable to the development of post-Stalinist socialist legality, although they did not cite the West German experience, presumably because expression of such receptivity would have been precluded for ideological reasons. However, the similar circumstances of West Germany and the Soviet Union in the 1950s, during which time both were seeking a restoration of legality after totalitarian rule, suggest parallels between the aspirations of personality rights advocates in both countries. In this regard, it is noteworthy that an effort—ultimately unsuccessful—was made in West Germany in the late 1950s to codify the precepts of personality rights protection contained in the decisions of the West German Supreme Court.

In the Soviet Union too, personality rights advocates met with strong opposition. These advocates drafted a chapter of norms for comprehensive protection of personal non-property rights, but only one survived the legislative process to become part of the 1964 Civil Code of the Russian Soviet Federated Socialist Republic: "Defense of Honor

---

[95] In 1957, the Union Republics regained the right to enact their own civil codes.

and Dignity."[105] In addition, as a part of copyright law, a "Right to One's Own Image" was placed in the Code.[107]

Article 7 provided a civil cause of action for defamation based on three elements, all of which remain part of the current system: dissemination, defamatory meaning, and falsity. Two important considerations governed the questions of remedies and the standard of liability. First, because article 7 protected nonmaterial interests, the prevailing view among Soviet jurists was that money damages should not be made available to successful plaintiffs and that the sole remedy should be retraction. The successful opponents of moral damages viewed them as inconsistent with article 7's restorative goals. Second, the individualistic acquisitiveness represented by money damages was discordant with the communal ethos. Damages were available to plaintiffs, but only to the extent that they could show actual material loss resulting from the defamatory publication.

As to the standard of liability, in contrast to the general Soviet legal principle that liability for material damages arose only upon a finding of the defendant's intent or negligence, the standard of liability in article 7 cases was liability without fault. The rationale for this absence of a fault-based standard was the fact that the moral damages remedy was unavailable.

In practice, article 7 was subject to the intrusion of external, public values in two ways. The first was the use by the Communist Party of extra-legal means to discourage defamation actions or to influence the outcome of particular cases, a method which could effectively be employed to shield the state- and Communist Party-controlled press. The second was the intrusion of communal values into interpretation and application of the law in ways that limited the opportunities for redress available to plaintiffs. This process of limitation was the result of judicial and scholarly interpretation on two important questions: defamatory meaning and critical commentary.

---

[105] This code was adopted in conformity to the USSR Fundamental Principles enacted in 1961. In the Soviet federal system, all-Union Fundamentals of Legislation, enacted by the federal parliament, set forth the norms to be implemented in the codes of the various republics.

[107] Technically, this provision did not relate to personality rights, since a right to one's own image was viewed as a property interest related to copyright. The provision is included in this discussion, however, because of its similarity to a right to privacy, and because under the 1995 Civil Code it would clearly fall into that category. Article 514 stated in full:

> Protection of the interests of a citizen depicted in a work of pictorial fine arts. The publication, reproduction, or dissemination of a work of pictorial fine arts in which another person is depicted is permitted only with the consent of the person depicted or, after his death, with the consent of his children and surviving spouse. No such consent is required when these actions are carried out in the interests of State or society, or when the person depicted has posed for the author for a fee.

This provision, if interpreted broadly, would have had considerable impact on the press, because it could have governed the widespread use of cartoons and caricatures (most of them negative) meant to portray particular individuals.

The definition of "defamatory meaning" was limited to the scope of the directives in section 5 of the 1961 Communist Party Program, so that whether a statement was to be judged legally injurious to a plaintiff's reputation was to be viewed from the perspective not of a "reasonable person" but from that of a "right-thinking" member of society who adheres to the Rules of Socialist Community Life and Communist Morality. This approach to "defamatory meaning" was articulated by the Civil Chamber of the USSR Supreme Court in 1964:

> Defamatory, within the meaning of Section 7 of the Principles, is not just any negative information disseminated [by the defendant], but only such which is deserving of a negative evaluation by society, from the point of view of law, of the rules of socialist community life, and of the ethical principles of our own society.

Thus, article 7 as interpreted by the USSR Supreme Court did not provide an unconditional right to protection of an individual's reputation when injured by a false statement. The simple fact of injury, in the eyes of a "reasonable person," was not sufficient to create a presumption of injury to reputation. Rather, a statement was injurious to reputation, and therefore defamatory, only if it accused the plaintiff of behavior violating a tenet of law or the Rules of Socialist Community Life or Communist Morality, as understood by one who adheres to those norms. For example, a false statement that a man owned a house was not defamatory, even though he demonstrated that he was denied an apartment in a government housing project as a result. In another case, a magazine article's description of a scholar's work as "incoherent" was not deemed defamatory.

In this way, the scope of article 7 protection was narrowed and broad categories of offensive expression made exempt from its reach. Research indicated that under the interpretation of "defamatory meaning," most actionable cases involved statements concerning a limited range of activities, primarily those involving interpersonal relations in the home and workplace. Of particular note here, in light of developments in the 1990s, is that questions of offensive expression within the context of open political debate—such as in the mass media—were not included, and almost undoubtedly were not even contemplated.

The scope of article 7 was also limited regarding statements of opinion or commentary, where the regime's directive that the press engage in public criticism to further communal values operated to insulate some of the most highly visible forms of expression from liability. Concern about application of article 7 to commentary formed the basis for much of the press' vocal opposition to adoption and implementation of article 7. The amount of insulation to be afforded critical commentary—such as whether a defendant would be required to prove the truth of underlying facts—was a controversial topic among Soviet jurists. The debate put in stark form the question of how much public value the legal system should assign to mass information and commentary, particularly in light of the fact that the law allowed, and the system encouraged, such expression. For the most part, in the case law, this issue was resolved by the courts in favor of mass media defendants, on grounds that plaintiffs' claims of defamatory meaning were unfounded on public interest grounds.

As for the right of protection of one's own image, article 514 contained an explicit reservation for depictions "carried out in the interests of the State or of society . . . ." Thus, practices such as the widespread dissemination of the likenesses of persons charged with anti-social acts (such as intoxication or riding public transportation without tickets) were not actionable. Indeed, as pointed out by Levitsky, this exception tended to swallow the rule as it related to publications by the mass media, since such activity was intended to instruct the general public.

Not satisfied with the limited possibilities offered by existing law, personality rights advocates continued their efforts throughout the 1970s and 1980s, pressing for recognition of new protected interests, including a right to protection against offensive truthful statements, and introduction of a moral damages remedy. Citing examples from the legislation of other socialist countries, the advocates of moral damages argued that theoretical concerns about the incompatibility of monetary compensation for non-material harm should give way to money damages as a form of "compensation" or "satisfaction" (with a certain punitive element as well).

B. Post-1990

1. The Triumph of Private Law

Enactment of Russia's current system of personality rights protection marks the culmination of the long campaign by personality rights advocates. Their success is attributable in large part to the congruity of their goals with the larger reform movement for a restoration of Russia's place in the civil law tradition. Grounded in the principles of that tradition, it is part of the resurgence of private law which has taken place in the 1990s, of which the 1995 Civil Code is a leading example, and which is linked to aspirations of development of a "civil society." Thus, personality rights protection has been shorn of its communal ethos and infused with a new set of values geared to Civil Society values and the marketplace: individual autonomy; moral damages as the leading remedy; the addition of business reputation as a protected interest; and the absence of public interest concerns external to civil legislation, such as those which had previously narrowed the scope of defamatory meaning or created a broad privilege for critical commentary.

2. The Absence of a Public Ideology

Coincident with Russia's reclamation of its place in the civil law tradition has been the evaporation of any notion that offensive expression has potential public value. Such a notion has been discredited in the 1990s in the wake of the rejection of Marxist-Leninist ideology and its emphasis on communal values.

In March 1991, the USSR Supreme Court revised the definition of "defamatory meaning" for purposes of article 7 interpretation, making a small deletion which discarded nearly thirty years of the ideological basis for determining actionable claims of civil defamation. In the new definition, the perspective from which the defamatory statement determination was to be made no longer included Rules of Socialist Community Life and Principles of Communist Morality.

> False communications that are defamatory are those that diminish the honor and dignity of a citizen or organization in public opinion or in the opinion of individual citizens in regard to observance of laws and moral principles of society (for example, communications about commission of dishonorable acts, unworthy behavior in the workplace or in the family, or communications discrediting productive-economic activity, reputation, and so on).

This new definition reflected the withdrawal of the ideologically-based communal ethos as a basis for law which occurred when the Soviet legislature in 1990 deleted the "leading role of the Party" from article 6 of the USSR Constitution.

The effect of these changes was to remove Marxist ideology and the regime's version of communal values from their place as the primary determinants of the "public value" of mass information and commentary, thereby curtailing any legal support for the press's duty to criticize. Without these ideological moorings, the role of the press was cut adrift from any "public interest" foundation. As a result, information as a "public value" in the 1990s no longer functions as a legal rationale and therefore has been rendered inapplicable to cases of personality rights protection.

The absence of a public ideology in civil defamation law is manifested in several significant ways. For one thing, the statutory and judicial criteria for measurement of moral damages do not include public interest factors. The absence of defenses other than the truth of the contested statement. In addition, it is particularly in cases regarding expressions of critical opinion in political debate that the absence of public interest considerations has been shown to have important implications. Prior to the 1990s, much public criticism—including that which was by any standard insulting or abusive—was insulated from legal sanctions on the grounds that it served a public purpose. Now, however, with the disappearance of public interest considerations, limitations upon civil actions for allegedly offensive statements of opinion have been removed.

In light of the current system's historical roots, however, it would be a mistake to assume blithely that these features are manifestations of authoritarianism or illustrative of a weakly-developed legal culture. Rather, Russia's current system is grounded in the civil law aspirations of nineteenth-century European liberalism, and the conviction that the strongest protection of individual autonomy rights is found in civil code codification. This ideology is marked by aversion to the infusion by outside forces, including the state, of public values outside those considered by the legislature.

As a result, legal dialogue in Russia has lacked any opportunity for consideration of the notion that offensive expression should be viewed as anything other than an actionable invasion of private interests. A key to understanding Russia's current system has been the absence of any procedural or substantive vehicle for infusion of public values other than through the communal ethos, including the duty to criticize imposed on the press, sought by the Soviet regime. At this point, Russian law does not recognize any other rationale to replace Marxist ideology as a "public interest" consideration. However, the structural prerequisites for such recognition now exist in Russia's new constitutional structure. The anticipated dialogue about consideration of a constitutional dimension in Russian personality rights protection law is the subject of [the following parts] of the article.

[IV]. Sources of Defamation Law

[The first three parts] of this article describe[] the statutory scheme which, as interpreted and applied by the ordinary courts,[1] serves as the sole source of Russian civil defamation law. This scheme, found in the 1995 Civil Code and the Mass Media Law, seeks to protect natural and juridical persons from defamatory expression without the intrusion of public interest considerations other than those recognized and codified by the legislature. This body of law has developed against the background of the resurgence of private law in Russia and post-Soviet Russian jurists' antipathy toward public interest concerns as a discredited notion corrupted by the Soviet regime.

Recently, however, another notion has been introduced into Russia's expanding dialogue concerning defamation law. It has been argued that certain public interest considerations, centering on the public value of free expression, must also be taken into account in the clash between personality rights and free expression interests. The Deputy Procurator-General's unsuccessful protest in early 1995 of the result in *Zhirinovskii v. Gaidar* was based on alleged infringement of constitutional free expression guarantees. Later in 1995, then-Russian Foreign Minister Andrei Kozyrev unsuccessfully sought the Russian Constitutional Court's invocation of the Constitution's free expression guarantees to invalidate the statutory basis for a civil defamation suit brought by Vladimir Zhirinovskii against him and a television broadcasting company. Not long after the *Kozyrev* decision, Justice Tamara Morshchakova, Deputy Chairman of the Constitutional Court, reportedly told a session of the Russian Supreme Court that while a right to protection of reputational interests is "unquestionable," the rights of freedom of speech and of the press must also receive protection. In an article which reported Justice Morshchakova's remarks and which focused primarily on a highly visible criminal defamation case, legal commentator Iurii Feofanov described the competing interests in

[1] The term *ordinary courts* will be used to include the Russian Federation Supreme Court and all lower appellate and first instance courts of general jurisdiction. It does not include Russia's specialized judicial branches—the Russian Federation Constitutional Court or the *Arbitrazh* courts which have jurisdiction over economic disputes. That jurisdiction now includes civil defamation cases involving business entities.

defamation actions by public officials against the press and discussed the public value of free expression in a democratic society.

Feofanov's commentary explored in greater depth certain themes sounded earlier by other observers. Lawyer and human rights activist Kronid Lyubarsky, commenting on the outcome in *Zhirinovskii v. Gaidar*, acknowledged the literal correctness of the Moscow appellate court's decision, but at the same time concluded that the court lacked "the least particle of civil responsibility." Another attorney, Leonid Rozhetskin, equating Russian defamation law to censorship, has written that the public's constitutional right to freedom of information "is stifled by the justified concerns of editors who feel that negative information will engender lawsuits."

These remarks reflect the confluence of two at times conflicting tendencies in Russian legal reform: the campaign to replace rule by administrative or extra-legal command with statutory supremacy, and the movement to subject even legislative action to conformity with fundamental norms. Both Feofanov and Lyubarsky are critical of court decisions in which Russia's defamation laws were applied against press defendants, even though the judges in these cases apparently acted independently and followed the applicable law, rather than extra-legal commands, in making their decisions. Their criticism is based on the conviction that adjudication of disputes involving expressive activity requires consideration of additional sources of law that introduce values beyond those recognized and codified by the legislature.

It is likely that further efforts will be made to convince courts to apply constitutional or international norms to Russian defamation law. Some of the impetus for such efforts will undoubtedly be provided by the example of other legal systems where attempts to include constitutional norms among the sources of defamation law have been successful. The immediate origins of such constitutionalization lie in decisions from the late 1950s and early 1960s by the West German Federal Constitutional Court [*Bundesverfassungsgericht*][22] and the United States Supreme Court.[23] Since then, the European Court of Human Rights and domestic courts in Japan, Canada, England, Spain, Hungary, India, and Australia have been among those which have also recognized the presence of a constitutional dimension in defamation law. The goal of these efforts has been to blur the distinction between private and public law. Proponents of constitutionalization have not sought to eliminate the protection of personality rights, yet they have claimed that it must at times be superseded by a public interest in furthering free expression.

[22] 7 BVerfGE 198 (1958) (*Luth*) and 12 BVerfGE 113 (1961) (*Schmid-Spiegel*), *translated in* Donald P. Kommers, The Constitutional Jurisprudence of the Federal Republic of Germany 368, 377 (1989). Neither of these cases involved civil defamation case law; however, *Luth* dealt with the crucial third-party effect issue, and *Schmid-Spiegel* with the question of the application of a public interest dimension in a criminal defamation case. These principles have since been applied in a number of civil defamation cases.

[23] New York Times Co. v. Sullivan, 376 U.S. 254 (1964). To the author's knowledge, this was the first direct application in any legal system of a constitutional norm in a civil defamation case.

[V]. The Constitutional Court's Decision in *Kozyrev*

In his complaint to the Constitutional Court, Andrei Kozyrev argued that article 29 of the Constitution should shield him from bearing the burden of proving the truthfulness of his statement, made over the air on television station NTV [Independent Television] in February 1994, that Vladimir Zhirinovskii holds "Fascist-like views." Specifically, his complaint called upon the Court to invalidate the civil code provisions supporting Zhirinovskii's civil defamation lawsuit because the absence in them of a fact/opinion distinction is inconsistent with paragraphs 1 and 3 of article 29.

In finding Kozyrev's complaint inadmissible, the Court paid close attention to the jurisdictional requirements of Russia's system of constitutional review. Operating under a system of constitutional control which combines elements of centralization and diffusion,[40] the Russian Federation Constitutional Court and ordinary courts are empowered to review those acts that fall within their respective competencies. Under that system, the Court has exclusive jurisdiction to declare parliamentary statutes invalid if they are deemed inconsistent with constitutional norms.[41] The Court's competence includes adjudication of constitutional challenges to legislation brought by individual complainants (such as Andrei Kozyrev) against whom the statute in question has been applied or will be applied in a concrete case. In addition, the Court may exercise judicial review upon referral to it of a concrete case by an ordinary court that has concluded that application of a particular statute violates the Constitution. In cases involving constitutional challenges to governmental acts other than legislation, however, the Court lacks jurisdiction; instead, such cases fall under the competence of Russia's ordinary courts. Reasoning that treatment of Kozyrev's complaint would entail examination of factual questions, the Court relied on article 3 of the Constitutional Court Statute to conclude that review of the issues raised was a matter only for the ordinary courts.

While ruling Kozyrev's complaint inadmissible, the Court nevertheless discussed several substantive issues. First, the Court questioned Kozyrev's assertion that the civil code provision in question was constitutionally suspect, given that it represented statutory implementation of article 23(1) of the Constitution, which guarantees protection of one's honor and good name.

---

[40] A centralized or "concentrated" system of judicial review, with exclusive jurisdiction in one specialized constitutional court, contrasts with a "diffuse system," such as in the United States, where courts of general jurisdiction are empowered to resolve constitutional issues.

[41] The Russian Parliament (officially, the "Federal Assembly," which is divided into two houses—the State Duma and the Federation Council) is not the only body empowered to enact federal legislative norms. For example, the President may issue decrees and directives which have general binding force throughout the Russian Federation ("normative presidential acts") so long as they comply with the Constitution and statutes enacted by Parliament. When requested to do so by other state bodies, but not by means of an individual citizen's complaint, the Constitutional Court is competent to review normative presidential acts. Because the norms governing defamation law are in statutory form in the 1995 Civil Code and the Mass Media Law, this study will focus on the legislature as the source of those rules.

At the same time, however, the opinion states that Kozyrev's complaint posed "an important and topical question": how in a specific case to reconcile the protection of an individual's honor and good name with "the interest of free discussion of political issues in democratic society?" Having thereby articulated recognition of a public interest element in the defamation calculus, the Court declared to the ordinary courts that it would be necessary for them to determine whether the statement in question in a specific case "fits in the sphere of political discussion," how to distinguish generally between assertions of fact and political value judgments, and whether it is possible to make an objective evaluation of the truth or falsity of the latter. So that the ordinary courts will correctly carry out their duty to "insure the requisite equilibrium between the constitutional rights to protection of one's honor and dignity and the freedom of speech," the Court suggested strongly to the Russian Supreme Court that it issue "guiding explanations" for resolution of the difficult questions posed by Kozyrev's complaint.[52]

While the Court's declarations on these substantive matters might be viewed as contradictory, the first suggesting that the statutory scheme does not implicate article 29 and the second asserting that it does, it is probably of little consequence since they are not legally binding.[53] Because of the nature of Russia's system of exclusive competencies over different categories of judicial review, the ordinary courts are not obligated to follow the Constitutional Court's declarations.[54] Thus, the only conclusive result of the *Kozyrev* decision is that one can say with certainty that the Constitutional Court will not for the foreseeable future be disposed to exercise jurisdiction over a constitutional complaint grounded in the purported unconstitutionality of the statutory scheme's lack of a fact/opinion distinction. Therefore, the Court has agreed that the questions of a constitutional dimension to defamation law, at least the fact/opinion problem, should be subject to a diffuse form of judicial review and law application analysis. As a result, Russia's ordinary courts will probably be the leading fora for consideration of possible constitutionalization of Russian defamation law—in other words, those questions

[52] It appears from the *Kozyrev* opinion that the Court has concluded that article 152 of the 1995 Civil Code is somehow constitutionally suspect. However, rather than treating this as a matter of statutory invalidity—an issue that falls squarely within the Court's competence—the Court appears to suggest that this is a matter of law application, and that any potential insufficiencies can be overcome by the ordinary courts' infusion of constitutional values into consideration of the differing fact situations presented by specific cases. Put another way, the Court is perhaps declining to engage in case-by-case balancing, particularly where two countervailing constitutional rights are asserted, as a jurisprudential method. To this author's knowledge, *Kozyrev* is the only case in which the Constitutional Court has considered a direct confrontation between competing rights guaranteed under chapter two of the 1993 Constitution.

[53] Given the Court's express statement that it found the complaint inadmissible pursuant to article 43(1) of the Constitutional Court Statute, it must be concluded that the opinion's statements about article 23(1) of the Constitution are without effect because they would constitute a determination on the merits and recognition that the complaint was admissible. The Court could have chosen to decide this matter as a question of substantive law, but chose not to.

[54] Whether they will choose to is certainly another question. At this time, the only action known to the author taken by the Supreme Court related to defamation law and the Constitution is that Court's dismissal of the protest in early 1995—prior to *Kozyrev*—in the *Zhirinovskii v. Gaidar* litigation.

identified by the Constitutional Court in *Kozyrev*, as well as others considered in this article, such as normativity and third-party effect. It is to those questions that we now turn.

[VI]. Textual Analysis: The Russian Constitution, the ICCPR, and Russian Civil Defamation Law

The provisions of article 29 in the Constitution and article 19 in the ICCPR guarantee the exercise of free expression. However, as is generally the case with such textual protections, they are sufficiently indeterminate[56] to allow the exercise of broad judicial discretion as to their construction and application. Before applying them as sources of law in a specific defamation case, a Russian court would have to resolve several issues. The first of these pertains to normativity—whether constitutional norms operate with direct effect as a source of enforceable rights and duties in litigation, and are therefore distinct from a declaratory political program. Moving closer to issues specific to defamation law, the court would also have to determine whether to recognize "third party effect," the notion that constitutional norms are applicable to legal relations even in the absence of state action. Finally, it is unclear whether the constitutional text mandates exclusion of all defamatory statements from its protection. Each of these issues—normativity, third-party effect, and exclusion of defamatory expression—will now be examined.

A. Normativity

This threshold question asks whether constitutional provisions serve as an independent source of rights and duties in a case before the courts, or whether they act solely as a declaration of political goals to be implemented by the legislature. Put another way, this question of the direct effect or applicability of constitutional norms is a choice between two variants, which I will call "legislative" and "judicial" normativity. The distinction centers on which branch will serve as the ultimate author of the specific parameters of indeterminate constitutional norms, so as to make them applicable to the facts of a specific case.

1. Legislative Normativity

Under legislative normativity, the legislature serves as the sole or primary agent of constitutional normativity—in other words, constitutional provisions lack direct effect until the enactment of statutes that implement and shape the contours of those indeterminate rights. Until the legislature acts, constitutional and international law provisions simply represent symbolic political programs and do not serve as sources of directly enforceable rights. This system of legislative normativity, which one commentator has described as characterized by the "sanctification of statutes,"

[56] Thomas Franck has defined *determinacy* as "the literary property of a rule: that which makes its message clear."

predominated in the continental civil law tradition until the post-World War II creation of constitutional justice systems, and has been a hallmark of English law for three hundred years.

Judicial normativity and the constitutionalization of an area of law such as defamation represent a fundamental departure from legislative normativity, which excludes the judiciary from a decision-making role beyond that of statutory application. The primary characteristic of judicial normativity is the concept of independent court review of governmental acts, using sources of law other than legislation.

Current Russian defamation law reflects a system that in its practical effect operates in accordance with the precepts of legislative normativity. The only determinacy to article 29 has been rendered by Parliament. For example, in defamation law article 29's contours have been specified in chapter 8 of the 1995 Civil Code and the Mass Media Law. Thus, it may be concluded that article 29 protection extends only to non-defamatory expression or to defamatory statements that are grounded in facts. The broader implications of such a viewpoint are that in the area of defamation law, the legislature commands almost total deference and has exclusive domain over the clarification of indeterminate constitutional human rights protection norms. Support for this conclusion lies in the Russian courts' treatment of defamation cases and in scholarly commentary. In *Zhirinovskii v. Gaidar*, for example, the courts relied entirely on the applicable Civil Code provisions, and according to a leading Russian constitutional scholar, commenting on article 29, statutory Civil Code and Mass Media Law provisions establish limitations on the exercise of article 29 rights.[68]

Legislative normativity represents a thread of continuity with the Soviet constitutional system, which in turn shared this characteristic with most pre-World War II European constitutional systems. A defining tenet of Soviet constitutional theory was that the legislature gave constitutional provisions determinate form and made them directly effective. Thus, the 1977 USSR Constitution was considered a hortatory political program that required the implementation of domestic legislation to give its provisions legal force. In this way, the free expression guarantees in the 1977 Constitution received normativity in 1990 with legislative enactment of the 1990 Press Law (abolition of censorship, for example) and in post-Soviet Russia, enactment of the Mass Media Law.

Although legislative supremacy was the goal of Soviet legal reformers, in reality the Communist Party's public interest concerns were applied to statutes in extra-legal fashion or by the judiciary effectuating Party commands such as those requiring conformity to the Rules of Socialist Community Life. In this way, the Soviet system differed from those pre-World War II European models that it so closely resembled in form. This situation led reformers in the late 1980s to press for the establishment of a law-based state where the legislature would in reality, and not just in constitutional theory, exercise exclusive constitutional normativity. In the mid-1990s, the question is

[68] E.A. Lukasheva, *Stat'ia 29* [*Article 29*], *in* Konstitutsiia Rossiiksoi Federatsii: Kommentarii 179 (B.N. Topornin ed., 1994).

whether such a legislative normativity approach is compatible with Russia's new constitutional order.

2. The Russian Constitution and Judicial Normativity

In the past two years, Russia has sought to put in place a constitutional order, based on the December 1993 Constitution, which identifies and guarantees human rights and is grounded in explicit textual recognition of judicial normativity. As to substantive rights, chapter 2 of the Constitution ("Rights and Freedoms of Man and Citizen") sets forth individual rights which are recognized and guaranteed in articles 19 through 54. Explicit provisions demonstrate that chapter 2 is intended to be more than a declaratory political program: articles 15(1) and 18 expressly provide that the constitutional norms, including the rights and freedoms recognized in chapter 2, shall have direct effect.

As to international norms such as those set forth in the ICCPR, the Constitution explicitly mandates the incorporation of agreements to which the Russian Federation is a party into the domestic "legal system"; however, it is unclear as to whether this formulation means that they are self-executing and therefore receive the same direct effect as constitutional norms themselves. The Russian Federation Statute on International Treaties, enacted in 1995, seeks to clarify the general issue, but does not provide guidance as to the treatment of the ICCPR. Under article 5(3) of the statute, an international agreement to which Russia is a party will be self-executing in domestic law unless the agreement itself requires enactment of implementing domestic legislation. However, this does not resolve the question of whether the ICCPR should be self-executing because consensus is lacking as to whether it is intended to be directly applicable and therefore leaves open the question of how to apply the criteria of article 5(3) of the Statute on Treaties.[83] As a result, it cannot be stated conclusively on the basis of the constitutional text or the applicable legislation that the ICCPR serves as a source of law which may be invoked before domestic courts in the absence of implementing legislation.[84] Meanwhile, however, the Russian Constitutional Court has applied or cited

[83] This disagreement centers on interpretation of article 2(2) of the ICCPR, which calls upon parties to the Covenant to adopt necessary measures "to give effect to the rights recognized" within its provisions in those cases where not already provided for in "existing legislative or other measures."

The question of direct applicability is distinct from that of the extent of a state-party's discretion to decide the means of implementing the ICCPR's terms in its domestic legal system; rather, it asks whether as a matter of international obligation a state-party is required to make the agreement self-executing under their domestic law.

[84] The same can be said regarding the ECHR, assuming that Russia decides to accede to it.

On February 8, 1996, the Committee of Ministers of the Council of Europe approved Russia's application to become the Council's 39th full member, on condition that Russia take several steps including accession to the ECHR. In anticipation of such approval, the Russian Federation State Duma in July 1994 proclaimed Russia's readiness to take such action. Due to the extensive jurisprudence of the European Court of Human Rights concerning ECHR article 10, accession to the ECHR will perhaps have a significant impact on Russian defamation law. However, since accession has not yet occurred at the time of this writing, such questions are beyond the scope of this article.

the ICCPR on at least two occasions, in decisions invalidating legislative acts, without expressly addressing the self-execution question.

In addition to having direct effect, the Constitution's norms are expressly made superior to all legislative acts or other domestic laws in the event of a conflict. The supremacy of chapter 2 rights is complemented by article 55(2), which prohibits "[l]aws which deny or diminish human and civil rights and freedoms . . . ." Provisions in treaties to which Russia is a party also are accorded higher rank in the legal hierarchy than are conflicting domestic laws. Statutes limiting the exercise of fundamental rights are invalid unless they conform to the specific requirements enumerated in article 55(3).

In institutional form, this human rights protection system is based on judicial normativity, with the Constitutional and ordinary courts empowered to exercise judicial review over those governmental acts that fall within their respective spheres of competency. In the event of a challenge to a statute based on its alleged non-conformity with international norms, meanwhile, it appears that the ordinary courts are authorized to refuse application of the statute, rather than required to refer it to the Constitutional Court. For the arbitration courts, this principle is expressly stated in the applicable statute. These questions are potentially significant in light of article 7(2) of the 1995 Civil Code, which states with certain exceptions that the Code's provisions are subordinate to conflicting norms in international agreements to which Russia is a party.

Both the Constitutional Court and the ordinary courts in 1995 demonstrated their willingness to exercise judicial review and give direct effect to constitutional norms. Since its resumption of activity in early 1995, the Constitutional Court has exercised its powers of concrete norm control in at least seven cases, invalidating provisions in the Housing Code, Criminal Procedure Code, and three other statutes. In the first five months of its activity in 1995, the Court received 3101 communications requesting that it take action. Of those, some 600 survived initial screening to be reviewed for admissibility, with some fifty petitions undergoing the Court's substantive review.

Among the ordinary courts, the Court of Appeals for Iaroslavl' Province, in two decisions affirmed by the Supreme Court's Civil Chamber in March 1995, which were in turn affirmed by the Supreme Court's Presidium four months later, relied on the direct effect provision of Constitution article 15(1) to invalidate acts by the Province's administrative organs. In addition, the Supreme Court's guiding explanations, issued on October 31, 1995, strongly endorse the normativity of constitutional norms and call upon lower ordinary courts to give them direct effect and supreme legal force over governmental acts, including legislation.

Despite these affirmations of judicial normativity, the specific area of Russian defamation law appears to straddle the gap between the reality of legislative normativity and the aspirations of judicial normativity. On the one hand, in practice it exhibits the characteristics of the former; on the other, it operates within a constitutional order that on a textual basis and in the Constitutional Court's actual exercise of judicial review is directed toward the latter. However, it may be concluded that nothing in current Russian law mandates a legislative monopoly on normativity. Therefore, if courts were to apply the Constitution and ICCPR as additional sources of law, giving articles 29 and 19 direct effect, such action would have a solid foundation.

3. Normativity in Private Relations: Third-Party Effect

Although constitutional norms might have direct effect as a general principle, they will not be imposed on private legal relations unless the courts recognize the principle of third-party effect, which has been characterized as "recognition of constitutional rights in private legal relationships." Opposition to this principle is based on the notion of strict separation of the public and private spheres. Put another way, the third-party effect question is an extension of the legislative versus judicial normativity "grand debate": it asks whether assessment of the effect of constitutional norms in relations between private parties is the exclusive domain of the legislature, with the result that a constitutional provision without legislative implementation may be construed to bind only the state.

This issue has been examined in a number of legal systems and is similar to the state action question in the United States.[107] When considered in the defamation law context, it has been accompanied by examination of the nature of constitutional free expression guarantees. In 1956, the Japanese Supreme Court rejected a defamation defendant's constitutional defense while ruling that the issues in the case "related only to private law." Two years later, the German Constitutional Court faced similar questions in its seminal *Luth* decision. While not a defamation case, *Luth* serves as the forerunner of the trend toward constitutionalization of this area of law, due to its treatment of the third-party effect issue.

Luth was decided amidst considerable controversy over the third-party effect issue. The issues in the case centered on the availability of injunctive relief to the plaintiff film producer and distributor against the defendant's published appeal, based on the plaintiff's Nazi past, for a boycott of the plaintiff's film. The trial court, upholding the plaintiff's claim based on article 826 of the German Civil Code, viewed the case as one involving solely private interests. The defendant responded with a complaint to the Constitutional Court, grounded in the free expression guarantees in article 5(1) of the Basic Law. In resolving the case, the Constitutional Court considered three options: (1) denial of the complaint, based on the inapplicability of the Basic Law to private law relations; (2) reversal of the civil court decision, giving direct effect to article 5(1); or (3) a middle ground retaining the fundamental aspects of the private law scheme, but requiring consideration of constitutional norms.

---

[107] The European Court of Human Rights implicitly recognized the principle in a recent determination that a large damages award in a civil defamation case was a violation of article 10 of the ECHR, even though article 10(1) guarantees the right to exercise freedom of expression "without interference by public authority." In United States First Amendment jurisprudence, unless "state action" is present, the free expression guarantees do not apply against acts by private persons. An important element in the landmark decision in *New York Times Co. v. Sullivan* was the United States Supreme Court's conclusion that state action is present in the judiciary's adjudication of civil defamation cases.

In the part of the decision most significant for the third-party effect question, the Court chose the third option. Acknowledging that German historical experience dictated that fundamental rights guarantees have their fullest impact against the State, the Court at the same time concluded that the reach of constitutional values must also extend to all legal relationships. Although the Court did not give those values direct effect, it adopted the concept of "reciprocal (or indirect) effect," whereby constitutional norms influence, rather than supersede, private values in a balancing analysis, and thereby rejected the notion of the private sphere's impermeability from public interests.

In Russia, as in Germany, the constitutional text does not appear to speak explicitly to the third-party effect question, and the issue apparently has not yet been directly addressed in a concrete case before the Russian courts. One commentator, meanwhile, has concluded that the Constitution unequivocally requires recognition of third-party effect, due to the language of article 17(3), which prohibits the exercise of human rights when it violates the rights of others. While such an interpretation is certainly plausible, it should be noted that the language of article 17(3) is similar to certain provisions of the German Basic Law that the German Constitutional Court did not find sufficient to require third-party effect in the *Luth* case. The Russian and German texts also contain similar provisions guaranteeing access to the courts in the case of claimed violations of rights, but in cases where the acts in question have been committed by public officials. However, what the German Basic Law lacks, and the Russian Constitution contains, is a more general guarantee of court access—a provision that when read in conjunction with article 17(3) would support application of third-party effect.

Under Russia's constitutional structure, another question is whether international law might decide the third-party effect issue. The German Constitutional Court did not consider the application of international law in *Luth*. In 1958, the ICCPR did not exist, and although West Germany was a party to the ECHR, that agreement had received little application. Moreover, the Basic Law is somewhat ambiguous regarding the domestic normativity of provisions in international agreements. Under the 1993 Russian Constitution, on the other hand, the ICCPR's norms, including the free expression provisions in article 19, are a direct part of the Russian legal system. As a result, the extent to which the ICCPR's norms apply to private relations in Russia should depend on whether those norms themselves are intended to operate with third-party effect.

Russian courts would not find abundant outside direction in attempting to determine whether the ICCPR addresses this problem because the effectiveness of the ICCPR depends upon agreed interpretation and uniform application, international law is the source of law for interpretation, and the Human Rights Committee has declared that its provisions are to be interpreted independent of any particular domestic legal system and of all dictionary definitions. The HRC provides interpretation through decisions in optional protocol cases and interstate complaints (none had been made by 1993), as well as "general comments" made pursuant to article 40(4). However, this leaves considerable room for interpretation of international law by domestic courts, since there is little definition of the contours of a number of the ICCPR's indeterminate norms, including those in article 19.

Although little interpretation has been made of the relevant ICCPR provisions, scholarly commentary supports the view that numerous ICCPR provisions, including article 19, are intended to have third-party effect. If so, this would be controlling in Russian law, due to article 15(4), even if it were to be determined that article 29 of the Constitution does not operate with third-party effect.

Outside the Constitution and ICCPR, the Russian Parliament itself perhaps has resolved the third-party effect question by including provisions in articles 2 and 7 of the 1995 Civil Code that act as "portals" into private law for the entry of public values in the form of constitutional and international norms. Stating that human rights and freedoms "are protected by civil legislation," article 2(2) appears to dictate that the 1995 Civil Code be interpreted and applied in conformity with constitutional norms: a provision of considerable potential significance in civil defamation law because of the opportunities for judicial interpretation and exercise of discretion in specific cases. Article 7(2) recognizes the direct effect of international treaties on private relations recognized in the Code, and their supremacy over conflicting statutory provisions, unless the treaty in question is deemed to require domestic implementing legislation.

More explicit than the so-called "general clauses" in German Civil Code sections such as 826, these provisions, which are set forth in the "General Part" of the 1995 Civil Code and therefore control the personality rights protection provisions of chapter 8, demonstrate legislative intent that the third-party effect should apply to private relations in most cases. Less conclusive is the question of whether article 7(2) requires giving the ICCPR third-party effect: although article 7(2) dictates that international norms generally are applicable to private civil relations and will supersede conflicting statutory provisions, it is possible that the ICCPR might fall under the exception for treaties that as a matter of international law require domestic legislative implementation. In this regard, however, it should also be noted that the Constitutional Court has cited or applied the ICCPR without considering the necessity of an implementation requirement.

In conclusion, literal textual analysis does not yield a clear-cut conclusion as to whether constitutional and international norms would be found to operate with third-party effect in Russian law. If confronted with this question, it is possible that a Russian court would go beyond the texts in order to resolve it, which might involve examination of the German Constitutional Court's decision in *Luth*. *Luth* was decided in a setting with interesting parallels to 1990s Russia. For example, both 1950s West Germany and 1990s Russia experienced a resurgence of private personality rights protection law that was viewed as essential to a legal order emerging from totalitarian or authoritarian rule, along with the creation of new constitutional courts with broad powers of judicial review. For this reason, among others, the German experience is perhaps of particular relevance to mid-1990s Russia.

In this regard, in addition to the German Court's analysis described above, a Russian court in an effort to reconcile those textual requirements that support third-party effect and the concerns of its opponents might draw upon distinctions made by the *Luth* court between different branches of private law, such as tort and contract. The German Court concluded that in contrast to contract law, where the substantive rules of private relations are created primarily by agreement between the parties, tort rules are creations of state policy-making enforced by the courts. As a result, they bear a strong element of mandatory state action, piercing the protective shell of autonomous private relations. This line of reasoning suggests that perhaps recognition of a third-party effect in Russian defamation law need not lead to substantial intrusion of public law into such areas as contract.

B. Defamation Law and Free Expression Guarantees

Recognition of third-party effect as a general principle would trigger the more specific inquiry into whether broad indeterminate constitutional guarantees of expressive activity do not protect defamatory statements and are therefore not to be included among the sources of defamation law. The core question in a court's examination of a defamation defendant's constitutional challenge would be whether application of the current statutory scheme would implicate the exercise of constitutional rights guaranteed in article 29 of the Constitution.

Article 29 sets forth broad guarantees of freedom of expression and communication. Each person is guaranteed freedom of thought and speech, and freely to seek, receive, transmit, produce, and disseminate information. No one may be compelled to express one's opinions and convictions or to renounce them. Finally, freedom of the mass information media is guaranteed, with censorship prohibited.

These rights, however, are not absolute. Express categorical restrictions on their exercise are found in article 29 itself, along with more ambiguous provisions that might be construed to permit the same result. Thus, certain content—propaganda or "hate speech" directed against groups—is categorically prohibited, and more generally protected communicative activities are limited to those that may be carried out by "any lawful method" [*liubym zakonnym sposobom*].

In addition, certain constitutional provisions outside article 29 could be interpreted to permit restrictions on the exercise of free expression. Personality rights are also protected by the Constitution, and therefore are among those that may not be violated by the exercise of other rights and freedoms. In order to resolve such clashes of countervailing constitutional rights, federal statutes may restrict the exercise of human rights and freedoms in order to protect the rights and lawful interests of other persons.

The question, then, is whether any of these provisions within or without article 29 operates to exclude false defamatory expression from article 29 protection. As to the enumerated categorical content restrictions in article 29(2), they do not include defamatory statements or other potential intrusions on individual personality interests.

Also, in contrast to instruments such as the German Basic Law, the South Korean Constitution, ECHR, and the ICCPR, explicit language restricting the exercise of expressive activity for the purpose of protecting personality rights is not found in any of article 29's provisions.

On the basis of the article 29 text, therefore, one Russian scholar has concluded that the only constitutional limits on freedom of expression are those content restrictions enumerated in article 29(2). However, two other Russian scholars have concluded that article 29(2) contains an implied term, incorporating ICCPR article 19(3)(a), which includes intrusion on personality interests, including reputation, among the abuses of freedom of expression that are outside the protective mantle of the article 29 guarantees. Neither author suggests that balancing of competing interests is required. This approach implies that article 29(2) is sufficiently indeterminate to require the placement of false defamatory expression into the same legal category as those types of content enumerated in article 29(2). It may be assumed that all actionable statements under the 1995 Civil Code and Mass Media Law would not have constitutional protection under this approach, because Russian law treats all defamatory statements as susceptible to objective determinations of truth or falsity.

The invocation by these authors of the ICCPR requires examination of ICCPR article 19(3)(a) to determine whether it can be read as a categorical exclusion. In contrast to article 29 of the Constitution, article 19(3) does provide that the exercise of expressive activity may be subject to certain restrictions, including those "for respect of the rights or reputations of others"; however, it qualifies this by requiring that "these shall only be such as are provided by law" and are "necessary" to accomplish these goals. The Human Rights Committee and commentators have interpreted the "necessity" requirement as imposing a heavy burden of justification upon a state seeking to restrict the exercise of free expression. While the HRC has not applied the "necessity" requirement in a defamation case, it has done so in examining a restriction imposed pursuant to article 19(3)(b). In a challenge to the Province of Quebec's restrictions on outdoor advertising in the English language, the HRC required Quebec to show that no alternative means were available for advancing its aims, and concluded that it had failed to do so.

In addition, the text, legislative history, and interpretation of ICCPR article 17 suggest that it does not dictate a categorical denial of protection for all defamatory statements, even those determined to be false. Article 17(1) requires that a state party guarantee legal protection against "unlawful attacks" on a person's honor and reputation. The legislative history of the ICCPR establishes that the term "unlawful attacks" was intended to limit the scope of this protection to intentional acts, lest legitimate commentary and criticism be suppressed.

For these reasons, although the term "unlawful attacks" in article 17(1) is open to interpretation, it is doubtful that the ICCPR can be employed, either as a matter of direct application or to inform the constitutional text, to exclude all defamatory statements, or even all false defamatory statements, from article 19 protection (protection from free expression determined to be false). The ICCPR is not sufficiently determinate to contain such an express categorical limitation.

Returning to the Constitutional text, several provisions might be relevant. Looking outside article 29, two commentators have suggested that offensive expression should be outside the parameters of article 29 because it implicates the guarantees of personality rights protection in articles 21(1) and 23(1), and therefore violates article 17(3). This appears to be the analysis used in that part of the *Kozyrev* decision where the Constitutional Court questioned the complainant's assertion that his article 29 rights were implicated by the statutory defamation scheme. However, articles 21 and 23 are also indeterminate in that they are silent regarding restrictions on expression, and article 17(3) also says nothing specific about defamation law. Although article 17(3) could be construed to exclude free expression guarantees from the defamation law calculus, it might just as readily be read to exclude all protection of personality interests when they clash with the exercise of article 29 rights. Another plausible construction of article 17(3) is that it calls for balancing of countervailing constitutional rights on a case-by-case basis rather than wholesale protection of one set of rights at the expense of the other.

Within article 29 itself, the inclusion of the indeterminate phrase "any lawful means" to qualify exercise of free expression rights in article 29(4) is perhaps problematic even well beyond the context of defamation law. This qualifying condition, which suggests a return to legislative normativity, is sufficiently ambiguous to support a determination that because the legislature has established remedies against false defamatory statements, their dissemination is automatically precluded. On the other hand, again, the text of article 29(4) is not sufficiently determinate to suggest that it refers to defamatory expression at all. In this regard, it should be noted that Professor Piatkina has concluded that "lawful means" operates solely to exclude dissemination of state secrets as defined by the legislature.

In sum, although article 29, particularly paragraph (4), is open to differing interpretations, it can be concluded that literal examination of the constitutional text does not dictate categorical exclusion of all defamatory expression from constitutional protection. As a result, it is likely that a judicial effort to resolve the constitutionalization question—whether the civil defamation scheme implicates the exercise of interests protected by article 29—would rest in the application of other methods of interpretation. In such an exercise, the Russian courts and legal community will perhaps be compelled to address the nature of free expression guarantees—a task beyond literal textual analysis.

[VII]. Beyond the Texts: Accommodation of Private and Public Values

If a court were to conclude that the relevant texts do not categorically exclude recognition of constitutional and international norms as sources of defamation law, this would be only the first step in resolving the clash of countervailing interests. A Russian court perhaps would consider methodologies, such as the categorical and balancing approaches, which other legal systems have used in attempting to complete this task. For example, the United States employs a categorical approach, calibrated to constitutionally relevant distinctions such as the status of a defamation plaintiff, while the German Constitutional Court and the European Court of Human Rights rely on ad hoc balancing methodology that identifies and prioritizes a range of factors specific to each individual case. Given in particular the constitutional guarantees afforded personality rights and constitutional limitations on restrictions on the exercise of fundamental rights, as well as the attraction of German models, it is likely that Russian jurists would be more inclined toward the latter approach rather than creation of strict categories.[184]

Regardless of the chosen methodology, recognition of a constitutional mandate to accommodate would entail identification of constitutionally relevant balancing factors or categories—for example, a distinction between critical opinion and assertions of fact. The Constitution itself perhaps provides a basis for distinguishing opinion and fact by setting aside a discrete provision guaranteeing protection of the former. Also of potential relevance to the Fascist cases in the Russian courts is the status afforded to public official plaintiffs in the United States and European Court of Human Rights. In the United States, the plaintiff's status as a public figure triggers an elevated standard of liability; under the ECHR, it requires the plaintiff to tolerate a higher degree of public criticism (in other words, greater weight is given to the public interest). The point, however, is that under both approaches the status of plaintiffs as public officials is deemed constitutionally relevant, whereas Russian law makes no such distinction, although in *Kozyrev* the Constitutional Court recently declared that one should be made.

An essential element of this inquiry into accommodation would be assessment of the nature of the article 29 and article 19 free expression guarantees—an exercise laden with value considerations. A conception of free expression guarantees as individual and private in nature would be consistent with what might be called a "civil society" model of defamation. The alternative view that free expression guarantees should also further public values would reflect a "democratic" model.

The Civil Society Model recognizes freedom of expression from unwarranted state interference (such as pre-publication censorship) as an individual private right, protected as an attribute of personality and means of promoting individual self-fulfillment. However, when balanced against protection of personality interests, the free expression guarantees must give way to a considerable extent. Current Russian defamation law reflects Parliament's implicit acceptance of this model: thus, free expression is not entirely without protection, since defamatory statements that a defendant can prove to be

[184] This appears to be the methodology suggested by the Constitutional Court to the ordinary courts in *Kozyrev*, although the Court's statements about article 23(1) make this a somewhat mixed message. Meanwhile, by declining to engage in something akin to case-by-case law application analysis, the Court is perhaps signaling that its limited jurisdiction precludes it from engaging in ad hoc balancing.

based upon true facts are exempt from liability.[192] Under this view, the nature of article 29 guarantees and the goals of the current statutory scheme are congruent.

Underlying the constitutionalization debate in other legal systems, however, has been a different vision of the nature of free expression guarantees—the Democratic Model—which views freedom of expression as dual in nature, imbued with a public dimension grounded in the essential value of information and ideas to a pluralistic democratic society. According to proponents of the Democratic Model, this public dimension must at times take precedence over protection of personality rights even when the defamatory statement cannot be proven to be true.

The differences in the free expression values recognized in the Civil Society and Democratic Models coalesce around assessment of the so-called "chilling effect"—the values served or impaired by the deterrent effect posed by the threat of sanctions, including moral damages, for dissemination of defamatory statements. In the Civil Society Model, free expression interests, while recognized, are simply outweighed by the competing individual personality interests that require a deterrent effect to make such protection effective. The Democratic Model, meanwhile, views the self-censorship inherent in the defamation law deterrence goal as the greater threat to democracy and therefore to society. This fundamental difference over deterrent effect lies at the core of the clash between private and public values in civil defamation law. If a Russian court were to opt for the Democratic Model, it would compete directly with Parliament in a contest over who will be the arbiter of the proper balance between public and private interests.

At the same time, however, it is possible that such an interaction might contain within itself an opportunity for reconciliation, in the form of both sides' shared interest in rejecting the intervention of state executive or administrative agencies as arbiters, as occurred in the Soviet system. In contrast to the extra-legal mechanisms employed in the Soviet era, constitutional norms under a Democratic Model would serve as a new vehicle for the entry of public values into private law. As a result, for perhaps the first time in Russian history the notion of "public interest" might not be synonymous with "state interest," and the ideology underlying application of public values would not be the discredited communal ethos, but pluralistic democracy.

[VIII]. Conclusion

In the early 1990s, advocates of press freedoms in Russia achieved two goals: legislative recognition of pluralism in mass media ownership, and the abolition of direct pre-publication censorship. Pursuit of these objectives, and their realization in statutory form, have been consistent with the individual self-fulfillment values which underlie Russia's civil defamation law.

---

[192] The defense of truth is not available in criminal law actions based on article 131 of the Criminal Code, nor would it be if "insult" is recognized as a civil cause of action.

The recognition and effectuation of this first generation of press rights, while illustrative of Russia's new departures in freedom of expression, did not exhaust the legal issues faced by the mass media relating to content regulation. One of the forms of post-publication regulation to emerge has been a civil defamation scheme weighted in favor of plaintiffs and featuring expanded civil remedies against false defamatory expression.

The basic elements of this scheme, although now grounded in the 1995 Civil Code, reflect Russia's institutional configuration in the several years prior to the adoption of the Russian Federation Constitution in 1993—a configuration marked by the legislature's exclusive definition of the contours of mass media rights and duties. In its exercise of these responsibilities, the legislature perceived rights of freedom of expression as defensive, serving individual, self-expression values. This two-part study has sought to identify the various elements that characterize this approach: Russia's roots in the civil law tradition and the attraction of continental European models; Russian jurists' quest for legality as manifested by the achievement of legislative supremacy; and hostility toward infusion of public interest concerns into private legal relations. The latter component, which distinguishes Russia from many of those continental legal systems that its civil jurists sought to emulate in the post-World War II period, was engendered in large part by the Soviet regime's use of extra-legal methods to thwart claims against state-controlled mass media which often employed offensive expression to further collectivist goals.

[The latter part] of this study has examined the legal setting which came into being in December 1993, in order to determine whether a foundation for a second generation of press freedoms is under construction—a constitutional basis for press activity grounded in a theory of free expression that emphasizes not only individual self-fulfillment, but also a public dimension. What distinguishes the post-1993 Russian legal system in this regard is not so much the text of article 29 of the Constitution, but rather the textual dismantling of legislative supremacy in the form of direct applicability and supremacy of constitutional norms, and the institution of judicial review as a means of constitutional control of governmental acts. As a result, it may be concluded that an institutional and textual basis for such constitutionalization exists; however, in practice Russian defamation law remains securely anchored in its solid pre-1993 foundations. Constitutional and international norms do not operate as independent sources of Russian defamation law, but instead serve at most as an expression of broad political principles. In a manner consistent with the principle of legislative normativity, they find their only application in the notion that legislative actions, such as the chapter 8 of 1995 Civil Code and the Mass Media Law, are an expression of the constitutional commands, and are consistent with them. The contours of article 29 remain solely as defined by the legislature, and perhaps reflect a preference among the Russian people for a system heavily weighted in favor of defamation plaintiffs.

It is anticipated, however, that litigants will continue to urge the Russian courts to include articles 29 and 19 among the sources of defamation law, and to apply them so as to invalidate certain provisions of the legislative scheme. This effort will receive further stimulus if, as expected, Russia accedes to the European Convention on Human Rights.

It is therefore a matter of considerable importance for the future development of Russian civil defamation law that it will evolve within a diffuse system of constitutional review, with ordinary first instance and appellate courts throughout the country, as well as the Russian Federation Supreme Court and perhaps the Arbitration Courts, empowered to decide questions raised by litigants seeking its constitutionalization. In its *Kozyrev* decision, the Russian Constitutional Court voiced recognition of a constitutional dimension in defamation law; however, the Court found itself compelled to refrain from subjecting the statutory scheme to judicial review and instead called upon the ordinary courts, particularly the Supreme Court, to fashion the proper methodology for resolving the clash of countervailing rights. On the one hand, this dispersal of power to the ordinary courts might result in an integration into Russia's system of judicial constitutional control that is deeper than that experienced by their counterparts in legal systems with concentrated review. On the other, it might hinder the attainment of uniformity and clarity in this body of law or result in inattention to the issues raised in the Constitutional Court's opinion. Thus far, the ordinary courts, in particular the Supreme Court as demonstrated in its denial of the protest in *Zhirinovskii v. Gaidar*, have not been inclined to consider the application of constitutional norms in concrete defamation cases; however, it is too early to know whether the Constitutional Court's entreaties in *Kozyrev* will persuade them to consider a new approach.

In such challenges, a question will be whether the 1993 Constitution adds anything new to the existing defamation law calculus. In this regard, examination of the issues expected to arise in a constitutional challenge demonstrates that the first issue—that of judicial normativity—can be resolved with little difficulty: the 1993 Constitution expressly introduced into Russian law the notions of direct effect and supremacy of constitutional and (somewhat less emphatically) international norms. Moreover, in their 1995 decisions invalidating a range of statutory provisions, the Constitutional Court and ordinary courts have demonstrated their ready acceptance of such constitutional normativity. The questions of third-party effect and literal exclusion of defamatory expression from the article 29 and article 19 guarantees are less amenable to simple answers; however, it can at least be said that the relevant texts provide significant support for the conclusion that the statutory defamation scheme implicates the exercise of constitutional rights.

If so, and a court were to examine a challenge on its merits, that judicial body probably would consider itself compelled to go beyond the literal text toward identification and articulation of the contours of the indeterminate provisions of articles 29 and 19. Such an exercise would almost undoubtedly entail examination of the nature of these indeterminate free expression guarantees: a prospective norm development function extending beyond concrete norm control. This inquiry—whether free expression guarantees have not only an individual dimension, but a public one as well—will go to the heart of the conflict between private and public interests inherent in defamation law. In this process, an element would be determination of the necessity, or lack thereof, of making constitutionally-relevant distinctions, such as between plaintiffs based on their status or between statements of fact and opinion. Such determinations would be heavily weighted in value judgments; for example, it is possible that a Russian court could recognize a public dimension in defamation law and at the same time conclude that under article 29 the public interest requires placement of a higher priority on deterring offensive expression in order to protect civic discourse than on fostering uninhibited free expression.

Whatever the outcome, consideration of such questions will necessitate examination and articulation of the values underlying free expression guarantees—a process that might have consequences beyond civil defamation itself. First, it might provide a means of reconciling the clash between the public and private spheres: the sensitive problem of "practical concordance." From one perspective, the current polarization between personality rights protection adherents and free press advocates can be viewed as a clash between competing visions of human rights protection—the former supportive of representative institutions' enactment of barriers against unwarranted state interference in private relations, and the latter of judicial organs applying constitutional and international norms as restraints on unbridled legislative supremacy. In this regard, the "portals" in the 1995 Civil Code might reflect legislative recognition of a potential compatibility between private and public interests that sweeps aside notions that civil autonomy is dependent upon absolute exclusion of public interest concerns, or that pursuit of private goals is inconsistent with the public interest. Put another way, perhaps the Civil Code portals reflect an implicit conclusion that the application of constitutional and international norms by judicial organs is not to be equated with intervention by state executive and administrative agencies as a threat to the goals of civil society.

Second, by triggering development of a theory of free expression, examination of a constitutional challenge to civil defamation law might increase the determinacy of articles 29 and 19 by opening the door to identification and articulation of their contours in other areas of press activity as well. An obvious example would be the Criminal Code provisions governing defamation and insult. In addition, if this exercise were to examine whether other areas involving expressive activity should be subject to pluralistic sources of law, it might extend to the informal attempts at intimidation or manipulation which Russian journalists frequently cite. Finally, if the courts were to some extent to adopt a Democratic Model of free expression, that determination might result in an examination of whether affirmative constitutional duties should be imposed on state institutions in areas such as public access to governmental activities and documents or the establishment of structural restrictions on ownership to reduce de jure or de facto state control or to promote media diversity.

It has not been the goal of this study to analyze future developments in Russian defamation law from the perspective of legal culture. Instead, it has been to identify the historical roots of the existing scheme, as well as those elements that characterize it today, and to speculate as to the institutional and textual grounds for the introduction of a public dimension into defamation law by means of the interpretation and application of constitutional and international norms.

At the same time, it must not be forgotten that many of these questions have arisen in an extraordinarily short time frame. In the past ten years the hierarchy of sources of Russian law has shifted swiftly and dramatically from a legal system marked by extra-legal Party supremacy, to a law-based state grounded in legislative normativity and supremacy, to a constitutional order featuring judicial review of governmental acts. The institutional anchors of this new system—the Constitution, new Constitutional Court, Constitutional Court Statute, ordinary courts with competence to exercise judicial review of certain governmental acts, and the 1995 Civil Code—are at most barely two years old. However, as evidenced by the work of the courts in 1995, the institutional basis for a system of constitutional review is now in place, and the Constitutional Court and ordinary courts are engaged in norm control and development.

Considerable concern has been voiced regarding the short-term prospects for this new constitutional order; instead, it has been said, constitutionalization must await the development of a legal culture receptive to such a process. If the concept of legal culture is understood as a long-standing historical tradition of constitutionalism and judicial review, or as one linked to pluralistic democracy, the example of a country such as post-World War II Germany suggests that such an assessment might be unduly pessimistic. Indeed, some authors have questioned the basis for viewing the existence of a "constitutional culture" as a prerequisite for constitutionalization. On the other hand, it is perhaps the case that successful constitutionalization, however that might be gauged, requires lengthy exposure to a Rechtsstaat or law-based state tradition of legality marked by legislative supremacy over administrative rule. In Russia, jurists have sought to instill such precepts into the legal system since the nineteenth century, including efforts beginning in the 1950s to establish a system of personality rights protection. Whether these efforts have been sufficient to provide a foundation for a transition to constitutionalism, and whether they themselves are compatible with notions such as the perceived need for a public dimension in defamation law, must await the evolution of Russia's constitutional order. Judicial examination of efforts to constitutionalize defamation law may be expected to play a part in that process.

E.

CHANGING INSTITUTIONS

Corporate Transformation of the Russian Media*

Elena Vartanova

Since 1991, when the Russian Mass Media Law introduced private ownership and freedom of entrepreneurship in the media, the print and audiovisual industries have undergone many changes. Although the Russian media have achieved a kind of economic stability, many media companies still struggle to survive, including regional, local and specialized publications, as well as some regional broadcasting companies. This paper has three major goals: to give a brief overview of the present ownership structures in the Moscow media market, to outline the basic economic freedoms and rights granted by the present laws to Russian media enterprises, and to trace the increasing influence of the Russian economic elite (banks and various industries) over the operations of the Russian media with the special emphasis on the "media-business-elite" relationship during the election campaigns of 1995 and 1996.

The Shift to the Market

Publishing newspapers, magazines and books yielded enormous profits for the Communist Party and the Soviet state in the USSR, but the media was never listed among the major Soviet profit-making industries. On the contrary, the press, TV, and radio were used by the Party and state to educate the public on the basics of Marxist-Leninist ideology. Some scholars argue that, in the Soviet model, the media fulfilled the function of a public relation agent, rather than that of a mediator among different groups and forces within society.

The Soviet media was owned by various official organizations. The Communist Party owned some newspapers and periodicals. The Soviet state-owned newspapers, periodicals, broadcast companies, and news agencies. Other public organizations owned their own print media and publications sponsored by numerous specialized professional organizations. The Party's control over media content and operations spanned all publications regardless of the owner. For instance, despite the fact that the state operated and financed all broadcast companies and news agencies, the Communist Party determined programming policy.

When market reform began to affect the mass media, journalists saw it as both a harmful and beneficial force. The promotion of media freedom was never associated with the development of market reform. So, for some journalists, the increased dependence on advertising, sponsors, and the market meant the loss of their democratic dreams. For others, it was the beginning of their "gilded age." They managed to

* Post-Soviet Media Law & Policy Newsletter, Sept. 5, 1996 (Supp.), at 5.

combine professional skills with entrepreneurship and managerial abilities, and many of the first media proprietors were journalists.

Recent statistics show the dominance of journalists among owners or shareholders of the Russian press. The number of "pure" private owners remains relatively small, about 8.6%. Of them, the number of businessmen and bankers is particularly limited; only 2.3% of all Russian newspapers proprietors are of the Russian financial and economic elite.

Still, the most widely presented form of ownership in the Russian newspaper market is a journalistic corporation. During the privatization of Russian newspapers after the 1991 coup, the ownership of many newspapers were transferred into the hands of their journalist employees. These statistics also reflect the existing difference between "owners" and "founders," who are described by the Russian Mass Media Law as persons applying for the registration of the mass medium. Currently, founders of the Russian local/regional media are journalist staffs or local/regional administrations.

Only 12.5% of local newspapers have been founded by political parties or public organizations. On the national level, the degree of party or public organizations among the founders is somewhat higher (20%). In large industrial cities, such as St. Petersburg, public organizations have founded more than one-third of all newspapers (38.7%).

A New Diversity

As a result of the intensive corporate transformations, a broad range of ownership modes have developed within the Russian media industry. The Moscow media market is one of the most diversified in Russia and provides various samples of ownership forms. Among media companies, one can identify:

- state-owned newspapers (*Rossiiskaia Gazeta* and *Rossiiskie Vesti*);
- state-owned broadcast companies (VGTRK);
- state-owned news agencies (ITAR-TASS and RIS);
- media companies owned by the city administration (MTK terrestrial TV-company and a cable television channel);
- open share-holdings (*Izvestiia* and *Komsomolskaia Pravda*);
- joint-stock companies with the participation of financial and industrial capital (Public Russian Television and ORT company);
- joint-stock media companies with foreign market expansion (Interfax news agency);
- horizontally integrated private joint-stock companies (*Kommersant* Publishing House); and
- private newspaper chains (*Argumenti i Fakti* Publishing House).

The emergence of diversified newspaper companies is the most general trend in the corporate transformation in the newspaper market. The first type of such companies are media companies with multi-sectoral integration. For many of them, political benefits from publishing newspapers outweigh the economic disadvantages. Market activity of diversified companies is ensured by re-channeling revenues from profitable non-media divisions such as insurance companies, banks, travel companies, and trade activities into the media, particularly newspapers.

An example of the second type of multi-sectorally integrated media companies is the *Moskovskie Novosti* newspaper company. After facing economic problems in the market of weekly publications, it looked for other profitable media sectors and made investments in radio by establishing a profitable FM station.

Kommersant Publishing House is an example of a horizontally integrated media company because it produces other related products. *Kommersant* publishes several financial newspapers, owns news, advertising and photo agencies, and other new diversified media companies. However, the sources for the initial investments into *Kommersant* are still unclear.

A Legislative Framework for Media and the Economy

Regulation of economic issues in post-Soviet Russia has been primarily concerned with financial support for the print media and the privatization of the broadcast media. The Russian Constitution and the Mass Media Law laid the grounds for a "hybrid ownership system and policy" with the legal co-existence of state and private ownership in the media. Freedom of economic activity and the right of private ownership are guaranteed by the Constitution (Part 4, Articles 8, 34, 35), while the Mass Media Law stresses the rights of every Russian citizen to establish a mass media enterprise and defines the rights and duties of various component parts of these enterprises. The Law gives the media independence from state and government intervention.

In many post-Socialist countries, the period of new legislation for the media was characterized by idealistic attempts to remove political, legal, and administrative constraints on media operations, and to guarantee free access to the market. Many previously unaddressed problems have caused heated discussion. One such problem is the contradiction between the "founder" and the position of the owner. According to the Mass Media Law, a foreigner cannot found a mass medium in Russia. This idea, of course, coincides with the rules of many Western countries that restrict the presence of foreign capital in national media ownership. However, the Russian Mass Media Law puts no limits on foreign capital buying a Russian media enterprise.

On the other hand, the Law states that the "founder" cannot interfere with the editorship, editor-in-chief, and journalists. A status agreement between the founder and editorship is required to cover a number of important points in their relations. Only in cases foreseen by the agreement may the founder interfere with editorial policy.

Unfortunately, in many Russian newspaper companies, the editor-in-chief, the founder, and the major shareholder is the same person, rendering the agreement useless.

The state has also secured its economic position in the media. It remains the major owner in the supply, production, and distribution sectors of the newspaper industry and maintains control over all newsprint production plants, technologically modern publishing houses, and distribution networks.

A lack of competition laws allows the state to continue to hold monopolies in key sectors of the media economy. The Duma continues to stress the need for a special legal system of financial support for non-profitable media enterprises. At an earlier stage, support was given through press subsides, followed by grants. However, uncertain selection principles led to a discrediting of this practice.

Market operations of the Russian media enterprises are determined by media laws as well as economic regulation. At present, the most important are the Value Added Tax Law (1991), Revenue-Tax Law (1992), and Customs-Tax Law (1993). In autumn 1995, the State Duma adopted several laws exempting media enterprises with educational and cultural output and some subscription and retail revenue operations from VAT. New laws also provide media enterprises with some benefits such as tax exemption for capital investments and advantages in the privatization of the production sector. At the Parliamentary hearings on the implementation of these laws, journalists and media executives stressed that many media companies are not able to use new benefits because of the unwillingness of the executive power. Without special provisions for executive bodies, laws would fail to fulfill their goals. The ambivalent policy of the Russian state still prevents normal market operations in the newspaper industry.

The Financial Elite, the Media, and Political Power

For many scholars, the question of ownership and more precisely of the owners' influence over medium contents is extremely important. In Russia, the uncertainty of the legal status of media owners increases their ability to influence media contents and operations.

The inefficiency of the modern Russian newspaper economy has strengthened newspapers' dependence on proprietors. The everyday operations of many newspaper companies conflict with the economy of scale. For instance, production of a million copies does not diminish, but rather increases marginal costs while failing to produce marginal revenues. This is contrary to the very nature of newspaper production. It is also more profitable to publish one thousand copies of an expensive magazine for an untargeted audience than one million copies of a popular daily due to the extremely high cost of postal distribution. This may also explain why the periodicals in big cities rely primarily on retail and other forms of inner-city distribution instead of home delivery.

Distortions of the economy of scale explain why advertising and normal marketing do not produce enough revenues for the newspaper industry, while sponsorship and investments from financial elite do. The owner is seen as the investor and has become the key figure in the economic survival of certain media forums.

Vitali Tretiakov, the founder and the editor-in-chief of the fifth Soviet independent daily *Nezavisimaia Gazeta*, which was temporarily closed because of debt in the summer of 1995, declared frankly, "to survive today the Russian newspaper needs to find a sponsor." It was his choice in autumn 1995 to add his newspaper to the growing media empire of Boris Beresovsky, the owner of the LogoVAZ corporation. Currently, LogoVAZ is one of the largest private shareholders of Public Russian Television ORT (8% shares + 8% of Obiedinennibank owned by LogoVAZ). Besides *Nezavisimaia Gazeta* and ORT, LogoVAZ had also invested in *Ogoniok* news magazine, improving its printing and changing its contents.

Russian banks are steadily increasing their investments in the media business as well. By building financial-media empires, the financial elite enters politics, thus suggesting a Russian model of media moguls. Of Moscow banks, several are seriously involved in the media business. Most group, owned by Vladimir Gusinsky, has activities in banking and real estate, but also controls NTV, a private television channel. Gusinsky has 77% of the shares while the journalists own 23% of the shares. Most Group also controls *7 Dnei*, a publishing company that publishes the daily *Segodnia*, news magazine *Itogi* (jointly with *Newsweek*), and TV-weekly *7 Dnei*. In addition, Most Group owns the popular Moscow FM station Echo of Moscow. Menatep group, which includes Menatep bank and a wide range of holdings in Russian industrial companies, bought a minority stake of Independent Media Publishing company. The latter publishes a number of popular English language publications and Russian editions of *Playboy*, *Cosmopolitan*, and *Good Housekeeping*. Onexsimbank bought the majority shares of *Ekspert* news magazine on condition that the publication would not be transferred to any other banks.

Some Russian scholars argue that while the long-term goal of such concentration might be the effective and profitable enterprises, short-term goals are determined by the political situation and quests for political power. The process of media concentration is partially politically motivated. The most vivid illustration may be found in operations of the powerful state-private corporation Gazprom. Gazprom's former head was former Prime Minister Victor Chernomyrdin. Recently, Gazprom announced its plans to buy a 30% stake in NTV. In addition, there are rumors that Gazprom owns significant share in *Komsomolskaia Pravda* and supports *Trud* newspapers, the two dailies with the largest circulation in Russia.

Developments in the regional and local press also demonstrate the emergence of political concentration. Newspapers that stand close to the local administrations receive numerous advantages, including indirect subsidies in the form of better and cheaper access to news agencies' information and support of print. The conversion of the old political elite into a new financial elite in many regions outside Moscow might help to predict the further direction of concentration in local newspaper markets.

Pass the Advil: Financial Woes of Russia's State Broadcasters*

Peter Krug

Russia's state broadcasting system, which guarantees the integrity of the country's "common information space," must remain the property of the state—so declared President Yeltsin on February 24, as he endorsed continued subsidies for print media.

These goals, however, are colliding with Russia's economic problems, creating difficult dilemmas for policymakers. The most dramatic effects are being felt in the state television and radio broadcasting system, with its four national television channels, radio networks, and more than eighty regional broadcasting companies, where budget cuts and subsidy reductions are producing programming changes and threatening severe reductions of air time. State broadcasters, which are almost totally dependent on the national budget because their advertising revenues are insignificant and which do not receive license fee monies, were recently warned by the Finance Ministry to prepare for 50% funding cuts.

The major problem is the cost of signal distribution. State broadcasters do not own or control the expensive system of satellites, transmitters, and other facilities needed to transmit signals over Russia's vast territory and beyond to other CIS countries; instead, the system is a monopoly of the Russian Communications Ministry. It is estimated that some 70-80% of state broadcasters' expenditures are to the Communications Ministry for signal distribution. In the past, massive government subsidies to the Communications Ministry cushioned the impact of these costs on state broadcasters. However, those subsidies have been drastically reduced in the last two years.

The Communications Ministry, meanwhile, chafes under the fact that the tariff rates paid by state broadcasters have not been changed since 1981, kept artificially low by the state subsidies. The Ministry would rather make room for independent broadcasters, who are viewed as capable of paying their bills and are not protected by the freeze on state broadcasters' tariff rates. As long ago as last July, Deputy Communications Minister Mikhail Yelizarov proposed that all state television companies—national and regional—have their air time slashed by at least 40%, stating that broadcasting should not take place during the morning, afternoon, or late evening. A successful result of this lobbying effort was the inclusion in President Yeltsin's December 18, 1993, decree on state broadcasting of a provision directing state broadcasters to submit within one month proposals to the Council of Ministers for the possible reduction of broadcasting time. To our knowledge, such proposals have not been made.

* Post-Soviet Media Law & Policy Newsletter, Feb. 28, 1994, at 1.

Whether independent broadcasters can afford to pay higher transmission rates is questionable. Last summer, the General Director of radio station Ekho Moskvi, Yurii Fedutinov, complained that tariffs for the use of transmitters in Moscow were three times higher than world standards, stating that it is three times cheaper to place a transmitter on top of the Empire State Building in New York than on the Ostankino tower in Moscow.

The most recent manifestation of these problems was the February 10 job action by communications workers—the engineers and technicians who operate signal transmission facilities—who shut down one-third of the country's transmitters for all or part of the day on February 10 in an effort to recover back wages unpaid since December. The effort, which—with the exception of Moscow—blacked out most state broadcasters' programming for much of the day, may have been successful: Prime Minister Chernomyrdin quickly promised to pay off the state broadcasters' debts (estimated at an equivalent to some $43-50 million) in stages during the first quarter of 1994.

Another result of the funding cutbacks is the widespread use of independent production companies' programming on Ostankino's Channel One. According to Irena Lesnevskaia, head of independent production company REN-TV, more than 75% of the programming on Ostankino's channel one is now produced by independent companies.

Of perhaps even more ominous import to some politicians is the airing of foreign programming. During a State Duma session on February 16, a deputy from Vladimir Zhirinovski's Liberal Democratic Party decried an Italian television company's purchase of air time and called upon Mikhail Poltoranin, chairman of the Duma's Committee on Information Policy and Communications, to explain "the consequences for the audience of the sale of broadcasting time to foreign television companies." In response, Poltoranin declared that the airing of "low-grade" Western films "does not improve the standards of morality in Russia" and enlarged upon this theme to denounce "privatization of our channels," a process which he described as "destruction of the common information space" in Russia.

Indeed, state broadcasters face growing competition from independent broadcasters. For example, Independent Television (NTV), with its 58 hours per week on Channel Four of programming which features foreign films, productions by independent domestic studios, and highly-regarded news programs, is reportedly increasing in popularity. Vladimir Gusinsky, the head of the Most banking consortium bankrolling NTV, recently predicted that NTV will be operating in the black within three to five years. In a Reuters interview, Gusinsky added that the Most group, which also owns the *Sevodnia* newspaper, is considering the purchase of several other newspapers and an ownership stake in a radio station (reportedly independent broadcaster Ekho Moskvi).

As a result of these developments, Russian policymakers are in a quandary as they ponder whether and how to shore up state broadcasting companies. As one commentator, Sergei Dorenko of Russian TV, put it in a February 9 broadcast: "At the moment the government refuses to allow state channels to become share-holding companies but neither does it finance them itself." The former approach is favored by Grigori Shevelev,

First Deputy Chairman of Ostankino. In a January 24 ITAR-TASS interview, Shevelev pointed out that it would be impossible for Ostankino to adapt to new market conditions when the government budget could satisfy less than half the company's financial requirements. He also rejected the idea of cutting back on air time, declaring that Ostankino is Russia's "national asset" and it is not possible "to lower the plank." In his opinion, the only solution is to turn Ostankino into a joint-stock company, presumably with state entities as at least some of the participants.

It is doubtful that this will be the approach taken by the State Duma, which apparently will soon be considering legislation to bolster the position of state broadcasters. Deputy Poltoranin has announced that a draft broadcasting law is being prepared and that the Information Policy Committee will hold hearings on the economic status of the mass media. Long a vocal advocate of significant state funding for Ostankino and Russian TV, Poltoranin is strongly opposed to privatization or conversion into joint-stock companies. He told the Duma on February 16 that Russia must maintain at least two state broadcasting companies, and that, if local budgets were to be saddled with supporting regional broadcasters, "we would thereby edge closer to the dismemberment of Russia." As for privatization, he criticized financial groups that want to translate their resources into political power by "brazenly" grabbing television time and channels, warning that "Russia's fate is at stake."

Poltoranin's views appear to be consistent with those of State Duma Chairman Ivan Rybkin. In a January 31 interview on Russian TV, Rybkin cited the independence of the mass media as an important goal, but added that they must receive financial support from the state rather than attempt to tackle their problems on their own. As an example of his thinking, he cited the BBC, which he had recently visited.

In Russia, Private Doesn't Mean Independent: Bankers and Oil Tycoons Use the Media as a Business Weapon*

Andrei Fadin

A short but fierce tussle between Russian banks over privatization of a state enterprise this summer exposed the flagrancy with which financial groups are using their newspapers and television stations to wage war on one another. The ostensible prize was an attractive piece of the state property pie—Svyazinvest, the largest Russian telecommunications holding—but what was ultimately at stake was the reallocation of property, financial might, and political influence. For the first time, a political offensive was waged by appeal to public opinion through the media rather than by the secret Kremlin intrigues of days gone by.

The blatant spread of propaganda through private newspapers and television is not entirely new in post-Soviet Russia. In the 1996 elections, the bankers who controlled the most media outlets were the main winners. Vladimir Gusinsky and Boris Berezovsky, businessmen who control the two main information empires in the country, are still reaping the benefits of the good press they gave Yeltsin and his crowd.

Gusinsky's media concern, owned by his Most bank group, consists of Independent Television (NTV), Ekho Moskvi radio, the daily newspaper *Segodnia*, and a weekly television guide called *Seven Days*. It also partly owns several publications, such as *Novaia Gazeta* and *Obshchaia Gazeta*. Boris Berezovsky, de facto head of the LogoVAZ concern and one of the richest people in Russia, managed to establish control over Russian Public Television (ORT), which reaches more than 100 million people, *Nezavisimaia Gazeta*, and *Ogoniok* magazine. Berezovsky and Gusinsky are consulted on practically every decision of national importance, and Berezovsky was appointed deputy secretary of the Security Council and Moscow's main negotiator with Chechnya.

Other members of the so-called Davos alliance, the seven largest banks that joined efforts to prevent a communist return to power in early 1996, later realized that having one's own press was an asset in the struggle for access to privatized state property. Vladimir Potanin, head of Oneksimbank, one of the most powerful Russian banks, became a deputy prime minister in Yeltsin's first post-election government. The appointment was widely considered a thank-you to the Davos alliance.

When he left the government, Potanin was much stronger than before. But his main achievement was his friendship with the powerful first deputy prime minister, Anatoli Chubais. With Chubais on its side, the financially and politically strengthened Oneksimbank could enter the battlefield of the financial giants: the sphere of oil, gas,

---

* Transitions, Oct. 1997, at 90-92.

and information. Under the previous tacit arrangement, every privatization was agreed upon by the main players, but now Oneksimbank was strong enough to outbid its competitors.

In preparation, Oneksimbank began creating its own information empire. It bought the best national daily newspaper, *Izvestiia*, established control over *Komsomolskaia Pravda*, *Ekspert* magazine, and several other Moscow publications, and founded a new business daily, *Russkii Telegraf*, to be launched as "the Russian *Wall Street Journal*" with $20 million over three years, enormous funding by Russian standards.

Clash of The Titans

The auction of the block of shares of the Svyazinvest state telecommunications holding was the battleground. The Davos alliance was an alliance no more. Potanin's main rivals, Gusinsky and Berezovsky, tried to pull all their political strings to reach a compromise at the Svyazinvest auction. But attempts to talk Chubais into making a secret deal failed. He was now in a position to insist and stated, "everything should be solved in an honest and open auction where the winner is the one who offers more. There will be no more covert deals. The budget needs money to pay debts to the army, teachers, and doctors." The bankers reportedly threatened to start a public campaign against Chubais on the television channels under their control, but he threatened them with the might of the state machine in return.

An even harder stand was taken by the new Kremlin favorite, the other first deputy prime minister, Boris Nemtsov, whose personal creed is the principle of open competition. "There will be no bandit capitalism and unfair privatization anymore. Everything will be done honestly," Nemtsov said.

Under those circumstances, Oneksimbank's rivals had no choice but to move the struggle to the public sphere. Using their connections at the top as well as their mass media outlets, they tried a pre-emptive strike. The weapons were public accusations of corruption, financial abuse, and theft. The banks publicized confidential and compromising information about their rivals. With the help of their cronies in the Kremlin, they initiated legal actions and searches.

The main battles took place in July and August. At first, the head of the Central Bank, Sergei Dubinin, accused two banking structures connected to Oneksimbank of gross mismanagement, causing a loss of millions of dollars to the budget. The head of one of the accused banks, influential ex-Deputy Finance Minister Andrei Vavilov, retaliated by giving the prosecutors' office materials compromising the head of the Central Bank. The public prosecutor's office and Prime Minister Viktor Chernomyrdin demanded a stop to the final sale to Oneksimbank of a controlling interest in a very lucrative company. Nevertheless, the deal went through, apparently with Chubais's support.

Having lost the battle in the corridors of power, Gusinsky and Berezovsky turned to the media to attack Potanin and Chubais. The weekly analytical television program "Vremia"—owned by Berezovsky—investigated Oneksimbank's machinations during the privatization of some state enterprises. Moderator Sergei Dorenko directly accused Potanin of swindling and stealing state money. The exposé generated a stream of materials compromising Alfred Kokh, the chairman of the State Privatization Committee.

ORT, NTV, Ekho Moskvi radio, *Nezavisimaia Gazeta*, *Novaia Gazeta*, *Segodnia*, and *Obshchaia Gazeta* concentrated on exposing corruption in the sphere of privatization—in most cases, through authentic and truly compromising materials. They paid special attention to the roles of Chubais, Kokh, and Nemtsov.

The focus of the campaign was that Oneksimbank received unfair privileges due to its "special relations" with the Chubais team. The media suggested—and proved in the case of Kokh—that the "special relations" had a purely financial dimension. Kokh had to resign and the Customs Committee account was taken from Oneksimbank. Nevertheless, Oneksimbank and its foreign partners won a twenty-five-percent stake at the Sviazinvest auction.

The Ownership Divide

Alas, the media failed to demonstrate the minimum of independence of opinion necessary for preserving self-respect and enjoying the confidence of the public. Moscow's main press outlets are divided into camps—not according to ideological or political orientation, but according to ownership. Independent commentary was evident only in such newspapers as *Kommersant Daily* and *Moskovskii Komsomolets* because their owners did not participate in the "clash of the titans."

The papers that were critical of Chubais and Potanin harped on the danger of concentrating so much power and money in one organization. Instead of the old oligarchy of seven major banks, one super-monopoly has emerged.

The opposite side interpreted the victory of Oneksimbank and the reformers' team as the victory of open market rules over secret political bargaining. *Izvestiia*, purged of "disloyal" journalists since it was bought by Oneksimbank, declared it a victory of national interests over private.

The criticisms on both sides are absolutely right. The irony is that the mutual accusations and exposures of the bank's presses somehow ensure a peculiar freedom of information. For ordinary Russians, though, that freedom is exhausting; in order to get the complete picture, you have to read at least half a dozen newspapers a day.

Television and Politics: The ORT Crisis*

Svetlana Kolesnik

Russia's mass media system is undergoing rapid change and has moved away from its centralized Soviet structure. In Russian broadcasting today, the main branches of the signal transmission industry and the broadcasting industry remain under state control. The state owns and operates about ninety regional television stations and two national broadcasting companies, the Russian Radio and Television Company (RTR, Channel 2) and the Federal Broadcasting Service "Russia" (St. Petersburg, Channel 5). In addition, Public Russian Television (ORT, Channel 1) is a stock company in which the state owns a 51% share. Russia has also developed a private broadcasting industry. 625 commercial companies, of which about 370 are included in the National Directory of Television Companies in Russia, are well-established. There are also two independent national channels, NTV and TV-6 Moscow. The private sector in Russian television is powerful enough to influence the structure of mass media throughout the country and has radically altered the relations between state bodies and broadcasting.

In many cases, television is independent from the state, though a detailed look at its role in the political life of Russia may call this observation into doubt. It is an expensive medium trying to survive with an underdeveloped advertising market. Advertising revenues are sufficient to cover production costs, but Russian television needs to improve its antiquated technical base and cannot exist without support from wealthy financial structures and the state.

Upon examining the current financial position of structures such as the financial group Most or the LogoVAZ company, it appears that they are profit-seeking. In reality, however, the striving of these companies for ownership in television is determined by the desire to preserve the current regime, which will guarantee the market economy and with which they have worked hand-in-hand in the process of privatization. Banks and financial groups have united resources with state bureaucrats in order to exert influence over the electorate. While this is less profitable than the banking business, it is the only medium able to reach almost every voter in Russia.

Because of the press crisis which has made many central publications inaccessible to readers in the center and in the provinces, television has become an influential tool for the "party in power." According to the *Izvestiia* Analytical Center, about thirty-three to fifty percent of voters are making their political choices under the pressure of the mass media. The data presented in the report further shows that press, radio, and television, at both the local and national levels, can exert direct influence over their respective audiences.

---

* Post-Soviet Media Law & Policy Newsletter, June 13, 1997, at 9.

The notion "central television" is a remnant of the USSR, when all national broadcasting came from Moscow. Even today the idea holds that a national channel can be established only with a base in Moscow. Moscow is the richest market and accumulates a large share of the country's financial potential. The struggle for radio and television frequencies covering the Moscow region is intense and involves powerful political and financial forces. In the case of REN-TV, it seems that its friendly relations with high ranking bureaucrats helped it gain control of Channel 49 last year and construct a national network.

There are nine television channels available in Moscow today, depending on one's location in the city, but they do not all have equal influence. Viewers of channels such as 49, 27, and 31 are not numerous. Channel 3 is partially financed by the Moscow government, and it sells the programming product to local stations around the country. The Federal Radio and Television Service "Russia" (St. Petersburg, Channel 5), which is produced in St. Petersburg, has the status of a national broadcaster, but is not paying for signal transmission into all regions due to the lack of state funding. Only four channels—two state supported (ORT and RTR) and two commercial channels (NTV (Channel 4) and TV-6, Moscow)—can now be called "central television."

Two years ago, the Television and Radio Company Ostankino (then ORT) and RTR experienced what some specialists described as a crisis in the system's character. The crisis was characterized by the absence of a precisely formulated political position, the loss of control over the different production companies that were part of the Channel, and Ostankino's failure to collect all of the revenue created by advertising because several programs, such as the morning show "UTRO," had a large amount of hidden advertisement and sponsor money transferred to the company budget.

Television's financial straits mirrored those of the Russian economy as a whole, and seemed at the outset to be the cause of the crisis. However, an analysis of the history of the company, which was created on the ruins of the USSR's Gosteleradio, reveals another cause of the crisis—the Channel became a victim of a struggle of political interest.

In a Decree issued on December 12, 1991, the President formulated a task force to reorganize the Channel. Shortly thereafter, different groups came forward with projects for creating a joint-stock company. The company VID, which represents the production ventures interest, was among the first to come forward. Aleksander Lubimov, the company director, proposed a project of "the people's television." Although the idea to invite ordinary citizens to hold shares in the company was attractive, the Russian federal legislation presented the possibility that someone might buy a controlling share. As the possibility of losing control over the main channel became real, the idea was opposed by many political forces and Russian television lost a crucial opportunity to become private.

By autumn 1992, the operative management of Channel 1, which reflects the pressure of production companies, attempted to propose another project, with the help of well-known Western firms. The project was waylaid by the government's unwillingness to pay the Western specialists. Soon after that, the company's managers came forward with their own project to form a stock company and to distribute shares among Ostankino personnel. Again, the project was stopped, this time by Goskomimuszhestvo's (the state agency responsible for privatization) structural transformation of the company, a transformation that proceeded from Goskomimuszhestvo's interests and that were unknown to the public. Soon thereafter, a press secretary at Goskomimuszhestvo received a very important position in the company. At the same time, the Ministry of Communication raised tariffs for signal transmission, and company debts grew to enormous proportions.

It appeared that state bodies were attempting to make the company work less effectively. Until the fall of 1994, the TV and Radio Company Ostankino, using the First Channel, was absolutely demoralized by incompetent operative management and by the chaotic restructuring conducted by Goskomimuszhestvo. At that time, it was impossible to speak about an independent political line of the company. The best news journalists had left Ostankino for new commercial companies such as NTV and TV-6, Moscow.

Under these conditions, the President signed the Decree about assignation of the Channel to a commercial structure called the Public Russian Television (ORT). The official goal was to get effective management of the Channel under state control, and different state bodies received 51% of the company's shares. The Board of Trustees was formed on December 4, 1994, with President Boris Yeltsin as its chairman. Among participants at the staff founders meeting, which took place on January 24, 1994, were stock companies—LogoVAZ received eight percent of the PRT shares, Gazprom received three percent, Mikrodin and several banks—Menatep, Nationalnii Credit, Stolichny, and Alfa Bank—each received five percent, and Obiedinenni Bank received eight percent of the PRT shares.

The last attempt to secure the production companies' interests, which were formulated by Ostankino journalists, was made by a famous anchorperson Vlad Listyev, who was appointed the General Director. After his assassination on March 1, 1995, however, the Association of Independent Television and Radio Companies, with three percent of the ORT shares, left the staff of founders. The state remained face-to-face with oil-gas business and financial structures.

The five-year-old romance of power and journalists on the First Channel was over. The control over the main channel in the country was taken by the state bureaucratic machine supported by commercial structures that formed industrial and political clans.

Can we say that ORT's financial situation has improved today? ORT's debts for signal transmission are still enormous, and it is unclear who is actually financing the company. Despite the company's explanations about the decisive role of LogoVAZ in financing ORT, LogoVAZ cannot take on all of ORT's expenses. Officially, the state is not supporting the company, but journalists are trying, with some success, to obtain money from unofficial state sources, and the presidential election campaign has produced several scandals in connection with campaign financing.

ORT has failed to stop the practice of using company programs for hidden advertisements and cannot stop the sponsors' money from flowing into the pockets of journalists. ORT cannot harmonize relations with production companies and does not pay them on time. As a result, several independent producers decided to leave ORT in 1997, among whom include the producers of the popular show for children "Utrenniaia Zvezda" (The Morning Star) and a thirty-five-year-old popular program for youth "The KVN."

On the other hand, ORT decided to discontinue the day segment of company programming by the International Television and Radio Company (MIR), which covers news of the CIS. The ORT declared that the company is not satisfied by MIR's low-rating programs. At the same time, MIR had not paid for the signal transmission. Taking into account ORT's debts, it is reasonable for ORT to omit MIR from its programming, but there are rumors that ORT will give MIR time for State Duma coverage.

On the eve of 1997, RTR (Channel 2) rejected the State Duma's proposal to cover Duma activity three times a week during prime time. The rejection contributed to the state's decision to provide only minimal funding to RTR. In 1996, RTR got only thirty percent of the promised budget money, and the chairman of the company asked that about 1.8 billion rubles be set aside in 1997. The question is: why did ORT decide to allocate money for covering the Duma?

It is necessary to emphasize that "the party in power" has changed during the last half of 1996, and it is safe to say that Duma communists are very close to that party now. As Gleb Pavlovksi has mentioned, "journalism is a service in Russia: maybe the only well developed sphere of service. It serves the central power." The ORT has proved its ability to work spectacularly for the "party in power" during the presidential campaign. In the last news show of 1996, the head of the ORT information service, Ksenia Ponomareva, emphasized that all forces of the company were devoted to the active forming of a positive image of the president, and that she could not understand the Western journalists' criticisms of the company for this practice.

At the same time, it seems that it is the intention of the current government to create a new version of the "national idea," and to influence national ideology through ORT's coverage of the former USSR. On the other hand, the government of the Russian Federation paid less attention to relations with former Soviet republics at the beginning of the nineties when the republics actively formed national states. Unfortunately, as a result, the Channel has almost lost the market of the former USSR.

ORT broadcasting was stopped in Ukraine on October 20, 1996. In early 1997 in Belarus, President Lukashenko threatened to follow the path that Ukraine took, though the channel is still popular. A sort of censorship has already been established in Belarus, and political and news programs were cut.

It looks like efforts to organize the informational space of the former USSR with the help of "MIR" have failed, and money was used as a simple explanation for a more complex problem.

It is impossible to avoid the problem of television management when speaking about the system of the state television crisis. The First Channel did not have skilled managers during difficult years because of the Soviet tradition of solving complicated tasks by dismissing highly ranked managers. From 1991 to 1996, the Channel had five Chairmen.

During the same period another state-owned and operated channel—the RTR (Channel 2) was headed by Oleg Poptzov. Despite several attempts to dismiss him, Poptzov was supported by journalists working in the company. On the eve of presidential elections, however, he was fired, marking the end of a period of revolutionary transformation of Russian television, which in many cases was inspired by journalists.

Oleg Poptzov represented the Khruschev-thaw generation and had a rare chance to be rewarded for the many years of political difficulties in the Brezhnev era. As a part of the intellectual elite of Russian representatives in the sixties, he took the thesis about the Fourth Estate too literally. Journalists like him were not satisfied playing the role of mediators and tried to become a part of the political process as deputies of the Supreme Soviet or the State Duma. In other words, they did not want to be reporters, they wanted to be newsmakers. Poptzov was not the most active representative of this group but, of course, he served the power structures that adhered to his own ideals. As a result, the position of the RTR Chairman was given to Eduard Sagalaev who represented the generation of reporters and businessmen that preferred to be in a middle-of-the-road position.

Sagalaev came to RTR as a founder, one of the main stockholders and the director of the private company TV-6, Moscow. Founded on principles adopted from American networks, the company is an economically effective venture that has now successfully achieved the status of a national broadcaster.

Despite the fact that ORT management has failed to solve many problems in the company, it has proved the company's loyalty to the President. During the meeting of the staff of founders in December 1996, the General Director, Sergey Blagovokin, was able to retain his position. This meeting was marked by the creation of a new structure—"ORT—the Banks Consortium," which is headed by Aleksander Smolenskii, the Stolichnii Bank Sberezhenii. The Consortium has united the Alfa Bank, the Menatep, the United Bank, and the Stolichii Bank Sberezhenii and has 38% of ORT's stock now.

The banks decided to remove the LogoVAZ label from ORT and to unite efforts to finance the Channel. It means that the reorganization of the company has entered a new stage, and the Russian public will have a chance to see if the creation of a financial pool normalizes the ORT situation that was created and directed mainly by political factors.

Mixed forms of property in television, competition between state and commercial companies, commercial supercompetition, the opposition of professional journalists to censorship, and the personal ambitions and political attitudes of key television figures guarantee that Russian television will not revert to a vertically governed system.

Local Media Legislation in Russian Provinces: An Old and Winding Road*

Andrei Richter

The theme of the Twenty-first Scientific Conference of the IAMCR is "The end of the nation?" with a question mark. The theme refers to the collapse of national boundaries in the age of digital communication as well as the transfer of media and mass communications regulations in Western societies from the national to the transnational level. The European Union and the Council of Europe have set universal standards on freedom of speech, access to information, mass communications and telecommunications regulations. They have addressed market rules and content for such communication.

Though Russia became a member of the Council of Europe in 1996 and ratified the European Convention on Human Rights this year, legislation of the Council has not had any impact on mass communication regulation. The decisions of the European Court of Human Rights are insignificant, if not irrelevant, for the Russian judiciary. At a recent media law conference sponsored by the Moscow Media Law and Policy Centre together with the School of Journalism of the Moscow State University, a judge of the Russian Supreme Court pointed out that, though the Constitution sets international treaties ratified by the Russian Federation over national law, the Court would never apply or recommend to the general courts European legislation unless Parliament made relevant specific changes in the national law. Since the Constitution is the law of direct action, it remains to be seen what will happen when someone challenges the national law in a court of justice.

Russian federal legislation on mass media is essentially very democratic and liberal. Some Western authors have even noted that the 1991 Law On the Mass Media gives journalists rights unheard of in Western societies. Compared to other Western countries, media law in Russia is peculiar because there is an array of local legislation as well as federal laws and decrees governing the press. All eighty-nine "subjects of the Federation"—that is, provinces, national republics, and cities of Moscow and St. Petersburg—have a constitutional right to issue laws regulating different media under their jurisdiction.

The current Constitution of the Russian Federation, hastily drafted and approved by a "popular polling" in December 1993, was intended to guarantee the presidential administration extremely wide powers in the wake of the clash between Yeltsin and the Supreme Soviet that September. Because of this, there are lapses in those parts of its text that have to do with power distribution in Russia, and division of authority between the federal and regional governments over the media is highly ambiguous.

---

* Post-Soviet Media Law & Policy Newsletter, Nov. 1, 1998, at 36.

Articles 72, 73, and 74 of the Constitution set lists of issues that come under jurisdiction of the federal authorities, regional authorities, or both. Article 72 puts defense of basic human rights and freedoms, including the right to seek, obtain, produce, and distribute information, as well as the so-called "federal information" and "federal communication" under exclusive federal regulation. On the other hand, article 73 states that issues of "education" (*vospitanie*) and "culture" are under the joint regulation of the national and regional authorities.

The ambiguity of the articles became clear when the Constitutional Court of Russia heard two appeals on the constitutionality of the federal statute On Advertising. One appeal stated that regulation of advertising is part of the regulation of culture and should therefore be under the common jurisdiction of the Federation and its "subjects." Another said that since advertising is not mentioned in the Constitution it should be under the jurisdiction of the regional authorities. The Court decided that whenever advertising law regulates issues of business, competition, and the right to access commercial information, it is under federal legislation alone. In regard to other issues, subjects of the Federation are free to introduce acts of their own.

In light of this case, certain issues listed in the Constitution as exclusively under federal regulation apply to the media field. Those issues are: scope of the citizens' right to obtain information, legal status of organizations (e.g., news organizations of the federal media), federal taxation, and criminal liability for violations in the mass media sphere. Protection of citizens' right to obtain information, issues other than federal taxation, registration and licensing, and administrative control of mass media and of relations with the state authorities and self-government bodies come under joint jurisdiction.

Joint jurisdiction means that regional governments can adopt statutes, acts, or other regulations in the same spheres as those of federal legislation, but such acts shall not contradict federal legislation. The following basic questions remain practically unresolved. First of all, what happens if the regional laws contradict Russian law adopted before the Constitution that is not "federal statutes" but "statutes of the Federation," or still effective USSR statutes? A 1968 decree on the procedures to review petitions of citizens is an example. In most cases, the local authorities ignore such laws with silent approval from the federal government. Second, can regional governments adopt their own acts before federal legislation is adopted in that area? For example, there is an array of local statutes that regulate broadcasting or issues of obscenity adopted in the last several years, but there are no statutes of the federal parliament on these matters.

Another problem with local legislation is that the legal grammar of the existing regional law is far from perfect. For example, the last group of regional statutes on indecency and obscenity contain several logistical gaps. Some of them permit sexual programming on terrestrial television only after 11:00 p.m. or midnight local time but do not state till what time the permission lasts. Till 10:59 p.m.? One of the statutes permits sale of pornographic magazines "away from streets with crowded pedestrian traffic." What does that mean from a legal point of view: "sell them in the woods"?

Local authorities use these legal gaps to gain control of the local media. They have also received encouragement from the Yeltsin administration in this regard. Boris Yeltsin addressed the regional governments during the peak of his confrontation with the USSR President in 1991 and said: "Take as much sovereignty as you can swallow!" The liberties thus gained were reinforced in the 1993 constitutional right to adopt local constitutions and statutes which Yeltsin gave the regions in exchange for loyalty during the coup. In addition, regional governments "widen" their scope of legal activity by negotiating treaties with the Federation on delegations of powers. In such cases, the treaties repeat constitutional provisions on areas of exclusive competence of the federal government, but favor the regions when interpreting the "gray areas" of the Constitution.

At the same time, regulation of the mass media in the regions is not so much about cultural peculiarities of the Ossetians or Yakuts, or how media should follow local traditions or religions. Rather, it is drafted and adopted to show the journalists who is in charge and who can give favors and impose penalties. It is no surprise that out of nine regional constitutions adopted by the "stateless nations" all repeat the federal Constitution's support of freedom of speech and expression, but only three prohibit censorship.

At least four subjects of the Federation have adopted their own mass media statutes. To a large extent, those acts mechanically repeat the Russian mass media statute of 1991 calling into doubt the whole rationale of such lawmaking. Local statutes also repeat many of the commonly recognized flaws and internal contradictions of the federal act. For example, like the federal statute, criminal liability of a citizen who abuses the law with the use of mass media and administrative responsibility of editorial offices are combined in one article.

While the regional acts seem to parrot the federal acts, a number of new restrictions are also included. For example, at least four statutes prohibit creation and distribution within the territory of the region of any mass media established by entities with an address outside the boundaries of the particular region without prior permission from the local authorities. Others demand a special accreditation or permission from the correspondents' bureaus of "outside" media for journalists if the journalists want to have the same status as local journalists. These provisions contradict article XIX of the Universal Declaration, article X of the European Convention, and the Russian Constitution.

In addition to the regional mass media statutes, local regulation of the mass media consists of acts that regulate the following areas: additional subsidies to the local media and relief from local taxes; regulation of licenses' allocation for the local broadcasters; regulation of access to information and accreditation of journalists; and regulation of obscenity, pornography, and erotic publications and programs.

The existence of local acts on subsidies to the press can be explained by competition between the executive and legislative branches of the government. The President and the Russian Parliament have been at odds or even in the state of open hostilities since early 1992. By providing different favors to journalists, one or the other has tried to prove its status as the guarantor of freedom of press and speech in Russia. These favors are usually attempts to lure the press to one side of a political duel. Incidentally, because of rivalry between the two branches, almost none of the numerous decrees and laws that provide the press with tax relief, reduced tariffs, and state subsidies are effective. The executive is never in a hurry to execute what the legislature adopts, and the Parliament does not allocate funds in the budget for the programs envisioned by the executive power. A similar trend is evident in the provinces where regional governors compete with local legislatures.

The remaining areas of legislation mentioned above are locally legislated because of the absence of federal laws on the subjects. It remains to be seen whether or not contradictions between local acts and federal acts yet to be passed will arise.

How can these contradictions be resolved? Legally there are two ways. The first way is when a federal authority, be it the office of the Prosecutor General or that of the Minister of Justice, complains to the regional legislature about existing contradictions, requesting them to amend certain pieces of regional legislation. The federal authorities have tried to do that with elections regulations but failed to achieve a positive result because local legislators disregarded their appeals. It is also difficult for the federal authorities to enforce a change in local laws.

The second way is through the court system. If, for example, a local legislation violates someone's rights, that person can petition the courts to have them restored to the extension provided by federal law. While the local courts are dependent of the local government and will probably turn down such a petition, the plaintiff can appeal to federal courts and eventually bring the case to the attention of the Supreme Court or the Constitutional Court. In order for this to occur Russian citizens or media outlets must have the time and resources to go along that long road. However, even if they do win the court battle it will satisfy the plaintiff alone, since the precedent will not necessarily bind other courts.

What we see today in the provinces of Russia is a Balkanization of media legislation, open or potential contradictions between federal and regional statutes with no clear way to resolve them under the current political climate. Violations of journalists' rights and restrictions on freedom of speech and the press are more common the further you go from Moscow. Loyalty to regional czars is crucial for a career in journalism. While the national media are accessible to the population in the regions they contain relatively scarce coverage of the local affairs. At the local level, the media, at least the traditional ones such as terrestrial broadcasting and daily press, are under the control of local authorities and may even suffer oppression. I believe that all this cannot be but a reason for concern for the international community.

IV.

Into the Putin Era

The Kremlin Strikes Back: The Reassertion of State Power over the Russian Media

Laura Belin

As many articles in this book have shown, the Russian state was the main threat to media independence in the early 1990s. Growing corporate ownership and financing of media outlets was the dominant trend of the mid-1990s. This accelerated after Boris Yeltsin's 1996 re-election campaign appeared to confirm that media could be powerful weapons in the battle for public opinion and that media ownership conferred a seat at the table of power in Yeltsin's Russia.[1] Recruiting journalists to support Yeltsin's re-election was easy, but the president's team had trouble keeping the media in line once the danger of a Communist revanche had faded. Owners and financiers used their media assets in political battles, and the Kremlin was frequently unable to impose a ceasefire, let alone compel privately-owned outlets to express the official viewpoint on political developments.[2]

At the same time, the approaching end of Yeltsin's presidency posed a huge problem for Kremlin operatives. Not only did Yeltsin's poor health rule out another vigorous election campaign, but the Constitutional Court ruled in October 1998 that he could not seek a third term. Prospects that the Kremlin could use fear of communism or promises of privatization spoils to forge a consensus over Yeltsin's successor appeared slim. Even worse, the August 1998 ruble crash and default shattered what little faith existed in the economic policies pursued by Russian governments in the 1990s, creating unprecedented pressure on Yeltsin to resign. He rode out the storm, but at a considerable political cost. In 1998, the State Duma twice rejected Yeltsin's efforts to reinstate Viktor Chernomyrdin as prime minister, and finally in September of that year the president bowed to pressure and appointed Yevgenii Primakov, a compromise figure.

As the 2000 elections approached, the president's circle of advisers was left with little chance of recreating the consensus among Russian political and business elites that

---

[1] Many Moscow-based print and electronic media changed hands in the late 1990s, and several new outlets were created. For a comprehensive record of changing media ownership during this period, see the series of reports on *Russian Media Empires* by Floriana Fossato and Anna Kachkaeva for Radio Free Europe/Radio Liberty. The most recent version of the report can be found at http://www.rferl.org/nca/special/rumedia6/index.html. The previous versions can be found in English and Russian at http://www.rferl.org/nca/special/.

[2] More detailed analysis of the "information wars" of the late 1990s can be found in Laura Belin (with Floriana Fossato and Anna Kachkaeva), *The Distorted Russian Media Market*, *in* Business and the State in Contemporary Russia (Peter Rutland ed., 2000); Laura Belin, *Political Bias and Self-Censorship in the Russian Media*, *in* Contemporary Russian Politics: A Reader (Archie Brown ed., 2001) [hereinafter Contemporary Russian Politics]. See also Ivan Zassoursky, Mass-Media vtoroi respubliki (1999), especially appendix 2 ("Istoriya odnoi informatsionnoi voiny").

aided Yeltsin in 1996, and they desperately needed a strategy to elect a successor who would, in the words of influential businessman Boris Berezovsky, ensure the "continuity of power." That successor was found in Vladimir Putin, and his rise to power accompanied efforts to increase the influence of state-owned media and to enhance the state's power over private media. During the year following Putin's election in March 2000, such policies continued as the authorities sought to consolidate their influence over how the news was reported.

The first part of this article will examine media policies in the latter part of Yeltsin's second term, through the 2000 presidential election. The remainder will cover media policies during Putin's first year as president.

Electing Yeltsin's Heir

Although Yeltsin proclaimed himself a democrat, he appeared to have little patience for the uncertain outcomes that accompany genuinely democratic elections. He never hesitated to employ the levers of power, including state influence over media, to try to obtain the desired results from various elections and referenda.[3] Similarly, he felt entitled to install a presidential successor of his own choosing. During his two terms, he groomed but later rejected several possible candidates for the role, including Viktor Chernomyrdin, Boris Nemtsov, and Sergei Stepashin.

The search for an heir assumed more urgency in 1999, after damaging reports appeared in Russian and Western media concerning alleged bribery in Yeltsin's administration. The reports mentioned credit cards and foreign bank accounts allegedly used by the president and his daughters and paid for by companies doing business with the Kremlin. Yeltsin's desire to select his own successor thus reflected more than a typical incumbent's concern for his legacy or place in history. Like those around him implicated in the corruption allegations, Yeltsin needed a winning candidate who could be relied on not to pursue criminal prosecution of the president or members of his "family."[4]

Elections to the State Duma, the lower house of the parliament, would take place in December 1999, and the presidential election was scheduled for June 2000. The Duma elections were therefore a test of strength for competing political forces on the eve of the presidential campaign.[5] Since September 1998 Primakov had consistently topped

---

[3] Many contributions to this book illustrate that point. For more information on media coverage of the 1993 elections and referenda, see Ellen Mickiewicz, Changing Channels: Television and the Struggle for Power in Russia (1997).

[4] In the summer of 1999, NTV commentator Yevgenii Kiselev popularized the use of the term "family" to describe Yeltsin's coterie of advisers and associates as well as those literally related to the president.

[5] On how the 1999 parliamentary campaign was merely the first stage of the process of choosing Yeltsin's successor, see Andrei Raskin, *Television: Medium to Elect the President*, *in* Russian Media Challenge (Kaarle Nordenstreng et al. eds., 2001).

opinion polls, and a strong showing for Primakov's electoral bloc would confirm his status as the man to beat in the presidential race.

During the 1995 parliamentary campaign, the Kremlin's media strategy consisted of little more than disproportionate air time and friendly coverage for favored electoral blocs on state-controlled television networks.[6] There was no sophisticated media strategy comparable to what emerged during the 1996 presidential race. But the Kremlin implemented a range of policies to shape the results of the 1999 parliamentary elections.

Building Up the State's Media Arsenal

Efforts to increase the state's capacity to manage media coverage predated Yeltsin's troubles with Primakov and even the August 1998 crisis. The roots of the policy lay in the "information wars" of 1997 and 1998, during which the Kremlin appeared to have few weapons at its disposal.[7] Fully state-owned Russian Television (VGTRK, more commonly known as RTR) remained loyal to the government, but it was a distant third in Russian television market. Its broadcast reach on Channel 2 covered almost the entire country, and therefore its potential audience was second only to fifty-one-percent state-owned Russian Public Television (ORT), the Channel 1 broadcaster. But RTR news and analysis programs consistently had much lower ratings than similar programs on ORT or the private network NTV, which broadcast to about seventy percent of Russian territory. Chairmen of RTR branches in the regions were often beholden to the local governor or republican president, whose views sometimes differed from those of political leaders at the federal level.

RTR was also in poor shape financially. State funding repeatedly fell far short of the level theoretically allocated in the federal budget. Advertising revenues were insufficient to help the network cover its costs or upgrade obsolete equipment. Under four different chairmen during the 1990s, RTR was plagued by what could charitably be termed financial mismanagement.[8] Two audits of the network's finances uncovered evidence of kickbacks and corruption as well.[9]

---

[6] On media coverage of the 1995 parliamentary elections, see the report written by monitors for the European Institute for the Media; Laura Belin & Robert W. Orttung, The Russian Parliamentary Elections of 1995: The Battle for the Duma ch. 6 (1997); Sarah Oates & Laura Roselle, *Russian Elections and TV News: Comparison of Campaign News on State-Controlled and Commercial Television Channels*, 5 Harvard International Journal of Press/Politics 30 (2000).

[7] Ivan Zassoursky, *Media and Power: Russia in the Nineties*, *in* Russian Media Challenge, *supra* note 5, at 79-80; Zassoursky, Mass-Media vtoroi respubliki, *supra* note 2, at 121-24. Zassoursky cites an interesting unpublished paper prepared by Gleb Pavlovsky's Foundation for Effective Politics in May 1998, when massive protests by coal miners were used in the information war to undermine the government of Prime Minister Sergei Kirienko.

[8] Sometimes senior managers entered RTR into contracts on terms unfavorable financially to the network. For instance, there were persistent allegations that the network's exclusive advertising contract with the Video-International agency starved RTR of revenues. Video-International founder Mikhail

The first important step toward recentralizing management of state-owned media was a May 1998 presidential decree. It created a huge media holding company, including RTR, state-owned regional television stations, and the television and radio broadcasting towers that had previously fallen under the jurisdiction of the Ministry of Communications. The decree was the brainchild of Mikhail Lesin, founder of the Video-International advertising agency that produced Yeltsin's 1996 campaign commercials and the number two man at RTR, appointed to that post by Yeltsin soon after the 1996 elections.

Lesin's fingerprints were also evident in a July 1999 presidential decree creating the Ministry for the Press, Television and Radio Broadcasting, and Mass Communications (the "Press Ministry"). It was immediately clear that the Press Ministry would exert more influence on state policy than the State Press Committee and the Federal Service on Television and Radio Broadcasting, which had both inherited functions of the Press and Information Ministry after that body was dissolved in early 1994. Yeltsin put Lesin in charge of the new ministry, which had such a broad scope of responsibilities that some Russian journalists began calling it the Ministry of Truth. Nearly a year later, Lesin remarked that "for a long time state media developed and were managed rather chaotically. It is clear that the state is trying to unify all these resources and control the developments."[10]

Making Peace with Corporate Media

If Kremlin operatives were to influence prevailing media coverage of the 1999/2000 electoral cycle, they would need more than the support of state-controlled media. Consequently, a major goal of media policy in 1999 was securing the allegiance of Russia's media moguls. Above all, that meant reaching an understanding with Boris Berezovsky. Paradoxically, although the state held a fifty-one-percent stake in the Channel 1 broadcaster, ORT, Berezovsky wielded more influence over editorial policy at the network than any government or Kremlin official.[11] He paid the salaries of top ORT

Lesin was first deputy chairman of RTR when the deal was struck. *See* Obshchaya gazeta, Jan. 6, 2000; Novaya gazeta, Jan. 3, 2000.

[9] On the Audit Chamber's first investigation of RTR, launched in 1997, see Kommersant-Daily, Feb. 13, 1998; Izvestiia, Feb. 17, 1998. On the Audit Chamber's 2000 report on RTR, see Obshchaya gazeta, Jan. 25-31, 2001; Obshchaya gazeta, Feb. 15-21, 2001; Russia Journal, Feb. 17-23, 2001.

[10] Interview with Lesin on Radio Free Europe/Radio Liberty's Russian Service, June 14, 2000, *quoted in* Floriana Fossato & Anna Kachkaeva, *Russian Media Empires VI*, Radio Free Europe/Radio Liberty, Sept. 2000, *available at* http://www.rferl.org/nca/special/rumedia6/index.html.

[11] For instance, Berezovsky spoke regularly with Sergei Dorenko about the contents of his "analytical program" on ORT. See a transcript of one such telephone conversation (which Dorenko admitted was accurate), published in Novaya gazeta, Dec. 16-19, 1999. Similarly, ORT commentator Aleksandr Nevzorov claimed he spoke to Berezovsky almost daily. See Vremya-MN, June 1, 1999, at 3. A transcript of one such conversation appeared in Novaya gazeta, Dec. 20-23, 1999. *See also* Jen Tracy, *Berezovsky: My Media Wars Can End*, Moscow Times, Dec. 23, 1999.

journalists and executives,[12] made important hiring decisions and negotiated contracts on behalf of the network.[13] Berezovsky also held a controlling stake in the private network TV-6 and financed the operations of several publications, notably *Nezavisimaya Gazeta*.[14]

Berezovsky had used his media holdings to attack senior government officials in 1997 and 1998, after a high-profile privatization sale went against him. But by 1999, he and the Kremlin were natural allies again. During Primakov's tenure as prime minister, prosecutors pursued criminal investigations into firms linked to Berezovsky, and those cases posed the most serious threat to Berezovsky's influence in years.[15] His incentive to cooperate with the Kremlin increased further in the summer of 1999, when Primakov (who had by then been sacked by Yeltsin) joined forces with Moscow Mayor Yurii Luzhkov, a longtime nemesis of Berezovsky's.[16] A triumph for Primakov or Luzhkov in the 2000 presidential election would not only reduce Berezovsky's status but could lead to a long spell in prison or exile. Fatherland—All Russia, the opposition alliance headed by Primakov and Luzhkov, had the backing of many powerful politicians, both in Moscow and in the regions. In response, Berezovsky helped Kremlin officials create a pro-government bloc called Unity, which recruited regional leaders who opposed Luzhkov.

Berezovsky was back on the team, but Kremlin operatives had more work to do in order to resurrect the media alliance at the center of the 1996 presidential campaign. NTV had been a crucial element of Yeltsin's successful strategy in 1996 and was one of Russia's most influential private networks. Thanks to a series of helpful presidential decrees over the years, along with substantial loans backed by the government or para-statal institutions, NTV broadcast to a much larger audience, for many more hours a day, than it had in 1996. Winning back its loyalty was therefore a high priority for the upcoming electoral cycle. In June 1999, Yeltsin's chief of staff Aleksandr Voloshin and then Prime Minister Sergei Stepashin met privately with Vladimir Gusinsky to try to secure the backing of NTV and other outlets in Gusinsky's Media-Most empire. NTV journalists later claimed that Voloshin offered Gusinsky $100 million if his media outlets

---

[12] Floriana Fossato & Anna Kachkaeva, *Russian Media Empires V*, Radio Free Europe/Radio Liberty, Aug. 1999, *available at* http://www.rferl.org/nca/special/rumedia5/index.html.

[13] Vremya-MN, Dec. 7, 1999, at 4.

[14] For more on Berezovsky's acquisition of a controlling stake in TV-6, see Fossato & Kachkaeva, *Russian Media Empires V*, *supra* note 12.

[15] Berezovsky spent several weeks abroad in early 1999, as the authorities pursued several criminal investigations connected to his business dealings. He returned to Moscow in April only after then-Interior Minister Sergei Stepashin indicated that he would not act on a warrant issued for Berezovsky's arrest. *See* RFE/RL Newsline, Apr. 19, 1999.

[16] Media linked to Berezovsky had long been exceptions to the general rule that Moscow-based outlets did not attack the powerful mayor. By the same token, media close to Luzhkov, such as the daily *Moskovsky komsomolets* and the TV-Center network, had repeatedly publicized damning allegations about criminal activity by Berezovsky.

would support the Yeltsin team politically;[17] Kremlin officials denied the charge and accused Gusinsky of using threats in order to secure more money for his media operations.[18] (The August 1998 ruble devaluation had severely damaged the finances of NTV and other arms of the Media-Most empire.)

Whatever was on offer that day, Gusinsky refused the deal. He had long worked closely with Luzhkov,[19] who was by now firmly in opposition to Yeltsin. When persuasion failed, economic pressure commenced. State-controlled Vneshekonombank had loaned Media-Most some $42 million in 1998, but in the summer of 1999 the bank refused to extend the loan and demanded repayment in cash.[20] A furious "information war" between NTV and media loyal to the Kremlin ensued. ORT led the charge, asserting that NTV was pursuing a political agenda in order to be freed from large debts accumulated by Media-Most. Berezovsky himself appeared on ORT's prime-time news program to accuse NTV of undermining Russia's economic stability.[21] For its part, NTV publicized new corruption allegations involving members of the Yeltsin "family," including Voloshin and Pavel Borodin, the longtime head of the Kremlin's property department. During the Sunday analytical program *Itogi*, NTV's star anchor Yevgenii Kiselev also alleged that Kremlin operatives were seeking to punish the network for disloyalty.

Information Warfare

Information wars were a recurring phenomenon in Russian politics during the late 1990s, but as the sophisticated media campaign waged before the 1999 Duma elections progressed it began to eclipse all previous information wars in terms of ferocity.[22] State-owned media and fellow travelers, especially media financed by Berezovsky, promoted Vladimir Putin, the little-known prime minister appointed in August, and the pro-government Unity bloc. Whereas the Communist Party bore the brunt of the media assault in 1996, this time Fatherland—All Russia was assigned the role of bogeyman,

[17] Itogi (NTV), Nov. 14, 1999; Segodnya, Nov. 11, 1999.

[18] Voloshin told his side of the story in an interview published in *Komsomolskaya Pravda* on August 3, 1999. For Stepashin's version, see his interview published in *Segodnya* on November 12, 1999. He suggested that, although no one explicitly offered Gusinsky money in exchange for political support, Voloshin hinted that Media-Most's problems were related to the fact that several Gusinsky-owned media outlets were working "against the president."

[19] Gusinsky's Most Bank earned a fortune in the 1990s handling accounts for the Moscow city government. A controversial raid on the bank by the Presidential Security Service in December 1994 was widely interpreted as a Kremlin attack on Luzhkov.

[20] Although Vneshekombank acted within its legal rights, it is notable that the bank did not ask ORT to repay a $100 million loan it had issued to ORT in late 1998, when that network was on the brink of bankruptcy.

[21] Fossato & Kachkaeva, *Russian Media Empires V*, *supra* note 12.

[22] For detailed reports on media coverage during the Duma campaign, see the series of *RFE/RL Russian Election Reports*, which can be found at http://www.rferl.org/elections/russia99report/archives.html.

with the goal of demolishing the prospects for either Primakov or Luzhkov to win the presidency.

The scale of the media campaign against Fatherland—All Russia was staggering. The opposition bloc's leaders were depicted as incompetent, devious, hypocritical, and corrupt. Commentators suggested they were willing to break the law, commit murder, undermine the Russian economy, and jeopardize the military campaign in Chechnya, all in order to achieve their own narrow political objectives.[23] Particularly damaging allegations appeared in so-called "analytical programs" on ORT and RTR, whose hosts came to be known as "information killers." Ordinary newscasts and special programs also routinely cast Fatherland—All Russia leaders in an unfavorable light. For instance, during the final week of the campaign RTR broadcast programs four evenings in a row alleging that Moscow city authorities "close[d] their eyes" to widespread criminal activities in the capital. Primakov and Luzhkov were rarely given any opportunity, let alone equal time, to respond to such charges on the air.[24] Publications linked financially to Berezovsky also attacked Primakov, Luzhkov, and other prominent figures in the opposition bloc.

While some charges against Fatherland—All Russia were grounded in fact or at least contained a grain of truth, others were based on empty speculation or outright fabrication.[25] In retrospect, it is clear that the authorities were not much bothered by the heinous acts attributed to leaders of the opposition bloc. Despite the numerous allegations of crime and corruption in Moscow and St. Petersburg, for instance, law enforcement agencies showed virtually no interest in investigating, let alone prosecuting, any officials implicated in the media reports. Further evidence that the campaign propaganda did not reflect the Kremlin's genuine concerns emerged in January 2000, when Unity and the Communist Party forged an alliance, with Putin's blessing. A common refrain of official media coverage during the campaign had been that Fatherland—All Russia and Communist leaders were plotting a secret alliance, with potentially disastrous consequences for Russian political stability.

In theory, the law on parliamentary elections prohibited journalists and media outlets from engaging in "campaign agitation," defined as attempts to encourage citizens

---

[23] A more thorough analysis of the campaign against Fatherland—All Russia can be found in Laura Belin, *State TV Wages Unprecedented "Information War,"* RFE/RL Russian Election Report, Dec. 17, 1999. *See also* Raskin, *supra* note 5.

[24] However, Primakov did appear on Aleksandr Lyubimov's prime-time ORT program *Zdes i seichas* on November 16, 1999. He also denounced the information war against his electoral bloc in comments broadcast on state-owned Radio Mayak on November 12, 1999.

[25] One example of unfounded speculation can be found in Laura Belin, *Two Views of Primakov's Visit to Paris*, RFE/RL Russian Election Report, Dec. 10, 1999, *available at* http://www.rferl.org/elections/russia99report/tvreports.html. In a different report aimed at exposing the incompetence/unpreparedness of the Moscow police, RTR broadcast some allegedly recent footage taken as part of an Interior Ministry investigation. In fact, some of the footage had appeared two or three years earlier on NTV and TV-6. *See* Izvestiia, Nov. 27, 1999.

to vote for or against a given candidate.[26] But while the Central Electoral Commission sought to apply that part of the electoral law,[27] only the Press Ministry had the authority to issue formal warnings to media outlets.[28] Lesin announced early in the campaign that his ministry would not enforce the ban on agitation.[29] In fact, Lesin flouted the spirit of the law when he appeared on the RTR program "Zerkalo" two weeks before voting day to criticize a political advertisement produced by Fatherland—All Russia. (In what must be one of the most creative "dirty tricks" perpetrated in a Russian election campaign, ORT and RTR aired that paid advertisement only alongside copycat commercials designed to diminish its impact.[30]) The Press Ministry eventually did issue warnings to ORT and TV-Center during the final week of the campaign. ORT's was for discrediting Fatherland—All Russia, while TV-Center's was for promoting the opposition alliance.[31]

The newcomer Unity, which offered no clear ideology or program, received massive favorable publicity on Channels 1 and 2. Quantitative and qualitative analysis of the air time devoted to various blocs on ORT and RTR revealed bias in favor of Unity but not the full extent of its advantages.[32] The Kremlin's proxy benefited indirectly from a huge amount of coverage that showed Putin in a positive light (Putin endorsed Unity about a month before the election). In addition, sympathetic coverage of the military campaign in Chechnya boosted the government's popularity and created many opportunities to showcase Minister for Emergency Situations Sergei Shoigu, the top candidate on Unity's party list.[33]

---

[26] A good critique of Russian electoral rules relating to the media is Daphne Skillen, *Otsenka Federal'nogo zakona 'O vyborakh Prezidenta Rossiiskoi Federatsii' v chasti regulirovaniya deyatel'nosti SMI*, *in* SMI I predstoyashchie vybory prezidenta Rossii v 2000 godu (2000). The book is a publication of the International Foundation for Electoral Systems (IFES). Russian commentators also found fault with that portion of Russian electoral law. *See* Izvestiia, Nov. 2, 1999; Segodnya, Nov. 5, 1999; Kommersant-Daily, Nov. 13, 1999.

[27] *See* Raskin, *supra* note 5, at 95-96; S. Bolshakov and E. Ishchenko, Novyi 'Bloknot Agitatora': ili osobennosti pravovogo regulirovaniya predvybornoi agitatsii v izbiratel'noi kampanii po vyboram prezidenta Rossiiskoi Federatsii v 2000 godu (2000); interview with Sergei Bolshakov in Vremya-MN, Jan. 26, 2000.

[28] The Central Electoral Commission asked the Press Ministry to hold ORT and Sergei Dorenko accountable for allegations aired against Primakov on Dorenko's programs of October 17 and 24, 1999. *See* Kommersant-Daily, Nov. 2, 1999.

[29] Vremya-MN, Nov. 3, 1999; Kommersant-Daily, Nov. 3, 1999. *See also* Laura Belin, *Legal Prohibition of Media 'Agitation' a Dead Letter*, RFE/RL Russian Election Report, Nov. 5, 1999.

[30] *See* Laura Belin, *Fatherland—All Russia Stakes Campaign on Primakov . . . as State-Run Networks Seek to Reduce Impact of His Words*, RFE/RL Russian Election Report, Dec. 17, 1999.

[31] Kommersant-Daily, Dec. 15, 1999, at 3. Skillen argued that the Press Ministry did not act even-handedly, since TV-Center's alleged misdeeds were minor compared to those of ORT, while RTR received no warning from the Press Ministry. *See* Skillen, *supra* note 26.

[32] European Institute for the Media, Final Report on Media Coverage of the Parliamentary Elections in the Russian Federation (1999) [hereinafter EIM Final Report], *available at* http://www.eim.org/.

[33] Raskin, *supra* note 5, at 107. *See also* Laura Belin, *NTV Criticizes Shoigu's 'Cynical' Campaign Tactics*, RFE/RL Russian Election Report, Nov. 19, 1999.

Compared to how the top two television networks treated Fatherland—All Russia, the Communists got off easily during the 1999 campaign. However, despite commanding more popular support than any other political party, the Communist Party was arguably short-changed in newscasts on all networks, as it had been during the 1995 parliamentary campaign.

One remarkable development during the 1999 campaign was the determination of several television networks to boost the prospects of Vladimir Zhirinovsky and his Zhirinovsky Bloc, formed in October after Zhirinovsky's Liberal Democratic Party of Russia was denied access to the ballot.[34] Although Zhirinovsky was initially reviled by the Russian journalistic community, in the mid- to late 1990s it became clear that his oppositionist stance was for public consumption only. On key votes in the Duma, his faction consistently supported the Kremlin, inspiring the media campaign to help him clear the five-percent barrier for representation in parliament.[35] During numerous appearances on ORT, RTR, and Berezovsky-controlled TV-6, Zhirinovsky played a role similar to Aleksandr Lebed's in 1996: he not only promoted himself but did his best to trash the Kremlin's designated bogeyman.[36]

The Union of Right Forces also received disproportionate news coverage on major television networks, but that was less surprising than the friendly coverage afforded to Zhirinovsky. An alliance of many prominent former government officials, the Union of Right Forces was the ideological heir to Russia's Choice in 1993 and Russia's Democratic Choice in 1995. In their day, both of those blocs received more media coverage than most of their political rivals.[37]

Other television networks tried to compensate for the bias of networks controlled by the state and Berezovsky. TV-Center, mostly financed by the Moscow city authorities, aggressively promoted Fatherland—All Russia,[38] as did several Moscow newspapers. To a lesser extent, NTV devoted sympathetic coverage to Fatherland—All Russia,[39] while its news and analysis programs cast a skeptical eye toward Unity.[40] But

---

[34] *And Then There Were 26*, RFE/RL Russian Election Report, Dec. 10, 1999.

[35] Monitoring conducted by the European Institute for the Media showed that Zhirinovsky and the LDPR received disproportionate coverage on ORT and RTR. *See* EIM Final Report, *supra* note 32.

[36] *See* Laura Belin, *State TV Kinder Than Ever to Zhirinovsky*, RFE/RL Russian Election Report, Dec. 3, 1999. During the final two weeks before the first round of the 1996 election, televised interviews with Lebed often contained lengthy criticism of the Communist Party.

[37] Belin & Orttung, *supra* note 6; Oates & Roselle, *supra* note 6.

[38] Fatherland—All Russia received more air time on TV-Center than all other major political parties combined. See EIM Report and results of monitoring conducted by the Agency for Regional Political Research (ARPI), *available at* http://www.monitoring.ru. Luzhkov regularly appeared on hour-long prime-time programs and was the subject of a fawning "political portrait" during the final week of the campaign. *See* Laura Belin, *TV-Center: All Luzhkov, All the Time*, RFE/RL Russian Election Report, Dec. 17, 1999; Izvestiia, Nov. 27, 1999.

[39] The EIM monitoring revealed that NTV's newscasts contained much more coverage of Fatherland—All Russia bloc than similar programs ORT or RTR. Moreover, references to Fatherland—All Russia on ORT and RTR were largely negative, while references on TV-Center and NTV were largely positive or

neither NTV nor TV-Center could match the audience reach of ORT and RTR. Throughout the campaign, ORT's "Sergei Dorenko Show" consistently gained higher ratings than NTV's *Itogi*, which aired at the same time on Sunday evenings.

The European Institute for the Media concluded that media coverage of the 1999 parliamentary campaign was "considerably worse" than coverage of the 1995 Duma elections. The institute's report particularly faulted ORT and RTR for failing to meet their public-service obligations and thereby undermining the public's "ability to come to a well-informed conclusion about who deserves their confidence."[41]

Leaving Nothing to Chance

The results of the Duma elections could hardly have pleased the Kremlin more. Unity, which had not even existed until a few months before voting day, finished a close second to the Communist Party with nearly a quarter of the party-list voting.[42] Fatherland—All Russia, which in the summer had seemed likely to place first or second in the party-list voting, placed a distant third. Smaller electoral blocs promoted by pro-Kremlin media did well, with the Union of Right Forces and the Zhirinovsky Bloc both clearing the five-percent hurdle.

Most important, the results took Primakov and Luzhkov out of the running for the next presidential election. Commentators almost unanimously attributed Unity's strong showing to Putin's coat-tails. Regional leaders and other politicians who had backed Fatherland—All Russia during the Duma campaign quickly began to gravitate toward Putin. That process accelerated after Yeltsin's surprise resignation on New Year's Eve made Putin acting president and forced an early presidential election. The December 1999 election thus produced a broad consensus among political and economic elites over the identity of Russia's next president. The "continuity of power" was assured.

In contrast to the task facing Yeltsin's handlers in 1996, Kremlin operatives did not have a mountain to climb during the 2000 presidential campaign. Putin looked virtually unbeatable; the main question was whether he would win outright in the first round or defeat Communist leader Gennadii Zyuganov in a runoff. But anyone who expected official media to assume a neutral stance in the absence of a tough fight was quickly proved wrong. While Putin did not use the free air time to which he was entitled

---

neutral. NTV's deputy editor in chief Vladimir Kulistikov told EIM monitors that the network deliberately tried to give more air time to groups that were poorly represented on state television networks. EIM report, excerpted in *Sreda*, Jan. 2000, at 9.

[40] *See, e.g.*, Laura Belin, *NTV Links Unity to Corruption*, RFE/RL Russian Election Report, Dec. 17, 1999.

[41] EIM preliminary report on media coverage of the 1999 parliamentary elections, released on 20 December 1999.

[42] Of the 450 seats in the State Duma, half was filled by proportional representation based on the results of the party-list voting. The other half was filled by individual candidates who gained a plurality of the vote in 225 single-member districts.

and ran no paid commercials, major television newscasts did plenty of campaigning on his behalf.[43] Extensive coverage of his activities and the military campaign in Chechnya played to his strengths. In addition, ORT and RTR correspondents repeatedly depicted campaign activities as demeaning rituals for politicians trying to sell themselves, which subtly elevated the acting president to a higher level of statesmanship.[44]

Having faced a barrage of media criticism in 1996, Zyuganov received comparatively gentle coverage the second time around. The shift reflected official confidence that the Communist leader posed no electoral threat to Putin. It was also consistent with the Kremlin's support for the deal Unity struck with the Communist Duma faction in January 2000. Zyuganov's activities received far less air time than Putin's during the campaign, but Channels 1 and 2 aired several interviews with him. RTR even broadcast a mostly favorable documentary about the Communist leader less than a week before the presidential election, which would have been unthinkable in 1996.[45]

While the presidential campaign did not involve information warfare on a scale with the firepower directed against Fatherland—All Russia, ORT and RTR attacked Yabloko leader Grigorii Yavlinsky on many fronts during the final week before election day.[46] Yavlinsky had no chance of winning, but the Kremlin wanted a decisive victory for Putin in the first round, and some political analysts thought a strong showing for Yavlinsky could force Putin into a runoff against Zyuganov.

A secondary target was the marginal candidate Yurii Skuratov, whom Yeltsin sacked as procurator-general in 1999. News reports and commentaries on ORT and RTR repeatedly mocked him, devising various pretexts to remind voters of Skuratov's famous dalliance with two prostitutes.[47] Although Skuratov barely registered on opinion polls, undermining his credibility served a political purpose, since he had threatened to reveal damaging information about high-level corruption involving the Yeltsin "family." For good measure, ORT and RTR aired several reports discrediting a small-scale campaign that encouraged Russians to check the "against all candidates" box on election day.[48]

---

[43] *See* Laura Belin, *How State Television Aided Putin's Campaign*, RFE/RL Russian Election Report, Apr. 7, 2000.

[44] *Id.*

[45] Laura Belin, *When Is Equal Time Not Equal Time?*, RFE/RL Russian Election Report, Mar. 24, 2000.

[46] Laura Belin, *ORT Launches Wide-Ranging Assault on Yavlinskii*, RFE/RL Russian Election Report, Mar. 24, 2000.

[47] *See* Laura Belin, *State TV Seeks to Discredit Skuratov*, RFE/RL Russian Election Report, Mar. 17, 2000.

[48] Laura Belin, *State TV Pushes for First-Round Putin Victory*, RFE/RL Russian Election Report, Mar. 24, 2000. Although voting "against all candidates" was a valid option on the ballot, the Central Electoral Commission advanced the unconvincing argument that encouraging citizens to vote against all candidates was somehow unlawful. *See* Bolshakov & Ishchenko, *supra* note 27, at 12.

Keeping Up the Pressure on Alternative Media

Using the state's media arsenal was only part of the strategy to ensure a smooth path to victory for Putin. Since his popularity had skyrocketed in tandem with support for the military campaign in Chechnya,[49] officials expended considerable effort to keep Russian news coverage of the fighting "on message."[50] This task was easy when fighting in the breakaway republic first resumed, because aside from a handful of newspapers such as *Novaya Gazeta*, most print and broadcast media devoted favorable coverage to the "anti-terrorist campaign."[51] However, the tone of coverage on NTV and TV-Center shifted noticeably in November and December 1999, with many reports expressing skepticism about official casualty estimates and some questions about the prospects for winning the war.[52] (Oleg Dobrodeev, who was general director of NTV at the time, alleged much later that NTV increased its negative coverage of the military campaign in Chechnya in late 1999, hoping the Kremlin would respond by urging Media-Most's creditors to forgive large debts.[53]) After the December parliamentary elections, media criticism of Russian military tactics increased. NTV broadcast footage of Russian troops looting a "liberated" village in the aftermath of an alleged massacre. In January 2000 several prominent newspapers, including *Izvestiia*, *Komsomolskaya Pravda*, and *Moskovsky Komsomolets*, also began to express skepticism about official casualty estimates and the wisdom of Russian military strategy.[54]

Putin's team wanted to avoid a repeat of the experience from 1995, when opinion polls showed that official reports on the war lost credibility in light of conflicting reports in privately-owned newspapers and electronic media. Putin put former Yeltsin press secretary Sergei Yastrzhembsky in charge of managing information about Chechnya. Soon after his appointment, Yastrzhembsky suggested that journalists had a patriotic duty

---

[49] Putin's approval rating was very low in August 1999, the month he was appointed, and remained in single digits in September. It increased sharply in October and November, when the fighting in Chechnya intensified. *See* Yitzhak M. Brudny, *Continuity or Change in Russian Electoral Patterns? The December 1999-March 2000 Election Cycle*, *in* Contemporary Russian Politics, *supra* note 2, at 173 table 11.6.

[50] For a comparison of Russian policies to influence media coverage during the two Chechen wars, see Oleg Panfilov, *Ot VITsa k RITsu*, December 1999.

[51] Many Moscow-based journalists were sympathetic to the Chechen fighters during the first war from 1994-1996, but a spate of kidnappings (including a few murders) of journalists in the breakaway republic made Russian journalists more likely to take a hard line against Chechen independence.

[52] Semen Liberman found that coverage of Chechnya by major television networks was very similar in September and October 1999, but in November and December coverage on NTV and TV-Center diverged from the tone of ORT and RTR coverage. See the articles by Liberman in *Sreda* in October and December 1999.

[53] Dobrodeev made that assertion and several other embarrassing allegations about the political agenda behind NTV's news reporting in an open letter published in *Izvestiia* on April 9, 2001.

[54] Lev Lurie, *The Russian Media Turns*, *in* Institute for War & Peace Reporting Caucasus Reporting Service, no. 14, Jan. 2000.

to assist the war effort: "When the nation mobilises its forces to solve some task, that imposes obligations on everyone, including the media."[55]

Heavy restrictions on journalists' movements in Chechnya, along with special accreditation requirements, helped keep correspondents from straying far from Russian military encampments.[56] Although journalists could pay bribes to circumvent those restrictions, the ordeal of Radio Liberty correspondent Andrei Babitsky provided a cautionary tale.[57] Secretly detained by Russian security forces in mid-January 2000, he spent several weeks in custody with no opportunity to contact his family, employers, or a lawyer. In the early days following Babitsky's disappearance, Yastrzhembsky pointedly commented that Russian authorities could not vouch for his safety, since he lacked the proper accreditation. Putin later accused Babitsky of "working for the bandits" and doing things "more dangerous than firing from machine guns."[58] To further discourage media from presenting Chechen points of view, Deputy Press Minister Mikhail Seslavinsky announced in March 2000 that the authorities would consider interviews with senior Chechen officials to be violations of the law on terrorism.

Warnings from a ministry might appear to be a mere slap on the wrist, but they carried potentially grave consequences. Under a new interpretation of the rules, adopted in 1999,[59] license operators that received multiple warnings from the Press Ministry lost the right to have their broadcast licenses renewed automatically. (Representatives of private television networks opposed that and other aspects of the new licensing procedure, but the ministry did not accommodate their concerns.[60]) Lesin caused an uproar by announcing in late February 2000 that licenses held by TV-Center and ORT, which each had received two warnings, would be reviewed in May, when their terms were to expire. Executives at TV-Center and ORT accused Lesin of manipulating the

---

[55] Yastrzhembsky was interviewed in *Kommersant* on January 21, 2000.

[56] NTV correspondent Yurii Lipatov said military officials barred NTV correspondents from the press pool in Chechnya after the network broadcast an unsanctioned interview with a Russian officer. Reuters, Jan. 23, 2000; Jen Tracy, *Kremlin Tells Press to Toe the Line*, Moscow Times, Jan. 25, 2000.

[57] Comprehensive coverage of Babitsky's detention and subsequent trial on the charge of using false documents can be found at http://www.rferl.org/nca/special/babitsky. Archives of reports on Babitsky are also available on the websites of the Glasnost Defense Foundation (www.gdf.ru), the Center for Journalism in Extreme Situations (www.cjes.ru), and the Committee to Protect Journalists (www.cpj.org).

[58] A lengthy interview with Putin appeared in *Kommersant* on March 10, 2000. While discussing the Babitsky case, the acting president, who received a law degree at university in the 1970s, argued that one should "observe the laws of your country if you are counting on the same laws being observed with respect to you."

[59] In the absence of a federal law on television and radio broadcasting, many rules concerning licensing matters could be changed by decrees and government or ministerial directives. *See* Andrei Richter, *Media Regulation: Foundation Laid for Free Speech*, *in* Russian Media Challenge, *supra* note 5 [hereinafter Richter, *Media Regulation*].

[60] *See* Vedomosti, Nov. 10, 1999; Rossiiskaya gazeta, Nov. 26, 1999. Some commentators accused the Press Ministry of charging excessive fees for participating in auctions for broadcast licenses. Portions of those fees contributed substantially to the ministry's budget. *See* Vremya-MN, Oct. 12, 2000; Obshchaya gazeta, Nov. 2, 2000.

licensing procedure to influence both networks' news coverage during the presidential campaign, and many commentators shared their interpretation.[61]

While not in danger of losing its broadcast license, NTV faced intense financial pressure. Video-International, the advertising agency founded by Lesin, ended its exclusive contract with the network in late 1999, forcing NTV to create its own division for selling advertisements.[62] In early 2000 the network's transmission fees were doubled.[63] Parent company Media-Most managed to repay its debt to Vneshekonombank, in part by selling a 4.5-percent stake in NTV and the TNT network to an obscure U.S.-based company. But soon after, Gusinsky and his colleagues found themselves battling a different adversary. The gas monopoly Gazprom, a major shareholder in NTV and Media-Most, had benefited from NTV's support during its own conflicts with government,[64] but the company did not return the favor in NTV's hour of need. Shortly after meeting with Putin in February, Gazprom's chief executive criticized NTV's coverage of Chechnya. The following month, the gas monopoly demanded reimbursement for a $211-million loan it repaid on behalf of Media-Most. Because the state was the largest shareholder in Gazprom, the company had incentive to avoid a confrontation with Putin, who might restructure the monopoly or bring about the dismissal of senior executives after his near-certain election.[65]

The Kremlin's attempts to shape coverage on alternative television networks during the presidential campaign met with limited success. Content analysis revealed that reports about Putin dominated newscasts on NTV and TV-Center, as was the case for ORT and RTR.[66] That was hardly surprising, given the incumbency advantages Putin held as acting president. Media analyst Semyon Liberman concluded that NTV and TV-Center began to depict Putin in a more favorable light in February once Primakov definitively took himself out of the presidential race.[67] One of TV-Center's hard-hitting

---

[61] Obshchaya gazeta, Mar. 9, 2000; *see also* J.A. Dunn, *The Commercialisation of the Russian Mass Media*, *available at* http://www2.gla.ac.uk/slavonic/jdtampere.htm (conference paper presented at the Sixth World Congress of ICCEES in Tampere, Finland in July-August 2000).

[62] For more discussion of the Russian advertising market and Video-International's move away from NTV, *see* Fossato & Kachkaeva, *Russian Media Empires VI*, *supra* note 10.

[63] Although NTV executives characterized the fee increase as persecution, it was in fact merely the undoing of a favor Yeltsin had bestowed on the network. A deal made during the 1996 campaign and cemented in a January 1998 presidential decree guaranteed NTV the right to pay far lower transmission fees than those charged to other private television networks.

[64] This was especially true when the Kirienko government tried to force Gazprom to pay its tax arrears in July 1998. *See* Belin, *The Distorted Russian Media Market*, *supra* note 2.

[65] Despite Gazprom's political loyalty to Putin, a longtime associate of the president's replaced Rem Vyakhirev as Gazprom's chief executive in May 2001, one month after NTV finally came under Gazprom's control.

[66] *See* the European Institute for the Media's Final Report on the 2000 presidential election in the Russian Federation, *available at* http://www.eim.org/.

[67] Sreda, Mar. 2000.

programs turned its fire predominantly on Berezovsky rather than Putin himself.[68] Yet NTV commentator Yevgenii Kiselev continued to criticize Putin,[69] and the acting president remained a frequent target on NTV's satirical programs "Kukly" and "Itogo."

Putin's First Year

With Putin's first-round election victory in March 2000, the main goal driving efforts to strengthen state power over the media had been achieved. However, the new president did not back away from election-season strategies to tame the media. On the contrary, Putin's administration intensified efforts to enlist media support and to intimidate media outlets that did not fall into line. Sentiments expressed by Putin and others in his camp suggested that the Kremlin viewed media's proper role as one of supporting official policies, thereby helping strengthen the Russian state.[70]

Sorting Out Major Television Networks

Item number one on the media policy agenda was consolidating state influence over news content on major television networks. Fully state-owned RTR continued to support Putin faithfully. Oleg Dobrodeev, whom Putin appointed RTR chairman in early 2000, defended the network's editorial policy on the grounds that "at this stage, the interests of society and the president coincide."[71] RTR was the only network Kremlin operatives fully trusted. During the crisis surrounding the sinking of the Kursk nuclear submarine in August 2000, only RTR correspondents and cameras were allowed near the site of the disaster.[72]

TV-Center, created as a vehicle for Luzhkov, faced a struggle to keep broadcasting once the Moscow mayor's presidential ambitions were dead. Despite a court ruling striking down the Press Ministry's second warning to the network (which had served as the official justification for not extending the license), the ministry refused to cancel the auction for the use of the frequency. After repeated delays and backroom negotiations

---

[68] Raskin, *supra* note 5, at 112. TV-Center's decision to pull its punches against Putin confounded the expectations of many Moscow journalists that media sympathetic to Luzhkov and Primakov would hype compromising information about Putin during the presidential race.

[69] Laura Belin, *Top NTV Manager Delivers Harsh Assessment of Putin*, RFE/RL Russian Election Report, Mar. 17, 2000.

[70] In a commentary posted to the pro-Kremlin website strana.ru on September 28, 2000, presidential adviser Gleb Pavlovsky lamented the fact that media trends during the 1990s had deprived the government of "its legitimate tools for spreading information." Lesin and other Press Ministry officials spoke of the need to protect the state from media "aggression." Press Release, World Press Freedom Committee, July 14, 2000, *quoted in* RFE/RL (Un)Civil Societies, July 20, 2000.

[71] As quoted in RFE/RL Newsline, July 14, 2000.

[72] Russia's Union of Journalists issued a statement protesting the preferential access granted to RTR. RFE/RL Newsline, Aug. 21, 2000.

between Lesin and Luzhkov, TV-Center retained its license.[73] It was not clear what Luzhkov promised in return.[74]

Like TV-Center, NTV bet on the "wrong" horse during the 1999 campaign, and the network's troubles worsened after the presidential election. Gusinsky tried to raise funds to repay Media-Most's debts, but a deal to sell Most Bank fell through in April 2000 when Putin reportedly intervened to stop the sale from going ahead.[75] Four days after Putin's inauguration the following month, armed police raided Media-Most's headquarters and confiscated documents.[76] (In the year to come, various law enforcement agencies conducted more than two dozen searches of Media-Most and affiliated companies.) Gusinsky was arrested in June on embezzlement charges related to the acquisition of a St. Petersburg television company, but he was released after three days in custody.[77] Meanwhile, the financial squeeze continued, as Gazprom's subsidiary Gazprom-Media continued to press for repayment of large loans to Media-Most. It did not help matters that Gazprom-Media head Alfred Kokh had an axe to grind against NTV, having lost a powerful cabinet post three years earlier partly because of the network's news coverage.[78]

Kremlin officials and Gazprom executives repeatedly claimed that the problems confronting Gusinsky's media empire had nothing to do with settling political scores or silencing an opposition voice. Rather, they asserted, events were driven by the dispassionate enforcement of criminal laws and Gazprom's legitimate efforts to assert its rights as a creditor and minority shareholder. Media-Most's debts were real enough, and the criminal allegations made against Gusinsky and his associates were by no means implausible. Still, claims that Media-Most's troubles had nothing to do with politics strained credulity. In late July, the authorities abruptly dropped criminal charges against Gusinsky, after he agreed to sell a controlling stake in Media-Most to Gazprom.[79] Suspicions arose immediately that the two developments were linked, but evidence of the authorities' determination to secure a management change at Media-Most emerged only

---

[73] For more details about the competition for the frequency used by TV-Center, see Fossato & Kachkaeva, *Russian Media Empires VI*, *supra* note 10.

[74] Floriana Fossato, *Luzhkov's TV Station Back in Favor*, Radio Free Europe/Radio Liberty, July 7, 2000.

[75] David Hoffman, *Putin's Actions Belie Promise on Tycoons: 'Strange Decisions' Reveal Favoritism Despite Vow to Bring Equality*, Washington Post, May 7, 2000.

[76] Tax police were involved in the raid, but Federal Security Service officials initially suggested the criminal investigation was related to illegal wiretapping allegedly conducted by Media-Most's private security service.

[77] For more on the circumstances surrounding Gusinsky's arrest, see Sophie Lambroschini & Floriana Fossato, *Gusinskii's Arrest Has Several Goals*, RFE/RL Newsline, June 16, 2000; *see also* Fossato & Kachkaeva, *Russian Media Empires VI*, *supra* note 10.

[78] Laura Belin, *Ten Ironies of the NTV Saga*, RFE/RL Russian Political Weekly, Apr. 16, 2001.

[79] Law enforcement officials had insisted for months that they had strong evidence backing the criminal case against Gusinsky, so the sudden decision to drop charges with little explanation raised eyebrows.

in September. Russian media reported that Lesin signed a secret "protocol No. 6" to the July agreement, promising that criminal cases against Gusinsky and his associates would be dropped if Gusinsky sold Gazprom a controlling stake in Media-Most.[80]

From self-imposed exile, Gusinsky renounced the deal he had reached with Gazprom. Putin steadfastly refused to take a public stand on what Kremlin officials characterized as a simple business dispute between Media-Most and its creditor.[81] But despite the clear abuse of power involved in "protocol No. 6"—after all, ordinary negotiations between debtors and creditors do not involve official pledges to shelve criminal investigations—the president did not sack Lesin or Prosecutor-General Vladimir Ustinov.

Shortly after the terms of "protocol No. 6" became public, Gazprom-Media sued Media-Most for non-repayment of loans and alleged breach of contract. Within days the Prosecutor-General's Office opened a new criminal investigation into whether Media-Most officials had illegally transferred property abroad. In early October, several state-controlled lending institutions announced plans to sue Media-Most for unpaid loans as well. Russian authorities sought Gusinsky's arrest through Interpol, and Spanish authorities detained him in December 2000.[82] Although officials again denied that any political agenda lay behind the criminal cases, a double standard was evident. An Audit Chamber investigation in 2000 uncovered evidence of massive financial abuses at the politically loyal RTR during the 1990s. However, no criminal cases were pursued against current or former top executives at RTR—neither when the Audit Chamber's secret report was written, nor when details from it leaked in early 2001.[83] Perhaps not coincidentally, Lesin was the number two man at the state-owned network when much of the alleged malfeasance took place.

It proved difficult to hold ranks in the face of great political and economic pressure. NTV was weakened by attrition during 2000, as prominent managers and journalists took jobs at state-controlled media entities. The most breathtaking departure was that of Dobrodeev, NTV's founding news director and longtime general director of the network, who resigned in late January 2000.[84] Several well-known journalists followed Dobrodeev to RTR after Putin appointed him chairman of that network.[85]

---

[80] Excerpts from "protocol No. 6" appeared in *Izvestiia* on September 19, 2000.

[81] For example, Putin's press secretary said the president "considers it wrong to interfere in a conflict between two commercial organizations." *See* RFE/RL Newsline, Sept. 27, 2000. As the conflict neared its climax in April 2001, Putin insisted that he did not have the right to intervene in a dispute between a debtor and creditors. RFE/RL Newsline, Apr. 10, 2001.

[82] A panel of Spanish judges refused to extradite Gusinsky to Russia in April 2001.

[83] *See* Obshchaya gazeta, Jan. 25-31, 2001; Obshchaya gazeta, Feb. 15-21, 2001; The Russia Journal, Feb. 17-23, 2001.

[84] At the time, Dobrodeev said little about his reasons for leaving, but he elaborated on his differences with Gusinsky in an open letter published in *Izvestiia* on April 9, 2001.

[85] Among them was Yelena Masyuk, NTV's star correspondent during the first war in Chechnya.

NTV's most skilled technician defected to RTR in October, and the network's news director left to head the state-owned news agency RIA-Novosti the same month.

Meanwhile, Gazprom pursued various legal tactics against Media-Most and sought to take control of NTV, in which it owned a minority stake.[86] When the small American company which had purchased a 4.5-percent stake in NTV a year earlier sided with Gazprom, the gas monopoly was able to call a special shareholders' meeting to appoint new management for NTV.[87] Journalists staged on-air protests for ten days, refusing to recognize the new management. But Gazprom representatives accompanied by armed guards ultimately took over the NTV headquarters on the night of April 13-14, 2001, leading to a mass exodus of journalists and staff.[88]

If the campaign against NTV suggested that opposition media might face reprisals, a parallel campaign to force Berezovsky out of his influential position at fifty-one-percent state-owned ORT showed that taking the "right" stand during the parliamentary and presidential elections did not guarantee an easy ride either. Although Berezovsky had done as much as anyone to facilitate Putin's rise to power, the new president's team appeared to lack confidence in his loyalty.[89] ORT held on to its license when the Press Ministry held an auction in May 2000 for the use of the Channel 1 frequency, but tension soon emerged between Berezovsky and his protégé. Prosecutors revived investigations into alleged embezzlement at companies linked to Berezovsky.[90] Newspapers financed by the businessman began to criticize Putin more frequently, as Berezovsky sought to form an opposition political movement and his close associate Igor Shabdurasulov resigned as first deputy head of the presidential administration.[91]

The conflict escalated following the Kursk disaster, when ORT news and analysis programs, including Dorenko's popular weekly show, contained some harsh assessments of Putin's actions. Stung by unfavorable news coverage, Putin repeatedly sought to shift blame for the crisis onto wealthy financial backers of media outlets, who, he charged, used "unscrupulous" means to turn the tragedy to their political or financial advantage. Speaking on nationwide television, Putin said that people "on the front lines defending the sailors turned out to be the same people who for a long time facilitated the

---

86 Gazprom's battle against Media-Most involved a confusing array of lawsuits and countersuits filed by different entities in various countries.

87 NTV journalists and Media-Most managers charged that the shareholders' meeting was illegal and did not recognize the new management.

88 See Belin, *Ten Ironies of the NTV Saga*, *supra* note 78.

89 Even though media influenced by Berezovsky supported Putin's presidential bid, some Russian political commentators speculated in early 2000 that Berezovsky's media were subtly working against Putin, hoping to deny him a first-round victory. *See, e.g.*, Andrei Ryabov, *Berezovsky—Novyi Suslov?* Vek, January 28-February 1, 2000. *See also* Laura Belin, *Analyst Predicts Media Campaign to Force Second Round*, RFE/RL Russian Election Report, Mar. 3, 2000.

90 For more background on the conflict that prompted Berezovsky to begin negotiations to sell his ORT shares, see Fossato & Kachkaeva, *Russian Media Empires VI*, *supra* note 10.

91 RFE/RL Newsline, July 17, 2000.

disintegration of the army, navy and the state."[92] In a closed meeting with grieving relatives of the sailors, Putin accused television networks of "lying" and said of those driving the media coverage, "Their logic is simple. Very simple. To work on a mass audience and in that way show the military leadership [and] the political leadership of the country that we need them . . . that we should be afraid of them, yield to them and let them go on robbing the country, army and navy. That is the true goal behind their actions."[93]

In early September, Berezovsky accused a Kremlin official of threatening him with prison if he did not relinquish his minority stake in ORT.[94] Soon after, ORT's general director took Dorenko's program off the air[95] and fired the top two executives in ORT's news department, who had been hand-picked by Berezovsky.[96] In order to avoid giving up his ORT shares,[97] Berezovsky tried to place them in a trust to be managed by a diverse group of journalists, but the scheme fell through.[98] In January 2001 he finally sold his shares in the network.[99] Information about the terms of the sale was sketchy,[100]

---

[92] Interview broadcast on Russian Television (RTR), Aug. 23, 2000.

[93] A transcript of the closed meeting between Putin and relatives of Kursk sailors was published in *Kommersant-Vlast* on August 29, 2000.

[94] *See* Berezovsky's open letter to Putin, published in *Novye Izvestiia* on September 5, 2000.

[95] Dorenko claimed that ORT's general director, Konstantin Ernst, met daily with Putin's chief of staff, Aleksandr Voloshin. He also said that Putin had phoned him three times during the summer of 2000 seeking a guarantee of his loyalty. See Dorenko's interview on Ekho Moskvy on September 9, 2000, and his interview published in *Vremya novostei* on September 14, 2000.

[96] Before they took senior jobs at ORT in May 1999, Tatyana Koshkareva and Rustam Narzikulov penned most of the sharp attacks on government ministers published in *Nezavisimaya gazeta* (financially dependent on Berezovsky) during the 1997 and 1998 "information wars."

[97] In 2000, Berezovsky and Russian commentators routinely referred to the 49-percent stake in ORT that was "controlled by" him, but only part of the privately held ORT stock formally belonged to companies under his control. When ORT was created in late 1994, entities linked to Berezovsky (LogoVAZ and the Obedinennyi Bank) were each allowed to acquire 8 percent of ORT shares. LogoVAZ later purchased Gazprom's 3-percent stake in ORT, while Obedinennyi Bank joined a consortium of banks that collectively owned the remaining 38 percent of privately held ORT shares. That consortium authorized Berzovsky's ally Igor Shabdurasulov to represent their interests. *See* Vedomosti, Sept. 19, 2000.

[98] For details about Berezovsky's abortive attempt to form a "Teletrust," see Vedomosti, Oct. 17, 2000; Vedomosti, Dec. 8, 2000; Obshchaya gazeta, Sept. 21, 2000; Obshchaya gazeta, Oct. 5, 2000; Vremya novostei, Sept. 5, 2000. In one revealing remark published in *Nezavisimaya gazeta* on September 6, 2000, Shabdurasulov indirectly confirmed that Berezovsky previously gave orders to ORT news staff, saying that as soon as Berezovsky handed over his shares to the Teletrust, "he will no longer be dictating to ORT, [its] journalists, [or] management" how to cover the news.

[99] Speaking to the Internet publication Grani.ru on April 18, 2001, Berezovsky said he sold his ORT shares "under the strongest pressure," noting that he made the final decision to sell on the same day his close business partner Nikolai Glushkov was arrested. A summary of that interview was published at http://lenta.ru/russia/2001/04/18/interview/.

[100] Influential businessman Roman Abramovich, Berezovsky's longtime ally who remained on good terms with the Kremlin under Putin, served as middleman in the buyout. Berezovsky asserted that the

but the implications were clear: state officials once again became the dominant force in shaping editorial policy at Channel 1.

Having fallen out with Putin, Berezovsky offered to help his longtime adversary Gusinsky. He made clear that disgruntled NTV staff would be welcome at TV-6, in which he held a controlling stake.[101] In fact, NTV's star anchor Kiselev became general director of TV-6 the day after Gazprom-appointed managers took control of NTV offices.[102] It was a move steeped in irony; once bitter enemies, Berezovsky and Gusinsky had cooperated between 1996 and 1998. But since 1999, Berezovsky and various ORT reporters and commentators had repeatedly sought to discredit Gusinsky and undermine the credibility of NTV and other Media-Most entities.[103] Some analysts questioned Berezovsky's motives in offering assistance to NTV.[104] Others predicted that if he was sincere about providing a venue for alternative news coverage, Berezovsky would eventually be forced out of TV-6, which broadcast to nearly 70 Russian cities.[105] Actions taken by a private pension fund affiliated with LUKoil, the partly state-owned oil company, fueled that speculation. That pension fund, LUKoil-Garant, held a minority stake in TV-6 and filed several lawsuits seeking not only to nullify personnel decisions adopted at TV-6 shareholders' meetings, but also to liquidate the network entirely.[106]

Many NTV personnel who did not join TV-6 went to work for Media-Most's cable network TNT, which had 260 partner stations broadcasting in more than 500 Russian cities and towns. TNT picked up many of NTV's popular politically-oriented programs. However, the network had its own problems with the tax police.[107] Two days after Gazprom completed its takeover of NTV, Russian tax police pursued criminal charges against senior TNT staff.[108] The Press Ministry issued a formal warning to TNT

---

shares would end up in state hands. *See* interview with Berezovsky published in *Kommersant* on January 11, 2001.

[101] Interview with Berezovsky on Ekho Moskvy on April 13, 2001.

[102] *See* Belin, *Ten Ironies of the NTV Saga*, *supra* note 78.

[103] Gusinsky and NTV sued Berezovsky for comments he made in September 1999, when he accused Gusinsky and NTV of having ties to Chechen terrorists. Nezavisimaya gazeta, Jan. 11, 2000. See also ORT's "Vremya with Pavel Sheremet" on November 6, 1999, November 13, 1999, and November 27, 1999 and "The Sergei Dorenko show" on January 22, 2000 (an interview with Berezovsky), January 29, 2000, March 4, 2000, May 13, 2000, May 27, 2000, and June 17, 2000.

[104] See Jamestown Foundation's "The Fortnight in Review" on April 27, 2001.

[105] *See* WPS Monitoring Agency Political Forecasts, *Putin and the Oligarchs: Or, Some Consequences of the NTV Affair*, Apr. 2001, *available at* http://www.wps.ru. Berezovsky alleged that Kremlin operatives were trying to use the oil company LUKoil to buy up all of his media assets (*see* http://lenta.ru/russia/2001/04/18/interview/), but a LUKoil representative denied the allegation in an interview with gazeta.ru on April 19, 2001.

[106] In June 2001 the Moscow Arbitration Court rejected two lawsuits by LUKoil-Garant seeking to declare TV-6 shareholders' meetings illegitimate. As of this writing, LUKoil-Garant's lawsuit seeking to liquidate TV-6 is pending.

[107] In January 2001, the tax police went to court to try to force the liquidation of TNT. Segodnya, Jan. 11, 2001.

[108] Ekho Moskvy, Apr. 16, 2001.

soon after, potentially clearing the way toward refusing to extend the cable network's broadcast license (or threatening to do so, as was done with respect to TV-Center).[109] The Ekho Moskvy radio station, also part of the Media-Most empire, came under pressure as Gazprom went to court successfully to claim a controlling stake in the station as compensation for unpaid debts, and prosecutors searched the radio station's offices in connection with a criminal investigation.[110]

A joke circulating in Moscow in August 2000 told of the following notice posted to a message board: "Pending the successful implementation of Putin's reforms, I will trade two television sets for a good radio receiver."[111] Although state officials did not gain complete control over television news reporting, policies to rein in the major networks certainly diminished pluralism during Putin's first year in office.[112] Speaking in April 2001, Kremlin spin doctor Yastrzhembsky rejected claims that NTV had been Russia's only alternative source of news. He characterized both TV-6 and TV-Center as "opposition" networks,[113] an assessment few analysts shared, coming just a week after TV-Center's founding father Luzhkov had agreed to merge his Fatherland party with the Kremlin's proxy, Unity.

New Doctrine and Law

The Putin administration's media strategy had aims much broader than changing personnel or programming at a few television networks. On several fronts officials sought to change the legal environment in which all Russian media operated.

One important development was the approval of an Information Security Doctrine. Proposals to adopt that doctrine originated in 1995 but were not followed through during Yeltsin's presidency.[114] Putin, a KGB veteran who appointed many veterans of the security services to high-ranking posts, proved more committed to the idea of staving off "information threats" to national security. Russia's Security Council approved the

---

[109] Yastrzhembsky said the warning, based on coverage on a TNT affiliate in Nizhnii Novgorod, would "serve as a lesson for those who engage in political blackmail." See several stories posted on gazeta.ru, including the one posted on May 10, 2001, *available at* http://www.gazeta.ru/2001/05/10/-minpe4atiper.shtml. For Media-Most officials' comments on the matter, see http://www.ntv.ru/russia/-10May2001/tnt_most_print.html.

[110] Sophie Lambroschini & Francesca Mereu, *Ekho Moskvy May Be Next in Line for Gazprom Takeover*, Radio Free Europe/Radio Liberty, May 9, 2001.

[111] The joke alluded to the Soviet-era habit of turning to foreign radio stations (as opposed to officially-sanctioned television) for "real" news.

[112] A few weeks after the takeover, Peter Baker observed that NTV "has not offered the sort of crusading Chechnya coverage it was known for in the past. Those who have compared newscasts have found it hard to distinguish the new NTV's reports out of the battered Chechen capital, Grozny, from those on the official state channels." Baker, *To Russia, With Capital*, Washington Post, May 14, 2001.

[113] Yastrzhembsky made the comments in an interview with Vek on April 20, 2001, as quoted in *Jamestown Foundation Monitor* on April 24, 2001.

[114] *Nezavisimaya gazeta*, June 24, 2000.

Information Security Doctrine in June 2000, and Putin signed the document in September of that year.

Andrei Richter, Director of the Moscow Media Law and Policy Center, summarizes the main idea of the doctrine as "the need to increase governmental control over the flow of information by establishing a legal basis for such control."[115] The doctrine calls for balancing the individual's constitutional right of access to information against the interests of society and the state. Society's interests include "ensuring the interests of the individual . . . , promoting democracy, . . . achieving and maintaining accord in society, and promoting Russia's spiritual revival," while the state is interested in "creating conditions for the harmonious development of the Russian information infrastructure, for the exercise of constitutional human and civil rights and freedoms in the field of obtaining information and using it for the purposes of ensuring the stability of the constitutional order, sovereignty and territorial integrity of Russia, political, economic and social stability, the unconditional ensuring of legality, law and order . . . ."

The main assumptions underlying the doctrine—that information can harm society and that unrestricted flows of information are therefore dangerous—recall the "Defense of Democracy Theory" Frances Foster describes as shaping Russian policy toward the media during the autumn of 1993.[116] The Information Security Doctrine contains a lengthy list of perceived security threats, many of which echo concerns shaping the Defense of Democracy Theory. As Foster writes, that theory views the public's right to information as a right to receive "constructive" information.[117] It emphasizes the potential destabilizing effect of information, in particular the potential for "irresponsible" dissemination of information to discredit the government, deligitimize the state, or exacerbate divisions in society.

Although the Information Security Doctrine acknowledges the need to "guarantee freedom of mass information and the prohibition of censorship," it endorses policies that are inconsistent with those principles.[118] For instance, in order to counteract "abuses" of freedom of information, the doctrine endorses legal acts to prohibit media "distortion" and the "deliberate circulation of false information." International media watchdog groups unanimously condemn "false news" provisions, which are applied in many countries to suppress press freedom.

---

[115] Richter, *Media Regulation*, *supra* note 59, at 125.

[116] Frances H. Foster, *Information and the Problem of Democracy: The Russian Experience*, 44 American Journal of Comparative Law 243 (1996) [hereinafter Foster, *Information and the Problem of Democracy*].

[117] In this spirit, Deputy Security Council Secretary Vladislav Sherstyuk explained the justification for the Information Security Doctrine as follows: "The experience of recent years shows that certain citizens and society as a whole do not receive a sufficient amount of necessary and truthful information about the activities of state authorities, their plans and intentions." Taken from an interview with Sherstyuk published in *Nezavisimoe voennoe obozrenie* on October 13-19, 2000.

[118] Victor Yasmann, *The Roots of Putin's Attack on Media Freedom*, RFE/RL Security Watch, Aug. 7, 2000; Richter, *Media Regulation*, *supra* note 59.

In addition, the Information Security Doctrine seeks to broaden the power of state bodies to keep certain types of information out of the public domain, concerning not only military topics but also some economic and ecological issues.[119] Such restrictions appear to contradict the spirit, if not the letter, of the 1993 Law on State Secrets, which lists types of information that cannot be classified—including information about catastrophes that threaten the health and safety of citizens.[120]

The official reaction to the sinking of the Kursk, the first crisis of Putin's administration, suggests that the political fallout deepened the authorities' determination to curb unflattering media coverage of disasters. The RTR program "Press Club," which had aired live since its inception in the early 1990s, was taped after the Kursk sank, so that embarrassing comments by participating journalists or politicians could be edited out before broadcast.[121] The show has not returned to a live format since. Alluding to the Kursk tragedy, Gleb Pavlovsky, a senior adviser to Putin, wrote shortly after the president signed the Information Security Doctrine that "[t]he lesson of August 2000 is that technological catastrophes may grow into media-orchestrated challenges to national security in general. As technological crises become further aggravated by communicative political performances, they are transformed into major crises on a national scale, which is completely inadmissible for the government."[122]

Although the Information Security Doctrine carried no legal force on its own, it was far more than a symbolic gesture. Soon after signing the document, Putin expanded the list of federal officials who were allowed to classify information, adding the heads of several ministries dealing with economic policies.[123] The Press Ministry has drafted amendments to Russia's fundamental media law, effective since February 1992, in order to bring it in line with the doctrine.[124] Among other things, Lesin has advocated licensing requirements and mandatory re-registration for print media,[125] which would give

---

[119] Statement by the watchdog group Article 19 on the Information Security Doctrine, issued on September 26, 2000. Foster writes that, in 1993, officials employed principles of the Defense of Democracy Theory to justify limiting public access to information. The theory holds that secrecy can be essential for preserving a democratic system, especially during periods of crisis.

[120] Mikhail Fedotov, *SMI v otsutstvii Ariadny*, *in* Zakonodatel'stvo Rossiiskoi Federatsii o sredstvakh massovoi informatsii 249-50 (1996). An electronic version of that book can be found on the website of the Moscow Media Law and Policy Center at http://www.medialaw.ru/publications/index.htm.

[121] Yevgenia Albats, *Cry for Russia's Lost Press Liberty*, Guardian, May 11, 2001. Albats notes that *Press Club* has retained certain production elements likely to give viewers the misleading impression that they are watching a live broadcast.

[122] Pavlovsky's commentary on the information security doctrine was posted on the pro-Kremlin website strana.ru on the day the site opened, September 28, 2000. This quotation appears as it was translated into English and distributed on Johnson's Russia List on September 28, 2000.

[123] *RFE/RL Security Watch*, Oct. 2, 2000.

[124] As of May 2001, the State Duma has not yet approved those amendments. Since a majority of Duma deputies belong to factions supporting the president, it seems likely that the parliament will approve Kremlin-backed amendments to media law, although some of them might be altered in the Information Policy Committee.

[125] For background on Lesin's plans in this area, see RFE/RL Newsline, June 12, 2000.

bureaucrats more discretion than the press registration process outlined in existing media law. Press advocates fear that by issuing multiple warnings to opposition-minded newspapers, the Press Ministry would be able to suspend a newspaper's publishing license for political reasons, without seeking a court order. (The 1992 mass media law requires a court order in order to shut down a registered media outlet.) Lesin's ministry has also been working on registration rules for Internet publications.[126]

Meanwhile, the Kremlin has heeded the Information Security Doctrine's call to "strengthen state mass information media and expand their possibilities for bringing reliable information to Russian and foreign citizens in a timely manner." In September 2000, presidential adviser Pavlovsky launched a website, strana.ru. While not formally subordinate to the government or Kremlin, the website presented the official viewpoint on various political issues.[127] Strana.ru recruited journalists from across the country, paying its stringers more than they could earn working for local media. In the spring of 2001 the Kremlin was rumored to be planning to create a nationwide newspaper which, like strana.ru, would show unfailing loyalty to the president without being officially linked to the government or presidential administration.[128] (As of this writing, no such newspaper had appeared.) As for better communication with foreigners, Lesin announced in early 2001 that the Press Ministry was considering plans to improve Russia's image abroad by running advertisements in U.S. media.[129]

In another move to facilitate transmission of "reliable information," Putin revoked regional leaders' power to select top personnel at state-owned regional television networks. In September 2000, he signed a decree granting the presidential representatives in Russia's seven federal districts the authority to appoint the chief executives of RTR's regional branches.[130] Similarly, a new procedure for distributing regional press subsidies appeared likely to increase the federal authorities' leverage over local newspapers at the expense of regional political bosses. That change predated the Information Security Doctrine, however; in January 2000 Putin signed a law mandating that subsidies to local print media be paid directly from the federal budget. Whereas

---

[126] Richter, *Media Regulation*, *supra* note 59, at 123. For background on early proposals to regulate the Internet, see Floriana Fossato, *Russia: Government Rethinks Internet Control*, Radio Free Europe/Radio Liberty, Feb. 7, 2000; Floriana Fossato, *Russian Authorities and the World Wide Web*, Radio Free Europe/Radio Liberty, Mar. 2000, *available at* www.rferl.org/nca/special/-rumedia5/babitsky2.html.

[127] An official statement on the day of its launch depicted strana.ru as a way for the authorities to "bring the [official] position and the motivation of their actions to the principal groups in society." *V strane nachinaetsya novyi vek novostei*, *available at* http://www.infonet.nnov.ru/nnews/arch/-mess.phtml?mess_id=35534. *See also* Yevgenia Albats, *Out with Old Media, in with New*, Moscow Times, Oct. 5, 2000; Victor Yasmann, *The Kremlin Propagandist Drive into Internet*, RFE/RL Security Watch, Sept. 25, 2000.

[128] The Press Ministry took over supervision of the official government newspaper *Rossiiskaya gazeta* in October 2000, but officials quickly abandoned hopes of transforming that publication into a newspaper with mass appeal.

[129] *See* Vedomosti, Feb. 28, 2001; Vremya-novostei, Feb. 28, 2001.

[130] Nezavisimaya gazeta, Sept. 29, 2000; Kommersant, Sept. 29, 2000.

regional authorities previously controlled how federal funds were divided locally, the federal government's Press Ministry would in the future supervise the payment of subsidies.[131]

Journalists' advocates in Russia and abroad sharply criticized the Information Security Doctrine.[132] However, their objections failed to dent the Kremlin's resolve to implement the doctrine's recommendations. Policies to increase the state's capacity to get the official message out reflected a vision of the media as a conduit between the state and citizens, serving primarily to emphasize official accomplishments. By the same token, policies to limit journalists' access to information and impose new licensing requirements threatened to undermine the media's ability to serve as a watchdog or "fourth estate."[133]

Chilling Effects

In Russia, as in many other countries, the law on paper can differ dramatically from the law in practice. Several policies during Putin's first year as president increased pressure on media outlets, either directly or directly, without altering any existing laws.

The authorities remained concerned about news coverage of the "anti-terrorist operation" in Chechnya. The Russian military continued to enforce strict controls over journalists' movements, using intimidation to keep journalists from crossing the border between Ingushetia and the breakaway republic. Oleg Panfilov, a close observer of infringements on journalists' rights since the early 1990s, commented in June 2000 that official disinformation, along with illegal threats by officers to revoke journalists' accreditation, had made it "impossible to work in Chechnya."[134] In fact, it was not impossible for Russian correspondents to work there, but avoiding trouble with the authorities required journalists to stay near federal military installations and to report exclusively on the lives of Russian soldiers serving in Chechnya.[135]

Problems arose for journalists whose reporting diverged from the acceptable topics, and for their employers. The Press Ministry followed through on its pledge to issue warnings regarding interviews with senior Chechen officials. Outlets that received warnings on those grounds included *Kommersant*, *Novaya Gazeta*, *Nezavisimaya Gazeta*,

---

[131] Izvestiia, Jan. 13, 2000, at 1; Rossiiskaya gazeta, Jan. 13, 2000, at 5.

[132] Igor Yakovenko, secretary general of Russia's Union of Journalists, told Interfax on September 14 that the doctrine was "written in a spirit very much at odds with the principles of freedom of expression and openness." *See* RFE/RL Newsline, Sept. 15, 2000.

[133] The conception of the media's role as a conduit for the state rather than a watchdog is another key element of the Defense of Democracy Theory described by Foster in *Information and the Problem of Democracy*. Foster, *Information and the Problem of Democracy*, *supra* note 116.

[134] Panfilov was interviewed in Russkaya mysl, June 8-14, 2000. He noted that Russia's 1992 media law requires a court order to revoke a journalist's accreditation.

[135] According to *Novaya gazeta* correspondent Anna Politkovskaya, who was speaking at a London event sponsored by Article 19, Amnesty International, and the Freedom Forum on May 2, 2001.

and NTV. The warnings cited the 1997 Law On Terrorism and/or the 1992 Law On the Mass Media, which prohibited appeals to violence and the propaganda of war. However, the legal justification for applying those statutes as the Press Ministry did was questionable.[136] Journalists argued that Russians were entitled to hear alternative views and that the published interviews with Chechen separatists did not contain illegal appeals for a violent overthrow of Russia's constitutional structure.[137]

It is hardly surprising that the federal authorities would try to limit Chechen leaders' access to media. But Russian journalists could get into plenty of trouble without interviewing high-ranking Chechen officials. *Novaya Gazeta* correspondent Anna Politkovskaya was detained by Russian officers in February 2001 while trying to cover the war's impact on the civilian population.[138] They accused her of using falsified accreditation documents and expelled her from Chechnya. As she later recounted, military officers considered coverage of civilian suffering just as dangerous as reporting the Chechen rebels' point of view.[139] A few days after Politkovskaya was compelled to leave Chechnya, Putin signed a decree conferring honors on 22 journalists working for state-owned media in Dagestan, the republic neighboring Chechnya. His decree praised their "high professionalism and objectivity in reporting events in the republic," but the information center Glasnost-Kavkaz, affiliated with the Russian human rights organization Glasnost, characterized the journalists' work as "the zealous dissemination of information [emanating from] Kremlin propagandists."[140]

The selective application of the law was a recurring theme of the Putin presidency, and media policies were no exception to the rule.[141] As mentioned above, the vigorous pursuit of criminal investigations of Gusinsky and Media-Most entities contrasted sharply with the reluctance to investigate those responsible for alleged wrongdoing at RTR.[142] The editorial offices of the bimonthly *Novaya Gazeta* received frequent visits from tax

---

[136] See a commentary produced by the Moscow Media Law and Policy Center, published in the March 2001 issue of *Zakonodatelstvo i praktika Mass-Media* (http://www.medialaw.ru). The commentary argued that, in theory, applying the 1992 media law was somewhat less problematic than applying the law on terrorism, but the way the Press Ministry issued warnings in practice raised serious legal questions.

[137] *Nezavisimaya gazeta* published the Press Ministry's warning, along with a short rebuttal to it, on March 3, 2001.

[138] For more details about the Politkovskaya case, see the archives of reports on the websites of the Glasnost Defense Foundation (www.gdf.ru) or the Committee for Journalism in Extreme Situations (www.cjes.ru).

[139] Politkovskaya was speaking at the May 2, 2001, event in London. *See supra* note 135.

[140] According to a story published by the Glasnost-Kavkaz Daily News Service on February 27, 2001, and distributed on an e-mail list run by the Moscow-based Center for Journalism in Extreme Situations.

[141] *See* Archie Brown, *Evaluating Russia's Democratization*, *in* Contemporary Russian Politics, *supra* note 2.

[142] Similarly, even as Russia requested Interpol's assistance in arresting Gusinsky, in December 2000 the Procurator-General's Office closed its investigation of the Mabetex case, a bribery and corruption scandal allegedly involving many prominent members of the Yeltsin "family." Prosecutors likewise showed little interest in investigating reports concerning massive alleged fraud and embezzlement involving senior Gazprom executives. *See* Financial Times, May 25, 2001.

inspectors. Besides opposing the second Chechen war from the start, *Novaya Gazeta* published many stories that irritated the Kremlin, raising questions about corruption in high circles and about the possible role of the security services in apartment-building bombings attributed to Chechens in autumn 1999.

Izvestiia, one of the first Moscow newspapers to experience the pitfalls of attracting corporate investors, learned in December 2000 that even newspapers that generally supported Putin's policies might face sanctions if they stepped out of line.[143] *Izvestiia* was by no means an opposition newspaper during Putin's rise to power. In fact, it was among the major publications that declined to co-sponsor a special edition of *Obshchaya Gazeta*, which protested the detention of Andrei Babitsky.[144] At the same time, *Izvestiia* was a steadfastly anti-communist newspaper; it published several pieces criticizing Putin's decision to restore the Soviet-era national anthem. The Kremlin's property management department soon filed a lawsuit challenging the newspaper's ownership of its headquarters on Pushkin Square.[145] (The building was one of Yeltsin's gifts to *Izvestiia* in the early 1990s, when the newspaper was caught in the power struggle between the president and the parliament.[146]) The editors understood the implicit message and made a "political decision" to spike a column by Yevgenia Albats about opposition to the Soviet anthem.[147] According to Albats, "the lawsuit was frozen, but not withdrawn—just in case the paper made another wrong move in Kremlin politics."[148]

Other methods of intimidation were aimed at crippling media outlets financially. Politkovskaya alleged that Kremlin officials contacted companies that advertised in *Novaya Gazeta*, threatening them with tax inspections if they continued to place advertisements in the opposition newspaper.[149] The flip side of this policy was the generous Press Ministry budget for grants allocated for "socially important projects" with little transparency or input from media professionals.[150]

Violent attacks on journalists were an all too common problem in Russia throughout the post-Soviet period, and the pattern continued during Putin's first year in

---

[143] *See* Laura Belin, *Changes in Editorial Policy and Ownership at Izvestiia*, appendix to *Politicization and Self-Censorship in the Russian Media*, paper given at the November 1997 conference of the American Association for the Advancement of Slavic Studies. The appendix can be found at http://www.rferl.org/nca/special/rumediapaper/appendix2.html.

[144] The special edition of *Obshchaya gazeta* was published on February 16, 2000. For a list of the diverse group of media outlets that co-sponsored the publications and the big names that were conspicuously absent, *see* RFE/RL Newsline, February 17, 2000.

[145] Yevgenia Albats, *Press: As Free as Putin Says*, Moscow Times, Jan. 16, 2001.

[146] Frances H. Foster, Izvestiia *as a Mirror of Russian Legal Reform: Press, Law, and Crisis in the Post-Soviet Era*, 26 Vanderbilt Journal of Transnational Law 675 (1993).

[147] Albats, *Cry for Russia's lost press liberty*, *supra* note 121.

[148] *Id.*

[149] Comments at the May 2 event in London. *See supra* note 135.

[150] Yelena Rykovtseva, *Vedomstvo so mnogimi nulyami: Kak Ministerstvo pechati vorochaet millionami*, Obshchaya gazeta, Nov. 2, 2000. The Press Ministry refused to release a complete list of grant recipients.

office. Journalists were assaulted in many Russian regions, and while no evidence directly linked the crimes to the authorities, the victims tended to be affiliated with opposition media, and the assailants were rarely found or prosecuted. In Moscow, one *Novaya Gazeta* journalist was fatally wounded in a May 2000 beating, and another correspondent from that newspaper had his face slashed later that year, after discussing his investigative reporting on an NTV program.[151]

Conclusion

During his first year as president, Putin expressed support for media freedom many times, but his administration's policies conveyed a different attitude. His televised address to the parliament in July 2000 encapsulated the mixed message. Putin acknowledged that "Russian democracy simply cannot survive and civil society cannot be created without genuinely free media," but he decried the political use of media by owners and sponsors, which, he argued, sometimes "transforms [media] into means of mass disinformation and means for battling the state."[152] Kseniya Ponomareva, a former ORT news director who was one of Putin's image-makers during the 1999/2000 electoral cycle, commented that Putin's rapid rise to power left him without "the thick skin that every public politician should develop." She added that Putin "is no enemy of free speech. He simply finds absurd the idea that somebody has the right to criticize him publicly."[153]

The policies implemented by Putin's administration did not eliminate alternative viewpoints in the Russian media. A few opposition outlets stayed in business, and even the large-circulation daily *Komsomolskaya Pravda* expressed doubts about the official explanation for the sinking of the Kursk.[154] But the "chilling effects" were real. Moscow journalists swapped stories of self-censorship and a general reluctance to offend Putin. Stories portraying the president in a negative light appeared less often, and were less harsh, than was the case during most of Yeltsin's presidency.

Media advocates sounded the alarm repeatedly. On World Press Freedom Day in May 2001, international organizations cited Russia in "name and shame" campaigns.[155] Russia's Union of Journalists warned that "[a]ttacks on freedom of speech in Russia are becoming more and more persistent and refined" and that the press is "persistently"

---

[151] Reports on the fatal beating of Igor Domnikov and the attack on Oleg Lur'e can be found on the websites of the Glasnost Defense Foundation (www.gdf.ru), the Center for Journalism in Extreme Situations (www.cjes.ru), and Radio Free Europe/Radio Liberty (www.rferl.org).

[152] Putin's address was televised on RTR on July 8, 2000.

[153] Interview with Ponomareva in *Kommersant* on March 26, 2001, *quoted in* Moscow Times, Mar. 27, 2001.

[154] *See, e.g.*, Komsomolskaya pravda, Feb. 24, 2001.

[155] Putin appeared on the Committee to Protect Journalists' list of 10 enemies of a free press, and Russia was among 30 countries listed in a similar report by Reporters Without Borders.

portrayed as an "enemy."[156] But although the union sought to draw attention to the threats to media freedom, it was unable to persuade journalists to form a united front to combat those threats.[157]

Putin paid virtually no political price for his administration's media policies. More than a year after his election, opinion polls indicated that a solid majority of the population continued to support him. In contrast, public trust in media was extremely low.[158] The widespread reliance of media on wealthy individuals or industrial groups may help explain the lack of opposition to policies that squeezed them. Putin and his allies sought to frame their efforts as a campaign against corrupt businessmen as opposed to a deliberate attempt to reduce pluralism in the media. With both houses of parliament willing to support almost all of Putin's initiatives, there was no institutional opposition to the reassertion of state power over the media either. That lack of public resistance, combined with the apparent success of the Kremlin's media strategy during the 1999 and 2000 elections, suggested that Putin's approach to media issues is unlikely to change much in the coming years.

---

[156] The statement issued by the Russian Union of Journalists on May 3, 2001, was quoted by the Ekho Moskvy news agency.

[157] In July 2000, following a survey of journalists, the Union of Journalists released a list of "enemies of the Russian press," topped by Press Minister Lesin. *See also* Floriana Fossato, *Russian Journalists Not United to Defend Press Freedom*, RFE/RL Newsline, July 12, 2000. On the lack of journalistic solidarity concerning NTV's predicament in early 2001, see Galina Chermenskaya, *After the Battle*, Jamestown Foundation Prism, May 2001.

[158] Fossato, *Russian Journalists Not United to Defend Press Freedom*, *supra* note 157.

A Brief Chronology of Russian Media Law and Policy During the Yeltsin Years

Bethany Davis Noll

This timeline covers the period from 1990, when the Law On the Press and Other Mass Media was first passed in the USSR, to the beginning of Russian President Vladimir Putin's administration. The events listed here are chosen because of their relevance to the many articles published in this volume. This timeline is by no means a complete list. Instead, it is intended as a brief overview of the events during Yeltsin's administration that affected the freedom of Russian media in the 1990s, including the passage of laws and decrees, political events, and journalist casualties.

Date	Event or Decree
08/01/1990	USSR Law On the Press and Other Mass Media enters into force. Censorship is abolished.
1991	Moscow's Second Channel announces independence from the USSR authorities.
01/10/1991	Gorbachev suggests to the Parliament that ban on censorship be suspended temporarily because of events in Lithuania. Deputies vote to enforce milder measures and encourage "objectivity" in the media.
06/12/1991	Russian Federation declares sovereignty.
08/19/1991	Communist coup attempt takes place.
11/22/1991	Supreme Soviet adopts the Universal Declaration of Human Rights, stating that the Declaration will be adopted into the Russia Constitution and that all existing legislation will be "brought into conformity" with the Declaration. *See* Rossiskaia Gazeta, Dec. 25, 1991.
12/27/1991	The State Duma adopts Federal Law On the Mass Media.
02/08/1992	Federal Law On the Mass Media enters into force.
2/20/1992	Russian Federation Presidential Decree On Additional Measures of Legal and Economic Protection for the Periodical Press and State Book Publishing is issued. Certain measures are taken to mitigate market reforms. *See* Frances Foster's article, Izvestiia *as a Mirror of Russian Legal Reform: Press, Law, and Crisis in the Post-Soviet Era*, in part I, section II of this volume.

02/25/1993	Igor Malashenko resigns as deputy chairman of Ostankino TV company, due to frustration over Russian Federation Law On the Mass Media, which does not provide him with complete freedom.
03/29/1993	Russian Federation Presidential Decree On Measures to Provide Freedom of Speech at Government Television, Radio and Information Services is issued. The Decree requires the Supreme Soviet to close down Federal Information Center and to form supervisory councils.
04/25/1993	Referendum asking for confidence in President Yeltsin and his socio-economic policies is held. The results give the President a new mandate to pursue his policies.
05/27/1993	Constitutional court upholds the power of the Parliament to create supervisory councils over two state television stations.
07/09/1993	The State Duma adopts Federal Law On Copyright and Neighboring Rights.
07/21/1993.	The State Duma adopts Federal Law On State Secrets.
08/23/1993	*Pravda* and five other pro-Communist newspapers—*Sovetskaya Rossiya, Glasnost'*, *Rabochaya Tribuna, Moskovskaya Pravda*, and *Leninskoe Znamya*—are suspended.
09/23/1993	The President dissolves the Parliament by decree.
10/04/1993	*Pravda*, *Den*, and *Sovetskaya Rossiya* are closed. Pre-publication censorship is established.
10/6/1993	Pre-publication censorship is lifted.
10/10/1993	NTV, first independent TV station, airs for the first time. Igor Malashenko serves as NTV's director.
10/14/1993	A permanent ban is placed on thirteen newspapers.
10/29/1993	The Statute On Information Guarantees is passed. It provides for an Information Arbitration Tribunal to temporarily oversee election campaign in the media.
12/1993	The Ministry of Information of the Russian Federation is divided into *Roskompechat* (Press Committee) and the Federal Service on Radio and TV Broadcasting.
12/01/1993	"600 Seconds" TV program is closed because of anchor Alexander Nevzorov's reported support of the coup.
12/03/1993	"600 Seconds" ban is lifted due to popular outcry.
12/12/1993	The Constitution of the Russian Federation is adopted.

12/18/1993	Russian Federation Presidential Decree No. 2206 On Urgent Measures to Support State Television and Radio Broadcasting is issued.
12/31/1993	Russian Federation Presidential Decree No. 2334 On Supplementary Guarantees of Citizens' Rights to Information is issued.
12/31/1993	Russian Federation Presidential Decree No. 2335 On the Presidential Judicial Chamber for Information Disputes is issued, making the Information Arbitration Tribunal permanent under the new name.
01/10/1994	Decree No. 15 of the Government of the Russian Federation Issues Ensuring Publication and Dissemination of Mass Media Information and Printed Matter is issued.
02/10/1994	Communication workers temporarily shut down a third of the country's transmitters, demanding payment of back wages.
04/28/1994	Treaty of Public Accord is concluded.
06/10/1994	Russian Federation Presidential Decree No. 1183 On Consumer Protection Against Unfair Advertising is issued.
06/11/1994	Russian Federation Presidential Decree No. 1233 On Protection of Investor's Interests is issued.
07/29/1994	MMM pyramid scheme collapses. Many investors lose their life savings.
09/02/1994	Yeltsin fires Boris Mironov, chairman of Press Committee, for nationalist remarks. Yeltsin appoints Vladimir Volodin.
09/15/1994	Vladimir Zhirinovsky sues Yegor Gaidar for calling him a fascist and wins on the grounds that the statement was false.
10/17/1994	Dmitry Kholodov, a *Moskovsky Komsomolets* journalist who was investigating theft and illegal arms trading in the army, is murdered by a bomb hidden in his briefcase.
11/08/1994	Yuri Korolyov, a photo journalist for *Deloviye Lyudi*, is killed.
11/30/1994	Russian Federation Presidential Decree On Improving the Use of Channel One (Moscow) Television and Its Distribution Network is issued. Ostankino joins Public Russian Television joint-stock company with 51% of stock.
01/13/1995	The State Duma adopts Federal Law On Rules for the Coverage by State Mass Media of the Activity of Bodies of State Power.
02/16/1995	The State Duma adopts Federal Law On Communications.
02/17/1995	Russian Federation Presidential Decree No. 616 Guarantees of Citizens' Right to Protection of Health in the Spread of Advertising is issued.

02/20/1995	The State Duma adopts Federal Law On Information, Informatization, and Protection of Information.
03/01/1995	Vladislav Listyev, head of Ostankino, is murdered.
04/25/1995	*Rossiskaia Gazeta* prints draft presidential decree, announcing creation of the United Federal Agency on the State Information Policy of the Russian Federation (*Gosinform*) out of Press Committee and the Federal Television and Radio Broadcasting Service. Paper accuses the President of setting up a "propaganda machine."
06/17/1995	Natalya Alyakina, a Russian journalist for *German Rufa News Agency*, is killed in Budennovsk by Russian soldiers after she passes through a checkpoint.
07/18/1995	The State Duma adopts Federal Law On Advertising.
07/19/1995	Articles 21, 29, 30 of the Federal Law On the Mass Media are amended.
08/15/1995	Russian Federation Government Decree No. 941 On Licensing of Activity Involving Public Screening of Cinema and Video Films is issued.
08/20/1995	1995 Election Regulations for State Television and Radio Companies are issued.
09/20/1995	Election Regulations for State Television and Radio Companies No. 18/149P are adopted.
11/15/1995	The State Duma adopts Federal Law On the Introduction of Additions to Part I of the Civil Code of the Russian Federation.
11/24/1995	The State Duma adopts Federal Law On Economic Support of District (Municipal) Newspapers.
12/01/1995	The State Duma adopts Federal Law On the State Support of the Mass Media and Book-Publishing in the Russian Federation.
01/09/1996	Dagestan Hostage Crisis begins in town of Kizlyar.
01/26/1996	Oleg Slabynko, producer of "Moment of Truth" television show, is shot to death.
2/1996	President Yeltsin fires Oleg Poptsov, chairman of the All-Russia Television and Radio Company, reportedly because of publishing critical book, *A Chronicle of the Times of Tsar Boris* [*Khronika vremyon tsarya Borisa*] and because of outspoken reportage on Chechnya. *See* Marina Shakina, Nezavisimaya Gazeta, Feb. 17, 1996, at 1-2, *reprinted in* Current Digest of the Post-Soviet Press, Mar. 13, 1996, at 3.
02/08/1996	Russia becomes a member of the Council of Europe.

02/20/1996	President Yeltsin signs Federal Law On the Introduction of Additions to Part I of the Civil Code of the Russian Federation, which the State Duma adopted on November 15, 1995.
02/26/1996	Felix Solovyov, a free-lance photographer who has published a portfolio on the Russian mafia for *Bild am Sonntag* in Germany, is shot in Moscow.
03/11/1996	Victor Pimenov, a cameraman for Vaynakh (a pro-Moscow Chechen TV station), is killed in Grozny while filming the aftereffects of the Chechen's March 6-9 raid on the city.
03/24/1996	Igor Malashenko, director of NTV, joins Yeltsin's re-election campaign staff.
03/30/1996	Nadezhda Chaikova, a journalist for *Obshchaya Gazeta* who was known as a fearless reporter on controversial topics surrounding the war in Chechnya, is killed in Gekhi, Chechnya.
05/9/1996	Nina Yefimova, a contributor to *Vozrozhdeniye*, is killed in Leninsky District of Grozny, reportedly because of stories on crime in Chechnya.
05/12/1996	Viktor Mikhailov, a crime reporter for *Zabaikalsky Rabochy* in southeastern Siberia, is killed in Chita.
07/04/1996	The State Duma adopts Federal Law On Participation in International Information Exchange.
08/11/1996	Ramzan Khadzhiev, head of the Northern Caucasus bureau of ORT (Russian Public Television), is killed while leaving Grozny.
01/01/1997	New code goes into effect to replace 1960 Criminal Code, targeting copyright violations and economic crimes.
08/25/1997	Russian Federation Presidential Decree On Improving State TV Broadcasting in the Russian Federation is issued.
09/19/1997	The State Duma adopts Federal Law On Basic Guarantees of Electoral Rights and the Right of Citizens of the Russian Federation to Participate in a Referendum.
12/19/1997	State Duma Decree No. 2028 On State Regulation of the Activities of the NTV Television Company and Other Non-State Television and Radio Companies is issued.
12/22/1997	Decree On the Information Telegraph Agency of Russia is issued.
3/1998	ORT accepts governmental Public Council as supervisor that issues recommendations. The Council is not supposed to interfere in running the station. *See New ORT Head Rejects Merger or Nationalization*, BBC Worldwide Monitoring, Oct. 16, 1998

03/18/1998	State Duma Decree No 2294 On the Activity of Certain Russian Television Companies is issued.
05/05/1998	Russia adopts the European Convention on Human Rights.
06/08/1998	Larisa Yudina, editor-in-chief of *Sovetskaia Kalmykia Segodnia* (the only opposition paper in Russian Republic of Kalmykia), is killed in Kalmykian capital Elista.
07/31/1998	Alva TV, an Izhevsk TV company, has its license revoked for violating the Copyright Law and for airing Paramount Pictures and Twentieth Century Fox movies. *See Izhevsk TV Station Closed for Copyright Violations*, BBC Worldwide Monitoring, Aug. 5, 1998.
08/06/1998	Russian Federation Government Decree No. 895 On Approval of the Statute on Payment for the Use of the Radio Frequency Spectrum in the Russian Federation is issued.
08/19/1998	The ruble collapses and Russia partially defaults on its debt. A wide-scale economic crisis ensues.
09/25/1998	The State Duma adopts Federal Law On Licensing of Certain Types of Activities.
09/28/1998	Head of VGTRK (All-Russian State Television and Radio Broadcasting Company) agrees with Communist leader Gennady Zyuganov to create a supervisory council over Channel 2, Russia TV.
10/15/1998	At "The European Council and European Law Standards Guaranteeing Freedom of the Media" seminar, Russia ranks as the worst country in the world for the murder and persecution of journalists. *See* Segodnya, Oct. 15, 1998, at 2.
03/17/1999	The State Duma passes the Draft Federal Law On a Higher Council for the Defense of Morality in Television and Radio Broadcasting in the Russian Federation.
03/30/1999	The State Duma amends Federal Law On Basic Guarantees of Electoral Rights and the Right of Citizens of the Russian Federation to Participate in a Referendum.
03/31/1999	President Yeltsin vetoes Draft Federal Law On a Higher Council for the Defense of Morality in Television and Radio Broadcasting in the Russian Federation.

06/20/1999	"Sovershenno Sekretno [Top Secret]," a politically outspoken and controversial television show, is pulled off the air. Officials at RTR, the state television network, say it is because of the relentless mud-slinging. However, President of "Sovershenno Sekretnno," Artyom Borovik, states that officials are trying to silence critical media in lieu of the upcoming parliamentary elections. *See* Oksana Yablokova, *RTR Cancels TV Show That Dug Dirt on Politics*, Moscow Times, June 24, 1999.
06/24/1999	The State Duma adopts Federal Law On Elections of the Deputies of the State Duma of the Federal Assembly of the Russian Federation.
12/19/1999	Parliamentary elections are held in the midst of a heavily biased media environment. *See* Michael Wines, *Russia Voting After Rancorous Campaign, but All's Just Prelude to Main Bout Next Year*, New York Times, Dec. 19, 1999, at 30.
12/31/1999	The State Duma adopts Federal Law On Elections of the President of the Russian Federation.
12/31/1999	President Yeltsin resigns, appointing Vladimir Putin as Acting President.
01/17/2000	Police apprehend Alexander Khinshtein, a *Moskovsky Komsomolets* journalist, who has published critical articles on the Chechen War. They attempt to take him to a psychiatric clinic outside of Moscow for testing concerning his 1997 driver's license application. *See A Bruised Press*, Economist, Feb. 12, 2000.
02/03/2000	Russian forces hand over to the Chechens Andrei Babitsky, a *Radio Free Europe/Radio Liberty* correspondent who was detained in January. *See A Bruised Press*, Economist, Feb. 12, 2000.
02/29/2000	Andrei Babitsky is freed. He tells of torture of Chechens by Russian forces at detention camp in Chernokozovo. *See* Daniel Williams, International Herald Tribune, Mar. 1, 2000, at 4.
03/09/2000	Artyom Borovik, head of the Sovershenno Sekretno television production company, dies in a plane crash.
04/18/2000	*Izvestiia* reports that Dmitry Ayatskov, governor of the Saratov region, has censored an article critical of him in the *Izvestiia* published in his region on April 14, 2000. *See* Sarah Karush, St. Petersburg Times, Apr. 21, 2000.
05/11/2000	Masked men raided Media-Most, headquarters for privately owned media outlets such as Ekho Moskvy and NTV. Russian journalists, along with international observers, unite to protest raid.

06/03/2000	Russian Federation Presidential Decree On Structure of Presidential Administration is adopted. The Presidential Judicial Chamber of Information Disputes is abolished.
06/13/2000	Vladimir Gusinsky, head of NTV, is arrested for fraud. He is freed on June 16, 2000, after local and international uproar.
4/2001	After a long legal battle, state-dominated gas company Gazprom takes over NTV by calling in its loans to the network. Vladimir Gusinsky, the company's owner, flees Russia on fraud charges in November 2001.
1/22/2002	Court orders liquidation of TV-6 owned by self-exiled Boris Berezovsky on the grounds that it is technically bankrupt. Only three major networks remain—all controlled through various ways by the state.

PART II

DOCUMENTS

I.

Decisions and Recommendations from the Judicial Chamber for Information Disputes

On Violations of the Russian Federation Constitution's Norms on Equality of Women, March 11, 1994, No. 5*

The Women's Union of Russia and Union of Lawyers submitted statements to the Judicial Chamber for Information Disputes regarding violations by some of the print media of the Russian Federation Constitution's norms on equality of women.

After examining these claims, the Judicial Chamber for Information Disputes has determined that:

Advertisements for the First Voucher Fund (published in the January 13-19, 1994, issue of *Finansovye Izvestiia* and in issue No. 4 (January 1994) of *Ekonomika i Zhizn'*) and advertisements for the Alpha Bank (published in the February 18, 1994, issue of *Izvestiia TV*) announced competitions for vacant positions in these organizations. The positions were: securities specialists, lawyers, accountants, secretary-"referent," and chair of the board of directors of a bank. These advertisements stipulated that only men would be allowed in the competitions.

Such limitation by gender was a flagrant violation of article 19 of the Russian Federation Constitution, which provides that "men and women have equal rights and freedoms and equal opportunities for their realization." It also contravened article 16 of the Russian Federation Labor Code, pursuant to which it is impermissible "in any form, directly or indirectly, to limit rights or to establish direct or indirect gender-based preferences in employment." In addition, it violated the United Nations Convention of December 18, 1979, on Liquidation of All Forms of Discrimination with Respect to Women (ratified by the USSR Supreme Soviet Presidium on December 19, 1980), which provides that men and women have the right to "equal opportunities in hiring, including the application of equal criteria for selection in hiring."

The Judicial Chamber takes notice that *Ekonomika i Zhizn'* published the following announcement: "The newspaper's Editorial Office takes no responsibility for the content of this advertisement." Such a general disclaimer does not comply with article 57 of the Russian Federation Law On the Mass Media. This article contains a comprehensive list of the only information, infringing citizens' rights and legal interests, for the dissemination of which editorial offices, editors-in-chief, and journalists bear no responsibility. Thus, according to this article, editorial offices and editors-in-chief are responsible for the content of advertisements published in the mass media. At the Judicial Chamber session, a representative of *Izvestiia*, M.G. Khazin, stated that *Izvestiia* would refrain from publishing such advertisements in the future.

---

* Post-Soviet Media Law & Policy Newsletter, Oct. 15, 1994, at 5. Translated by Natalia Dronova and Frances Foster from *Rossiiskaia Gazeta*, Mar. 22, 1994, at 4.

Based on the above stated facts and in accordance with articles 4 and 12 of the Statute on the Judicial Chamber for Information Disputes, the Judicial Chamber has decided:

1. To recognize that dissemination by the mass media of announcements and materials, including advertisements, that are aimed at any direct or indirect limitation of rights or that establish direct or indirect gender-based preferences for employment is a gross violation of the equality of men and women, which is established in the Russian Federation Constitution, other legislative acts, and commonly recognized norms of international law.

2. To reprimand the editors-in-chief of *Izvestiia* (Iu. N. Golembiovskii), *Finansovye Izvestiia* (D.A. Murzin), and *Ekonomika i Zhizn'* (Iu. V. Iakutin) for publishing the above advertisements.

3. To recommend that mass media editorial offices verify that published advertisements are in conformity with the Russian Federation Constitution and other Russian Federation legislative acts.

Chairman of the Judicial Chamber

A.B. Vengerov

On Advertisements Disseminated by the Mass Media That Are Hazardous to Life and Health, May 5, 1994, No. 1*

The Russian Federation Presidential Chamber for Information Disputes has examined the issue of dissemination of advertisements that are dangerous for life and health.

It analyzed publication of advertisements of alcoholic beverages and tobacco products in March-April 1994 issues of the newspapers *Ekstra-M*, *Ekspress-Reklama*, *Moskovskii Komsomolets*, *Kommersant*, *Kommersant Daily*, *Delovoi Mir*, *Tsentr Plus*, *Rossiiskaia Gazeta*, *Komsomol'skaia Pravda*, and other publications. The Judicial Chamber also studied information regarding advertising of alcoholic beverages and tobacco products on television—by the television company NTV, the tele-radio companies Moskva and Sankt-Peterburg-5th Channel, the VGTRK, and the 1st Channel Ostankino.

The Judicial Chamber heard the expert conclusions of a group of specialists headed by M.N. Maleina, the Chairman of the Russian Federation State Committee on Anti-Monopoly Policy and Support for New Economic Structures (N.E. Fonareva), the representative of the Russian Federation Ministry of Health (G.B. Tkachenko), and the representatives of the mass media (B.A. Piliatskina (*Izvestiia*), I.M. Podzigun (Ostankino), A.S. Politkovskaia (*Obshchaia Gazeta*), L.V. Grechkina (*Moskovskii Komsomolets*), Iu. M. Nekrasov (*Delovoi Mir*), R.I. Alibegov (Otkritoe Radio), A.O. Shchekelev (MTK Moskva), and others).

The Judicial Chamber has determined that:

The mass media have widely disseminated advertisements of alcoholic beverages and tobacco products, which are explicitly prohibited by article 19, clause 2 of the Fundamentals of Russian Federation Legislation On Protection of Citizens' Health. The editorial staff of the print media and tele-radio companies profit from such advertising.

Moreover, the mass media do not always observe article 7, clause 4 of the Russian Federation Law On Certification of Products and Services. This article prohibits the advertisement of products that must be certified, but have not received such certification.

Also, the mass media do not always fulfill the requirements of article 43, clause 8 of the Fundamentals of the Russian Federation Legislation On Protection of Citizens' Health. This article prohibits propaganda of methods for prevention, diagnosis, and treatment, as well as medicinal remedies that have not been properly tested as required by law. The mass media also advertise various healers, psychics, sorcerers, and other

* Post-Soviet Media Law & Policy Newsletter, Sept. 10, 1994, at 4. Translated by Natalia Dronova and Frances Foster from *Rossiiskaia Gazeta*, May 14, 1994, at 4.

persons who claim to be specialists in non-traditional methods of treatment but do not have the appropriate permits to do so. In fact, the Russian Federation Ministry of Health has failed to control such persons and the advertising of their unlawful activities.

During the Judicial Chamber hearing, representatives of the mass media that violated article 19, clause 2 of the Fundamentals of Russian Federation Legislation On Protection of Citizens' Health (regarding advertisement of alcoholic beverages and tobacco products) presented various reasons to justify the established practice of dissemination of prohibited, improper advertisements.

These reasons included: the financial hardship of many individual mass media outlets, especially tele-radio companies; the blanket prohibition of advertisements, which should be replaced by a system that would only limit such advertisements and allow them to appear at specified times (for example, as on Ostankino from 11:00 p.m. on); the failure to distinguish between advertisements and commercial announcements (information); the lack of a Russian Federation Law On Advertisements; the absence of norms regarding responsibility for violation of article 19, clause 2 of the Fundamentals of Russian Federation Legislation On Protection of Citizens' Health, and so on.

The Judicial Chamber could not agree with such arguments.

Protection of Russian citizens' health remains a priority and is set forth in existing law. It is impermissible to adopt administrative normative acts that contradict or "correct" this legislation. It is easy to distinguish advertisements from mere announcements of the sale of alcohol and tobacco products. Advertisements popularize and extol the quality and accessibility of the products and encourage consumption of these products by various methods.

Russian legislation includes some legal remedies that could cover the most obvious cases of dissemination of prohibited advertisements. In particular, article 49 of the Russian Federation Civil Code may be used for this purpose. This article provides that, under certain conditions, all profits from a transaction may be confiscated by the state if such a transaction is declared void because its purpose contradicts the interests of society.

During the Judicial Chamber hearing, B.G. Tkachenko, the representative of the Russian Federation Ministry of Health presented extensive data revealing that smoking has become an alarming problem in Russia and showing the increase in fatalities from smoking and the rise in numbers of teenaged and women smokers (including pregnant women), etc.

The Judicial Chamber placed special emphasis on the fact that advertisement of foreign alcohol and tobacco products has increased significantly in the Russian mass media, at the very time that these same advertisements are not carried in the manufacturing countries. Therefore, foreign producers of alcohol and tobacco products are using advertisements, especially those in the Russian mass media, to turn Russia into a market for the sale of their products, despite the legislation for protection of Russian citizens' health.

In light of the above-stated facts and in conformity with articles 20 and 21 of the Statute on the Judicial Chamber, the Judicial Chamber recommends:

1. Mass media dissemination of advertisements of alcohol and tobacco products, for whatever reason, should be considered a violation of article 19, clause 2 of the Fundamentals of Russian Federation Legislation On Protection of Citizens' Health.

2. It is important to draw the attention of the mass media to the fact that, according to article 7, clause 4 of the Russian Federation Law, On Certification of Products and Services, in entering into a contract for advertisement of a product that requires certification, the mass media must verify that the advertising party has obtained the appropriate certificate. In the absence of such certificate of compliance, the mass media should not enter into a contract for advertisement of a product that requires certification.

3. It is necessary to take into consideration the fact that the results of testing new methods of prevention, diagnosis, treatment, and medicinal preparations should be reported by the mass media in a manner consistent with article 43, clause 8 of the Fundamentals of Russian Federation Legislation On Protection of Citizens' Health. Prior to final formulation of such results, the mass media may report only the facts of such testiness and research. This information should not be accompanied by conclusions regarding the progressiveness, effectiveness, uniqueness, and other alleged advantages of new methods of treatment and medicinal preparations (i.e., they should not be advertised).

It is impermissible to allow advertisement of activities by persons who claim to be specialists in non-traditional methods of treatment (so-called healers, psychics, sorcerers, fairies, etc.) but do not have the appropriate permits to engage in such activity.

4. It is necessary to draw the attention of the Russian Federation Ministry of Health and procuratorial organs to their failure to use legal remedies to prevent violation of article 19, clause 2 of the Fundamentals of Russian Federation Legislation On Protection of Citizens' Health. These remedies include in particular article 49 of the Russian Federation Civil Code, which, as stated above, provides that all profits from a transaction may be confiscated by the state if the purpose of such a transaction is against the interests of the state and society.

5. It is necessary to examine proposals presented during this hearing by representatives of the mass media. These proposals may be used in drafting the Law On Advertisements and in improving legislation on protection of citizens' health. It is advisable to accelerate the drafting of the Russian Federation Law On Advertisements.

The Judicial Chamber decided to send all information regarding established cases of violation of the legislation on protection of citizens' health to the Russian Federation Ministry of Health for the application of concrete sanctions against the violators.

Chairman of the Judicial Chamber

A.B. Vengerov

On Violations of Legal and Ethical Norms in Conducting the Paid Game "05" with the Use of the Mass Media, June 2, 1994, No. 16*

The Russian Federation Presidential Judicial Chamber for Information Disputes received a complaint from a journalist, N.N. Belotserkovskaia, claiming that she was defrauded and sustained losses that could reach in excess of 100,000 rubles as a result of the so-called game "05." This game was conducted by the form "DIOS" and advertised on the NTV channel by D.A. Dibrov.

The Judicial Chamber studied publications in newspapers that criticized the rules and conditions of the game "05."

After examining these materials and documents specifically requested by the Judicial Chamber, the Chamber has determined that:

The organization and operation of the paid game "05" as well as its advertisement by the journalist D.A. Dibrov on his Sunday program on the NTV television company's channel was in direct fraud of its participants. This game flagrantly violated the information rights of citizens . . . .

Organizations and operation of the paid game "05" had no legal basis. The actual lottery was designated as a TV-contest. There was no license to operate this game. Its organizers' contracts regarding technical and financial provisions were made in gross violation of Russian Federation legislation.

ATV journalist D.A. Dibrov advertised the game "05" on his NTV channel program at the same time that he was a founder for the Joint-Stock Partnership "DIOS," which organized the game "05." Thus, D.A. Dibrov used his status as a journalist for advertising his own commercial enterprise without the required registration of his advertising activity.

D.A. Dibrov did not participate in the Judicial Chamber hearing even though he was informed of it in a timely manner and twice agreed to be present.

Based on the above stated facts and in accordance with articles 8, 10, and 12 of the Statute on the Russian Federation Presidential Judicial Chamber for Information Disputes, the Judicial Chamber has decided:

1. To draw the attention of mass media editorial offices (editors-in-chief) to the fact that organization, operation, and advertisement of paid games must be in strict compliance with the requirements of Russian Federation legislation. They should not

* Post-Soviet Media Law & Policy Newsletter, Oct. 15, 1994, at 5. Copyright © 1994 Natalia Dronova and Frances Foster. Reprinted by Permission. Translated by Natalia Dronova and Frances Foster from *Rossiiskaia Gazeta*, June 8, 1994, at 3.

allow violations of citizens' information rights and should not promote fraud and deception.

2. To recommend that the leadership of the NTV TV-company take measures to prevent further abuses by journalists of their professional status in order to advertise commercial projects that are ethically questionable and illegal.

3. To reprimand TV-journalist D.A. Dibrov for advertising the unlawful game "05" on his program "Sunday Evening with D.A. Dibrov."

All materials regarding legal violations that were uncovered during investigation of the unlawful paid lottery "05"'s organization and operation should be sent to procuratorial organs for a legal assessment of the activity of the game's organizers, including D.A. Dibrov.

4. To commend the constructive reaction of the GP MGTS [a Moscow telephone company], which took the initiative to stop the game "05" and to return all money to citizens.

Chairman of the Judicial Chamber

A.B. Vengerov

On the Legal Nature of ITAR-TASS Materials, October 14, 1994, No. 4*

The Russian Federation Presidential Judicial Chamber for Information Disputes received a request from ITAR-TASS General Director V.N. Ignatenko to provide clarification of the following questions:

1. Is an information product (report, commentary, video, photographic materials, etc.) that is created by the collective of an agency and disseminated to consumers of information copyrightable?

2. Does ITAR-TASS have the right to use a copyright sign and place it on its information products?

3. Can news agencies and mass media organizations collect money for an ITAR-TASS information product when they adapt it to fit their specific conditions and regional features?

In accordance with article 21 of the Statute on the Russian Federation Presidential Judicial Chamber for Information Disputes, as confirmed by the Russian Federation Presidential Decree No. 228 of January 31, 1994, the Judicial Chamber makes the following recommendations:

1. In accordance with article 7 of the Russian Federation Law On Copyright and Related Rights, literary, audio-visual (including video films and other film and television productions), and photographic works are copyrightable.

Pursuant to article 8 of said Law, reports about events and facts that are of an informational nature are not subject to copyright. If the material goes beyond a report of an "informational nature," that is, it contains commentary or analysis or is the product of some other creative activity of the author, then it is subject to copyright.

2. In accordance with article 14 of the Russian Federation Law On Copyright and Related Rights, ITAR-TASS has exclusive rights to a work that was created by an author in the course of fulfilling employment duties and tasks, if the contract between ITAR-TASS and the author does not provide otherwise.

Pursuant to article 9 of this Law, the holder of an exclusive copyright is entitled to use a copyright sign.

3. In accordance with article 16 of the Russian Federation Law On Copyright and Related Rights, material copyrighted by ITAR-TASS can be reproduced in an adapted form only with its permission.

---

* Post-Soviet Media Law & Policy Newsletter, Dec. 10, 1994, at 16. Translated by Frances Foster from *Rossiiskaia Gazeta*, Oct. 22, 1994, at 5.

If an editorial office of another mass media organ lawfully adapts ITAR-TASS material (with additional commentary, analysis, etc.), it can collect fees as stipulated in a contract with respect to such adaptations.

Chairman of the Judicial Chamber

A.B. Vengerov

On the State of Freedom of Mass Information in the Maritime Krai, December 13, 1994, No. 35*

Many journalists and newspaper editors have addressed petitions and statements to the Russian Federation Presidential Judicial Chamber for Information Disputes and the Russian Federation Press Committee regarding violations of freedom of mass information in the Maritime Krai. They point to violations of journalists' rights of access to information, rude and insulting attitude towards them of various administrative personnel, interference with the professional activity of editorial offices, suspension of a series of publications, persecution of journalists due to disagreement with their political positions, etc.

These facts are indicated in the statements and petitions of the journalists N. Barabash, N. Ostrovskaia, V. Shkrabov, G. Medvedov, and others. A statement by the Political Council of the "Russia's Democratic Choice" party, signed by party chairman E. Gaidar, also draws the Judicial Chamber's attention to violations of freedom of mass information in the Maritime Krai.

In accepting all these appeals, petitions, and statements for examination, the Judicial Chamber and the Russian Press Committee proceed from the high social significance of freedom of mass information, which is guaranteed in the Russian Federation Constitution, and the need to defend the rights and legitimate interests of journalists. The Judicial Chamber and the Russian Press Committee consider freedom of mass information as a most important component of democracy and an indicator of the state of society. The status of freedom of mass information in the Maritime Krai—a component of the Russian Federation that is resolving important and complex social, economic, and ecological problems—should be examined comprehensively and objectively, with regard to the significance of the results of this examination for other regions of Russia. After hearing the report of the deputy chairman of the Russian Press Committee (A.B. Morgun) and the speeches of journalists (G.M. Medvedeva, I.A. Kots, E.V. Gorchenkov, L.G. Artemova and others); editors-in-chief (I.G. Grebneva (*Arsen'evskie Vesti*), V.V. Bakshin (*Vladivostok*), and V.P. Shkrabov (*Krasnoe Zvezda*)), representatives from the Krai administration (S.I. Novoselov, T.B. Vadil'eva, and I.V. Buivol), the head of the Vladivostok State Television and Radio Company (B.V. Maksimenko), the head of the Regional Inspectorate for Protection of Freedom of the Press and Mass Information (V.N. Savchenko), State Duma Deputy Iu. N. Iakovlev, representative of the radio station VVC (A.V. Kalanchinskii), and Dal'press employees (Iu. A. Bondarenko and R.K. Abbasova) and after familiarizing itself with the letters of N. Barabash and Iu. Mokeev, numerous documents, newspaper clippings, and the statement of V.I. Cherepkov and other persons, the Judicial Chamber has established:

* Post-Soviet Media Law & Policy Newsletter, Feb. 27, 1995, at 2. Copyright © 1995 Frances Foster. Reprinted by Permission. Translated by Frances Foster from *Rossiiskaia Gazeta*, Dec. 27, 1994, at 4.

There have indeed been instances in the Maritime Krai of flagrant violation of freedom of mass information.

Publication of the regional newspaper *Krasnoe Znamia* and the Maritime Krai weekly *Arsen'evskie Vesti* was in fact suspended. The Krai administration, interfering with the professional independence of the newspaper *Krasnoe Znamia*, impeded the work of editor-in-chief V.P. Shkrabov and, exceeding its authority, attempted to remove him from his position. Only after examination of this dispute by the Judicial Chamber on October 14, 1994, did the administration, in accordance with the decision, acknowledge its wrongful conduct, cease its obstruction of the newspaper's publication, and withdraw from the position of founder. At the present time, the newspaper continues publication.

According to the statements of many session participants, the deputy chief of the Krai administration (I.P. Lebedinents) rudely insulted journalists he found objectionable, impeded their access to information, put pressure on them, and "generally failed to conform to the functions entrusted to him as curator of the krai mass media" both in his knowledge and level of legal and political culture.

Iu. A. Bondarenko, the general director of the Dal'press State Publishing and Printing Complex, is playing a negative role in guaranteeing freedom of mass information in the Maritime Krai. Taking a selective approach to various publications, he impeded publication of the newspapers *Krasnoe Znamia* and *Arsen'evskie Vesti* and made illegitimate demands of editors-in-chief. In particular, contrary to the provisions of part 2 of article 19 of the Russian Federation Law On the Mass Media, Iu. A. Bondarenko demanded that the editorial office of *Krasnoe Znamia*, which had already been registered as a mass information medium by an authorized registering organ (the State Regional Inspectorate for Protection of Freedom of the Press and Mass Information), undergo supplementary registration as an enterprise. This was despite the fact that the editorial office's charter indicated that its fundamental purpose was solely publication of the newspaper and that the editorial office has no other purposes connected with commercial activity.

At the very height of the subscription campaign, the Dal'press State Publishing and Printing Complex prevented publication of a number of central newspapers.

B.V. Maksimenko, general director of the Vladivostok State Television and Radio Company, suspended television reporter G.M. Medvedeva for five months without sufficient cause. Her subsequent dismissal as part of a staff reduction was ruled illegal by judicial decision.

In March of this year, the Judicial Chamber was forced to intervene and make a corresponding recommendation with respect to the conflict between the head of the All-Russia State Television and Radio Company's Far East Bureau (M.B. Voznesenkii) and the administrations of the Maritime Krai and the city of Vladivostok, which had restricted the journalist's professional rights.

Unfortunately, in the Maritime Krai, as also in a number of other Russian regions, journalism is becoming a dangerous profession. Unknown persons abducted and tortured the young journalist A. Sadykov. The Russian Television correspondents' center in Vladivostok came under fire.

Much is still unclear about the situation concerning the change in leadership of the newspaper *Utro Rossii.* Former editor Iu. Mokeev maintains that at a meeting of mass media leaders, the head of the Krai administration, "not being fastidious in his choice of words, gave 'Utro Rossii' and its journalists a dressing down and declared that the newspaper would not be published until there was a change in its leadership and direction."

It is significant that after Iu. Mokeev's forced resignation, all the problems (lack of paper, etc.) that had made publication of the newspaper impossible—according to Iu. Bondarenko, Dal'press general director—were immediately "resolved." It is also noteworthy that the suspension of *Utro Rossii* coincided with the campaign for election of deputies to the Krai Duma.

Thus, after evaluating the adduced facts and journalists' numerous appeals at various instances for protection of their professional rights, the Judicial Chamber is forced to affirm that many of the problems involved in the realization of freedom of mass information in the Maritime Krai are the result of the Krai authorities' inability or unwillingness to establish an equal, civilized dialogue with the press and remain within the framework of the law and ethical norms.

At the same time, the Judicial Chamber observes that exposés regarding the state of freedom of mass information in the Maritime Krai are, in several instances, unjustifiably summary in nature and their conclusions often not supported by evidence. A notable example is the report prepared by the "Russia's Democratic Choice" party's group of experts, who worked in the Maritime Krai.

In this connection the Judicial Chamber also observes that, despite invitation, neither the party leader, E. Gaidar, nor representatives deemed it necessary to participate in the hearings and explain their position and that this conduct is, to a lesser degree, unethical.

In consideration of the above and guided by articles 4, 9, 10, and 13 of the Statute of the Russian Federation Presidential Judicial Chamber for Information Disputes, the Judicial Chamber has decided:

1. To demand of the Maritime Krai administration (E.N. Nazdratenko) strict compliance with the norms of the Russian Federation Constitution and the Russian Federation Law On the Mass Media regarding guarantees of freedom of mass information and the professional rights of journalists.

2. To propose that the Maritime Krai administration consider the suitability of I.P. Lebedinets for his position as deputy chief of the Krai administration.

3. To recommend that the Russian Federation Press Committee study the advisability of continued use of Iu. A. Bondarenko in the position of general director of the Dal'press State Publishing and Printing Complex.

4. To draw the attention of V.B. Maksimenko, general director of the Vladivostok State Television and Radio Company, to the fact that it is impermissible to violate legal and ethical norms in the leadership of a journalists' collective.

5. To publish this decision in *Rossiiskaia Gazeta*.

Chairman of the Judicial Chamber

A.B. Vengerov

On Defense of Freedom of Mass Information in Connection with the Events in Chechnya, December 26, 1994, No. 11*

The dramatic events of recent days in Chechnya are being accompanied by cases of flagrant violation of journalists' rights of access to comprehensive and reliable information, impermissible pressure on journalists, instructing them how and what to write on the events in Chechnya, and other deviations from the Russian Federation Constitution's provisions on freedom of mass information and prohibition of censorship.

The Judicial Chamber declares that no one and nothing can revoke the direct effect of the Russian Federation Constitution, including provisions on freedom of speech and the right of citizens to receive reliable and objective information.

At the same time, said right of citizens also assumes comprehensive press coverage of the real goals and motives of measures adopted by the Russian Federation President, Russian Government, MVD organs, and armed forces to ensure operation of the Russian Federation Constitution on the territory of the Chechen Republic and the restoration of constitutional order.

The Judicial Chamber declares that, within the limits of its competence and established means, it will defend freedom of mass information and rights of journalists and at the same time appeal to them to weigh every word and to try to differentiate facts from opinions, analysis from emotion, and the interests of Russia from the interests of various political forces.

The Judicial Chamber calls on citizens and Russian military forces in the conflict zone to observe strictly the rights and legitimate interests of journalists and to render them maximum assistance in fulfillment of their professional duty.

The Judicial Chamber is deeply grieved over the tragic casualties in Chechnya and the death of American journalist Cindy Elbaum and expresses condolences to the nearest and dearest of the deceased.

Chairman of the Judicial Chamber

A.B. Vengerov

---

* Post-Soviet Media Law & Policy Newsletter, Feb. 27, 1995, at 17. Translated by Frances Foster from *Rossiiskaia Gazeta*, Dec. 30, 1994, at 4.

On the Appeal of N.E. Fonareva, Deputy Chairman of the Russian Federation State Committee on Antimonopoly Policy and Support of New Economic Structures, February 21, 1995, No. 6(43)*

The Judicial Chamber for Information Disputes received an appeal from N.E. Fonareva, Deputy Chairman of the Russian Federation State Committee on Antimonopoly Policy and Support of New Economic Structures, requesting an examination of mass media dissemination of inaccurate information regarding the draft Federal Law On Advertisements, introduced in the State Duma by the Russian Federation Government, and of tendentious and biased publications devoted to analysis of this draft.

After studying numerous publications presented by the claimant that discussed the draft law and after hearing the accounts of N. Fonareva, representatives of newspaper editorial offices, advertising agencies, and other interested parties (Iu. Iakutin, B. Piliatskin, A. Politkovskaia, V. Filippov, N. Osipova, I. Krylov, N. Vainonen, I. Glebov, and others) at the February 21, 1995, session, the Judicial Chamber has determined:

The appearance in the mass media of a series of publications on the draft advertising law is well-founded. It is also understandable that the press is concerned about what the law on advertising will look like and its consequences for economic reform, the establishment of a market economy, and the formation of an economic base for independent mass media.

In this connection, as N. Fonareva also confirmed in her statement, the opinion of editorial offices and journalists, including criticism, demands due attention and consideration in drafting and adopting the draft Federal Law On Advertisements. It can contribute to improvement of the law.

At the same time, this critique and the accompanying references to the text of the draft law, other official documents, and legal norms on advertising must be objective, accurate, and professional.

However, a number of mass media publications regarding the draft Federal Law On Advertisements do not meet these requirements. They contain inaccurate information about the text of the draft law and individual provisions, contravene norms of Russian legislation, and include statements that insult the drafters.

For example, the press disseminated insulting allegations that the drafters were seeking to prepare a law that would enable state officials to fill their own pockets (I. Krylov, *Moskovskaia Pravda*, February 14, 1995).

Publications carelessly misstated the draft law's ban on mass media advertisement of tobacco products and alcohol, which, incidentally, is also contained in existing Russian

* Post-Soviet Media Law & Policy Newsletter, July 27, 1995, at 7. Translated by Frances Foster from *Rossiiskaia Gazeta*, Mar. 23, 1995, at 5.

legislation (the Russian Federation Fundamental Principles on Protection of Citizens' Health, the Russian Federation Presidential Decree of February 17, 1995, No. 161), as a total prohibition on advertisement of these products (A. Dmitriev, *Moskovskie Novosti*, No. 64, December 18-25, 1994; I. Krylov, *Ekonomika i Zhizn*, No. 1, January 1995). I. Krylov was especially active in his critical interpretation of the ban on advertisement of alcoholic beverages and tobacco products. He asserted that this contradicted world experience. However, he omitted to mention that article 15(1) of the European Convention on Transfrontier Television (Strasbourg, May 5, 1989) prohibits the advertisement of tobacco products and contains strict limitations on advertisement of alcoholic beverages of all types.

Several publications used legal terms incorrectly ("censorship," "system of judicial expertise," etc.) with the goal of discrediting individual provisions of the draft law and their conceptual basis (I. Glebov, *Tsentr-Plus*; V. Piliatskin, *Izvestiia*, etc.).

This type of publication, which contained unreliable, inaccurate information, could cause readers to have a negative impression of the draft Federal Law On Advertisements and also of the intentions of the state organs that prepared the draft law.

In examining N. Fonareva's appeal, the Judicial Chamber does not encroach in any way on the competence of other state organs, especially the legislature. It considers the subject of the Antimonopoly Committee's appeal—that several publications insulted the honor and dignity of Committee employees.

The sole subject of Judicial Chamber examination in this case was the accuracy and objective interpretation in mass media discussions of the draft Federal Law On Advertisements.

In light of the foregoing and guided by article 9 of the Statute on the Judicial Chamber, the Judicial Chamber has decided:

1. To recognize that, along with legitimate and constructive criticism of the draft advertising law, several mass media organs, including the aforementioned, provided distorted versions of the actual text of the law, incorrect use of legal terms, and groundless allegations regarding negative intentions of the drafters. Their objective was to create insufficient public support for the goals and content of the draft law.

2. To direct the attention of mass media editorial offices to the need to be more careful in verifying facts and information in the preparation and publication of materials that evaluate drafts of normative, legal acts, including the draft Federal Law On Advertisements.

3. To publish this decision in *Rossiiskaia Gazeta*.

Chairman of the Judicial Chamber

A.B. Vengerov

On the Appeal by the State Duma of the Russian Federation Federal Assembly Regarding the VGTRK Television Program "Newspaper Histories" ("Fascism in Russia. Who?") of February 22, 1995, March 15, 1995, No. 7(44)*

The Russian Federation Presidential Judicial Chamber for Information Disputes received an appeal from the State Duma of the Federal Assembly reporting that, at the February 24, 1995, session of the State Duma, deputies assessed several segments of the VGTRK television program "Newspaper Histories" ("Fascism in Russia. Who?") as being of a provocative and inciting nature, and promoting the kindling of national enmity and hatred. The appeal requested that the Judicial Chamber examine the case and take measures within its competence.

After studying the videotranscript of the February 22 program "Newspaper Histories" presented by VGTRK, newspaper articles to which the program referred ("From KGB to LDPR. Career of a Nazi"—*Moskovskie Novosti*, September 4-11, 1994; "RNE Intends to Come to Power Soon"—*Nezavisimaia Gazeta*, February 10, 1995), and a number of other publications and materials and after hearing in judicial session the parties' representatives (I.I. Zablotskii, E.A. Shcherbinskii, E.V. Tuinov), the program's authors (O. Iu. Vakulovskii, T.S. Bondarenko); the representatives of VGTRK and the Oblik television company (E.V. Dmitrieva, T.V. Men'shikova); the representative of the "Sirena" corporation (N.P. Zarubina); and other interested parties, the Judicial Chamber has determined:

The appearance in the mass media of materials exposing Russian fascism was justified. The Judicial Chamber has addressed this subject often. In its decisions On Mass Media Publications Fostering Social and National Intolerance (July 14, 1994); On the Appeal to the Judicial Chamber by State Duma Chairman of the Russian Federation Federal Assembly I.P. Rybkin Regarding the VGTRK Television Program "Great Scandal" (November 25, 1994); On Ia. Mogutin's Publication *Chechen Knot. 13 Theses.* in *Novyi Vzgliad* (February 21, 1995), and in several other decisions, the Judicial Chamber has stressed the high degree of social danger presented by dissemination of hate speech, nationalistic and extremist views, and use of the mass media for these goals.

Accordingly, the Judicial Chamber has observed that existing legislation establishes conditions for battling the dissemination of propaganda regarding the superiority of one nation over another, their incitement of social discord, national enmity and hatred, and the formation on this illegal basis of a para-military organization that displays the essential features of fascism. The essence of the matter is to fulfill the laws of Russia. The Judicial Chamber has also called attention to the fact that slogans of

* Post-Soviet Media Law & Policy Newsletter, July 27, 1995, at 7. Translated by Frances Foster from *Rossiiskaia Gazeta*, Mar. 29, 1995, at 13.

national revival, strengthening of statehood, and patriotism have nothing in common with fascism, which represents a real social danger.

The Judicial Chamber shares the concern of the public, including the authors of the "Newspaper Histories" television program, about the spread of fascism in Russia today.

The full title of the television program ("Fascism in Russia. Who?") and also the authors' text are testimony to the aim of its creators to show Russian fascism in the faces and actual carriers of fascist ideology and practice and the motive forces and forms of fascism.

To a certain degree this was successful. For example, the television program showed the rock group "Krek," which openly and with impunity demonstrated to its audience its fascist nature. This confirmed that in Russia fascism is a normal, natural phenomenon. The program convincingly showed the pro-fascist character of the armed group "Vervol'f" [Werewolf], against which legal security organs have taken appropriate measures.

In the authors' opinion, the figure that personified and at the same time exposed Russian fascism was a certain A. Vedenkin, as the alleged "financial genius of Zhironovskii," "deputy leader of the RNE Barkashov," deputy "minister of defense" Achalov, "KGB officer."

The Judicial Chamber considers the broadcast of the "Russian fascism" program timely and justified. The program alarmed the public and became grounds for urging authorities to take action. These were positive consequences of journalistic investigation.

At the same time, however, the program used insufficiently verified and even refuted facts, especially regarding the purchase by A. Vedenkin and Co. of a 90% share of the international technology corporation Sirena. This caused damages to the corporation.

In reaching this decision within its competence the Judicial Chamber takes into consideration the fact that the procuracy has brought criminal proceedings against A. Vedenkin and that the LDPR faction thus far has not refuted in accordance with established procedures the allegation that Vedenkin is an active participant in party activities.

Based on the above-stated facts, the Judicial Chamber has decided:

1. To recognize that the television program "Newspaper Histories" was not of a provocative and inflammatory character and that its authors did not violate Russian legislation.

2. To draw the attention of the authors of the "Fascism in Russia. Who?" television program to the fact that the use of insufficiently verified and inaccurate information is impermissible.

3. To take into consideration the readiness of VGTRK to correct its admitted mistake regarding the "Sirena" corporation.

4. To observe that under current conditions it is necessary to develop legislation on the struggle against fascism, including providing legal accountability for use and propagandizing of fascist attributes and symbols.

5. To publish this decision in *Rossiiskaia Gazeta*.

Chairman of the Judicial Chamber

A.B. Vengerov

On the Appeal by the State Duma of the Russian Federation Federal Assembly Regarding S. Parkhomenko's Publication *We Must Choose Better* in the Newspaper *Segodnia*, May 11, 1995, No. 13(50)*

The Russian Federation Presidential Judicial Chamber for Information Disputes has received an appeal from the State Duma of the Russian Federation Federal Assembly, reporting that at its April 12, 1995, session the State Duma assessed S. Parkhomenko's publication *We Must Choose Better* in *Segodnia*, no. 65 (April 8, 1995) as insulting not only State Duma deputies but also the voters.

After examining the publication and hearing from State Duma deputies (T.A. Astrakhankina and V.N. Volkov), representatives of the State Duma apparatus (I.I. Zablotskii; E.A. Shcherbinskii; N.A. Sautin), the editor-in-chief of *Segodnia* (D.V. Ostal'skii), the author (S.B. Parkhomenko), and the secretary of the Moscow Union of Journalists (I.S. Simanchuk), the Judicial Chamber has determined:

In issue no. 65 of April 8, 1995, *Segodnia* published material from its parliamentary correspondent S. Parkhomenko, which was entitled *We Must Choose Better*. This article contained, in particular, the following statements: "We will remain alone face to face with our parliament. And we must somehow live in the future under the laws written in that farce. We will have to send our children off to the army—in accordance with the procedure just approved by that crowd of buffoons. We will have to pay taxes—at the rate just determined at that clowns' ball."

It was this very paragraph, along with several other phrases and definitions, that evoked a sharply negative reaction from State Duma deputies.

The Judicial Chamber, first of all, confirms the right of journalists to provide a critical assessment of the activity of state organs, organizations, officials, and deputies as well. This right represents the practical fulfillment of the principle of freedom of mass information, which is established in the Constitution.

At the same time, it is absolutely impermissible to abuse freedom of mass information. In carrying out his professional activity, a journalist is duty-bound to respect the rights, legitimate interests, and honor and dignity of citizens and organizations. It is impermissible to violate ethical norms and to use untruthful information.

The Judicial Chamber considers S. Parkhomenko's article as falling within that very category of publications that violate the law and requirements of professional ethics.

* Post-Soviet Media Law & Policy Newsletter, July 27, 1995, at 8. Translated by Frances Foster from *Rossiiskaia Gazeta*, May 23, 1995, at 12.

The author, by using such words as "farce, clowns, and buffoons" to characterize the activities of the entire membership of the State Duma, violates legal and ethical norms. The publication also contained other inappropriate expressions and untruthful information. Moreover, it disparaged the features of several laws adopted by the Duma in a superficial and unfounded manner.

The Judicial Chamber cannot agree with the editor-in-chief's (D.V. Ostal'skii) and author's (S.B. Parkhomenko) explanations for this information dispute. Publication of materials in a so-called author's column, if it represents an abuse of mass information, does not relieve either the author or the editor-in-chief from liability. Moreover, it does not follow from the context of the article that the sharply negative evaluation related to individual State Duma sessions or the activity of individual deputies. In an impermissibly general form, the article directly presented the parliament as a farce and all deputies as clowns and buffoons.

The Judicial Chamber also notes with regret that S. Parkhomenko's article turned out to be only one in a series of publications, which often appear in the mass media, that are biased and insulting to the young institutes of statehood of democratic Russia.

Taking into consideration the above-stated facts and guided by articles 8-10 of the Statute on the Russian Federation Presidential Judicial Chamber for Information Disputes, the Judicial Chamber has decided:

1. To recognize that, in publishing *We Must Choose Better* in *Segodnia* on April 8, 1995, the author and editor-in-chief violated articles 49 and 51 of the Russian Federation Law On the Mass Media.

2. To reprimand the editor-in-chief D.V. Ostal'skii and the journalist S.B. Parkhomenko.

3. To publish this decision in *Rossiiskaia Gazeta.*

Chairman of the Judicial Chamber

A.B. Vengerov

On the Appeal by the Editorial Board and the Editor-in-Chief of *Vecherniaia Ufa*, Ia. B. Khusainov, Regarding the Legality of Advertisements Published in the Newspaper, May 25, 1995, No. 14(51)*

The Russian Federation Presidential Judicial Chamber for Information Disputes has received appeals from the editorial board and editor-in-chief of the newspaper *Vecherniaia Ufa*, Ia. B. Khusainov, regarding the legality of advertisements published in the newspaper, which relate to the sale of alcoholic beverages and the activity of the Bashkir Special Commodities-Raw Materials Exchange (BSTSB).

After studying documents and materials presented by the claimant and hearing from the deputy editor-in-chief of *Vecherniaia Ufa* (R.B. Faizrakhmanov), the chief specialist of the R.B. State Inspectorate for Protection of Freedom of the Press and Mass Information (V.S. Orlov), the R.B. Deputy Minister for the Press and Mass Information (A.M. Sultangariev), the head of the State-Legal Administration of the R.B. President (I.A. Adigamov), the claimant's representative (V.A. Vinogradov), and Russian Federation Duma Deputy A.N. Arinin, the Judicial Chamber has determined:

1. The R.B. State Inspectorate for Protection of Freedom of the Press and Mass Information found violations of the law on advertisement of alcoholic beverages in the publications presented by the editorial board and editor-in-chief Ia. B. Khusainov and ordered the removal of these violations. After examining these publications, the Judicial Chamber observes that several of these publications do indeed contain advertisements of alcoholic beverages (references to the "lowest prices" and "highest quality" of advertised products, with corresponding pictures as well). The State Inspectorate's order regarding these publications is lawful.

Other publications regarding the sale of alcoholic beverages do not contain such characteristic features of advertisements (for example, the March 23, 1995, advertisement for the Dasko firm). This information complies with article 437(1) of the Russian Federation Civil Code as an offer to an indefinite class of persons regarding the purchase of goods. It does not constitute an infringement of existing legislation.

The Judicial Chamber also takes into consideration the fact that publication of such offers (those that do not contain characteristic features of advertisements) for the sale of goods, including alcoholic beverages, assists in supplying an economic base for the normal activity of the mass media.

2. In accordance with the Bashkir Republic Presidential Decree on Examining the Legality of the Creation and Activity of the BSTSB, the Ufa City Soviet as founder of

* Post-Soviet Media Law & Policy Newsletter, July 27, 1995, at 9. Translated by Frances Foster from *Rossiiskaia Gazeta*, June 1, 1995, at 6.

Vecherniaia Ufa (and other newspapers) and the R.B. Ministry of Press and Information were asked to examine the responsibility of the leaders of these publications for the losses sustained by legal and physical persons as a result of the insulting remarks about the BSTSB that appeared in many of the newspaper's advertisements.

In their appeal, the claimants express disagreement with a similar evaluation of *Vecherniaia Ufa*'s advertising activity. They raise questions about the lawfulness of advertisements that relate to the BSTSB's activity.

The Judicial Chamber does not agree with the claimants' arguments and notes that the publications violate article 36(2) of the Russian Federation Law On the Mass Media, which provides that "the editorial office does not have the right to collect payment for placing advertisements under the guise of informational, editorial or author's material." It was the very absence of any indication that the publications were advertisements that promoted the communication of misinformation to readers about the BSTSB's activities, the exchange's financial characteristics, and the like.

Moreover, the publications violated professional journalistic ethical norms, such as those established in the contracts with the head of the exchange regarding the organization and development of an advertising campaign with the exchange's guarantee to organize trips abroad for editorial office employees.

3. A legal evaluation of the Bashkir Republic Presidential Decree, the legal responsibility of the editorial office, other questions of a property nature, and questions regarding the participation of other organizations in causing the damages that resulted from the BSTSB's activities are not within the Judicial Chamber's competence and should be resolved according to established legislative procedure.

Based on the above-stated facts and guided by articles 8 and 9 of the Statute on the Judicial Chamber, the Judicial Chamber has decided:

1. To recognize as legal the newspaper's publications regarding sale of alcoholic beverages that did not contain the characteristic features of an advertisement.
2. To reject the rest of the claimants' appeal to the Judicial Chamber.
3. To publish this decision in *Rossiiskaia Gazeta.*

Chairman of the Judicial Chamber

A.B. Vengerov

Joint Recommendation of the Presidential Judicial Chamber for Information Disputes and the Union of Russian Journalists on the Freedom of Mass Information and the Responsibility of Journalists, June 15, 1995*

The mass media's attainment of legal independence from authorities and from state interference in the professional activity of journalists is recognized as the most notable result of democratic transformation. The press has become an influential social force. It is no accident that, along with the familiar phrase "as is the people, so is the government" it has been asserted that "as is the press, so is society." This imposes on journalists and leaders of editorial staffs and publishing houses a responsibility that is not merely formal and on the books, but moral and political.

This was the very subject of the hearing that was jointly held by the Judicial Chamber for Information Disputes and the Russian Union of Journalists on June 15, 1995. The result was elaboration of a recommendation that comprehends a wide range of problems.

The goal of the recommendation is as follows: in view of the very important political events that the elections for parliament and president will constitute and in light of the complex political situation, to draw the attention of journalists and mass media leaders to their duty to provide the populace with full, objective, and truthful information about everything occurring in the country and the world and to give professional and honest analysis of this information.

Under conditions of competition and a still incomplete market for information, many journalists and editorial staffs disregard the most elementary norms of the Law On the Mass Media. Untruthful information has been widely disseminated. Sometimes, this is done deliberately. More often, it occurs in the heat of competition for readers and viewers. At times, this is the result of an elementary failure to verify the accuracy of information. Often, it is due to a lack of access to information, which has been covered up by the administration. Even reliable publishers commit violations with unverified reports and deliberate distortion of factual material for the sake of sensational presentation. They do so by hushing up unprofitable facts and overemphasizing sensational facts. Indeed, this irresponsible attitude towards reliability of information has prompted the abolition in many mass media of verification departments and bureaus. All this leads to gross violations of legislation and disregard for norms of professional ethics and damages the interests of society.

---

* Post-Soviet Media Law & Policy Newsletter, Sept. 27, 1995, at 9. Translated by Frances Foster from *Rossiiskaia Gazeta*, July 11, 1995, at 6.

The Law On the Mass Media clearly stipulates the range of publications for the content of which editorial staffs are not liable. Yet, the heads of many mass media organs arbitrarily expand this category to include author's columns, special pages, and individual contributions. They shift liability for the content to the authors personally or to subsidiary editorial staffs. This practice is contrary to the Law On the Mass Media. Mass media editors and editorial staffs bear full responsibility for all published materials, with the exception of those specifically named in the law.

Competition and pursuit of sensation have led to domestic journalism losing such traditional and popular genres as satires, pamphlets, and psychological essays. In their place are hastily cooked up items, containing undisguised crudeness and insults to the point of using an "abnormal lexicon." In-depth and often dangerous journalistic investigation attracts the attention of readers and viewers. But usually accompanying this are ersatz commentaries, dubious versions, and irresponsible prognoses, concocted for ratings, as well as innumerable lists of the "richest" and "most influential" people. Very often such publications are not based on serious sociological research. Their goal is to inflate authority or to discredit political rivals. Such publications do not always contravene legal norms, but crudely flout journalistic ethics and discredit the mass media in the eyes of the populace. Several publishers, abusing mass information, sink to the level of all-out persecution of prominent politicians and officials without any concern for the authenticity of facts.

It is outside the traditions of responsible journalism to implant a cult of violence, racial superiority, and pornography, to relish horrors, and to spread propaganda for the occult and mysticism. Nonetheless, this is precisely the type of material many mass media use in their efforts to gain popularity. Other publishers have developed an enthusiasm for pornography, catering to people's base nature. Not to mention the so-called "special" publishers, popular and circulation newspapers, which without cause or limits savor "klubnichka." They pay no regard to the pernicious effect this has on the morality of society. Protection of the moral health of children and adolescents demands self-restraint and also the development of legal principles in this sphere.

At present, courts are overwhelmed with claims from citizens whose honor and dignity was insulted in print or on the air. In principle, such methods of defense are a normal phenomenon. However, the quantity of cases indicates that the mass media, which endlessly speak about human rights, with ease and extraordinary irresponsibility trample on these rights. They mix reputation with mud and do not hesitate to use deliberate slander. Battling diktat of authorities, several publishers themselves use their influence to secure diktat of the press. Freedom of mass information is often understood as unbridled freedom of the mass media. In the process, many publications "skillfully" exploit the legislative norm regarding the right not to disclose sources of information. If they lose in the courts, then they resort to worthless cliches: libel on the first page under a garish headline — the refutation appearing in fine print at the end and, what is more, accompanied by insulting commentaries. At the same time, there are appeals to courts about threats from certain officials, who for the slightest criticism of them literally terrorize journalists. At times, these threats become means to work on newspapers.

Advertisements fill the press and air like hallucinations. Because they produce large amounts of money, they have begun to dictate the subject matter of publications in many cases. Concealed advertisements constitute a major source of enrichment. The relationship between advertisers and publications is complex and completely unregulated by legislation. Many editorial staffs attempt to decline responsibility for advertisements, an action that is contrary to law. Although to a lesser extent than previously, impermissible advertisement of alcoholic beverages and tobacco products continue in the mass media.

The amount of "bought" materials has increased, as has low-quality and at times obviously unscrupulous advertising. The authors of these texts bestow a "dubious benefit" upon both advertisers and themselves. They destroy the interest and confidence of readers, viewers, and listeners in both advertisements and media. They do not take into account the fact that the production of high-quality advertisements is a special, complex activity that has nothing in common with journalism as it is usually understood. According to the standards of civilized journalism it is absurd for one person to be both journalist and advertising agent.

The intensification of interethnic conflicts has raised difficult legal and ethical questions for the mass media. It should be taken into consideration that even the slightest lack of balance in a publication's coverage or analysis of these problems can seriously influence the exacerbation of ethnic tension and perhaps cause a social explosion. Here, as nowhere else, caution and careful consideration are essential. Unfortunately, several publications take openly chauvinistic and nationalistic positions, which are fraught with the most ruinous consequences. Aspects of the relations between nationalities and the interaction between federal authorities and Federation subdivisions must be carefully weighed on a pharmacist's scales since a mistake in the dosage can make a publication a poison rather than a cure.

Freedom of speech and independence of the mass media place on a completely different level the interrelationship between press and authorities. Unreliability, incompleteness, and distortion of information very often result from the inaccessibility of sources of information. Only parliament is sufficiently open to the press. As far as the presidential structures, government circles, and administrative offices are concerned, however, they are sealed off from journalists; they are more closed than the former party committees.

Press centers, press services, press secretaries, and others of their ilk have been established everywhere. In theory, they were intended to facilitate journalists' access to information. In practice, they have turned into insurmountable barriers and supply only the information that is of interest to the given structure. And naturally journalists overcome these barriers by any means, including bribing officials and openly purchasing information. If these methods are beyond them, they resort to fabrication and conjecture.

The procedure for supply of information by press services as well as the procedure for accreditation of journalists is unregulated by legislation. This is a serious detriment to objective and complete coverage of events. It is essential to strengthen immediately the legislative bases for journalists' access to information and citizens' rights to information and to implement other measures, including economic measures, to support the press.

These "recommendations" are a verification of the state of affairs on the information market. They do not purport to have any regulatory status. Their chief goal is to draw the attention of journalists to their responsibility to society and once again to emphasize the necessity of observing the Constitution and the Law On the Mass Media and to urge the creation and realization in practice of ethical codes.

Judicial Chamber

A.B. Vengerov

Union of Journalists

V.L. Bugdanov

On the Appeal by the State Duma Deputy Chairman A. Chilingarov Regarding the Publication of *Should the Icebergs Be Sold?* in *Moskovskaia Pravda* on June 16, 1995, July 13, 1995, No. 20(57)*

State Duma Deputy Chairman A. Chilingarov has appealed to the Judicial Chamber for Information Disputes regarding B. Vyucheiskii's publication of *Should the Icebergs Be Sold?* under the "Voter's Opinion" rubric in *Moskovskaia Pravda* on June 16, 1995.

The claimant contends that said publication is untrue and contains a set of defamatory fabrications designed to discredit his political, social, and professional reputation and also to discredit the authority of legislative power.

After hearing the testimony of State Duma Deputy Chairman A.N. Chilingarov, State Duma Deputy Iu. P. Ivanov, Vice President of the Russian Association of Polar Explorers Iu. A. Khabarov and after examining B. Vyucheiskii's publication and other materials, including a letter from the governor of the Nenets Autonomous Region V.A. Vyucheiskii, the Judicial Chamber has established:

B. Vyucheiskii's article *Should the Icebergs Be Sold?* published under the "Voter's Opinion" rubric contains a negative analysis of the social-political activity of A.N. Chilingarov and also unfavorable evaluations of several of his personality traits.

The information cited as the basis for a certain Voter's Opinion, however, did not receive any substantiation whatsoever at the Judicial Chamber session.

The Judicial Chamber, as it states later in this decision, notes especially the unprincipled and inconsistent position of the editorial staff of *Moskovskaia Pravda*, which published the untruthful and biased article but avoided open and public discussion in Judicial Chamber session of the bases for the information cited in the article.

Taking into consideration the stated facts and in accordance with article 45(2) of the Russian Federation Constitution and articles 9, 10, and 12 of the Statute on the Russian Federation Presidential Judicial Chamber for Information Disputes, the Judicial Chamber has decided:

1. To recognize that the publication *Should the Icebergs Be Sold?* in *Moskovskaia Pravda* was based on unreliable and false information and represented an abuse of the mass media, as stipulated in article 59(2) of the Russian Federation Law On the Mass Media, and a violation of ethical norms.

---

* Post-Soviet Media Law & Policy Newsletter, Sept. 27, 1995, at 10. Copyright © 1995 Frances Foster. Reprinted by Permission. Translated by Frances Foster from *Rossiiskaia Gazeta*, July 20, 1995, at 6.

2. To reprimand *Moskovskaia Pravda* editor-in-chief Sh. S. Muladzhanova for the publication of B. Vyucheiskii's article *Should the Icebergs Be Sold?*

3. To propose that the editorial board of *Moskovskaia Pravda* examine the issue of disciplinary action against members of the editorial staff who prepared said article for publication.

4. To publish this decision in *Rossiiskaia Gazeta.*

5. To recommend that *Moskovskaia Pravda* editor-in-chief Sh. S. Muladzhanova publish this decision in *Moskovskaia Pravda.*

Chairman of the Judicial Chamber

A.B. Vengerov

On the Appeal by Moscow Oblast' Duma Deputy R. Ia. Murashkovskaia Regarding the Legality of the TOO Klin Television's Activity in Preparing and Disseminating Information of a Pre-election Nature, July 13, 1995, No. 21(58)*

The Russian Federation Presidential Judicial Chamber for Information Disputes has received an appeal from Moscow Oblast' Duma Deputy R. Ia. Murashkovskaia, supported by the "New Regional Policy" deputy's group of the Russian Federation Federal Assembly's State Duma. The appeal relates to a series of broadcasts by the TOO Klin Television that, according to the claimant, were of a pre-election agitation nature.

After examining materials presented to the Judicial Chamber, familiarizing itself with videotapes of the cited broadcasts and hearing testimony from State Duma Deputy A.A. Murav'eva, Klin Television Company Poisk official S.G. Sharapova, *Serp i Molot* newspaper editor-in-chief Z.C. Maksimova, and the TOO Klin Television director Iu. V. Samsonov, the Judicial Chamber has established:

On May 20, 1995, the TOO Klin Television broadcast a recording of a meeting between the leader of the State Duma LDPR faction, V.V. Zhirinovskii, and residents of the city of Klin. V.V. Zhirinovskii's entire speech clearly manifested characteristics of pre-election agitation. It contained calls to vote in the forthcoming elections for candidates from the Liberal-Democratic Party of Russia and pejorative comments about possible competitors. Moreover, the speaker spoke rudely about the State Duma Deputy from Klin, A.A. Murav'eva.

The recording of this meeting subsequently was used repeatedly on Klin Television broadcasts.

On June 5 and 20, 1995, on broadcasts of the TOO Klin Television "Priamoi Efir," State Duma Deputy V.A. Marychev appealed to television viewers to vote in the forthcoming elections for the director of the TOO Klin Television Iu. V. Samsonov. For this purpose, he used expressions of the following type: "Samsonov, as future candidate for deputy," "Our chief task is to choose Samsonov as State Duma deputy," "If Samsonov brings in (the LDPR) 7 thousand votes . . ."

The Judicial Chamber notes that the character and conditions for pre-election agitation are established in the Federal Law On Basic Guarantees for Electoral Rights of Russian Federation Citizens. According to the meaning of this law, pre-election agitation comprehends "Activity of Russian Federation citizens and social organizations in the preparation and dissemination of information that has the goal of inducing voters to

* Post-Soviet Media Law & Policy Newsletter, Sept. 27, 1995, at 11. Translated by Frances Foster from *Rossiiskaia Gazeta*, July 28, 1995, at 5.

participate in voting for or against some or other candidates (slates of candidates)." article 26 of the same law stipulates that "Pre-election agitation begins on the date of registration of candidates and ends on the day before the elections."

Thus, said broadcasts of the TOO Klin Television were contrary to the norms of the Law On Basic Guarantees for Electoral Rights of Russian Federation Citizens since they had the characteristics of pre-election agitation.

Acknowledging the fact that the Klin Television channel televised topics that were of the nature of pre-election agitation, its director Iu. V. Samsonov plead ignorance of the requirements of article 26 of the Russian Federation Law On Basic Guarantees for Electoral Rights of Russian Federation Citizens. In the Judicial Chamber's opinion, however, this cannot serve as a basis for relieving Iu. V. Samsonov from liability.

The Judicial Chamber also notes that such ignorance of the rules for pre-election agitation can result in misinformation of the populace, deception of potential voters regarding the dates and procedure for nomination and registration of deputy candidates, and their participation in the election campaign.

The Judicial Chamber believes that the leadership and journalists of the TOO Klin Television were obliged to consider legislative requirements in the preparation of said broadcasts and to adopt necessary measures for preventing unlawful (premature) pre-election agitation.

Taking into consideration the great social-political significance of rigorous compliance by the mass media with election legislation and guided by articles 8 and 10 of the Statute on the Russian Federation Presidential Judicial Chamber for Information Disputes, the Judicial Chamber has decided:

1. To recognize that the content of the TOO Klin Television broadcasts of May 20 and June 5 and 20, 1995, with the participation of State Duma deputies V.V. Zhirinovskii and V.A. Marychev contravenes the requirements of the Russian Federation Federal Law On Basic Guarantees for Electoral Rights of Russian Federation Citizens in the part on commencement of pre-election agitation.

2. To propose that the Russian Federation Television and Radio Service examine the issue of whether the TOO Klin Television has complied with the conditions of its broadcasting license.

3. To send this decision to the Russian Federation Central Electoral Commission.

4. To publish this decision in *Rossiiskaia Gazeta*.

Chairman of the Judicial Chamber

A.B. Vengerov

On the Appeal by the Russian Federation Federal Assembly State Duma Deputy V.N. Lysenko Regarding Inaccurate Information Broadcast on the "Vremia" Program (ORT), September 22, 1995, No. 27(64)*

The Russian Federation Presidential Judicial Chamber for Information Disputes has received an appeal from Russian Federation Federal Assembly State Duma Deputy V.N. Lysenko.

His statement points out that despite repeated appeals to journalists, they continue to omit the first name of Deputy Nikolai Lysenko in their reports. In doing so, especially in stories about Deputy Nikolai Lysenko's unethical conduct in the State Duma, they cause significant moral injury to the electoral bloc "Pamfilova-Gurov-Lysenko" and to Deputy V.N. Lysenko personally. According to the statement, such expressions were disseminated on the "Vremia" program (ORT) at 9 p.m. and on "Segodnia" at 10 p.m. on September 11, 1995.

Prompt correction (refutation) of factual errors disseminated by the mass media, which are of societal interest, is within the Judicial Chamber's competence.

After examining the presented materials and hearing the testimony of Russian Federation Federal Assembly State Duma Deputy V.N. Lysenko, his representative (A.V. Kligman), the representatives of the ORT and NTV television companies (A.B. Orfenov and I.V. Minaev), and the Secretary of the Russian Federation Union of Journalists (I.S. Simanchuk), the Judicial Chamber has established:

On September 11, the "Vremia" (ORT) program broadcast information about a fight in the halls of a State Duma session. In its reference to Nikolai Lysenko as one of the fight participants, the broadcast did not use his first name. This information in essence misinformed the television viewers because there are two State Duma deputies named Lysenko-Nikolai and Vladimir. Print publications also allowed such incomplete information about V.N. Lysenko. As for the "Segodnia" (NTV) program, a survey of its videocassettes revealed no incomplete and inaccurate information.

The Judicial Chamber considers that the "Vremia" (ORT) program contained incomplete information. Such incomplete information can cause television viewers, radio audiences, and readers to have an inaccurate impression of which deputy is the topic of discussion. It can cause moral injury to V.N. Lysenko and to the bloc he heads.

During the consideration of this information dispute, there were questions raised about the need to observe legal and ethical norms in mass media references to the

* Post-Soviet Media Law & Policy Newsletter, Nov. 27, 1995, at 9. Translated by Frances Foster from *Rossiiskaia Gazeta*, Sept. 30, 1995, at 4.

surnames of political, state, and public figures and the impermissibility of using their surnames in a disparaging fashion.

In light of the foregoing and guided by points 4, 9, and 10 of the Statute on the Russian Federation Presidential Judicial Chamber for Information Disputes and article 19 of the Russian Federation Civil Code, the Judicial Chamber has decided:

1. To recognize that the story on the State Duma fight, broadcast on the September 11, 1995 "Vremia" (ORT) program, presented viewers with incomplete and inaccurate information, which violated Deputy V.N. Lysenko's right to his name (Article 19 Russian Federation Civil Code).

2. To recommend that mass media editorial offices in their references to people with the same surnames use the full name and other identifying personal characteristics and that television broadcasts must include a picture of the person under discussion.

3. To rectify on a "Vremia" program in the near future the inaccurate information regarding V.N. Lysenko, which has societal significance.

4. To publish this decision in *Rossiiskaia Gazeta.*

Chairman of the Judicial Chamber

A.B. Vengerov

On Violations in A.G. Nevzorov's "Wild Field" Program of June 30, 1995, of the Constitutional Rights of Convicts Imprisoned in Institution US-20/2, October 19, 1995, No. 32(69)*

The Russian Federation Presidential Judicial Chamber for Information Disputes has received appeals from N.L. Vorontsova and other women convicts who are currently imprisoned in the general regime colony US-20/2. They assert that A.G. Nevzorov's program "Muckraking" of the "Wild Field" series (June 30, 1995) flagrantly violated the right to inviolability of private life.

The Judicial Chamber notes that, indeed, articles 23 and 24 of the Russian Constitution provide that everyone has the right to inviolability of private life and that collection, storage, use, and dissemination of information related to an individual's private life without his/her consent are impermissible.

Moreover, according to article 49, part 1, ¶ 5 of the Russian Federation Law On the Mass Media, a journalist must obtain the consent of the citizen or his/her legal representative for dissemination in the mass media of information related to the private life of that citizen.

After examining the statements of N.L. Vorontsova and other convicts, familiarizing itself with the videotapes of the "Wild Field" television program ("Muckraking" broadcast), studying other materials, and hearing the testimony of N.L. Vorontsova, "Russian Public Television" representative M.M. Martirosova, and Russian Federation MVD representative V.I. Orlov, the Judicial Chamber has established:

A.G. Nevzorov's broadcast disseminated information about several aspects of the daily life of convicts imprisoned in the general regime colony US-20/2 located in the Leningrad oblast'. It devoted special attention to the distinctive features of the sexual behavior of women prisoners. It made broad generalizations about the ways of life characteristic, in the author's opinion, of every Russian women's correctional labor institution, without exception.

In organizing television filming for the "Muckraking" broadcast ("Wild Field" program), A.G. Nevzorov made a request to film on a completely different topic. He promised to observe steadfastly the right of a convict to consent to being filmed and if such consent was refused to use the technique of anonymous filming—without the individual's face, surname, and first name.

However, in preparing this television broadcast, he flagrantly violated these promises. Without their consent, he filmed N.L. Vorontsova, G.S. Krupskaia, E. Iu. Kupriianova, and other female convicts who were subjects of the broadcast. In a series of

* Post-Soviet Media Law & Policy Newsletter, Nov. 27, 1995, at 9. Translated by Frances Foster from *Rossiiskaia Gazeta*, Oct. 31, 1995, at 6.

broadcast episodes it was absolutely clear that those included in the footage did not wish to be objects of journalistic attention.

The broadcast groundlessly attributed to the entire population of institution US-20/2 (and also, as the author claimed, all residents of similar institutions) certain forms of sexual orientation and modes of behavior.

Close-up shots of women (who ended up in footage purely at the whim of the journalist) as a backdrop for unambiguous commentary and frank interviews, as well as the entire context of the broadcast, gave prisoners grounds to take personally A.G. Nevzorov's unfounded assertions.

The claimants justly point to the possible adverse consequences of this broadcast for women with husbands, children, parents, etc., outside prison. The dissemination of such information weakens moral principles and has the potential to cause tangible moral injury and destroy family relations.

The Judicial Chamber has also established that, according to the contract for delivery of the "Wild Field" television program, the creative enterprise "600 seconds," headed by A.G. Nevzorov, is answerable for all complaints by third parties about the program. Yet, as is stipulated in this very same contract, the concept, theme, and scenario are approved in advance by appropriate officials of Russian Public Television. Moreover, ORT has the power, with A.G. Nevzorov's consent, to make necessary editorial changes in filmed material. In this way, it has control over the program's compliance with Russian Federation legislative requirements.

However, in this case, the company's leadership did not exercise its rights and did not fulfill the control functions it is assigned by contractual terms and Russian legislation.

The Judicial Chamber notes that in general the aspiration of journalists to cover the truly complex and urgent problems related to confinement of citizens, who are serving a term of imprisonment, deserves support. What is more, openness of the Russian penitentiary system to the mass media, and thus to public opinion, and penitentiary leaders' support for this situation are essential conditions to ensure that generally accepted principles and norms are observed in the prison system. The right of a journalist to collect and disseminate information, including information about the penitentiary system and its actual problems, is recognized and guaranteed by Russian legislation. However, realization of this right must not become the grounds and excuse for infringing the constitutional rights of citizens, including prisoners, to inviolability of private life.

In this regard, the Judicial Chamber considers it also necessary to note the intolerable inaction by several employees of institution US-20/1 during A.G. Nevzorov's illegal filming.

The Judicial Chamber notes that despite repeated invitations journalist A.G. Nevzorov without valid reason refused to participate in the hearing and explain his actions. It regards the fax he sent as an attempt to replace one question with others and to avoid objective analysis of his broadcast.

Based on these findings and guided by articles 4 and 30 of the Statute on the Russian Federation Presidential Judicial Chamber for Information Disputes, the Judicial Chamber has decided:

1. In light of journalist A.G. Nevzorov's flagrant violation of legal and ethical norms in his "Muckraking" broadcast (of the "Wild Field" series), to recommend that the ORT leadership examine without fail the question of canceling its contract for dissemination of the "Wild Field" program and to send this decision to the ORT leadership.

2. To reprimand journalist A.G. Nevzorov for his flagrant violation of the constitutional and ethical norms that protect the inviolability of citizens' private life.

3. To draw the attention of Russian Public Television General Director S.E. Blagovolin to the need to strengthen control over television programs' observance of citizens' rights and legal interests.

4. To recommend that the Russian Federation Ministry of Internal Affairs adopt measures to prevent future violations of convicts' constitutional rights during filming in prisons.

5. To publish this decision in *Rossiiskaia Gazeta*.

Chairman of the Judicial Chamber

A.B. Vengerov

On Several Cases Involving Violation of Election Campaign Rules, December 9, 1995, No. 3(14)*

The election campaign has entered the final stage. The final week of the period allocated for election campaigning can be decisive in determining the political preference of voters.

How sound these preferences turn out to be depends to a considerable degree on the mass media and on strict observance of election campaign rules and procedures.

The legislator has guaranteed candidates and electoral associations various conditions for access to the mass media. On the whole, these norms are observed.

However, the Judicial Chamber has received numerous appeals from participants in the electoral process complaining of some violation or other of the election campaign rules on the part of television and radio companies.

An utterly intolerable situation occurred in Moscow. The Moskva television and radio company, whose founders include a government organ (*Moskomimushchestvo*) and who as a result is required to provide free airtime to Moscow candidates for deputy, categorically refuses to fulfill this legislative norm and disregards the lawful demands of the Moscow City Electoral Commission and the Judicial Chamber.

Complaints against the All-Russian Television and Radio Company are also piling up. Several of their leaders have "forgotten" about the legal orders contained in point 1.3 of the Russian Federation Central Electoral Commission's Instruction On the Procedure for Allocation of Airtime on State Television and Radio Company Channels . . . .

No one, of course, has deprived journalists, including employees of state television and radio companies, of the right to provide commentary on the election campaign. But what does this right, which is safeguarded by law, have in common with the unexpected appearance on the "Gentlemen" program by the leader of the "Forward Russia" electoral association, V. Fedorov, with his political anecdotes (VGTRK, November 24, 1995)? Or the constant references to the association "Our Home Is Russia" on the "Brain-ring" program (ORT, November 11 and 18, 1995)?

Under what category of election campaigning can one place the hour program on S. Kovalev, one of the leaders of the "Russia's Choice—United Democrats" bloc, which aired on the GTRK, "Petersburg-5th Channel"? There are a sufficient number of such examples to demonstrate that television and radio company leaders have clear political preferences and just as clear disrespect for the law.

---

* Post-Soviet Media Law & Policy Newsletter, Jan. 31, 1996, at 17. Translated by Frances Foster from *Rossiiskaia Gazeta*, Dec. 14, 1995, at 6.

The criticisms of many candidates for deputy and voters about the content of state television news programs are justified. The frequent appearances on these programs by the head of the Russian government, who is also the leader of an electoral association, have gone beyond the bounds of the permissible.

Unfortunately, again and again it is established that candidates for deputy mandates themselves disregard electoral legislation requirements and ethical norms. Many of these issues have already been the subject of examination by the Judicial Chamber and the Central Electoral Commission. Yet, they appear anew.

For example, during the December 6 election airtime of ORT, the head of the Liberal-Democratic Party of Russia, V.V. Zhirinovskii, proposed his method for "implementing order" in the Caucasus: "If even a single shot is fired from any village, if even one Russian soldier is wounded or killed (if you vote for the LDPR), I will give the order to destroy that village! We will destroy 5-6 villages, burn them down completely with napalm, and then there will be no war."

Is this not incitement of nationalist hatred and a gross violation of the Constitution? For his "weapon of retribution" (against women, the elderly and children!), Zhirinovsky has chosen napalm, the use of which has long been denounced and outlawed by the world community.

Another monopolist of the "Russian idea"—N.N. Lysenko, leader of the National-Republican Party of Russia—who has declared himself to be virtually the only person concerned with the interests of the Russian people, proposed a similarly simple and "effective" prescription for the crime problem (aired on Russian television on November 29, 1995). The solution, it turns out, is simply to remove from the Russian territory the "mafia hordes of the Transcaucasian and Central Asian Republics." To support his position, N. Lysenko referred to a certain young Moscow sociological association unknown in sociological circles and cited farfetched statistics that go beyond the bounds of common sense: 60-90% of the most serious crimes in Russia are allegedly committed by those very "immigrants." Of course, he failed to mention the overall level of criminality and its social and legal aspects.

The Judicial Chamber considers it necessary to point out that the election campaign is likely to "continue" even after December 17—in the form of the already numerous lawsuits concerning violations of the election campaign rules.

In evaluating the course of the election campaign, the Judicial Chamber declares its intention to use all means to eliminate violations of election legislation and to hold violators legally accountable for their actions.

In sending this statement to the Central Electoral Commission, electoral associations and blocs, and the mass media, the Judicial Chamber expects that, in the time remaining until the election, all participants in the electoral process will rigorously observe legislative requirements and will not create by their actions grounds for casting doubt on the results of the people's expression of its will.

Chairman of the Judicial Chamber

A.B. Vengerov

On the Publications by E.V. Limonov (Savenko), *Hand Grenade at Croats* and *Black List of Peoples*, in the Newspaper *Limonka*, Nos. 13 and 16 (1995), April 4, 1996, No. 7(90)*

In accordance with article 20 of the Statute on the Russian Federation Presidential Judicial Chamber for Information Disputes, the Judicial Chamber has examined the content of the publications by E.V. Limonov (Savenko), *Hand Grenade at Croats* and *Black List of Peoples*, in the newspaper *Limonka*, Nos. 13 and 16 (1995).

Having familiarized itself with said newspaper materials and having heard the testimony of *Limonka* editor-in-chief E.V. Limonov (Savenko), the secretary of the Union of Moscow Journalists (I.S. Simanchuk), the representative of the Russian Federation Press Committee (N.I. Novikov), and experts (V.A. Shnerel'man, M.A. Mel'nikov, A.A. Malinovskii), and the expert assessment of S.K. Roshchin, the Judicial Chamber has established:

In proclaiming and guaranteeing freedom of thought, speech, and mass information, the Russian Federation Constitution also prohibits propaganda or agitation that incites social, racial, nationalist, or religious hatred and enmity (art. 29).

Propaganda of war, in whatever form, is also prohibited by law and is recognized as a criminal act.

The articles by *Limonka* editor-in-chief E.V. Limonov (Savenko), *Black List of Peoples* and *Hand Grenade at Croats* (reprinted by the newspaper *Novyi Vzgliad* and published as an insert in the newspaper *Moskovskaia Pravda*), contain features that insult entire peoples: Chechens, Czechs, Slovaks, Latvians, Croats, and several others. These publications flagrantly violate legal and ethical norms.

For example, in the publication *Black List of Peoples*, the author discussed the "collective guilt of peoples" and "bad peoples," "substantiating" and justifying Stalinist repression against Chechens, Ingush, and Crimean Tatars. He asserted that Stalin was right to punish minority peoples for their war crimes committed as allies of Hitler's Germany. And this was despite the fact that in contemporary Russia all repressed peoples have been legally rehabilitated and the crimes of Stalin and his allies against these peoples have been unequivocally and sharply condemned. Thus, editor-in-chief E.V. Limonov (Savenko) violated article 4 of the Russian Federation Law On Rehabilitation of Repressed Peoples, which prohibits agitation or propaganda for the purpose of impeding rehabilitation of repressed peoples.

---

* Post-Soviet Media Law & Policy Newsletter, May-June 1996, at 7. Copyright © 1996 Frances Foster. Reprinted by Permission. Translated by Frances Foster from *Rossiiskaia Gazeta*, Apr. 11, 1996, at 6.

Attempting to provide historical support for the thesis that there exist "bad" peoples, E.V. Limonov (Savenko) resorted to substitution of concepts. He claimed that acts by war criminals who were individual representatives or groups from one nationality or another were crimes by entire peoples.

Citing the events of the Russian Civil War and, in particular, the history of the so-called "Czechoslovakian corps," the author went so far as to say that this corps' actions "more than justified a decade of future invasions of the Czech Republic and Slovakia." That is, following the logic of E. V. Limonov (Savenko), responsibility for actions committed seventy years ago by a thousand people ought to be borne by millions of their grandchildren and great-grandchildren.

The author directs analogous threats against the pre-Baltic states ("the terrible and powerful neighbor once in a bad mood will hit you in the head").

In essence, E.V. Limonov (Savenko) is an advocate of revenge and mass terror, raised to the level of state policy.

Moreover, the journalist is an apologist for the insane, misanthropic "theory" that there is an almost genetic predisposition of certain peoples to manifest features such as cruelty and malice on a mass scale and regular basis. For example, in *Hand Grenade at Croats*, he observes that the Croats are "an exceptionally savage people" and concludes with the following wish: "Let their children be born without fingers." Here too the author changes the responsibility of war criminals, which necessarily attaches, into the responsibility of women, the elderly, and children who were guilty of nothing whatsoever.

In the Judicial Chamber's opinion, dissemination of such information by the editorial office and editor-in-chief of the newspaper *Limonka* was illegal and immoral. It represented a violation of article 4 of the Russian Federation Law On the Mass Media—abuse of freedom of mass information in the form of an incitement of nationalist hatred and enmity and propaganda of war.

Such publications in the Russian press also damage the international reputation of the Russian Federation. They are contrary to the international treaty obligations of Russia, its policy of good relations with its neighbors and cooperation, and its programs for peaceful political resolution of the most critical problems of today, especially settlement of military conflicts.

During the hearing, editor-in-chief E.V. Limonov (Savenko) stated that he actually supported the views expressed in these publications. The appearance of the article *Black List of Peoples* was associated with his emotional assessment of the events in the city of Budennovsk. He also explained that he did not consider the legislation violated by dissemination of his publication to be mandatory in its application, since this legislation could be revised in the future.

However, the Judicial Chamber does not regard the arguments of E.V. Limonov (Savenko) as justifying dissemination of said publications.

The Judicial Chamber observes that circulation of such materials through republication in other publications also promotes incitement of nationalist hatred and discord.

Considering the foregoing and guided by articles 8, 10, 11, and 12 of the Statute on the Russian Federation Presidential Judicial Chamber for Information Disputes, the Judicial Chamber has decided:

1. To send the materials of this case to the Russian Federation Press Committee and propose that it issue an official warning to the editorial office of the newspaper *Limonka* regarding the editorial office's violation of article 4 of the Russian Federation Law On the Mass Media in publishing the articles *Hand Grenade at Croats* and *Black List of Peoples* in *Limonka*, Nos. 13 and 16 (1995).

2. To send the materials of this case to the Moscow procuracy to examine whether *Limonka* editor-in-chief E.V. Limonov (Savenko) can be held legally responsible.

3. To publish this decision in *Rossiiskaia Gazeta*.

Chairman of the Judicial Chamber

A.B. Vengerov

On the Application of the Principle of Presumption of Innocence in Journalists' Activity (On an Inquiry from the Moscow Media Law and Policy Center), December 24, 1997, No. 3(10)*

The Judicial Chamber for Information Disputes under the President of the Russian Federation has received from the Moscow Media Law and Policy Center a letter of inquiry as to whether the principle of presumption of innocence as it is used in law may act as a limit to the professional activity of a journalist who is not an official.

The reason for this inquiry was the fact that the State Duma of the Federal Assembly of the Russian Federation had passed at the first reading the Bill On Television and Radio Broadcasting, Paragraph 1 of article 18 of which lays down that "broadcasters shall be obliged: . . . not to spread any information that may violate a presumption of innocence or predetermine a court decision . . . ."

After examining this inquiry, the Judicial Chamber has come to the following conclusion:

In the Russian legal system, the generally accepted legal principle of presumption of innocence is explicitly stated in part 1, article 49 of the Constitution of the Russian Federation.

Under the rule of this article, the accused (i.e., the person charged with an offence by the procedure set out in the Criminal Procedure Code of the RSFSR) is presumed to be innocent until and unless his guilt has been proven under the federal law and adjudged by a valid verdict of a court.

The Judicial Chamber, however, maintains that only those government bodies and government officials that are empowered to impose limitations on human and civil rights and liberties are responsible for observing the principle of presumption of innocence in the sense set out in the constitutional rule.

Only courts of justice can decide whether anyone guilty of a crime or offence and determine all legal consequences they shall suffer.

Now, where journalists are conducting their own investigations or reporting pre-trial investigation in a criminal case, they are in fact realizing their freedom of communication as a constitutional right, on the one hand, and fulfilling their professional duty by informing the public of issues of public interest, on the other hand.

Journalists are not persons empowered to restrict anyone's rights and liberties. For this reason, opinions of any journalist broadcast on television or radio or published in

* Post-Soviet Media Law & Policy Newsletter, Jan. 15, 1998, at 36. Translated by Andrei Richter.

any periodical cannot, by virtue of the constitutional rule referred to above, legally affect anyone's right to plead not guilty.

For the same reasons, it seems illegitimate to demand broadcaster "not to spread any information . . . that may predetermine a court decision." Indeed, only a court of justice can establish anyone's guilt. But this cannot be taken as a ground for restricting the rights of journalists or any other persons (including representatives of the prosecution and the defense, victims, suspects and others) to expound their views on any aspects of a pre-trial investigation or trial proceedings, except where statements made by any of the aforesaid persons in the media contain signs of any of the offences as provided for in Chapter 31 (Offences against Justice) of the Criminal Code of the Russian Federation.

The Judicial Chamber maintains, then, that the provision of the bill that the rights of journalists to publish and broadcast information must be restricted on the ground that they thereby may violate a presumption of innocence or may predetermine a court decision is in fact an unjustified attempt to narrow significantly the range of the freedom of communication set down by the Constitution of the Russian Federation.

Applied in practice, a rule worded like this one would in fact amount to a ban on journalist investigations and comment on pre-trial investigations and trial proceedings in cases of significant public interest.

The Judicial Chamber maintains that the whole body of journalists' responsibilities as established by the law to check the truth of the information they publish or broadcast, respect the right, legitimate interests, honor and dignity of individuals and institutions, and not to use the media for disclosing secrets protected under the law (including the secrets of legal investigation, and secrets of correspondence and telephone conversations) seems sufficient to provide the protection (judicial protection as well) of the rights and legitimate interests of individuals and institutions against possible abuses of the freedom of communication.

Given all this, the Judicial Chamber is addressing the Committee for Information Policy and Communications of the State Duma of the Russian Federation's Federal Assembly with a recommendation that discussion of the rule in part 1, article 18 of the Bill On Television and Radio Broadcasting should be resumed, taking into consideration all the arguments suggested herein.

Igor Yeremin

Deputy Chairman

Judicial Chamber

II.

STATUTES AND DECREES

Constitution of the Russian Federation (Excerpts)

December 12, 1993

Article 15.

1. The Constitution of the Russian Federation shall have supreme legal force and direct effect, and shall be applicable throughout the entire territory of the Russian Federation. Laws and other legal acts adopted by the Russian Federation may not contravene the Constitution of the Russian Federation.

2. Organs of state power and local self-government, officials, citizens and their associations must comply with the laws and the Constitution of the Russian Federation.

. . . .

4. The commonly recognized principles and norms of the international law and the international treaties of the Russian Federation shall be a component part of its legal system. If an international treaty of the Russian Federation stipulates other rules than those stipulated by the law, the rules of the international treaty shall apply.

Article 17.

1. The basic rights and freedoms in conformity with the commonly recognized principles and norms of international law shall be recognized and guaranteed in the Russian Federation and under this Constitution.

2. The basic rights and freedoms of the human being shall be inalienable and shall belong to everyone from birth.

3. The exercise of rights and freedoms of a human being and citizen may not violate the rights and freedoms of other persons.

Article 18.

The rights and freedoms of man and citizen shall have direct effect. They shall determine the meaning, content and application of the laws, and the activities of the legislative and executive branches and local self-government, and shall be secured by the judiciary.

Article 21.

1. The dignity of the person shall be protected by the state. No circumstance may be used to justify its diminution.

. . . .

Article 23.

1. Each person shall have the right to the inviolability of private life, personal and family secrecy, and protection of one's honor and good name.

. . . .

Article 29.

1. Each person is guaranteed freedom of thought and speech.

2. Propaganda or agitation exciting social, racial, national or religious hatred and enmity is not permitted. Propaganda of social, racial, national, religious or language supremacy is prohibited.

3. No one may be compelled to express his or her opinions and convictions or to renounce them.

4. Each person has the right freely to seek, receive, pass on, produce and disseminate information by any lawful method. The list of information constituting a state secret is determined by federal law.

5. The freedom of mass information is guaranteed. Censorship is prohibited.

Article 55.

. . . .

2. Laws which deny or diminish human and civil rights and freedoms shall not be enacted in the Russian Federation.

3. Human and civil rights and freedoms can be curtailed by federal law only to the extent to which it may be necessary for the purpose of protecting the foundations of the constitutional system, morality and the health, rights and legitimate interests of other individuals, or of ensuring the country's defense and the state's security.

Article 125.

. . . .

4. The Constitutional Court of the Russian Federation, proceeding from complaints about violations of constitutional rights and freedoms of citizens and requests from courts shall review the constitutionality of the law applied or due to be applied in a specific case in accordance with procedures established by federal law.

Federal Law No. 2124-1
On the Mass Media

December 27, 1991

***As Amended on* January 13, 1995, June 6, 1995, July 19, 1995, December 27, 1995, March 2, 1998, May 24, 2000, *and* July 7, 2000**

Chapter I. General Provisions.

Article 1. Freedom of Mass Communication.

In the Russian Federation, the retrieval, receipt, production and dissemination of mass communication, the foundation of mass media, the possession, use and disposal of these media, the manufacture, acquisition, storage and use of technical facilities and equipment, raw and auxiliary materials designed for the production and spread of products of mass information media; shall not be restricted unless prescribed by the legislation of the Russian Federation on mass media.

Article 2. Mass Media: Basic Notions.

For purposes of the present Law:

- *mass communication* shall be understood to mean printed, audio and audio-visual and other messages and materials intended for an unlimited range of persons;
- *mass media* shall be understood to mean a periodical printed publication, a radio, television or video program, a newsreel program, and any other form of periodical dissemination of mass information;
- *the periodical printed publication* shall be understood to mean a newspaper, magazine or journal, almanac, bulletin, any other publication with a constant name, current issue and coming out at least once in a year;
- *mass media products* shall be understood to mean the total print or part of the total print of the separate issue of a periodical printed publication, a separate issue of a radio, TV or newsreel program, the total print or part of the total print and audio or video recording program;
- *the dissemination of mass media products* shall be understood to mean the sale (subscription, delivery or distribution) of periodical printed publications, audio and video recording programs, broadcasting of radio and TV programs, demonstration of newsreel programs;
- *specialized mass media* shall be understood to mean such mass media for the registration or dissemination of whose products the present Law provides for special rules;

- *mass media editor's office* shall be understood to mean an organization, institution, enterprise or a private citizen and association of private citizens, which produce and issue mass media;
- *the editor-in-chief* shall be understood to mean a person heading the editorial staff (regardless of the name of the post) and taking final decisions on the production and issue of mass media;
- *the journalist* shall be understood to mean a person who edits, creates, collects or prepares messages and materials for the editor's office of a mass medium and is connected with it with labor and other contractual relations or engaged in such activity, being authorized by it;
- *the publisher* shall be understood to mean a publishing house or any other enterprise (entrepreneur) who is responsible for material and technical supplies of the production of mass medium products and also a legal entity or a private citizen who is the functional equivalent of the publisher and for whom this activity is not the key one or does not serve as the main source of income;
- *the distributor* shall be understood to mean a person who disseminates mass medium products under the agreement with the editor's office and publisher or on any other legal grounds.

Article 3. Inadmissibility of Censorship.

No provision shall be made for the censorship of mass information, that is, the demand made by officials, state organs, organization, institutions or public associations that the editor's office of a mass medium shall get in advance agreement on a message and materials (except for the cases when the official is an auditor or interviewee) and also for the suppression of the dissemination of messages and materials and separate parts thereof.

No provision shall be made for the creation and financing of organizations, institutions, organs or offices whose functions include the censorship of mass information.

Article 4. Inadmissibility of Misuse of the Freedom of Mass Communication.

No provision shall be made for the use of mass media for purposes of committing criminally indictable deeds, divulging information making up a state secret or any other law-protective secret, calling for the seizure of power, violently changing the constitutional system and the state integrity, fanning national, class, social and religious intolerance or strife, propagating war, and also for the spreading of broadcasts propagandizing pornography or the cult of violence and cruelty.

It shall be prohibited to use—in the television, video and cinema programs, in documentary and feature films, and also in information computer files and in the programs of the processing of information texts belonging to special mass information media concealed in-sets influencing the subconscious of human beings and/or affecting their health.

It shall be prohibited to disseminate in mass media, as well as in via computer networks information on the means, methods of development, production and use, places of trade of narcotics, psychotropic substances and their precursors, propagating of any advantages of use of separate narcotics, psychotropic substances, their analogues and precursors with the exception of advertising of narcotic means and psychotropic substances, included in lists II and III in accordance with the Federal Law On Narcotic Means and Psychotropic Substances—in mass media, targeted for the medical and pharmaceutical workers, as well as any other information, dissemination of which is prohibited by federal laws.

Article 4 of the present Law was amended by Federal Law No. 114-FZ of July 19, 1995. The third paragraph was added by Federal Law No. 90-FZ of May 24, 2000.

Article 5. Legislation on Mass Media.

The legislation of the Russian Federation on mass media consists of the present Law and other legislative acts promulgated in accordance with it, and also of legislative acts on mass media adopted by the Republics within the Russian Federation.

If an inter-state agreement concluded by the Russian Federation provides for the organization and functioning of mass media the rules different from those established by the present Law, the rules of the inter-state agreement shall be applicable.

Article 6. The Application of the Law.

The present Law shall be applicable to mass media founded in the Russian Federation and to those set up beyond its borders only in respect of the dissemination of their products in the Russian Federation.

Legal entities and citizens of other States and stateless persons shall enjoy the rights and bear the duties envisaged by the present Law on a par with the organizations and citizens of the Russian Federation, unless otherwise stipulated by law.

Chapter II. Organization of Mass Media Activity.

Article 7. Founders.

An individual, association of individuals, enterprise, institution, organization or a state body may be a founder (or co-founder) of a mass medium.

The following persons and bodies may not act as founders:

- a private citizen who has not reached 18 years of age, an individual who serves his or her order punishment in places of confinement according to the court's sentence, or an insane person recognized as legally unfit by a court of law;
- an association of private citizens, enterprise, institution and organization whose activity is banned by law;

- a citizen of another State or a stateless person who is not domiciled in the Russian Federation.

  Co-founders shall act jointly as a mass media founder.

Article 8. Registration of a Mass Medium.

The mass medium editor's office shall carry on its activity after its registration.

The application for the registration of a mass medium whose products are intended for the dissemination chiefly:

- in the entire territory of the Russian Federation, beyond its borders and in the territory of several Republics within the Russian Federation, several territories and regions shall be submitted by its founder to the Ministry of the Press and Information of the Russian Federation;
- in the territory of a Republic within the Russian Federation, a territory, region, district, town, other populated locality, ward, and a micro-district—shall be submitted by its founder to the respective territorial bodies of the State Inspectorate for the Protection of Freedom of the Press and Mass Information under the Ministry of the Press and Information of the Russian Federation.

A notification about the receipt of an application with the indication of its date shall be sent to the founder or the person authorized by it therefor. The application shall be subject to consideration by the registration body within a month since the said date.

A mass medium shall be deemed to be registered since the issue of a registration certificate.

The founder shall retain the right of putting out its mass medium's products during one year since the day of the issue of the registration certificate. If this term is missed, the registration certificate shall be recognized as null and void.

Article 9. Inadmissibility of a Repeated Registration.

A registered medium may not be registered for the second time by the same or different registration body.

If a court of law ascertains the fact of a repeated registration, the first registration shall be recognized.

Article 10. The Application for Registration.

The application for the registration of a mass medium shall indicate:

- information about the founder (or co-founders) provided for by the present Law;
- the name of a mass medium;
- language (languages) to be used;
- address of its editor's office;
- a form of periodical dissemination of mass communication;

- the supposed area of the spread of products;
- approximate topics and/or specialization;
- the supposed periodicity of issue and maximum extent of a mass medium;
- sources of financing;
- information about the mass media in which the applicant is a founder, owner, editor-in-chief in the editorial office or distributor.

The document certifying the payment of a registration fee shall be appended to the application.

It shall be forbidden to make any other demands during the registration of mass media.

Article 11. Re-registration and Notification.

The replacement of a founder, the change of co-founders and the alteration of the name, language, and form of the periodical dissemination of mass communication, the area where the mass medium products are spread shall be allowed subject to the re-registration of this mass medium.

Mass media shall be re-registered in the same order as they are registered.

A mass medium whose activity is terminated by decision of a court of law shall not be re-registered.

If the editorial office changes its place of location, alters the periodicity of its issue and maximum size, the founder shall be obliged to notify in written form the registration body within a month.

Article 12. Release from Registration.

No registration is required for the following mass media:

- the mass information media founded by the organs of legislative, executive and judicial power to publish nothing but their official communications and materials, normative and other acts;
- periodicals with a total print of less than one thousand copies;
- radio and television programs disseminated through cable networks, limited by the premises and area of one governmental institution, educational establishment industrial enterprise or organization that has not more than ten subscribers;
- audio- and video-programs spread in recording with a total printing of not more than ten copies.

Article 13. Refusal of Registration.

The refusal of registration of a mass medium is possible on the following grounds alone:

- if an application is filled on behalf of a private citizen, association of individuals, an enterprise, institution or organization not possessing the right of instituting mass media in keeping with the present Law;
- if information indicated in an application does not correspond to the reality;
- if the name, approximate topics and/or the specialization of a mass medium represent an abuse of the freedom of mass communication in terms of the first part of Article 4 of the present Law;
- if the respective registration body or the Ministry of the Press and Information of the Russian Federation has registered earlier a mass medium with the same name and form of dissemination of mass communication.

A notification about the refusal of registration shall be forwarded to the applicant in written form with the indication of the grounds for the refusal provided for by the present Law.

The application for the registration of a mass medium shall be returned to the applicant without consideration, with the indication of a ground for the return:

- if the application has been filed with the violation of the requirements of the second part of Article 8 or the first part of Article 10 of the present Law;
- if the application on behalf of the founder has been filed by the person who has no authority for this;
- if a registration fee has not been paid.

The application shall be accepted for consideration after the removal of violations.

Article 14. The Registration Fee.

A registration fee shall be collected for the issue of a registration certificate in the order and amounts defined by the Government of the Russian Federation. A higher registration fee shall be established for mass media specializing in the issue of communications and advertising and erotic materials, while a reduced registration fee shall be introduced for mass media specializing in the issue of communications and materials intended for children, adolescents and disabled persons and used for educational, cultural and enlightening purposes.

In case of a refusal of registration and equally of a refusal to undergo registration the applicant shall have the right to obtain refund for the registration fee during three months beginning with the date of receipt of a registration application indicated in the notification. The document testifying to the payment of a registration fee shall be a ground for the return of money in the place of its payment. At the request of the applicant the note ("Not registered") shall be made on this document by the registration body.

Article 15. Recognition of a Registration Certificate as Null and Void.

A certificate of the mass medium registration may be recognized as null and void exclusively by a court of law in civil proceedings upon the statement by the registration body or the Ministry of the Press and Information of the Russian Federation only in the following cases:

- if a registration certificate has been obtained by fraud;
- if a mass medium does not appear (does not go on air) for a term exceeding one year;
- if the statutes of an editorial office or the agreement replacing them has not been adopted and/or has not been approved during three months since the first publication or airing of the given mass medium;
- if the given mass medium has been registered for the second time.

The registration fee shall not be subject to return upon the recognition of a registration certificate as invalid.

Article 16. Termination or Suspension of Activity.

The functioning of a mass medium may be terminated or suspended only by decision of its founder or by a court of law in civil proceedings at the suit filed by the registration body or the Ministry of the Press and Information of the Russian Federation.

The founder shall have the right to terminate or suspend the functioning of a mass medium exclusively in cases and in the order envisaged by the statutes of the editorial office or the agreement concluded between the founder and the editorial office (or editor-in-chief).

Repeated (during twelve months) breaches by the editorial office of the requirements of Article 4 of the present Law, on whose occasion the registration body or the Ministry of the Press and Information of the Russian Federation has made written warnings to the founder and/or the editorial office (or editor-in-chief) and likewise the non-execution of the court's ruling on the suspension of the mass medium shall be grounds for the termination of the activity of the mass medium by the court of law.

Only the need for the security for a suit, envisaged by the first part of this Article may serve as a ground for suspension by a court of law of the activity of a mass medium. The termination of the functioning of a mass medium shall entail the invalidity of the certificate of its registration and the statutes of the editorial office.

Article 17. Accrual of Rights and Duties.

The rights and duties of the founder and the editorial office stipulated by the present Law shall emerge since the time of registration of a mass medium, while those envisaged by the statutes of the editorial office shall emerge since the time of their approval. The founder, editorial office, publisher or distributor may in addition institute mutual rights and duties on a contractual basis. The provisions of the statutes and agreements shall not run counter with the present Law and other legislative acts of the Russian Federation.

Article 18. The Status of a Founder.

The founder shall approve the statutes of an editorial office and/or conclude an agreement with the editorial office (or editor-in-chief) of a mass medium.

The founder shall be free to oblige the editorial office to feature free of charge or within the specified period a message or material on his or her behalf (the statement of the founder). The maximum scope of the founder's statement shall be determined by the statutes of an editorial office, its agreement or any other contract concluded with the founder. The founder shall be liable for claims and suits connected with his or her statement. If the fact that the said message or material belongs to the founder has not been stipulated by the editorial office, the latter shall act as a co-defendant.

The founder shall have no right to interfere in the activity of a mass medium, except for the cases provided for by the present Law, the statutes of its editorial office or the agreement concluded between the founder and the editorial office (or editor-in-chief).

The founder may transfer his or her rights and duties to a third person with the consent of the editorial office and the co-founders. If the founder—the association of private citizens, the enterprise, institution, organization, state body—is liquidated or reorganized, its rights and duties shall transfer in full to the editorial office, unless otherwise provided for by its statutes.

The founder may act as an editorial office, publisher, distributor or owner of the editorial office's property.

Article 19. The Status of an Editorial Office.

The editorial office shall carry on its activity on the basis of its professional independence.

The editorial office may be a legal entity or an independent business subject organized in any form admitted by the law. If the office of a registered mass medium is organized as an enterprise, it shall also be subject to registration in accordance with the legislation of the Russian Federation on enterprises and business activity and shall be free to carry on in a statutory manner a different activity not banned by the law in addition to the production and issue of a mass medium.

The editorial office shall be exempted from tax payments during two years since the day of the first publication (airing) of a mass medium. The re-registration of a mass medium shall not influence the estimation of the given period. If the founder has ceased the functioning of a mass medium until the expiration of said period, payments shall be collected in full amount for the entire term.

The editorial office may act as a founder of a mass medium, publisher, distributor or owner of the editorial office's property.

The editorial office shall be directed by the editor-in-chief, who discharges his or her powers on the basis of the present Law, the office's statutes or the agreement concluded between the founder and the editorial office (or editor-in-chief). The editor-in-chief shall represent the editorial office in his or her relations with the founder, publisher, distributor, private citizens, their associations, enterprises, institutions, organizations and state organs, and also in court. He or she shall bear responsibility for the fulfillment of the requirements made on the activity of a mass medium by the present Law and other legislative acts of the Russian Federation.

Article 20. The Statutes of an Editorial Office.

The statutes of a mass medium's editorial office shall be adopted at the general meeting of the collective of journalists (the editorial office employees on the staff) by a majority vote in the presence of not less than two thirds of its membership and shall be endorsed by the founder.

The statutes of the editorial office shall define:

- the mutual rights and duties of the founder, editorial office and the editor-in-chief;
- the powers of the collective of journalists, the editorial office employees on the staff;
- the order of appointment (election) of the editor-in-chief, editorial board and/or other organs of management of the editorial office;
- the grounds and order of termination and suspension of the functioning of a mass medium;
- the transfer and/or preservation of the right to the name, other legal consequences of the change-over of the founder, changes in the composition of the co-founders, the termination of the mass medium's activity, the liquidation or reorganization of the editorial office, and the alteration of its organizational structure and legal status;
- the order of confirmation and alteration of the statutes of the editorial office, and also other provisions envisaged by the present Law and other legislative acts.

Pending the confirmation of the statutes of the editorial office and also in case when the latter consists of less than ten persons, its relations with the founder, including the questions listed in Items 1-5 of the second part of the present Article, may be determined by the agreement between the founder and the editorial office (or editor-in-chief) that replaces the statutes.

The statutes of the editorial office organized as an enterprise may be simultaneously the statutes of the given enterprise. In this case the editorial office's statutes shall correspond to the legislation on enterprises and business activity.

The copy of the editorial office's statutes or the agreement that replaces then shall be forwarded to the registration body not later than three months since the day of the first publication (airing) of the given mass medium. In this case the editorial office shall be entitled to specify which information contained in its statutes or the agreement that substitutes the latter constitutes a commercial secret.

Article 21. The Status of a Publisher.

The publisher shall implement its rights and bear its duties on the basis of the present Law, the Federal Law on the Procedure of Giving Information About the Activity of the Bodies of State Power in the State Mass Media, the legislation on publishing business, enterprises and entrepreneurial activity.

The publisher may act as a founder of a mass medium, editorial office, distributor or owner of its property.

Federal Law of the Russian Federation No. 6-FZ of January 13, 1995, amended the first part of Article 21 of this Law.

Article 22. Agreements.

The agreement concluded between the co-founders of a mass medium shall determine their mutual rights, duties, responsibility, the order, terms and the legal consequences of changes in the composition of the founders, and the procedure for the adjustment of disputes between them.

The agreement concluded between the founder and the editorial office (or editor-in-chief) shall determine the production, property and financial relations between them: the order of assignment and use of monetary resources on the upkeep of the editorial office, the allocation of profit, the formation of funds and the compensation for losses, the obligations of the founder to provide proper production, welfare, living and working conditions of the editorial office's employees. Every co-founder or all the co-founders together may act as a party to the agreement with the editorial office.

The agreement concluded between the editorial office and the publisher shall determine the production, property and financial relations between them, the mutual distribution of the right of publication, the obligations of the publisher for the material and technical supply of the production of the mass medium items, and the responsibilities of the parties.

The founder, editorial office (or editor-in-chief) and the publisher may also conclude other agreements between themselves, and with the distributor as well.

Article 23. News Agencies.

The status of the editorial office, publisher, distributor and the legal treatment of mass media shall also extend to the news agencies in the process of applying the present Law.

A bulletin, newsletter, any other publication or program with a permanent name set up by a news agency shall be registered in the order prescribed by this Law.

When messages and materials of a news agency is disseminated by another mass medium, reference to the news agency shall be obligatory.

Article 24. Other Mass Media.

The rules introduced by this Law for periodical printed publications shall be applicable to the periodical dissemination with a total print of 1,000 and over copies of the texts formed with the aid of computers and/or kept in their databanks or databases, and also to any other mass media whose printed output is spread in the form of messages, materials and pictures.

The rules introduced by this Law for radio and TV programs shall be applicable to the periodical dissemination of mass communication through teletext and videotext systems and other telecommunication networks, unless otherwise provided for by the legislation of the Russian Federation.

Chapter III. Mass Communication.

Article 25. The Order of Dissemination.

Private citizens, their associations, officials, enterprises, institutions, organizations and state agencies shall not be allowed to prevent the lawful dissemination of mass communication products.

The dissemination of mass communication products shall be deemed to be commercial, if payments are made for them. Products designed for non-profit dissemination shall have the note "gratis" and may not be an object of commercial circulation.

The demonstration of video recordings in living quarters and also the taking of single copies of them, unless a payment is made directly or indirectly, shall not be regarded as the dissemination of mass communication products in the meaning of the present Law.

The retail sale of periodical publications, including sale from hand to hand, shall not be liable to limitations, except for the publications provided for by the present Law. The retail sale of the total print of periodicals in places which are not of public resort—in special premises or in other facilities where a special regime has been instituted by their owner or the person authorized to manage his or her property—shall be allowed only with the consent of said persons.

In case the editorial office, publisher or distributor violates the author's property or personal non-property rights and in other cases provided for by the law, the dissemination of mass communication products may be terminated by decision of a court of law.

Article 26. Airing.

Mass communication products shall be disseminated only after the editor-in-chief permits publication or airing.

Article 27. Publisher's Imprint.

Every issue of a periodical printed publication shall contain the following information:

- the name of the publication;
- the founder (or co-founders);
- the full name of the editor-in-chief;
- the ordinal number of the issue and the date of its appearance and for newspapers also the time of signing for press (under the adjusted schedule and actual time);
- postal index for publications distributed by post offices;
- total circulation;
- price or the note "free-market price" or "grants";
- the addresses of the editorial office, publisher and the printing house.

With every airing of a radio or TV program and during the uninterrupted broadcasting at least four times a day the editorial office shall be obliged to announce the program name.

Every copy of audio-, video- or newsreel program shall contain the following information:

- the program name;
- the date of appearance (or run) and the issue number;
- the name and initials of the editor-in-chief;
- total circulation;
- the editorial office and its address;
- price or note "free-market price" or "grants."

Reports and materials of a news agency shall be accompanied with its name.

If a mass medium is not released from registration, the import shall also indicate the registration body and the respective registration number.

Article 28. Total Circulation.

The total circulation of a periodical printed publication, an audio-, video- and newsreel program shall be determined by the editor-in-chief by agreement with the publisher.

The confiscation and also the destruction of the circulation or the part thereof shall be allowed only by the decision of a court of law that has entered into force.

A circulation fee shall be instituted for mass media specializing in the production of advertising or erotic products and collected in the order determined by the Government of the Russian Federation.

Article 29. Deposit Copies.

Obligatory free deposit copies of periodicals, including those released from registration on the strength of Article 12 of the present Law shall be sent upon the manufacture of the initial issue of the print by the editorial office to the founder (or co-founders), the body that has registered the given mass medium, the Ministry of the Press and Information of the Russian Federation, the Scientific and Production Association of the All-Union Book Chamber, the Lenin State Library of the USSR, the Saltykov-Shchedrin State Public Library, the Library of the Supreme Soviet of the Russian Federation and the Library of the President of the Russian Federation.

The Ministry of the Press and Information of the Russian Federation shall have the right to oblige the editorial offices to send paid copies to other institutions and organizations as well.

Article 30. The Federal Television and Radio Broadcasting Commission.

The Federal Television and Radio Broadcasting Commission shall elaborate the state policy in the field of licensing radio and TV broadcasting and pursue it both directly or through the territorial TV and radio broadcasting commissions.

The order of forming and operating the Federal Television and Radio Broadcasting Commission and territorial commissions shall be determined by the Law of the Russian Federation.

Federal Law No. 87-FZ of June 6, 1995, On Amending the Law of the Russian Federation on Mass Media amended Article 30 of this Law.

Article 31. Licenses for Broadcasting.

Broadcasting licenses shall be issued by the Federal Television and Radio Broadcasting Commission and territorial commissions.

The broadcasting licenses shall give to its holder the right to disseminate mass media products registered in keeping with the present Law by using the technical means of air or cable television or radio broadcasting, including that owned by him or her subject to the observance of the license terms.

If there is no technical possibility of broadcasting with stated characteristics or with those related to them, the broadcasting license shall not be issued.

The broadcasting license may be denied on the grounds provided for by the competition terms, if applications are considered on a contest basis.

The concession of a broadcasting license to another person shall be allowed only with the consent of the body that has issued it with the appropriate reissuing of the license.

The amount and order of collecting the payment for a broadcasting license, and also for the reissuing of the license, shall be established by the Government of the Russian Federation.

Federal Law No. 87-FZ of June 6, 1995, On Amending the Law of the Russian Federation on Mass Media amended paragraph 1 of Article 31 of this Law.

Article 32. Cancellation of a License.

A license shall be cancelled in the following cases:

- if it was received by fraud;
- if license terms have been repeatedly broken or the rules for disseminating radio and TV programs, provided for by the present Law, have been violated, in connection with which warnings have been made in written form;
- if the broadcasting commission has ascertained the fact of concealed concession of a license.

The laws of the Russian Federation may provide for additional grounds for the cancellation of licenses.

The license shall be cancelled by decision of the body that has granted it or by the Federal Television and Radio Broadcasting Commission.

When a license has been cancelled, the payment for it shall not be returned.

Article 33. Radio and Television Jamming.

The creation of jamming that prevents the sure reception of radio and TV programs, that is, the spread of radio, TV and other technical signals in the frequency band in which broadcasts are made under the license, shall entail responsibility in keeping with the legislation of the Russian Federation.

Industrial jamming arising during the operation of technical devices in the course of economic activity shall be removed at the expense of the persons owning or managing the source of this jamming.

Article 34. The Storekeeping of Radio and TV Broadcasting Materials.

In order to obtain evidence of importance for the proper adjustment of disputes, the radio and TV program sections shall be obliged:

- to preserve the materials of their own broadcasts recorded and aired;
- to fix broadcast that has gone on air in their registration log;

  The registration log shall indicate the date and time of going on air, the topic of a broadcast, its author, announcer and participants.

  The terms of storekeeping shall be as follows:

- for broadcast materials—not less than one month since the day of going on air;
- for the registration log—not less than one year since the date of the latest entry in it.

Article 35. Obligatory Reports.

The editorial office shall be obliged to publish free of charge and in the prescribed period:

- the court's decision that has come into force and contains the demand for its publication in a given mass medium;
- the report on the functioning of an editorial office, received from the body that has registered the given mass medium.

The editorial offices of the mass media founded by state agencies shall be obliged to publish on the demand of these agencies their official reports in the order regulated by their statutes or the agreements that replace them, and also other materials whose publication in these mass media is provided for by the legislation of the Russian Federation.

The state mass media must publish information and materials of the federal bodies of state power and of the bodies of state power of the entities of the Russian Federation in the procedure established by the Federal Law On the Procedure of Giving Information About the Activity of the Bodies of State Power in the State Mass Media.

The editorial offices of the state mass media must release (broadcast) without delay and free of charge upon the demand of the State Fire-Fighting Service of the Ministry of the Interior of the Russian Federation operational information on issues of fire safety.

Federal Law of the Russian Federation No. 6-FZ of January 13, 1995, introduced the third part to Article 35 of this Law.

Federal Law of the Russian Federation No. 211-FZ of December 27, 1995, introduced the fourth part to Article 35 of this Law.

Article 36. Advertisement Distribution.

Dissemination of advertising in mass media shall be carried on according to the rules set by the legislation of the Russian Federation on advertising.

As formulated in the Federal Law of the Russian Federation No. 30-FZ of March 2, 1998.

Article 37. Erotic Publications.

A mass medium specializing in erotic reports and materials shall be understood to mean for purposes of the present Law a periodical edition or a program, which in general and systematically use public interest in sex.

The distribution of the issues of specialized radio and TV erotic programs without signal coding shall be allowed only from 11 p.m. to 4 a.m., local time, unless otherwise stipulated by the local administration.

The retail sale of the products of mass media specializing in erotic reports and materials shall be allowed only in sealed transport packages and specially designed premises, the arrangement of which is determined by the local administration.

Chapter IV. Relations of Mass Media with Private Citizens and Organizations.

Article 38. The Right to Information.

Through mass media private citizens shall have the right to the operative receipt of authentic information about the activities of state organs and organizations, public associations and their officials.

State organs and organizations, public associations and their officials shall submit information about their activities to mass media in reply to the inquiries of editorial offices or broadcasting sections, and also by holding press conferences, circulating reference and statistical materials and other forms.

Article 39. Information Inquiry.

The editorial office or broadcasting section shall have the right to request information about the activities of state organs and organizations, public associations and their officials. The request for information is possible both in oral and written form. This information shall be submitted by the heads of said organs, organizations and associations, their deputies, press service workers or other persons authorized within their terms of reference.

Article 40. Refusal to Submit Information and Delayed Information.

Refusal to submit requested information is possible if only the latter contains the data comprising a state, commercial or any other secret specially protected by the law. A notification about the refusal shall be handed over to the representative of an editorial office within three days since the day of the receipt of the inquiry about said information.

The notification shall indicate:

- the reasons why requested information cannot be separated from the information comprising a specially law-protected secret;
- the official who refuses to submit information;
- the date of decision-taking on the refusal.

A delay in submitting requested information is possible, if the required data cannot be presented within seven days. A notification about the delay shall be handed over to the representative of an editorial office within three days since the day of receipt of the written inquiry of information.

The notification shall indicate:

- the reasons why the requested information cannot be presented within seven days;
- the date on which requested information will be presented;
- the official who fixes the delay;

- the date of decision-taking on the refusal.

Article 41. Confidential Information.

The editorial office shall not have the right to divulge in distributed reports and materials the information submitted by a private citizen with the proviso of keeping this information secret.

The editorial office shall be obliged to keep the source of information secret and shall not have the right to name the person who has submitted information with the proviso of non-divulgence of his or her name, except for the case when the corresponding demand came from a court of law in connection with the case it disposes of.

The editorial office shall not have the right to divulge in distributed reports and materials the information, that directly or indirectly points to the identity of a minor who committed a criminal offence or is suspected in doing it, as well as one who committed a juvenile delinquency or a misdemeanor, without permission of the minor and his/her legitimate representative.

The editorial office shall not have the right to divulge in distributed reports and materials the information, that directly or indirectly points to the identity of a minor who is found a victim, without permission of the minor and/or his/her legitimate representative.

The third and fourth paragraphs were added by Federal Law No. 110-FZ of July 7, 2000.

Article 42. Author's Works and Letters.

The editorial office shall be obliged to observe the rights to the used works, including copyrights, the rights of publication and other intellectual property rights. The author or any other person who possesses the right to a work may stipulate the special terms and character of using the work he or she presents to the editorial office.

The letter addressed to an editorial office may be used in reports and materials of the given mass medium, unless its meaning is distorted and the provisions of this Law are violated. The editorial office shall not be obliged to answer the letters sent by private citizens and to send these letters to the organs, organizations and officials which are competent to consider them.

No one has the right to oblige the editorial office to publish the work, letter or any other communication it has declined, unless otherwise provided for by law.

Article 43. The Right of Refutation.

A private citizen or organization shall have the right to demand from the editorial office disproof of information that does not correspond to the reality and denigrates their honor and dignity and that was spread by the given mass medium. The same right shall belong to the lawful representatives of the person, if he or she has no opportunity of demanding refutation. If the editorial office of a mass medium does not possess evidence of the fact that the information it has disseminated corresponds to the reality, it shall be obliged to refute this information in the same mass medium.

If a private citizen or organization has submitted the text of refutation, this text shall be subject to dissemination provided it complies with the requirements of the present Law. The radio or television program section, which is obliged to spread the refutation, may enable the person or the representative of the organization who demands the refutation to read out his or her own text and transit it in transcription.

Article 44. The Order of Refutation.

The refutation shall indicate which information does not correspond to the reality, when and how it was spread by the given mass medium.

Refutation published in a periodical printed publication shall be set up with the same type and featured under the heading "Refutation," as a rule, in the same place where the refuted report or material is placed. Over radio and television the refutation shall be transmitted at the same time of a day and, as a rule, in the same broadcast that the refuted report or material is transmitted.

The scope of refutation may not exceed twice as much the scope of the reflected fragment of the report or material. It shall not be demanded that the text of the refutation be shorter than one standard page of the typewritten text. The refutation transmitted over radio or television shall not take up less airtime than is required for the announcer to read out one standard page of the typewritten text.

The refutation shall follow:

- in mass media that are to be published or go on air at least one time in a week during ten days since the receipt of the demand about the refutation or of its text;
- in other mass media, in the prepared or in the text planned issue.

During one month since the day of receipt of the demand for refutation or its text the editorial office shall be obliged to notify in written form the interested person or organization about the supposed time-limit of the dissemination of the refutation or about the refusal of its spread with the indication of the grounds for the refusal.

Article 45. Grounds for the Refusal of Refutation.

The refutation may be refused, if the respective demand or the submitted text of the refutation:

- represents the abuse of the freedom of mass communication in the sense of the first part of Article 4 of the present Law;
- contradicts the court's decision that has entered into legal force;
- is anonymous.

The refutation may be denied:

- if somebody disproves the information that has been disproved by the given mass medium;

- if the demand for refutation or the submitted text was received by the editorial office upon the expiration of one year since the day of the spread of the refuted information by the given mass medium.

The refusal of refutation or the infringement of the order established by the present Law may be appealed against with a court of law during one year since the day of the spread of the refuted information in accordance with the civil procedure legislation of the Russian Federation.

Article 46. The Right to Answer.

A private citizen or organization, in respect of whom a mass medium has spread information that runs counter to the reality or impinges on the rights and lawful interests of the citizen, shall have the right to give the answer (commentary or report) in the same mass medium.

The rules contained in Articles 43-45 of the present Law shall be applicable to the answer or refusal to this reply.

The answer to the reply shall be featured at least in the next issue of a mass medium. This rule shall not extend to editorial commentaries.

Chapter V. The Rights and Duties of the Journalist.

Article 47. The Rights of the Journalist.

The journalist shall have the right:

- to look for, inquire, receive and spread information;
- to visit state organs and organizations, enterprises and institutions, the press organs or press services of public associations;
- to be received by officials in connection with the inquiry of information;
- to get access to documents and materials, with the exception of their fragments containing information comprising a state, commercial or any other specially law-protected secret;
- to copy, publish, announce or reproduce by any other method documents and materials subject to the observance of the requirements of the first part of Article 42 of the present Law;
- to make recordings with the use of audio- and video-equipment, photography and cine-photography, except for the cases provided for by law;
- to visit specially protected places of natural disasters, accidents and catastrophes, mass disorders and mass gatherings, and also localities where a state of emergency is declared; to attend meetings and demonstrations;
- to verify the authenticity of the information he or she has received;
- to set forth his or her personal judgments and assessments in reports and materials intended for dissemination under his or her signature;

- to refuse to prepare under his or her signature reports and materials inconsistent with his or her convictions;
- to remove his or her signature put under the report or material whose content was distorted, in his or her opinion, in the process of editorial preparations or to ban or stipulate in any other way the conditions and character of using this report or material in keeping with the first part of Article 42 of the present Law;
- to spread reports and materials he or she prepared under his or her signature, under pseudonym or without any signature.

The journalist shall enjoy other rights granted to him by the legislation of the Russian Federation on mass media.

Article 48. Accreditation.

The editorial office shall have the right to file its application with a state organ, organization, and the organ of a public association for the accreditation of its journalists to them.

State organs, organizations, institutions and organs of public associations shall accredit said journalists, provided the editorial offices observe the accreditation rules established by these organs, organizations, and institutions.

The organs, organizations, and institutions which accredited journalists shall be obliged to notify them in advance about their meetings, conferences and other events, to supply them with verbatim reports, minutes and other documents, and to create favorable conditions for making entries.

The accredited journalist shall have the right to attend the meetings, conferences and other events held by the accrediting organs, organizations, and institutions, except for the cases when decisions have been taken to hold closed gatherings.

The journalist may be deprived of his or her accreditation, if he or she and the editorial office have infringed upon the accreditation rules or information which denigrates the honor and dignity of the organization that accredited the journalist and which runs counter to the reality, which fact has been confirmed by the court's decision that has entered into legal force.

The mass media offices' own correspondents shall be accredited in keeping with the requirements of this Article.

Article 49. The Duties of the Journalist.

The journalist shall be obliged:

- to observe the statutes of the editorial office with which he or she maintains labor relations;
- to verify the authenticity of the information he or she supplies;

- to satisfy the requests of the persons who submitted information concerning the indication of its source, and also the authorization of a cited pronouncement, if it is made public for the first time;
- to preserve the confidential character of information and/or its source;
- to receive the consent of a private citizen or his or her lawful representatives (except for the cases when it is necessary to protect public interests) to the spread in a mass medium of information about his or her personal life;
- to inform private citizens and officials about audio- and video-recording, photography and cine-photography upon the receipt of data from these persons and officials;
- to inform the editor-in-chief about possible suits and the presentation of other claims envisaged by law in connection with the spread of the communication or material prepared by him;
- to decline the assignment given to him by the editor-in-chief or his or her editorial office, if its fulfillment involves the infringement of law;
- to produce as soon as required the identity card issued by his or her editorial office or any other document that certifies his or her identity and rights, when he or she carries on professional activities.

The journalist shall also bear other duties established by the legislation of the Russian Federation on mass media.

In his or her professional activities the journalist shall be obliged to respect the rights, lawful interests, the honor and dignity of private citizens and organizations.

The State shall guarantee for the journalist, who carries on his or her professional activities, the protection of his or her honor, dignity, health, life and property as a person discharging his or her civil duty.

Article 50. A Hidden Record.

The dissemination of reports and materials prepared with the use of hidden audio- and video-recording, photography and cine-photography shall be allowed in the following cases:

- if this does not infringe upon the constitutional rights and freedoms of man and citizen;
- if this is necessary to protect public interests and if measures have been taken to prevent a possible identification of outside persons;
- if the record is demonstrated by decision of a court of law.

Article 51. Inadmissibility of Abusing the Journalist's Rights.

The rights of the journalist stipulated by this Law shall not be used with the purpose of the concealment or falsification of publicly important information, the spread of rumors under the guise of authentic reports, the collection of information in favor of an outside person or organization, which is not a mass medium.

It shall be forbidden to use the journalist's right to spread information with the aim of discrediting private citizens or particular categories of private citizens exclusively on account of sex, age, race, nationality, language, religion, profession, place of residences and work, and also of political convictions.

Article 52. The Special Status of Journalists.

The professional status of journalists established by the present Law shall extend to:

- staff workers of the editorial offices engaged in editing, writing, collecting or preparing communications and materials for newspapers with a large circulation and other mass media whose products are disseminated exclusively within one enterprise (association), organization or institution;
- authors who are not connected with the editorial office or section of a mass medium by labor or other contractual relations but are recognized by it as its free-lance authors or non-staff correspondents when they fulfill the editorial office's assignments.

Chapter VI. Interstate Cooperation in the Sphere of Mass Communication.

Article 53. Interstate Treaties and Agreements.

Interstate cooperation in the sphere of mass communication shall be effected on the basis of treaties and agreements concluded by the Russian Federation.

The editorial offices, sections and the professional associations of journalists shall take part in international cooperation in the sphere of mass communication on the basis of agreements concluded with individuals and legal entities from other States, and also with international organizations.

Article 54. The Dissemination of Foreign Information.

Citizens of the Russian Federation shall be guaranteed unimpeded access to reports and materials of foreign mass media.

The reception of programs of direct TV broadcasting shall be limited except in cases provided for by interstate treaties and agreements concluded by the Russian Federation.

To disseminate its products, the foreign periodical printed publication, which is not registered in the Russian Federation, has the place of the permanent stay of its founder or editorial office beyond the Russian Federation, and which is financed by foreign States, legal entities or individuals, shall be obliged to receive the permit of the Ministry of the Press and Information of the Russian Federation, unless the procedure for dissemination is established by the interstate agreement concluded by the Russian Federation.

Article 55. Foreign Correspondents.

The representative office of foreign mass media shall be set up in the Russian Federation with the permission of the Ministry of Foreign Affairs of the Russian Federation unless otherwise provided for by the interstate agreement concluded by the Russian Federation. The foreign representative offices of mass media registered in the Russian Federation shall be set up in the order prescribed by the legislative acts of the Russian Federation and the host country, unless otherwise provided for by the interstate agreement concluded by the Russian Federation.

Foreign correspondents who stay in the Russian Federation shall be accredited by the Ministry of Foreign Affairs of the Russian Federation in keeping with Article 48 of the present Law.

Foreign correspondents, not accredited in the Russian Federation in a statutory manner, shall enjoy the rights and bear the duties as representatives of a foreign legal entity. The following persons shall be released from the obligatory accreditation to carry on professional activities in the Russian Federation:

- foreign correspondents accredited earlier in the USSR or in the sovereign States incorporated in it;
- correspondents of mass media registered earlier by the state organs of the USSR or the sovereign States incorporated in it.

The professional status of the journalist established by the present Law shall extend to the correspondents accredited in the Russian Federation, regardless of their citizenship. The Government of the Russian Federation may introduce retaliatory restrictions with regard to mass media correspondents of the State where there are special limitations on the professional activities of the journalists of the mass media registered in the Russian Federation.

Foreign correspondents of the mass media registered in the Russian Federation, shall enjoy, regardless of their citizenship, the rights and duties of the journalist established by the present Law, unless such enjoyment runs counter to the legislation of the host country.

Chapter VII. Responsibility for Breaching the Legislation on Mass Media.

Article 56. Placement of Responsibility.

The founders, editorial offices and sections, distributors, state agencies, organizations, institutions, enterprises and public associations, officials, journalists, and the authors of disseminated reports and materials shall bear responsibility for breaching the legislation of the Russian Federation on mass media.

Article 57. Absolution from Responsibility.

The editorial office, editor-in-chief and journalist shall bear no responsibility for the dissemination of information that does not conform to the reality and denigrates the honor an dignity of private citizens and organizations or infringes on the rights and lawful interests of individuals or represents an abuse of the freedom of mass communication and/or the rights of the journalist:

- if this information is available in binding reports;
- if this information was received from news agencies;
- if this information is contained in the reply to its inquiry either in the materials of the press-services of state organs, organizations, institutions, enterprises, and organs of public associations;
- if this information is the literal reproduction of the fragments from the speeches of People's Deputies at the congresses and sessions of Soviets of People's Deputies, delegates of congress, conferences and plenary meetings of public associations, and also from the official statements by the office-bearers of state organs, organizations and public associations;
- if this information is to be found in the author's works that go on air without preliminary recording or in the texts not subject to editing in keeping with the present Law;
- if this information is the literal reproduction of reports and materials or of their fragments disseminated by another mass medium, which can be ascertained and called to account for a given breach of the legislation of the Russian Federation on mass media.

Article 58. Responsibility for the Infringement on the Freedom of Mass Communication.

The infringement of the freedom of mass communication, that is, the prevention by individuals, officials of state organs and organizations, and public associations of the lawful activity of the founders, editorial offices, publishers and distributors of mass media products, and also by journalists by means of:

- censorship;
- interference in the activity and breach of the professional independence of the editorial office;
- illegal termination or suspension of the functioning of a mass medium;
- breach of the right of the editorial office in reply to the inquiry and receipt of information;
- illegal seizure and also destruction of the print or part thereof;
- compulsion of journalists to spread information or to refuse to spread it;
- establishment of limitations on the contracts with journalists and transfer of information to them, except for the data comprising a state, commercial or any other specially law-protected secret;
- breach of the rights of journalists established by the present Law

shall entail criminal, administrative, disciplinary or any other responsibility in accordance with the legislation of the Russian Federation.

The identification of organs, organizations, institutions or officials whose functions cover censorship of mass communication shall entail the immediate termination of their financing and their liquidation in the order prescribed by the legislation of the Russian Federation.

Article 59. Responsibility for Abusing the Freedom of Mass Communication.

Abuses of the freedom of mass communication expressed in the breaches of the requirements of Article 4 of this Law shall entail criminal, administrative, disciplinary or any other responsibility in conformity with the legislation of the Russian Federation.

Abuses of the rights of the journalists expressed in the breaches of the requirements of Article 50 and 51 of this Law shall entail criminal or disciplinary responsibility in accordance with the legislation of the Russian Federation.

Article 60. Responsibility for Other Breaches of the Legislation on Mass Media.

The following breaches of the legislation of the Russian Federation on mass media shall entail criminal, administrative, disciplinary or any other responsibility in keeping with the legislation of the Russian Federation:

- the foundation of a mass medium through a false person, the receipt of information about registration or of a license for broadcasting by fraud, the hidden concession of a license, the evasion of the payment of a circulation or increased registration fee, and the illegal receipt of privileges instituted for specialized mass media;
- the illegal manufacture of products of mass media without their registration or after the adoption of a decision on the termination or suspension of their activities, the evasion of re-registration, and also the presentation of requirements not provided for by the present Law during registration;
- the prevention of the spread of mass media products put out on the lawful grounds, the introduction of illegal restrictions on the retail sale of the printing of a periodical publication;
- the illegal dissemination of products of mass media without their registration or after the adoption of a decision on the termination or suspension of their activities, or without the permission to be published (or to go on air), the illegal commercial dissemination, and the broadcasting without a license or with the infringement of license terms;
- the violation of the rules for spreading obligatory reports, advertisement, erotic publications and programs;
- the violation of the order of declaring imprints, submitting deposit copies of books and journals and of storing TV and radio broadcasting materials;
- the creation of jamming that prevents the stable reception of radio and TV programs.

Article 61. The Order of Appeal.

In accordance with the civil and civil procedure legislation of the Russian Federation the following actions may be appealed with a court of law:

- the refusal to register mass media, the violation by the registration body of the order and terms of registration and other illegal actions of the registration body;
- the decision of the commission for TV and radio broadcasting on the cancellation of a license for broadcasting;
- the refusal to submit requested information or the delay in its submission, or the non-observance of the requirements of Article 40 of this Law by officials, press-service workers of state organs, organizations, institutions, enterprises, and the organs of public associations;
- the refusal to accredit journalists, their deprivation of accreditation, and also the infringement of their rights.

If the court of law recognizes the appealed decision or action (inaction) as illegal, it shall pass its decision on the validity of a complaint and the duty to remove the committed infringement and compensate the losses, including the lost income incurred by the founder, editorial office or section, and the license holder.

Article 62. Compensation of Moral Damage.

The moral (non-property) damage inflicted to a private citizen as a result of the spread by a mass medium of information running counter to the reality and denigrating the honor and dignity of the person or causing to him any other non-property damage shall be compensated by decision of a court of law by the mass medium, and also by the guilty officials and private citizens in the amount estimated by this court.

Russian Federation Presidential Decree No. 2334 On Additional Guarantees of Citizens' Rights to Information*

December 31, 1993

Proceeding from the premise that the right to information is one of man's fundamental rights;

Striving to broaden the real opportunities for citizens and their associations to participate actively in the management of state and public affairs and to assist the development of local self-government;

To guarantee that citizens freely receive information about the activity of the bodies of legislative, executive, and judicial power;

Based on Articles 29(4) and 80(2) of the Russian Federation Constitution, I decree:

1. That the Presidential Commission on Legislative Proposals shall develop a draft Russian Federation Law On the Right to Information and present it to the President of the Russian Federation for submission to the Federal Assembly as a priority legislative initiative.

2. That until the appropriate federal law has been adopted, the norms set forth by this decree shall remain in effect.

3. That the activity of state bodies, organizations and enterprises, public associations and officials shall be carried out on the principles of information openness, as expressed in:

- citizens' access to information of public interest or affecting citizens' personal interests;
- citizens being systematically informed of proposed or adopted decisions;
- the exercise of control by citizens over the activity of state bodies, organizations and enterprises, public associations and officials and over decisions made by them in connection with the observance, protection and defense of citizens' rights and legal interests.

4. That information programs of state radio and television broadcasting companies shall inform citizens without fail of the principal provisions of legal acts and decisions of state bodies on fundamental domestic and foreign policy questions on the day they are issued.

5. State television and radio broadcasting companies shall produce a series of broadcasts (programs) explaining the activity of federal legislative, executive and judicial bodies and presenting the essence of the decisions made, using leading specialists, experts, and drafters of the relevant documents to work on such programs.

* Rossiiskaia Gazeta, Jan. 10, 1994, at 4.

The length and frequency of the broadcasting of such programs shall be determined autonomously by the leaders of state television and radio broadcasting companies.

6. The activity of federal legislative, executive, and judicial bodies shall receive equal coverage in the programs of state television and radio broadcasting companies.

The Presidential Judicial Chamber for Information Disputes shall supervise the objectivity of the coverage of such activity.

7. Guided by Article 15(4) of the Russian Federation Constitution, mass media coverage of the Federal Assembly shall follow Resolution No 820 (1984) of the Council of Europe Parliamentary Assembly on Relations Between State Parliaments and Mass Media (Collected Acts of the Russian Federation President and Government, 1993, No. 15, Article 1340), keeping in mind the limited number of television channels:

As a rule, the content of deputies' speeches in debates on draft legislation shall be brought to the attention of their voters via publication in the print media;

A greater number of articles of an educational nature about parliamentary activity shall be published.

The provisions of Resolution No 820 (1984) shall apply to relations between other federal bodies of state power and the mass media, and this includes establishing the following principles which shall apply to all federal bodies for the production of live and recorded television and radio broadcasts:

- the need for a television or radio broadcasting company to obtain consent to make a transmission from a session of the relevant federal body of state power;
- the timely notification of television and radio broadcasting companies about the proposed consideration of the most important questions of public interest;
- decisions as to the time (length) of broadcasts and their form (live or recorded) shall be made by television and radio companies.

8. The Russian Federal Service for Television and Radio Broadcasting shall strengthen supervision over television and radio companies' strict observance of the Russian Federation Law On the Mass Media.

9. This decree comes into force the moment it is signed.

Russian Federation Presidential Decree No. 2335 On the Presidential Judicial Chamber for Information Disputes[*]

December 31, 1993

With a view toward guaranteeing citizens' right to information secured in Article 29 of the Russian Federation Constitution, the observance of their legal interests in this sphere, and the effective fulfillment by the President of the Russian Federation of the constitutional duty to act as guarantor of human and civil rights and freedoms, I decree the following:

1. To recognize the constructive activity of the Information Arbitration Tribunal which was formed for the period of the 1993 election campaign, and to rule that its powers ended on December 31, 1993, following the conclusion of the 1993 election campaign.

2. Using the positive experience of the Information Arbitration Tribunal, to create a permanent Judicial Chamber for Information Disputes under the President of the Russian Federation, keeping in mind that this Judicial Chamber is not part of the system of federal courts of the Russian Federation.

3. To establish that the basic functions of the Judicial Chamber are:

- to assist the President of the Russian Federation in defending rights and freedoms in the mass information sphere;
- to guarantee the objectivity and authenticity of news reporting;
- to guarantee the principle of equality in the mass information sphere;
- to guarantee the protection of the moral interests of children and adolescents in the mass media;
- to guarantee the principle of pluralism in informational and socio-political television and radio programs;
- to resolve disputes about the allocation of radio and television air time between factions in the Federal Assembly;
- to correct factual errors in mass media news reports affecting public interests;
- to issue warnings to mass media in accordance with Article 16 of the Russian Federation Law on the Mass Media in the absence of the Russian Federation Ministry of Press and Information.

4. To appoint Anatoli Borisovich Vengerov as Chairman of the Presidential Judicial Chamber for Information Disputes.

5. To appoint members of the Presidential Judicial Chamber for Information Disputes.

---

[*] Rossiiskaia Gazeta, Jan. 10, 1994, at 4.

6. The Chairman of the Judicial Chamber shall submit within three weeks a draft statute governing the Presidential Judicial Chamber for Information Disputes for adoption according to established procedure.

7. To provide support for the Judicial Chamber's activity, to form a secretariat of the Presidential Judicial Chamber for Information Disputes as a working apparatus with the status of department within the administration of the President of the Russian Federation. The leader of the administration of the President of Russian Federation is to approve the structure and numerical strength of the working apparatus.

8. This decree enters into force the moment it is signed.

The Treaty of Public Accord

April 28, 1994

Today Russia needs public accord as never before. The tasks facing society are too complex and too difficult for its resources to be dissipated in political antagonism. Dialogue, the search for points of contact and common ground, and reasonable compromises must be the basic standard in public and political life.

It is our common aim to make the Russian Federation a flourishing state, enjoying a high level of authority in the international arena, a state inhabited by free people, proud of their history and looking towards the future with confidence. This aim can be achieved only through a public accord that grows out of respect for the dignity of the human being, for different political convictions and for national, cultural and religious traditions.

For the sake of public accord, the president of the Russian Federation, the Federation Council of the Federal Assembly of the Russian Federation, the State Duma of the Federal Assembly of the Russian Federation, the Government of the Russian Federation, the constituent parts of the Russian Federation, the Public Chamber under the president of the Russian Federation, political parties, trade unions other public associations and religious associations (henceforth referred to as the parties to the treaty), acting in accordance with the constitution and laws of the Russian Federation, placing common interests higher than group, party, departmental and religious interests, ruling out the possibility that the problems arising in society can be resolved through violence, whatever form it may take, conclude the present treaty.

Chapter I. Attaining Political Stability in Society.

1. The parties to the treaty pledge to abide strictly, in their activities, by the primacy of human rights and freedoms, respect for the rights of peoples, the principles of democracy, the law-governed state, the division of powers and federalism.

The parties to the treaty proceed from the view that the political life of society must develop within the framework of the Constitution of the Russian Federation.

The parties to the treaty consider that the only amendments that should be made to the constitution are those that will be conducive to stabilizing the situation in society. To this end, the parties to the treaty will make use of conciliation procedures when drawing up proposals. The parties to the treaty consider the main areas for amending the constitution to be: strengthening human rights guarantees; improving the system for the division of powers; local self-government; and the development of federalism.

The parties to the treaty undertake not to initiate political campaigns in favor of holding early elections, not envisaged by the constitution, to the federal bodies of power.

2. The Federation Council and the State Duma undertake to pass, in the near future, legislation on elections, laws on the referendum, parties, citizens' right of association and laws laying down the procedure for staging rallies, processions and demonstrations.

3. The parties to the treaty pledge to take all necessary measures to ensure stability within the country, without which it is impossible to emerge from the economic crisis.

The organizers of rallies and demonstrations, and local bodies of power and law-enforcement bodies accept moral and political, as well as legal, responsibility for ensuring that these actions are peaceful in nature and that they are conducted in strict accordance with current legislation.

4. The parties to the treaty consider that the president of the Russian Federation and the leaders of federal state bodies must maintain a constant dialogue with society, political parties, movements and other public associations.

5. The parties to the treaty consider that the grandeur of Russian history, with its heroic and tragic pages, obliges one to avoid simplified or insulting appraisals of the past and to prevent the distortion of historical fact.

6. The parties to the treaty pledge to do their utmost to promote the strengthening of Russia's international authority and defense capability, and the conducting of a unified foreign policy for the country.

. . . .

Chapter III. Consolidating the Federal Structure.

1. The president of the Russian Federation, the Federation Council, the State Duma and the Government and the constituent parts of the Russian Federation pledge to adopt measures to:

- strengthen the unity of the Russian Federation's economic, political and legal space;
- organize and support a unified labor market through rigorous observance of labor legislation and of international treaties and conventions concluded by the Russian Federation;
- coordinate the activities of the bodies of power of the constituent parts of the federation regarding the accomplishment of tasks that are beyond the scope of individual regions, and harmonize the actions of federal bodies of power and the bodies of power of the constituent parts of the federation regarding the accomplishment of national tasks;
- compensate the regions if the federal bodies of power, within the limits of their jurisdiction, take decisions that lead to a diminution of the revenue or an increase in the expenditure of the regional budgets.

2. The Federation Council and the State Duma pledge, within the current year, to pass federal laws: on a more detailed delimitation of the objects of jurisdiction and

powers between the Russian Federation and its constituent parts; on general principles for organizing the representative and executive power of the constituent parts of the federation.

3. The parties to the treaty stress that it is possible for the constituent parts of the federation to exercise their rights only if the state integrity of Russia and its political, economic and legal unity is ensured.

4. The parties to the treaty acknowledge the need to extend the economic independence of the constituent parts of the federation by strengthening the tax base of their budgets and by federal guarantees of a per capita minimum of budget support for a region from the federal grant fund.

The constituent parts of the federation confirm their responsibility for collecting federal taxes on their territory and forwarding the money to the federal budget.

5. In order to strengthen local self-government, the Federation Council and the State Duma pledge to draw up and pass federal laws that establish:

- general principles for the organization of local self-government bodies;
- guarantees of the independence of the local self-government bodies in dealing with matters of local importance;
- support for local self-government by an independent tax base and by the right to fix norms for payments to its own budget, given guarantees of a budgetary minimum from the state;
- the right of local self-government bodies to take part in tackling pan-regional and pan-Russian problems.

Chapter IV. Ethnic Relations.

1. The parties to the treaty undertake:

- to support the equal rights of all peoples to their ethnic development;
- to support ethnic cultures and languages;
- to support ethnic associations, unions, societies and other ethnic and cultural groups;
- to provide for the development of a multiethnic Russian society in which there is dialogue, peaceful settlement of conflicts, where no territorial claims are made within the state and where force is not used to settle disputes, expect where this becomes a necessary measure by the state following a violation of human rights;
- to set up the mechanisms needed to implement the Law on the Rehabilitation of Repressed Peoples.

2. The parties to the treaty are called upon to observe strictly the principle that the base of power throughout the Russian Federation is its multiethnic people. No single ethnic group has an exclusive right to control territory, the institutions of power or resources.

3. The parties to the treaty stress the need to protect the interests of minority peoples. The implementation of socio-economic changes in areas where they have traditionally resided should be accompanied by a range of measures to preserve the cultural, historical and natural environment of these peoples.

4. The parties to the treaty deem it necessary to heighten state and public monitoring of the observance of human rights in the sphere of ethnic relations and to prevent and curb any manifestations of discrimination along ethnic, racial and religious lines.

5. The state authorities recognize their obligation actively to protect the rights and interests of Russians living in other states, to accept and accommodate Russians who are compelled to resettle in Russia, providing them with comprehensive support.

Chapter V. The Safety of the Citizen and Society.

1. The parties to the treaty regard ensuring the personal safety of citizens and the fight against organized crime and corruption as a task of the utmost importance.

The Federation Council and the State Duma pledge during the current year to create the necessary legislation, including that required to strengthen the law-enforcement bodies.

2. The parties to the treaty, in line with the Constitution of the Russian Federation, oppose the creation by political parties, movements and public associations of any armed and paramilitary formations, and favor their immediate disbandment should such formations exist.

3. The parties to the treaty consider attempts to draw the power structures of the state into supporting political programs and demands to be unlawful and immoral.

4. The parties to the treaty consider an urgent task the working out of specific measures in the following areas:

- strengthening and raising the efficiency of the work of the state's power structures in accordance with the real demands for ensuring the security of the citizen and the state;
- providing legal and material backup for the work of the state's power structures and establishing civil control over them, including the reform of legal proceedings in the military, shaping personnel policy and ensuring the openness of budget expenditure in accordance with international norms;
- ensuring rigid control over the movement of freight and individuals across borders with the purpose of eliminating the illegal export of material and cultural treasures, and the import of weapons, drugs and ecologically dangerous cargoes;
- creating the necessary material conditions and stepping up the responsibility of the law-enforcement bodies for ensuring legality and law and order;
- improving the environment in ecologically unfavorable areas.

5. In order to formulate an agreed state policy in the sphere of security the parties to the treaty consider it advisable that the chairmen of the Federation Council and the State Duma should participate in the work of the Russian Federation Security Council and that the chairmen of the corresponding committees of Federal Assembly chambers should be recruited to work in interdepartmental commissions of the Federation Council.

6. The bodies of state power provide for the possibility of participation by the political parties, movements, public associations in working out a concept for national security.

Chapter VI. Morality, Science, Education and Culture.

1. The parties to the treaty stress that love for the fatherland, freedom and moral duty to society, creative labor, all the values common to the whole of mankind, spiritual and moral traditions of the multiethnic people of the Russian Federation should become the basis for its revival. The parties to the treaty pledge to uphold, in word and deed, the norms of moral behavior in politics, the economy and public life. A special role in this belongs to the mass media, education, scientific and cultural institutions, to religious organizations, the efforts of which should be supported by the state and society.

2. The parties to the treaty pledge to conduct an agreed policy in the field of the moral, spiritual, cultural, patriotic and aesthetic education of children and young people. To seek out the possibilities for stimulating the creativity of children and young people, physical education and sport, for organizing leisure activities for children and teenagers, for which the relevant actions of public associations and other organizations should be encouraged.

3. Bodies of state power in constituent parts of the federation pledge to assist in preserving the system of free, complete secondary, secondary specialized and vocational and technical education, as well as not to permit the existing level of financing for higher education to be reduced; to encourage the creation of nonstate higher education establishments to train specialists for vitally important spheres of the economy, public life, science, culture and education.

4. The treaty signatories will take all necessary measures to overcome the crisis in science in our country. Scientific potential accumulated is the property of Russian society.

Federal bodies of power pledge that they will seek funds to finance scientific and cultural establishments to a sufficient level.

5. The Federation Council and State Duma undertake to adopt laws which will secure tax and other privileges for scientific, cultural, educational and public health establishments and organizations for veterans and the disabled as well as a law on charity work and charitable organizations.

6. Parties to the treaty undertake to assist in the creation of a nationwide fund to support Russian talent, whose activities will be financed by state forces and public, commercial and other structures.

7. Federal power bodies undertake to draw up an all-Russian program to secure cultural and other links with ethnic Russians living abroad and their public associations.

Chapter VII. On the Implementation of the Present Treaty.

The president of the Russian Federation will hold regular meetings with representatives of organizations and establishments which have signed the treaty to discuss the most important issues connected with implementing the present treaty.

A Conciliation Commission is being set up to carry out coordination work on a permanent basis. The commission consists of plenipotentiary representatives of the president of the Russian Federation, the Government, the Federation Council, the State Duma, the Public Chamber under the president of the Russian Federation, the political parties, the trade unions, other public associations and the Cossacks.

The Conciliation Commission organizes the work of conferences, "round tables" and temporary working groups made up of representatives of the parties to the treaty and prepares questions for meetings with the president of the Russian Federation.

Appendices and protocols will be drawn up to develop the treaty; they will make its individual provisions more specific and will be an integral part of the treaty after they have been signed by the parties to the treaty.

The parties to the treaty stress that this treaty must be implemented strictly on the basis of the existing constitution and laws of the Russian Federation.

Chapter VIII. The Responsibility of the Parties Which Have Signed the Present Treaty.

The parties which have signed the present treaty acknowledge their great responsibility to society for fulfilling the commitments which they have undertaken.

The Conciliation Commission monitors the observation of the provisions set out in this treaty.

Full information is to be made available so that the mass media can cover fulfillment of the treaty by its signatories.

Chapter IX. The Procedure for Signing the Treaty.

The treaty is being signed by the president of the Russian Federation, the chairman of the Federation Council of the Federal Assembly, the chairman of the State Duma of the Federal Assembly, the chairman of the Government, heads of republics, heads of administrations, leaders of representative bodies of power in the constituent parts of the Russian Federation or their plenipotentiary representatives, and by leaders of groups, political parties and public associations represented in the State Duma, trade unions and their associations, religious associations, the Public Chamber under the president of the Russian Federation, and by leaders of the Russian Academy of Sciences and the Cossacks—after which the treaty is open for signing by others.

Chapter X. The Duration of the Treaty and Conditions Under Which Others Can Join It.

This treaty is being concluded for a period of two years and can be extended with the consent of the signatories.

The treaty is open for signing by representatives of public associations throughout the period of its validity.

Chapter XI. Final Provisions.

The parties to the treaty are unanimous that the establishment of public accord in Russia is a process in which all forces in society which adhere to the principles of this treaty are invited to take an active part.

The parties to the treaty appeal to all constructive forces of the Russian Federation to support this treaty and assist in its implementation. The parties to the treaty express confidence that in two years problems can be overcome, the country can be brought out of economic crisis, the life of Russians can be improved and the prerequisites for a growth in prosperity can be created.

Russian Federation Presidential Decree On Improving the Use of Channel One (Moscow) Television and Its Distribution Network

November 30, 1994

For the purposes of developing independent television broadcasting and ensuring guarantees of freedom of speech and mass information, I resolve:

1. to accept the proposal by the Russian state television and radio company Ostankino, agreed with the Russian federal television and radio broadcasting service, on this television and radio company joining the Public Russian Television joint-stock company as a cofounder, with 51 per cent of shares under federal ownership;

2. to establish that from the moment it is founded the Public Russian Television joint-stock company will broadcast on channel one (Moscow) television and also on the Moscow Global satellite television system;

3. to extend to the Public Russian Television joint-stock company the legal management framework established for the All-Russian State Television and Radio Broadcasting Company ["Russia" TV channel]. Payment of services provided to the Public Russian Television joint-stock company by state communications enterprises and the television technical center are to be made according to rates set for state television and radio broadcasting companies.

4. The government of the Russian Federation is instructed:

- to ensure within a month from the day the Public Russian Television joint-stock company is founded that it is issued with broadcasting licenses and licenses for communications activity in the field of television and radio broadcasting in accordance with established procedure;
- to ensure transmission from February 1, 1995, of programs of the Public Russian Television joint-stock company on channel one (Moscow) television, and also on the Moscow Global satellite television system, while maintaining existing conditions for the distribution of programs;
- within a month from the day the Public Russian Television joint-stock company is founded, to adopt a decision on the legal management framework, established in clause three [above], on issues within the competence of the Government of the Russian Federation.

5. This decree comes into force on the day it is signed.

Civil Code of the Russian Federation (Part One) (Excerpts)

January 1, 1995

Article 1. Basic Principles of Civil Legislation.

1. Civil legislation shall be based on the recognition of the equality of the participants in the relations which it regulates, the inviolability of property, the freedom of contract, the inadmissibility of arbitrary intervention by anyone whomsoever into private matters, the necessity for unhindered implementation of civil rights, and the provision for restoration of violated rights and their judicial protection.

2. . . . .

Civil rights may be limited on the basis of federal law, and only in that measure to which this is necessary for purposes of protecting the principles of the constitutional order, morality, health, or the rights and lawful interests of other persons, or ensuring the defense of the country and the security of the state.

Article 2. Relations Regulated by Civil Legislation.

. . . .

2. Inalienable human rights and freedoms and other non-material benefits are protected by civil legislation, unless otherwise dictated by the essence of these non-material benefits.

Article 7. Civil Legislation and Standards of International Law.

1. Generally accepted principles and standards of international law and international treaties of the Russian Federation are, in accordance with the Constitution of the Russian Federation, an integral part of the legal system of the Russian Federation.

2. International treaties of the Russian Federation are directly applied to relations specified in points 1 and 2, article 2 of this Code, except for cases when it follows from an international treaty that enactment of implementing domestic legislation is required for such application.

If an international treaty of the Russian Federation establishes different rules than those which are provided in the civil legislation, the rules of the international treaty are applied.

Article 150. Non-material Benefits and Their Protection.

1. Life and health, dignity of the individual, personal inviolability, honor and one's good name, business reputation, inviolability of personal life, personal and family privacy, right to unrestricted movement, choice of place of habitation and residence; right to one's name; right of authorship and other personal non-property rights and other non-

material benefits belonging to a citizen from birth and by virtue of the law, are inalienable and not transferable by other means. In the cases and in the order created by law, personal non-property rights and other non-material benefits belonging to a deceased person may be exercised and protected by other persons, including by the heirs of the holder of said rights.

2. Non-material benefits are protected in accordance with the present Code and also by other laws in the cases and in the order provided by them, as well as in those cases and to those limits in which the use of methods of protection of civil rights (article 12) stems from the essence of the violated non-material right and character of consequences of this violation.

Article 151. Compensation of Moral Damages.

If moral damages (physical or moral suffering) have been inflicted upon a citizen by actions which violate his or her personal non-property rights or which encroach upon other non-material benefits belonging to the citizen, as well as in other cases specified by law, the court may impose upon the violator the obligation of monetary compensation for the inflicted damages.

In determining the amounts of compensation of moral damages, the court takes into consideration the degree of fault of the violator and other circumstances deserving of attention. The court must also consider the degree of physical and moral suffering associated with the individual peculiarities of the person upon whom the damages were inflicted.

Article 152. Protection of Honor, Dignity and Business Reputation.

1. A citizen has the right to demand in court a retraction of information which defames his or her honor, dignity or business reputation, if the person who has spread such information cannot prove that it corresponds to reality.

At the demand of interested persons, the protection of honor and dignity of a citizen after his or her death is permitted.

2. If the information defaming the honor, dignity or business reputation of a citizen is distributed in the mass media, it must be retracted in these same mass media.

If the said information is contained in a document originating from an organization, such document is subject to replacement or repeal.

The order of retraction in other cases is established by the court.

3. A citizen in regard to whom the mass media publishes information which infringes upon his or her rights or legally protected interests has the right to publish his or her rebuttal in the same mass media.

4. If a court ruling is not implemented, the court has the right to impose a fine upon the violator, collected in the amount and in accordance with the procedure specified in the procedural legislation and payable to the income of the Russian Federation.

Payment of the fine does not absolve the violator of the responsibility of fulfilling the action specified by court ruling.

5. A citizen in regard to whom information defaming his or her honor, dignity or business reputation has been disseminated has the right, along with retraction of such information, to demand compensation of losses and moral damages inflicted by its dissemination.

6. If it is impossible to determine the identity of the person who disseminated the information defaming the honor, dignity or business reputation of a citizen, the person in regard to whom such information was disseminated has the right to appeal to court with a petition on recognizing the distributed information as not corresponding to reality.

7. The rules of the present article on protection of the business reputation of a citizen are respectively applied also to the protection of the business reputation of a legal entity.

Federal Law No. 15-FZ On Communications[*]

February 16, 1995

The present Federal Act shall establish the legal principles for activity in the field of communications under the jurisdiction of the Russian Federation (Federal communications, hereinafter "communications"), and shall determine the powers of the organs of state power in regulating the aforesaid activity, and also the rights and duties of natural and legal persons taking part in the aforesaid activity or making use of communications services.

Federal communications shall include all networks and facilities of electric and postal communications in Russian Federation territory (except for in-house and technological communications networks).

Chapter I. General.

Article 1. Purposes of Communications.

Communications shall be an integral part of the producer and social infrastructure of the Russian Federation and shall function in its territory as an interconnected economic-and-production complex designed to satisfy the requirements of citizens, organs of state power (administration) defense, security, and law and order in the Russian Federation, and of natural and legal persons in the services of electric and postal communications.

Communications facilities, together with computer facilities, shall constitute the technical basis for maintaining the process of collection, processing, accumulation and dissemination of information.

Development of communications and stable operation thereof up to a high quality standard shall be key conditions for the development of the society and the activity of the state.

Article 2. Basic Terms Used in Federal Act.

For the purposes of the present Federal Act, use shall be made of the following basic terms:

- *electric communications*—any transmission or receipt of digits, signals, written text, images, and sounds along wire, radio, optical and other electromagnetic systems;
- *postal communications*—receipt, processing, carriage and delivery of postal mailings, and remittance of monies;

[*] Adopted by the State Duma on January 20, 1995.

- *electric-communications networks*—technological systems ensuring one or more types of transmission: telephone, telegraph or facsimile transmission of data and other types of documentary communications, including exchange of information between computers, television, sound and other types of radio and wire broadcasting;
- *interconnected Russian Federation communications network*—a complex of technologically conjugate networks of electric communications in Russian Federation territory maintained by an overall centralized administration;
- *general-use communications network*—a component part of the interconnected network of Russian Federation communications available for use to all natural and legal persons, whose services these persons cannot be denied;
- *departmental communications networks*—electric-communications networks of ministries and other Federal bodies of executive power created for the satisfaction of producer and special requirements, with outlets to the general-use communications network;
- *in-house and technological communications networks*—electric-communications networks of Federal bodies of executive power, and also of enterprises, institutions and organizations created for the administration of in-house activity and technological processes without outlets to the general-use communications network;
- *segregated communications networks*—electric-communications networks of natural and legal persons without outlets to the general-use communications network;
- *communications enterprises, institutions and organizations ("communications enterprises")*—legal persons, irrespective of form of ownership, providing electric or postal communications services to natural and legal persons as core activity;
- *state-owned communications enterprise*—a communications enterprise held in Federal ownership or the ownership of Russian Federation subject;
- *communications operator*—a natural or legal person having the right to provide electric or postal communications services;
- *communications services*—the product of activity in the receipt, processing, transmission and delivery of postal mailings or electric-communications messages;
- *communications users*—natural and legal persons using communications services;
- *license*—a document establishing the powers of natural and legal persons, in conformity with the present Federal Act and other legal enactments, for activity in the field of communications;
- *certificate*—a document confirming that duly identified communications equipment or services accord with the requirements of normative documents;

- *terminal*—technical facilities linked up to subscriber lines and used by subscribers in the formation of electric-communications signals for transmission or reception along communications channels of information required by subscribers;
- *communications facilities (means of communication)*—technical facilities used in the formation, processing, transmission or reception of electric-communications messages or postal mailings;
- *postal mailings*—letters and postal cards, postal wrappers, packages, parcels, postal containers, and printed editions in appropriate packaging.

Article 3. Ambit of Federal Act.

The present Federal Act shall apply to relations connected with activity in the provision of services and performance of works in the field of communications involving participation by the organs of state power, communications operators, individual persons in office, and users of communications.

With respect to communications operators located outside the Russian Federation and effecting their activity in conformity with the legislation of foreign states, the present Federal Act shall apply only in the part of regulation of the rules under which they provide communications services in Russian Federation territory.

Article 4. General Regulation in Communications.

The present Federal Act shall determine the basic provisions on communications in the Russian Federation.

Relations in the field of communications not regulated by the present Federal Act shall be regulated by other Federal acts and other legal enactments issued in the Russian Federation, and also by laws and other normative legal enactments of Russian Federation subjects within the limits of their powers.

Normative enactments and orders issued by Federal bodies of executive power in the field of communications on matters of regulating the administration of communications networks, technical-organization maintenance of stable functioning of communications networks, and technical operation of communications facilities shall be binding on all natural and legal persons providing communications services or making use thereof, irrespective of their location or form of ownership.

Responsibility for the overall regulation of communications in the country shall be borne by the Russian Federation Government and duly authorized Federal bodies of executive power in the field of communications.

Article 5. Principles of Activity in Communications.

Activity in the field of communications shall proceed on the basis of:

- equality of the rights of natural and legal persons to participation in activity in the field of communications and use of the results thereof;

- harmonization of the interests of the Russian Federation and of Russian Federation subjects;
- freedom of transmission of messages along electric-communications networks and facilities, freedom of postal mailings and transit of mail throughout Russian Federation territory;
- concern for the interests of communications users;
- development of entrepreneurial activity and restriction of monopolistic activity where different forms of ownership of communications networks and facilities exist;
- guarantee of reliability and governability of communications, with due account of its network technological specifics, on the basis of a single set of standards in Russian Federation territory, in accordance with the recommendations of the International Electric Communications Union and the World Postal Union;
- guarantee of priority of production of communications facilities in the Russian Federation, in accordance with state scientific and technical policy;
- introduction of world achievements in the field of communications, attraction and use of foreign material and financial resources and of advanced foreign hardware and managerial experience;
- promotion of broader international cooperation in the field of communications and development of world-wide communications;
- controllability and accountability of communications enterprises to the Federal bodies of executive power;
- release of the Federal bodies of executive power in the field of communications from economic functions.

In conformity with Article 56 of the Russian Federation Constitution and of Article 13 of the present Federal Act, under a state of emergency throughout Russian Federation territory or in various parts of it, in the manner established by Federal constitutional law, the effect of paragraphs one and three of part one of the present Article may be limited.

Chapter II. Communications Networks.

Article 6. Russian Federation Interconnected Communications Network.

The interconnected communications network of the Russian Federation shall be a complex of technologically conjugate communications networks in general use and departmental electric-communications networks in Russian Federation territory maintained by a common centralized administration, irrespective of departmental affiliation or form of ownership.

Development and improvement of the Russian Federation interconnected communications network shall be effected with due account of the technological unity of all the networks and electric-communications facilities, in the interests of their complex use, enhanced efficiency and greater stability of functioning.

In conformity with the Federal program of development of the Russian Federation interconnected communications network out of the Federal Budget and the budgets of Russian Federation subjects, the state shall give support to communications enterprises in implementing Federal and regional programs, and in effecting measures to make the Russian Federation interconnected communications network more reliable and to create a mobilization buffer stock of communications equipment and cable products to ensure the development of every type of communications networks within the aforesaid network.

Article 7. General-Use Communications Network.

The communications network in general use, as a component part of the Russian Federation interconnected communications network, shall be designed for the provision of communications services to all natural and legal persons in Russian Federation territory, and shall include all the electric-communications networks under Russian Federation jurisdiction, except segregated and departmental communications networks, irrespective of affiliation or form of ownership. The responsibility for the functioning and development of this general-use communications network shall be borne by the Federal bodies of executive power in the field of communications.

In the construction and equipment of the general-communications network, account shall be taken of the need to make the aforesaid network reliable at impact of destabilizing factors.

Article 8. Departmental Communications Networks, Segregated Communications Networks of Natural and Legal Persons.

Departmental communications networks shall be set up and function to meet the producer and special requirements of the Federal bodies of executive power, and shall be managed and operated by these organs. Departmental communications networks may also be used to provide communications services to the population and to other users of communications. Conjugation of departmental communications networks with the general-use communications network shall be made on a contractual basis, provided the technical facilities and installations of departmental communications networks are in accord with the requirements and technical standards established for the general-use communications network, under a license received in conformity with Article 15 of the present Federal Act.

Segregated communications networks in Russian Federation territory may be created by any natural and legal persons, including foreign investors having recognized legal status. The requirement of licensing in conformity with Article 15 of the present Federal Act shall apply to activity in providing communications services by the operators of segregated communications networks.

Where segregated communications networks are conjugated with the general-use communications network, the aforesaid networks shall pass into the category of general-use communications networks.

The rules for the conjugation of departmental and segregated communications networks with the general-use communications network shall be established by the Russian Federation Government.

Article 9. Communications Networks for Requirements of Administration, Defense, Security, and Law and Order in the Russian Federation.

Governmental communications shall be provided by expressly authorized agencies designated by the Russian Federation President. The aforesaid agencies shall provide the organs of state power and organizations with special types of communications, safeguarding state secrets within the limits of their powers. The rights and duties of the agencies of the aforesaid communications shall be determined by Russian Federation legislation.

Communications for the requirements of defense, security and maintenance of law and order in the Russian Federation shall be provided by the communications agencies of the respective Federal bodies of executive power. They shall have the right, without damage to their core activity, to use the networks and communications facilities in their management to transmit or receive messages of communications users for commercial purposes. In such case, the requirement of licensing in conformity with Article 15 of the present Federal Act shall apply to the provision of communications services.

Channels of the general-use communications network and of departmental communications networks for the requirements of administration, defense, security and maintenance of law and order in the Russian Federation shall be made available by way of rental, in the manner specified by Russian Federation legislation.

The rules of preparation and use of the general-use communications network for the requirements of administration, defense, security and maintenance of law and order in the Russian Federation shall be determined by Russian Federation legislation.

The Federal bodies of executive power in the field of communications, the communications agencies of other Federal bodies of executive power, and communications operators, irrespective of form of ownership, shall have the duty to guarantee priority provision of communications channels for the requirements of administration, defense, security and maintenance of law and order in the Russian Federation, and to take priority and urgent measures for the replacement or repair of communications channels in the event of damage thereof.

Article 10. Postal Communications.

Postal communications under Russian Federation jurisdiction shall be a single technological network of institutions and transport facilities ensuring the reception, processing, carriage and delivery of postal mailings, remittance of monies, and also organizing, on a contractual basis, the forwarding, delivery and dissemination of the periodical press and delivery of pensions, aids and other specified-purpose payments.

The freedom of postal mailings and transit of mail shall be guaranteed throughout Russian Federation territory.

The state institutions of postal communications, special communications, and the Federal courier and messenger service shall constitute a single postal territory for the mutual exchange of postal mailings.

The activity of postal communications in the Russian Federation and of the Federal courier and messenger service shall be regulated by Federal laws.

Postal communications shall also include the subdivisions of the courier and messenger service and postal communications of the Russian Federation Ministry of Defense.

The state shall, out of the funds of the Federal Budget, provide economic support for the development and functioning of postal communications and give social protection to the employees thereof.

The services of postal communications may be rendered by nonstate postal communications enterprises under license issued in the established manner.

Chapter III. Administration in Communications.

Article 11. System of Federal Bodies of Executive Power in Communications.

Administration of activity in the field of communications shall be effected in conformity with the present Federal Act by Federal bodies of executive power in the field of communications united in a single system, in the established manner. The aforesaid organs shall, within the limits of their powers, bear responsibility for the state and development of all types of communications.

The structure and organization of the activity of the Federal bodies of executive power in the field of communications shall be determined by statutes confirmed by the Russian Federation Government.

With the object of implementing the present Federal Act, the tasks of the Federal bodies of executive power in the field of communications within the single system shall be the following:

- drafting of proposals for state policy in the field of communications and implementation thereof, general regulation in the field of communications;
- intersectoral coordination on a collegial basis of the functioning and development of electric communications;
- organization and exercise of state supervision and control of activity in the field of communications;
- drafting of proposals for state policy in the field of assignment and use of the radio-frequency spectrum and implementation thereof;

- drafting of development programs in the field of postal communications and implementation thereof.

Article 12. Regulation of Use of Radio-Frequency Spectrum and Orbital Positions of Communications Satellites.

The state shall have exclusive right in regulating the use of the radio-frequency spectrum and of the orbital positions of communications satellites.

Development and implementation of policy and procedures in the assignment of the radio-frequency spectrum, effective use of radio frequencies and orbital positions of communications satellites, in accordance with Russian Federation interests, with due account of international treaties and agreements of the Russian Federation, shall be ensured by the Russian Federation Government.

With the object of effecting the electromagnetic compatibility of radio-electronic facilities, the Russian Federation Government shall establish the rules of the assignment of radio frequencies, special conditions for the development, design, construction, acquisition, operation and import from abroad of radio-electronic facilities and high-frequency devices, and shall also determine the complex of measures for protection of radio reception against industrial radio interference.

Communications facilities, including those used for the purposes of TV and radio broadcasting, and other technical facilities which are sources of electromagnetic radiation shall be subject to registration in the manner established by the Russian Federation Government.

Frequency assignments to communications enterprises may be altered for the purpose of ensuring state administration, defense, security and maintenance of law and order in the Russian Federation, with compensation to communications enterprises of any damages arising from the switch to other frequencies.

Article 13. Operation of Communications Networks in Emergency Situations and Under State of Emergency.

Operation of communications networks in emergency situations shall be effected in conformity with Russian Federation legislation by the Federal bodies of executive power in the field of communications, in cooperation with the communications-operation centers of governmental organs, the Russian Federation Armed Forces, the Federal bodies of executive power in the field of civil defense, emergency situations and liquidation of the effects of natural disasters, and also of other Federal bodies of state power having management of departmental communications networks.

During natural disasters, quarantines and other emergency situations, as specified by Russian Federation legislation, duly authorized state agencies shall have the right to make priority use, and also to suspend the activity of any networks and communications facilities, irrespective of departmental affiliation or form of ownership.

For the purpose of coordinating operations in liquidating circumstances caused by the introduction of a state of emergency, special ad hoc communication agencies may be set up, under Russian Federation state-of-emergency legislation, to which the respective powers may be transferred, fully or in part, of the Federal bodies of executive power in the field of communications and communication agencies of Russian Federation subjects in the territory covered by the state of emergency.

Losses incurred by nonstate communications enterprises, where the communications networks and facilities of these enterprises are used in the cases enumerated in part two of the present Article, shall be indemnified out of the funds of the respective budgets.

Article 14. Interaction of Communications Enterprises with Agencies Conducting Operative Investigation.

Communications enterprises and communications operators, irrespective of departmental affiliation or form of ownership, operating in Russian Federation territory shall have the duty, in conformity with Russian Federation legislation, in the development, creation and operation of communications networks, to render assistance and to enable agencies conducting operative investigation to carry out operative-investigation measures on communications networks, and to take measures to prevent the disclosure of organizational and tactical methods used in conducting the aforesaid measures.

In the event of use of communications facilities for criminal purposes inflicting harm on the interests of the individual, the society and the state, duly authorized state agencies shall have the right, in conformity with Russian Federation legislation, to suspend the activity of any networks and means of communication, irrespective of departmental affiliation or form of ownership.

Article 15. Licensing of Activity in Communications.

The activity of natural and legal persons involving provision of communications services shall be effected on the basis of a license duly obtained and processed for this purpose, in conformity with the present Federal Act.

The types and terms of validity of licenses, the conditions of issue, suspension or termination thereof, and also other matters in licensing shall be regulated by Russian Federation legislation.

Issue, alteration of conditions or extension of the validity of licenses for the right of activity in the field of communications, and also termination of licenses shall be effected by the Russian Federation Ministry of Communications, in conformity with the present Federal Act and the statute of licensing in the field of communications, as confirmed by the Russian Federation Government.

Issue of licenses for activity in the field of communications for the purposes of television and radio broadcasting, and also assignment of frequencies entered on the schedule of frequencies used and planned to be used for the purposes of television and radio broadcasting shall be effected under license for broadcasting, without arrangement of bidding by the Russian Federation Ministry of Communications, in conformity with

Russian Federation legislation, on application by natural and legal persons having possession, use and disposal of communications facilities designed for the purposes of television and radio broadcasting, or having an intention to assume the rights of possession, use and disposal of communications facilities designed for the purposes of television and radio broadcasting.

No license shall be required where a network:

- is designed for in-house or technological purpose;
- is used to provide communications services exclusively for the requirements of administration, defense, security and maintenance of law and order in the Russian Federation, as specified in Article 9 of the present Federal Act;
- is concentrated in a single complex of premises or several complexes adjacent to each other, or is installed on motor-transport vehicle, vessel, aircraft or other type of transport.

A license or any of the rights it gives may be transferred, fully or in part, by one legal person to another legal person only upon receipt of a new license by the latter.

Natural and legal persons conducting activity in the field of communications without license or in breach of the rules of the use thereof shall bear liability under Russian Federation legislation.

Illegal acts by a Federal organ of executive power in the field of communications in matters of licensing activity in the field of communications may be appealed against in court of law or court of arbitration.

Article 16. Certification of Communications Facilities.

All communications facilities used in the interconnected Russian Federation communications network shall be subject to mandatory audit (certification) in terms of accordance with standards, other norms and technical requirements.

Communications services supplied along the general-use communications network may also be subject to certification.

Certification of communications facilities in the Russian Federation shall be effected by the Federal bodies of executive power in the field of communications, with the help of duly authorized testing centers (laboratories) accredited in the established manner with the Federal bodies of executive power in the field of standardization, metrology and certification.

Upon completion of the certification procedure, a certificate shall be issued in the established format for each specimen of communications facilities by the Federal organ of executive power in the field of communications.

The certification procedure shall be determined by Russian Federation legislation.

Persons in breach of the rules of certification of communications facilities shall bear liability, as established by Russian Federation legislation.

Chapter IV. Principals of Economic Activity in Communications.

Article 17. Ownership of Networks and Communications Facilities.

Communications enterprises shall be set up and shall function in Russian Federation territory on the basis of a single economic space, diversity of forms of ownership, and in conditions of competition.

Networks and means of communication in the Russian Federation may be held in Federal ownership, in the ownership of Russian Federation subjects, in municipal ownership, and also in the ownership of natural and legal persons acting as communications operators, including foreign organizations and foreign citizens.

The schedule of networks and means of communications which may be held only in Federal ownership shall be determined by Russian Federation legislation.

Article 18. Alteration of Form of Ownership of Communications Networks and Facilities.

Alteration of form of ownership of communications networks and facilities held in federal ownership shall be made in the manner provided for by Russian Federation legislation.

Foreign investors may take part in the privatization of state-owned and municipal communications enterprises on the terms and conditions determined by Russian Federation legislation.

Alteration of the form of ownership of communications networks and facilities shall be allowed only where such alteration does not disrupt the technological regime of the functioning of communications networks or infringe the rights of natural and legal persons using communications services.

Article 19. Investments in Development of Communications and Financing of Activity Thereof.

Investments in the development of communications shall be effected in conformity with Russian Federation legislation on investment activity.

Decisions on state investments in the development of communications in the Russian Federation out of the funds of the Federal Budget shall be taken on the basis of Federal state programs for the development of communications, in the manner established by Russian Federation legislation.

Federal state programs for the development of communications shall be drawn up by the Federal bodies of executive power in the field of communications, with due account of proposals of Russian Federation subjects, and shall be confirmed by the Russian Federation Government.

The organs of state power of Russian Federation subjects and the organs of local self-government shall determine, on the basis of socio-economic development plans for the respective territories, the lines of investment and shall draw up programs for the use thereof in the development of communications effected out of the funds of the respective budgets.

Financing of activity in the field of communications out of the funds of the Federal Budget shall be effected on the basis of Federal state programs for the development of communications, and shall be provided for as a separate line in Federal Budget appropriations.

Expenditures on financing activity in the field of communications for the requirements of defense, security and maintenance of law and order in the Russian Federation shall be provided for in Federal Budget appropriations as part of the expenditures, respectively, on the maintenance of defense, security, and law and order.

Natural and legal persons taking part in implementing projects for the development and maintenance of communications may be granted, in the established manner, guarantees, easy credits, and tax and other benefits.

Foreign investments in the field of communications may be guaranteed in conformity with Russian Federation legislation on foreign investments.

Article 20. Competition in Communications.

The Federal bodies of executive power in the field of communications, acting together with the Federal bodies of executive power in the field of antimonopoly policy and support of new economic structures, shall have the duty to encourage and promote fair competition in the provision of communications services through application of normative documents and fulfillment of the terms and conditions of licensing under Russian Federation legislation.

Communications operators shall bear Russian Federation statutory liability for use of their position or for commission of any other acts in restraint or prevention of competition.

Article 21. Tariffs for Communications Services.

Tariffs for communications services shall be established on a contractual basis.

In the cases specified by Russian Federation legislation, tariffs may be regulated by the state for some types of communications services rendered by communications enterprises.

Emergency calls for operative services (fire prevention, police, first aid, gas-repair service, mountain-rescue service, and the like) shall be made by all natural and legal persons free of charge.

Charges for internetwork connections shall be established on the basis of contracts, conditions and provisions agreed between the respective communications enterprises. Disputes on these matters shall be heard in court of law or court of arbitration.

Chapter V. Relations Between Communications Enterprises, Organs of State Power, Organs of Local Self-Government, Organizations and Enterprises.

Article 22. Relations Between Communications Enterprises, Organs of State Power and Organs of Local Self-Government.

In the planning and development of cities and other populated localities, residential areas and complexes, individual buildings and structures, the organs of architecture, town-building and town-planning shall have the duty to provide for the construction of premises to house communications enterprises, in accordance with existing standards.

In the design and construction of individual buildings and structures, separate premises shall be provided, as the need arises, for the housing of means of communication, in accordance with existing standards.

The organs of state power of Russian Federation subjects and the organs of local self-government shall have the duty to provide communications enterprises, by way of lease, with individual premises in existing (or under-construction) residential or other buildings subject to technological norms, in the manner determined by the organs of state power of Russian Federation subjects.

Employees of communications enterprises working and living in rural localities shall be supplied, by the organs of local self-government, with dwelling premises, fuel, land and other facilities and other social benefits, as established for the workers of agricultural enterprises in the given locality.

Article 23. Use of Lands in Operations to Develop Communications Networks.

Communications lands shall include land parcels made available, in the established manner, to natural and legal persons engaged in the provision of communications services into ownership or conveyed by the owners thereof into permanent of fixed-term use, including lease.

The rules for provision of land parcels, establishment of safeguarded zones or cuttings in forests, and the regimes for the use thereof shall be determined by Russian Federation legislation.

At termination of activity in the field of communications by the persons specified in part one of the present Article, termination of rights to land parcels shall be effected on the grounds and in the manner established by land legislation.

The size of land parcels, including safeguarded zones and cuttings in forests, made available to the persons specified in part one of the present Article shall be determined in accordance with the allotment norms of lands for this type of activity and technical-design documentation confirmed in the statutory manner.

The natural and legal persons specified in part one of the present Article shall be entitled to effect, in the established manner, construction of communications buildings and structures on land parcels made available for these purposes, and also to make use, in conformity with Russian Federation legislation, of the immovable property located thereon. The aforesaid persons shall also be entitled to effect construction of communications structures on the roofs of buildings, pylons, bridges, in collectors, underground and railway tunnels, and on other engineering facilities, and also to set up and service communications equipment, by agreement with the owners and users, including leaseholders (tenants) of the aforesaid land parcels, buildings or structures. Owners and users, including leaseholders, shall be entitled to deny communications enterprises the right to carry out the aforesaid works only on the grounds specified by law and other legal enactments issued in the Russian Federation. In the event of any dispute, the matter may be settled in court of law or court of arbitration.

Transfer or remodeling of communications structures caused by new construction, expansion, reconstruction of populated localities and individual buildings, roads and bridges, development of new lands, rearrangement of land-improvement systems, and mining for minerals shall be effected by the prime builder at his or her own expense, in accordance with the standards and technical conditions of the holders or users of networks and means of communication. In such case, any increase in the capacity of the means of communication shall be effected at the expense of communications enterprises.

Upon completion of works on a land parcel, in a building or structure, the communications enterprise or prime builder shall have the duty, at his or her own expense, to return the land parcel, building or structure to its original state or to indemnify the owner, user or leaseholder for any damages caused.

In the event of withdrawal of a land parcel or onset of the right of limited use of another's land parcel and other immovable property (servitude/easement) in the performance of design works, the buyout price, and also the charge for the use of the parcel and other immovable property shall be established in the manner determined by Russian Federation legislation.

Article 24. Protection and Safeguarding of Communications.

Facilities and Structures, Radio-Frequency Spectrum

and Orbital Positions of Communications Satellites

Communications facilities and structures, the radio-frequency spectrum, and the orbital positions of communications satellites shall be under the protection of the state.

The rules for the protection of communications facilities and structures and of the radio-frequency spectrum shall be established by the Russian Federation Government.

With the object of providing protection for the established procedure in the use of the radio-frequency spectrum and of the orbital positions of communications satellites, Russian Federation legislation may establish restrictions on the production and importation into the Russian Federation of radio-electronic facilities creating above-normal interference for the functioning of electromagnetic systems.

Natural and legal persons allowing damage to communications facilities and structures or unauthorized connection to communications networks and facilities, breaches of the established order of manufacture, acquisition, importation, use and registration of radio-electronic facilities and high-frequency devices, or use of frequencies for the operation of any radio-electronic facilities and high-frequency devices, and also those creating above-normal interference for television and radio reception shall bear liability in the manner established by Russian Federation legislation, including indemnification of any possible costs arising in the repair of any damage and compensation of communications enterprises for benefits forgone.

Article 25. Liquidation of Effects of Accidents in Communications Networks.

Liquidation of the effects of accidents in communications networks shall be effected by the appropriate state services, with the participation of communications operators.

The organs of Federal executive power, the organs of state power of Russian Federation subjects, and the organs of local self-government shall, without delay, render to communications enterprises assistance in liquidating the effects of any accidents occurring in communications networks, assigning, where necessary, manpower, transport and other facilities, with subsequent payment therefor out of the funds of the respective communications enterprises or, by decision of the organs of state power, out of the funds of the respective budgets.

Performance of works in liquidating the effects of accidents in communications networks shall not require the consent of the owner (holder, tenant) of the land parcel, building or structure where the means of communication are located. Any losses caused to the owner (holder, tenant) shall be subject to indemnification at the expense of the respective communications enterprise. The communications enterprise compensating the losses shall be entitled to make a claim in recourse on the person causing the damage.

Works in liquidating the effects of accidents in communications networks shall include restoration and reconstruction of the means of communication damaged in consequence of the accidents, and also performance of the requisite nature-protection measures.

Compensation to communications operators and to other natural and legal persons of any damage caused by an accident in communications networks shall be effected out of insurance funds or at the expense of the person causing the damage.

By decision of the Federal bodies of executive power, the organs of state power of Russian Federation subjects or the organs of local self-government, indemnification to communications operators and to other natural and other legal persons of any damage caused by accidents in communications networks may also be effected out of the funds of the respective budgets.

Article 26. Use of Transport Vehicles.

Postal communications enterprises shall have the right to carry mail, under contract, along all the routes and lines of railway, sea, river, air and motor-road transport under escort of postal communications employees or to assign such mail for carriage on the responsibility of transport organizations.

No transport enterprise may refuse to conclude a contract for the carriage of mail along regular inter-city and international routes used by its transport vehicles.

In the performance of urgent technical-repair works in the restoration of damaged networks and means of communication, transport vehicles shall be made available to communications enterprises by the owners of the transport vehicles, as a matter of priority.

Transport vehicles belonging to communications enterprises may bear special symbols and may not be used, without the consent of communications enterprises, for rendering services or performing works not proper to activity in the field of communications.

Chapter VI. Rights of Communications Users.

Article 27. Right to Use Communications.

All users of communications in Russian Federation territory shall have an equal right to transmit messages along the networks of electric and postal communications.

No user of communications in Russian Federation territory may be denied access to the services of the general-use communications network.

Users and operators of communications shall have the right to connect to the general-use communications network their own communications networks and terminals equipment, in compliance with the connection conditions established by the Russian Federation Government and issued to the communications operators concerned or specified in the license.

Connection to communications networks shall be allowed only of duly certified means of communication.

Article 28. Quality of Communications.

Communications operators shall have the duty to provide users with communications services corresponding in quality to the standards, technical norms, certificates and conditions of contract for the provision of communications services.

Article 29. Priority in Use of Communications.

The owners of communications networks and facilities shall have the duty to give absolute priority to all messages concerning the safety of human life at sea, on land, in the air and in outer space, performance of urgent measures in the field of defense, security and protection of law and order in the Russian Federation, and also to messages about major accidents, disasters, epidemics, epizootics and natural calamities.

Article 30. Benefits and Advantages in Use of Communications.

Benefits and advantages in terms of priority, procedure of use and size of fee for communications services in the use of electric and postal communications may be established for some categories of officials of state organs, diplomatic and consular representatives of foreign states, representatives of international organizations, and also for some groups of citizens.

The schedule of benefits, and also of the categories of persons in office and citizens with the right to benefits and advantages shall be determined by Russian Federation legislation and normative legal enactments of Russian Federation subjects, and also by international treaties and agreements of the Russian Federation.

In the provision of benefits in payment for communications services under the present Federal Act or other legal enactments issued in the Russian Federation, and also of normative legal enactments of Russian Federation subjects, compensation of incomes short-received by communications enterprises shall be made out of the funds of the Federal Budget or of the budget of the respective Russian Federation subject.

In other cases in the provision of benefits in payment for communications services, compensation of incomes short-received by the communications enterprises shall be made by the natural or legal person establishing the benefits, out of his or her own funds.

The rules for compensation to state communications enterprises of shortfall incomes resulting from the application of benefits and regulated state tariffs shall be determined by the Russian Federation Government and by the organs of state power of Russian Federation subjects.

Article 31. Protection of Rights of Communications Users.

Protection of the rights of users of communications to have a supply of services of electric and postal communications of proper quality, to receive information on such services and on their performers, and also the mechanism for the exercise of these rights shall be regulated by Russian Federation legislation.

Normative legal enactments of Russian Federation subjects regulating relations in the field of communications in conformity with the powers of Russian Federation subjects may not limit the rights of users of communications, as established by the respective Federal laws.

Article 32. Secrets of Communications.

Secrets of correspondence, telephone conversations, postal mailings, telegraph and other messages transmitted along the networks of electric and postal communications shall be protected by the Russian Federation Constitution.

All communications operators shall have the duty to keep the secrets of communications.

Information on postal mailings and messages transmitted along electric-communications networks, and also these mailings and messages themselves may be issued only to the senders and addressees or to their legitimate representatives.

The tapping of telephone conversations, scrutiny of electric-communications messages, delay, inspection and seizure of postal mailings and documentary correspondence, receipt of information thereon, and also other restriction of communications secrets shall be allowed only on the basis of a judicial decision.

Persons in office and other persons, and communications employees in breach of the aforesaid provisions, shall be held to liability in the manner established by Russian Federation legislation.

Article 33. Safety of Postal and Other Mailings.

Communications operators shall bear liability for the safety of accepted postal and other mailings, and for the delivery thereof to the place of destination by the appointed time.

The schedule of objects prohibited for forwarding by post shall be established by the Russian Federation Government.

State postal communications enterprises shall have the right to seize postal mailings whose content is prohibited for forwarding, and also to destroy or to permit the destruction of postal mailing whose content creates a hazard to the life and limb of postal employees or third parties, where such hazard cannot be eliminated in other ways.

Article 34. Postal Mailings with Declared Value.

The sender of a postal mailing shall be entitled to declare its value within the limits of the value of the enclosure.

In the event of loss or damage of postal mailing with declared value, the communications operator shall indemnify the sender for the damages, in conformity with Russian Federation legislation.

Chapter VII. Specific Aspects of Provision of Communications Services.

Article 35. Use of Languages and Alphabets in Activity of Communications Enterprises.

Throughout Russian Federation territory, official dispatch of business in electric and postal communications networks shall be effected in the Russian language, as the state language of the Russian Federation.

The addresses of the sender and the addressee of telegrams and postal mailings forwarded within the borders of the Russian Federation must be done in the Russian language, and the addresses of the sender and the addressee of telegrams and postal mailings forwarded within the borders of the territories of republics within the Russian Federation may be done in the state language of the respective republic within the

Russian Federation, with a repetition of the addresses of the sender and the addressee in the Russian language.

The text of telegrams must be written in the letters of the Russian or the Latin alphabet in any language.

International messages transmitted along electric and postal communications shall be processed in the languages determined by the provisions of the international treaties and agreements of the Russian Federation.

Article 36. Standard (Registry-and-Report) Time in Communications.

In the conduct of activity in the field of communications, use shall be made of the registry-and-report time—Moscow standard time—in the technological processes of dispatch and receipt of communications and information at communications enterprises, irrespective of their location in Russian Federation territory.

In international communications, the standard (registry-and-report) time shall be determined by the international treaties of the Russian Federation.

Chapter VIII. Liability in Conduct of Communications Activity.

Article 37. Liability in Conduct of Communications Activity.

The Federal bodies of executive powers, the organs of executive power of Russian Federation subjects, the organs of local self-government, and also natural and legal persons in breach, in the conduct of activity in the field of communications, of the present Federal Act, other Federal Acts, and also other legal enactments adopted in the Russian Federation shall bear liability in the manner established by Russian Federation legislation.

Communications operators shall bear material liability for the loss or damage of valuable postal mailings, shortage of postal-mailing enclosures within the limits of the declared value, distortion of the text of telegrams altering the meaning thereof, nondelivery of telegram or delivery of telegram to addressee upon the expiration of 24 hours from the time of filing thereof, in the amount of the paid-up charge for the telegram (with the exception of telegrams addressed to populated localities without electric communications).

The amount of liability for nonperformance or improper performance by state postal-communications enterprises of their duties in the forwarding or delivery of other registered postal mailings shall be determined by Russian Federation legislation.

At breach by communications user of the rules of operation of terminals equipment of electric-communications network, use of uncertified equipment on the network, and also at delayed payment of communications services, the communications operator shall have the right to suspend access by the communications user to the electric-communications network, pending elimination of the defects, except in the cases specified in Article 29 of the present Federal Act, with indemnification by the communications user of any income losses incurred by the communications operator and with compensation of any harm caused to the communications operator because of damage to or idling of equipment.

Employees of state communications enterprises shall bear material liability to their communications enterprises for loss or delay of delivery of all types of postal mailings and telegraph dispatches, shortage or damage of enclosures of postal mailings allowed (caused) through their fault, in the amount of the material liability borne by the communications enterprise to the consumer, where other liability measure is not provided for by the respective Federal law.

The communications operator shall not bear liability for nonperformance or improper performance of obligations in the dispatch or receipt of messages or in the forwarding or delivery of postal mailings, where it is proved that such nonperformance or improper performance of obligations occurred through the fault of the communications user or in consequence of the effect of force majeure (act of God).

Article 38. Claims and Lawsuits Procedure.

At nonperformance or improper performance of obligations in the rendering of communications services or performance of works in the field of communications, the communications user shall be entitled to file claims on the communications operator rendering the services or performing the works, including a claim for indemnification of damage.

Claims shall be filed in writing and shall be subject to mandatory registration, in the statutory manner.

Claims shall be filed within the following time periods:

- claims involving nonrendering, delayed rendering or inferior-quality rendering of communications services or nonperformance or improper performance of works in the field of electric communications (except claims on telegraph messages)—during six months;
- claims involving nondelivery, delayed delivery, damage or loss of postal mailings—during six months;
- claims involving nondelivery, delayed delivery or distortion of telegraph message—during one month.

Written replies to claims must be given within the following time periods:

- claims specified in paragraph one of part three of the present Article—during two months;
- all types of other-town postal mailings—during two months;
- local postal mailings—during five days;
- telegraph dispatches—during one month.

For claims involving subscription and delivery of newspapers, magazines and other printed periodicals, the time periods for the filing of claims and for consideration thereof shall be one year for legal persons. For natural persons, the time periods for filing claims on the aforesaid grounds shall be determined by Russian Federation legislation on matters in the protection of consumer rights.

Where a claim is rejected fully or in part, or where no reply is received within the established period therefor, the claimant shall have the right to take action in a court of law or a court of arbitration.

Lawsuits involving the sending or receipt of postal mailings or telegraph dispatches may be brought either against the communications operator accepting the postal mailing or telegraph dispatch, or against the communications operator at the point of destination of the mailing or dispatch.

Article 39. Indemnification of Damage.

Indemnification of damage caused in the conduct of activity in the field of communications shall be made either voluntarily or under decision of a court of law or a court of arbitration, in the manner established by Russian Federation legislation.

Chapter IX. Settlement of Disputes over Matters in Communications Activity.

Article 40. Settlement of Disputes in Communications.

Disputes arising in the conduct of activity in the field of communications between communications enterprises, and also between communications users and communications enterprises, shall be settled in the manner established by Russian Federation legislation.

Where a communications enterprise conducts urgent works in the restoration of communications structures located on agricultural land or other parcels of land not having communications-land status, in the event that the owner (holder, tenant) of the land parcel and the communications enterprise fail to reach agreement on the amount of indemnification of damage due or where the owner (holder, tenant) refuses to take part in drawing up the respective deed, these circumstances may not serve as an obstacle to the conduct of restoration works and shall not relieve the owner of the communications structures from indemnification of the damage caused.

Article 41. Settlement of Disputes in Use of International Communications Networks.

Disputes in matters of activity in the field of communications arising between communications enterprises located in Russian Federation territory and in the territory of foreign states shall be settled in the manner established by the respective international treaties and agreements of the Russian Federation.

Chapter X. International Cooperation.

Article 42. International Cooperation.

The Russian Federation shall promote the development of international cooperation in the field of communications, and also the solution of problems in the legal regulation of activity in the field of communications.

International cooperation in the field of communications shall be effected on the basis of the international treaties and agreements of the Russian Federation.

In international activity in the field of communications, the Federal organ of executive power in the field of communications shall act as the communications administration and shall, within the limits of the powers provided for by the international treaty, represent and protect the interests of the Russian Federation in the field of electric and postal communications in interaction with the communications administrations of other countries and international communications agencies, and shall also coordinate international activity in the field of communications effected by all the natural and legal persons of the Russian Federation.

Foreign organizations and citizens conducting activity in the field of communications in Russian Federation territory shall enjoy the use of the legal regime established for the natural and legal persons of the Russian Federation, to the extent to which the aforesaid regime is made available by the respective state to the natural and legal persons of the Russian Federation.

Article 43. Law Applied to International Cooperation in Communications.

The natural and legal persons of the Russian Federation taking part in effecting international projects in the field of communications shall conclude contracts with foreign organizations and citizens, in conformity with Russian Federation legislation, unless these contracts provide for the application of the legislation of another state.

Chapter XI. Entry into Force of Federal Act

Article 44. Entry into Force of Federal Act.

The present Federal Act shall enter into force on the day of its official promulgation.

Russian Federation Presidential Decree No. 161 On Guarantees of Citizens' Right to Protection of Health in the Spread of Advertising

February 17, 1995

Regarding the constitutional guarantees of protection of the health of the Russian Federation population as the basis for ensuring active longevity for each person, pending adoption of a Federal act on advertising, I hereby decree:

1. Advertising in the mass media of the following shall not be allowed:

- alcoholic drinks and tobacco products contrary to the interests of protection of the health of citizens and in violation of the requirements of part two of Article 19 of the Fundamentals of Russian Federation Legislation on Protection of the Health of Citizens;
- methods of prophylactics, diagnostics, treatment, medical technologies and medicinal preparations which have not been duly tested or approved in the established manner, as prohibited by part eight of Article 43 of the Fundamentals of Russian Federation Legislation on the Protection of the Health of Citizen;
- healers, ESP experts and other persons claiming to be specialists in treatment by folk- medicine methods and other traditional methods and not in possession of the requisite permits under Articles 56 and 57 of the Fundamentals of Russian Federation Legislation on Protection of the Health of Citizens;
- products subject to obligatory certification but not having the appropriate certificate, in conformity with part four of Article 7 of the Russian Federation Certification of Goods and Services Act.

2. For the advertisements specified in Clause 1 of the present Directive, the persons disseminating, inserting and making advertisements shall bear liability in conformity with Article 169 of the Russian Federation Civil Code, and everything received by them under transactions involving such advertisements shall be exacted into the revenue of the Russian Federation for the purposes of public health care.

3. The organs of the procurator's office, together with the Russian Federation Ministry of Public Health and Medical Industry and public health agencies of Russian Federation subjects, shall bring claims under law suits against the editorial boards of the mass media and persons disseminating, inserting and making advertisements, for exaction into the revenue of the Russian Federation for the purposes of public health care of everything received by them under transactions from advertisements disseminated in violation of the requirements of Russian Federation legislation.

4. The Russian Federation government shall, within the period of three months:

- consider the matter of compliance with Russian Federation legislation on the guarantees of citizens' right to protection of health in the dissemination and spread of advertising by the editorial boards of mass media and by persons disseminating, inserting and making advertisements;
- establish the rules of use for the purposes of public health care of the monies exacted into the revenue of the Russian Federation, in conformity with Clause 2 of the present Directive.

5. The present Decree shall take effect upon its promulgation.

Federal Law No. 108-FZ On Advertising*

July 18, 1995

Chapter I. General Provisions.

Article 1. Purposes and Sphere of Application of This Federal Law.

1. This Federal Law shall regulate relations arising during the process of production, placement and distribution of advertising on the markets of goods, work, services (hereinafter—goods) of the Russian Federation, including the markets of banking, insurance and other services connected with the use of monetary means belonging to citizens (physical persons) and legal entities, and also securities markets.

The purposes of this Federal Law are to defend against unfair competition in the field of advertising, and to avert and cease inappropriate advertising capable of misleading advertising consumers or causing harm to the health of citizens, the property of citizens or legal entities, harm to the environment or to the honor, merit or business reputation of the indicated persons, and advertising that encroaches on the interests of society and the principles of humanity and morality.

2. This Federal Law is also applicable when activities completed outside the boundaries of the Russian Federation by legal entities or citizens of the Russian Federation in the field of advertising lead to the limitation of competition, or the misleading of legal entities and physical persons on the territory of the Russian Federation, or lead to other negative consequences in the goods markets of the Russian Federation.

3. This Federal Law extends to foreign legal entities and to foreign citizens and persons without citizenship (individual entrepreneurs registered according to the established procedure) who produce, place and disseminate advertisements on the territory of the Russian Federation.

4. This Federal Law does not extend to political advertisements.

5. This Federal Law does not extend to announcements by physical persons, including those made through the mass media, that are not related to conducting entrepreneurial activity.

Article 2. Basic Concepts.

For the purpose of this Federal Law the following basic concepts shall apply:

- *advertising/advertisement*—distribution of information about a physical person or legal entity, goods, ideas or projects (advertising information) in any form with the

* Adopted by the State Duma on June 14, 1995. Signed by President Yeltsin on July 18, 1995.

help of any media, which is intended for an indeterminate group of persons and is aimed at forming or supporting interest in such physical persons, legal entities, goods, ideas and projects and facilitating the sale of goods, ideas and projects;

- *inappropriate advertising*—unfair, unauthentic, unethical, knowingly untrue and other advertisements that violate the requirements regarding their content, timing, location and method of dissemination as established by the legislation of the Russian Federation;
- *counter-advertising*—a refutation of inappropriate advertising disseminated for the purpose of counteracting its consequences;
- *advertiser*—a legal entity or physical person who is the source of advertising information for the production, placement and subsequent distribution of advertising;
- *advertisement producer*—a legal entity or physical person conducting entire or partial preparation of advertising information into a form ready for distribution;
- *advertisement distributor*—a legal entity or physical person that places and/or distributes advertising information by means of supplying and/or using property, including the technical means of radio broadcasting, television broadcasting as well as communications channels, transmission time and by other means;
- *advertising consumers*—legal entities and physical persons to whose attention advertising is directed, or may be directed, and who are or may be affected correspondingly as a consequence of advertising.

Article 3. Legislation of the Russian Federation on Advertising.

The legislation of the Russian Federation on advertising consists of this Federal Law and other federal laws passed in accordance with it.

Relationships arising during the process of production, placement and distribution of advertising may be regulated also by directives of the President of the Russian Federation, normative legal acts of the government of the Russian Federation and normative legal acts of federal executive agencies issued in accordance with this Federal Law.

Article 4. Author's Right and Related Rights to Advertising.

Advertising may, fully or partially, be the objects of author's right and related rights. In this case, author's right and related rights are subject to defense in accordance with the legislation of the Russian Federation.

Chapter II. General and Specific Requirements of Advertising.

Article 5. General Requirements of Advertising.

1. An advertisement must be recognizable without specialist knowledge or the application of technical means clearly as advertising immediately at the moment of its presentation regardless of the form or the media used for its dissemination.

The use of radio, television, video, audio and film products, as well as the use of printed products of a non-advertising nature for the purpose of attracting the attention of an advertising consumer to a distinct make (model, article) of good or to the manufacturer, user, or seller for the formation and support of interest in it without the appropriate prior communication of this (in particular, by noting "with rights of advertising") is not permitted.

If radio, television, video, audio, film or printed products are distributed in parts (series), notice of the advertisement must also be repeated for the corresponding number of parts (series).

Mass-media information organizations are not permitted to take payments for placing advertising in the guise of informational, editorial or authored material.

2. Advertising on the territory of the Russian Federation shall be disseminated in the Russian language and, at the discretion of the advertiser, additionally in the official languages of the republics and native languages of the peoples of the Russian Federation. This statute does not apply to radio broadcasts, television broadcasts or printed publications produced exclusively in the official languages of republics or in the native languages of peoples of the Russian Federation or in foreign languages, nor to registered trade marks (service marks).

3. Advertisements for goods and for the advertiser itself is not permitted if the activity of the advertiser requires special permission (a license) but such permission (license) has not been received. Advertising for goods whose production is forbidden in accordance with the legislation of the Russian Federation is also not permitted.

4. Advertisements for goods subject to mandatory certification must be accompanied by the notice "subject to mandatory certification."

5. Use in advertising of objects of exclusive rights (intellectual property) is permitted according to the procedure provided for by the legislation of the Russian Federation.

6. Advertising must not incite citizens to violence against the population or to aggression, excite panic, or incite citizens to dangerous actions capable of bringing harm to the health of physical persons or threatening their safety.

7. Advertisements must not incite actions that violate environmental protection legislation.

Article 6. Unfair Advertising.

Unfair advertising is advertising that:

- discredits legal entities or physical persons who do not use the advertised good;
- contains incorrect comparisons of the advertised good with the good (goods) of other legal entities or physical persons, or contains pronouncements or images which discredit the honor, merit or business reputation of a competitor (competitors);
- misleads the consumer in regard to the advertised good by means of imitation (copying or mimicry) of a general concept, text, advertising formula, images, musical or sound effects, the use in the advertisement of other goods, or by abusing the trust of a physical person or his or her inexperience, including in connection with the advertisement's lack of part of the relevant information.

Unfair advertising is not permitted.

Article 7. Unauthentic Advertising.

An advertisement is unauthentic if it contains information that does not correspond to reality in relation to the following:

- those characteristics of a good, such as its nature, content, method and date of preparation, use, consumer characteristics, conditions for application, the presence of certification of conformity, certification marks and marks of conformity to state standards, quantity or place of origin;
- the presence of a good on the market and the possibility of its purchase in the indicated volume, period of time and place;
- the cost (price) of the good at the moment of dissemination of the advertisement;
- additional conditions of payment;
- supply, exchange, return, repair and servicing of a good;
- security guarantees, the period of service and the period of validity;
- exclusive rights to the results of intellectual activity and equivalent means of individualization of the legal entity, the individualization of products and the fulfillment of work or services;
- the right to use state symbols (flags, coats of arms, anthems) and symbols of international organizations;
- official recognition, the receipt of medals, prizes, diplomas and other awards;
- supplying information on methods for acquiring an entire series of a good, if the good is a part of a series;
- results of research and experimentation, scientific terms and citations from technical, scientific and other publications;
- statistical information that should not be presented in a way that exaggerates its validity;
- reference to any kind of recommendation or to the approval of a legal entity or physical person, including reference to obsolete recommendations;

- use of terms in the superlative, including through the use of such words as "the most," "only," "best," "absolute," "sole" and other such words, if it is impossible to confirm them documentarily;
- comparison with another good (goods) and with the rules and regulations of other legal entities or physical persons;
- reference to any kind of guarantee to the consumer of the advertised good;
- the actual amount of demand for a good;
- information about the advertiser itself.

Unauthentic advertising is not permitted.

Article 8. Unethical Advertising.

1. An advertisement is unethical if:

(a) it contains textual, visual, or audible information that violates the generally accepted norms of humanity and morality through the use of offensive language, comparisons and images in relation to race, nationality, profession, social category, age group, sex, language, or the religious, philosophical, political or other beliefs of physical persons;

(b) it denigrates objects of art of national or international merit;

(c) it denigrates state symbols (flags, coats of arms, anthems), the national currency of the Russian Federation or other state or religious symbols;

(d) it denigrates any kind of physical person or legal entity, any kind of activity, or any profession or good.

Unethical advertising is not permitted.

2. Physical persons or legal entities who gain knowledge of the production or distribution of advertising containing information that denigrates his/her/its honor, merit or business reputation have the right to apply for protection of their violated rights through the appropriate court or arbitration court according to the procedure set out by the legislation of the Russian Federation, and also have the right to demand that the advertiser retract such advertising in the same way the advertising was first distributed if the advertiser does not fulfill this demand voluntarily.

Article 9. Knowingly False Advertising.

A knowingly false advertisement is one that helps the advertiser (advertisement producer, advertisement distributor) intentionally to mislead an advertising consumer.

Knowingly false advertising is not permitted.

Article 10. Subliminal Advertising.

The use of radio, television, video, audio, film and other products, as well as dissemination by other means for subliminal advertising, meaning advertising that has an unconscious influence on the perception of the consumer, including through the use of special video equipment (double sound recording) and other means, is not permitted.

Article 11. Particulars of Advertisements on Radio and Television Programs.

1. The following radio and television programs shall not be interrupted by advertising:

- children's and religious programs;
- not more than once every 15 minutes and for not more than 45 seconds in educational programs;
- without the agreement of the copyright holder for radio-plays and feature films;
- live programs on the air, according to the list established by the Federal Law On the Procedure for Covering the Activities of State Authorities in the State Mass Media;
- any programs with a transmission time of less than 15 minutes;
- more than twice in any programs with a transmission length of between 15-60 minutes.

2. When using advertising as an on-screen addition, including by means of a "running line," the size of such advertisements must not be more than 7% of the area of the frame.

3. The dissemination of an advertisement for exactly the same good and, equally, the dissemination of an advertisement about an advertiser must not take place more than twice, with a total time period of not more than two minutes during every hour of air time, on a radio or television program on one frequency broadcasting.

4. Advertising must not exceed 25% of the broadcast volume of each twenty-four hour period on radio and television programs that are not registered as specializing in information and materials of an advertising nature.

Article 12. Particulars of Advertisements in Periodically Printed Publications.

Advertisements must not exceed 40% of the volume of one edition of a periodically printed publication that does not specialize in information and materials of an advertising nature.

Article 13. Particulars of Advertisements in Cinema, Video and Information Services.

1. Interrupting the demonstration of a film with advertisements, except during breaks between series (parts), in cinema and video services is not permitted.

2. Advertising may be presented in telephone information services only after communicating the information that the subscriber has requested.

3. Advertisements may be presented in payable telephone information services, computer or other services only with the agreement of the subscriber. The cost

of such advertising must not be included in the cost of the information requested by the subscriber.

Article 14. Particulars of Outdoor Advertisements.

1. The distribution of advertising in urban and rural settlements and other territories may done through posters, stands, illuminated boards and other technical means of stable territorial placement (outdoor advertisements) according to the procedures provided for under Clauses 2 and 3 of this Article. Outdoor advertisements must not bear similarities to road signs and indicators, must not impede their visibility and must not impair the safety of traffic movement.

2. Distribution of outdoor advertisements in urban and rural settlements and in other territories is allowed contingent upon receipt of permission from appropriate local self-government agencies, in agreement with:

(a) for designated areas of land and roadside zones of highways outside the territory of urban and rural settlements: the appropriate management agencies for highways and the territorial subdivision of the state auto inspectorate of the federal executive agency of internal affairs;

(b) for urban and rural settlements: the territorial subdivision of the state automobile inspectorate of the federal executive agency of internal affairs;

(c) for designated areas of railroad: the appropriate management agency for railroads.

Payment for granting permission to distribute outdoor advertisements in consideration of the requirements laid out in Clause 1 of this Article shall be established by the appropriate local self-government agency with the agreement of the appropriate agencies as indicated herein. The amount of the payment must not exceed the amount of the expense incurred for conducting the work of granting permission to distribute outdoor advertisements, determining the locations of their placement and controlling the condition of the outdoor advertisement and technical means for their stable territorial distribution.

3. Distributing outdoor advertisements through installations on a territory (including on the territory of cultural monuments, ritual objects and protected natural areas), buildings, facilities or other objects, and determining the amount of and procedure for payments to be made for distributing the indicated advertisement shall be done on the basis of an agreement with the owner of the property or the person with proprietary rights to the property, if not otherwise stated by law or agreement in regard to the person with proprietary rights to the property, and contingent upon permission as provided for under Clause 2 of this Article.

Article 15. Particulars of Advertisements on Transport Means and Postal Services.

1. Distributing advertisements on transport means shall be done on the basis of agreements with the owners of transport means or with persons with proprietary rights

to the transport means, if a law or agreement does not provide otherwise in relation to the person with proprietary rights to the property.

Cases of limitation and prohibition of distributing advertisements on transport means for the purpose of ensuring the safety of traffic movement shall be determined by the authorized agency controlling the safety of traffic movement.

2. Distributing advertisements on postal services shall be carried out only with the permission of the federal executive authority to whose jurisdiction questions of postal communications are referred. The procedure for granting this permission and the amount of payment charged shall be established by the indicated body. The said payment must not exceed the cost of conducting the work of granting the permission for the dissemination of an advertisement. Payment shall be made to the federal budget in full.

Article 16. Particulars of Advertisements for Various Types of Goods.

1. Advertisements for alcoholic drinks, tobacco and tobacco products disseminated by any method must not:

- contain demonstrations of the process of smoking or the use of alcoholic drinks, and must not create the impression that the use of alcohol or the action of smoking has any important significance for attaining social, sporting or personal success, or for improving physical or psychological condition;
- discredit abstinence from using alcohol or from smoking, contain information on any positive therapeutic property of alcohol, tobacco or tobacco products or represent the high content of properties in the product as a merit;
- appeal directly to minors or use images of physical persons under 35 years of age, or use the opinions or participation of persons who are popular among minors and persons under 21 years of age;
- be disseminated on radio or television programs between 7 am and 10 p.m. local time;
- be disseminated in any form on radio or television programs, cinema or video services or in printed publications for minors;
- be disseminated on the first or last pages of a newspaper or on the first or last pages or covers of a magazine;
- be disseminated at children's, scholastic, medical, sporting or cultural organizations, or within 100 meters of them.

The dissemination of advertisements for tobacco and tobacco products in all cases must be accompanied by a warning on the dangers of smoking. For radio and television programs, the said warning must be given not less than 3 seconds of air time, and in other forms of dissemination of an advertisement, the warning must be not less than five percent of the total area (expanse) of the advertisement.

2. Advertisements for medicaments, products with a medicinal purpose and medical technology that do not have permission for production and/or sale, and

advertisements for methods of treatment, prevention, diagnosis, and rehabilitation that do not have permission for the furnishing of such services as granted by the federal executive authority in the field of health care are not permitted, including in cases where a patent has been received for an invention in this field.

Advertisements for medicines issued on the prescription of a doctor and advertisements for products with a medicinal purpose and medical technology, the use of which requires specialist training, shall be allowed upon consideration of the requirements provided for in the first paragraph of this clause, only in printed publications intended for use by medical and pharmaceutical employees.

3. Advertisements for all types of weapons, armaments and military technology are not permitted, with the exception of advertisements for war and service weapons, armaments and military technology as named in the list of military products, the export and import of which is carried out in the Russian Federation pursuant to a license, and also permitted civilian weapons, including those for hunting and sport.

Advertisements for civilian weapons, armaments and military technology that are on the list of military products, the export and import of which is carried out in the Russian Federation pursuant to a license, are not permitted if the indicated advertisement directly or indirectly discloses the technological production or methods of military and specialized application of weapons, armaments or military technology.

The dissemination of advertisements for permitted civilian weapons including hunting and sporting weapons is permitted only in periodically printed publications specializing in the dissemination of advertisements and in other periodically printed publications intended for users of permitted civilian weapons, and in places where hunting and sporting weapons are used.

The dissemination of advertisements for permitted civilian weapons through electronic means of mass media shall be permitted only after 10 p.m. local time.

Advertisements for fighting and service weapons and for armaments and military technology that are contained on the list of military products, the import and export of which is carried out in the Russian Federation pursuant to a license, shall be permitted only in publications indicated in the Law of the Russian Federation On Weapons, and also in specialist exhibitions, sales and fairs held according to the procedure established by the Government of the Russian Federation.

Article 17. Particulars of Advertisements for Financial, Insurance and Investment Services, and for Securities.

In respect of the production, placing and dissemination of advertisements for financial (including banking), insurance, investment and other services connected with the use of monetary means of legal entities and physical persons, and also of securities, the following is not permitted:

- citing in the advertisement quantitative information that does not bear a direct relation to the advertised services or securities;

- guaranteeing the size of dividends on common inscribed shares;
- advertising securities before the registration of their issue prospectus;
- presenting any kind of guarantee, promise or proposal on the future effectiveness (profitability) of activity, including by means of announcing the growth in the value of a security;
- failing to mention even one of the conditions of the agreement if an advertisement discusses the conditions of an agreement.

Article 18. Social Advertising.

1. Social advertisements represent social and state interests and have the purpose of achieving a charitable goal.

Social advertisements must not refer to commercial organizations or individual entrepreneurs, or definite makes (models, articles) of their goods, or makes (models, articles) of goods that are the result of the entrepreneurial activity of a non-commercial organization.

2. The activity of legal entities and physical persons in the production and dissemination of social advertisements carried out free of charge and the transfer of property, including monetary means, to another legal entity or physical person for the production or dissemination of social advertisements are recognized as being for charitable aims and use of privileges provided under legislation.

3. Advertisement distributors that are organizations of the mass media are obliged to disseminate social advertisements presented by advertisers within a limit of five percent of air time (of the general printed area) per year as used within the framework established for advertising by the legislation of the Russian Federation on advertising.

Advertisement distributors that are not organizations of the mass media are obliged to disseminate social advertisements within a limit of five percent of the annual cost of services supplied by them for the dissemination of advertisements.

Advertisement producers are obliged to supply services for the production of social advertisements within the framework of five percent of the annual volume of advertisements produced by them.

Conditions concerning the timing of placement and means of dissemination of social advertisements as proposed by advertisers shall be obligatory for advertisement distributors if the advertiser applies to the advertisement distributor not later than one month prior to the proposed period of dissemination of the social advertisement.

Payment for the production, placement and dissemination of social advertisements shall take place on the basis of an agreement.

In the event of an increase in the volume of orders for production, placement or dissemination of social advertisements above the established limits of air time, printed area, production volume, placement and dissemination of such advertisements and in the event of disagreements, the order of production, placement and dissemination of social advertisements shall be determined according to the order of receipt by the advertisement producer and advertisement distributor of the offer of the advertiser.

4. Any activities of an advertisement producer and advertisement disseminator that impede the production, placement or dissemination of a social advertisement within the limits established in clause 3 of this Article are not permitted. In the event such activities take place, they will be subject to appeal in court in the due procedure.

Article 19. Sponsorship.

For the purpose of this Federal Law the term sponsorship means the making by a legal entity or physical person (sponsor) of a contribution (in the form of property, the results of intellectual activity, the furnishing of services or the performing of work) to the activities of another legal entity or physical person (sponsored person) on the condition of dissemination of sponsored advertisements about the sponsor or its products.

Sponsorship contributions are recognized as payment for advertising, and the sponsor and the sponsored person are respectively the advertiser and advertisement disseminator.

A sponsor does not have the right to interfere in the activities of the sponsored person.

Article 20. Defense of Minors in the Production, Placement and Dissemination of Advertisements.

1. During production, placement and dissemination of advertisements, for the purpose of defending minors from any abuse of their vulnerability or lack of experience, the following is not permitted:

- discrediting the authority of parents and teachers or undermining a minor's trust in them;
- suggesting directly to minors that they convince parents or other persons to acquire advertised goods;
- attracting the attention of minors to the notion that the possession of this or that good gives them some kind of advantage over other minors, and also to the notion that a lack of these goods results in the opposite effect;
- mixing into the advertisement textual, visual or audible information that shows minors in dangerous places or situations;
- underestimation of the level of experience necessary for a minor to use a good. In the event that the results of the use of a good is shown or described, the advertisement must give information on what is actually attainable for minors of the age group for which the good is intended;
- the creation in minors of an unrealistic (distorted) idea of the cost (price) of a good for minors, in particular by means of the application of the words "only," "all of"

and so forth, and by means of a direct or indirect indication that the advertised good is attainable within any family budget.

2. Textual, visual or audible use of examples of minors in an advertisement not directly relating to a good for minors is not permitted.

Chapter III. Rights and Responsibilities of Advertisers, Advertisement Producers and Advertisement Disseminators.

Article 21. Time Period for Holding Advertising Materials.

The advertiser, advertisement producer and advertisement distributor are obliged to retain materials or copies containing advertising matter, including all ensuing changes, for a period of one year from the day of last dissemination of the advertisement.

Article 22. Availability of Advertising Information for the Development and Dissemination of an Advertisement.

1. The advertisement producer and advertisement distributor have the right to demand, and the advertiser shall be, in such event, obliged to provide documented proof of the authenticity of the advertised information.

2. If the activity of the advertiser is subject to licensing, then upon advertising a corresponding good, and also upon advertising the company itself, the latter is required to present, and the advertising agent and the advertising disseminator are required to request, presentation of the corresponding license or an appropriately certified copy of it.

Article 23. Responsibility of the Advertisement Producer to Notify the Advertiser of Circumstances That May Have Violated the Legislation of the Russian Federation on Advertising.

The advertisement producer must in a timely manner notify the advertiser of the fact that compliance with the demands of the latter may lead to the violation of the legislation of the Russian Federation on advertising.

If the advertiser, despite a timely and substantiated warning by the advertisement producer, does not change its demand (demands) for a given advertisement, or fails to submit, at the request of the advertisement producer, documented proof of the authenticity of the information to be contained in the advertisement, or fails to remove other items that may make the advertisement inappropriate, then the advertisement producer may, in the established procedure, terminate its agreement and demand a full compensation for losses, if the agreement does not provide otherwise.

Article 24. Submitting Information to Executive Authorities.

Advertisers, advertisement producers and advertisement distributors must, at the request of federal executive authorities (their territorial agencies) empowered to control the observance of the legislation of the Russian Federation on advertising submit within the established time period authentic documents, oral or written explanations, video and audio recordings and any other information necessary for the implementation of the legislation on advertising provided for by the Russian Federation.

Article 25. Public Offer to Conclude an Agreement in Advertising.

1. The consequences of accepting an advertisement for an invitation to make offers, or public offers (a public offer to conclude an agreement in an advertisement) shall be determined in accordance with the civil legislation of the Russian Federation.

2. The advertiser must specify the duration period of the advertisement acting as an invitation to make offers if the advertisement lists at least one of the essential conditions, as well as those advertisements that act as public offers.

3. If the advertiser declines to conclude an agreement after receiving, in the established order, acceptance from the person to whom such a public offer was addressed, then such person has the right to turn to the courts or arbitration courts with demands to conclude the agreement and to receive reimbursement for expenses caused by an unfounded refusal to conclude an agreement by an advertiser.

Chapter IV. State Control and Self-Regulation in the Area of Advertising.

Article 26. Rights of the Federal Anti-Monopoly Agency for State Control in the Area of Advertising.

1. The federal anti-monopoly agency (its territorial agency) shall control, within the bounds of its competence, the observance of the legislation of the Russian Federation on advertising. This agency (its territorial agency):

- shall warn and put a stop to facts of improper advertisement by legal entities or natural persons;
- shall issue to advertisers, advertisement producers and advertisement distributors written instructions to discontinue violations of the legislation of the Russian Federation on advertising, and decisions on producing counter-advertisements;
- shall send materials on the violation of the legislation of the Russian Federation on advertising to the agency that issued the license, in order to resolve a matter regarding suspension or early revocation of the license for the corresponding type of activity;
- shall send to the public prosecutor's office and other authorities within its jurisdiction materials needed for a decision on whether to start a criminal proceeding on the basis of the violations in the area of advertising.

2. The federal anti-monopoly agency (its territorial agency) shall have the right to make claims in the courts or arbitration courts, as well as in the interest of an indeterminate group of advertisement consumers in connection with the violation of legislation of the Russian Federation on advertising by advertisers, advertisement producers and advertisement distributors, and on recognizing the invalidity of transactions connected with improper advertisements.

3. When making claims in the courts or arbitration courts, the federal anti-monopoly agency and its territorial agencies are exempt from paying state duties.

4. Federal executive authorities, authorized in accordance with the legislation of the Russian Federation, within their competence to take measures to protect consumer rights and suppress unfair competition, shall have the right to conclude agreements with advertisers, advertisement producers and advertisement distributors for observing the rules and customs of advertising practices.

Article 27. Right of Access to Information.

1. Officers of the federal anti-monopoly agency (its territorial agency), in order to fulfill the functions entrusted to them in controlling the observance of the legislation of the Russian Federation on advertising, shall have the right to unimpeded access to all necessary documents and other materials of advertisers, advertisement producers and advertisement distributors.

2. Information comprising commercial secrets and received by the individuals mentioned in Clause 1 of this Article is not to be made public.

In the event such confidential information is made public, the losses incurred as a result shall be compensated by the federal anti-monopoly agency (its territorial agency) in the procedure established by legislation.

3. Persons mentioned in Clause 1 of this Article shall be allowed access to organizations conducting activities connected with the use of information comprising state secrets in the procedure established by the legislation of the Russian Federation.

Article 28. The Rights of Self-Regulatory Agencies in the Field of Advertising.

1. Self-regulatory agencies in the field of advertising, i.e., social organizations (societies), associations and unions of legal persons, shall:

- participate in the development of the rules on advertising, including draft laws and other normative acts;
- conduct independent examination by advertising experts on the subject of establishing its (their) conformity to the requirements of legislation of the Russian Federation on advertising, and shall forward corresponding recommendations to advertisers, advertisement producers and advertisement distributors;
- be used by the federal anti-monopoly agency (its territorial agency) when it is fulfilling its duties of regulating the observance of the legislation of the Russian Federation on advertising;
- forward to the public prosecutor's office materials and turn to the federal executive authorities in connection with violations of the legislation of the Russian Federation on advertising.

2. Self-regulatory agencies in the field of advertising have the right to make claims in courts or arbitration courts in the established procedure in the interests of

advertising consumers, including an undetermined group of advertising consumers, in the event their rights as provided for by the legislation of the Russian Federation are violated.

After satisfying a claim in regard to an undetermined group of advertisement consumers, the courts or the arbitration courts shall require the offender to bring the decision of the court or arbitration court to the attention of the indicated consumers by means of mass information or otherwise, in the time period determined by them.

Chapter V. Counter-Advertising and Responsibility for Improper Advertising.

Article 29. Counter-Advertising.

1. If the fact of a violation of the legislation of the Russian Federation on advertising has been established, then the offender must produce a counter-advertisement within the time period determined by the federal anti-monopoly agency (its territorial agency) that made the ruling in regard to the counter-advertisement. The expenses incurred for the counter-advertisement shall be the sole responsibility of the offender.

2. In the event the offender does not produce a counter-advertisement within the specified time period, then the federal anti-monopoly agency (its territorial agency) that made the ruling in regard to the counter-advertisement shall have the right to make a decision on the full or partial suspension of the offender's advertisements until the day the offender finishes distributing the counter-advertisement.

In addition, the agency that made the ruling to suspend the offender's advertisements in full or in part must notify all parties of this fact who are under contract with the offender to produce, place and distribute its advertisements immediately.

3. The dissemination of a counter-advertisement shall be handled in the same manner and for the same duration, space, placement and in the same order as the refuted advertisement. The content of the counter-advertisement shall be agreed upon with the federal anti-monopoly agency (its territorial agency) that established the fact of the violation and made an appropriate decision regarding its rectification.

In specific cases, in respect to the decision made by the federal anti-monopoly agency (its territorial agency) which made the ruling on the counter-advertisement, substitutions may be made regarding the means of dissemination, duration, space, place and order for implementing the counter-advertisements.

Article 30. Responsibility of the Advertiser, Advertisement Producer, and Advertisement Distributor.

The advertiser bears responsibility for violating the legislation of the Russian Federation on advertising in respect of the contents of the information submitted for the creation of an advertisement, unless it is proved that the violation occurred at the fault of the advertisement producer or the advertisement distributor.

The advertisement producer bears responsibility for violating the legislation of the Russian Federation on advertising in respect of the execution, production, and preparation of the advertisement.

The advertising distributor bears responsibility for violating the legislation of the Russian Federation on advertising in respect of the duration, place and the means of placing the advertisement.

Article 31. Responsibility for Violating the Legislation of the Russian Federation on Advertising.

1. Legal entities or persons (advertisers, advertisement producers and advertisement distributors) bear civil responsibility in accordance with the legislation of the Russian Federation for the violation of the legislation of the Russian Federation on advertising.

Persons whose rights and interests are violated as a result of improper advertisements have the right to turn to the courts or the arbitration courts in the established procedure with claims, including claims for the reimbursement of losses, lost profits, damage caused to health and property, compensation for moral damage, and public retraction of inappropriate advertisements.

Persons with claims seeking compensation for damages to health, property, dignity, honor and business reputation caused by improper advertisement shall be exempt from the payment of state duties.

2. Improper advertisement, or refusal to counter-advertise, or non-submission of information in the determined time period at the request of the federal anti-monopoly agency (its territorial agency) shall result in administrative responsibility in the form of a warning or a penalty in an amount of up to 200 times the minimum wage, as determined by federal law.

Improper advertisement, repeated within a year of the imposition of administrative deductions and penalties for the same activity, shall be considered a criminal offence in accordance with the legislation of the Russian Federation.

Knowingly false advertising, produced for the purpose of receiving profits (earnings), that causes considerable harm to the state or the public interest or to the rights and interests of persons regulated by law shall be considered a criminal offence in accordance with the legislation of the Russian Federation.

3. The federal anti-monopoly agency (its territorial agency) shall have the right to impose fines on advertisers, advertisement producers and advertisement distributors in the amount of 5,000 times the minimal wage established by federal law for failure to stop within the determined time period violations of the legislation of the Russian Federation on advertising and decisions on producing counter-advertisements.

The amount of fines payable by advertisers, advertisement producers or advertisement disseminators in accordance with this Federal Law shall be entered into the appropriate budgets as follows:

(a) 40 percent—to the federal budget;

(b) 60 percent—to the budgets of the subjects of the Russian Federation on the territory where the legal entity or individual entrepreneur (the advertiser, advertisement producer or advertisement distributor) is registered.

Penalty amounts shall be withheld by the courts if the payments are not made voluntarily.

The payment of a fine shall not relieve an advertiser, advertisement producer or advertisement distributor from fulfilling a court order to stop violating the legislation of the Russian Federation on advertising or from a ruling on producing a counter-advertisement.

4. The advertiser, advertisement producer or advertisement disseminator has the right to turn to the courts or arbitration courts with an application to recognize as fully or partially invalid the decision of the federal anti-monopoly agency (its territorial agency) in accordance with the legislation of the Russian Federation.

Filing such an appeal shall not excuse the filer from fulfilling the demands of the order or the decision of the federal anti-monopoly agency (its territorial agency), unless the courts or arbitration courts make a decision to suspend the fulfillment of such order or decision.

Chapter VI. Closing Provisions.

Article 32. International Agreements of the Russian Federation in the Field of Advertising.

If an international agreement of the Russian Federation has established other rules on advertising different from the ones provided by this Federal Law, then the international rules shall be observed.

Article 33. On Implementation of This Federal Law.

1. This Federal Law shall come into force on the day of its official publication.

2. The effectiveness of Article 16(1) of this Federal Law, in respect of advertisements for alcohol, tobacco and tobacco products in television programs, shall be repealed as of January 1, 1996, and advertisements for these goods in television programs shall not be allowed from that moment on.

3. It is proposed that the President of the Russian Federation introduce normative legal acts promulgated by him in accordance with this Federal Law.

4. The Government of the Russian Federation is authorized:

(a) to prepare suggestions on updating legislative acts of the Russian Federation in accordance with this Federal Law;

(b) to bring normative legal acts of the Government of the Russian Federation into conformity with this Federal Law.

Russian Federation Government Decree No. 941 On Licensing of Activity Involving Public Screening of Cinema and Video Films

September 15, 1995

1. The present Statute shall establish the rules for the licensing of activity involving the public screening of cinema and video films in cinemas, on television or by means of other technical devices, and effected by legal persons, irrespective of their legal-organization form, and also by natural persons doing business without formation of a legal person.

2. The license shall be an official authorization document certifying the right to conduct activity involving the public screening of cinema and video films and regulating the conditions for effecting this activity on the basis of compliance with the license conditions and Russian Federation legislation.

3. The licensing shall be effected by the organs of executive power of Russian Federation subjects on the basis of the present Statute and in conformity with Russian Federation legislation.

4. The effect of the license shall not apply to other persons engaged in activity together with the license-holder, including activity under contract of cooperation, or to legal persons whose founder (one of whose founders) is the license-holder.

5. Licenses shall be issued for a period of three to five years, unless a shorter period is requested in the application for obtaining a license.

Prolongation of license validity shall be made in the manner established for the receipt thereof.

6. Consideration of applications for the issue of licenses and the issue of licenses shall carry a charge.

7. The Russian Federation Committee for Cinematography shall:

- keep a single register of license-holders effecting the public screening of cinema and video films, and shall create an information databank on the basis thereof;
- provide methodological, information and consultation assistance to the organs of executive power of Russian Federation subjects in the arrangement and conduct of licensing activity by them.

8. In order to obtain a license, the applicant shall file an application for the issue of a license, which shall state the following:

- for legal persons—title and legal-organization form, juridical address, and banking requisites;
- for natural persons—full name, passport data (series, number, when issued and by whom), and place of residence;

- type of activity;
- period of license validity.

9. The following shall be attached to the application:

- copies of founding documents (where these are not notarized, with presentation of the originals);
- a copy of the certificate of state registration of the legal person;
- a document confirming payment for consideration of the application;
- a tax agency statement confirming entry on the records or a certificate of state registration of the natural person as an entrepreneur, duly stamped by the tax agency;
- findings by agencies of the Sanitation and Epidemiological Service and State Fire-Prevention Service on correspondence of the cinema or of the cinema or video-film unit with the stated requirements;
- a document containing information on the qualification of specialists handling the work of the cinema or video-film projection equipment.

An application for the issue of a license shall be accepted for consideration only where all the above-listed documents are available.

10. All documents filed for obtaining a license shall be registered.

Demand that the applicant present documents other than those specified in the present Statute shall be prohibited.

11. A decision on the issue or on denial of issue of a license shall be made within 30 days of the day of receipt of the application with all the requisite documents.

Where the need arises for an additional, including independent, expert examination, the decision shall be made within the period of 15 days from the day of receipt of the expert findings, but not later than 60 days from the day of the filing of the application with all the requisite documents.

In certain cases, depending on the complexity and volume of the materials subject to expert examination, the period for deciding whether to grant or deny issue of issue of a license may be additionally prolonged up to 30 days.

12. A license shall be issued after presentation by the applicant of a document confirming payment of the required fee.

13. Notice of denial of issue of a license shall be served on the applicant in writing within the period of three days after the decision with an explanation.

The following shall be grounds for denial of issue of a license:

- presence of unauthentic or distorted information in the documents filed by the applicant;

- negative expert findings establishing a discrepancy between the filed documents and the conditions required for carrying on the respective type of activity or safety conditions.

14. In conducting the licensed activity, the license-holder shall have the duty:

(a) to comply with the norms established by Russian Federation legislation in the field of entrepreneurial activity, protection of the rights of consumers, copyright and allied rights, and also technical-organization and technological requirements pertaining to the quality of public screening of cinema and video films and safety in servicing audiences;

(b) to have the following documents for cinema and video films of the Russian Federation, foreign or joint production intended for public screening:

  - a contract for acquisition of rights to use the screened cinema and video films;
  - a notarized copy of the distribution certificate or a copy of the distribution certificate attested by the state register of cinema and video films of the Russian Federation Committee for Cinematography presented by the owner of the cinema or video film, containing information on age-group limitations and ways of dissemination of the film.

15. License-holders operating in cinemas or with the use of cinema and video-film units shall have the duty:

- to observe the rules for providing cinema and video services to the population;
- to keep a mandatory record of the cash received through cinema tickets, in accordance with the normative acts in effect;
- to have a certificate of quality (technical passport) confirming correspondence of the cinema and video materials with the requirements of technical-normative documentation.

16. Activity on the basis of a license issued by an organ of executive power of a Russian Federation subject may be effected on the territory of other Russian Federation subjects after registration of such license by the organs of executive power of the respective Russian Federation subjects, in the manner established by Russian Federation Government Decree No. 1418 of December 24, 1994, on the Licensing of Some Types of Activity.

17. Upon liquidation of a business person or upon lapse of the validity of a certificate on the state registration of a natural person as an entrepreneur, the license issued to him shall lose its legal force.

18. In the event of reorganization or change of title of a legal person or of legal address, alteration of passport data or place of residence of a natural person, or loss of license, the license-holder shall have the duty, within the period of 15 days from the day of such reorganization (alteration, loss), to file an application for reprocessing of the license.

Reprocessing of a license shall be made in the manner established for the receipt thereof.

Pending reprocessing, the license-holder shall conduct his or her activity on the basis of the earlier-issued license.

19. Upon loss of a license, a duplicate shall be issued with the marking "Duplicate" on the blank license.

20. The fee for the issue of a license (or duplicate thereof) shall be determined in the light of the costs arising for the organ of executive power of the Russian Federation subject authorized to conduct licensing activity, according to the rules of establishing the license fee, as worked out by the Russian Federation Ministry of Economics and the Russian Federation Ministry of Finance.

21. In the event of adoption of a decision or denial of issue of a license, the charge for consideration of the application shall not be subject to refund.

22. For prolongation, and also for reregistration of a license (in the event of changes in the conditions of license validity), the license fee shall be the same as for the issue of a license.

23. License blanks shall have a degree of protection on the level of bearer securities, a registration series and number, and shall be documents of strict accountability.

24. Acquisition, recording and safekeeping of license blanks shall be effected by the organs of state power of Russian Federation subjects authorized to conduct licensing activity.

25. An organ of executive power of Russian Federation subject authorized to conduct licensing activity shall suspend the effect of a license or cancel it in the following cases:

(a) filing by the license-holder of an application to that effect;

(b) discovery of unauthentic data in the documents submitted for obtaining the license;

(c) nonfulfillment by the license-holder of directives or orders of state organs or suspension by these organs of the activity of a business person, and also a natural person doing business without formation of a legal person, in conformity with Russian Federation legislation;

(d) liquidation of business person or lapse of the validity of a certificate on the state registration of a natural person as an entrepreneur;

(e) breach by the license-holder of the conditions of license validity.

26. The organ of executive power of the Russian Federation subject authorized to conduct licensing activity shall suspend the effect of a license registered in its territory and issued by the organ of executive power of another Russian Federation subject, in the event of nonfulfillment by the license-holder of the requirements laid down for conducting the corresponding type of activity in the given territory.

The agency issuing the license shall inform Russian Federation State Tax Service agencies and the license-holder of the suspension of the validity of a registered license, in writing, within the period of three days from the day of adoption of the respective decision.

27. A license shall be subject to surrender to the organ of executive power of the Russian Federation subject authorized to conduct licensing activity within the period of 10 days from the day of receipt by the license-holder of the notice of cancellation thereof.

28. In the event of a change in the circumstances entailing suspension of license validity, the license validity may be revived.

A license shall be deemed revived upon adoption of a corresponding decision by the organ of executive power of the Russian Federation subject authorized to conduct licensing activity, of which it shall, not later than within three days from the day of adoption of the decision, notify the license-holder and Russian Federation State Tax Service agencies.

29. Suspension of license validity may also be effected by other agencies vested with this right under Russian Federation legislation.

30. Organs of executive power of Russian Federation subjects authorized to conduct licensing activity shall keep a register of issued, registered, suspended and cancelled licenses, and shall, within the period of 14 days after issue (registration, suspension, cancellation) of a license, address the corresponding information to the Russian Federation Committee for Cinematography for entry of the information on the single register of license-holders engaged in the public screening of cinema and video films.

31. Control of compliance with the conditions provided for by the issued licenses shall be exercised by the organs of executive power of Russian Federation subjects authorized to conduct licensing activity.

Other state agencies vested with the right of control under Russian Federation legislation may also be involved in the work of verifying compliance with the conditions of conducting the licensed type of activity.

32. The requirements of the agencies ensuring, within the limits of their competence, control of compliance with the conditions of conducting licensed activity shall be binding on the license-holders.

Controlling agencies shall have the right to request the organs of executive power of Russian Federation subjects to suspend the validity of a license or to cancel it.

33. In the event of breach of the conditions stated in the license, a directive shall be issued on elimination of the discovered breaches, with an indication of the period for liquidation thereof.

Pending elimination of the breaches, the validity of the license may be suspended.

34. Upon repeated breach of the conditions for the conduct of licensed types of activity, the organs of executive power of Russian Federation subjects authorized to conduct licensing activity shall be entitled to cancel the license.

In this event, the license-holder shall have the right to file another application for receipt of a license for the respective type of activity only upon expiration of one year from the day of cancellation of the license.

35. The suspension or cancellation of license validity shall be made known to the license-holder in writing not later than three days from the day of adoption of the decision.

36. Decisions and acts of the organs of executive power of Russian Federation subjects authorized to conduct licensing activity may be appealed against in judicial proceedings.

37. Heads and officers of the organs of executive power of Russian Federation subjects authorized to conduct licensing activity shall bear liability for breach or improper performance of the established rules for the conduct thereof.

Election Regulations for State Television and Radio Companies No. 18/149-P*

September 20, 1995

On the Procedure for Granting Air Time on Channels of State TV and Radio Companies to Electoral Associations, Electoral Blocs and Candidates for Deputy of the State Duma of the Federal Assembly of the Russian Federation and Publication of Election Campaign Materials in Periodicals with Government Participation

Chapter I. General Provisions.

1. These Regulations were issued in compliance with the requirement of the Federal Law On Basic Guarantees of Electoral Rights of Citizens of the Russian Federation, the Federal Law On Elections of Deputies of the State Duma of the Federal Assembly of the Russian Federation, the Law of the Russian Federation On the Mass Media and cover the procedure for and conditions of election communication.

2. Electoral associations, electoral blocs and candidates for deputy have the right to communicate via non-governmental mass media provided that all participants in the electoral process observe basic principles established by the Federal Laws. Electoral propaganda activities must be financed exclusively via electoral funds of electoral associations, electoral blocs or candidates for deputy.

These Regulations shall not establish a procedure for election communication via non-governmental mass media.

3. In the period of election campaign, governmental mass media and their officers and creative workers in their reports, materials and broadcasts shall abstain from any form of support or bias towards any electoral associations, electoral blocs or candidates for deputy, and their election programs.

4. The following terms are used in these Regulations:

- *election communication*—activities of citizens, electoral associations, electoral blocs, candidates for deputy and other subjects of the electoral process provided for by these Regulations for the preparation and the dissemination of information established by the Law through the mass media in order to persuade voters to vote for or against one or another candidate or a Federal list of candidates;
- *kinds of election communication*—a speech, interview, press conference, election debates, "round tables" or political advertisement;
- *speech*—a personal message (monologue) of a representative of electoral association or electoral bloc or a candidate for deputy addressed to voters stating

* Approved by the Central Election Commission of the Russian Federation. Translated by the International Foundation for Electoral Systems.

his or her election program if such a message is delivered beyond the framework of other kinds of election communication;

- *interview*—answers by a candidate for deputy or a representative of electoral association or electoral bloc to questions asked in a personal meeting with a journalist (journalists);
- *press-conference*—a statement by a representative of an electoral association or electoral bloc or a candidate for deputy of his or her own election program before representatives of the press, TV and radio, including answers to questions asked by journalists;
- *election debates*—comments by two or more representatives of electoral associations or electoral blocs or candidates for deputy on a wide range of vital social problems, including messages related to election programs (platforms) or the contending candidates, electoral associations, or electoral blocs made at a public exchange of opinions and questions;
- *"round table"*—an exchange of opinions, questions and answers between representatives of electoral associations, electoral blocs, candidates for deputy, and representatives of the mass media, TV and radio audiences, and readers held within the framework of election propaganda campaign;
- *political advertisement*—information and materials (announcements, slogans, video/audio clips, etc) on electoral associations, electoral blocs or candidates for deputy communicated through the mass media by subjects of electoral process involving the use of means and methods particular for advertisements in contrast to other information types and genres (emotional effect prevailing over meaning, arresting sentences, laconicism stressing the main advantages of the advertised subject) and accepted as the features of advertisement by the Federal Laws and mass media practice for the purpose of shaping public opinion for the benefit of electoral associations, electoral blocs or candidates for deputy;
- *information program*—TV and radio program periodically broadcast by TV and radio companies and containing information on current events and news;
- *state TV and radio company*—a TV and radio company founded (or co-founded) by a government authority;
- *all-Russia state TV and radio company* (hereinafter *STRC*)—a state TV and radio company whose zone of regular and continuous coverage encompasses half or more than half of the subjects of the Russian Federation;
- *regional TV and radio company* (hereinafter *RTRC*)—a state TV and radio company whose zone of regular and continuous coverage encompasses less than half of the electoral districts but at least a territory within administrative borders of a subject of the Russian Federation;
- *municipal TV and radio company*—a TV and radio company founded (or co-founded) by a local government authority whose zone of regular and continuous

coverage is within one or more administrative territories of a subject of the Russian Federation;

- *periodical with government participation*—a publication founded (or co-founded) by a government authority, government enterprise, institution, organization or publication which are fully or partially financed (minimum 25%) from the Federal budget or a budget of a subject of the Russian Federation;
- *a municipal periodical*—a publication founded (or co-founded) by a local government authority, municipal enterprises, institutions, organizations or publication which are fully or partially financed (minimum 25%) from the local budget.

5. The list of all-Russia TRCs and periodicals with government participation shall be published by the Central Election Commission of the Russian Federation as submitted by the Federal TV and Radio Service of the Committee for Printed Media of the Russian Federation while the list of regional TRCs and municipal periodicals by election commissions of the subjects of the Russian Federation as submitted to mass media by relevant regional TRCs no later than October 15, 1995.

Chapter II. The Procedure for Granting Air Time on Channels of State TV and Radio Companies.

1. Electoral associations or electoral blocs that are registered in the federal list of candidates with the Central Election Commission of the Russian Federation for election communication shall have the right to use the All-Russia and regional TRCs. Moreover, a regional group of candidates (by subjects or groups of subjects of the Russian Federation) shall be serviced only by those regional TRCs whose zone of regular and continuous coverage is within the administrative borders of the relevant subjects of the Russian Federation.

2. Candidates for deputy at single mandate electoral districts for the purpose of election communication shall have the right to use regional TRC and municipal TV and radio companies.

The order of granting air time to candidates for deputy at the channels of municipal TV and radio companies shall be regulated by district election commissions in accordance with the Federal Laws on election and accounting for basic provisions of these Regulations.

3. Electoral associations, electoral blocs and candidates for deputy shall be entitled to free and paid air time on the channels of All-Russia and regional TRCs respectively on an equal basis in terms of amount of air time, broadcasting slot, amount and order of payment for air time and other conditions.

4. TV and radio companies shall publicly announce (or declare) the amount of payment for provided air time no later than October 15, 1995.

In the period of elections, TV and radio companies shall have the right to establish a different rate of payment for air time in the event of changes in respective state-regulated prices and rates.

5. Electoral associations and electoral blocs shall be granted free air time on channels of All-Russia TRCs in the period from November 15 to December 15, 1995.[1]

6. All-Russia state TV and radio companies shall be obliged to provide electoral associations and electoral blocs during weekdays with at least 30 minutes of air time between 7 and 10 a.m. and 30 minutes of air time between 6 and 11 p.m. with due regard to the time zone broadcasting in various regions of the Russian Federation.

7. The ground to provide free air time on the channels of All-Russia TRCs to an electoral association or electoral bloc that has registered in the federal list of candidates shall be the document confirming the registration of the federal list of candidates nominated by the association or the bloc and a written request of the authorized representative of an electoral association or electoral bloc to the executive of the relevant TV and radio company to be submitted no later than on the third day of the registration of the candidate list.[2]

8. Air time shall be granted to an electoral association or electoral bloc free of charge on the channels of the All-Russia TRCs in accordance with the schedule approved by the Central Election Commission of the Russian Federation.

The schedule for granting air time shall be prepared by the executives of All-Russia TRCs. The specific date and time of broadcasting shall be determined by the results of the lot held by the authorized representatives of electoral associations or electoral blocs in the presence of members of the Central Election Commission of the Russian Federation, representatives of All-Russia TRCs, members of the Judicial Chamber for Information Disputes and shall be approved by the Central Election Commission of the Russian Federation upon completion of registration of Federal lists of candidates but no later than November 5, 1995.

9. Candidates for deputy and regional groups of candidates of electoral associations or electoral blocs shall be entitled to free air time on the channels of regional TRCs in the period of November 15 to December 15, 1995.[3] Each candidate and each regional group shall be entitled to equal air time under similar conditions.

10. The ground to provide free air time to a candidate for deputy on the TV and radio shall be an identification document of a candidate for deputy and his or her written request to the executive of the relevant TV and radio company to be submitted by the candidate no later than on the third day after his or her registration with the district election commission as a candidate for deputy.

---

[1] A ten-day period from the date of the schedule for granting air time to the day of broadcasting is established as required by organizational and technical activities to be performed by All-Russia TRCs.

[2] This provision shall be applicable from October 19, 1995, after publication of the list of All-Russia TRCs by printed media.

[3] A five-day period from the date of the schedule for granting air time to the day of broadcasting is established as required by organizational and technical activities to be performed by regional TRCs.

11. The ground to provide free air time to a regional group of candidates of an electoral association or electoral bloc shall be a document confirming registration of a Federal list of candidates and a written request by the authorized representative of the electoral association or electoral bloc to the executive of the respective regional TRC to be submitted through the regional group no later than on the third day after registration of the Federal list of candidates.[4]

12. In the event a regional TRC is technically incapable of granting free air time to each candidate or each regional group of candidates, the relevant election commission of the subject of the Russian Federation shall, within schedules set by these Regulations, approve a schedule for election debates or "round tables" between candidates or regional groups of candidates to ensure that equal conditions to each candidate for deputy or each regional group of candidates is provided under similar conditions.

13. Air time on the channels of regional TRCs shall be provided free-of-charge to candidates for deputy, regional groups of candidates of an electoral association or electoral bloc in compliance with the schedule approved by the relevant election commission of the subject of the Russian Federation.

The schedule for granting air time shall be prepared by the executives of the relevant regional TRC. The specific date and time of broadcasting shall be determined by the results of the lot held by the election commission of the subject of the Russian Federation among candidates and representatives of regional groups in the presence of members of the election commission of the subject of the Russian Federation and representatives of the regional TRC, and shall be approved by the relevant election commission of the subject of the Russian Federation upon completion of registration of candidates for deputy or Federal lists of candidates and publication of the schedule for granting air time to electoral associations or electoral blocs but no later than November 10, 1995.

14. Schedules for granting free air time to electoral associations, electoral blocs and candidates for deputy shall be made public by state-owned mass media free of charge in compliance with Article 35 of the Law of the Russian Federation On the Mass Media no later than on the second day upon approval of the schedule by the relevant election commission.

15. A concerned party may appeal to the relative election commission or court against the refusal of the executives of TV and radio companies to grant free air time to an electoral association, electoral bloc or a candidate for deputy in violation of the equality principle in the use of mass media for election communication set by law.

The aforesaid bodies shall be entitled to oblige the executives of such TV and radio companies to grant free air time guaranteed by law to electoral association, electoral bloc or a candidate for deputy.

---

[4] Provisions established in paragraphs 2.10 and 2.11 shall be applicable from October 19, 1995, after publication of the list of regional TRCs by printed media.

16. An electoral association, an electoral bloc, or a candidate for deputy shall in accordance with the kind of election communication agreed with the TV and radio company and within the framework of broadcast time granted free of charge independently determine the contents of information and composition of their representatives (or participants).

17. The expenses of the All-Russia and regional TRCs related to the granting of free air time to electoral associations, electoral blocs or candidates for deputy shall be indemnified from the relevant budget (federal budget or the budget of a subject of the Russian Federation).

18. An electoral association, an electoral bloc, or a candidate for deputy shall be entitled to get, under a contract concluded with All-Russia and regional TRCs, additional paid air time that shall not exceed the amount of free air time granted. The amount of free and paid air time granted by regional TRC shall be correlated depending on their technical and program capacity. The air time shall be paid for by electoral associations, electoral blocs and candidates exclusively from their own electoral funds.

19. Electoral associations, electoral blocs and candidates for deputy shall be granted air time for a fee on the channels of All-Russia and regional TRCs in the period specified in paragraphs 2(5) and 2(9) of these Regulations.

20. An electoral association, electoral bloc or a candidate for deputy willing to get paid air time on the channels of All-Russia and regional TRCs shall submit to the relevant TV and radio company a written request (electoral associations or electoral blocs to regional TRC through regional groups of candidates) for paid air time for election communication and a document confirming registration of the Federal list of candidates or candidates for deputy no later than on the third day after registration of the Federal lists of candidates or candidates for a single mandate electoral districts.[5]

Paid air time shall be granted to an electoral association, an electoral bloc, a candidate for deputy, or a regional group of candidates on the channels of the state-owned TV and radio companies in accordance with schedules drawn up by the management of the relevant All-Russia and regional TRCs no later than November 13, 1995.

The specific dates and time of the broadcasting shall be determined on the basis of submitted requests and on the results of the lot held by the management of a TV and radio company. The schedule shall be published by printed media no later than on the second day upon its completion.

21. Contracts between electoral associations, electoral blocs, candidates for deputy and TV and radio companies for granting paid air time shall contain the following terms and conditions: kind of election communication, broadcast time, the amount of granted time, the amount and procedure of payment for granted air time and other

[5] This provision shall be applicable from October 19, 1995, after publication of the list of periodicals with state participation by printed media.

conditions. Payment shall be made before granting of air time. Air time shall not be granted unless payment is confirmed by the relevant documents.

22. TV and radio companies shall keep track of free and paid air time granted to electoral associations, electoral blocs and candidates for deputy for election communication and inform about the granted air time as requested by relevant election commissions in writing and deliver to them the relevant contracts.

23. TV and radio programs containing election propaganda shall not be interrupted by commercials for goods, work and services. Free TV and radio programs containing election propaganda shall not be interrupted by election propaganda broadcast for a fee, nor shall TV and radio programs involving a particular electoral association, electoral bloc or candidate for deputy be interrupted by TV and radio programs involving other participants in the election communication.

24. TV and radio programs containing election communication materials of electoral associations or electoral blocs while being broadcast on the channels of one federal TV and radio company shall not overlap with the broadcast time of the similar TV and radio programs of another federal TV and radio company.

25. TV and radio programs containing election propaganda materials of regional groups of candidates of electoral associations, electoral blocs and candidates for deputy while being broadcast on the channels of regional TV and radio companies shall not overlap with the broadcast time of the similar TV and radio programs broadcast on the channels of federal TV and radio companies.

Regional TRCs shall not overlap with their broadcasts the programs containing election communication of electoral associations or electoral blocs broadcast on the channels of federal TRCs.

26. An electoral association, an electoral bloc, or a candidate for deputy who was granted the broadcast time for the election debates or "round table" shall be entitled to:

- organize and hold debates or "round table" at the time agreed upon with the TV and radio company;
- determine, together with other organizers of election debates and "round tables," the procedure for conducting the event;
- participate in the election debates or "round tables" organized by other electoral associations, electoral blocs or candidates for deputy unless other participants of the debates or "round tables" are against it.

27. Organizers of election debates or "round tables" shall be obliged to announce the subject matter(s) of the forthcoming debates between representatives of electoral associations, electoral blocs and candidates for deputy through the mass media in advance.

28. The TV and radio company shall appoint a mediator in election debates or "round tables" and shall notify the participants when publishing the schedule for granting broadcast time.

The mediator of election debates or "round table" shall ensure that the participants observe the procedure agreed upon prior to the event, request a reply from representatives of the electoral association, electoral bloc or candidates for deputy to a question asked by other participants of election debates or "round table" or by TV and radio audiences.

The mediator in the election debate or "round tables" shall not be entitled to:

- violate the procedure set by the organizers of election debates or "round table";
- limit the speaking time of a representative of electoral association, electoral bloc or a candidate for deputy unless otherwise provided for by the procedure agreed upon by the participants of the election debates or "round table" or unless it is caused by the expiration of air time allocated for this program;
- give preferences to any of the participants of election debates or "round tables."

29. A participant in election debates or "round tables" shall be obliged to:

- observe the procedure set for the debates or "round table";
- hold discussion in compliance with ethical standards, refrain from insulting, fraudulent, defamatory statements addressed against other participants;
- follow reasonable requests of the mediator.

30. Political advertisement disseminated by electoral associations, electoral blocs and candidates for deputy through the channels of federal and regional TRCs shall be identifiable, i.e., shall contain clear indication of the electoral association, electoral bloc or a candidate for deputy in whose interests it is disseminated.

Broadcast time of a political advertisement for one electoral association, electoral bloc or a candidate for deputy shall not exceed 10 per cent of the total broadcast time granted to them.

Under the applicable laws, an electoral association, an electoral bloc, or a candidate for deputy and the relevant TV and radio company shall be responsible for observance of requirements to political advertisements.

31. In broadcasting information programs reflecting events related to the election campaign TV and radio companies shall not give preferences to a particular electoral association, electoral bloc or candidate for deputy. No political advertisement shall be incorporated in a commercial within information programs or in any other commercials.

32. If a TV and radio company intends to broadcast a speech, press conference, interview, election debates or "round table" not live or edited, it shall be obliged to record the program live within the allocated time of broadcast.

33. All TV and radio programs containing election communication shall be broadcast with parallel video/audio recording which shall be held by the TV and radio

company within six months from the date of broadcast of the above programs and shall be made available to the relevant election commission no later than within three days from the date of the request.

Chapter III. The Procedure for Publications of Propaganda Election Materials in the Federal and State Periodicals.

1. Electoral associations or electoral blocs who are registered in the list of candidates for deputy with the Central Election Commission of the Russian Federation shall be entitled to use the federal state periodicals for purposes of election communication.

Candidates for deputy in single mandate electoral districts shall, for the purposes of election communication, be entitled to use periodicals with state participation as well as municipal periodicals that disseminate materials in the territory or part of the territory of the relevant subject of the Russian Federation (or group of subjects of the Russian Federation).

2. The order of publication of election communication materials of regional groups of candidates from electoral associations, electoral blocs or candidates for deputy in periodicals with state participation as well as the order of publication of election communication by candidates for deputy in municipal periodicals shall be established by district election commissions in accordance with Federal Laws on elections and basic provisions of these Regulations.

3. Propaganda materials of electoral associations, electoral blocs or candidates for deputy on the pages of the said periodicals shall be published with and without fees and on equal conditions in terms of space, place, time of edition, rate of payment for a printed area and other conditions.

4. Each electoral association, electoral bloc or candidate for deputy shall be entitled to free publication of election communication materials in periodicals in the period of November 5 to December 15, 1995.

Each electoral association, electoral bloc or candidate for deputy shall be entitled to a minimum of one free publication of election communication materials in periodicals.

The volume of publications for candidates registered in a single mandate district in one periodical may not exceed five, and the publications for electoral associations or electoral blocs registered in the federal lists of candidates may not exceed ten per cent of the total volume of the edition.

5. The ground for the free publication of election communication materials of electoral associations, electoral blocs or candidates for deputy shall be a document confirming the registration of the federal list of candidates, identification document of a candidate for deputy and a written request of an authorized representative of the electoral association, electoral bloc or a candidate for deputy in the name of the Editor-in-Chief (or Editor) of the relevant periodical submitted no later than on the third day after the

registration of the federal list of candidates or candidate in a single mandate electoral district.[6]

6. The schedules for free provision of printing space to electoral associations, electoral blocs and candidates for deputy shall be approved by relevant election commissions after the completion of the registration of the federal list of candidates but no later than November 5, 1995.

The schedule for free-of-charge publication of election communication materials shall be prepared by the editorial board of the periodical according to the results of the lot conducted by the editorial board of the periodical among authorized representatives of electoral associations, electoral blocs or candidates for deputy in the presence of members of the relevant election commission and the editorial board of the periodical.

7. The denial of the board of editors of a periodical to publish free election communication materials submitted to the board in the established procedure, and violation by the board of the equality principle for the use of the mass media by electoral associations, electoral blocs or candidates for deputy may be appealed against to the relevant election commission or court.

The aforesaid bodies shall be entitled to oblige the board of editors of the relevant periodical to publish free election propaganda materials of electoral association, electoral blocs or candidate for deputy.

8. Expenses of periodicals with state participation related to free publication of election communication materials of electoral associations, electoral blocs or candidates for deputy shall be financed from the relevant budget (federal budget or budget of the subject of the Russian Federation).

9. Additional paid column space in newspapers (or magazines) shall be provided to electoral associations, electoral blocs or candidates for deputy by the relevant editorial boards of periodicals under contracts concluded between them. Expenses for additional printing space shall be financed by electoral associations, electoral blocs or candidates for deputy by means of own election funds. Payment shall be made prior to provision of column space. Additional column space in newspapers (or magazines) shall not be provided unless there are documents confirming payment for additional column space.

Periodicals with state participation that published paid propaganda materials of an electoral association, electoral bloc, or a candidate for deputy shall not be entitled to refuse to provide the space under the same conditions.

10. Editorial boards of periodicals with state participation shall keep track of free and paid publication of election communication materials by electoral associations, electoral blocs or candidates for deputy and inform the relevant election commissions on provision of space in newspapers (magazines) and make available the relevant contracts as requested by the relevant election commissions in writing.

---

[6] This provision shall be applicable from October 19, 1995, after publication of the list of All-Russia and regional TRCs by printed media.

11. Political advertisement disseminated by electoral associations, electoral blocs or candidates for deputy through periodicals shall be identifiable, i.e., shall contain clear indication of the electoral association, electoral bloc or candidate for deputy in whose interests it is disseminated.

Space in a newspaper (or magazine) provided to an electoral association, electoral bloc or candidate for deputy for purposes of a political advertisement shall not exceed 10 per cent of the total space granted to them.

Under the applicable laws, an electoral association, electoral bloc or candidate for deputy and the relevant periodical shall be responsible for observance of requirements to political advertisements.

12. An electoral association, electoral bloc or candidate for deputy shall within the framework of the law independently determine the form of election communication and contents of information. Contents of the submitted materials shall not be changed without agreement with the authors.

13. Printed media founded by representative, executive, judicial authorities as well as by local governments exclusively for purposes of publishing official statements and materials, normative and other acts shall not be entitled to publish election materials containing propaganda by electoral associations, electoral blocs or candidates for deputy.

Chapter IV. Organization of Control, Settlement of Disputes, and Responsibility.

1. The Central Election Commissions of the Russian Federation, election commissions of subjects of the Russian Federation and district election commissions shall exercise control over observance of the procedure for election communication set by the federal legislation and these Regulations.

The aforesaid election commission shall be entitled to form groups to exercise control over observance by the participants of the electoral process of the procedures and rules for election communication through mass media. The groups shall consist of members of the relevant election commission including those with deliberate vote as well as experts in the spheres of law and journalism. The results of checks-up, conclusions and proposals regarding applications and complaints shall be submitted by the control groups to the relevant election commission for consideration.

2. In the event of violation of the procedure established for election communication, election commissions shall be entitled to require the competent bodies to check such actions and may appeal to a court requiring to nullify the decision on the registration of the federal lists of candidates and candidates in a single mandate election districts.

3. Election commissions shall be entitled to organize hearing of the reports by the mass media executives concerning the observance of the requirements of the legislation and these Regulations and, within the limits of their competence, to make binding decisions.

Mass media executives shall make available the information on the use of broadcast time and newspaper space by electoral associations, electoral blocs or candidates for deputy as requested by the relevant election commission within three days from the date of the request.

4. In the event of violation of the provisions of these Regulations by representatives of the mass media, the executives of the mass media may upon a reasonable request of the relevant election commission suspend journalists, creative workers and officials of the publishing house for the period of election campaign from the work related to the coverage of election campaign.

5. Electoral associations, electoral blocs, candidates for deputy or other participants of electoral process may appeal, to the relevant election commission or court, the actions made in violation of the procedure for election communication through the mass media set by law and these Regulations.

6. In compliance with the Federal legislation, the Judicial Chamber for Information Disputes shall consider and settle the information disputes of public importance that resulted from the violation of the procedure and the rules of election communication with the mass media set by law and these Regulations, ensure the observance of the principle of political pluralism, equal access to the mass media by electoral associations, electoral blocs and candidates for deputy.

The Judicial Chamber shall consider, as first priority, the disputes upon request of the Central Election Commission of the Russian Federation, electoral associations, electoral blocs, All-Russia TRCs and periodicals with state participation.

7. The Judicial Chamber shall be entitled, proceeding from the results of consideration of the disputes over information related to election communication, to propose to the Central Election Commission of the Russian Federation to submit for consideration to the relevant court the problem of nullification of the decision to register a federal list of candidates or candidates for deputy in a single mandate electoral district.

8. The hindering of the right of electoral associations, electoral blocs or candidates for deputy for free conduct of election communication and the abuse of the right to conduct communication resulted in dissemination of reports and materials inconsistent with the reality and that damage the honor, dignity and business reputation of representatives of electoral associations, electoral blocs, candidates for deputy, and their agents shall entail disciplinary, administrative or criminal penalties provided for by the federal legislation.

Federal Law No. 191-FZ On the State Support of the Mass Media and Book-Publishing in the Russian Federation*

December 1, 1995

The present Federal Law shall regulate the procedure for the State support of mass media and book-publishing and for the privatization of the enterprises ensuring their functioning, and shall be directed towards securing the citizens' constitutional right to obtain full and objective information.

Chapter I. Basic Concepts.

Article 1. Basic Concepts Used in the Present Federal Law.

For purposes of the present Federal Law these shall be understood:

- *state support of the mass (information) media*—the totality of the organizational, technical-organizational, legal, economic and any other measures established by the State for the purposes of securing the rights of citizens to obtain objective information and to exercise the freedom of speech and for the purposes of ensuring the independence of the mass media;
- *mass information*—printed, audio, audiovisual and any other messages and materials intended for an indefinite circle of persons;
- *a mass (information) medium*—a periodical printed publication, a television, radio, video or cinema newsreel program, or any other form of periodic dissemination of mass information;
- *a periodical printed publication*—a newspaper, magazine, almanac, bulletin, or any other publication having a permanent title, a current number and coming out at least once a year;
- *a television, radio, video and cinema newsreel program*—the totality of periodic audio or audiovisual news and materials (transmissions); it has a permanent title and comes out (input on the air) at least once a year;
- *products of mass media*—a circulation or a past thereof of an individual issue of a periodical printed publication, an individual release of a television, radio or cinema newsreel program, a circulation or a part thereof of an audio or video recording of a program;
- *dissemination of mass media products*—a sale (subscription, delivery, distribution) of periodical printed publications, audio or video records of programs,

* Adopted by the State Duma on October 18, 1995. Approved by the Federation Council on November 15, 1995.

transmission (broadcasting) of television and radio programs, and showing of cinema newsreel programs;

- *an editorial board of a mass medium*—an organization (regardless of the form of ownership) conducting the production and release of a mass medium;
- *a publishing house*—an enterprise of the State form of ownership or an organization of any other form of ownership, conducting the preparation, production and release of books and any other printed products;
- *a polygraphic enterprise*—an enterprise of the State form of ownership or an organization of any other form of ownership conducting the material-and-technical support of the release of newspapers, books and magazines;
- *a television and radio broadcasting organization (a television and radio (broadcasting) company, TRBC)*—an organization conducting the production, montage, arrangement in time and dissemination, with the use of electromagnetic waves (through the air, cable, wire and any other electromagnetic systems) of sound (radio broadcasting), of visual and audiovisual (television broadcasting) mass information and of data intended to be received directly by television viewers and radio listeners;
- *a transmitting center (TC)*—radio and television transmitting centers (RTTC), radio centers (RC) and any other telecommunications organizations which furnish, among other things, the services in the dissemination of television and/or radio programs prepared by the television and radio broadcasting organizations;
- *an information agency*—an organization conducting the selection and operational dissemination of information;
- *an organization for dissemination of periodical printed publications*—an organization conducting the realization of periodical printed publications both in the Russian Federation and in the States;
- *a monopolist*—an enterprise or an organization considered to be such in accordance with the antimonopoly legislation;
- *a mass medium of advertising character*—a mass medium in which advertising exceeds 40 per cent of the volume of an individual issue of a periodical publications, and in television and radio programs, 25% of the volume of broadcasting;
- *a mass medium of erotic character*—a periodical printed publications or a television or radio program which by and large and systematically make use of the interest in sex.

Chapter II. Tax, Customs, Currency and Other Financial Regulation.

See also Federal Law No. 188-FZ of November 30, 1995, On Amending Certain Laws of the Russian Federation on Taxes. According to Article 10 of the present Law, Article 2 shall be effective from January 1, 1996, until December 31, 1998.

Article 2. Tax Regulation.

There shall be exempted from the value added tax the turnover in the realization of the products of the mass media, the book products connected with education, science and culture, and also the editorial, publishing and polygraphic activity in the output of the book products connected with education, science and culture, or of newspaper or magazine products.

There shall be exempted from the value added tax the services in the transportation, loading, unloading and reloading of the periodical printed publications and book products connected with education, science and culture.

There shall not be subject to taxation the profit obtained by the editorial boards of the mass media, by publishing houses, information agencies, television and radio companies, by organizations for the dissemination of periodical printed publications and book products, and by transmitting centers, the profit from the output and dissemination of the products of the mass media and book products connected with education, science and culture in the part transferred to the federal budget.

There shall not be subject to taxation the profit obtained by the polygraphic enterprises and organizations from the rendering of services in the output of the book products connected with education, science and culture, and of the products of the mass media in the part transferred to the federal budget.

There shall not be subject to taxation the profit obtained by the editorial boards of the mass media, by publishing houses, information agencies, television and radio broadcasting companies and by organizations for the dissemination of periodical printed publications and book products and assigned by them to finance the capital investments in their main field of activity. The non-taxable share of the profit assigned for those purposes shall not be restricted.

According to Article 10 of the present Law, Article 3 shall be effective from January 1, 1996, until December 31, 1998.

Article 3. Customs Regulation.

See also Federal Law No. 185-FZ of November 25, 1995, On Supplementing the Law of the Russian Federation on the Customs Tariff.

The periodically printed publications and the book products connected with education, science and culture imported into and exported from the customs territory of the Russian Federation by the editorial boards of the mass media and by publishing houses shall be exempted from the customs duty and the fees connected with the import and export. Paper, polygraphic materials and polygraphic carriers, the audio and video information, the technological and engineering equipment imported into the customs territory of the Russian Federation by the editorial boards of the mass media, by publishing houses, information agencies, television and radio broadcasting companies, polygraphic enterprises and organizations and used by them for the output of the products of the mass media and book products connected with education, science and culture shall be exempted from the customs duty. According to Article 10 of the present Law, Article 4 shall be effective from January 1, 1996, until December 31, 1998.

Article 4. Currency Regulation.

The editorial boards of the mass media, publishing houses, polygraphic enterprises and organizations, television and radio broadcasting companies, information agencies, and organizations for the dissemination of periodical printed publications shall be exempted from the obligatory sale of the currency returns received from the export of the book products connected with education, science and culture, and newspaper, magazine, audio and video products, if the latter are used to acquire equipment and materials necessary for the output of the products of mass media and book products connected with education, science and culture, and for the expansion of the said output. According to Article 10 of the present Law, Article 5 shall be effective from January 1, 1996, until December 31, 1998

Article 5. Other Financial and Economic Regulation.

The editorial boards of the mass media, publishing houses, information agencies, television and radio broadcasting companies shall use the services of the organizations of the postal, telegraphic and telephonic communication at the rates stipulated for the budgetary organizations.

The editorial boards of the mass media, publishing houses, polygraphic enterprises and organizations, information agencies, television and radio broadcasting companies, organizations for the dissemination of periodical printed publications, and transmitting centers shall pay the rent of the premises in the buildings that are federally owned at the tariffs and rates not exceeding those established for the organizations of the sphere of culture.

The editorial boards of the mass media, publishing houses, information agencies, and television and radio broadcasting companies shall be given under their economic management the premises which they own or use in the process of their production and economic activity.

Article 6. Peculiarities of the Tax, Customs, Currency and Other Financial Regulation.

The privileges stipulated by Articles 2-5 of the present Federal Law shall not apply to the books and periodical printed publications of advertising and erotic character and to the mass media of advertising and erotic character.

The privileges stipulated by Articles 2-5 of the present Federal Law shall be applied in the procedure and on the terms which are determined by the relevant legislative acts of the Russian Federation on the tax, customs, currency and budgetary issues.

Chapter III. Peculiarities of the Privatization of the Enterprises Ensuring the Publication of Newspaper, Magazine and Book Products.

The privatization of the enterprises ensuring the publication of newspaper, magazine and book products shall be carried out in accordance with the existing legislation of the Russian Federation on privatization, taking into account the peculiarities established by the present Federal Law.

Article 7. Restrictions on Privatization.

There shall not be subject to privatization the publishing houses and polygraphic enterprises referred exclusively to the objects of the federal ownership:

- the polygraphic enterprises that are monopolists on the all-Russian market of goods (services);
- the polygraphic enterprises equipped with high technologies for the output of highly artistic and high-quality printed products;
- the publishing houses that are monopolists on the all-Russia market of goods (services);
- the monopolist enterprises that ensure the functioning of the polygraphic branch.

The publishing houses and polygraphic enterprises falling within the effect of the present article may be transformed into joint-stock companies in the procedure stipulated by a decision of the Government of the Russian Federation no earlier than three years after from the day when the present Federal Law enters into force.

Article 8. Peculiarities of the Privatization of the Publishing Houses and Polygraphic Enterprises Referred to the Objects of the Federal Ownership.

The polygraphic enterprises which are situated on the territory of the entities of the Russian Federation, are referred to the objects of the federal ownership and are monopolists in the production of newspaper, magazine and book products on the territory of a relevant entity of the Russian Federation, and also the polygraphic enterprises comprising the system of decentralized printing of newspapers and magazines, shall be transformed into joint-stock companies.

- 25.5 per cent of the shares shall be assigned to the federal ownership for a period of three years.
- 24.5 per cent of the ordinary shares shall be given free of charge to the polygraphic enterprise that are being transformed into joint-stock companies.
- 50 per cent of the ordinary shares shall be given free of charge to juridical persons: the editorial boards of the mass media and the publishing houses that release products at a given polygraphic enterprise and are being transformed into open joint-stock companies or are such companies. The blocks of shares shall be distributed among them proportionally to the volumes of the released products in kind.

The editorial boards of the mass media, the publishing houses and polygraphic enterprises may sell a part of the shares, attracting the investors at their choice, on condition that the field of their activity is preserved.

The editorial boards of the mass media and the publishing houses releasing the products of advertising or erotic character shall not be admitted to the allotment of shares by a closed subscription.

Article 9. Procedure for the Privatization of the Publishing Houses and Polygraphic Enterprises That Are Not Monopolists or Have Been Transferred to the Ownership of the Entities of the Russian Federation.

The privatization of the publishing houses and polygraphic enterprises that are federally owned and are not monopolists and of the publishing houses and polygraphic enterprises that have been transferred to the ownership of the entities of the Russian Federation shall be carried out in accordance with the present Federal Law and the regional programs of privatization.

Chapter IV. On the Procedure for the Entering into Force of the Present Federal Law.

Article 10. The Time for the Entering into Force of the Present Federal Law.

The present Federal Law shall enter into force as of the day of its official publication.

Articles 2-5 of the present Federal Law shall enter into force as of January 1, 1996, shall be effective until December 31, 1998, and shall lose force as of January 1, 1999.

Articles 7-9 of the present Federal Law shall enter into force as of the day of its official publication and shall be effective until the Federal Assembly of the Russian Federation approves the State Program of the Privatization of State and Municipal Enterprises in the Russian Federation.

Article 11. On the Bringing of the Normative Acts in Conformity with the Present Federal Law.

To recommend the President of the Russian Federation and assign the Government of the Russian Federation to bring their legal acts in conformity with the present Federal Law.

Russian Criminal Code
(Excerpts)

As Amended on **April 13, 1996**

Article 130. Defamation.

1. Defamation, that is, the dissemination of fabrications known to be false which defame another person, shall be punished by imprisonment not exceeding one year, by correctional labor not exceeding one year, by a fine not exceeding twice the minimum monthly wage index, by imposition of a duty to make amends for the harm, by public reprimand, or by application of measures of public influence.

2. Defamation in a published or otherwise reproduced publication or means of mass information, or in an anonymous letter, or by a person previously convicted of defamation, shall be punished by correctional labor not exceeding two years, or by a fine not exceeding twenty times the monthly minimum wage index as well as deprivation of the right to assume certain professional responsibilities.

3. Defamation combined with an accusation of a crime against the state or other grave offence shall be punished by imprisonment not exceeding five years.

Article 131. Insult.

1. Insult, that is, the intentional diminution of the honor and dignity of a person, expressed in indecent form, shall be punished by correctional labor for a term not exceeding six months, by a fine not exceeding the minimum monthly wage index, by imposition of a duty to make amends for the harm, by public reprimand, or by application of measures of public influence.

2. Insult in a printed publication or means of mass information, or insult inflicted by a person previously convicted of insult, shall be punished by correctional labor not exceeding two years or by a fine not exceeding twenty times the minimum monthly wage index as well as deprivation of the right to assume certain professional responsibilities.

Russian Federation Presidential Decree On Improving the State TV Broadcasting in the Russian Federation

August 25, 1997

In order to strengthen the role of the state electronic mass media, to develop a single comprehensive national information sphere, and to restore the cultural and educational role of state TV in the Russian Federation, I resolve that:

1. The government of the Russian Federation, the All-Russia State TV and Radio Broadcasting Company (VGTRK) and the Mayor's Office of St. Petersburg should set up a state mass medium: the All-Russian State TV Channel Kultura.

2. VGTRK should set up the main editorial office of the All-Russian State TV Channel Kultura within the company's overall structure.

3. The chief editor of the All-Russian State TV Channel Kultura should be appointed or dismissed by the president of the Russian Federation.

4. The board of trustees of the All-Russian State TV Channel Kultura should be formed in order to assist the channel with fulfilling its functions.

5. The Council for Art and Culture under the President of the Russian Federation should prepare within a month a draft decree on the board of trustees of the All-Russian TV channel Kultura and also submit some proposals on its composition.

6. Broadcasts of the All-Russian TV channel Kultura should begin on November 1, 1997, on [UHF] channel 33 in Moscow and on appropriate channels in other cities and Regions of the Russian Federation (with the exception of St. Petersburg and Leningrad Region), which have been used for transmitting broadcasts of the St. Petersburg Channel 5 State Radio and Television Company.

7. A Russian Federation government proposal, in accordance with the St. Petersburg Mayor's Office and the Leningrad Region administration, should be adopted on the re-organization of the St. Petersburg Channel 5 State Radio and Television Company by way of its being turned into a public joint-stock company, named the St. Petersburg Radio and Television Company. The Russian Federation government should hand over to the City of St. Petersburg property owned by the state and assigned to the St. Petersburg Channel 5 State Radio and Television Company, as the property of the City of St. Petersburg on the condition that the St. Petersburg Mayor's Office incorporates this property in the authorized capital of the St. Petersburg Radio and Television Company public joint-stock company and it should give the City of St. Petersburg 51 per cent of the shares in the joint-stock company.

8. It should be established that the St. Petersburg Radio and Television Company will broadcast television and radio programs in St. Petersburg and in Leningrad

Region on frequencies previously allocated to the St. Petersburg Channel 5 State Radio and Television Company.

9. The VGTRK should provide for the transmission of programs on culture and art by the St. Petersburg Radio and Television Company, lasting no less than three hours a day, on the Kultura TV channel's daily broadcasting program.

10. The State Committee of the Russian Federation on Communications and Information should, jointly with the Russian Federal Television and Radio Broadcasting Service, ensure that the programs of the All-Russian State TV Channel Kultura are disseminated in the City of St. Petersburg and in Leningrad Region as well as in other constituent parts of the Russian Federation which are unable to receive the television channel's programs for technical reasons.

11. The VGTRK should ensure that the All-Russian State TV Channel Kultura is financed from income received by the company from commercial activities, funds attracted and funds from the federal budget.

12. The Russian Federation Finance Ministry and the Russian Federal Television and Radio Broadcasting Service should ensure that the VGTRK allocates additional funds in 1997, including funds to pay for the services of communications enterprises for distributing the programs of the All-Russian State TV Channel Kultura.

13. The Russian Federal Television and Radio Broadcasting Service should ensure that licenses for radio and television broadcasting are issued and revised, in line with this decree.

14. The Russian Federation government should bring all of its legislative acts into line with this decree by October 1, 1997.

15. The Russian Federation President's Main State Law Directorate should table proposals on amendments to the Russian Federation president's acts in connection with this decree coming into force, by October 1, 1997.

16. This decree comes into force on the day it is signed.

State Duma Decree No. 2028 On State Regulation of the Activities of the NTV Television Company and Other Non-State Television and Radio Companies

December 19, 1997

In order to stabilize the social and political situation in the Russian Federation, domestic television is called upon to reflect the opinion of political, religious, ethnic and other groups of the population and create the requisite conditions for the preservation of ethnic culture.

But the NTV television company is pursuing an active policy of blowing up conflict situations and stirring up political confrontation in society. Lies and distortion of the facts are used to manipulate public opinion. Abusive language has become the norm in television programs.

Contrary to the traditions and customs of the peoples of the Russian Federation, the NTV television company continues to produce and purvey erotic and pornographic material unchecked. Believers' religious feelings are being patently ignored and efforts are being made to set Russia at loggerheads with its immediate neighbors.

For the purposes of state regulation of the activities of the NTV television company and other non-state television and radio companies, the Russian Federation Federal Assembly State Duma decrees that:

1. The Russian Federation government be recommended to:

- step up monitoring of the NTV television company's and other non-state television and radio companies' compliance with the terms of broadcasting licenses, and impose tough sanctions on those who contravene the aforementioned terms;
- review the terms of the contract with the NTV television company with a view to establishing new, higher tariffs for relaying signals via state radio relay transmitting centers;
- devise normative legal acts making it incumbent on the relevant federal executive authorities, when issuing broadcasting licenses, to conclude contracts with television and radio companies making it incumbent on them in their work to take account of ethnic traditions; when drawing up the broadcasting network, maintain the ratio between domestic and foreign works of art and culture (songs, musical works, films), giving priority to Russian culture; following international practice, show concern for Russia's integrity and security;
- conclude similar contracts with all television and radio companies currently operating on Russian Federation territory;

- strictly monitor non-state television and radio companies' observance of the norms of Russian Federation legislation.

2. The State Duma Committee on the Budget, Taxes, Banks and Finance and the State Duma Committee on Information Policy and Communications are to devise a draft law regulating the taxation of non-state television and radio companies.

3. The State Duma Committee on Information Policy and Communications is to be instructed on the basis of this decree and Russia Federation legislation to devise a draft law, including additional grounds for revoking a non-state television or radio company's broadcasting license, and submit it to the State Duma for its consideration.

State Duma Decree No 2294
On the Activity of Certain Russian Television Companies

March 18, 1998

The strengthening of public morality and respect for the historically conditioned norms of culture and the inalienable right of citizens to freedom of conscience and freedom of religion are the immutable cornerstones of Russian society as enshrined in the Russian Federation constitution and in Russian Federation legislation.

However, certain Russian television companies, above all NTV [Independent Television], taking advantage of the imperfection of legislation, are through their activity inflicting damage on public morality, showing output of a frankly cynical, indecent and offensive character and effectively propagandizing pornography and the cult of violence and cruelty, which are capable of inducing people to commit crimes.

In accordance with Article 6, Point 3 of the Federal Law On Freedom of Conscience and Religious Associations, the inadmissibility of deliberately offending citizens' feelings in connection with their attitude to religion is an essential condition for citizens to exercise their constitutional right to freedom of conscience and freedom of religion. Despite this, and despite public protests, on November 9, 1997, the NTV television company showed the director Martin Scorsese's film "The Last Temptation of Christ," which, according to the statement of His Holiness the Patriarch of Moscow and All Russia Aleksiy II, offended the religious beliefs of Russia' s millions of Orthodox Christians.

With the aim of protecting public morality and citizens' right to freedom of conscience and freedom of religion the Russian Federation Federal Assembly State Duma decrees:

1. The State Duma Committee for Legislation and Judicial and Legal Reform and the State Duma Committee for the Affairs of Public Associations and Religious Organizations are hereby instructed to organize the preparation of draft laws providing for stricter measures of liability for propagandizing pornography or the cult of violence and cruelty, and also for deliberately offending—publicly or in the mass media—citizens' feelings in connection with their attitude to religion.

2. The State Duma Committee for Information Policy and Communications is hereby instructed to organize the preparation of a draft law on amendments and additions to the Russian Federation Law On the Mass Media, stipulating in this draft law the following additional grounds for annulling television broadcasting licenses:

- the showing or output of a cynical, indecent or offensive character;
- the use in disseminated output of non-standard vocabulary and offensive expressions;

- the showing or output containing the detailed depiction of scenes of cruelty and violence and the committing of crimes;
- the dissemination of output in which outrage against objects of religious veneration is committed, thereby offending citizens' beliefs in connection with their attitude to religion.

3. It is proposed that the Russian Federation government:

- elaborate a system of standards, which should be based on historically conditioned traditional norms of morality, culture and language, and to which the output of Russian television companies, irrespective of their form of ownership, should correspond.
- elaborate statutory legal acts in which compliance with the aforementioned standards is stipulated as one of the conditions for issuing a TV broadcasting license;
- monitor more stringently the compliance with Russian Federation legislation by Russian TV companies, irrespective of their form of ownership;
- instruct the Russian Federal Service for Television and Radio Broadcasting:
  - to reword the licenses of all Russian television companies irrespective of their form of ownership in accordance with the aforementioned statutory legal acts;
  - to issue a written warning to the NTV television company for showing on November 9, 1997, the director Martin Scorsese's film "The Last Temptation of Christ" in violation of Article 3 of the Federal Law On Freedom of Conscience and Religious Associations," which forbids interference with a citizen's exercise of his or her right to freedom of conscience and freedom of religion involving deliberate offence to citizens' feelings in connection with their attitude to religion.

4. The attention of the leadership of Russia's television companies, irrespective of their form of ownership, is drawn to the inadmissibility of abusing the freedom of information through the dissemination of output propagandizing pornography and the cult of violence and cruelty or offending citizens' feelings in connection with their attitude to religion.

5. This decree is to be sent for publication in *Rossiyskaya Gazeta*.

6. This decree comes into force from the day of its adoption.

Statute on Payment for the Use of the Radio Frequency Spectrum in the Russian Federation

August 6, 1998

1. The present statute establishes the basic principles of and general conditions for payment for the use of the radio frequency spectrum, frequency appropriation, and the radio frequency channel (hereinafter referred to as the radio frequency spectrum) for all organizations, irrespective of their form of ownership, and individual entrepreneurs who use radioelectronic equipment on the territory of the Russian Federation for commercial purposes in order to render the communications services envisioned by the decree of the government of the Russian Federation of June 2, 1998, No. 552, On Introducing Payment for the Use of the Radio Frequency Spectrum.

2. The radio frequency spectrum shall be exclusively a state resource. Payment for the use of the radio frequency spectrum shall be established separately for each permit for the use of the radio frequency spectrum. The transfer of the use of the radio frequency spectrum to organizations, irrespective of their form of ownership, or to individual entrepreneurs for possession or indefinite continuous use shall be prohibited.

3. The right of an organization, irrespective of its form of ownership, or an individual entrepreneur to use the radio frequency spectrum may not be transferred to other individuals or legal entities unless otherwise stipulated by normative legal acts of the Russian Federation.

4. The amount of the fee for use of the radio frequency spectrum shall be established annually.

5. Organizations, irrespective of their form of ownership, and individual entrepreneurs using radio frequency spectrums, whose permits for their use have not been obtained on a competitive basis, must before September 1, 1998, make the annual payment set in the amount of twice the rate for services for administration of the use of the radio frequency spectrum developed by the service for government oversight over communications in the Russian Federation and approved by the federal service of Russia for regulation of natural monopolies in the area of communications in compliance with the decree of the government of the Russian Federation of March 7, 1997, No. 265, On Regulation of Rates for Communications Services and Approval of the Basic Provisions for State Regulation of Rates for Services of Generally Accessible Electronic Communications on the Federal and Regional Levels.

Payment for the use of the radio frequency spectrum shall be made to agencies of the service for state oversight of communications in the Russian Federation annually or quarterly, in equal portions no later than the fifth day of the first month of the quarter.

Said payment shall be distributed as follows:

Fifty per cent shall be forwarded as reimbursement for costs of the state service for oversight over communications in the Russian Federation for administration of the use of the radio frequency spectrum.

Fifty per cent shall be forwarded to the state budget.

Agencies of the state service for oversight over communications in the Russian Federation shall make a point of transferring the corresponding amounts to the federal budget no later than three days after they are received.

6. Violation of the procedure envisioned by the present statute for making payments for the use of the radio frequency spectrum shall be grounds for suspension of the license to grant communications services involving the use of the radio frequency spectrum.

Federal Law
On Basic Guarantees of Electoral Rights and the Right of Citizens of the Russian Federation to Participate in a Referendum

September 19, 1997

***As amended on* March 30, 1999**

Chapter VII. Campaigning During Elections and Referenda.

Article 39. General Terms and Conditions of the Access of Candidates, Electoral Associations, Electoral Blocs, and Referendum Initiative Groups to Mass Media.

Mass media outlets whose founders (or co-founders) are state or municipal bodies, organizations, establishments, or who are financed completely or partially from the relevant budget (federal budget, budget of Subject of Russian Federation, or local budget) or at the expense of the bodies of local self-government as well as those enjoying tax and other exemptions, if compared with other mass media, shall provide equal conditions of election campaigning to registered candidates, electoral associations, and electoral blocs.

The mass media which do not come under the provisions of Clause 1 of this Article may provide air time and space in printed media to registered candidates, electoral associations, electoral blocs, and referendum initiative groups on a contractual basis. Candidates, electoral associations, and electoral blocs shall pay for air time and printed matter on equal terms and on conditions exclusively through the appropriate electoral funds. In cases provided by federal constitutional laws, federal laws, and laws of Subjects of Russian Federation, a referendum initiative group shall pay for air time and printed matter through a referendum participation fund.

Article 40. Terms and Conditions for Campaigning Through Electronic Mass Media.

Registered candidates, electoral associations, electoral blocs, and referendum initiative groups shall be entitled to free air time on the channels of TV and radio companies coming under the provisions of Clause 1 of Article 39 of this Federal Law and engaged in TV and radio broadcasting in the territory wherein elections or a referendum is to be held. The said air time shall be provided during the prime periods when TV and radio programs are viewed and listened to by the greatest number of people. The total free air time provided by each Russian national TV and radio company for campaigning in elections for federal bodies of state power shall be not less than one hour during work days. The total free air time provided by each regional TV and radio company for election campaigning in elections to federal bodies of state power and in elections for bodies of state power of Subject of Russian Federation shall be not less than 30 minutes during work days and no less than one-fourth of the total broadcasting time if the total broadcasting time of the TV and radio company is less than two hours. The said free air time shall be equally distributed among registered candidates, electoral associations and electoral blocs.

Not less than one-third of the total free air time shall be given to candidates, electoral associations, and electoral blocs for joint discussions, roundtables and similar propaganda events. This part of free air time shall be equally accessible to all registered candidates, electoral associations, and electoral blocs.

TV and radio companies coming under the provisions of Article 39, Clause 1 of this Federal Law regarding the level of elections shall reserve paid air time for election campaigning of candidates, electoral associations, and electoral blocs. This air time shall be made available for a fee on a contractual basis to candidates, electoral associations, and electoral blocs at their request. The fee shall be the same for all candidates, electoral associations, and electoral blocs and announced no later than the day on which nomination of candidates (or lists of candidates) begins or no later than ten days after announcement of the voting day in a referendum. Each candidate, electoral association, or electoral bloc shall be entitled to a part of the total reserved air time given by division of this time by the total number of registered candidates (or electoral associations or electoral blocs). The total reserved air time shall not be less than the total free air time provided in accordance with Clause 1 of this Article.

The provision of air time to registered candidates, electoral associations, electoral blocs, public associations, and referendum initiative groups on the channels of the state TV and radio companies coming under the provisions of Article 39, Clause 1 of this Federal Law shall be regulated by federal constitutional laws, federal laws, and laws of Subjects of Russian Federation.

Expenses incurred by state municipal TV and radio companies in connection with the free allocation of air time to registered candidates, electoral associations, electoral blocs, and initiative groups for referendum shall be covered by current funding from the budget.

Article 41. Terms and Conditions for Campaigning Through Printed Mass Media.

Periodicals coming under the provisions of Article 39, Clause 1 of this Federal Law and distributed in the territories wherein elections and referenda are to be held, with the exception of publications founded by bodies of state power and bodies of local self-government exclusively for publication of official reports and materials, normative and other acts, shall provide space for materials submitted by candidates, electoral associations, electoral blocs, and referendum initiative groups. The total minimum space of this kind and the ratio between its parts provided by periodicals free of charge at the expense of their current budget financing and on a paid basis shall be established by federal constitutional laws, federal laws, and laws of Subjects of Russian Federation. Specialized publications (children's, technical, scientific and others) may refuse to publish any propaganda materials whatsoever provided they completely abstain from any participation in the election campaign, preparation and holding of referenda.

The provisions of Clause 1 of this Article shall not apply to periodicals founded by registered candidates, electoral associations, electoral blocs, referendum initiative groups and electoral associations comprised in electoral blocs.

Draft Federal Law On A Higher Council for the Defense of Morality in Television and Radio Broadcasting in the Russian Federation*

Vetoed by President Yeltsin on March 31, 1999

Television broadcasting and radio broadcasting in the Russian Federation are free.

Censorship is prohibited by the Constitution of the Russian Federation. Freedom of television broadcasting and radio broadcasting can be limited by federal law only to the degree that is necessary in the interest of defending the fundamentals of the constitutional system, morality, health, and the rights and legal interests of citizens, and of guaranteeing the defense of the country and the safety of the state.

This Federal Law is aimed at the defense of morality in television and radio broadcasting in the Russian Federation.

Chapter I. General Provisions.

Article 1. The Subject of Regulation of This Federal Law.

This Federal Law defines the capacity of the Higher Council for the defense of morality in television and radio broadcasting in the Russian Federation (the Council), the status of the Council's members, the procedure for its formation and activity, and its relationship with other law-making bodies.

Article 2. Definitions.

Definitions used in this Federal Law:

- *morality*—a system of ethical norms and rules of behavior established in society on the basis of traditional spiritual and cultural values, particularly the concepts of goodwill, honor, dignity, duty, conscience, and fairness;
- *television and radio broadcasting*—distribution with the use of electromagnetic waves of television, audio programs, and additional information in open or encoded form, implemented by airwaves or by freely accessible cable network, intended for individual reception by an unlimited audience;
- *broadcaster*—a legal entity regardless of the form of ownership or an individual registered as an entrepreneur, performing television and/or radio broadcasting on the basis of a broadcast license;
- *territorial broadcaster*—a broadcaster performing television and/or radio broadcasting on the territory of one of the geographical-administrative territories of the Russian Federation;

* Adopted by the State Duma and approved by the Federation Council on March 17, 1999.

- *regional broadcaster*—a broadcaster performing television and/or radio broadcasting on the territory of two or no more than half of the geographical-administrative territories of the Russian Federation;
- *all-Russian broadcaster*—a broadcaster performing television and/or radio broadcasting on the territory of more than half of the geographical-administrative territories of the Russian Federation.

Chapter II. The Council.

Article 3. Goals and Tasks of the Council.

1. The Council, in the framework of its competency, in accordance with Article 7 of this law, controls the compliance of broadcasters with the requirements of federal legislation of the Russian Federation.

The Council does not have the right to demand that broadcasters and mass media coordinate in advance their announcements or materials or to prohibit the distribution of announcements and materials or their separate parts.

2. The Council's activity is aimed at:

(a) protection of morality, cultural values, family, motherhood, fatherhood, and childhood;

(b) reinforcement of love and respect for the Fatherland, faith in good-will and fairness;

(c) development of the national traditions and languages of the peoples populating the Russian Federation;

(d) development of state policy in the sphere of television and radio broadcasting.

3. In the interest of defending morality, the Council issues warnings to broadcasters, uses other measures of influence on broadcasters established by this Federal Law in the case of distribution by broadcasters of television programs, radio programs, and other mass information, the contents or aims of which are:

- to provoke commission of capital crimes or to create a feeling in the viewer's mind that such crimes go unpunished;
- to directly threaten the security of individuals or the state;
- to propagandize or inflame social, racial, national and religious hatred, enmity or superiority;
- to propagandize war, cruelty, and violence;
- to do damage to the physical or mental health of citizens, the mental or moral development of children, or to arouse the possibility for such damage;
- to debase the dignity of human identity;
- to violate the generally accepted norms of Russian language as the state language of the Russian Federation;

- to violate the generally accepted norms of humanity and morality, historically developed through the foundations of the family.

4. The Council will annually issue diplomas of honor to those broadcasters that facilitate the reinforcement of morality, love and respect for the Fatherland, faith in good will and fairness.

The name of the diploma of honor of the Higher Council and its resolution are to be confirmed by the Council.

Article 4. Procedure for Formation and Functioning of the Council.

1. The Council is a constantly acting state organ comprised of twelve members, three of whom are appointed by the President of the Russian Federation, three by the State Duma, three by the Federation Council, and three by the Government of the Russian Federation. The appointment of members of the Council will take place within two months from the day that this law takes effect.

2. The Council passes the Regimen for the Higher Council.

For selection of a chairman of the Higher Council, no fewer than seven members of the council must be present at the meeting. The chairman of the Higher Council is chosen by secret vote by a majority of votes of the members of the Council taking part in the vote. For approval of a decision by the Council on the issuing to a broadcaster of a warning or on the use against a broadcaster of measures of influence, no fewer than three members of the Council must be present at the meeting of the Council. The decision is approved by a simple majority of votes. If the votes for and against are even on a given decision, the vote of the chairman is the deciding vote.

3. The Council reviews questions presented by:

- the President of the Russian Federation;
- the Federation Council or the State Duma, formulated in the appropriate resolutions;
- committees and commissions of the Federation Council and State Duma;
- members of the Federation Council and deputies of the State Duma;
- the Government of the Russian Federation;
- state organs of administrative-geographical entities of the Russian Federation;
- one or more members of the Council.

The Council has the right to review questions presented by other legal entities or individuals.

The Council takes issues under review only within the period of twenty days following the airing of the television or radio program in question, and only if the claim contains information about a violation of morality by a specific broadcaster.

The decisions of the Council made on claims, on the basis of the notions of the Council, must be published in print media, the founders (or co-founders) of which are state organs, and must be distributed by the broadcaster that claim concerns.

4. The Council will publish an annual report on its work, which must be published in print media, the founders (or co-founders) of which are state organs.

5. The Council is a legal entity.

The Council will have an apparatus at its disposal, which shall be appointed and dismissed by decision of the Council.

The property needed by the Council for performance of its activity will be found in the operating department and is considered federal property.

In the framework of its estimate of expenses, the Council sets the staff schedule of its apparatus.

The rights, duties and responsibilities of the members of the Council's apparatus, and the conditions for their entrance into state service are determined by federal laws, other legal acts on federal state service, and Russian Federation legislation on labor.

6. Location of the Council: Moscow.

Article 5. Members of the Council.

1. A member's term on the Council is six years, and a member cannot be removed except in cases stipulated by this Federal Law.

The appointment of a member of the council in the framework of the quotas established by this Federal Law is implemented within two months from the day of the end of a term of a member of the Council.

2. The term of a member of the Council can be preemptively curtailed by decision of the body that appointed him in the event of:

- the member's written announcement of resignation;
- declaration of a guilty verdict by a court regarding the member;
- pronouncement by a court that the member is incapable of performing his or her duties or absent without explanation;
- limitation by a court of the capacity of the member;
- declaration by a court that a member is dead;
- death of the member.

A new member of the Council is appointed to the open position in the framework of the quotas established by this Federal Law within two months from the moment of the preemptive curtailment of the term of the previous member.

3. A member of the Council cannot carry out any professional activity, paid or unpaid, except for instructive, scientific, or other creative work.

4. Material guarantees of independence of members of the Council, connected with salary, medical, social and other provisions and services, are established as they

apply to corresponding guarantees stipulated by laws and other legal acts of the Russian Federation for people holding state positions in the Russian Federation.

Article 6. Financing of the Council.

Funds for maintaining the Council are stipulated in the federal law on the federal budget for the given year.

The Council shall develop the estimate of its expenditures and send an account of its fulfillment to the President of the Russian Federation, the Federation Council, the Duma, and the Government of the Russian Federation.

Article 7. The Competency of the Council.

1. The Council, on the basis of claims taken under consideration in accordance with Point 3 of Article 4 of this federal Law, in the framework of its competency, controls (including the use of recordings of television and radio programs after their airing) the compliance of aired television and radio programs and other mass information with the requirements of legislation of the Russian Federation.

2. The Council performs the following activities:

- upon inquiry by the President of the Russian Federation, houses of the Federal Parliament of the Russian Federation, the Government [cabinet of ministers] of the Russian Federation, or the Ministry of Justice of the Russian Federation, shall give in the framework of its competency recommendations for development of state policy in the sphere of television and radio broadcasting and offer analysis and expertise to the situation in the sphere of television and radio broadcasting;
- shall bring in state organs and experts for receipt and analysis of information in the framework of its competency;
- in the manner established by the Regulations of the Higher Council, shall within one month of broadcasters' requests give conclusions on the compliance of films, TV programs, radio programs, and other mass information planned for distribution with the requirements of this Federal Law;
- shall call to its meetings representatives of television and radio broadcasters for receipt of information regarding their activity;
- shall demand from television and radio broadcasters, within the statute of limitations established by legislation of the Russian Federation, copies of television and radio programs and other information necessary for review of claims stipulated in Point 3 of Article 4, information that the broadcaster is obligated to present to the Council free-of-charge within a period of ten days.

3. The Council shall prepare for the Government of the Russian Federation recommendations on the presentation to broadcasters of privileges established by federal laws.

4. Upon review of a claim stipulated in Point 3 of article 4 of this Federal Law, the Council, in the event of its establishment of the fact of distribution by a

broadcaster of television or radio programs or other mass information defined by Point 3 of Article 3 of this law, shall have the right to issue the broadcaster the appropriate warning, and to take the following measures against the broadcaster that has been warned:

(a) imposition of a fine in the manner established by Article 8 of this Federal Law;

(b) presentation to a court of a claim for the annulment of the license for broadcasting, in connection with the violation by the broadcaster of licensing requirements and conditions;

(c) appeal to the appropriate body or other responsible entity for the removal of the head of the broadcaster from his or her post.

5. The Council shall notify a broadcaster in violation of this Federal Law of the warning issued to him and explain the reasons for the decision.

6. In the event that there are indications that a violation found by the Council during review of a claim is of a criminal nature, the Council shall refer it to law-enforcement agencies.

7. A decision by the Council to take measures against a broadcaster can be appealed by the broadcaster in a judicial proceeding within a period of one month from the time the decision is made.

Article 8. Administrative Responsibility of the Broadcaster for Violation of Morality.

1. Performance by a broadcaster of broadcasting with a violation of licensing requirements and conditions, in the form of distribution of television programs, radio programs, or other mass information provoking the commission of criminally punishable acts; creating a feeling in the viewer's mind that such crimes go unpunished; directly threatening the security of individuals or the state; propagandizing or inflaming social, racial, national and religious hatred, enmity or superiority; propagandizing war, cruelty, and violence; doing damage to the physical or mental health of citizens or the mental or moral development of children or arousing the possibility for such damage; debasing the dignity of human identity; violating the generally accepted norms of Russian language as the state language of the Russian Federation; or violating the generally accepted norms of humanity and morality, historically developed on the foundations of the family—entails imposition of a fine of 10 to 500 minimum wages for territorial broadcasters, 100-5,000 minimum wages for regional broadcasters, and 1,000-50,000 for national broadcasters.

2. Issues of administrative infractions stipulated in point 1 of this article are reviewed by the Council within the framework of its competency.

3. Trials regarding administrative infractions stipulated in Point 1 of this article, and the fulfillment of resolutions on the imposition of administrative penalties in such trials is carried out by the procedure established by the Russian Federation Administrative Infraction Code.

4. In the event of non-payment by a broadcaster of a fine in the period established by Article 285 of the Russian Federation Administrative Infraction Code, forced fulfillment of the resolution of the imposition of the fine is carried out by the procedure established by federal legislation.

5. The amount of the fine paid by territorial broadcasters in accordance with this Federal Law is paid into the budget of the administration of the territory of the Russian Federation on which the broadcaster broadcasts.

The amount of the fine paid by regional broadcasters in accordance with this Federal Law is paid in equal parts into the budgets of the territories of the Russian Federation on which the broadcaster broadcasts.

The amount of the fine paid by a national broadcaster in accordance with this Federal Law is paid into the federal budget.

Chapter III. Conclusion.

Article 9. On the Enactment of This Federal Law.

This Federal Law shall take effect on November 1, 1999.

Article 10. On the Introduction of Legal Acts in Accordance with This Federal Law.

Offer the President of the Russian Federation and instruct the Government of the Russian Federation to introduce their legal acts in accordance with this Federal Law.

Russian Federation Presidential Decree On the Structure of the Presidential Administration*

June 3, 2000

Guided by paragraph "I" of Article 83 of the Russian constitution, I resolve:

1. That the administration of the Russian President be formed, which is to be made up of the President's chief of staff, his or her deputies and other officials, as well as the following independent sub-units:

- The Russian President's Main Territorial Directorate (on the basis of the Russian President Territorial Directorate, the Russian President's Directorate for Coordinating the Work of the Russian President's Plenipotentiary Representatives in the Russian regions and the President's Directorate for Local Government Issues, which are being wound up);
- The Russian President's Main Home Policy Directorate (on the basis of the President's Home Policy Directorate, the Russian President's Political Planning Directorate, the Russian President's Public Relations land Culture Directorate, which are being wound up):
- Russian Security Council staff;
- The Russian President's Main Control Directorate;
- The Russian President's Main State Law Directorate;
- The Russian President's Chief of Staff Secretariat;
- The Russian President's Foreign Policy Directorate;
- The Russian President's Personnel Directorate;
- The Russian President's Economic Directorate;
- The Russian President's Expert Directorate;
- The Russian President's State Awards Directorate;
- The Russian President's Citizenship Directorate;
- The Russian President's Pardons Directorate;
- The Russian President's Protocol Directorate;
- The President's Press Service Directorate;
- The Russian President's Organizational Work Directorate;
- The Office of the Russian President;
- The Russian President's Directorate for Information Supply and Documentation;
- The Russian President's Directorate for Dealing with Appeals by the Public;

* Interfax News Agency, June 3, 2000.

- The Russian President's Information Research Service (with the status of a directorate) which is made up of the Russian President's information researchers;
- Directorate of the President of the Russian Federation for the Affairs of Cossacks;
- Personnel of the Russian President's plenipotentiary representatives in federal districts.

2. That the Judicial Chamber for Information Disputes under the Russian President should be wound up.

3. That it be established that the Russian President's chief of staff has 10 deputies, including two first deputies.

4. That it be established that the Russian President's administration also includes the following officials:

- plenipotentiary representatives of the Russian President in the Federation Council of the Russian Federal Assembly, in the State Duma of the Russian Federal Assembly and in the Russian Constitutional Court;
- the Russian President's press secretary;
- the head of the Russian President's Protocol;
- the head of the Russian President's Office;
- the Russian President's advisers;
- the Russian President's senior information researcher (heads Russian President's Information Research Service).

5. That the Russian President's chief-of-staff should within a month approve the structure and staff numbers of independent sub-units of the Russian President's administration enumerated in paragraph one of this decree; implement other organizational and staff measures ensuing from this decree.

6. That the Russian President's State Law Directorate should within two months submit proposals to bring the Russian President's regulations in line with this decree.

That this decree comes into force on the day it is signed.

Doctrine of the Information Security of the Russian Federation

Approved by the Security Council on June 23, 2000

The Doctrine of the Information Security of the Russian Federation is the body of official views on the goals, tasks, principles and main directions of ensuring the information security of the Russian Federation.

This Doctrine provides the basis for:

- the shaping of the state policy of ensuring the information security of the Russian Federation;
- preparation of propositions on improving the legal, methodological, scientific-technical and organizational support of the information security of the Russian Federation;
- development of target-specific programs of ensuring the information security of the Russian Federation.

This Doctrine elaborates the concept of the national security of the Russian Federation with reference to the information sphere.

Chapter I. Information Security of the Russian Federation.

Article 1. The National Interests of the Russian Federation in the Information Sphere and the Securing Thereof.

The present stage in the development of society is characterized by the growing role of the information sphere which represents a combination of information, the information infrastructure, the agents that gather, form, disseminate and use information as well as the system of regulating the social relations arising from this. The information sphere, being a pivotal element in the life of society, exerts a strong influence on the state of the political, economic, defense and other components of the security of the Russian Federation. The national security of the Russian Federation depends to a substantial degree on ensuring the information security, a dependence that will increase with technological progress.

Information security of the Russian Federation refers to the protection of its national interests in the information sphere that are determined by the balance of the interests of the individual, society and the state.

The interests of the individual in the information sphere consist in the exercise of the constitutional rights of man and citizen to have access to information, to use information in the pursuit of activities allowed under the law, for the purpose of physical, spiritual and intellectual development as well as in the protection of the information that ensures personal security.

The interests of society in the information sphere consist in ensuring the interests of the individual in that sphere, in strengthening democracy, in creating a rule-of-law social state, in achieving and maintaining social harmony and spiritual renewal of Russia.

The interests of the state in the information sphere consist in creating conditions for harmonious development of the Russian information infrastructure, for the exercise of the constitutional rights and freedoms of man and citizen in obtaining information and using it for the purpose of ensuring the immutability of the constitutional system, the sovereignty and territorial integrity of Russia, political, economic and social stability, in unconditionally ensuring legality, law and order, and promoting equal and mutually beneficial international cooperation.

Based on the national interests of the Russian Federation in the information sphere, the strategic and current tasks are determined in the domestic and foreign policy of the state aimed at ensuring information security.

Four main components of the national interests of the Russian Federation in the information sphere can be identified.

The first component of the national interests of the Russian Federation in the information sphere includes respect of the constitutional rights and freedoms of man and citizen in obtaining and using information, spiritual renewal of Russia, the preservation and strengthening of the moral values of society, the traditions of patriotism and humanism, the cultural and scientific potential of the country.

To achieve this it is required:

- to use the information infrastructure more effectively in the interests of social development, consolidation of the Russian society and the spiritual revival of the multinational people of the Russian Federation;
- to improve the system of forming, storing and rational use of the information resources which constitute the basis of the scientific, technological and spiritual potential of the Russian Federation;
- to secure the constitutional rights and freedoms of man and citizen to freely search for, obtain, transfer, produce and disseminate information by any legal methods, and to obtain authentic information on the state of the environment;
- to ensure the constitutional rights and freedoms of man and citizen to personal and family secrets, the secret of correspondence, telephone conversations, postal, telegraph and other messages, to the protection of one's honor and good name;
- to strengthen the mechanisms of legal regulation of relations in the protection of intellectual property, to create conditions for compliance with the restrictions on access to confidential information established under the federal laws;
- to guarantee freedom of mass information and a ban on censorship;
- not to allow propaganda and agitation that contribute to the kindling of social, racial, national or religious hatred and hostility;

- to enforce a ban on the collection, storage, use and dissemination of information on the private life of a person without that person's consent and other information to which access is limited under the federal legislation.

The second component of the national interests of the Russian Federation in the information sphere comprises information support of the state policy of the Russian Federation in bringing to the Russian and international public accurate information on the state policy of the Russian Federation, its official position on socially significant events in Russian and international life, with the provision of public access to open state information resources.

To achieve this it is required:

- to strengthen the state mass media, to expand their potential for providing Russian and foreign citizens with authentic information in a timely manner;
- to intensify the shaping of open state information resources and to husband them more effectively.

The third component of the national interests of the Russian Federation in the information sphere includes the development of modern information technologies, a domestic information industry, including an industry of informatization and telecommunications means, providing for the needs of the internal market with its products and putting these products in the world market as well as ensuring the accumulation, storage and effective use of national information resources. Under present-day conditions it is only on this basis that the problem of creating science-intensive technologies, technical modernization of industry and multiplying the achievements of the domestic science and technology can be solved. Russia must occupy a worthy place among world leaders in the microelectronics and computer industry.

To achieve this it is required:

- to develop and improve the infrastructure of the single information space of the Russian Federation;
- to develop the national industry of information services and use the state information resources more effectively;
- to develop the production in the Russian Federation of competitive means and systems of informatization and telecommunications, to broaden the participation of Russia in international cooperation of the producers of such means and systems;
- to ensure state support of national fundamental and applied research and development in the sphere of informatization and telecommunications.

The fourth component of the national interests of the Russian Federation in the information sphere comprises protection of information resources against unauthorized access, ensuring the safety of information and telecommunications systems both already deployed and being created on the territory of Russia.

To this end it is required:

- to enhance the security of information systems, including communications networks, above all, the security of primary communications networks and information systems of the federal bodies of state power, the bodies of state power of the subjects of the Russian Federation, the financial and credit and banking spheres, the sphere of economic activities as well as the systems and means of informatization of armaments and military equipment, the systems of control of troops and weapons, environmentally hazardous and economically critical production facilities;
- to intensify the development of the domestic production of hardware and software to protect information and methods to monitor the effectiveness thereof;
- to ensure the protection of data constituting a state secret;
- to broaden the international cooperation of the Russian Federation in the field of development and safe use of information resources and countering the threat of the unleashing of confrontation in the information sphere.

Article 2. Types of Threats to the Information Security of the Russian Federation.

In terms of their general thrust the threats to the information security of the Russian Federation are divided into the following types:

- threats to the constitutional rights and freedoms of man and citizen in spiritual life and information activities, to individual, group and social consciousness and the spiritual revival of Russia;
- threats to the information security of state policy in the Russian Federation;
- threats to the development of the national information industry, including the industry of means of informatization and telecommunications, to the meeting of the domestic market demands in its production and to the emergence of these products in the world market as well as to ensuring the accumulation, storage and effective use of national information resources;
- threats to the security of information and telecommunications means and systems, both already deployed and being created on the territory of Russia.

The following may be the threats to the constitutional rights and freedoms of man and citizen in the field of spiritual life and information activities, to individual, group and social consciousness and the spiritual revival of Russia:

- the adoption by the federal bodies of state power, the bodies of state power of the subjects of the Russian Federation of regulatory legal acts that infringe upon the constitutional rights and freedoms of citizens in spiritual life and information activities;
- the establishment of monopolies on the creation, obtaining and dissemination of information in the Russian Federation, including through the use of telecommunications systems;

- obstruction, including by criminal structures, of the exercise by citizens of their constitutional rights to personal and family secrets, the secret of correspondence, telephone conversations and other messages;
- irrational and excessive restrictions on the access to publicly vital information;
- illegal use of special means of influence on individual, group and social consciousness;
- non-compliance by federal bodies of state power, the bodies of state power of the subjects of the Russian Federation, the bodies of local government, organizations and citizens with the requirements of the federal law regulating the relations in the information sphere;
- unlawful restriction of access of citizens to open information resources of the federal bodies of state power, the bodies of state power of the subjects of the Russian Federation, the bodies of local government, open archive materials and other open socially significant information;
- disorganization and destruction of the system of accumulation and storage of cultural values including archives;
- violation of the constitutional rights and freedoms of man and citizen in the realm of mass information;
- the ouster of Russian information agencies and mass media from the internal information market and the strengthening of dependence on the spiritual, economic and political spheres of social life in Russia on foreign information structures;
- depreciation of spiritual values, the promotion of specimens of mass culture based on the cult of violence, on spiritual and moral values that contradict the accepted values of Russian society;
- the lowering of the spiritual, moral and creative potential of the Russian population which would significantly complicate the preparation of labor resources for the introduction and use of the latest technologies, including information technologies;
- manipulation of information (disinformation, concealment or distortion of information).

The following may be the threats to the information support of the state policy of the Russian Federation:

- monopolization of the information market in Russia and its individual sectors by domestic and foreign information entities;
- the blocking of the activities of state mass media in informing the Russian and foreign audiences;

- poor information support of the state policy of the Russian Federation due to a shortage of skilled personnel, the lack of a system of forming and implementing the state information policy.

The following may be the threats to the development of the domestic information industry, including the industry of the means of informatization and telecommunications and to the needs of the internal market for its products and the entry of these products into the world market as well as to ensuring the accumulation, storage and effective use of the national information resources:

- obstructing the access of the Russian Federation to the latest information technologies, mutually beneficial and equal participation of Russian producers in the world division of labor in the industry of information services, means of informatization and telecommunications, information products as well as the creation of conditions for greater technological dependence of Russia in the field of modern information technologies;
- the purchase by the bodies of state power of imported means of informatization and telecommunications even as domestic analogs exist which are not inferior to foreign specimens in terms of their characteristics;
- the ouster of Russian producers of means of informatization and telecommunications from the domestic market;
- growing outflow of specialists and holders of intellectual property rights abroad.

The following may be the threats to the security of information and telecommunications means and systems, both already deployed and being created on the territory of Russia:

- unlawful collection and use of information;
- non-compliance with the technology of information processing;
- the introduction to the hardware and software products of components performing functions not stipulated in the documentation covering these products;
- the development and dissemination of programs that disrupt the normal functioning of information and telecommunications systems, including the systems of information protection;
- the break-up, damage, radio-electronic suppression or destruction of the means and system of information processing and telecommunications;
- tampering with password and key systems protecting computerized systems of information processing and transmission;
- the compromising of keys and means of cryptographic protection of information;
- leakage of information through technical channels;
- the introduction of electronic devices to intercept information into technical means of the processing, storage and transmission of information through communication

channels as well as into the offices of the bodies of state power, enterprises, institutions and organizations irrespective of the form of ownership;

- destruction, causing damage to, breaking up or stealing of machine and other information carriers;
- interception of information in data transmission networks and communication lines, decoding of such information and imposition of false information;
- the use of uncertified domestic and foreign information technologies, means of information protection, means of informatization and telecommunications in the creation and development of the information infrastructure in Russia;
- unauthorized access to information contained in data banks and bases;
- violation of lawful restrictions on the dissemination of information.

Article 3. Sources of Threats to the Information Security of the Russian Federation.

The sources of threats to the information security of the Russian Federation are divided into external and internal ones. The external sources include:

- the activities of foreign political, economic, military, intelligence and information structures aimed against the interests of the Russian Federation in the information sphere;
- the desire of some countries to dominate and infringe upon the interests of Russia in the world information space and to oust it from the external and internal information markets;
- growing international competition for the possession of information technologies and resources;
- the activities of international terrorist organizations;
- the widening of the technological lead of the main world powers and the buildup of their potential to counteract the creation of competitive Russian information technologies;
- the activities of space, air, sea and land technical and other means (types) of intelligence of foreign states;
- the development by a number of states of the concepts of information warfare envisaging the creation of dangerous means of influencing the information spheres in other countries of the world, the disruption of the normal functioning of information and telecommunications systems, the information resources and gaining unauthorized access to them.

Internal sources include:

- the critical state of the domestic industry;
- the unfavorable crime situation accompanied by the tendency of the merger of state and criminal structures in the information sphere, the gaining of access by criminal structures to confidential information, the growing influence of organized

crime on the life of society, the decline in the level of protection of the legitimate interests of citizens, society and the state in the information sphere;

- inadequate coordination of the activities of the federal bodies of state power and the bodies of state power of the subjects of the Russian Federation in the development and implementation of a single state policy in ensuring the information security of the Russian Federation;
- insufficiently developed regulatory legal framework regulating the relations in the information sphere as well as inadequate law enforcement;
- insufficient development of the institutions of civil society and insufficient state control over the development of the information market in Russia;
- inadequate financing of measures to ensure the information security of the Russian Federation;
- insufficient economic strength of the state;
- a decline in the effectiveness of the system of education and upbringing, insufficient number of qualified workers in the field of ensuring information security;
- inadequate efforts of the federal bodies of state power and the bodies of state power of the subjects of the Russian Federation to inform society of their activities, explain the decisions taken and form open state resources and develop a system of citizens' access to them;
- Russia's lag behind the leading countries of the world in terms of informatization of the federal bodies of state power and the bodies of state power of the subjects of the Russian Federation and bodies of local self-government, the credit and finance sphere, industry, agriculture, education, health, the services and welfare of citizens.

Article 4. The State of the Information Security of the Russian Federation and the Main Tasks in Ensuring It.

In recent years the Russian Federation has implemented a set of measures to upgrade its information security.

The creation of the legal framework for information security has begun. The Law of the Russian Federation On State Secret, the Basic Principles of the Legislation of the Russian Federation on the Archive Fund of the Russian Federation and Archives, the federal laws On Information, Informatization and Information Protection, On Participation in International Information Exchange and a number of other laws have been adopted and work has begun to create the mechanisms of their implementation and to prepare draft laws regulating social relations in the information sphere.

Measures have been implemented to ensure information security in the federal bodies of state power, the bodies of state power of the subjects of the Russian Federation, in enterprises, institutions and organizations irrespective of the form of ownership. Work has gotten underway to create a protected information and telecommunications special-purpose system in the interests of the bodies of state power.

Contributing to success in ensuring the information security of the Russian Federation are the state system of information protection, the system of protecting state secrets, the system of licensing activities in protecting state secrets and the system of certification of information protection means.

At the same time an analysis of the state of the information security of the Russian Federation shows that its level does not quite correspond to the needs of society and the state.

The present-day political and social-economic conditions in the country tend to exacerbate the contradictions between the needs of society to expand free exchange of information and the need to preserve certain regulated restrictions on its dissemination.

The conflicting and undeveloped legal regulation of social relations in the information sphere leads to serious negative consequences. Thus, inadequate legal regulation of the relations in using the possibilities of constitutional restrictions on media freedom in the interests of protecting the foundations of the constitutional system, morality, health, the rights and legitimate interests of citizens, ensuring the country's defenses and the security of the state substantially hampers the maintenance of the necessary balance between the interests of the individual, society and the state in the information sphere. Inadequate legal regulation of relations in the field of mass media makes it more difficult to form competitive Russian information agencies and mass media on the territory of the Russian Federation.

Denial of citizens' rights to access information and manipulation of information provoke a negative reaction of the population which in some cases destabilizes the social and political situation in society.

The rights of citizens to privacy, personal and family secrets, the secret of correspondence enshrined in the Constitution of the Russian Federation do not, in practice, have adequate legal, organizational and technical support. The protection of data on natural persons (personal data) gathered by the federal bodies of state power, the bodies of state power of the subjects of the Russian Federation and the bodies of local self-government is unsatisfactory.

There is no clarity in the implementation of the state policy in the shaping of the Russian information space, the development of the system of mass information, organizing international information exchange and integration of the Russian information space into the world information space, which creates conditions for the ousting of Russian information agencies and mass media from the internal information market and the distortion of the structure of international information exchange.

State support of the activities of Russian information agencies in promoting their products in the foreign information market is inadequate.

The situation surrounding the safety of data constituting state secrets is deteriorating.

The human resource potential of the scientific and production collectives operating in the field of creating means of informatization and telecommunications has been seriously depleted by the wide-scale drift-away of the best-qualified specialists from these teams. The domestic information technology lag forces the federal bodies of state power, the bodies of state power of the subjects of the Russian Federation and the bodies of local self-government, in creating their information systems, to purchase imported technology and bring in foreign firms, which increases the probability of unauthorized access to the information being processed and the dependence of Russia on foreign producers of computer and telecommunications hardware and software.

The massive introduction of foreign information technologies in the activities of individuals, society and the state as well as wide-scale use of open information and telecommunications systems and the integration of the domestic information systems and international information systems increases the threats of the use of the "information weapon" against the information infrastructure of Russia. Work to counteract these threats in an effective and comprehensive manner is not coordinated well enough and is poorly financed. Not enough attention is paid to the development of space intelligence and radio-electronic warfare means.

The current state of affairs in the field of ensuring the information security of the Russian Federation requires that the following tasks should be addressed without delay:

- the development of guidelines of the state policy in ensuring the information security of the Russian Federation as well as measures and mechanisms involved in implementing such policy;
- the development and improvement of the system of ensuring the information security of the Russian Federation which follows a single state policy in the field, including the improvement of the forms, methods and means of identifying, assessing and forecasting threats to the information security of the Russian Federation as well as a system of counteracting such threats;
- the development of federal target programs of ensuring the information security of the Russian Federation;
- the development of criteria and methods of assessing the effectiveness of the systems and means of ensuring the information security of the Russian Federation as well as certification of such systems and means;
- improving the regulatory legal framework for ensuring the information security of the Russian Federation, including mechanisms for the exercise of citizens' rights to obtain and access information, the forms and methods of the implementation of the legal standards pertaining to the interaction between the state and the mass media;
- determining the responsibility of the officials of the federal bodies of state power, the bodies of state power of the subjects of the Russian Federation, the bodies of local self-government, legal entities and citizens for complying with the requirements of information security;

- coordinating the activities of the federal bodies of state power, the bodies of state power of the subjects of the Russian Federation, enterprises, institutions and organizations irrespective of the form of ownership in ensuring the information security of the Russian Federation;
- developing the scientific and practical principles of ensuring the information security of the Russian Federation with due regard for the current geopolitical situation, the political and social-economic conditions in Russia and the reality of the threat of the use of the "information weapon";
- developing and establishing mechanisms for the formation and implementation of the national information policy of Russia;
- developing the methods to make more effective the participation of the state in the shaping of the information policy of state-owned television and radio broadcasting organizations and other state-owned mass media;
- ensuring the technological independence of the Russian Federation in key areas of informatization and telecommunications that determine its security, in the first place in the development of specialized computer technology, for specimens of weapons and military equipment;
- developing modern methods and means of protecting information, ensuring the security of information technologies, above all, those used in the systems of control of troops and weapons, environmentally hazardous and economically important production facilities;
- developing and improving the state system of information protection and the system of protecting state secrets;
- the creation and development of a modern protected technological basis of state control in peacetime, in emergency situations and in wartime;
- broadening the interaction with international and foreign bodies and organizations in addressing the scientific-technical and legal issues of ensuring the security of information transmitted via international telecommunications system;
- ensuring conditions for vigorous development of the Russian information infrastructure, the participation of Russia in the processes of establishment and use of global information networks and systems;
- the creation of a uniform system of training personnel in the field of information security and information technologies.

Chapter II. Methods of Ensuring the Information Security of the Russian Federation.

Article 5. General Methods of Ensuring the Information Security of the Russian Federation.

The general methods of ensuring the information security of the Russian Federation are divided into legal, organizational-technical, and economic.

The legal methods of ensuring the information security of the Russian Federation include the development of the legal acts regulating the relations in the information sphere and regulatory methodological documents on ensuring the information security of the Russian Federation. The most important areas of this activity are:

- introducing amendments and additions to the laws of the Russian Federation regulating the relations in ensuring information security for the purpose of creating and improving the system of ensuring the information security of the Russian Federation, eliminating internal contradictions in federal legislation, the contradictions related to international agreements to which the Russian Federation has acceded and the contradictions between the federal laws and the laws of the subjects of the Russian Federation as well as for the purpose of specifying the legal norms which envisage liability for violations in the field of ensuring the information security of the Russian Federation;
- legislation to separate the powers in the field of ensuring the information security of the Russian Federation between the federal bodies of state power, bodies of state power of the subjects of the Russian Federation, identifying the goals, tasks and mechanisms of the participation of non-governmental associations, organizations and citizens in these activities;
- development and adoption of regulatory legal acts of the Russian Federation which envisage the responsibility of legal entities and natural persons for unauthorized access to information, its unlawful copying, distortion and illegal use, deliberate dissemination of false information, unlawful disclosure of confidential information, the use of in-house information or information containing commercial secrets for criminal or selfish purposes;
- defining more clearly the status of foreign information agencies, mass media and journalists as well as investors if foreign investments are attracted into the development of the information infrastructure of Russia;
- passing legislation to confirm the priority of the development of national communications networks and domestic production of communications satellites;
- defining the status of the organizations that render the services of global information and telecommunications networks on the territory of the Russian Federation and legal regulation of the activities or these organizations;
- developing a legal framework for creating regional structures ensuring information security in the Russian Federation.

The organizational and technical methods of ensuring the information security of the Russian Federation are:

- the establishment and improvement of the system of ensuring the information security of the Russian Federation;
- intensifying the law-enforcement activities of the federal bodies of executive power, the bodies of executive power of the Russian Federation, including

prevention and stopping of violations in the information sphere as well as detection, exposure and punishment of the individuals who have perpetrated crimes and other offences in this sphere;

- developing, using and improving the means of information protection and methods to monitor the effectiveness of these means, the development of protected telecommunications systems and making the special-purpose software more reliable;
- creating systems and means to prevent unauthorized access to the information being processed and special actions that cause the breakup, destruction and distortion of information as well as a change in operating procedures of the systems and means of informatization and communication;
- revealing the technical devices and software which pose a threat to the normal functioning of the information and telecommunications system, preventing the interception of information in technical channels, the application of cryptographic means to protect information in the process of storage, processing and transmission via communication channels, monitoring compliance with the special information protection requirements;
- certification of the means of information protection, licensing of activities in the field of protecting state secrets, standardization of the methods and means of information protection;
- improving the system of certification of telecommunications equipment and software in management information systems based on information security requirements;
- controlling the actions of the personnel in protected information systems, and training personnel in the field of ensuring the information security of the Russian Federation;
- creating a system of monitoring the indicators and characteristics of the information security of the Russian Federation in key spheres of life and the activities of society and the state.

The economic methods of ensuring the information security of the Russian Federation include:

- developing the programs of ensuring the information security of the Russian Federation and determining the procedure of financing them;
- improving the system of financing of the works to implement the legal and organizational-technical methods of information protection, creating a system of insurance of natural persons and legal entities against information risks.

Article 6. Special Features of Ensuring the Information Security of the Russian Federation in Various Spheres of Social Life.

The information security of the Russian Federation is a component of the national security of the Russian Federation which is relevant to the protection of the national interests of the Russian Federation in various areas of the life of society and the state. Threats to the information security of the Russian Federation and methods of ensuring it are common to all these spheres.

Yet in each of these spheres there are special features of ensuring information security stemming from the specific nature of the objects of security, the degree of their vulnerability to the threats to the information security of the Russian Federation. In each area of the life of society and the state, along with the common methods of ensuring the information security of the Russian Federation, special methods and forms may be used in accordance with the specific factors that influence the state of the information security of the Russian Federation.

(a) In the Economic Sphere.

Ensuring the information security of the Russian Federation in the economic sphere plays the key role in ensuring the national security of the Russian Federation.

The areas of the economy most exposed to the threats to the information security of the Russian Federation are:

- the system of state statistics;
- the credit and financial system;
- information and accounting computerized systems in the divisions of the federal bodies of executive power which ensure economic activities of society and the state;
- the systems of accounting at enterprises, institutions and organizations irrespective of the form of ownership;
- the system of collecting, processing, storage and transmission of financial, exchange, tax and customs information and information on the foreign economic activities of the state as well as enterprises, institutions and organizations irrespective of the form of ownership.

The transition to market relations in the economy has brought to the internal Russian market of goods and services a multitude of domestic and foreign commercial entities which produce and consume information, means of informatization and information protection. Uncontrolled activities of these entities in creating and protecting the systems of gathering, processing, storage and transmission of statistical, financial, exchange, tax and customs information pose a real threat to the economic security of Russia. Similar threats arise from uncontrolled involvement of foreign firms in the creation of such systems because it offers favorable conditions for unauthorized access to confidential economic information and for the monitoring of the processes of its transmission and processing by foreign special services.

The critical state of the enterprises of the national industries which develop and produce means of informatization, telecommunications and information protection leads to wide-scale use of corresponding imported means which threatens to make Russia technologically dependent on foreign states.

Computer crime involving the breaking of criminal elements into computer systems and the networks of banks and other credit institutions poses a serious threat to the normal functioning of the economy.

The inadequate regulatory legal framework that spells out the liability of agents in the economy for providing false information or concealing information on their commercial activities, the consumer qualities of their goods and services, the results of their economic activities, investments and so on, impedes the normal functioning of economic entities. At the same time substantial economic damage to economic entities may be caused by the disclosure of commercial secrets. In the systems of gathering, processing, storage and transmission of financial, exchange, tax and customs information unlawful copying of information and its distortion as a result of deliberate or accidental violations of the technology of work with information and unauthorized access to information pose the greatest danger. This applies to the federal bodies of executive power which form and disseminate information on the foreign economic activities of the Russian Federation.

The main measures to ensure the information security of the Russian Federation in the economic sphere are:

- organizing and exercising state control over the creation, development and protection of the systems and means of gathering, processing, storage and transmission of statistical, financial, exchange, tax and customs information;
- drastic restructuring of the system of the state statistical reporting to ensure authenticity, completeness and protection of information by introducing strict legal liability of officials for the preparation of the basic information, organization of control over the activities of such persons and the statistical information processing and analysis services as well as by limiting the commercialization of such information;
- the development of national certified means of protecting information and the introduction thereof in the systems and means of gathering, processing, storage and transmission of statistical, financial, exchange, tax and customs information;
- the development and introduction of national protected system of electronic payments on the basis of smart cards, the systems of electronic money and electronic trade, standardization of such systems as well as the development of a regulatory legal base for the use thereof;
- the development of the regulatory legal framework of information relations in the economic sphere;

- the improvement of the methods of selecting and training personnel to work in the systems of gathering, processing, storage and transmission of economic information.

(b) In the Sphere of Internal Politics.

The most important objects of ensuring the information security of the Russian Federation in the sphere of internal politics are:

- constitutional rights and freedoms of man and citizen;
- the constitutional system, national harmony, the stability of state power, the sovereignty and territorial integrity of the Russian Federation;
- open information resources of the federal bodies of executive power and the mass media.

In the sphere of internal politics the following are the key threats to the information security of the Russian Federation:

- violation of the constitutional rights and freedoms of citizens in the information sphere;
- inadequate legal regulation of the rights of various political forces to use the mass media to propagate their ideas;
- dissemination of disinformation on the policy of the Russian Federation, the activities of the federal bodies of state power and the events taking place in and outside the country;
- the activities of non-governmental associations aimed at violent change of the foundations of the constitutional system and breakup of the integrity of the Russian Federation, fomenting of social, racial, national and religious hostility, and disseminating these ideas in the mass media.

The main measures in ensuring the information security of the Russian Federation in the sphere of internal politics are:

- creating a system of counteraction to the monopolization by domestic and foreign structures of the components of the information infrastructure, including the market of information services and the mass media;
- stepping up counter-propaganda activities aimed at preventing the negative consequences of the dissemination of disinformation about the internal policy of Russia.

(c) In the Sphere of External Policy.

The key objects of ensuring the information security of the Russian Federation in the sphere of external policy are:

- the information resources of the federal bodies of executive power implementing the external policy of the Russian Federation, the Russian missions and organizations abroad, the missions of the Russian Federation to international organizations;

- the information resources of the missions of the federal bodies of executive power which implement the external policy of the Russian Federation on the territories of the subjects of the Russian Federation;
- the information resources of the Russian enterprises, institutions and organizations subordinate to the federal bodies of executive power implementing the foreign policy of the Russian Federation;
- the blocking of the activities of the Russian mass media to explain to the foreign audiences the goals and main guidelines of the state policy of the Russian Federation and its opinion on socially significant events in Russian and international life.

Among the foreign threats to the information security of the Russian Federation in the sphere of foreign policy the following are the most dangerous:

- the information influence of foreign political, economic, military and information structures on the development and implementation of the Russian foreign policy strategy;
- dissemination abroad of disinformation on the foreign policy of the Russian Federation;
- the violation of the rights of Russian citizens and legal entities in the information sphere abroad;
- attempts at gaining unauthorized access to information and to influence the information resources and the information infrastructure of the federal bodies of executive power which implement the foreign policy of the Russian Federation, the Russian missions and organizations abroad, the missions of the Russian Federation to international organizations.

Among the internal threats to the information security of the Russian Federation in the sphere of external policy the following are the most dangerous:

- violations of the established procedure of gathering, processing, storage and transmission of information at the federal bodies of executive power which implement the foreign policy of the Russian Federation and the enterprises, institutions and organizations within their jurisdiction;
- the information and propaganda activities of political forces, non-governmental associations, mass media and individuals which distort the strategy and tactics of the foreign policy activities of the Russian Federation;
- insufficient provision of information to the population on the foreign policy activities of the Russian Federation.

The main measures ensuring the information security of the Russian Federation in the sphere of foreign policy are:

- developing the guidelines of the state policy in improving the information support of the foreign policy of the Russian Federation;
- development and implementation of a complex of measures to strengthen the information security of the information infrastructure of the federal bodies of executive power which implement the foreign policy of the Russian Federation, Russian missions and organizations abroad and the missions of the Russian Federation to international organizations;
- the creation for Russian missions and organizations abroad of conditions for work to neutralize the disinformation being disseminated there on the foreign policy of the Russian Federation;
- improving the information support of the work to counteract the violations of the rights and freedoms of Russian citizens and legal entities abroad;
- improving the information support of the subjects of the Russian Federation on matters of foreign policy activities within their jurisdiction.

(d) In the Field of Science and Technology.

The most important objects of ensuring the information security of the Russian Federation in the field of science and technology are:

- the results of fundamental, exploratory and applied scientific research potentially vital for scientific, technological, social and economic development of the country including the information whose loss may cause damage to the national interests and prestige of the Russian Federation;
- discoveries, unpatented technologies, industrial prototypes, usable models and experimental equipment;
- scientific and technological personnel and the system of their training;
- the systems of controlling sophisticated research complexes (nuclear reactors, particle accelerators, plasma generators and others).

Among the main external threats to the information security of the Russian Federation in the field of science and technology are:

- the intention of developed foreign states to gain unlawful access to the scientific and technological resources of Russia in order to use the results obtained by Russian scientists in their own interests;
- creating advantages in the Russian market for foreign scientific and technological products and the desire of developed countries to limit the development of the scientific and technical potential of Russia (by purchasing the shares of advanced enterprises with subsequent change of their core business, retaining export and import restrictions and so on);
- the policy of Western countries aimed at continued destruction of the common scientific and technological space of the states—members of the Commonwealth of Independent States inherited from the USSR by reorienting their scientific and

technical links and some of the more promising scientific collectives to the Western countries;

- stepping up the activities of foreign state and commercial enterprises, institutions and organizations in the field of industrial espionage with the participation of intelligence and special services.

Among the main internal threats to the information security of the Russian Federation in the field of science and technology are:

- the persisting difficult economic situation in Russia leading to a dramatic reduction in the funding of scientific and technical activities, temporary decline in the prestige of science and technology, the leakage of ideas and cutting-edge developments abroad;
- the inability of the enterprises in the national electronics industry to produce, on the basis of the latest micro-electronics achievements and advanced information technologies, competitive science-intensive products that would ensure an adequate level of technological independence of Russia from foreign countries which leads to forced wide-scale use of imported hardware and software in creating and developing the information infrastructure in Russia;
- serious problems in the field of patent protection of the results of scientific and technological activities of Russian scientists;
- difficulties in implementing measures to protect information, especially in privatized enterprises, scientific and technological institutions and organizations.

A realistic way to counter the threats to the information security of the Russian Federation in the field of science and technology is to improve the laws of the Russian Federation regulating relations in this field and the mechanisms of their implementation. To this end the state must seek to create a system of evaluation of the possible damage from the threats to the key objects of ensuring the information security of the Russian Federation in the field of science and technology, including independent scientific councils and independent expert organizations that work out recommendations for the federal bodies of state power and bodies of state power of the subjects of the Russian Federation on how to prevent unlawful or ineffective use of the intellectual potential of Russia.

(e) In the Spiritual Sphere.

Ensuring the information security of the Russian Federation in the spiritual sphere aims to protect the constitutional rights and freedoms of man and citizen connected with the development, growth and behavior of the individual, freedom of mass information, the use of the cultural, spiritual and moral heritage, historical traditions and norms of social life, with the preservation of the cultural legacy of all the peoples of Russia, realization of the constitutional restrictions of the rights and freedoms of man and citizen in the interests of preserving and strengthening the moral values of society, the traditions of patriotism and humanism, the health of citizens, the cultural and scientific potential of the Russian Federation, and ensuring the defense capability and security of the state.

Among the main objects of ensuring the information security of the Russian Federation in the sphere of spiritual life are:

- the dignity of the individual, freedom of conscience, including the right to freely choose, hold and disseminate religious and other convictions and to act in accordance with them, freedom of thought and expression (with the exception of propaganda or agitation that incite social, racial, national or religious hatred or hostility) as well as the freedom of literary, artistic, scientific, technical and other types of creativity and teaching;
- freedom of the mass media;
- privacy, personal and family secrets;
- the Russian language is a factor of spiritual unity of the peoples of multinational Russia, the language of communication between the peoples of the states—members of the Commonwealth of Independent States;
- the languages, moral values and cultural heritage of the peoples of the Russian Federation, large and small;
- objects of intellectual property.

The greatest danger in the sphere of spiritual life is posed by the following threats to the information security of the Russian Federation:

- distortion of the system of mass information both by monopolizing the mass media and by uncontrolled expansion of the foreign media sector in the domestic information space;
- the deterioration and decay of the objects of the Russian cultural heritage, including archives, museum collections, libraries and architecture monuments due to underfinancing of corresponding programs and activities;
- possible disruptions of social stability, damage to the health and threat to the lives of citizens due to the activities of religious associations that preach religious fundamentalism as well as totalitarian religious sects;
- the use by foreign special services of the mass media operating on the territory of the Russian Federation to damage the defense capability of the country and the security of the state and to disseminate disinformation;
- the inability of the contemporary civil society in Russia to inculcate to the young generation and maintain in society the socially vital moral values, patriotism and a sense of civic responsibility for the destiny of the country.

The main areas in ensuring the information security of the Russian Federation in the sphere of spiritual life are:

- the development of the fundamentals of a civil society in Russia;

- the creation of social and economic conditions for the creative activities and the functioning of cultural institutions;
- working out civilized forms and methods of social control over the shaping, in society, of spiritual values that meet the national interests of the country, the fostering of patriotism and a sense of civic responsibility for the destinies of the country;
- improving the legislation of the Russian Federation that regulates the relations regarding constitutional restrictions of the rights and freedoms of man and citizen;
- state support of measures to preserve and revive the cultural heritage of the large and small peoples in the Russian Federation;
- the formation of legal and organizational mechanisms for ensuring the constitutional rights and freedoms of citizens, raising their legal awareness in order to counteract conscious or unconscious violation of such constitutional rights and freedoms in the spiritual sphere;
- developing effective organizational and legal mechanisms to ensure the access of the mass media and citizens to unclassified information on the activities of the federal bodies of state power and non-governmental associations, ensuring the provision of authentic data on socially significant events in social life distributed through the mass media;
- developing special legal and organizational mechanisms to prevent unlawful information and psychological influences on the mass consciousness, uncontrolled commercialization of culture and science and to ensure the preservation of the cultural and historical values of the large and small peoples of the Russian Federation, rational use of the information resources of society that constitute part of the national heritage;
- introducing a ban on the use of air time in the electronic media to distribute the programs that propagate violence and cruelty and anti-social behavior;
- countering the negative impact of foreign religious organizations and missionaries.

(f) In National Information and Telecommunications Systems.

The main objects of ensuring the information security of the Russian Federation in national information and telecommunications systems are:

- the information resources containing data classified as state secrets and confidential information;
- the means and systems of informatization (computers, information and computer complexes, networks and systems), software (operational systems, database management systems and other systemic and applied software support);
- management information systems, the systems of communication and data transmission that receive, process, store and transmit limited-access information and their informative physical fields;

- the technical means and systems that process publicly accessible information and are located in the premises in which limited-access information is also processed as well as the actual premises intended for the processing of such information;
- the premises intended for the conduct of secret negotiations as well as negotiations in the course of which limited-access data are mentioned.

The main threats to the information security of the Russian Federation in the national information and telecommunications systems are:

- the activities of the special services of foreign states, criminal communities, organizations and groups, unlawful activities of individuals aimed at gaining unauthorized access to information and controlling the functioning of information and telecommunications systems;
- the forced use, due to the lag of the domestic industry, or imported software and hardware in the creation and development of information and telecommunications systems;
- the violation of the established procedure of gathering, processing and transmitting information, deliberate actions and errors of the personnel of information and telecommunications systems, malfunctions of the hardware and breakdowns in software support in information and telecommunications systems;
- the use of means and systems of informatization and communications that are uncertified in terms of safety requirements as well as of means of protection of information and control of their effectiveness;
- the involvement in work to create, develop and protect information and telecommunications systems of organizations and firms that hold no state licenses for engaging in these types of activities.

The main areas of ensuring the information security of the Russian Federation in the national information and telecommunications systems are:

- preventing the interception of information from premises and objects as well as information transmitted through communications channels by technical means;
- ruling out unauthorized access to the information being processed or stored in hardware;
- preventing the leakage of information through technical channels arising in the process of operating the hardware for its processing, storage and transmission;
- preventing special software and hardware interventions causing the breakdown, destruction, distortion of information or malfunctions in the work of the informatization means;
- ensuring information security when hooking up national information and telecommunications systems to external, including international, information networks;

- ensuring the safety of confidential information at the interface of information and telecommunications systems with varying degrees of protection;
- detecting information intercept devices planted into objects and the electronic hardware.

The main organizational and technical measures to protect the information in national information and telecommunications systems are:

- the licensing of the activities of organizations in the field of information protection;
- attestation of the objects of informatization for compliance with the requirements of information protection in the conduct of works connected with the use of data that constitute a state secret;
- certification of the means of protecting information and controlling the effectiveness of their use as well as the protection of information against being leaked via the technical channels of the systems and means of informatization and communication;
- the introduction of territorial, frequency, energy, spatial and temporal limitations on the regimes of the use of the hardware subject to protection;
- creation and use of information and computerized systems of management in the protected version.

(g) In the Sphere of Defense.

The objects of ensuring the information security of the Russian Federation in the defense sphere are:

- the information infrastructure of the central military control bodies and the military control bodies of all the services of the Armed Forces of the Russian Federation, formations, units and organizations constituting the Armed Forces of the Russian Federation, scientific research institutions of the Defense Ministry of the Russian Federation;
- the information resources of defense industry enterprises and research institutions that fulfill state defense contracts or deal with defense problems;
- the hardware and software of computerized systems of control of the troops and weapons, arms and military equipment provided with informatization means;
- information resources, systems of communication and the information infrastructure of all other troops, military units and agencies.

The external threats that pose the greatest danger to the objects of ensuring the information security of the Russian Federation in the defense sphere are:

- all types of intelligence activities of foreign states;
- information and technical intervention (including radio-electronic warfare and breaking into computer networks) by potential enemies;

- sabotage activities by the special services of foreign states pursued through information and psychological methods;
- the activities of foreign political, economic and military structures directed against the defense interests of the Russian Federation.

The internal threats which pose the greatest danger to the said objects are:

- violation of the established procedure of gathering, processing, storage and transmission of information in the staffs and institutions of the Ministry of Defense of the Russian Federation and at defense enterprises;
- intentional actions as well as errors of the personnel of special information and telecommunications systems;
- unreliable functioning of special-purpose information and telecommunications systems;
- possible information and propaganda activities that undermine the prestige of the Armed Forces of the Russian Federation and their combat readiness;
- unresolved problems of protecting the intellectual property of the defense enterprises leading to a leakage abroad of very valuable state information resources;
- problems of social protection of servicemen and their families.

The above internal threats will become particularly dangerous if the military and political situation deteriorates.

The main specific areas in improving the system of ensuring the information security of the Russian Federation in the defense sphere are:

- systematic identification of threats and their sources, the structuring of the goals of ensuring information security in the defense sphere and identification of corresponding practical tasks;
- certification of the general and specialized software, applied software packages and means of information protection in existing and yet-to-be-created management information systems intended for military purposes and in communications systems containing computer technology elements;
- constant improvement of the means of protecting information against unauthorized access, the development of protected systems of communication and troop and weapons control, and enhancing the reliability of specialized software;
- improving the structure of the functional bodies of the system of ensuring information security in the sphere of defense and coordination thereof;
- improving the devices and methods of strategic and operational camouflage, intelligence and radio-electronic warfare, the methods and means of counteracting information-propaganda and psychological operations of the potential enemy;
- the training of specialists in the field of ensuring defense information security.

(h) In the Law-enforcement and Judiciary Spheres.

Among the more important objects of ensuring information security in the law-enforcement and judiciary spheres are:

- the information resources of the federal bodies of executive power that perform law-enforcement functions, the judiciary bodies, their information and computer centers, scientific research institutions and educational establishments containing specialized data and operational data for service use only;
- information and computer centers and their information, technical, software and regulatory support;
- the information infrastructure (information and computer networks, control points, and communication hubs and lines).

The external threats posing the greatest danger for the objects of ensuring information security in the law-enforcement and judiciary spheres are:

- the intelligence activities of the special services of foreign states, international criminal associations, organizations and groups connected with the gathering of information that reveals the tasks, plans, technical equipment, operating methods and location of the special units and bodies of the Ministry of Interior of the Russian Federation;
- the activities of foreign state and private commercial structures seeking to gain unauthorized access to the information resources of the law-enforcement and judiciary bodies.

The internal threats posing the biggest danger to the above-mentioned objects are:

- violation of the established procedure of gathering, processing, storage and transmission of information contained in the card indexes and computerized data banks and used to investigate crimes;
- inadequate legislative and regulatory framework for information exchange in the law-enforcement and judiciary spheres;
- the lack of a uniform methodology of gathering, processing and storage of operational detective, reference, criminological and statistical information;
- failure of hardware and malfunctions of software in the information and telecommunications systems;
- intentional actions as well as errors of the personnel directly engaged in the creation and maintenance of card indexes and computerized data banks.

Along with the widely used general methods and means of information protection specific methods and means of ensuring information security in the law-enforcement and judiciary spheres are used.

Chief of them are:

- the creation of a protected multi-tiered system of integrated banks of operational-detective, reference, criminological and statistical data on the basis of specialized information and telecommunications systems;
- raising the standard of professional and specialized training of the users of information systems.

(i) In Emergency Situations.

The most vulnerable objects in terms of ensuring the information security of the Russian Federation in emergency situations are the system of decision-making on operational actions (reactions) connected with the development of such situations and the liquidation of their consequences as well as the system of gathering and processing information on the possible occurrence of emergency situations.

Of particular significance for the normal functioning of the said objects is ensuring the security of the national information infrastructure in the event of accidents, catastrophes and natural disasters. Concealment, delay in disclosing and distortion and destruction of operational information, unauthorized access to such information of individuals or groups of persons may cause both human casualties and create various difficulties in cleaning up the aftermath of an emergency situation connected with the special character of the impact of information in extreme conditions: the agitation of large masses of people who experience mental stress; rapid emergence and spread of panic and unrest on the basis of rumors, false or inaccurate information.

In these specific conditions information security is ensured among other things by:

- developing an effective system of monitoring hazardous objects whose malfunction may give rise to emergency situations and prediction of emergency situations;
- improving the system of informing the population about the threats of emergency situations, and the conditions in which they arise and develop;
- making more reliable the systems of processing and transmission of information that support the activities of the federal bodies of executive power;
- predicting the behavior of the population under the impact of false or inaccurate information on the possible emergency situations and working out measures to assist large masses of people in such situations;
- developing specialized measures to protect information systems that ensure control of environmentally hazardous or economically important production facilities.

Article 7. The International Cooperation of the Russian Federation in the Field of Ensuring Information Security.

The international cooperation of the Russian Federation in the field of ensuring information security is an inseparable component of political, military, economic, cultural and other types of interaction among the countries that form the world community. Such cooperation should contribute to enhancing the information security of all the members of the world community, including the Russian Federation.

A distinctive feature of the international cooperation of the Russian Federation in ensuring information security is that it proceeds in the context of sharper international competition for the possession of technological and information resources, for dominance in the markets, amid continued attempts to create a structure of international relations based on unilateral decisions on key problems of world policy, counteracting the strengthening of Russia's role as an influential center in the emerging multiple world, and the widening technological lead of the main world powers and the buildup of their potential for creating an "information weapon." All this may lead to a new phase in unleashing the arms race in the information sphere, a growing threat of foreign intelligences penetrating into Russia through agents and operational-technical means, including the use of a global information infrastructure.

The main areas of international cooperation of the Russian Federation in the field of information security are:

- banning the development, proliferation and application of "information weapons";
- ensuring the security of international information exchanges, including the security of information when being transmitted via national telecommunications channels;
- coordinated activities of law-enforcement bodies of the countries of the world community in preventing computer crime;
- preventing unauthorized access to confidential information in international banking telecommunications networks and world trade information support systems, the information of international law-enforcement organizations fighting transnational organized crime, international terrorism, the spread of narcotics and psychotropic substances, illegal trade in arms and fissile materials as well as trade in people.

In pursuing international cooperation in the field of ensuring information security the Russian Federation should pay particular attention to the problems of interaction with the states—members of the Commonwealth of Independent States. To pursue such cooperation in the main areas indicated above it is necessary to ensure Russia's active participation in all the international organizations active in the field of information security, including in the sphere of standardization and certification of the means of informatization and information protection.

Chapter III. Main Provisions of the State Policy of Ensuring the Information Security of the Russian Federation and Priority Measures to Implement It.

Article 8. Main Provisions of the State Policy of Ensuring the Information Security of the Russian Federation.

The state policy of ensuring the information security of the Russian Federation lays down the guidelines for the activities of the federal bodies of state power and bodies of state power of the subjects of the Russian Federation in this field, the procedure of fixing their duties in protecting the interests of the Russian Federation in the information sphere within their specific areas of activity and is based on maintaining a balance of the interests of the individual, society and the state in the information sphere.

The state policy of insuring the information security of the Russian Federation is based on the following main principles:

- compliance with the Constitution of the Russian Federation, the laws of the Russian Federation, the universally recognized principles and norms of international law in pursuing the activities to ensure the information security of the Russian Federation;
- openness in the performance of the functions of the federal bodies of state power and bodies of state power of the subjects of the Russian Federation and non-governmental associations which implies informing the public of their activities with due regard for the limitations established under the laws of the Russian Federation;
- equal rights of all the participants in the process of information exchange regardless of their political, social and economic status based on the constitutional right of citizens to free search for, access to, transfer, production and dissemination of information by any lawful method;
- priority development of domestic modern information and telecommunications technologies, the production of hardware and software capable of improving the national telecommunications networks, their integration into global information networks for the purpose of meeting the vital interests of the Russian Federation.

The state, in the process of implementing its functions of ensuring the information security of the Russian Federation:

- carries out an objective and comprehensive analysis and forecasting of the threats to the information security of the Russian Federation and develops measures to ensure it;
- organizes the work of legislative (representative) and executive bodies of state power of the Russian Federation to implement the set of measures aimed at preventing, countering and neutralizing the threats to the information security of the Russian Federation;
- supports the activities of non-governmental associations aimed at providing the population with objective information on socially significant phenomena in the life of society and at protecting society from distorted and inaccurate information;
- controls the development, creation, elaboration, use, export and import of the means of information protection through their certification and licensing of information protection activities;
- pursues the required protectionist policy with regard to producers of informatization and information protection means on the territory of the Russian

Federation and takes measures to protect the internal market from the penetration of inferior-quality means of informatization and information products;

- helps natural persons and legal entities to gain access to world information resources and global information networks;
- formulates and implements the state information policy of Russia;
- organizes the development of the federal program to ensure the information security of the Russian Federation combining the efforts of state and non-governmental organizations in this field;
- contributes to the internationalization of global information networks and systems and to the integration of Russia in the world information community on terms of equal partnership.

Improving the legal mechanisms for the regulation of social relations arising in the information sphere is a priority area of state policy in the field of ensuring the information security of the Russian Federation.

This implies:

- assessment of the effectiveness of the use of existing legislative and other regulatory acts in the information sphere and working out a program of improvement thereof;
- creating organizational and legal mechanisms to ensure information security;
- determining the legal status of all the agents in the information sphere, including the users of information and telecommunication systems, and determining their responsibility for compliance with the laws of the Russian Federation in this field;
- establishing a system of gathering and analyzing data on the sources of threats to the information security of the Russian Federation as well as the consequences of the implementation thereof;
- development of regulatory legal acts to determine the organization of investigation and legal process involving facts of unlawful actions in the information sphere as well as the procedure for eliminating the consequences of such unlawful actions;
- defining crimes and offences taking into account the specific features of criminal, civil, administrative, and disciplinary responsibility and including corresponding legal standards in the criminal, civil, administrative, and labor codes and the legislation of the Russian Federation on the civil service;
- improving the system of training the personnel used in the field of ensuring the information security of the Russian Federation.

The legal support of the information security of the Russian Federation should be based, above all, on compliance with the principles of legality, the balance of the interests of the citizens, society and the state in the information sphere.

Compliance with the principles of legality requires from the federal bodies of state power and bodies of state power of the subjects of the Russian Federation, in dealing with conflicts arising in the information sphere, to strictly abide by the legislative and other regulatory acts regulating the relations in this sphere.

Compliance with the principle of the balance of interests of the citizens, society and the state in the information sphere implies the existence of legislation fixing the priority of these interests in various areas of the life of society as well as the use of various forms of public control over the activities of the federal bodies of state power and bodies of state power of the subjects of the Russian Federation. Provision of guarantees of the constitutional rights and freedoms of man and citizen pertaining to the information sphere is the key task of the state in the field of information security.

Developing the mechanisms of legal support of the information security of the Russian Federation includes measures of informatization of the legal sphere as a whole.

For the purpose of identifying and harmonizing the interests of the federal bodies of state power, bodies of state power of the subjects of the Russian Federation and other agents in the information sphere and of working out the necessary decisions, the state supports the formation of public councils, committees and commissions with broad representation of non-governmental associations and assists in organizing their effective work.

Article 9. Priority Measures to Implement the State Policy of Ensuring the Information Security of the Russian Federation.

The following are the priority measures in implementing the state policy of ensuring the information security of the Russian Federation:

- development and introduction of the mechanisms of enforcing the legal standards regulating the relations in the information sphere as well as preparing a concept of legal support of the information security of the Russian Federation;
- development and introduction of the mechanisms to enhance the effectiveness of state supervision of the activities of the state-owned mass media and the implementation of the state information policy;
- adoption and implementation of federal programs to form generally accessible archives of the information resources of the federal bodies of state power and bodies of state power of the subjects of the Russian Federation, to enhance the legal awareness and computer literacy, to develop the infrastructure of the common information sphere of Russia, to counter in a concerted manner the threats of information warfare, to create safe information technologies for the systems used in the performance of vital functions of society and the state, to stop computer crime, to create a special-purpose information and telecommunications system in the interests of the federal bodies of state power and bodies of state power of the subjects of the Russian Federation, to ensure the country's technological independence in the creation and operation of oriented-oriented information and telecommunications systems;

- development of a system of training the personnel used in the field of ensuring the information security of the Russian Federation;
- harmonizing the domestic standards in the field of informatization and information security of management information systems, general-purpose and special-purpose information and telecommunications systems.

Chapter IV. Organizational Basis of the System of Ensuring the Information Security of the Russian Federation.

Article 10. Main Functions of the System of Ensuring the Information Security of the Russian Federation.

The system of ensuring the information security of the Russian Federation is intended to implement the state's policy in this sphere.

The main functions of the system of ensuring the information security of the Russian Federation are:

- developing the legal framework for ensuring the information security of the Russian Federation;
- creating conditions for the exercise of the right of citizens and non-governmental associations to pursue lawful activities in the information sphere;
- determining and maintaining the balance between the need of citizens, society and the state for free exchange of information and the necessary restrictions on the dissemination of information;
- assessing the state of the information security of the Russian Federation, identifying the sources of internal and external threats to information security, determining priority areas of preventing, countering and neutralizing such threats;
- coordinating the activities of the federal bodies of state power and other state bodies called upon to ensure the information security of the Russian Federation;
- controlling the activities of the federal bodies of state power and bodies of state power of the subjects of the Russian Federation, state and inter-agency commissions engaged in ensuring the information security of the Russian Federation;
- preventing, identifying and stopping the offences and crimes involving encroachment on the lawful interests of the citizens, society and the state in the information sphere, on the legal process over crimes in this area;
- developing a domestic information infrastructure as well as the industry of telecommunications and information means, making them more competitive in the internal and external markets;
- organizing the development of federal and regional programs to ensure information security and coordinating activities in implementing the same;

- pursuing a uniform technical policy in the field of ensuring the information security of the Russian Federation;
- organizing fundamental and applied research in ensuring the information security of the Russian Federation;
- protecting the state information resources, above all, in the federal bodies of state power and bodies of state power of the subjects of the Russian Federation and defense enterprises;
- controlling the creation and use of information protection means through mandatory licensing of activities in this sphere and certification of information protection means;
- improving and developing a single system of training the personnel to work in the field of ensuring the information security of the Russian Federation;
- pursuing international cooperation in the field of ensuring information security and representing the interests of the Russian Federation in corresponding international organizations.

The competence of the federal bodies of state power and bodies of state power of the subjects of the Russian Federation and other bodies included in the system of ensuring the information security of the Russian Federation and its subsystems is determined by federal laws and regulatory legal acts of the President of the Russian Federation and of the Government of the Russian Federation.

The functions of the bodies coordinating the activities of the federal bodies of state power, bodies of state power of the subjects of the Russian Federation and other government bodies that form the system of ensuring the information security of the Russian Federation and its subsystems are determined by specific regulatory acts of the Russian Federation.

Article 11. Main Elements of Organization of the System of Ensuring the Information Security of the Russian Federation.

The system of ensuring the information security of the Russian Federation is part of the system of ensuring the national security of the country.

The system of ensuring the information security of the Russian Federation is based on the delimitation of the jurisdiction of the bodies of legislative, executive and judiciary branches of power in this sphere and the jurisdictions of the federal bodies of state power and bodies of state power of the subjects of the Russian Federation.

The main elements of the organization of the system of ensuring the information security of the Russian Federation are: the President of the Russian Federation, the Federation Council of the Federal Assembly of the Russian Federation, the State Duma of the Federal Assembly of the Russian Federation, the Government of the Russian Federation, the Security Council of the Russian Federation, the federal bodies of executive power, inter-agency and state commissions established by the President of the Russian Federation and the Government of the Russian Federation, the bodies of executive power of the subjects of the Russian Federation, the bodies of local self-government, the judiciary bodies, public associations and citizens involved, under the laws of the Russian Federation, in ensuring the information security of the Russian Federation.

The President of the Russian Federation, within his or her constitutional powers, supervises the bodies and resources to ensure the information security of the Russian Federation; sanctions actions to ensure the information security of the Russian Federation; under the laws of the Russian Federation forms, reorganizes and abolishes the bodies and resources subordinate to him or her for ensuring the information security of the Russian Federation; identifies in his or her annual addresses to the Federal Assembly state policy priorities in ensuring the information security of the Russian Federation as well as measures to implement this Doctrine.

The houses of the Federal Assembly of the Russian Federation, proceeding on the basis of the Constitution of the Russian Federation and upon submission of the President of the Russian Federation and the Government of the Russian Federation, form the legislative framework in the field of ensuring the information security of the Russian Federation.

The Government of the Russian Federation, within its powers and consistent with the priority areas in ensuring the information security of the Russian Federation formulated in the annual addresses of the President of the Russian Federation to the Federal Assembly, coordinates the activities of the federal bodies of executive power and the bodies of executive power of the subjects of the Russian Federation and, as well as the activities in the process of the formation, under established procedure, of the draft federal budget for the corresponding years, and envisages the allocation of funds required to implement the federal programs in this field.

The Federation Council of the Russian Federation works to identify and assess the threats to the information security of the Russian Federation, promptly prepares draft decisions of the President of the Russian Federation to prevent such threats, develops suggestions in the field of ensuring the information security of the Russian Federation as well as suggestions on updating certain provisions of this Doctrine, coordinates the activities of the bodies and resources to ensure the information security of the Russian Federation, controls the implementation by the federal bodies of state power and bodies of state power of the subjects of the Russian Federation of the decisions of the President of the Russian Federation in this field.

The federal bodies of executive power ensure compliance with the laws of the Russian Federation, the decisions of the President of the Russian Federation and the Government of the Russian Federation in the field of ensuring the information security of the Russian Federation; within their competence, develop regulatory legal acts in this field and properly submit them to the President of the Russian Federation and the Government of the Russian Federation.

The inter-agency and state commissions established by the President of the Russian Federation and the Government of the Russian Federation address, consistent with their powers, the tasks of ensuring the information security of the Russian Federation.

The bodies of executive power of the subjects of the Russian Federation interact with the federal bodies of executive power on issues of compliance with the laws of the Russian Federation, the decisions of the President of the Russian Federation and the Government of the Russian Federation in the field of ensuring the information security of the Russian Federation as well as on the issues of implementing federal programs in this field; jointly with the bodies of local self-government, take measures to enlist the cooperation of citizens, organizations and non-governmental associations in addressing the problems of ensuring the information security of the Russian Federation, submit to the federal bodies of executive power proposals on improving the system of ensuring the information security of the Russian Federation.

The bodies of local self-government ensure compliance with the laws of the Russian Federation in the field of ensuring the information security of the Russian Federation.

The bodies of judiciary power administer justice on cases of crimes involving encroachments on the lawful interests of the individual, society and the state in the information sphere, and provide legal defense of citizens and public associations whose rights have been violated in connection with activities to ensure the information security of the Russian Federation.

The system of ensuring the information security of the Russian Federation may include subsystems (systems) geared to the solution of local tasks in this sphere.

. . . .

The implementation of priority measures to ensure the information security of the Russian Federation listed in this Doctrine implies the development of a corresponding federal program. Individual provisions of this doctrine with regard to certain spheres of the activity of society and the state may be specified in corresponding documents approved by the President of the Russian Federation.

III.

Reports and Other Publications

Russian Newspaper Crisis Recovery Program*

Robert Manoff *Robert Coalson*
Conrad Hohenlohe *Vladimir Svetozarov*

The National Press Institute ["NPI"] believes that it is possible to resuscitate the non-state regional newspaper industry in the wake of the present crisis and lay the foundations for a stable, viable newspaper industry in Russia. In order to do so, it is necessary for non-state newspapers—with the guidance and assistance of Western media professionals—to work together in a concerted fashion to (1) increase revenues by increasing advertising market share and circulation, (2) decrease costs through more efficient management, (3) improve the legal and regulatory environment through lobbying and legal and tax reform, and (4) improve journalistic practices and standards and heighten their sense of public responsibility to the public.

With these goals in mind, the National Press Institute has developed its Newspaper Crisis Recovery Program, a comprehensive set of initiatives to revive and further develop the independent press. Each of the priority initiatives described below is being proposed as an addition to NPI's ongoing programs described above, many of which already address some of the management, revenue, and journalistic issues that are highlighted below. But the crisis has made it imperative to establish a new level of commitment to resolving such issues. What is more, each of the 29 is designed to address the longer-term structural problems of the independent regional press, problems (as noted above) that were evident well before the crisis and that have been exacerbated since. Each of these initiatives also conforms to the principles (outlined above) that underlie all of NPI's work and which it believes should guide all future media assistance.

Moreover, it is important to note that these initiatives vary greatly in their complexity and cost and have been designed to be implemented with resources of varying magnitude. In fact, any one of them could be implemented successfully by itself. However, inasmuch as newspapers are facing a fundamentally sectoral crisis, it is NPI's belief that a comprehensive response on a sectoral scale will be required to successfully respond.

The 29 initiatives are briefly described below. It should be noted that given the dynamic nature of the crisis and NPI's continuing work to identify points of leverage in responding to it, this list is merely suggestive. The Newspaper Crisis Recovery Plan will evolve as the economic, journalistic, and political conditions in the country continue to unfold.

It should also be noted that, as it has in the past, NPI is committed to drawing upon a broad array of expertise from a variety of media organizations in the United States, Europe, and elsewhere. Over the last years, the National Press Institute has cooperated with hundreds of media organizations, newspapers, NGO's, and governmental and multilateral institutions, and this Newspaper Crisis Recovery Program is predicated on mobilizing similar resources in the future. A small sample of the organizations that NPI has worked with includes: the American Press Institute, the Newspaper Association of America, the National Newspaper Association, the *Flint Journal*, the *San Jose Mercury News*, Sister Cities International, the International Center for Journalists, Citizens' Democracy Corps, the World Association of Newspapers, the International Federation of Journalists, Internews, the European Institute for the Media, the Baltic Media Center, the European Journalism Center, the Union of Journalists of Russia, the All-Russian Union of Editors and Publishers, the All-Russian Union of Small and Medium-Size Businesses, Moscow State University, the Media Development Loan Fund, and the Glasnost Defense Foundation.

I. Revenue-Enhancement Projects

Although Russia's advertising market has collapsed since August, it must be helped to recover over the next few years. Otherwise, the survival of the independent press will simply not be possible. As advertising recovers, non-state newspapers must be in a position to gain a much larger share of national advertising than they had before the crisis and they must be ready to pursue local retail advertising far more aggressively than they ever have before. NPI offers the following projects to increase newspaper revenue:

A. National Advertising Representation

In Russia, up to 80 percent of all advertising budgets are spent in Moscow. This high degree of concentration makes it essential that local newspapers be actively and aggressively represented in Moscow and that they take every possible measure to make it easy and attractive for Moscow-based advertisers and agencies to place advertisements in regional papers. To date, this simply has not happened and, as a result, national advertising in regional newspapers has been minimal.

For the last several months, the National Press Institute has studied how the Newspaper Association of America works to increase national advertising in local newspapers in the United States. NPI believes that equivalent programs can be productively developed in response to Russian conditions. Because of the extremely high degree of centralization of the advertising market in Russia, in fact, such programs can be far more important in Russia than they are in Western countries.

Accordingly, the National Press Institute will create a national advertising representation to work aggressively to increase the advertising market share of regional newspapers. Specifically, it will:

1. Train regional newspaper advertising staffs on working with national-level advertisers. This will involve creating an effective alliance between regional newspapers and the staff of the national representation. One of the major factors suppressing advertising revenue in the regions is that regional newspapers have never been effectively trained to market themselves to national advertisers and meet the advertisers' specific needs. While national advertising representations have been tried halfheartedly in the past, this key ingredient of training has been missing. NPI will make training the advertising departments of regional newspapers a major focus of the national advertising representation. Part of the training process will be the collection and dissemination of information on national advertisers' needs and strategies.

2. Establish standard advertising formats and cost-per-thousand ad rates to facilitate the purchase of bulk and national advertising in regional papers throughout the country. Measures taken to create standard formatting will go a long way to encourage a larger share of national advertising in regional newspapers.

3. Assist and train member newspapers in planning, promoting, and producing supplements and special editions with the goal of increasing national advertising. Special supplements, currently underutilized in Russia, can be a primary source of very targeted advertising revenue, especially if coordinated on a national level. A team of special advertising consultants will be sent to all members of the national representation to ensure that marketing documents as well as actual supplements and editions are produced. The advertising representation will also coordinate the work of member newspapers producing supplements on similar themes to enable them to share editorial materials and reduce costs.

4. Conduct research and produce materials that will demonstrate to advertisers the effectiveness of newspaper advertising compared to advertising in other media. The NPI advertising representation would act as the newspaper industry's advocate in the advertising and marketing communities and would work with local newspapers to address the concerns of advertisers and marketers (on issues such as the accurate reporting of circulations, for example). It would serve as a conduit of information exchange between regional newspapers and Moscow-based marketers.

5. Develop the concept of cooperative advertising in Russia. Cooperative advertising is a mechanism by which national advertisers share advertising costs with local retailers and distributors. The advent of cooperative advertising markedly increased the newspaper share of national advertising revenue in the West and can work as well in Russia if a national newspaper representation is created to coordinate and encourage the practice.

The creation of a national advertising representation for regional newspapers is a considerable undertaking. Major program costs will include personnel in Moscow and the regions, equipment, travel, telecommunications, and production costs of marketing materials.

Should this project be implemented, it has the potential to reform the industry and enable it to emerge from the present crisis stronger and more viable than before. The project is designed to open up a major new revenue stream for the industry, and, as the Russian advertising market recovers from the crisis, the NPI national advertising representation should become increasingly self-sustaining.

B. Public Service Announcement Placement

NPI has developed a project that will help newspapers during the current crisis period, while at the same time promoting values, behaviors, and information that is important to the economic and political transformation in the country, as well as for the immediate well-being of the Russian people.

NPI, in conjunction with sponsoring organizations, will buy regional newspaper advertising space and then use the space for public service announcements. As a result, newspapers will receive a small but steady flow of advertising revenue, while at the same time the Russian public will be presented with critical information on a range of issues—health, environment, education, nutrition, conflict resolution, political participation, tolerance, etc.—that will either assist the public directly or promote the values of an open society. Such public service announcements can also help to promote, directly and indirectly, the work of Russia's struggling NGOs. Such announcements will also encourage the standardization of advertising formats (see No. 2 above) and will establish the concept of public service announcements in Russia for the future.

C. Local Advertising Sales

Despite the potential importance of national advertising as a revenue source for regional newspapers in Russia, it is certain that local retail and classified advertising will remain the most significant source of income, as it is for newspapers in other large countries. With local advertising, newspapers have considerable competitive advantages over other media in terms of cost, immediacy, and effectiveness.

Historically, however, Russian newspapers have failed to acquire the local market share that they should have. As a result, in many cities local television stations have even captured a significant share of the classified advertising market, running text-only announcements across the bottom of the screen during entertainment programming.

The present crisis has served in many cases as a wake-up call to regional newspaper publishers. The time is ripe for a concentrated effort to improve the sales and service capabilities of local newspaper advertising sales agents, and also to improve the efficiency of newspaper advertising departments. With the goal of improving local advertising markets, NPI is undertaking or plans shortly to undertake, with appropriate funding, the following programs:

1. NPI will organize direct, in-depth training in local advertising sales. NPI will establish a considerable training program on the ground, bringing Western sales

techniques and attitudes directly into newspaper advertising departments around Russia. Sales agents must be trained in the use of worksheets, in time management, in making sales calls, in advertising design, and in all other related skills.

2. NPI will publish manuals to give concrete guidance to newspapers in developing local advertising. As an immediate reaction to the present crisis, NPI has already undertaken the translation of *The Great Ad Venture: How to Succeed in Newspaper Advertising Sales*, a practical handbook for newspaper advertising sales agents published by the Newspaper Association of America and used widely in the West. This manual emphasizes the importance of understanding the client's needs, of selling solutions to the client's marketing problems, and of countering objections that inexperienced advertisers may have to the concept of newspaper advertising. It includes worksheets to enable advertising sales agents to assist clients in developing an annual advertising plan to match their budgets and projected sales. NPI is seeking to translate and publish a number of practical manuals on newspaper marketing, circulation control, and classified advertising from Western sources.

3. NPI will promote the development and distribution of specialized computer software. Advertising managers must be given the tools to effectively manage their agents. In 1997, the National Press Institute provided consulting to the independent newspaper *Zvezda in Perm* to create elementary computer software for managing advertising accounts. This software has been successfully used since then to keep track of payments for advertising, to track the work of sales agents and to effectively plan sales calls. Such software is used every day in every Western newspaper, but is rarely encountered in Russia. NPI is seeking to refine this software and provide it to as many independent newspapers as possible, together with the training necessary to use it effectively. Not only will this software greatly improve the efficiency of individual advertising departments, it will also enable media assistance organizations to more easily track developments and patterns in local retail advertising markets, to analyze developments throughout the industry, and to respond accordingly.

D. Printing Presses

The National Press Institute has argued for many years that the poor quality of newspaper printing in Russia (about 80 percent of all newspaper printing in Russia is still done with letterpress technology) is a major obstacle to attracting advertisers. What is more, the continuing state monopoly of newspaper printing is a powerful lever to apply economic and political pressure on independent newspapers.

Among assistance providers working in Russia, the National Press Institute (with funding from USAID) has taken the lead in addressing this problem. In 1997, NPI installed a modern newspaper printing press in Volgograd for a group of independent local newspapers. Since that time, this press has become a major revenue source for these newspapers and provides the only full-color newspaper printing in southern Russia.

As a result of this project, the first of its kind in Russia, the National Press Institute has the capacity to manage such projects, handling the logistics on the ground, assessing the needs of the Russian partner and the suitability of the site. In Volgograd, the National Press Institute and its partner, the American newspaper consulting firm Boles, Morgan and Canino, created a complete program of technical and management training that enabled the Russian partner to quickly and effectively take over management of this printing business.

Improving the quality of newspaper printing in Russia is an expensive and complex proposition. However, the newspaper industry will never be able to achieve its revenue potential from either advertising or circulation, to control costs, or to ensure its independence without a major investment in printing technology.

In the current crisis, the direct purchase of printing presses is simply not a realistic option. However, NPI continues to promote other ways of getting printing presses into the hands of regional newspapers, specifically loans for the leasing or leasing-to-own of printing presses. For example, NPI is encouraging infrastructure-development funds such as that associated with the Sakhalin-2 oil field project to include independent newspaper printing as a crucial element of infrastructure that is being established under the project. NPI has also begun working with Rybinsk Poligrafmash, Russia's only domestic manufacturer of newspaper printing presses, to improve their products and make them more affordable for Russian newspapers. A printing press is not just a machine; it is a business in itself. NPI, therefore, in conjunction with its American and Volgograd partners, would like to create a domestic training facility to provide a full range of technical training on printing and pre-press production and, equally important, to train press managers in effective marketing and financial control of a small printing business.

II. Cost-Containment Projects

In addition to efforts to increase their revenue, regional newspapers must undertake organized measures to reduce and control costs across the board. In doing so, they can benefit enormously from Western management practices and from increased cooperation among themselves.

A. Information Exchange and Best Practices

Russian regional newspapers operate without full information about market conditions and opportunities, and they remain isolated from other newspapers facing identical circumstances. As a result, they do not optimize their choices, and they often improvise stopgap measures to address problems that others have already creatively solved.

1. NPI will organize the systematic collection and publication of best management practices among Russian regional newspapers so that editors and publishers can learn from each other's innovations. In the wake of the August crisis, independent

newspaper managers undertook many anti-crisis measures, some effective and others not. NPI immediately began exchanging anecdotal information on management practices through its research into the crisis, through a crisis-related list-serve that was created in October, and through its annual Newspaper Management Conference (held in Moscow, November 11-14, 1998). This work needs to be systematized and continued in a regular, organized fashion in order to have maximum impact. Therefore, NPI seeks to create a monthly newspaper management newsletter to serve as a vehicle for newspapers to share innovative solutions to management problems, as well for NPI to disseminate cost-containment procedures that it will develop on its own in cooperation with international media organizations. Such a publication should evolve into a practical, regular professional publication for newspaper managers. The present crisis is the perfect time to cultivate in Russian managers the habit of learning from one another and to promote greater professionalism among managers throughout the industry.

2. Isolated regional newspapers are often not aware of current market conditions and opportunities. NPI will continue to publicize important economic information to enable regional newspapers to take advantage of the best prevailing opportunities. For example, after the crisis NPI began to collect and publicize information on newsprint prices, a simple undertaking which is helping newspapers identify the cheapest sources of newsprint in a wildly erratic market. NPI believes that such price monitoring, by increasing the transparency of markets for the goods and services that newspapers consume in quantity, can promote market stability and, thereby, help reduce costs and facilitate planning and budgeting on the part of newspaper managers.

B. Crisis-Management Consulting

Russian regional newspaper managers can learn much from the experience of newspaper professionals in other countries that have experienced similar economic collapses. Such experience can transfer valuable practical lessons that Western or Russian managers would not be able to provide.

Together with the World Association of Newspapers, NPI seeks to considerably expand its use of consultants with experience working in similar economic conditions. Newspaper managers from Indonesia, the Philippines, Latin America, and other parts of the world have a wealth of directly and immediately relevant experience that can help Russian publishers emerge from the present crisis stronger and more confident than before. In addition to learning to cope with the present crisis, Russian managers can be exposed to management techniques from around the world that can serve them far into the future. After coordinating this "emergency first aid" in the form of on-site consultations for select newspapers and national and local workshops, NPI will disseminate broadly the most useful suggestions through its publications, consulting, training programs, and Internet Media Service.

C. Improved Financial Management

Haphazard financial management has crippled the development of the commercial press in Russia for many years. In some respects, newspapers have suffered from the present crisis more than they might have because poor financial information hampered decision-making. Improving Russian newspaper management has been and continues to be a key priority, a fact that the crisis should not obscure. NPI's past work in this area has focused primarily on a combination of direct on-site consulting, publications, and training workshops throughout the country. It now plans to augment these activities with the following:

1. In order to help overcome the lack of financial management experience, NPI will develop and widely apply a CD-ROM-based newspaper management simulation. The simulation will make it possible for newspaper managers to undergo a five-year cycle of business decisions in a few days of intensive training. The American Press Institute has used such a management simulation very effectively for a number of years. The simulation would enable NPI to educate thousands of managers over a relatively short period of time at a low per-participant cost.

2. NPI's study of regional newspapers indicates that very few publishers receive even monthly cash-flow reports and startlingly few make effective use of available computers for financial management. For this reason, NPI will facilitate the development of financial-management software capable of generating quick and accurate cost and revenue reports for newspaper managers. This software, together with a package of training materials and a training program, could markedly improve managers' ability to evaluate and improve company performance.

3. At the same time, the widespread use of such a financial-management package, which could help to gather financial information in a standardized format, would enable NPI to monitor and report on industry averages for key costs such as newsprint, office supplies, labor, printing, etc. Such reports would themselves become another financial-management tool for Russian publishers, allowing them to compare their company performance with national standards.

D. Legal Consulting and Assistance

Russian newspaper managers are caught in an extremely perilous legal environment, partially regulated by business law and partially regulated by media law. Moreover, because of the isolation of regional newspapers from one another, there has been no accumulation of experience in legal affairs and no study of available precedents. This, of course, places commercial newspapers in very vulnerable circumstances as local authorities use the tax inspectorate or other agencies to apply pressure to keep them in line. Complex laws governing newspaper "founders," ownership, and control present major obstacles to newspapers wishing to assert or establish their independence. The lack of legal expertise also hampers newspapers in contractual negotiations and other settings.

1. Regional newspapers could clearly benefit enormously from a centralized, practically oriented commercial law service dedicated to assisting newspapers in availing themselves of the tax exemptions to which they are already entitled and, in general, in entering into commercial arrangements on the most advantageous terms.

2. State-founded newspapers that seek to become independent by breaking away from the state agencies that are associated with them present a unique legal category in Russia and absolutely nothing to date has been done to assist them. In many cases, the most responsible and progressive journalists in a given city have been denied the Western assistance that they need and deserve on the grounds that a state agency is listed among the founders of the publications for which they work and cannot be removed. NPI believes that competent legal assistance and pressure from commercial newspaper publishers across the country could help state-founded newspapers become legally independent and develop into mature community voices. Specifically, NPI could arrange subsidized or low-cost consulting with leading legal experts, including members of Russia's official Arbitration Chamber for Information Disputes who have worked with NPI in the past to preserve particular independent newspapers.

3. NPI will also arrange legal assistance for newspapers seeking to wholly or partially merge operations, which would benefit the industry as a whole. NPI can also assist groups of newspapers to create management and ownership structures for jointly owned printing and production equipment. NPI would base such agreements on the Joint Operating Agreements which have been undertaken among U.S. newspapers, although of course Russian legal, financial, and other conditions would clearly necessitate adaptations to the Russian environment.

E. Purchasing Cooperative

On their own, scattered around the largest country on Earth and with relatively small purchasing power, Russian regional newspapers are often at the mercy of suppliers of newsprint and other goods and services. NPI will pursue two related ideas:

1. For several years, the National Press Institute has been studying the feasibility of creating a purchasing cooperative among independent regional newspapers. Such cooperatives have been very successful in helping non-chain newspapers in the United States bargain with newsprint and other vendors on the same terms as large newspaper groups. By pooling demand and making it possible for newspapers to bargain together, such cooperatives can secure significant reductions in the cost of newsprint, computer equipment, subscriptions to news services and the like. A purchasing cooperative could also bargain with Western manufacturers of popular computer software for a group license for all members at a significantly lowered cost (the National Press Institute has already approached the manufacturer of QuarkExpress, a leading newspaper-design software package, with such a request). The creation of a purchasing cooperative

would be a landmark in the process of encouraging non-state publishers to work together. This cooperative could also be used to provide direct assistance through subsidizing the purchase of necessary equipment and materials, if that were deemed necessary. Because participation in the cooperative would constitute a form of self-empowerment among publishers, this kind of assistance would be more productive than the direct grants that have sometimes been provided in the past.

2. Such a purchasing cooperative could also serve as an ideal vehicle for distributing loans for the purchase of newsprint. By taking advantage of bulk purchasing, borrowers could be certain that they were getting the best possible price and lenders could be assured that the loans were actually used for the purchase of newsprint.

III. Projects to Strengthen Democratic Politics, Civil Society, and an Open Policy Process

At this moment of economic, political, and, indeed, psychological crisis for Russia, it is even more critical than ever that the media be able to fulfill their function as the preeminent source of business and economic information for democratic politics, as the facilitator of an open policy process, as a reliable source of business information, as a watchdog against official corruption and mismanagement, as a promoter of civil society, and as a responsible force for tolerance. The crisis has clearly impaired the media's ability to fulfill these roles. For that reason, a crisis program must address these key journalistic and professional issues if it is going to address the country's most pressing economic and political challenges, as it must.

It must be stipulated that the weakness of Russian newspapers stems in part from the fact that readers, as a rule, have a low regard for their journalistic standards and integrity. Although falling circulations over the last ten years can be mostly attributed to Russia's economic troubles, newspapers have done surprisingly little to make themselves essential to their readers. As a result, they have been unable to attract sufficient advertising to secure financial viability. The National Press Institute believes that improving journalism standards and techniques is not only a matter of social responsibility but also one of financial survival.

The National Press Institute advocates the creation of practical journalism programs that are designed to strengthen Russian democracy while also serving to cement the bond between readers and their local newspapers. Such programs, in fact, have been a staple of NPI's sectoral approach to media assistance since it was established early in this decade. However, NPI believes that Russia's underdeveloped civil society and the general passivity of the average Russian citizen continue to present a major obstacle to newspaper development (as well, of course, as to Russian democracy itself). Disengaged and unempowered citizens have no need for newspapers. For that reason, NPI has encouraged newspapers to cover and work with local citizens groups and NGOs and has served as a platform for well over 1,000 NGO press conferences and briefings.

In the context of the present crisis, it is absolutely critical that the journalistic capacity of the news media to play a constructive role in the political, economic, and social life of the country be restored and, indeed, dramatically enhanced. As elections approach, as nuclear and foreign policy challenges become more acute, and as the public threatens to lose patience with market economics and democratic politics, the challenges of informing the public and helping to shape the policy process have never been more formidable or significant. Initiatives to ensure and enhance coverage of specific issues will include the following:

1. Non-state local newspapers are the only serious defense against the rampant government and business corruption that is crippling Russia's social and economic transformation. Moreover, newspapers that have been most active in exposing local corruption in recent years have naturally faced the greatest political and economic hostility from local administrations. Unfortunately, however, much coverage of local corruption has been irresponsible and inflammatory. It has contributed to the undermining of public confidence in Russia's transition. NPI will develop, at its School of Media Management and Journalism, a major investigative journalism program, with a special focus on the complex reportorial, legal, ethical, and safety issues involved in reporting corruption.

2. Inaccurate, partisan, opaque election coverage threatens the integrity of the democratic system itself. Only thorough, accurate, balanced, and transparent coverage of election campaigns can ensure a result which reflects the interests of Russia's citizens. The scheduled 1999 parliamentary and 2000 presidential elections will be absolutely critical in determining Russia's future for years and even decades to come. Many media are already looking to these elections as a sure source of windfall income in return for favorable coverage, as has proven to be the case in previous elections. Such behavior by the media threatens to undermine these critical elections and to leave the media weak and compromised in the post-election environment. In order to promote professional and transparent campaign coverage, NPI will organize a targeted series of activities to provide training, support, and a number of incentives and disincentives. Specifically, it will organize regional training workshops, on the model of those NPI workshops that proved successful on a small scale in 1993, 1995, and 1996. It would establish prizes for accurate, informative, and balanced coverage. It would also publicize cases of paid political advertising under the guise of impartial journalism, in order to help establish a professional ethos militating against such behavior.

3. The lack of sustained and constructive public policy discussions about Russia's economic situation in the period before August of this year is in part a result of the media's inconsistent coverage of business and economic issues. Too often, speculation substitutes for fact and political intrigue substitutes for business reporting. Reporting on such issues is not just a way of informing the public, but it is, more important, itself a key element of a functioning economic system. Without a media sector capable of facilitating the free flow of information and a culture of transparency, it is impossible to develop a healthy economic system. For that reason, NPI will enhance

its programs to train reporters covering business and economic development, at both the national and regional levels.

4. Public apathy and an alarming disconnect with the political system that purports to represent citizens' interests contribute both to the growth of corruption and also to the increasing willingness to tolerate authoritarian rule in Russia. The media are the one institution best placed to facilitate the re-involvement of Russian citizens in public and political life, which is a key element in the establishment of democratic processes. As in the U.S., where the Civic Journalism movement has created healthy controversy within the journalism profession, NPI would promote open debate among Russia's leading media figures on the role of the media in promoting citizen involvement. NPI would work with targeted newspapers to provide models of coverage that promote involvement and activism rather than apathy and frustration.

5. In order to help promote a legal environment conducive to media independence, NPI established the Freedom of Information Commission in 1995 as Russia's first project to promote free access to government-held information. Russia's tradition of official secrecy and government control of the media has inhibited the development of a freedom of information movement, but independent media will never be able to enforce government accountability and adequately inform Russia's population without freedom of information laws, mechanisms, institutions, and routines. NPI, separately and in conjunction with the now-independent FOI Commission, will organize a range of programs—from lobbying and monitoring projects to educational programs and publications—to promote the development and effective implementation of FOI norms. In conjunction with the other projects outlined here, such FOI work will strengthen the independence of Russia's media and enhance their ability to promote government accountability.

6. The media in Russia play a major role in shaping relations among Russia's diverse ethnic, religious, and national groups. Perhaps more than any other single institution, the media have the ability to help avoid the increased tensions that seem likely to accompany increasing economic hardship. NPI, which has been working with the media for several years on the problems of reporting ethno-national conflict, will continue to work in several key areas—particularly in the volatile Northern Caucasus and in Moscow among the mainstream media—where altered media behavior can have an impact. Specific projects will include joint reporting projects, editorials and programming, training workshops, and research and monitoring designed to focus journalists' attention on the importance of balanced and responsible coverage.

7. Helping the media survive the current crisis also means helping the media report in depth on the key causes and effects of the crisis. The financial crisis and political struggles have overshadowed the steepest peacetime decline in life expectancy in modern history. A crumbling healthcare system and lingering environmental problems and dangers are in large measure to blame. While Russia does not have the resources to address all of the issues which confront it, aggressive and thorough reporting of these

problems can help focus scarce resources on the most threatening of them—such as the tuberculosis outbreak in Russia's penal system. NPI, through its School and its Center for Cyberjournalism, will offer a range of training opportunities and informational resources to help journalists tackle these complex and sensitive issues in an aggressive and responsible way.

8. As the crisis deepens, worldwide concern over the fate of Russia's nuclear arsenal and research facilities grows. Aggressive, accurate, and sophisticated Russian reporting on nuclear issues is critical both to an informed policy debate and to international understanding of prevailing conditions. NPI will continue its long-standing program of working with Russia's leading nuclear and security reporters to help them improve their coverage—through a combination of informational assistance, individual consulting, and institutional support.

The projects briefly outlined here constitute an attempt to sketch out a comprehensive sector-wide approach to helping newspapers work through the present crisis, work together to address the structural problems that crippled them even before the crisis, wean themselves from debilitating state subsidies, establish their independence, and at the same time ensure that the journalistic product is sufficiently informative, balanced, and sophisticated to meet the urgent needs of the struggling Russian democracy.

The initiatives previewed in this Newspaper Crisis Recovery Plan entail markedly different levels of financial and institutional commitment, and will produce markedly different results if they are implemented singly, or in concert, as part of a sectoral rescue package. They are presented here, however, in the interest of suggesting both how vast the undertaking must be if it is to have an impact, and also how even single, modest, targeted initiatives can achieve measurable and important results.

This NPI plan will continue to evolve in response to economic and political conditions and the expressed desires of Russia's newspaper publishers and journalists. As it does so, the National Press Institute welcomes comments and suggestions from all those interested in the fate of the press in a democratic Russia.

Regional Newspapers and the Russian Crisis*

Robert Coalson
Vladimir Svetozarov

In order to begin assessing the impact of the [1998 economic] crisis in Russia on privately owned regional newspapers, the National Press Institute (NPI) conducted an informal survey of regional newspaper publishers [between September 2 and September 9, 1998]. The results demonstrate clearly the vulnerability of regional newspapers to such financial shocks and, hence, their general inability to properly inform Russian society during times of crisis. As soon as the crisis broke, newspapers went into crisis mode, immediately laying off staff, reducing frequency and volume, canceling subscriptions to outside news sources, etc. The survey also demonstrates clearly the intimate connection between private newspapers in Russia and the development of local small business.

The ultimate effects of this crisis undoubtedly depend on its duration and on measures taken by national and local governments. However, it is clear that the landscape of the regional media has changed for the worse. Plans for capital improvements and investment have been wiped out. Newspaper managers have begun learning the dangerous lesson that dependence on advertising revenue can be less reliable than dependence on political patronage.

Brief Description of the Non-State Regional Press Before the Crisis

Even before the present crisis, privately owned newspapers in Russia faced an unenviable situation. Some key features of the Russian regional media are:

- Private newspapers face unfair competition from state-subsidized competitors who undermine reader confidence in the media in general.
- Because of state subsidies and sponsorship by commercial interests and political parties, Russia is heavily saturated with dependent and low-quality newspapers. Journalistic and management talent are hopelessly diluted among the huge numbers of newspapers.
- Private newspapers are almost all dependent on state-controlled monopolies for printing and distribution. They are unable to control their own deadlines or print runs. The state-controlled distribution systems limit the times of the year when newspapers can accept new subscribers; they also limit the number of single copies available for retail sale.

- Private newspapers work in an environment that is generally hostile to small business. There are no tax incentives to advertise in newspapers. Small business owners are generally unsophisticated about advertising and have very small advertising budgets to begin with.
- Private newspapers face intense pressure from local businesses and political interests to run hidden advertising (favorable reporting for which the reporter and/or editor receive under-the-table payments), which further undermines reader confidence in the press.
- Development in Russia has been largely centered on Moscow and has not filtered into the regions. It is estimated that 75 percent of all money spent on advertising in Russia is spent in Moscow.
- Private newspapers face intense pressure from major financial groups in Moscow and from dominant local business interests to influence their editorial content.
- Private newspapers in Russia are generally managed by journalists who have little experience running their newspapers as businesses.

Brief Description of the Crisis

The present crisis in Russia has three components. First, there has been a general devaluation of the ruble from a rate of about 6 to the dollar at the end of August, to a peak of about twenty-eight to the dollar during the period in which the survey was conducted, to a level of about twelve to the dollar at the time this report was written. The uncertainty about the exchange rate had dramatic consequences on the Russian economy as a whole, since it remains heavily dependent on imported consumer goods. The collapse of the ruble set off panic buying of basic goods throughout the regions, emptying store shelves. Importers suspended business and many stores insured themselves by raising prices even more than the exchange fluctuations would justify.

The general economic crisis was further exacerbated by a partial collapse of the banking system. The Russian government's decision to stop payments on government bonds and debt instantly made a number of leading banks insolvent. Commercial transactions were all but halted and individual depositors were unable to withdraw their funds. The suspension of SBS-Agro Bank, which has been very active in the regions over the last couple of years, has been especially acutely felt.

Finally, the dismissal of Prime Minister Sergei Kirienko and the attempt to replace him with former Prime Minister Viktor Chernomyrdin led to a tense standoff between President Yeltsin and the State Duma. This standoff meant that the government was paralyzed and unable to respond effectively to the economic crisis. The confirmation of Yevgeni Primakov as prime minister on September 11 gives hope that further political crisis, at least, has been averted, although the Communist Party continues to plan for mass protests on October 7 and several other Duma factions have already announced their opposition to the new government.

Effects of the Crisis on the Regional Press

Effects on Revenues. Most regional newspapers in Russia continue to receive most of their revenues from subscriptions and single-copy sales. The most dramatic effect of the crisis was to devalue the rubles that had been received for subscriptions for the period from July-December. Most newspapers responded by purchasing as much newsprint as possible, which may have contributed to the price increase of newsprint. The few newspapers that had been trying to save money in order to make capital improvements saw these efforts erased.

Surprisingly, none of the newspapers responding reported significant increases in single-copy sales, even though one would expect that more citizens would be interested in getting news about the crisis. Although the Russian distribution system makes it difficult to say for certain what the effect has been (because distributors file reports only monthly), the general sense is that retail sales have remained steady or fallen slightly.

The subscription campaign for the first half of 1999 began in most cities in August. Although no specific information is available yet, most respondents anticipated that the crisis would negatively impact subscriptions for this period. Since the campaign is already underway and subscription prices have already been announced, newspapers are reluctant to announce increases, although maintaining the old prices will be virtually impossible.

The effects of the crisis on local newspaper advertising markets have been dramatic. Many advertising contracts already signed for September and October have been cancelled. Overall advertising has been reduced by thirty to fifty percent. Payments for advertising run in August have been lost or delayed due to the banking crisis. Many retailers have cancelled advertising simply because the rush to purchase goods has made advertising unnecessary. In Nizhni Novgorod, the business-oriented newspaper *Birzha* (*The Market*), which has long been known as one of Russia's most successful advertising-supported newspapers, reported an immediate reduction in revenues of at least thirty percent.

Effects on Costs. Almost all of the newspapers responding to the survey reported immediate and dramatic increases in their basic production costs, although these increases were different in different parts of the country. Papers in St. Petersburg reported that the cost of newsprint rose fifteen to twenty percent, while in Vyatka and Nizhni Novgorod prices roughly doubled. The cost of printing at state-controlled printing presses also rose from fifteen to thirty percent in most locations. All newspapers reported that they either anticipate further increases or have already been notified that such increases are coming. It is likely that price levels will even out across the country over time.

There is some evidence that the price increases hit different papers differently even within a single city. In the Urals city of Chelyabinsk, for instance, the daily *Vecherni Cheliabinsk* (*Evening Chelyabinsk*) reported that the cost of printing had risen thirty-three percent, while its cross-town competitor *Cheliabinski Rabochi* (*Cheliabinsk Worker*) reported no increase at the same printer. It is likely that price levels will even out across the country over time.

Only two of the newspapers surveyed, *Gorodskie Vesti* (*City News*) in Volgograd and *Stavropolskie Gubernskie Vedomosti* (*Stavropol Regional News*) own their own printing presses. Both reported that the cost of imported plates, film, and ink had been raised but that they were still printing from old stocks. *Stavropol Regional News* reported that they had actually signed on new printing clients because of price increases at the competing state press.

How Newspapers Have Responded

The financial condition of Russian newspapers was so weak even before the crisis that they were forced to take immediate and drastic steps as soon as events began unfolding. No newspaper reported having sufficient cash reserves to allow it to continue functioning normally even through the first week of the crisis. Even Moscow-based publications and those owned by the foreign company Independent Media (*Moscow Times* and *St. Petersburg Times*) have resorted to Draconian measures in response to the crisis.

For the most part, newspapers have reacted mechanically and defensively. Immediate steps were taken to reduce costs. One newspaper in Novosibirsk reported that it had suspended publication. Others sent the majority of their staff home on unpaid leave.

Many newspapers, even some of the nation's most prestigious regional papers such as *Chelyabinsk Worker* and *Uralski Rabochi* (*Urals Worker*) in Yekaterinburg, reported reduced frequency and/or volume. In short, at the very time when Russians most sorely need information from non-government sources, regional newspapers have been providing steadily less.

Many newspapers report attempts to cut costs by canceling subscriptions to national news services and access to the Internet and electronic mail. These actions also undoubtedly increase the isolation of regional newspapers and reduce the effectiveness of their coverage of the crisis. The number of regional newspapers with online editions will no doubt soon decrease, reducing the availability of information from the regions and the exchange of information among them. Most newspapers report efforts to spend all available cash by purchasing as much newsprint as possible.

Proactive Responses. Very few newspapers have done anything proactive in order to minimize the impact of the crisis. A business-oriented newspaper in St. Petersburg has used its regular system of city-wide posters to advertise the slogan "An Anti-Crisis Packet in Every Issue of *Delovoi Peterburg*." The effects of this campaign on single-copy sales are not yet clear.

The English-language *St. Petersburg Times* is offering advertisers a 50 percent discount for advertisements which *express confidence about the future.* Playing to advertisers' vanity, the paper headlines the offer: "A special offer for companies wanting to confirm that they're standing firmly on their feet!" The paper is also publishing house advertisements with quotations from experts in advertising about the need to continue advertising even during times of economic difficulty.

Other newspapers report that they are attempting to reduce advertiser anxiety about the exchange rate by offering guaranteed rates for advertisements in October and even November. Undoubtedly, as the initial crisis passes and immediate measures are taken, more newspapers will no doubt begin acting along these lines.

An Unusual Case. Stavropol Regional News filed an extremely uncharacteristic report. This paper was the only respondent which, in addition to publishing a newspaper, also owns a commercial retail store. Because of the prevalence of barter advertising in Stavropol, this newspaper opened a small store in 1995 which is wholly owned by the newspaper and which sells a wide range of items acquired by barter for advertising space. Over the last couple of years, this store has developed into a significant profit center for the company and has given the paper greater flexibility in accepting barter advertising.

Since the present crisis broke, the store has reported a dramatic increase in sales as a result of hoarding. Moreover, a significant number of advertising clients that might have cancelled payment for advertisements run in August offered instead to pay by barter, meaning that this revenue was not lost as it was for other papers responding to the survey. Finally, because advertisers know this paper's friendly attitude toward barter advertising, contracts for September and October have been largely continued so far. *Stavropol Regional News* reports far fewer cancellations of contracts than other regional papers.

Banking Crisis and Political Crisis

None of the newspapers responding reported direct negative consequences either as a result of the collapse of the banking system or as a result of the standoff between Yeltsin and the Duma. Although many newspapers reported delayed payments from advertisers with accounts in frozen banks, none of the papers themselves seem to have lost access to their accounts. Because of previous crises in the regional banking systems, local publishers have learned which banks are the most reliable.

Most papers report that local political authorities have also been paralyzed and slow to react to the crisis generally. There have been no reported attempts to influence coverage or gain influence over the financially weakened newspapers. The newspaper *Zolotoi Rog* (*The Golden Horn*) in Vladivostok reports that, as a result of the crisis, the commercial company that owns shares of the paper may be forced to sell. The paper's publisher fears that the local administration may be the only organization in a position to purchase the shares.

As one indicator of things to come, the report of *Vyatski Nabludatel* (*The Vyatka Observer*) in Kirov may be instructive. On September 1, the publisher of this paper received a telephone call from the director of the press office of the mayor's office. He was asked to come to the mayor's office to discuss coverage of local efforts to handle the unfolding crisis *in order to avoid unnecessarily worrying the public*. The publisher declined the invitation, and nothing more has come of it to date.

Measures to Be Taken

All respondents agree that the crisis is systemic and that no easy solutions are to be found. Newspapers that receive large portions of their revenue from advertising are particularly vulnerable and point to Russian government tax policies that hamper the development of local small business and local small manufacturing. However, a number of concrete steps were suggested:

Renew the Law on Support for the Mass Media. The current law granting tax exemptions to the mass media is set to expire at the end of the year, and there is considerable fear that it will not be extended. Every single respondent to the survey indicated that securing the extension of these exemptions is the most important thing that can be done to support them at present. Specifically, this law exempts the mass media from the twenty percent VAT, as well as a variety of other taxes and duties. If they are discontinued, for instance, the cost of newsprint and printing will automatically increase by a further twenty percent. Publishers note that the chances of continuing these exemptions are reduced as pressure on the Russian government to quickly increase tax revenues increases. Any lobbying effort on this issue must convince lawmakers that supporting the regional press will stimulate local economies and ultimately increase tax revenues.

Increase Access to Information. Although many papers are reducing their access to outside information, most publishers feel an increased need for contact beyond their regions in order to learn more about the crisis and about its effects on other newspapers. They request assistance in securing access to news services at reduced cost. They request that the price of newsprint be regularly monitored and reported. They suggest that ideas for responding to the crisis be monitored and distributed. They support the idea of a national conference of non-state newspaper publishers and many indicate renewed interest in a national publishers' association.

Increase Access to Moscow-Based Advertising Revenues. Although the crisis has resulted in a serious decline in advertising around the country, regional publishers note that their interests are poorly represented and lobbied among national advertisers and advertising agencies in Moscow. They note that 75 percent of all advertising spending in Russia is determined in Moscow and urge the development of mechanisms to increase regional newspapers' share in that spending.

Prognoses

It is clear that the present crisis represents a long-term setback for privately owned newspapers in Russia. Just how grave a setback certainly depends on how long the crisis lasts and what measures are taken to manage it. If the new government responds by implementing inflationary measures, limiting convertibility of the ruble or nationalizing sectors of the economy, the threat to Russia's private newspapers would be great. If, on the other hand, the government undertakes to stimulate local economic development (by providing tax incentives to advertise in local newspapers, for instance) and to eliminate subsidies to state-controlled media organs, the ultimate effects of the crisis could actually be positive in that measure.

It is certainly quite possible that the crisis will lead to efforts on the national and local levels to increase state control over the media. Many publishers themselves are responding to the crisis with calls for extending subsidies. Some fear that state agencies will take over as commercial sponsors seek to divest themselves of media properties. In this regard, the situation will differ dramatically from region to region.

The crisis will also most likely force many publications to close down. Since Russia presently has far too many newspapers for the size of its market, this is not necessarily undesirable. However, it is clear that private and locally owned newspapers will be the first to close: state-controlled mouthpieces will no doubt remain, and the negative consequences for the development of civil society are clear.

The crisis has demonstrated most definitely the links between Russia's most reliable and responsible local newspapers and the fate of local small business. Publishers were only just beginning to trust the idea that newspapers can and should be supported largely by advertising revenues. One likely effect of the crisis will be to undermine this crucial psychological breakthrough. Publishers who were only just beginning to spend more time with local Chambers of Commerce than in the smoke-filled rooms of the local mayor's office will be tempted to return to tried and true methods.

The crisis has demonstrated the financial vulnerability of the regional press. If the Russian government undertakes to squeeze tax revenues out of local small business, the consequences will be extremely dire for the media. In very short order, the result will be the end of local economic diversification, the end of small-scale industrial production in the regions and increased economic and political dependency on Moscow. With it, Russia's newborn independent press will collapse. As Herbert Hoover said in 1928: "Free speech does not live many hours after free industry and free commerce die."

1998 Country Report on Human Rights Practices in Russia*

U.S. Department of State

The Constitution provides for freedom of speech and of the press. However, while the Government generally respects these provisions, reports of government pressure on the media continue, particularly when coverage deals with corruption or criticism of the authorities. Federal, regional, and local governments continued to exert pressure on journalists by depriving them of access to information, using accreditation procedures to limit access, removing them from their jobs and bringing libel suits against them, and violating their legal rights. Oleg Panfilov of the Glasnost Defense Fund (GDF), a nongovernmental organization which tracks violations of journalists' rights, estimates that between 250 and 300 lawsuits and other legal actions were brought by the Government against journalists and journalistic organizations during the year in response to unfavorable coverage of government policy or operations. In most of these cases, a government body or individual (often with links to a figure in power) accused journalists of damaging its (or his or her) "reputation and honor." In some instances, judges found for the journalists, but in the vast majority of such cases, the Government succeeded in either intimidating or punishing the journalist. Typically, judges seemed unwilling to challenge powerful federal and local officials. Stiff fines for journalists were a common result of these proceedings; jail terms occasionally were handed down, as well. According to the Committee to Protect Journalists these rulings had a "chilling effect on investigative journalism," and such rulings reinforce the tendency toward self-censorship. On occasion journalists were attacked physically and even murdered, leading a number of Russian newscasters to characterize journalism as Russia's "most dangerous profession."

Private media continued to proliferate, and by the first half of 1998, some 20 new newspapers were being registered by the Russian press committee each week. Magazines totaled about 2,000. The major print media organizations represent a broad political spectrum and provide readers with a variety of information; however, because Russian media generally are not financially self-sufficient, they are subject to manipulation by the Government and by companies that are their majority shareholders. These financial entities manipulate the media at times to further their own political and financial goals. Journalists and editors admit that the political and business interests of major shareholders are paramount, causing journalists to practice self-censorship. Prominent human rights activist Sergey Kovalev has stated that, in these circumstances, "the Russian media are free but not independent."

---

* This excerpt is taken from the section on Freedom of Speech and of the Press from the *U.S. State Department Country Report on Human Rights Practices in Russia* released by the Bureau of Democracy, Human Rights, and Labor on February 26, 1999.

The concentrated structure of the ownership of major media does not encourage editorial independence. Private companies began investing heavily in the media market in 1997, even though the media generally are not yet profitable. The most powerful companies, such as Lukoil, Gazprom, and a number of banks, fought for influence in the Moscow media market and began to invest in media in the provinces.

The resulting concentration of ownership of major Russian media organizations increased in 1998. The economic crisis that began in August exacerbated the problem, weakening the financial positions of most news organizations, thereby increasing their dependence on financial sponsors and, in some cases, the federal and regional governments. Many businesses began to struggle, and as a result, advertising revenues decreased for nearly every major media organization in the country, in some cases as much as 50 percent in late August and September alone. Consequently, many media organizations saw their tenuous financial independence disintegrate. The economy was unable to sustain such a large number of media organizations (in particular, there were far too many newspapers for the size of the market).

These phenomena affected regional media organizations, those based outside Moscow, to an even greater degree. With prices up sharply, newspapers in regions in which the average family's monthly income was rarely over $100 (1000 rubles) became even less affordable. The National Press Institute (NPI), a nonprofit organization dedicated to the development and maintenance of a free press, reported in September that "the landscape" for the regional media had "changed for the worse." Newspaper managers found that their dependence on advertising revenue could be less reliable than dependence on political patronage. Reliance on political patronage, in turn, resulted in the deterioration of journalistic objectivity. As the NPI report noted, private newspapers faced intense pressure from major financial groups in Moscow and from dominant local business interests to influence their editorial content. There was also widespread concern that state agencies would attempt to take over impoverished media organizations as commercial sponsors sought to divest themselves of these properties.

In a number of key respects, private media organizations across the country remained dependent on the Government as well. According to the GDF, four-fifths of all print media organizations continued to rely on state-controlled concerns for paper, printing, and distribution; these companies lacked their own equipment. Moreover, the cost of printing at state-controlled printing presses rose from 15 to 30 percent in most locations with the onset of the financial crisis. The GDF collected considerable evidence that throughout the year, the Government continued to manipulate these prices from time to time in an effort to apply pressure on private media rivals; the GDF notes that this practice was more common outside the Moscow area than in the capital itself.

Independent and semiindependent television stations continued to develop, and the number of small private radio stations, mostly in the large cities, continued to increase. However, television companies faced government economic pressure similar to that experienced by the print media. Many stations were forced to rely on the State (in particular, regional committees for the management of state property) for access to airwaves and office space.

Both private print and broadcast media, like other enterprises, were vulnerable to unpredictable changes in the policy and practice of tax collection. (Tax avoidance is extremely widespread, both among commercial enterprises and individuals.) In August, federal tax authorities sought to shut down *Novaya Gazeta*, a Russian daily known for its relative independence and aggressive reporting on corruption at high levels, on the pretext of alleged improprieties in the organization's internal accounting. *Novaya Gazeta* continued to publish.

In some instances, the private media faced more direct challenges from the Government. The State owns and controls some major media organizations, such as the national television station RTR, the radio stations Mayak and Radio Rossii, the newspapers *Rossiyskaya Gazeta* and *Parlamentskaya Gazeta*, and the news agencies ITAR-TASS and RIA-Novosti. At the regional and local levels, governments operated a much higher percentage of the media than in Moscow; in many cities and towns across the country, government-run media organizations were the only media outlet, according to the GDF. Thus, in an increasing number of media markets, citizens received information only from government-owned sources.

In May the Government took steps to strengthen its control over the state media—and to a certain extent, to increase its leverage over other, private broadcast organizations—by consolidating its central and local television and radio companies into an enlarged and potentially more powerful holding company, the All-Russia Television and Radio Company (known by its Russian acronym, VGTRK). The VGTRK began to manage the sites that transmit the broadcasts of private television channels. The head of the VGTRK is appointed by and answers to the President.

On more than one occasion, senior government officials, including in one case President Yeltsin, voiced "expectations" or "suggestions" to media representatives and government officials that clearly were intended to change the way the media operated.

Local governments, also, applied pressure on media based within their jurisdictions. Radio Free Europe/Radio Liberty noted in a 1998 report on the Russian media that the mayor of Moscow, Yuriy Luzhkov, could exert pressure on distribution companies, on paper suppliers, or on the corporate parents of "any media enterprise deemed to be objectionable," and that Luzhkov had used his power "to ensure a largely compliant press in his hometown."

There were many instances in which authorities disregarded and challenged the right of journalists to investigate and publish stories. In late January, President Yeltsin signed a decree "on the List of Information that Constitutes a State Secret," widening the scope of privileged information that legally could be withheld from the public. Information pertaining to the development, production, storage, and disposal of nuclear ammunition, for example, was included explicitly in the language of the decree, with the result that it has now become much more difficult—in fact illegal—for citizens residing near disposal sites to publicize through the media the increased health risks and environmental degradation. According to this decree, information on the preparation and conclusion of international treaties, as well as information in certain economic categories, falls within the domain of state secrets.

The controversy about military journalist Grigory Pasko continued during the year. Attorneys for Pasko, an active duty officer in the Russian Pacific Fleet, claimed he is being persecuted for his environmental activism. Pasko was arrested in November 1997 on charges of revealing state secrets. He had been working on a freelance basis with Japanese television network NHK and Japanese newspaper *Asahi Shinbun* to expose environmental dangers posed by the activities of the Russian Pacific Fleet, including the dumping of liquid radioactive nuclear wastes from nuclear submarines in the Sea of Japan. Pasko has remained in detention since his arrest, spending much of that time in solitary confinement. He faces a maximum of 18 years in prison if convicted.

In April Russian poet and journalist Alina Vitukhnovskaya faced trial for allegedly selling $40 (400 rubles) worth of drugs. At the time of her arrest, in October 1994, she was researching newspaper articles on drug use by the children of Moscow's political and business elite. In January she was sent to a psychiatric institute for tests of her sanity. Two months later, she was released when the tests found her normal. Her lawyers contended that Vitukhnovskaya was deprived of food and sleep at various points during the course of the trial; she endured what these attorneys described as "torture" at the hands of the legal authorities. Both her attorneys and the international PEN group charged that Vitukhnovskaya was being harassed for her investigative reporting.

In mid-July, the Constitutional Court rejected an appeal by well-known journalist Irina Chernova against sections of federal law on operational-investigative activities. As a correspondent for *Komsomolskaya Pravda* in 1994 and 1995, Chernova published several articles criticizing the Volgograd police. She subsequently was followed and detained in 1995 without being told the grounds on which she was being investigated; reportedly, police officers also tried to blackmail her by threatening to release pictures and videotapes of her engaged in sexual acts. The Constitutional Court found that the disputed articles in the law either were not relevant to Chernova's case or did not violate her rights.

Journalists publishing critical information about local governments and influential businesses, as well as investigative journalists writing about crime and other sensitive issues, were subjected to threats, beatings, and even murder.

According to the CPJ, murders and beatings of journalists were "routine" in Russia, and in particular, journalists who pursued investigative stories on corruption and organized crime found themselves at greatest risk. Police seldom found the perpetrators of crimes against journalists. The GDF's midyear report indicated that in the first half of the year, it recorded 602 actions against, or with negative ramifications for, journalists, the majority of which were related to their work as journalists (this figure included numerous legal actions and decisions with a bearing on the rights of journalists.) Sixteen killings of journalists, proved or presumed to be directly related to the journalistic work of the victims, and 10 other bodily assaults on the heads of news and media organizations were reported by the press and media NGO's.

On March 16, journalists Timur Kukuyev and Yuriy Safronov, who were working for the national ORT television station, were harassed and beaten by a group of men dressed in paramilitary uniforms as they tried to film at the Dagestani-Chechen border. The assailants destroyed the crew's camera and confiscated their video footage. Dagestani border guards who were stationed nearby reportedly failed to intervene. Later that evening, unidentified men severely beat Kukuyev, warning him against filming "on foreign territory" in the future; on March 9, the ORT had broadcast a story that showed paramilitary formations on Dagestani territory near the Chechen border. The attack on Kukuyev, which resulted in his hospitalization for broken ribs, a concussion, and a badly disfigured face, represented the tenth such attack on journalists in Dagestan in the last 2 years.

In April, Aleksey Nevinitsyn, the editor in chief of the *Zolotoye Koltso* newspaper in Yaroslavl, was beaten badly. Prior to the beating, "zolotoye koltso" had published a series of articles that documented corruption in the ranks of the local administration; specifically, a top municipal official in the pharmaceutical administration was purchasing medical supplies for the city from a company owned by the official's son. As a result of the articles, the mayor of Yaroslavl fired the senior official and a number of lawsuits were brought against *Zolotoye Koltso*, though municipal judges found in favor of the newspaper. Nevinitsyn—and, privately, other witnesses—stated that the man who brutally beat him was the son of the fired official; however, the witnesses were reluctant to come forward. As a result, no formal investigation of the beating was initiated and no one was charged with the crime.

On May 27, police raided the offices of Radio Titan, the only independent radio station in the Republic of Bashkortostan, and arrested its manager and news director, Altaf Galeyev. The police also rounded up and beat staff members and supporters. The police assault on Radio Titan came in the wake of the station's airing of interviews with three opposition candidates for president of the republic who had been banned from participating in the June 14 elections. Police also seized the station's equipment and detained the entire staff before releasing them the next day. Galeyev still is being held for "hooliganism" and "illegal use of firearms" for firing several shots in the air with a handgun when police stormed the radio's offices. Two days earlier, Radio Titan had quoted several Moscow-based newspapers that alleged corruption on the part of Bashkir President Murtaza Rakhimov. Radio Titan staff members maintained that as a result of these and other similar broadcasts, local authorities had made several attempts to silence the station by shutting off the electricity, telephone lines, and water supply.

In June Larisa Yudina, editor of the *Sovetskaya Kalmykia Segodnya* opposition newspaper, was killed, apparently in retaliation for investigating reports of corrupt business practices by regional officials. She disappeared on June 7. On that day she had been planning to meet a source who had promised to give her evidence of financial improprieties by local firms involved in an effort by Kalmyk president Kirsan Ilyumzhinov to set up an offshore economic zone in the republic. On June 8, she was found dead with multiple stab wounds and a fractured skull. For years Yudina had been harassed and threatened because of her exposes of local corruption and opposition to the hard-line rule of president Ilyumzhinov. Before her death, Yudina's application for press credentials had been rejected; she had been fired from her position; and her automobile had been confiscated. For several years, Yudina had been forced to print her newspaper in a neighboring oblast after president Ilyumzhinov allegedly prohibited local printing presses from publishing it. The investigation continues. The Russian procurator arrested four individuals in connection with the murder. Two of the suspects had close ties to President Ilyumzhinov. One of those arrested was Ilyumzhinov's personal representative in Volgograd. Officials in the republic denied any involvement in the murder. Yudina's death triggered a widespread reaction in Russian and international media and human rights circles, and it was perhaps the most widely publicized case in a year replete with assaults on journalists.

On August 21, Anatoliy Levin-Utkin, deputy editor of the St. Petersburg weekly, *Yuridichesky Peterburg Segodnya*, was beaten to death in apparent reprisal for his work as a journalist. Levin-Utkin also was robbed of his money and his briefcase, in which he was carrying materials that he had gathered for the next installment of a series of investigative articles on rivalries between major local financial and political figures. The local procurator's office investigated the murder, but by the end of September, there were no arrests. Many observers believe that the killing was directly related to the investigative work Levin-Utkin was undertaking; the customs service and the secret services were subjects of his research.

Journalists maintained and strengthened associations to defend their rights and monitor governmental abuse.

Murmansk human rights activist Oleg Pazyura was arrested in May 1997. He was charged with libel, contempt of court, and threatening public officials. At his trial in January, Pazyura was found guilty, but the judge immediately granted him amnesty.

In 1997 the Editor in Chief and a correspondent of the Irkutsk paper, *Zemlya: Novyy Poryadok*, were accused of accepting a bribe of $20,000. These individuals were subsequently released on grounds of insufficient evidence. Reportedly new incriminating evidence emerged during the year, and the two are once again under the threat of arrest. Some observers of the case stated that the charges represented an attempt by local authorities to trump up charges in order to suppress the ultranationalist activities of the newspaper for which the two journalists worked. The matter remained unresolved at year's end.

Communist members of the Duma attempted to deflect public outcry over their anti-Semitic statements by blaming the broad condemnation that they received on a smear campaign by the media. At a November 5 joint press conference at the Duma with Communist Party leader Gennadiy Zyuganov, the head of the Moscow Municipal Committee of the Communist Party, Aleksandr Kunayev, publicly called for a campaign against Moscow-based television journalists whom he accused of "active and conscious complicity with the present regime and criminal activities." He declared that he would seek the resignation of a number of leading television journalists.

In 1997 Duma Deputy Vladimir Zhirinovskiy, leader of the Liberal Democratic Party of Russia (LDPR) faction, and his bodyguards physically attacked Moscow television journalist Yulia Olshanskaya and Valeriy Ivanov, a cameraman from the 2X2 television channel. As of the end of 1997, the case against Zhirinovskiy's bodyguards was still pending. During the year, the case was dropped; no one was prosecuted for the beatings.

Violations of journalists' rights in Chechnya, rampant in 1997, decreased markedly during the year, according to the Glasnost Defense Fund. Nonetheless a number of serious abuses were reported. For example, the Maskhadov Government took actions against opposition television stations. In May acting prime minister Shamil Basayev ordered the confiscation of transmitter equipment used by opposition leader Salman Raduyev. The Chechen authorities tried to restrict reporting critical of President Maskhadov's administration.

On July 22, authorities in the republic of Chechnya declared a "state of emergency" and banned the activities of all non-Chechen state television and radio companies and newspapers and magazines. During the state of emergency, only state-owned television channels were permitted to broadcast programs. The authorities announced that they would strip the broadcast rights and confiscate the equipment of any media organization that attempted to violate this order. A Chechen military official explained that the decision to close down the independent media was taken because these media spread "unreliable and often provocative and biased information," which destabilized the social and political situation in the republic.

The Government respects academic freedom.

Commentary on 1998 U.S. State Department Country Report on Human Rights Practices in Russia*

Manana Aslamazyan
Internews Russia

The analysis of the state of Russian journalism and its relationship with the authorities given in this report is quite thorough. It is very difficult to add anything to the specific facts about violations of journalists' rights and pressure applied by the authorities. However, it seems to me that the report gives little attention to the organizational and economic changes that have been taking place in Russian mass media in recent years, which have a significant effect on the level of Russian journalism.

These changes are so rapid that neither participants in the process nor analysts are able to seriously grasp what is taking place. On the whole, the mass media and propaganda system previously subordinate to the state have been extricated from direct, total control by the state, which has been left with only a regulatory function.

Mass media in Russia have become an element of the market economy. They are naturally becoming subject to the laws of the market and are striving to win wider markets. The mass media market is undergoing a process of concentration and amalgamation.

Under such conditions, the weak are forced out of the market, while the strong gain additional advantages. In such harsh competitive conditions, mass media cannot exist without outside support, as the advertising market in its current state cannot support the existing media market. Under these circumstances, mass media are beginning to seek support wherever possible: public institutions, state structures, private capital, etc.

The intensification of the process of consolidation within the mass media market is accompanied by increasing financial opacity within the media, which is still the norm in Russia. This opacity, which is found in the advertising market as well, prevents us from making a positive appraisal of the perspectives for freedom of speech in Russia. Furthermore, the situation in the regions is very different from that in the center: while it is still perhaps somehow possible to understand the situation with the central media, the situation in the regions is extremely complicated and unclear.

On the whole, the chasm between the conditions of central and regional media continued to grow in 1998. Many blame this on the financial crisis, which definitely intensified the difficult financial position of regional media. Some analysts believe that, before the crisis, there was a tendency in the mass media market toward becoming a financially and politically independent business, but the new political confrontation in

* Post-Soviet Media Law & Policy Newsletter, July 15, 1999, at 6.

society and the crisis of August 1998 again pushed the media into the embrace of state structures and politicians.

It is well known that flagrant application of political pressure on the media is a thing of the past. However, according to a survey conducted by the Mass Media Law and Policy Center, 90% of the heads of regional television and radio companies admit that the media reflect somebody's point of view, be it that of the owner, executive or legislative government bodies, the regional governor, etc. Furthermore, almost all of them know precisely which publications serve which interests.

For regional mass media, 1998 was characterized by their division into three groups. The first group is comprised of private media that exist parallel to government bodies and support themselves through advertising (local, as a rule). The second group is made up of media founded by local government bodies and supported by financing from regional or city budgets and affiliated commercial structures. The third group, state television and radio companies, hold a very distinctive position. Such companies do not receive very much money from regional budgets. They are all part of a unified state production-technical complex.

Local management of state television and radio companies usually consider themselves separate and independent from local government. On the whole, the desire of authorities at all levels to have their own publications and have influence over the editorial policy of all other media in the region is a nationwide tendency that has intensified over the past year. In particular, local authorities are cultivating a tendency to distance themselves from Moscow as the center of political instability and incomprehensible political games and to intensify their role as the protector of regional interests.

Regional leaders long ago understood that it is easy to blame everything on Moscow, including their own miscalculations, their own negligence, and the corruption of the local apparatus. And while in no way should this excuse the lack of talent in the federal government, it must be admitted that the cultivation of "regional separatism" has become a real fact of contemporary Russian life. Naturally, media cannot but be exposed to the effects of these local tendencies.

Local authorities frankly fear Moscow's expansion into regional media markets. This expansion, which was sharply curtailed after August 1998, has both positive and negative ramifications for regional mass media. And while the negative aspects are easily recognized, a positive aspect could be considered the protection of local media by their Moscow partners against pressure from local authorities.

1998 was also characterized by the formation of Russian information empires. Their distinguishing characteristic was the open symbiosis of business and politics. In my view, this symbiosis is of a less candid character in the West. It is difficult, for example, to imagine that during the New York mayoral campaign informational empires were formed with the participation of state funds.

In addition to the excessive politicization of Russian media, Russian media empires have another characteristic that distinguishes them from Western corporations: they are all located in Moscow and divide the regions up amongst themselves. It can be stated beyond a shadow of a doubt that during the second half of 1998 there was a sharp acceleration of the concentration of media properties via the formation of large companies capable of large-scale investment in new technologies, large expenditures on production of new programs, quick transfer of funds from one subsidiary or division to the other, etc. This integration could take on any number of forms: multimedia corporations (publishing, radio, television); multi-sector conglomerates where business from other economic sectors are incorporated into media holdings; or vertical and horizontal alliances in which one owner controls all stages of production and distribution of information.

The leading role in this process is being taken by media moguls who secure broadcasting and publishing through large investments, thereby securing monopolistic positions for themselves on the media market. However, this was the tendency of 1998. In 1999, as these lines are written, the picture has changed, but that is a subject for further investigation.

1998 World Press Freedom Review on Russia*

International Press Institute

The obstacles facing the media in Russia are manifold: assassination is still tragically used to good effect to silence unwanted voices; cases of intimidation and harassment are commonplace; the 'oligarchs' blithely manipulate the media for personal gain; and a Communist-led Duma introduces legislation to censor and control.

Murder has shown itself to be the preferred method of censorship in at least five cases in Russia this year.

On June 8, Larissa Yudina, editor-in-chief of the daily *Sovietskaya Kalmykia*, was kidnapped and murdered in Elista, the capital of the Russian Republic of Kalmykia. On the evening of June 7, an unknown person claiming to be a representative of the Agency for Co-development, reporting to the President of Kalmykia, had made an appointment with the journalist. He was to give her documents on the misappropriation of funds, which implicated the President of the Republic, Kirsan Ilyumzhinov. The next morning her body was found with several stab wounds in a dam in the town. Yudina was also regional vice-president of the opposition party Yabloko. Her newspaper was in constant conflict with President Ilyumzhinov, who is also an influential businessman. *Sovietskaya Kalmykia* has published numerous articles criticising his authoritarianism and denouncing the corruption and misappropriation of funds under his presidency. For the past eighteen months, Yudina had also been inquiring into a company connected to President Ilyumzhinov, called Aris, which granted tax exemptions to firms setting up in an off-shore area of the republic. In her newspaper she claimed that the practice was accompanied by bribes paid by firms to the Kalmykian President. *Sovietskaya Kalmykia*, the only opposition newspaper in Kalmykia, has often been threatened with closure by authorities. Since 1993, Yudina had also received numerous threats due to her articles on the wealth and personality of President Ilyumzhinov.

Two suspects arrested in connection with the Yudina murder confessed to the crime in June. Sergei Vaskin, a former aide to Kalmykian President Kirsan Ilyumzhinov, and Tyurbi Boskomdzhiev, Ilyumzhinov's representative in Volgograd Oblast, were charged with premeditated murder. Authorities are still searching for a third suspect in the case. Investigators believe Yudina's murder was linked to her journalistic activities in *Sovetskaya Kalmykia Segodnya* which is the only local newspaper that criticises Ilyumzhinov. President Yeltsin remarked that "not everything" relating to the investigation can be shared with law enforcement officials in Kalmykia.

---

* Post-Soviet Media Law & Policy Newsletter, February 15, 1999, at 39.

On 21 August, Anatoly Levin-Utkin, deputy editor-in-chief of *Yuridichesky Peterburg Segodnya*, was reportedly assaulted by two unknown assailants on the porch of his house in St. Petersburg. He was found unconscious, suffering from serious head injuries. The journalist's briefcase, containing material for the next paper's issue, as well as photo equipment and exposed film, were missing.

On August 24, following neurosurgery, Levin-Utkin died from his injuries without having regained consciousness. According to neurosurgeon Sergei Yevdokimov, the nature of the journalist's injuries give reason to assert that he was murdered.

Yuridichesky Peterburg Segodnya, which had only commenced publishing three weeks prior to the murder, had published two articles on corruption in St. Petersburg's banking circles. According to GDF, the banking management—the focus of articles to have been published in the next issue—demanded that the newspaper name its sources for the articles. Previously, the vehicle carrying the previous issue of the newspaper had been detained by militia, allegedly under false pretext.

CPJ reported that on March 31, 56-year old Ivan Fedyunin, a reporter with the local *Bryanskie Izvestia* newspaper, was murdered. Fedyunin was stabbed to death in his apartment. Fedyunin's colleagues at the *Bryanskie Izvestia* said that he had recently published articles concerning the alleged criminal activities of local companies involved in renovating apartments. As a reporter for the "politics" department of the paper, Fedyunin covered the activities of the Duma, the local legislative body, as well as on current regional and national political events.

On May 2, Major Igor Lykov was shot twice at point-blank range in his apartment in Saratov (southeast of Moscow). Lykov had repeatedly published articles in the local and Moscow press concerning corruption and unlawful actions in the law-enforcement bodies, GDF reported. He was repeatedly punished for publishing the articles, including having nine criminal suits brought against him and twice being dismissed from the militia service. After a number of articles by Lykov on the methods of recruiting militia agents were published in the local press, there was an attempt to accuse him of divulging State secrets.

On January 30, Vladimir Zbaratski, a staff member of ITAR-TASS news agency was murdered on Mosrilmovskay Street, Moscow, as he was returning home from his office late at night.

Several other journalists met with violent deaths in Russia in 1998 and the crimes are currently under investigation to determine whether the killings were related to the journalists' professional activity.

Laws and decrees relating to the media have played a significant role in the political debates this year.

Chief editors of over 30 publications signed an appeal in October urging the State Duma not to adopt proposed amendments to the Mass Media Law.

The draft law expands the list of grounds for closing media outlets and increases the number of officials who have the right to do so. If the law is adopted, the appeal says, supervisory councils will appear in the editorial offices and these will be, in essence, censoring councils. Moreover, under the pretext of combating monopolies, the authors of the draft law propose restricting the broadcasting of television channels and radio stations to one constituent part of the federation which, the media chiefs say, will lead to the closure of nation-wide television and radio companies.

Overall, the adoption of such a law will mean an increase in the control exercised by state bodies over the state media and possibly arbitrary control by bureaucrats over the private media, and can only have irreparable consequences for freedom of speech in the country, the appeal says.

Communist Party officials launched a public campaign against television media, pledging to establish a "public committee" to draw up accusations. The move came on November 7, the anniversary of the 1917 Bolshevik revolution, RFE/RL reported. Earlier that week State Duma Deputy and Communist Party faction member Aleksandr Kuvaev accused several prominent television journalists of "maiming and raping public consciousness" and "collaborating with the regime and its crimes against society," the *Moscow Times* reported. Hearings were held in the Duma on "problems of morality, social harmony and censorship on Russian television channels." The Duma, which has a Communist Party majority, referred euphemistically to censorship devices as "ensuring psychocultural safety measures."

Communist Party leader Gennady Zyuganov recently told reporters that while the Communist Party does not require that state television be "nationalised", it must improve its compliance with the nation's media law. Zyuganov added that his party will continue to push for the establishment of supervisory boards in the mass media. He also told a press conference that his party will demand that the leadership of All-Russia State Television and Radio Broadcasting Company be replaced.

Meanwhile, the Duma overrode a Federation Council veto of a law on privileges for the media, thereby extending breaks on value-added tax and profit tax for media holdings for another three years. It failed, however, to override a bill on customs tariffs that would have extended a similar exemption for the same period. As a result the price of newspapers and magazines printed outside Russia might rise two to three times.

A controversial decree, "On Forming a Production-Technological Complex of State-Owned Electronic Mass Media" was signed on July 27.

The heads of a number of Russian private TV companies protested at the advantages given to the state-controlled Russia TV by the reorganisation of the state broadcasting company, VGTRK. Among other things, VGTRK will enjoy tax breaks and exemptions, and it will run—and charge for the use of—the regional transmission centres used by its rivals, giving it a virtual monopoly on signal distribution and the possibility of realising large profits from the charges it makes for the use of its facilities. The other television companies claim that the new law gives VGRTK an unfair advantage and is inconsistent with articles 8 and 27 of the constitution.

ITAR-TASS news agency reported that a total of 99 state TV and radio broadcasting companies, as well as other organisations, were being transformed into federal state unitary enterprises which would be VGTRK affiliates. Mikhail Shvydkoy—VGTRK's recently-appointed head who is directly answerable to Yeltsin—dismisses fears of undue state interference and said: "I'd quit rather than pull the plug on private broadcasters."

As the presidential election set for June 2000 looms closer, many see this initiative as a Kremlin attempt to jostle for a strong media position to enable it to effectively compete with rivals who already have a strong media presence—for example Moscow Mayor Yuri Luzhkov with his TV Centre consortium or Aleksandr Lebed, now governor of Krasnoyarsk region, who has been lent media support by Boris Berezovsky in the past.

When finally signed, the decree did not contain the particularly contentious suggestions of giving the VGTRK $860m in budget money in 1999 from foreign loan proceeds. Nor did it include the state enterprise Space Communications on the list of subsidiaries. Earlier in the year the RIA Novosti news agency, which has valuable properties all over the world, was attached to the VGTRK, changing its name to RIA Vesti.

Reports indicate that regional leaders, keen to hold on to media assets, transferred items of value from the books of the broadcasting stations while the decree was being debated. As a result, the VGTRK holding is considerably less valuable than it might have been.

President Yeltsin made an outspoken attack on Russian media tycoons in May, accusing them of censoring news for their own purposes. In a speech delivered to the International Press Institute World Congress in Moscow, Yeltsin said that objective, accurate reporting was being jeopardised by corporate ownership which openly interfered in editorial policy. He called it unreasonable and said he would be meeting the heads of the three main channels later in the week to express his indignation on this issue and, in particular, in connection with the "tone" of their coverage of the miners' strike.

The President likes to point his finger at the media at any opportunity. When he met with Vietnamese President Tran Duc Luong, the Vietnamese leader said Yeltsin looked "younger than in photographs," to which a smiling Yeltsin replied that the fault lay with the photographers, not his health.

The health of the President continues to make news around the world. He abandoned a Central Asia trip after appearing very weak this year and afterwards snapped at enquiring reporters, saying, "You do not even let me sneeze!"

While Yeltsin's treatment of the media is far from deferential, most pundits view him as a president who's willing to tolerate a free press and accepts this freedom is necessary in order for society to develop. The mounting fear is that his successor may not share these sentiments.

Russia's press was up in arms in September after Yevgeni Primakov, the recently appointed Prime Minister, banned members of his government from talking to the media until further notice. In a move that smacks of Soviet-era censorship, Primakov insisted that all press inquiries be channelled through the information department. Russia's leading *Kommersant Daily* called Primakov's moratorium an "iron curtain" and said it would be naïve to believe the Government's claim that the move is a temporary one. The newspaper points out that this kind of censorship is constitutionally illegal but that no legal action can be taken against Primakov because his decree was verbal rather than written.

The economic crisis that hit Russia this year has all but crippled the media. Newspaper production costs rose 70 percent in one month and the advertising market has virtually collapsed. Since the rouble plummeted, income from subscriptions is practically worthless. Thousands of media workers have lost their jobs or are working without pay. Media owners see the upcoming presidential elections as the possible glimmer of light at the end of the tunnel. For once the audience won't need money, just a valid voting card, to be attractive to advertisers.

Russia's ORT television station, 51 percent owned by the state and with the largest coverage of the former Soviet Union, is threatened with seizure because of unpaid debts of several million dollars. Bailiffs carried out an inventory in the luxurious offices of ORT's director-general and head of programmes in November. The bailiffs seized some equipment and Director General Igor Shabdurasulov announced that he had been ordered to hand over keys to the station's vehicles. ORT officials, predicting possible bankruptcy, see a political tinge to the legal moves being made against them, citing the company's anti-Communist stance.

"ORT's debts are of course very serious but everyone has debts these days. This is not a financial question, it is part of the pre-election campaign and the war to win television and media time," Sergei Mikhailov, a political analyst at the Russian Socio-Political Centre told Reuters.

Around the same time bailiffs were confiscating ORT's equipment, firemen were demanding that the influential Ekho Moskvy radio station be shut down for failing to comply with safety standards.

In November the state-owned RTR television pulled the plug on the Californian soap opera Santa Barbara. Bearing placards, a small group of middle aged women mounted a picket outside RTR in Moscow. RTR said the station was forced to take the programme off the air because of falling advertising revenues in the wake of the August financial crisis. An estimated 10.5 million people watched the programme every evening, making it by far the most popular soap on Russian television.

Duma chairman Gennadii Seleznev announced he will sue a St. Petersburg newspaper for accusing him of Russian Duma deputy Galina Starovoitova's murder in November. He told reporters that television is presenting Starovoitova's murder in "such a way as to promote the election campaigns of certain candidates to the St. Petersburg assembly".

Marina Kalashnikova, a journalist for *Kommersant Daily*, was reportedly sacked for criticising Russia's relationship with former Slovak Prime Minister Vladimir Meciar.

Kalashnikova wrote that Meciar has referred to Kremlin spokesman Sergei Yastrzhembskii as "Slovakia's ambassador in Russia". Yastrzhembskii apparently called Raf Shakirov, editor-in-chief of *Kommersant Daily*, and said that support for Meciar was in Russia's interests, and so demanded that all articles be written accordingly. Kalashnikova said she was reprimanded by her editor-in-chief but continued to write critical articles on Meciar's style of government.

Kalashnikova was refused entry into her office on March 23 and her work pass was confiscated. While she has not been officially dismissed, she is unable to work, her salary has been frozen and the paper's management refuse to meet with her.

Igor Rudnikov, editor-in-chief of the newspaper *Noviye Kolyesa* and deputy of City Council of Kaliningrad was assaulted on July 1 by an unknown person, who struck the journalist's head repeatedly with an iron tube wrapped in a sheet of polyethylene, injuring him seriously. Rudnikov's colleagues consider that the assault might be connected with his investigative reporting. GDF reported that the offices of *Noviye Kolyesa* have come under attack twice this year. On February 6, an explosion was set off outside the newspaper's office and on March 1, two Molotov cocktails were thrown into the editor-in-chief's office window.

The Glasnost Defence Foundation have documented numerous other instances of attacks against independent media leaders since the beginning of 1998, including the following:

On 2 January, an unknown person badly wounded Yakov London, vice-president of NTN-4 TV channel (Novosibirsk); on 21 January, unknown persons set fire to the car of Boris Fradkov, Director General of the Samara branch of Europe Plus radio station, and later he was threatened with murder in a phone call; on February 5, an armed attack was committed on the apartment of A. Baranov, editor-in-chief of the magazine *Stolichny Optovik* (Moscow); on 18 February, two unknown persons burst into the apartment of Anatoly Kovyrshin, editor-in-chief of the newspaper *Express-Reporter* and beat him; on 21 March, unknown persons beat Eduard Markevich, editor-in-chief of the newspaper *Noviy Reft* (Sverdlovsk region); on 11 April, Alexei Nevinitsin, editor-in-chief of the newspaper *Zolotoye Koltso* was beaten in Yaroslavl; on 22 April, Lyudmila Stakhovskaya, editor-in-chief of the newspaper *Zarya Timana* (Komi Republic) was beaten by unknown persons; on 30 April, Grigory Zabolotsky, editor-in-chief of the newspaper *Volgodonskaya Nedelya Plus* was threatened with physical violence; and on

May 15, Igopr Myasnikov, director of the newspaper *Volzhsky Bulvar* (Ivanovo region) was mortally wounded.

A journalist with the independent newspaper *Otechestvo*, Sergei Fufaev, was attacked by unknown individuals on August 14, in the city of Ufa in the Republic of Bashkortostan. Fufaev, who had received several threatening phonecalls in connection with his reporting, said one of the assailants told him: "You know what this is for."

The persecution of journalists by authorities and unknown individuals in the Republic of Bashkortostan has become more frequent, according to GDF reports. In January, the Neftekamsk City court, in examining the decision of the Ministry of Press and Information of Bashkortostan to revoke the licence of the privately-owned newspaper *Vecherny Neftekamsk*, ruled in favour of the ministry. In June, on the eve of presidential elections, broadcasts by Russian television in the republic were often tampered with by local TV companies. In addition, issues of Russian newspapers that criticised Murtaza Rakhimov, President of Bashkortostan, were unavailable for sale. Further harassment of the media included efforts to obstruct the work of the correspondent of the Russian TV programme "Vesti".

On July 2, in the city of Beloretsk, staff of the local economic crimes prevention unit confiscated 5,000 copies of the opposition newspaper *Otechestvo* from distributors. On August 7, in Ufa, Victor Shmakov, editor-in-chief of the independent newspaper *Vmeste*, was assaulted.

Timur Kukuyev and Yuri Safronov, members of a film crew for the local M-5 television station and stringers for the Russian public television company ORT in Makhachkala, Dagestan, were beaten by a group of men dressed in paramilitary uniforms as they tried to film at the Daghestani-Chechen border on March 13. Their attackers, CPJ reported, destroyed the crew's video camera and confiscated their videotapes. The crew members were not seriously injured, but they were shocked that the Daghestani border guards who witnessed the incident failed to intervene. On March 16, Kukuyev, the cameraman, was severely beaten in central Makhachkala by unidentified men who warned him against "filming anything else on a foreign territory in the future" as they assaulted him. He was admitted to a hospital with broken ribs, a concussion, and a badly disfigured face.

On May 11, Stanislav Kholopov, editor-in-chief of the weekly *Stolitza-C*, was stabbed twice with a knife near his home in Saransk (240 km south of Gorki) on April 16, RSF reported. He was immediately taken to hospital. A militia officer said that the attack could be linked to Kholopov's journalistic work. Local sources have indicated that the attack could have been prompted by articles written by Kholopov concerning the militia's use of torture, articles which have led to criminal cases being brought against regional high-ranking civil servants.

Sergei Bachinin, the editor-in-chief of the newspaper *Vyatskii Nablyudatel* in Kirov, was badly beaten by unknown assailants on July 1. He suffered severe concussion and other skull injuries.

Bachinin, who has been the victim of a variety of attacks in the past, believes the crime is linked to the editorial policy of Vyatskii Nablyudatel, which is critical of local authorities. Bachinin ran for mayor of Kirov in 1996 and was the main rival of the candidate who won that election.

On May 27, Police raided the offices of Radio Titan, the only independent radio station in the Republic of Bashkortostan, beating and rounding up staff members and supporters, CPJ reported. Employees and listeners had been keeping a round-the-clock vigil around the station's building, in anticipation of official reprisals after Radio Titan aired interviews with three opposition candidates who were barred from the June 14 presidential elections. Police seized the radio's equipment and detained the whole staff, including manager and news director Altaf Galeyev and Lilia Ismagilova, its executive director. Although Ismagilova and the others were released the next day, Galeyev was held for firing several shots in the air with a handgun when police stormed the radio's offices. On 4 June, Galeyev was charged with "hooliganism" and "illegal use of firearms" under article 213(3) of the Bashkir penal code. If found guilty, he faces a possible prison sentence of four to seven years.

Attacks on Radio Titan by the strong-arm regime of Bashkir President Murtaza Rakhimov, who exercises full control over the media, have been common since 1994, when Radio Titan began re-broadcasting Radio Liberty and Voice of America programmes. On May 25, Radio Titan quoted from several articles in Moscow newspapers revealing the allegedly corrupt practices of President Rakhimov's regime, his total control over the local oil industry and his tight grip on the media. Staff members maintain that, as a result of the broadcast, local authorities made several attempts to silence the station by shutting off the electricity, water supply and phone lines. After Galeyev called on listeners to defend his station, the government-controlled Russian Radio Ufa aired interviews with Rakhimov's press secretary and a psychiatrist, who questioned the "psychological health" of Radio Titan's reporters.

Grigori Pasko has been imprisoned since 20 November 1997 in Vladivostok. The charges against Pasko—a naval captain and correspondent for the newspaper of the Russian Pacific Fleet, *Boyevaya Vakhta*, who also operated on a freelance basis for some Japanese media outlets—are based on his publications in the Russian and Japanese media over a three-year period. These publications described the problem of nuclear waste caused by the deterioration of the condition of the Russian nuclear submarine fleet in the Far East, as well as other radioactive nuclear waste disposal problems that have created a major environmental danger. The authorities admit that none of the facts he published revealed state secrets or endangered national security. Moreover, all Pasko's contacts with the Japanese media were sanctioned or co-ordinated with the leadership of the Pacific Fleet, and all material published in the Fleet's newspaper were passed by the military censor. Nevertheless, the authorities argue that the net effect of his publications resulted in revealing a pattern whose exposure constitutes a challenge to Russian state security. Pasko's appeal was rejected in November.

Aleksandr Nikitin—writer, environmental activist and retired naval officer—Is currently facing high treason charges for drafting a report for the Norwegian environmental organisation Bellona Foundation on the dangers of nuclear contamination caused by Russia's Northern Fleet. His trial is on-going.

On July 24 all TV channels in Chechnya including private ones were shut down.

On the following day, the leadership of the Chechen Republic decided to let Russian RTR and ORT companies resume partial broadcasting in the republic, however, according to press secretary of the Chechen President Mayarbek Vachagayev, only non-political programme are to be allowed broadcast.

The decision to cease broadcasting by Russian mass media over the republic's territory was taken as the Chechen leadership found their interpretation of what is happening in the republic to be "preconceived, distorted and harmful."

According to Vachagayev, Russian mass media can fully resume broadcasting in Chechnya only after their leadership promise to truly cover events in the republic and offer their official apologies to the Chechen people. Vachagayev blamed Russian mass media correspondents accredited in Chechnya for betrayal of national interests and venality, and threatened to deny foreign correspondents accreditation if they do not stop carrying out orders by their agencies.

Seven journalists from the rebel republic of Chechnya who were seized on Christmas Day 1997 in the southern Russian region of Dagestan were released on January 2. The Chechen residents, working for Reuters, Worldwide Television News (WTN), Associated Press and two major Russian television networks, ORT and NTV, were reported missing after crossing into Dagestan to report on the aftermath of an attack on a Russian tank unit there. A group calling itself the People's Militia of Dagestan had said it was holding them and wanted ethnic Dagestanis being held hostage in neighbouring Chechnya to be freed in exchange for their release. However, ITAR-TASS news agency quoted the Dagestani Interior Ministry as saying their release had been unconditional.

The Moscow Arbitration Court on February 11 upheld a lawsuit brought by the private network NTV against the State Anti-Monopoly Committee, ITAR-TASS reported. In December 1997, the committee instructed the Communications Ministry to charge NTV commercial rates for using state-owned transmission facilities. Those rates would have more than doubled transmissions costs for the company, which since January 1996 had been charged government rates for transmission services.

The Prosecutor-General's Office officially charged retired Colonel Pavel Popovskikh with planning and taking part in the murder of journalist Dmitrii Kholodov, Interfax reported on February 12. On February 26, Major Vladimir Morozov, a paratrooper, was also charged with plotting Kholodov's assassination. Kholodov was killed by a booby-trapped briefcase in October 1994. Popovskikh formerly headed the intelligence department of the Airborne Troops. Sources in the Airborne Troops say investigators searched Popovskikh's office last year. They reportedly uncovered documents listing the names of journalists who were particularly critical of former Defence Minister Pavel Grachev and suggested actions to be taken against those journalists. Grachev was defence minister when Kholodov, who reported on military corruption, was murdered.

Valerii Kucher, the editor-in-chief of *Rossiiskie Vesti*, informed readers in a commentary in April that the newspaper is no longer the official publication of the presidential administration. Kucher promised that *Rosskiiskie Vesti* has been "de-ideologised" and will in future represent the interests of ordinary citizens and the middle class. He also said that owing to the loss of financing from the presidential administration, the newspaper has been forced to switch from daily to weekly publication for the time being. Kucher accused the Kremlin of failing to meet its financial obligations toward *Rossiiskie Vesti* and of trying to force the newspaper to publish only official materials.

Contributors

Laura Belin has written extensively on Russian politics and media issues since 1995, while working for the Open Media Research Institute and Radio Free Europe/Radio Liberty. She is completing a doctorate at the University of Oxford on *The Fall and Rise of State Power over the Russian Media.*

Melissa Dawson served as Law Clerk to Judge D.W. Nelson of the U.S. Court of Appeals for the Ninth Circuit. In 1987, she received her M.P.A. from the Woodrow Wilson School of Public and International Affairs at Princeton University. She received her J.D. in 1995 from Boalt Hall School of Law, University of California at Berkeley.

Andrei Fadin was a well-known Russian political journalist. In 1982, he was imprisoned with other intellectuals as a supporter of the Polish "Solidarnost." When perestroika began, they were released. After 1988, as a member of a group of left-wing intellectuals in Moscow, Fadin was very active in organizing the so-called Club "Perestroika." After the collapse of the Soviet Union, he has been working as a columnist at the *Obshaya Gazeta.* He tragically died in a car crash in November 1997 at the age of forty-four.

Frances H. Foster is Professor of Law at Washington University School of Law. She has been a Research Fellow at the East Asian Legal Studies Program at Harvard Law School, a visiting professor at Cornell Law School, a Fellow of Russian Research Center at Harvard University, and a member of the American Bar Association's Task Force on Cuban Technical Assistance. Professor Foster serves on the Board of Directors, the Long-Range Planning Committee, and the Nominating Committee of the American Society of Comparative Law. She is also a member of the editorial boards of several journals, including the *American Journal of Comparative Law*, Columbia University's *Parker School Journal of East European Law*, and formerly the *Post-Soviet Media Law & Policy Newsletter.* Her most recent publications include *The Family Paradigm of Inheritance Law* (in the *North Carolina Law Review*), *Linking Support and Inheritance: A New Model from China* (in the *Wisconsin Law Review*), and *Towards a Behavior-Based Model of Inheritance?: The Chinese Experiment* (in the *University of California at Davis Law Review*).

William G. Frenkel is a New York business lawyer with a decade-long experience of structuring, negotiating, and implementing cross-border investment, trade, and financial transactions in Russia, other former Soviet states, and Eastern and Central Europe. One of the areas of his international practice is Russian media and telecommunications law. He is Associate General Counsel to Metromedia International Telecommunications, Inc., which owns and operates television, radio, new media, and various telephony and telecommunications companies throughout the region. He is responsible for the legal aspects of their broadcasting, Internet, and other media-related activities. He is also an author of several books on the commercial, investment, and privatization regimes of Russia and Eastern Europe and numerous articles in legal and business publications.

Jamey Gambrell is currently a visiting scholar at the Harriman Institute of Post-Soviet Studies at Columbia University. Since 1985, she has been a guest lecturer at many universities and has written widely on contemporary Soviet-Russian art, culture, media and cultural politics. She is also a preeminent translator of Russian literature, having translated the works of Marina Tsvetaeva, Joseph Brodsky, and Tatyana Tolstaya, among others. She is a contributing editor to *Art in America* and has co-produced and written documentaries on Russian art and politics, most recently "Russia: Facing the Future," a production for the Carnegie Corporation's "Russia Initiative." Two of her translations will be published in the fall of 2002: Russian poet Marina Tsvetaeva's *Earthly Signs*, a volume of post-Revolutionary memoirs, and Tatyana Tolstaya's novel, *The Slynx*.

Svetlana Kolesnik is Associate Professor of Journalism at Moscow State University, where she conducts research on various aspects of television and broadcasting. She currently teaches courses on the history of international journalism and on contemporary foreign advertising at Moscow State University. As an expert advisor to the Russian National Association of Telebroadcasters, she has been involved in efforts to establish minimum standards for Russian TV audience surveys and has been monitoring the development of independent Russian television networks. Dr. Kolesnik has conducted research into programming policies of Russian television during the 1996 presidential election campaign. She is the Russian representative to the Council of Europe Commission on Violence in Electronic Media and a member of the group of experts to the Russian Duma Mass Media Committee.

Peter Krug is Associate Professor of Law at the University of Oklahoma College of Law. He joined the University of Oklahoma law faculty in 1991 after serving for six years as an associate with the law firm of Foley & Lardner in Madison, Wisconsin. Professor Krug teaches courses in communications law, comparative law, international business transactions, and public international law. He is a member of the Order of the Coif, the American Bar Association, and the International Law Section of the Oklahoma Bar Association. He is also the author of a number of publications on the topics of comparative mass media law, particularly in the former Soviet Union, and the Russian legal system.

Brian McNair is a reader and co-director of the Undergraduate Program at the Department of Film and Media Studies at the University of Stirling. He took degrees in Sociology (M.A., Ph.D.) and Comparative Communist Studies (M.Phil.) at Glasgow University before becoming a lecturer in media studies at the University of Ulster. Professor McNair's research interests include journalism, political communication, sexuality and the media, and the media of Eastern Europe and the former Soviet Union. His book publications include *Images of the Enemy* (1988), *Glasnost, Perestroika and the Soviet Media* (1991), *News and Journalism in the UK* (1994, 1996, 1999), *An Introduction to Political Communication* (1995, 1999), *Mediated Sex* (1996) and *The*

Sociology of Journalism (1998). He teaches on a variety of courses, including The Sociology of Journalism; Sex, Society and the Media; and The Media in Contemporary Britain.

Bethany Davis Noll is Development Officer and Publications Manager at the Programme in Comparative Media Law and Policy, Centre for Socio-Legal Studies, University of Oxford. Ms. Davis Noll graduated magna cum laude from Barnard College, Columbia University with a major in Russian Regional Studies. She is a founding member of Public Digital. Her publications include *Back in the U.S.S.R.: Films of the Soviet Sixties* in the March/April 2002 issue of *Books & Culture.*

Monroe E. Price is the founder and co-director of the Programme in Comparative Media Law and Policy, Centre for Socio-Legal Studies, University of Oxford. He is also the Joseph and Sadie Danciger Professor of Law and Director of the Howard M. Squadron Program in Law, Media, and Society at the Benjamin N. Cardozo School of Law, Yeshiva University. From 1982 to1991, he was Dean of Cardozo Law School. Professor Price was a member of the School of Social Science at the Institute for Advanced Study, Princeton in 2000-2001 and a Fellow of the Media Studies Center of the Freedom Forum in New York City in 1998. From 1967 to 1982, he was Professor of Law at UCLA. His recent and forthcoming books include *Media and Sovereignty: Law, Identity and Technology in a Global Environment* (MIT Press 2002); *Forging Peace: Intervention, Human Rights, and the Management of Media Space* (edited with Mark Thompson) (Edinburgh University Press 2002), and *Media Reform: Democratizing Media, Democratizing the State* (edited with Beata Rozumilowicz and Stefaan Vershult) (Routledge 2001).

Andrei Richter is an associate professor at the School of Journalism at Moscow State University and director of the Moscow Media Law and Policy Center. He is the editor of *Zakonodatelstvo i praktika sredstv massovoi informatsii* (*Law and Practice of Mass Media*) monthly journal and a trustee of the Glasnost Defense Foundation. Professor Richter holds a Ph.D. equivalent in Journalism from Moscow State University, completed a post-graduate study course at the School of Journalism at Moscow State University, and holds an M.A. equivalent in English Language and Literature, with distinction, from Kharkov State University, Ukraine. In 1991, he was a Visiting Research Scholar for the Media Studies Center of the Freedom Forum at Columbia University in New York City.

Elena Vartanova serves as professor and director of the Centre for Finnish-Russian Studies in Journalism, Mass Communication and Culture. She studied at the School of Journalism at Moscow State University (Ph.D. 1986; Dsc 1999). Professor Vartanova lectures on Media Economics, History of Business Journalism, Nordic Media System, and Contemporary Media Systems. She published two monographs and more than fifty articles in Russian and English and edited four books of research papers. She is a member of the International Council of the IAMCR and a member of executive board of the European Consortium for Communication Research (ECCR). In 1995-2000, she worked as an expert for the group of specialists on the impact of new technologies on democratic values and human rights.

Peter K. Yu is Acting Assistant Professor of Law, Executive Director of the Intellectual Property Law Program, and Deputy Director of the Howard M. Squadron Program in Law, Media & Society at the Benjamin N. Cardozo School of Law, Yeshiva University. He is also Research Associate of the Programme in Comparative Media Law & Policy at the Centre for Socio-Legal Studies, University of Oxford. Originally from Hong Kong, Professor Yu sits on the editorial board of GigaLaw.com and is a member of the Board of Editors of the *Journal of Copyright Society of the U.S.A.* He has written extensively on intellectual property, communications law, public international law, and the transition of legal system in China and Hong Kong. Professor Yu is the founding editor of the *Journal of Chinese Information Law, Technology & Society* and the editor of a book series on intellectual property and technology law. His recent and forthcoming books include *Reinventing U.S.-China Intellectual Property Policy: Forging a Sustainable Partnership in the Twenty-first Century* (forthcoming from Kluwer Law International) and *The Marketplace of Ideas: Twenty Years of* Cardozo Arts & Entertainment Law Journal (editor) (Kluwer Law International 2002).

Yassen Zassoursky is Dean of the School of Journalism and Professor of Journalism and Literature at Moscow State University. As a scholar, literary critic, and journalist, he has published numerous books and articles on theory and history of journalism and communication, and on literature. His research activities in media and communication concentrate on Information Society and the media, transitional media models, and comparative studies of Russian and American media systems. In 1995-1999, he was Chairman of the Commission of Broadcasting, which was responsible for licensing television and radio frequencies. He has coedited and coauthored a book of essays, *Beyond the Cold War* (Sage 1992), and two books on contemporary media, *Changing Media and Communication* (1998) and *Media, Communications, and the Open Society* (1999).